A DOCUMENTARY HISTORY OF

The Negro People in the United States

A DOCUMENTARY HISTORY

OF

The Negro People in the United States

1960–1968

Volume 7
From the Alabama Protests
to the Death of Martin Luther King, Jr.

Compiled and Edited by
HERBERT APTHEKER

Foreword by Angela Y. Davis

A Citadel Press Book
Published by Carol Publishing Group

#2966249

A Citadel Press Book
Published by Carol Publishing Group
Citadel Press is a registered trademark of Carol Communications, Inc.

Editorial Offices: 600 Madison Avenue, New York, N.Y. 10022
Sales & Distribution Offices: 120 Enterprise Avenue, Secaucus, N.J. 07094
In Canada: Canadian Manda Group, P.O. Box 920, Station U, Toronto,
   Ontario M8Z 5P9
Queries regarding rights and permissions should be addressed to
Carol Publishing Group, 600 Madison Avenue, New York, N.Y. 10022

Carol Publishing Group books are available at special discounts
for bulk purchases, sales promotions, fund-raising, or
educational purposes. Special editions can be created to
specifications. For details contact: Special Sales Department,
Carol Publishing Group, 120 Enterprise Avenue, Secaucus, N.J. 07094

Manufactured in the United States of America

10 9 8 7 6 5 4 3 2 1

Library of Congress Cataloging-in-Publication Data
(Revised for vol. 7)

Aptheker, Herbert, 1915–
   A documentary history of the Negro people in the
United States.

   Vols. have imprint: Secaucus, N.J. : Carol Pub. Group;
also have statement: A Citadel Press book.
   Contents [1. 1661–1910] — [2] 1910–1932 — [etc.] —
v. 7. From the Alabama protests to the death of Martin
Luther King Jr.
   1. Afro-Americans—History—Sources.   II. Title.
E185.A58   973′.0496073   51-14828
ISBN 0-8065-1542-2 (v. 7)

To the Memory
of
Louis Burnham

Contents

Foreword

This seventh volume of Herbert Aptheker's *Documentary History of the Negro People in the United States* marks the conclusion of the most comprehensive effort undertaken by any scholar to preserve, organize, and render accessible a vast assembly of voices reflecting more than three hundred years of African-American history. This great achievement bears witness to the continuity and depth of Dr. Aptheker's engagement with the history of a people whose impact on U.S. culture has been profound, multidimensional, and constantly changing. His work also attests to his own deep commitment to scholarship that invites reflection about new social possibilities—and suggests that oppressed and marginalized people can radically transform history.

The very magnitude and originality of Herbert Aptheker's research— he has authored and edited over fifty volumes and, in addition, has edited almost as many volumes of W. E. B. Du Bois's writings and correspondence—speaks for itself. It is the work of one of this century's foremost historians of the United States and of the African-American experience. As John Hope Franklin has acknowledged, "He was one of the openers in the movement to unearth Afro-American history and present it to the general public." For more than fifty years, Herbert Aptheker has been an exemplary public intellectual who creatively has used Marxist theory while developing antiracist scholarship and taking strong and radical public positions on contemporary social issues. As a consequence, he has encountered more obstacles in academia than any other scholar in this century. Although he has presented papers at universities throughout the country, anti-Communist policies have resulted in the withdrawal of all offers for a permanent faculty position. Having personally experienced a similar sort of academic repression during the late sixties, I was greatly encouraged by Herbert Aptheker to fight for my right to teach as a Communist. To a very great extent, then, I owe my present tenure at the University of California to Aptheker's unflinching principles, and I wish here to express my gratitude publicly.

Having been profoundly influenced both by Aptheker's scholarship and by his explicit engagement with antiracist projects, I am deeply honored to have been invited to contribute the preface to this work. I have known Herbert Aptheker and his wife, Fay, for most of my life. During my teenage years I knew him as the father of my friend during the earliest years of my own activism (Bettina Aptheker is now my colleague at UCSC), later as a comrade and mentor. Like many others who began to do research in African-American history before the development of a significant body of literature in that area, my own work was greatly facilitated by Aptheker's pioneering research.

Herbert Aptheker's principled defense of his right as an intellectual to affiliate himself with an international community attempting to work for radical social transformation has strong and creative resonances in his scholarship. His work has never been mere academic exercise. It is scholarship that truly has made a difference in the way we think and engage in radical struggles for change. Thus, his approach to history has sought to furnish incontrovertible evidence of the human capacity to resist systematic oppression. He meticulously has documented powerful U.S. traditions of resistance to racism from the era of slavery to the present. His documentation and analysis of human agency among black people consistently has contested ideological assumptions of black people's implicit consent to a social status of inferiority. As much as this idea may be accepted—and sometimes even fetishized today—it is important to remember that when Aptheker published *American Negro Slave Revolts*, it was highly subversive, especially in the work of a white scholar.

Aptheker's insistence on agency and resistance also contests notions of history as the exclusive work of heroic individuals. While he has not neglected heroes—in fact, he is responsible for research which has served as the foundation for the elevation of individuals like Nat Turner to heroic status—he has been equally concerned with the dailiness and ordinariness of African-American history. Thus, the actors in the history he presents us are working men and women and unacknowledged leaders as well as the officially anointed "great leaders." The present volume, which spans the years 1960–68, when Dr. Martin Luther King was assassinated, thus includes such documents as a travel journal by Betty Rice Hughes (a black woman who decided to test the desegregation of public transport) as well as articles and speeches by civil rights activists Ella Baker, Fannie Lou Hamer, and James Foreman, Communist party chairperson Henry Winston, grass-roots activist Unita Blackwell, and playwright Lorraine Hansberry. Publicly acknowledged leaders include Martin Luther King,

W. E. B. Du Bois, Malcolm X, Huey Newton, Stokely Carmichael, Langston Hughes, and James Baldwin.

Aptheker implicitly acknowledges the historical character of this history project that has spanned more than forty years. By preserving the title *A Documentary History of the Negro People in the United States*, he has retained a historical but now virtually obsolete designation for a people who now are generally known as African-Americans. It is with insightful irony, therefore, that he opens this seventh and last volume with an article discussing the appropriateness of the word *Negro*. The volume ends with James Baldwin's admonition that however complicated social conditions and black people's spontaneous responses to them, "we do have to be free." With these words, Herbert Aptheker brings this project—to which he has devoted much of his life's work—to a close. He thus reasserts for contemporary scholars and activists the challenge which he so successfully has met. We do have to be free.

Angela Y. Davis
University of California, Santa Cruz

Introduction

"Too long have others spoken for us," stated the editors in launching, back in 1827, the first newspaper produced by African-American people. That helped inspire volume 1 of *A Documentary History of the Negro People*, published in 1953.

Certainly by the late nineteenth century black people were speaking for themselves; how many have paid attention is another matter.

Once launched, volumes of this *Documentary* have appeared with fair regularity at twenty-year intervals. The present one, illustrating the tumultuous 1960s, concludes the effort for this editor. The source of the drama persists; others certainly will record its future acts, and perhaps a more happy note may be struck.

But more heroic and dramatic it will not be. Oppression produces resistance; resistance needs courage. Both have permeated African-American history. Some record of that reality is in these volumes.

Prefaces to the books have acknowledged the editor's indebtedness. Especially is the debt great to those makers of history who agreed to preface the volumes; foremost, the incomparable W. E. B. Du Bois and then the prince of black historiography, Charles H. Wesley; and thereafter the progenitor of the modern civil rights struggle, William L. Patterson. Following these pioneers and worthy of them were the younger scholars, Henry Louis Gates, Jr., and now Angela Y. Davis.

The struggle for dignity and liberty is unceasing. It rises and falls, but never does it end. So will it be in African-American history. Perhaps the twenty-first century will witness the end of the racism that has shamed and tormented the United States.

The conclusion of this effort suggests the propriety of acknowledging my great debt to the creators and sustainers of Citadel Press. They— originally Philip S. Foner, Morris Sorkin, and Allan Wilson—hazarded support for the editor not yet out of his twenties. Philip remained a few years and then left to devote himself to the creation of his remarkable contributions to historiography. Morris and Allan persevered; the latter, in particular, served as my sustainer. If there is another such warm relationship of author and publisher for some fifty years, that fact escapes me.

The present volume has had selfless assistance, again, from David Fathi. The aid rendered by Katharine Gelles has been simply indispensable.

For Fay—these many, many years—thank you.

Herbert Aptheker

A DOCUMENTARY HISTORY OF

The Negro People in the United States

THE NAME "NEGRO"

by Richard B. Moore

Richard B. Moore was a significant figure in the African-American community for over fifty years, beginning soon after World War I. He was a pioneer in urging that the term "Afro-American" replace that of "Negro." An example of his argumentation is an essay published in 1960.

What is the purpose of this word "Negro"? When you say this word is objectionable, some reach for a quotation from Shakespeare—"A rose by any other name would smell as sweet." A fine statement but taken completely out of context and miserably misapplied. Straight to the point indeed were the same author's apt and prescient lines in *Othello, The Moor of Venice* which treat directly on the significance of a name.

> Good name in man and woman, dear my lord,
> Is the immediate jewel of their souls.
> Who steals my purse steals trash; 'tis something, nothing;
> 'Twas mine, 'tis his, and has been slave to thousands;
> But he that filches from me my good name
> Robs me of that which not enriches him
> And makes me poor indeed.

The important thing about a name is the impression which it makes in the minds of others and the reactions which it invokes through the operation of the association of ideas. The purpose of the name "Negro" was to mark this people by virtue of their color for a special condition of oppression, degradation, exploitation, and annihilation. Has the term changed so much in all this time? To be sure, we no longer have chattel slavery, at least not the type the modern Europeans initiated. That has been abolished as a result of struggle, but we still have various kinds of oppression.

The record of history makes it abundantly clear that after the abolition of chattel slavery, the attempt was ruthlessly made to keep the freemen down at the bottom of society, still chained to the most laborious and menial tasks. In order to accomplish and to maintain this mode of oppression, the emancipated people were identified by their color and branded by the names "Negro," "Negress," "nigger," and the like for discrimination, segregation, and social ostracism.

Indeed, this campaign of caricature, ridicule, scorn, vilification, and debasement went even to the lengths of exciting gruesome lynchings and horrible massacres. Extermination and annihilation of people of African origin were openly incited, without any legal prohibition or governmental restraint, by such venomous writers as Hinton Rowan Helper in the book *Nojoque* published in 1867, who branded the "negro" in one chapter as "An Inferior Fellow Done For" and in another demanded "Removals— Banishments—Expulsions—Exterminations."

As a result of such monstrous incitements, over 40,000 Afro-American citizens were massacred during the Reconstruction period in the South by the Ku Klux Klan, the White Camelias, and such terrorist gangs. Many European-American citizens, who endeavored to uphold democratic rights for all, were also brutally murdered during this period of frightful reaction in the South from 1865 to 1876.

As late as 1905, the American Book and Bible House at St. Louis, Mo., published the book of Charles Carroll entitled "The Negro A Beast"— "but created with articulate speech and hands, that he may be of service to his master—the White man." Through poison pen and vicious picture, such as the *Birth of a Nation*, which is still being shown despite protest, the stereotype or image has been built up in the public mind of the "Negro," as at best a creature retarded by nature with the mentality of a child, and at worst a savage, bestial monster, who must be kept at bay while forced to labor for his "superiors," and who is ultimately to be destroyed. *This name "Negro," with all its vicious associations must therefore certainly be abolished.*

In the United States and the Caribbean, we have different forms of oppression. In the Caribbean the overwhelming majority of the population is of African descent and these people are still being denied their unalienable rights of self-determination and self-government. So the name "Negro" is being foisted upon them too. This offensive name is thus being spread through the Caribbean. When I was raised in the Caribbean, nobody considered this name "Negro" as being a fit name for him.

For those who say: "what is important is economic status; if you improve your economic status, you won't have to worry about your name!" I would state that you will have an extremely hard time improving your economic status if you do not change your name. To be sure, we need to improve our economic status, but who will ever begin to struggle to improve his or her economic status who has not within the driving force of human self-respect? If you are willing to accept the slave master's vile appellation "Negro," you are also willing to accept segregated slums at double rentals and all the disabilities that go with tenth-class citizenship. The term "Negro" was coined for helots, for hewers of wood and drawers of water who were held to be incapable of anything else. Have we forgotten Carlyle's ruthless dictum—"the 'Negro' is useful to God's creation only as servant"?

I thank whatever gods there be for a mother who, in my formative years, instructed me in this glorious, vital, and important understanding of self-respect. Said she to me over and over again: "My son, you are a person of worth. You do nothing that a person of worth would be ashamed of. You conduct yourself with respect, as a person of worth, and you command respect of others."

This is the ancient and honorable teaching which has come down to us from the sages of Egypt, in particular Amenemope, and before him Ptahhotep and others who gave the same wise and essential counsel. At the top of our letter-head, therefore, we have inscribed one of these quotations: "See to it that thou be respected of men."

In Africa there are many peoples who are still being oppressed by the vicious system of colonial conquest and domination. Out of this system came the predication of names such as "native," "munt," "Kaffir," and the like with all the contempt and degradation which go with them inevitably.

If there were any doubt, then what has happened in relation to the gruesome events in South Africa ought to clarify any murky misunderstanding that might exist. Consider those horrible massacres, beginning at Sharpeville, of hundreds of Africans, even mothers with babies on their backs, being shot down in the back by those illustrious examples of Christian Apartheid. It should then be clear how these loaded names "native," "Kaffir," "Negro," are used to excite and to store up hate and hostility in prejudiced minds, which are then easily incited to perpetuate such inhuman, bloodcurdling, and murderous deeds.

What did we see in the general press of the United States? Newspaper after newspaper, magazines, and radio commentators likewise, writing and speaking about the "Negroes" of South Africa and frequently palliating and excusing these atrocious crimes committed against the indigenous African people in the bestial and monstrous Hitler technique. Such callous extenuation reached down even to the lowest depths when the correspondent for *Life* magazine, Gene Farmer, in the issue of April 11, 1960, retailed and spread a disgusting, lying, and lethal canard about savage Africans wildly infuriated with drink who pulled a white Christian nun from an automobile and ate her even before she died!

Not so long ago, however, Mr. Alan Paton contributed an article to *The New York Times* published in its Magazine Section of April 10. This enlightening statement, entitled "As Blind As Samson Was," revealed the pathological mindset of the rulers of the Union of South Africa. Indeed it called to mind the fitting observation of the Greeks: "Whom the gods would destroy they first make mad."

Mr. Paton exemplifies the fact that not all Europeans think and feel as imperious slave masters and oppressors. On the contrary, some have been and are among the most stalwart fighters against such injustice and oppression. Mr. Paton writes and acts as one of these. The apartheid oppressors in South Africa not only arrested African leaders, but they also jailed a number of European leaders who had been standing up for the rights of the African people.

Explaining the attitude of the present apartheid minority ruler of the Union of South Africa, who, although a relatively recent immigrant from Holland, actually called himself the "Afrikaner," the "man of Africa," Mr. Paton revealed the following: "He even refuses to grant the black Africans the use of the word 'African'. The black African used to be a 'kaffir,' today he is a 'native' or a 'Bantu'."

Doubtless, Mr. Paton used the adjective "black" in order to identify the indigenous inhabitants of South Africa. But it must be pointed out here that this is a loose term which cannot be wholly separated from its racist overtones.

Observe that the apartheid usage dictates that "native" be written with a common "n." Clearly then the term "native" is a contemptuous name, and it carries with it ignominy, derogation, and hostility. Do you ever see *The New York Times* or any of these institutions of journalism referring to the European as a "native," or to American "natives," except when they mean the indigenous people of this country whom they have well nigh wiped out? In reference to themselves though, they are not "natives." The word "native" is proper for them only as an adjective, never as a noun or name. Nevertheless, they seem to think that the name "native" is proper for Africans and other indigenous people who are thus considered fit to be ruled, exploited, displaced, and even exterminated. See how the apartheid monsters are even now degenerating the good name Bantu which is African. They are associating it with ignominy and degradation.

Mr. Paton continued: "But he like the Afrikaner wants to be called a 'man of Africa.'" I submit now that the people of Africa, whose ancestors have inhabited this land from time immemorial, are the Africans. It is now altogether clear that the use of the term "Negro," like that of "native" and "Kaffir" and the like, is for the purpose of marking out the people for oppression, degradation, and destruction.

I wish to point out also that Africans generally resent the term "Negro." There are as many variations of color in Africa as there are in Europe or Asia, and yet the people of these two continents are always described as Europeans or Asians, or according to their nationality. The use of the term "Negro" in relation to Africans is an attempt to categorize and disparage them on the basis of American color prejudice.

Through the years, Afro-Americans have been uneasy about the name. Many have rejected it. The names of early organizations of people of African descent in this country speak for themselves. The Free African Society was instituted in Philadelphia by Richard Allen and Absalom Jones in 1787. Shortly thereafter the African Methodist Church was founded by the former in 1790 and the First (Episcopal) African Church of St. Thomas was established by the latter in 1794.

The African Lodge of Masons was set up by Prince Hall, whose *Address to the Lodge* in 1797 speaks of African and Ethiopian but never "Negro." The militant and powerful *Appeal* of David Walker, published in Boston in the year 1829, was addressed to the *Colored Citizens of the World*... but in particular to those of the United States of America.

The early poet Phillis Wheatley, who had been brought from Africa to Boston, wrote in 1772 of Africa and Ethiop, only once falling into the use of the name "Negroes." Obviously, however, this use was due to her Christian teaching and to the dominant American slave mores as the following pathetic appeal clearly shows.

> Remember, Christians, Negroes black as Cain
> May be refined, and join the angelic train.

However, the slave poet of North Carolina, George M. Horton, never mentioned this name of proscription in *The Hope of Liberty* which was published in 1829.

Likewise conscious and forthright in this respect were the *Sentiments of the People of Color* which were printed as an Appendix to the *Thoughts on African Colonization* written by a founder of the modern Abolitionist Movement, William Lloyd Garrison. Beginning with the resolution of the "people of color" of Philadelphia in 1817, the statements adopted by such people in New York, Boston, Baltimore, Washington, Brooklyn, Hartford, Middletown, New Haven, Nantucket, Pittsburgh, Wilmington, Harrisburg, Rochester, Providence, Trenton, Lyme, Lewistown, and New Bedford—all evidently show how widespread and total was the rejection of the use of the offensive name "Negro."

Lydia Maria Child's *Appeal in Favor of that Class of Americans Called Africans*, published in 1833, demonstrates a similar and growing consciousness among some of the most informed of the European-American Abolitionists.

William C. Nell's book, which is the first, shall we say, formal account of the contributions of Afro-Americans, is entitled *Colored Patriots Of The American Revolution*. Throughout this book the term "colored" is emphasized; the name "Negro" appears only in quotations or in a very few places under the obvious direct influence of other authors.

The first magazine published by persons of African descent in America was called *The Anglo-African Magazine*. For a long time, subsequently, there was a *Colored American Magazine* which eschewed the name "Negro." However, the term "colored" is too vague and cannot now be accepted as a proper designation.

The first comprehensive account of our journalistic enterprise was written by I. Garland Penn and entitled *The Afro-American Press*. William Monroe Trotter, editor of *The Guardian* and one of the great champions of human rights in these United States, banished the word "Negro" from the columns of his newspaper. Likewise, *The Chicago Defender* while under the editorial supervision of its founder, Robert S. Abbott, disdained the use of this epithet. Father Divine in the *New Day* has spoken and written against this term "Negro."

Significant and weighty is the record of the numerous National Conventions held by American citizens of African origin, from 1830 until 1892 when their names regrettably began to change. Never were these Conventions called "Negro." Seldom was this odious word used in speeches in these assemblies. Instinctively and consciously, the name denoting slave status and "free" inferiority was not applied to themselves in the Addresses which they made to the nation and to the world.

Consult *A Documentary History of the Negro People in the United*

States by Herbert Aptheker and read past the bold titles and headings inserted by the editor which parade the misnomer "Negro." Look into the official documents! You will read references to their organizations as "Colored Men," "People of Color," and so on—but no "Negro"! A striking example of this baneful tendency to read present harmful terms back into history is seen in the insertion of "Negro," first with brackets later even without, in the very title of the National Labor Union of 1870.

It would be well to mark the total absence of the degrading name "Negro" from the choice and fitly phrased wording of what is perhaps the most significant document of this entire period. The Call To Arms To Fight For Emancipation, which was made by the great Abolitionist leader Frederick Douglass, was particularly addressed: MEN OF COLOR, TO ARMS!

But by 1892 a backward trend was rising. The policy of "accommodation" to the requirements of reactionary oppressors was being shrewdly put over upon our people. The first self-styled *Negro* Conference was called by Booker T. Washington in 1892. The use of this name of indignity—Negro—was a symptom of the developing sickness of opportunism and of the increasing acceptance of inferior social and political status. This acceptance of a lower place for our people at the bottom of American society was unblushingly proclaimed by Booker T. Washington in his notorious "separate as the fingers" speech, delivered at the Atlanta Exposition in 1895.

As this spirit of acceptance of the bottom place possessed more of our people, the degrading name "Negro" became more common. But for a time it appeared that the name Afro-American would be wholly adopted. However, the climate of the time made it easy to take the path of least resistance, and so at last to our detriment the name "Negro" became dominant. Still conscious, however, of its degrading use, particularly with a common "n," some of the more thoughtful and manly of our leaders developed a campaign to secure its use with a capital letter.

One of our most influential newspapers still carries at its masthead the proper and honorable name Afro-American. Published first in Baltimore but extending its circulation on a national scale, this journal carries forward some of the best traditions of the press which came into being to voice and to defend the rights of a minority people suffering unjust oppression. This newspaper should now logically be in the forefront of the endeavor to get this name established on a national and international scale.

The chief organization, defending and promoting the general human rights of our people, appears to have been purposely named the National Association For the Advancement of Colored People. Its national organ, *The Crisis* magazine, was founded by the dean of Afro-American letters, Dr. W. E. B. Du Bois, who significantly projected this journal as "A Record of the Darker Races." This organization could ably serve the cause of removing prejudice by playing a leading role in the campaign to change the name "Negro." For such a change would direct thought to the vital aspects of this question, and help to create a state of mind and the social climate, which would certainly make easier the practical realization of the democratic rights of our people, and consequently those of all other citizens.

Allow me to consider the names which have been proposed as an alternative to "Negro." We have heard Ethiopian mentioned, but Ethiopia is now the recognized name of a specific nation and area in Africa and is not applicable to the whole of Africa. The term "colored" is vague, associated with false notions of "race," and lacking any definite connection with the good earth, or with an extensive historical record, or with a significant group culture. The names "Black Man," or "Black Race," have been suggested, but these are also loose, racist, color designations which have no basic, obvious, or unmistakable linkage with land, history, and culture. The name "African-American," although expressive of the essential fundamentals, is rather long and does not sound well. The repeated "eecan-eecan" sound diminishes its euphony.

There remains the name Afro-American. Please note that Afro-American could be written as one word without any hyphen, so that the objection to "hyphenated Americans" would not apply. A similar usage has been followed for some time now by enlightened Latin Americans who have fittingly replaced the noxious name "Negro" with the names Afroamericano, Afrocubano, Afrobrasileiro, and similar names compounded in the same way.

The name Afro-American properly recognizes and expresses our origin and connection with land, history, and culture. The word Afro-American proclaims at once our past continental heritage and our present national status. Besides being pleasant to the ear, this name Afro-American was devised by ourselves and is already in use to some extent. It should therefore be most easily and readily adopted by everybody.

All other minority groups in the United States of America are generally recognized in terms of the land or nation whence they came—all but the misnamed and proscribed "Negro." Thus we hear of Anglo-

Americans, Franco-Americans, Italo-Americans, Irish-Americans, Spanish-Americans, Chinese-Americans, and so on. Standing out alone and shamefully among all these Americans from these several countries and nations are the misnamed "Negro" Americans. They have come from nowhere!

All too often the desire to rid ourselves of this belittling name "Negro," is blocked by the defeatist thought: "How shall we ever be able to change it?" But this is not so difficult as it appears at first. In our time we have seen important changes made in the names of several peoples.

As Bishop Reginald Barrow has pointed out, the name of the people of Ghana was changed upon regaining their independence, and the name which had been imposed by European rulers, "Gold Coast," has been buried with the subject past. For centuries the Ethiopian nation was tagged "Abyssinia" by European powers and publicists. When the proper name Ethiopia was registered with the League of Nations, this misrepresentative "hybrid" name was decisively changed.

Similar changes of name have occurred among the Asian peoples. To mention only two: The people of Iran have put aside the name Persia. The name "Dutch East Indies" has been appropriately cast off and the honorable name Indonesia is now the accepted and proper name.

In our own hemisphere, it has been noteworthy that when the slaves of the former French colony of Saint Domingue succeeded in throwing off their yoke of subjection and emerged as a new nation in 1804, they took as a fitting name one which the indigenous people of that island had used in freedom and honor—Haiti.

The name "West Indies" was almost changed to "Caribbean." The organization which initiated the movement for "federation with complete self-government" called itself the *Caribbean* Labour Congress. The name Caribbean, derived from the indigenous people now almost wholly and sadly extinct, was projected in the draft for the constitution of the new nation. Unfortunately, however, the misnomer due to the error of Colón in assuming that he had reached the Indies has been reverted to and independence has not yet been achieved wholly.

It may still be objected, nevertheless, that all these examples of change of name do not really apply, since people of African origin in this country now lack the political power to enforce such a change. That is mistaken. Once this change of name is insisted upon by a majority of us, it will be accepted generally. The basic principle involved is actually the determination of any group of people to rid themselves of the stigma which a bad name carries and the recognition of their right to do so by other people. Directly in point is the change in the use of a common "n" to a capital "N" in writing the word "Negro" in English. This has been achieved widely, though not completely, as the result of effective action. Among the first important newspapers to adopt this change was *The New York Times*.

What is needed now is a clear recognition by the majority of American citizens of African ancestry that it is imperative to take a further and final step. By united action we must register this desire and will with those most influential in such a matter—the managers of the press and the directors of radio and television communications, educational institutions, religious bodies, fraternal, trade union, and other organizations, and governmental agencies. Fair-minded European-Americans will readily accede to such a request and others will be compelled to follow the decent and proper usage—Afro-American. Let us now call upon all who mould public opinion to reject the name "Negro" as wholly unsuitable, offensive, and insulting.

We are entitled to be called Americans, but some people desire to differentiate. If they must distinguish us, then in accordance with our human right, we will tell them what to call us—Afro-Americans. When all is said and done, dogs and slaves are named by their masters; free men name themselves!

"The Name 'Negro': Its Origin and Evil Use," first published by Afroamerican Publishers, New York, 1960; reprinted in W. Burghardt Turner and Joyce Moore Turner, eds., *Richard B. Moore: Caribbean Militant in Harlem: Collected Writings (1920–1972)* (Bloomington, Indiana University Press, 1988), pp. 231–39. Published in part.

2

THE REBELLION OF AFRICAN-AMERICAN STUDENTS: 1960

by Eyewitness Reports

Sit-downs as forms of protest against Jim Crow had appeared among black students in the 1940s and 1950s. Most were localized and short-lived. But in the spring of 1958 sit-ins against certain drugstores in Wichita, Kansas, lasted several weeks, and the segregation ended that summer. In the fall of 1958 sit-ins occurred in Oklahoma City with mixed results. Ronald Walters, later a professor at

Howard, was president of the youth chapter of the NAACP, which led the Wichita action; the Oklahoma City action also was initiated by the youth section of the NAACP, with Clara Luper as its adult adviser. Barbara Posey, a sixteen-year-old, was a driving force in that action. She is now Prof. Barbara Jones, of the economics department at Prairie View State University in Texas.

Those sit-ins, beginning February 1, 1960, by students at the A & T College in Greensboro, North Carolina, demanding service at a Woolworth lunch counter, proved to be inspiring. Their act was spontaneous, but it induced similar demonstrations throughout the South. Quickly, CORE and SCLC (Southern Christian Leadership Conference) became involved; most significant in this effort at expansion was the young, but already veteran, Ella Baker of the SCLC. This was the root of the creation, in 1961, of the Student Non-Violent Coordinating Committee (SNCC). Several firsthand reports of this historic sit-down movement follow: Tallahassee (A), Portsmouth (B), Nashville (C), Orangeburg (D), Baton Rouge (E).

[A]

TALLAHASSEE, FLORIDA

by Patricia Stephens, Florida A & M

I am writing this in Leon County Jail. My sister Priscilla and I, five other A & M students, and one high school student are serving sixty-day sentences for our participation in the sit-ins. We could be out on appeal but we all strongly believe that Martin Luther King was right when he said: "We've got to fill the jails in order to win our equal rights." Priscilla and I both explained this to our parents when they visited us the other day. Priscilla is supposed to be on a special diet and mother was worried about her. We did our best to dispel her worries. We made it clear that we want to serve out our full time.

Students who saw the inside of the county jail before I did and were released on bond, reported that conditions were miserable. They did not exaggerate. It is dank and cold. We are in what is called a "bull tank" with four cells. Each cell has four bunks, a commode, and a small sink. Some of the cells have running water, but ours does not. Breakfast, if you can call it that, is served at 6:30. Another meal is served at 12:30 and in the evening, "sweet" bread and watery coffee. At first I found it difficult to eat this food. Two ministers visit us every day. Sundays and Wednesdays are regular visiting days, but our white visitors who came at first are no longer permitted by the authorities.

There is plenty of time to think in jail and I sometimes review in my mind the events which brought me here. It is almost six months since Priscilla and I were first introduced to CORE at a workshop in Miami. Upon our return we helped to establish a Tallahassee CORE group, whose initial meeting took place last October. Among our first projects was a test sit-in at Sears and McCrory's. So, we were not totally unprepared when the south-wide protest movement started in early February.

Our first action in Tallahassee was on Feb. 13th. At 11:00 A.M. we sat down at the Woolworth lunch counter. When the waitress approached, Charles Steele, who was next to me, ordered a slice of cake for each of us. She said: "I'm sorry: I can't serve you" and moved on down the counter repeating this to the other participants. We all said we would wait, took out our books, and started reading—or at least, we tried.

The regular customers continued to eat. When one man finished, the waitress said: "Thank you for staying and eating in all this indecency." The man replied: "What did you expect me to do? I paid for it."

One man stopped behind Bill Carpenter briefly and said: "I think you're doing a fine job: just sit right there." A young white hoodlum then came up behind Bill and tried to bait him into an argument. Unsuccessful, he boasted to his friends: "I bet if I disjoint him, he'll talk." When Bill didn't respond, he moved on. A number of tough looking characters wandered into the store. In most instances the waitress spotted them and had them leave. When a few of them started making derisive comments, the waitress said, about us: "You can see they aren't here to start anything." Although the counters were closed 20 minutes after our arrival, we stayed until 2 P.M.

The second sit-in at Woolworth's occurred a week later. The waitress saw us sitting down and said: "Oh Lord, here they come again!" This time a few white persons were participating, secretly. They simply sat and continued eating, without comment. The idea was to demonstrate the reality of eating together without coercion, contamination, or cohabitation. Everything was peaceful. We read. I was reading the *Blue Book of Crime* and Barbara Broxton, *How to Tell the Different Kinds of Fingerprints*—which gave us a laugh in light of the arrests which followed.

At about 3:30 P.M. a squad of policemen led by a man in civilian clothes entered the store. Someone directed him to Priscilla, who had been chosen our spokesman for this sit-in. "As Mayor of Tallahassee, I am asking you to leave," said the man in civilian clothes.

"If we don't leave, would we be committing a crime?" Priscilla asked. The mayor simply repeated his original statement. Then he came over to me, pointed to the "closed" sign and asked: "Can you read?" I advised him to direct all his comments to our elected spokesman. He looked as though his official vanity was wounded but turned to Priscilla. We did too, reiterating our determination to stay. He ordered our arrest.

Two policemen "escorted" each of the eleven of us to the station. I use quotes because their handling of us was not exactly gentle nor were their remarks courteous. At 4:45 we entered the police station. Until recently the building had housed a savings and loan company, so I was not surprised to observe that our cell was a renovated bank vault. One by one, we were fingerprinted.

After about two hours, the charges against us were read and one of us was allowed to make a phone call. I started to call Rev. C. K. Steele, a leader of nonviolent action in Tallahassee whose two sons were involved in the sit-ins. A policeman stopped me on the grounds that Rev. Steele is not a bondsman. I heard a number of policemen refer to us as "niggers" and say we should stay on the campus.

Shortly, the police captain came into our cell and announced that someone was coming to get us out. An hour later we were released— through the back door, so that the waiting reporters and TV men would not see us and give us publicity. However, the reporters were quick to catch on and they circled the building to meet us.

We were arraigned February 22 and charged with disturbing the peace by riotous conduct and unlawful assembly. We all pleaded "not guilty!" The trial was set for March 3. A week prior to that date the entire A & M student body met and decided to suspend classes on March 3 and attend the trial. The prospect of having 3,000 students converge on the small courtroom was a factor, we believe, in causing a 2-week postponement.

Our biggest single demonstration took place on March 12 at 9 A.M. The plan was for FSU students, who are white, to enter the two stores first and order food. A & M students would arrive later and, if refused service, would share the food which the white students had ordered. It was decided that I should be an observer this time rather than a participant because of my previous arrest.

The white and Negro students were sitting peacefully at the counter when the mayor and his corps arrived. As on the previous occasion, he asked the group to leave, but when a few rose to comply, he immediately arrested them. As a symbolic gesture of contempt, they were marched to the station in interracial pairs.

After the arrests many of us stood in a park opposite the station. We were refused permission to visit those arrested. I rushed back to report this on campus. When I returned to the station, some 200 students were with me. Barbara Cooper and I, again, asked to visit those arrested. Again, we were refused.

Thereupon, we formed two groups and headed for the variety stores. The 17 who went to McCrory's were promptly arrested. The group headed for Woolworth's was met by a band of white hoodlums armed with bats, sticks, knives, and other weapons. They were followed by police. To avoid what seemed certain violence, the group called off the sit-in at Woolworth's and returned to the campus in an orderly manner.

We asked the president of the student body to mobilize the students for a peaceful march downtown. He agreed but first tried, without success, to arrange a conference with the mayor.

However, the mayor was not too busy to direct the city, county, and state police who met us as we neared the downtown area. There were 1,000 of us, in groups of seventy-five—each with two leaders. Our hastily printed posters said: "Give Us Our Students Back," "We Will Not Fight Mobs," "No Violence," "We Want Our Rights: We are Americans, Too."

As we reached the police line-up, the mayor stepped forward and ordered us to disperse within three minutes. But the police did not wait: they started shooting tear gas bombs at once. One policeman, turning on me, explained: "I want you!" and thereupon aimed one of the bombs directly at me.

The students moved back toward campus. Several girls were taken to the university hospital to be treated for burns. Six students were arrested, bringing the total arrests for the day to thirty-five. Bond was set at $500 each and within two days all were out.

The 11 of us arrested on February 20 were tried on March 17. There was no second postponement. The trial started promptly at 9:30. Five additional charges had been made against us, but were subsequently dropped. During the trial, Judge Rudd tried to keep race out of the case. He said it was not a factor in our arrest. But we realize it was the sole factor. The mayor in his testimony used the word "nigger" freely. We were convicted and sentenced to sixty days in jail or a $300 fine. All eleven had agreed to go to jail but three paid fines upon advice of our attorneys.

So, here I am serving a sixty-day jail sentence along with seven other CORE members. When I get out, I plan to carry on this struggle. I feel I shall be ready to go to jail again if necessary.

[B]

PORTSMOUTH, VIRGINIA

by Edward Rodman, Norcom High School

Life is and always has been unpredictable. Little did I or any one else know the startling effects the first sit-in at Greensboro would have on us in Portsmouth, Virginia. The only previous integration here had been on the buses, and, very recently, in the Public Library. The Negro youth of Portsmouth had good reason to be impatient.

Our story here begins on February 12th, Lincoln's birthday. Several girls decided to observe the occasion by staging a sit-in, in sympathy with the students of North Carolina. So, after school, the first sit-in of Portsmouth's history took place. There was no violence, but no one was served. We sat until the lunch counter at Rose's Variety Store closed.

Our group was a loosely-knit collection of high school students, each with the same ideal: "Equality for All." Frankly speaking, that is about all we had in common. We were lacking organization, leadership, and planning.

By February 15th, our numbers had increased considerably. We demonstrated at two stores at the Shopping Center. Again we met no obstruction—only a few hecklers, whose worst insults we passed off with a smile. Things were looking good. The newspaper and radio reporters were there getting our story.

Our spontaneous movement was gaining momentum quickly. We were without organization; we had no leader and no rules for conduct other than a vague understanding that we were not to fight back. We should have known the consequences, but we didn't.

I was late getting to the stores the following day, because of a meeting. It was almost 4:00 P.M. when I arrived. What I saw will stay in my memory for a long time. Instead of the peaceful, nonviolent sit-ins of the past few days, I saw before me a swelling, pushing mob of white and Negro students, news-photographers, T.V. cameras and only two policemen. Immediately, I tried to take the situation in hand. I did not know it at the time, but this day I became the sit-in leader.

I didn't waste time asking the obvious questions: "Who were these other Negro boys from the corner?" "Where did all the white hoods come from?" It was obvious. Something was going to break loose, and I wanted to stop it. First, I asked all the girls to leave, then the hoods. But before I could finish, trouble started. A white boy shoved a Negro boy. The manager then grabbed the white boy to push him out and was shoved by the white boy. The crowd followed. Outside the boy stood in the middle of the street daring any Negro to cross a certain line. He then pulled a car chain and claw hammer from his pocket and started swinging the chain in the air.

He stepped up his taunting with the encouragement of others. When we did not respond, he became so infuriated that he struck a Negro boy in the face with the chain. The boy kept walking. Then, in utter frustration, the white boy picked up a street sign and threw it at a Negro girl. It hit her and the fight began. The white boys, armed with chains, pipes, and hammers, cut off an escape through the street. Negro boys grabbed the chains and beat the white boys. The hammers they threw away. The white boys went running back to their hot rods. I tried to order a retreat.

During the fight I had been talking to the store manager and to some newspaper men. I did not apologize for our sit-in—only for unwanted fighters of both races and for their conduct. Going home, I was very dejected. I felt that this outbreak had killed our movement. I was not surprised the following day when a mob of 3,000 people formed. The fire department, all of the police force, and police dogs were mobilized. The police turned the dogs loose on the Negroes—but not on the whites. Peaceful victory for us seemed distant.

Next day was rainy and I was thankful that at least no mob would form. At 10:00 A.M. I received a telephone call that was to change our whole course. Mr. Hamilton, director of the YMCA, urged me to bring a few students from the original sit-in group to a meeting that afternoon. I did. That meeting was with Gordon Carey, a field secretary of CORE. We had seen his picture in the paper in connection with our recent campaign for integrated library facilities and we knew he was on our side. He had just left North Carolina where he had helped the student sit-ins. He told us about CORE and what CORE had done in similar situations elsewhere. I decided along with the others that Carey should help us organize a nonviolent, direct action group to continue our peaceful protests in

Portsmouth. He suggested that an all-day workshop on nonviolence be held February 20.

Rev. Chambers organized an adult committee to support our efforts. At the workshop we first oriented ourselves to CORE and its nonviolent methods. I spoke on "Why Nonviolent Action?" exploring Gandhi's principles of passive resistance and Martin Luther King's methods in Alabama. We then staged a socio-drama acting out the right and wrong ways to handle various demonstration situations. During the lunch recess, we had a real-life demonstration downtown—the first since the fighting. With our new methods and disciplined organization, we were successful in deterring violence. The store manager closed the counter early. We returned to the workshop, evaluated the day's sit-in, and decided to continue in this manner. We established ourselves officially as the Student Movement for Racial Equality.

Since then, we have had no real trouble. Our struggle is not an easy one, but we know we are not alone and we plan to continue in accordance with our common ideal: equality for all through nonviolent action.

[C]

NASHVILLE, TENNESSEE

by Paul Saprod, Fisk University

There were about thirty of us in the first group of sit-inners arrested in Nashville. It was approximately 1:30 P.M. on February 27. We were escorted from the store by police—not too gently. There were cheers from hundreds of people along the sidewalks. The cheers, I fear, were for the police, not for us.

During the few minutes it took the paddy wagon to get from the store to the city jail, I reflected on what a long way we had come since the idea of sit-ins first hit Nashville. The present action climaxes nearly two years of work by Jim Lawson of the Fellowship of Reconciliation, the Rev. Kelly Miller Smith of the Nashville Christian Leadership Conference, and Nashville CORE.

Back in 1958, following the opening of the new Cain-Sloan store with its segregated eating facilities, desegregation of restaurants became a prime objective. Starting last fall, Jim Lawson, as projects director of the NCLC, began holding training sessions on nonviolence, which were attended by Fisk and Tennessee A & I students. Although Nashville was almost completely unaware of it, test sit-ins were held at Harvey's department store on November 28, 1959 and at Cain-Sloan's on December 5. Hence, the movement which spread from Greensboro did not strike a vacuum when it hit Nashville.

The morning of February 10, Jim Lawson called me to say that CORE's field secretary Gordon R. Carey and the Rev. Douglas Moore had called him from Durham asking Nashville to help the North Carolina sit-ins. I told him I would talk with some of the students on campus. They were already quite excited over the North Carolina developments.

The next evening we were able to get together about fifty students from Fisk, A & I, and American Baptist Theological Seminary. We decided to go into action and the first sit-in took place February 13. About 100 students participated—at three stores: Woolworth's, McLellan's, and Kress's. We were refused service and remained seated until the stores closed. There was no hostility. Five days later, we tried again. This time 200 students took part and we were able to cover a fourth store, Grant's.

First sign of possible violence came on February 20, a Saturday, with school out and the white teenagers downtown. Some of them jeered at the demonstrators. At Walgreens, the fifth store to be covered, a boy got into a violent argument with a white co-ed from Fisk.

Police were present during all of these sit-ins, but did not make arrests or attempt to interfere with the demonstrators. Between February 20 and 27, however, a merchants' committee called upon Mayor Ben West to halt the sit-ins. He said city attorneys had advised him that anyone has the right to sit at a lunch counter and request service. However, he expressed the viewpoint that it is a violation of law to remain at a lunch counter after it has been closed to the public.

This set the stage for February 27, again a Saturday. Every available man on the police force had been ordered into the downtown area at the time of our demonstration. I was with the student group which went to Woolworth's. Curiously, no police were inside the store when white teenagers and others stood in the aisles insulting us, blowing smoke in our faces, grinding out cigarette butts on our backs and, finally, pulling us off our stools and beating us. Those of us pulled off our seats tried to regain them as soon as possible. But none of us attempted to fight back in any way.

Failing to disrupt the sit-ins, the white teenagers filed out. Two or three minutes later, the police entered and told us we were under arrest. To date, none of the whites who attacked us have been arrested, although Police Chief D. E. Hosse has ordered an investigation to find out why.

As might be expected, even the jail cells in Nashville are segregated. Two other white students and I were isolated from the others in a fairly large room, but we managed to join in the singing which came from the horribly crowded cells where the Negro students were confined.

There were eighty-one of us, in all, arrested that day. We hadn't been in jail more than a half hour before food was sent into us by the Negro merchants. A call for bail was issued to the Negro community and within a couple of hours there was twice the amount needed.

Our trials were February 29. The regular city judge refused on a technicality to handle the cases and appointed a special judge whose bias was so flagrant that Negro lawyers defending us were shocked. At one point, Z. Alexander Looby, a well-known NAACP attorney and City Council member, threw up his hands and commented: "What's the use!" During the two days I sat in court, every policeman who testified, under oath, stated that we had been sitting quietly at the lunch counters and doing nothing else.

The judge's verdict on disorderly conduct charges was "guilty." Most of us were fined $50 and costs. A few of the cases are being appealed as test cases. Next, we were all re-arrested on state charges of conspiracy to obstruct trade and commerce, but the district attorney general has expressed doubts as to the validity of this charge and to date no indictments have been returned by the grand jury.

On March 2 another sixty-three students were arrested at Nashville's two bus stations—Greyhound and Trailways. They too were charged with disorderly conduct and then conspiracy. It began to look as though we might well fill the jails. The next day, however, a new development occurred. At the urging of the Friends' Meeting, the Community Relations Conference, the Ministerial Association, and other groups, Mayor West appointed a seven-man bi-racial committee to try to work out a solution.

Although some Negroes expressed doubts about whether the committee was truly representative, we decided to discontinue the sit-ins temporarily to give it a chance to deliberate. However a boycott of the stores by the Negro community was started at this time. By March 25 we felt the committee had had sufficient time to answer what is essentially a moral problem and we took action again. This time we covered an additional drugstore, Harvey's, and Cain-Sloan's. Only four students were arrested—all at the drugstore. Police appeared to have received orders not to molest us.

This sit-in provoked a violent reaction from Governor Buford Ellington, who charged that it was "instigated and planned by and staged for the convenience of Columbia Broadcasting System." The charge stemmed from the fact that two CBS documentary teams had been with us for a week, filming our meetings and getting material for "Anatomy of a Demonstration." Of course, the idea that we would stage a sit-in purely for the convenience of cameramen is too ridiculous.

Meanwhile, the first breaks in the pattern had occurred. On March 16, four Negro students were served at the Greyhound bus station. . . .

The Mayor's committee announced it had been ready to report but, because of the March 25 sit-in, was unable to do so. On April 5 the committee recommended that for a ninety-day trial period the stores "make available to all customers a portion of restaurant facilities now operated exclusively for white customers" and that pending cases against the sit-in participants be dropped.

The plan of the Mayor's committee was rejected by the store management and by the student leaders. The students said "The suggestion of a restricted area involves the same stigma of which we are earnestly trying to rid the community. The plan presented by the Mayor's Committee ignores the moral issues involved in the struggle for human rights." We were not prepared to accept "integrated facilities" while "whites only" counters were maintained.

Demonstrations were resumed April 11.

One final note should be added about the effects of the sit-ins here. They have unified the Negro community in an unprecedented manner. The boycott proved effective in sharply curtailing seasonal Easter business in the variety stores. On April 19, within only a few hours after the bombing of Looby's home, over 2,500 demonstrators marched on City Hall. Adult leaders have assured us that, even if the students suddenly vanished from the scene, the action campaign would continue unabated. In Nashville, this is *not* a students-only struggle.

I could not close without reference to the academic freedom fight involving Jim Lawson, one of three Negro students at Vanderbilt's divinity school. He was expelled March 3 because of his "strong commitment to a planned campaign of civil disobedience." He did not actually participate in the sit-ins, but he has been our advisor and counselor throughout. His expulsion has touched off a storm of protest not only in Nashville but in academic and ministerial circles from coast to coast.

[D]

ORANGEBURG, SOUTH CAROLINA

by Thomas Gaither, Claflin College

On March 16 many newspapers throughout the world carried a photo showing 350 arrested students herded into an open-air stockade in Orangeburg, South Carolina.

I was arrested later in the day while marching in protest in front of the courthouse. I didn't realize until scrutinizing the stockade photo much later that the scene shown was unusual—to say the least—and would provoke questions from newspaper readers unfamiliar with the local scene.

What were all these well-dressed, peaceable-looking students doing in a stockade? Why weren't they inside the jail if they were under arrest? How come that such un-criminal-appearing youths were arrested in the first place?

The story begins about a month before when we students in the Orangeburg area became inspired by the example of the students in Rock Hill, first South Carolina city where lunch counter sit-ins occurred. We, too, feel that stores which graciously accept our money at one counter, should not rudely refuse it at another. We decided to request service at Kress's lunch counter.

But first, we felt that training in the principles and practice of nonviolence was needed. We formed classes of about forty students each over a period of three to four days. Our chief texts were the pamphlet "CORE Rules for Action" and Martin Luther King's inspirational book, "Stride Toward Freedom." In these sessions we emphasized adherence to nonviolence and discussed various situations which might provoke violence. Could each one of us trust our God and our temper enough to not strike back even if kicked, slapped, or spit upon? Many felt they could discipline themselves in violent situations. Others were honest enough to admit they could not and decided not to participate until they felt surer of themselves on this issue.

After the initial briefing session, two group spokesmen were chosen: one from Claflin College and one from South Carolina State College.

Their duty was to chart action plans for February 25. They checked the entrances of the Kress store and counted the number of stools at the lunch counter. The number of minutes it takes to walk from a central point on campus to Kress's was timed exactly. From our training groups, we picked forty students who felt confident in the techniques of nonviolence. After further training and some prayer we felt prepared for action.

At 10:45 A.M. on February 25, students from Claflin and South Carolina State left their respective campuses in groups of three or four, with one person designated as group leader. The groups followed three routes, walking at a moderate pace, which would ensure their arriving at the store simultaneously.

The first fifteen students went in and sat down at the lunch counter. After they had been there about a quarter of an hour, signs were posted saying that the counters were closed in the interest of public safety.

The first group then left and another group of about twenty students took their seats. The manager then started removing the seats from the stands. Each student remained seated until his seat was removed. A few students were jostled by police. A number of hoodlums were in the store, some of whom carried large knives and other weapons, unconcealed. However, no violence occurred. By closing time the seats were still off their stands and nobody was being served.

We returned to the store next day, following the same plan of action. At first the seats were still down but by 11:30 those at one end of the counter were screwed-on and some white people were served. We students stood along the rest of the counter until 3:30. By this time, additional students had joined us and we were several rows deep. At 4, the store closed.

The next day, Saturday, we decided against sitting-in. We had sought and obtained clearance from the chief of police to picket and we were prepared to start on Monday. However, no sooner had some twenty-five students started picketing than they were ordered to remove their signs or face arrest. They were informed that an antipicketing ordinance had been enacted that same day.

Inside the store, the counters were stacked with trash cans. Not more than two Negroes at a time were being permitted to enter. Each day our spokesmen checked the counter. Meanwhile some 1,000 Claflin and South Carolina State students were receiving training for the mass demonstrations which were to follow.

The first such demonstration started at 12:30 on March 1. Over 1,000 students marched through the streets of Orangeburg with signs saying:

"All Sit or All Stand," "Segregation is Obsolete," "No Color Line in Heaven" and "Down With Jim Crow."

Not long after reaching the main street, the marchers were met by a contingent of state police who requested identification of leaders and asked that the signs be taken down. The group leaders were informed that they would be held responsible for any outbreak of violence and that if this occurred, they would be charged with inciting to riot. There was no violence. Only two persons were arrested, and these were *not* participants.

After the March 1 demonstration, the lunch counters were closed for two weeks. With a view to strengthening our local movement and broadening it on a statewide basis, the South Carolina Student Movement Association was established. I was named chairman of the Orangeburg branch. We initiated a boycott of stores whose lunch counters discriminate.

March 15 was the day of the big march—the one in which 350 students landed in the stockade. The lunch counters had reopened the previous day and a sit-in was planned in addition to the march. Governor Hollings had asserted that no such demonstration would be tolerated. Regarding us, he said: "They think they can violate any law, especially if they have a Bible in their hands: our law enforcement officers have their Bibles too."

Of course, we were violating no law with our peaceful demonstration. As for the law enforcement officers having their Bibles, they may have them at home, but what they had in their hands the day of our demonstration were tear gas bombs and firehoses, which they used indiscriminately. The weather was sub-freezing and we were completely drenched with water from the hoses. Many of the girls were knocked off their feet by the pressure and floundered around in the water. Among the students thrown by the water were several physically handicapped students—one of them a blind girl.

Over five hundred students were arrested. One hundred and fifty filled the city and county jails. That's why some 350 were jammed into the stockade, surrounded by a heavy wire fence about seven feet high. The enclosure ordinarily serves as a chicken coop and storage space for chicken feed and lumber. There are two tall iron gates. It afforded no shelter whatsoever in the sub-freezing weather.

In contrast to the cold outside, students in the jail's basement were sweating in ninety-degree temperatures emanating from the boiler room. One student drenched from head to toe was locked in solitary in a cell with water three inches deep. Requests for dry clothing were denied. The Claflin College nurse who came to give first aid was halted at the court house entrance and literally had to force her way inside.

I was arrested with a group of some 200 students marching around the court house in protest over the earlier mass arrests. At first police told us we would be permitted to march if we kept moving in an orderly manner but then they announced that unless we returned to the campus at once we would be arrested. I was seized first as one of the leaders and was held in jail for four hours.

The trials of the arrested students started next day, a few students at a time. All were eventually convicted of "breach of the peace" and sentenced to thirty days in jail or $100 fine. The cases are being appealed to the higher courts.

Meanwhile, our action program proceeds. We are set in our goal and, with the help of God, nothing will stop us short of that goal.*

*On 1960 activity in Orangeburg, see Harvard Sitkoff, *The Struggle for Black Equality, 1954–1980* (New York: Hill & Wang, 1981), pp. 71–77.

[E]

BATON ROUGE, LOUISIANA

by Major Johns, Southern University

Some Negro university and college administrations have supported their students' lunch counter sit-ins or, at least, have remained neutral. Others have taken a stand in opposition to the students. Southern University in Baton Rouge and its president, Dr. Felton G. Clark, fall in this latter category.

Dr. Clark had the opportunity of taking a courageous position and becoming one of the world's most respected educational leaders. Instead, he chose to buckle-under to the all-white State Board of Education, which administers the university.

Early in March the Board issued a warning that any student participating in a sit-in would be subject to "stern disciplinary action." The sit-in movement had not yet spread to Baton Rouge but, as one law student expressed it: "When the Board spoke, it became a challenge to us and we could not ignore it." A representative student committee then met with Dr. Clark and asked, specifically, what would happen to students who sat-in. He replied that the Board had left him no alternative but to expel them.

On March 28 seven students sat-in at the Kress lunch counter. In less than twenty minutes they were arrested. Bond was set at the astronomical figure of $1,500 each. However, the money was promptly raised by the Negro community and the students were released. A mass meeting was held on campus at which students pledged support of the jailed sit-inners. The following day, nine more students engaged in sit-ins at Sitman's drugstore and at the Greyhound bus station. They remained in jail six days pending a court hearing and were released on bond April 4.

The day after the second arrests, 3,500 students marched through the center of town to the State Capitol, where we held an hour-long prayer meeting. As chief speaker, I attacked segregation and discrimination not only here in Baton Rouge but in other parts of the country.

I was unaware that this speech would sever my connections with the university before the day was over. That afternoon Dr. Clark returned from a conference in Washington and immediately cast his lot against the students. He summoned faculty members who were known to oppose the sit-ins and were furthest removed from really knowing the students. Immediately following this meeting, he announced the expulsion of seventeen students, the sixteen who had participated in the two sit-ins and myself.

This suddenly shifted the focus of the Baton Rouge student protest from lunch counters to the university administration. As Marvin Robinson, participant in the first sit-in and president of the senior class expressed it, we had a choice: "Which is the more important, human dignity or the university? We felt it was human dignity."

The students voted to boycott all classes until the seventeen of us were reinstated. Lines were tightly drawn: the students on one side, the administration, faculty, State Board of Education, and a group of hand-picked alumni on the other. We seventeen were no longer permitted on campus. But twice daily, in the morning and afternoon, we would address the students from the balcony of a two-story house across a railroad track from the campus. By using a loudspeaker we were able to make ourselves heard by the large groups of students assembled on the campus-side of the track. This went on for two days.

Unable to get the students back to class, administration officials started calling their parents and telling them that the student leaders were inciting to riot. This move boomeranged: it caused many parents to fear for their sons' and daughters' safety to the extent of summoning them home. The administration countered by announcing that any student who wanted to withdraw from the university and go home could do so. Such a sizable number of students applied at the registrar's office for withdrawal slips that the administration amended its ruling to the effect that these slips would have to be co-signed by parents.

Meanwhile certain persons in the community and on campus moved to negotiate a settlement. They initiated several meetings with administration officials. Dr. Clark admitted to friends that he had acted in haste, but remained adamant in refusing to re-admit the seventeen expelled students. Finally, he agreed to meet with eight of the student leaders. The meeting started at 5 P.M. on April 2 and lasted until 11:30. Throughout the 6½-hour meeting over 3,000 students sat in front of the building where the meeting was held. When the eight emerged, announced their decision to leave the university, but urged the other students to stay on and return to classes, there was an outcry. Some burst into tears, others shouted that they wanted to quit also. The student leaders reaffirmed their decision and gave assurance that they had reached it on their own after the administration had agreed not to dismiss anyone else.

The following morning, however, the administration broke its part of the agreement and expelled another student. The leaders thereupon called a meeting and urged that the students stay out of class. A local citizens' committee, which had raised bail bond money and had agreed to use some of it to help homegoing students pay their transportation, requested a meeting with Dr. Clark. The upshot was that the committee reversed itself and decided that money raised could be used only for bail bond and not for students' bus or rail fares home.

Jim McCain, CORE field secretary who had come to Baton Rouge to help us, tried to dissuade the committee from this decision, but without success.

"I tried my best to show them that helping the students to leave Southern, even if the university should close as a result, would strike a real blow at segregation," McCain said.

Withdrawal of the transportation funds was responsible for reducing considerably the total number of students who withdrew in protest. Nevertheless, the number who left on the weekend of April 2 was in the thousands. Of those, between 1,000 and 1,500 have not yet returned. As I write this, I do not know the exact number of students who permanently withdrew to protest an administration which serves segregation and discounts human dignity.

The protest movement by students at Southern will long be remembered in Baton Rouge. One instructor died, another had a heart attack and we are told that Dr. Clark is under medical care. It is reported by persons close to Dr. Clark that he has received several hundred letters and wires from all over the world—not one of them complimentary. Dr. Clark, I am sure, has lost many friends because of the position he has taken against his students. Until this protest, Southern University was an island unto itself. Dr. Clark was its president since 1938 and his father was its president from 1914 until 1938. Southern University will not be able to live by itself any longer. How far the community will proceed in continuing the movement which the students have started, only time will tell. But segregation in Baton Rouge has received a severe jolt.

CORE, *Sit-Ins: The Students' Report* (New York: 1960); reprinted in Gilbert Osofsky, ed., *The Burden of Race: A Documentary History* (New York: Harper, 1967), pp. 527–44. See also the letter by Ronald Waters in the *New York Times*, April 5, 1990.

3

SIT-INS AND THE NAACP

by the Editors of The Crisis

The official organ of the NAACP came to the defense of the burgeoning sit-in movement. A lead editorial in *The Crisis* stated:

Negro students in the South are justifiably in revolt against lunch-counter Jim Crow. To deny an American citizen access to a public lunch counter is senseless and demeaning. A Negro may patronize all the counters in national variety chains like Woolworth's, Grant's or Kress', but not the lunch counter or the soda fountain. In some places, he is allowed to eat at the lunch counter, but only if he stands. The moment he "sets" there is trouble, for the Southern white believes that seated Negroes are attempting to practice "social equality."

Whether he is educated or uneducated, whether he is rich or poor, the Negro knows very well the meaning of Jim Crow. For him it is ever present, an obscene daily reality. Even when intangible, he finds it dispersed through the whole atmosphere of the South. The Negro cannot eat a "hot dog" at a public lunch counter. He cannot eat a T-bone steak in a restaurant. He cannot drink a cup of coffee in a cafe. He cannot straw-sip a Coca-Cola at a soda bar. He cannot drink a Bromo-Seltzer for his headache in a drug store. He cannot eat his sandwich "in" even at a "greasy spoon"; he must take it "out." Whenever and wherever he tries to use a public eating facility he is faced with the bewilderment and the pain of refusal. He has to put up with the insolence of white waiters and clerks and managers. These are galling grievances. He is set apart. And though he may be thrifty, intelligent, and law-abiding, he is not allowed to live or work or play as others.

Mass Negro protests against these intolerable conditions began in Montgomery, Alabama, in December 1955, with the famous Montgomery bus strike. Negro students in five southern states—Virginia, North and South Carolina, Tennessee, and Florida—are continuing these mass protests against segregation in the form of "sit-in strikes," which were originated by NAACP youth members. The "sit-in strike" was first used by members of the Oklahoma City, Oklahoma, youth council in August 1958, against national variety stores in that city. Despite provocations to violence the youths maintained their dignity and self-control and won their fight. As a result lunch counters in variety and drugstores in Oklahoma City are now open to all.

Those Americans who genuinely believe in democracy for all should support these young people in every way possible. The NAACP has already called upon its branches to support them. And the Association has notified all branch leaders that these young people "have the cooperation and support of the NAACP, for they are legitimate expressions of citizens in a democracy." Furthermore, the NAACP stands ready "to defend, upon request, any of the young people who may become involved with the police or in court action as a result of their participation in this movement."

Crisis, March 1960, pp. 162–63.

4

THE BLACK PRESS WHEN THE "SIT-INS" BEGIN

by Benjamin F. Clark

A doctoral dissertation at Howard University in 1969 offered copious documentation of the response of the black press to the modern civil rights movement.

Typical was the coverage of the 1960 "sit-in" movement. Using the *Greensboro A & T College Register*, the author wrote:

The four North Carolina Agricultural and Technical College (A & T) freshmen who initiated the "sit-in" demonstrations in the 1960s had been planning to resist segregation for months. When and where they would resist had remained the major unanswered questions until Joseph McNeill was provoked to answer.

On January 31, 1960, McNeill was returning to A & T College in Greensboro from his home in Wilmington, North Carolina, when hunger forced him to try to secure food from the lunch counter of the Greensboro terminal. He was refused and told, "We do not serve Negroes." Upon discussing the incident with his roommate, Ezell Blair, Jr., a native of Greensboro, McNeill asked the question, "What can we do?" Then, answering his own question, he quickly responded, "Let's have a boycott. We should go in and ask to be served and sit there until they do."

The next morning McNeill, Blair, Jr., and two classmates, Franklin McClain of Washington, D.C., and David Richmond also of Greensboro, walked into the downtown Woolworth Store at approximately 4:30 P.M., purchased small items from a counter near the lunch bar, and then took seats at the lunch counter. According to the *Greensboro A & T College Register*, the following conversation transpired between Blair and the waitress: [February 5, 1960].

> BLAIR: 'I'd like a cup of coffee, please.'
> WAITRESS: 'I'm sorry. We don't serve colored here.'
> BLAIR: 'I beg to disagree with you. You just finished serving me at a counter only two feet from here.'
> WAITRESS: 'Negroes eat on the other end.'
> BLAIR: 'What do you mean? This is a public place, isn't it? If it isn't then why don't you sell membership cards? If you do that, then I'll understand that this is a private concern.'
> WAITRESS: 'Well you won't get any service here.'

> After this conversation, said Blair, the waitress left them and went to the other end of the counter.

[Contrasting responses of the general black press to the "sit-ins" in their initial phase were illustrated by the *Louisiana Weekly* (New Orleans) and the *Daily World* of Atlanta—EDITOR]

The *Louisiana Weekly* began coverage on the "sit-ins" as early as

February 13, 1960, when an article referred to the "sit-ins" as *sit down strike*. One week later an editorial appeared indicating that black and white patience was beginning to wear thin. Although *Weekly* editors took no clear position in this editorial, they did not reject the "sit-in" approach. By March 19, 1960, the *Weekly* made its stand explicit.

> The myth most often mouthed by Southern politicians, Negroes are satisfied with conditions as they are in the South, has been thoroughly and totally destroyed with the dramatic and sweeping suddenness of the lunch counter 'sit-downs' by college students throughout the South.
>
> By the large number of Negroes who have willingly gone to jail in the 'sit-down' demonstrations, it appears that they learned something from their African brothers. . . . Going to jail in the fight to uphold the principles of democracy and Christianity is no disgrace. It is a badge of honor and achievement. It means that the students have stood up like men and were counted. Freedom, dignity, and independence are seldom won without some sacrifice and the students involved in the 'sit-downs' are keenly aware of the fact.

Continuing to use the phrase "sit-downs" as opposed to "sit-in," the *Weekly* editors did not waver in their strong supportive position towards the sit-ins. Their denunciation of the actions of Southern University President Dr. Felton Clark, who expelled several students for participating, was demonstrative of their zealous support. The *Weekly* declared that Clark was out of step with other presidents and should reinstate the students (April 23, 1960).

Solidification of the [Atlanta] *Daily World*'s position came when riots broke out in Biloxi, Mississippi between demonstrators and whites over the desegregation of a twenty-eight mile beach front. In an April 30 editorial the *Daily World* explained its position in ultimate clarity.

> The city (Biloxi) today is like a dynamite keg which could be ignited and explode into a general race riot at any minute. We believe that all of this could have been prevented by wiser and more mature approaches to solve Biloxi's problem of removing discrimination in the use of recreational facilities.
>
> The legal test could have been arranged that would have placed the problem in the laps of the federal courts.
>
> There is no need for any group to take matters into their own hands in misguided attempts to gain civil rights, when these rights have already been guaranteed by the constitution of the United States and interpreted and confirmed by the courts.
>
> Such attempts merely create general ill-will and set up situations that

endanger the lives and property of everyone . . . the answer is to be found at the conference table, ballot box, and in the courts of law; to do otherwise is unsound, dangerous, and impractical.

Subsequently, the *Daily World*'s denunciation of picketing, sit-ins, and other pressure tactics brought it into conflict with the NAACP which urged blacks to use public pools and beaches immediately. The *Daily World* felt that test cases were all that would be needed because, they reasoned, the fate of any demonstrators will ultimately end up in the courts. Hence, the *Daily World* eventually became a voice in opposition to the "sit-ins."

Benjamin F. Clark, "The Editorial Reaction of Selected Black Newspapers to the Civil Rights Movement" (Ph.D. diss., Howard University, 1969). For the opposition to the sit-ins and other popular initiatives on the part of black publications in Mississippi, see James W. Silver, *Mississippi: The Closed Society* (New York: Harcourt, Brace and World, 1966), pp. 349–50.

5

RACIAL INTERMARRIAGE

by the Editors of The Crisis

A long-term executive secretary of the NAACP chose to divorce his African-American wife and marry a white woman. This second marriage deeply divided opinion among the leaders and members of the organization. Five years after his death, an editorial with the above title appeared in its official organ.

It required courage for the editors of *Social Progress* (published by the Department of Social Education and Action of the Board of Education of the United States Presbyterian Church in the United States of America) to devote their February issue to a symposium on racial intermarriage, a subject which, in the vernacular, is a "hot potato." A subject of concern to many whites who are not segregationists, and an obsessive bugaboo with all segregationists, interracial marriage has never been of concern to Negroes.

The SEA staff summarizes the marriage issue in this way:

On few issues is there so much heat and so little light. Yet the problem of intermarriage nearly always comes up when desegregation is earnestly and openly discussed, and even when the question is not actually raised, it lurks unspoken in the minds and hearts of many persons sincerely and positively concerned about race relations. When the meeting breaks up, the issue often arises in private conversations. And when it is brought out into the open, persons frequently gravitate toward one of three camps—the hotly opposed, the vehement defenders, and the inarticulately uncomfortable. Nearly everyone ends up with a stomach-ache.

The consensus of opinion, of both clergy and laity, North and South, is that Christian commitment does not preclude racial intermarriage; although John H. Marion feels that "in our present social climate, any Negro-white intermarriage as such would usually be imprudent." J. Metz Rollins, Jr., says he has "nothing against my daughter marrying a white man because I do not fear the 'bogeyman race-mixing.'" He feels it a matter of personal choice. John R. Bodo says it would depend on the man, not his race. Edler G. Hawkins remarks that the question posed by "racial intermarriage accurately anticipates . . . the recognition of the full humanity of the Negro, the fact of man's oneness under God." "Let's face it," warns Paul S. Wright "—the social climate of our country being what it is, and my personal life being so inextricably involved in it, I should not want my daughter to marry a Negro. . . . " Richard Siciliano writes: "It is my guess that advances in human relations will lead to more integration, and this inclusiveness will lead to more mixed marriages—and I think this is good."

What we need is much more open and objective discussion of this type. Racial intermarriage is an inflammable topic because the issues are seldom objectively discussed in the public prints. When seen in perspective it is not an issue at all. And *Social Progress* is to be congratulated for bringing it out into the open.

The Crisis, March 1960, p. 163.

6

AN APPEAL FOR HUMAN RIGHTS

by Atlanta University Students

Under the above title, students of the Atlanta University Center in Georgia, calling themselves the Atlanta Committee on Appeal for Human Rights, paid for the following advertisement in the Atlanta *Constitution* of March 9, 1960.

We, the students of the six affiliated institutions forming the Atlanta University Center—Clark, Morehouse, Morris Brown, and Spelman Colleges, Atlanta University, and the Interdenominational Theological Center—have joined our hearts, minds, and bodies in the cause of gaining those rights which are inherently ours as members of the human race and as citizens of these United States.

We want to state clearly and unequivocally that we cannot tolerate, in a nation professing democracy and among people professing Christianity, the discriminatory conditions under which the Negro is living today in Atlanta, Georgia—supposedly one of the most progressive cities in the South.

Among the inequalities and injustices in Atlanta and in Georgia against which we protest, the following are outstanding examples:

1. Education: In the Public School System, facilities for Negroes and whites are separate and unequal. Double sessions continue in about half of the Negro Public Schools, and many Negro children travel ten miles a day in order to reach a school that will admit them.
2. Jobs: Negroes are denied employment in the majority of city, state, and federal governmental jobs, except in the most menial capacities.
3. Housing: While Negroes constitute 32% of the population of Atlanta, they are forced to live within 16% of the area of the city.
4. Voting: Contrary to statements made in Congress recently by several Southern Senators, we know that in many counties in Georgia and other Southern states, Negro college graduates are declared unqualified to vote and are not permitted to register.
5. Hospitals: Compared with facilities for other people in Atlanta and Georgia, those for Negroes are unequal and totally inadequate.
6. Movies, Concerts, Restaurants: Negroes are barred from most downtown movies and segregated in the rest. Negroes must even sit in a segregated section of the Municipal Auditorium. If a Negro is hungry, his hunger must wait until he comes to a "colored" restaurant, and even his thirst must await its quenching at a "colored" water fountain.
7. Law Enforcement: There are grave inequalities in the area of law enforcement. Too often, Negroes are maltreated by officers of the law. An insufficient number of Negroes is employed in the law-enforcing agencies. They are seldom, if ever promoted. Of 830 policemen in Atlanta only thirty-five are Negroes.

7

THE CRY FOR FREEDOM

by Thurgood Marshall

At a mass meeting in Charlotte, North Carolina, on March 20, 1960, Thurgood Marshall—at this time director-counsel of the Legal Defense and Educational Fund of the NAACP—spoke as follows:

While the cry is against apartheid in South Africa, is for one man, one vote in Kenya, is for the right to register and vote in Mississippi and Alabama, the right to nondiscriminatory service in stores throughout the South, the right to nonsegregated education in the South or the ending of subtle segregation in the North, the cry for freedom is increasing in tempo throughout the world. Thus, the sit-in strikes of young people throughout the South is the latest evidence of this wave. We believe that those of us in the NAACP and other organizations who have fought so long in this fight must continue the type of leadership that brings about the lawful and orderly step-by-step march toward freedom from racial discrimination wherever it exists.

One writer, in commenting upon the situation in sit-in strikes says: "It seems rather ridiculous when you can buy a nice hat for eight or ten dollars in the store and yet you can't satisfy, without discrimination, the very fundamental need of your own hunger with a cup of coffee and a sandwich."

Thus young people, in the true tradition of our democratic principles, are fighting the matter for all of us and they are doing it in a most effective way. Protest—the right of protest—is basic to a democratic form of government. The right of petition; the right of assembly; the right of freedom of speech are so basic to our government that they are enshrined in the very first amendment to the Constitution. And the 14th Amendment says that no state shall throttle these freedoms.

These young people are just simply sick and tired of waiting patiently without protest for the rights they know to be theirs. Consequently, they settled upon the right of peaceful protests—and what is wrong with that?

As a result of these peaceful protests, the whole force of state government has been arrayed behind the private store owner to prevent peaceful protests. The students have been arrested on every possible type of criminal charge.

In some areas they are charged with trespassing because they refuse to leave the establishment; because they came on the property when told not to do so, or are charged with having threatened someone. Secondly, many of them have been charged with violation of fire department regulations such as blocking of aisles of a store despite the fact that no one has ever been charged with the same crime before;

Thirdly, some are charged with assault for refusing to move or allegedly brushing against someone;

Fourth, some are charged with failure to obtain licenses for public meetings or parades; and

Fifth, authorities have dragged out the old disorderly conduct procedure.

There will be many others thought up by lawyers well-paid and well trained in the law. And here we have once again the example of the full strength of a state government, paid for by white and black taxes, arrayed against young people solely because of their race and color.

In Orangeburg, South Carolina, 450 students were arrested walking down the street before they had even started to picket or to parade and everyone is to be tried in blocs of fifteen per day. This is obviously done in the hope of wearing our legal staff and our pocketbook down. We have news for them. We are prepared to stay in court after court, in city after city, and in state after state as long as they can stay there.

On Thursday, March 17, in Little Rock, Arkansas, fifteen students peacefully protesting were seized and fined $250, and sentenced to thirty days in jail.

Each of these instances can be cited in state after state wherever the protests have been made. To all of this, we have but one reply, even one word and the word is SHAME.

Whenever you read about it—

Whenever you hear about it—

Whenever you hear it discussed—say SHAME—SHAME on those who under the guise of states' rights or state law seek to throttle young people lawfully protesting.

Say SHAME on the white people of the South, the good white people, the so-called moderates who sit idly by and allow young people to be persecuted solely because of their race or color. And when you hear a

Negro who has been adequately brainwashed say that this is too much to do just to get a hamburger or a frankfurter, to him say SHAME. For this that the young people are doing is for the best interest of all of us and indeed for the country itself.

We have just completed a lawyers conference in Washington attended by lawyers handling the sit-in cases from Delaware to the Gulf of Mexico. We have compared notes. We have shared our legal thoughts, our legal briefs and legal procedures. We are as a unit. We are going to work in the most cooperative fashion. We are going to give to these young people the best legal defense available to them. Negroes and other Americans who believe in freedom will provide the bail money for them. Once again we are called upon to use our private resources, our private strength, and our private abilities to save the good name of this country.

The Crisis, May 1960, pp. 287–89; published in part.

8

SIT-INS AND PICKETS

by Mazette Watts

A mass meeting in support of the sit-in movement was held on April 6, 1960, on the campus of the University of Chicago. Speakers included Bernard Lee, president of the Alabama State University Student Organization, and Mazette Watts, a student at the same university. The effort described in Watts's speech, reproduced below, resulted in the expulsion of Lee, Watts, and seven other students.

First of all, I would like to say thanks to these people for coming out, and I would like to say that I know you want to hear what actually happened in Montgomery so as near as possible I'll try to tell you exactly what happened. My school is a very small school, like most things in the South controlled by the white people there. Actually, the governor of the state is the President. The president of my institution has been the president for thirty-seven years. We have no student body or government of any form; we have no voice in the policy of the school. The kids in the South feel a close kinship to other colleges and small universities, especially the Negro ones, because we feel that their problems are similar. When we discovered that the kids in Greensboro had made a move, we felt that we were obligated to show our hand. So a few of us got together and decided we would try to organize a little student movement where we would have our sit-downs.

At first it wasn't very successful; the students didn't seem to like the idea. But along with Bernard we worked very diligently and finally we got at least thirty-five students and went to Reverend Abernathy, President of the Montgomery Improvement Association, who directed the boycott in Montgomery. He called an emergency meeting of the Executive Board of the MIA in which they endorsed us and gave us support.

Well, we knew at this time that if we moved, it would have to be fast because the administration has a way of breaking up anything they want to. They have their spies everywhere and so forth. So, under the direction of the MIA we decided that instead of hitting the Woolworth Stores it would be nice if we would hit the courthouse. It's a new million-dollar building, and they have luncheon facilities for whites only. They have no provisions for the colored people of Montgomery.

This was on the twenty-fourth of February so we decided that the time for the move would be on the twenty-fifth. We organized ourselves and met on a small hill; and at 7:00 P.M. we moved on the courthouse, catching them by complete surprise. They were sitting there, just leisurely having their time; we walked into *their* courtroom,—the lunch counter that is. Now their first reaction was somewhat of terror. The police department of Montgomery that is the county, is located in the courthouse, and we have a lot of police officers standing around. The first reaction of one of them was to jump up to get his gun, without thinking. We marched right in, and the lady who was in charge panicked and said, "Will you please leave; I don't want any trouble. I understand your problem, but this is my place— will you just leave?" So we walked right in and we sat around, and the persons that were sitting there panicked and you'd think that Al Capone had just walked in. All of them jumped up and ran out. So she pleaded and begged and we laughed in her face—orderly, that is.

They finally discovered it was useless to ask us to leave, so at this time the chief of police was called; he walked in and said, "Did you ask these damn niggers to leave?"

She said, "Yes, I begged them."

So he said, "Well, call the wagon."

By this time the crowd had gathered and they were peeking in as though we were animals or something. The whole courthouse was in an uproar. The law enforcement agencies finally arrived—the city's law enforcement agencies—and they were about to make the blunder we had intended them to make. They were going to arrest us. It just happened that one man with a little sense was there, the Assistant Attorney General of the State of Alabama, and he told them, "You can't arrest these students; they haven't violated any laws."

After about 30 minutes of planning, they finally decided that they'd close the place down and we'd all have to leave. So they cut off the gas and lights and everything, and we got up to leave. Then they began to smile, and they said, "We have them now." We just walked straight down the hall and lined up on one side, and we began to use the white people's washroom. Well, they were back in a state of horror then.

By this time there were a lot of people gathered and the state investigators had been notified. The Sheriff came down, and Bernard was out talking while we were standing against the wall, and the Sheriff came and drew his nightclub on Bernard, and I dragged Bernard over in the hall somewhere to keep him from getting hit. We stood there, lined up against the wall like convicts, for approximately an hour. And the state investigators came and asked questions and wanted names. We couldn't refuse to give our names so we lined up in orderly fashion afterwards and walked back to our campus. By the time we arrived at campus, the newspapers had it on the front page and the kids were rejoicing and saying, why didn't you tell us, (all those we had told), and by this time everybody was in a state of panic. Law enforcement agencies were there and so forth, and they had photographers. Before this protest started, we had a drive going on to get young Negroes to vote and one of the persons who went down made a mistake in his application—you can fail the examination to become a registered voter in the State of Alabama by not dotting an 'i' or crossing a 't'. Things that small will keep you from the ballot. And he made the mistake in that he said—you see there was a question that was asked: "Was this the first time you had attempted to register in the State of Alabama as a voter?"—and he said yes. And for this, the State of Alabama indicted him for perjury. His trial was to be held the day after the sitdowns. So we decided, all 2,000 of us, at a meeting that night, that it would be nice if all of us could try to get in the courtroom although it wasn't much larger than the room we're sitting in now.

So we went down, and again they were waiting for us, and one of the police officers said, "We don't dare let all of these damn niggers in here," but someone had a little sense and tried to let in as many of us as possible, while the others lined up against the wall. And, incidentally, all the Negroes that were there, whether they were guilty or innocent, they were fined that day. They fined more Negroes and gave more 200-days away that day than I've ever seen them give away before. And after the proceedings were over we got up to leave, and the judge said: "It may be good that you stayed; you may have learned something here."

So we walked out and we went back to the campus, at which time we tried to have a rally; but the state investigators were there and they were standing around with the photographers and so forth, and the President of our institution came up and told us we couldn't assemble on our campus; "You can't have a mass meeting here, and you can't have a rally," he said. We thanked him and finished our rally, then moved off the campus. So they warned us there were no more rallies to be held on the immediate campus. So we obtained a church, the First Baptist Church, about a mile from the campus. The following night, after the trials, the police commissioner of Montgomery and the Mayor called for violence on the part of the white people. They had a TV telecast in which they told the Negro people of the community that "the white people here just won't stand this and if you persist in trying to incite riots we'll let them manhandle you."

Well, this gave everybody who wanted to whoop up some Negroes a chance, so the following day we held a meeting. They had heard we were coming to town, and there were approximately 200 bat-carrying white men patrolling the streets of Montgomery waiting for us to come, while we were in church having our meeting. A lady came up to the church and she was crying and so forth and she said, "Please don't go to town; they're beating up people down there." And incidentally, I'm sure most of you saw the picture of the man who had the bat drawn back. The man had hit the lady with his bat and he has been identified. I've known him for several years; he was indicted by a Grand Jury for the bombing of Reverend Abernathy's house. There has been no arrest; they have made no attempt to arrest this fellow.

Well, after the meeting, the downtown area was in an uproar and we proceeded to go back to our campus. By this time the adult community had become quite disturbed by the actions taken by the commissioner and outsiders so they decided they would have a march on the capitol. Again the police commissioner called for violence. Approximately 400 people that live in the community and 200 students made the march, and when we got there we were greeted by a mob of 5,000 calling us names and everything. So we went in the church and held our meeting after which we proceeded to march to the capitol. When we walked out of the door, the fire department had arrived; 5,000 whites jeering and hollering came on at us. The fire department directed the hoses at the 600 Negroes on the steps and we tried to advance on the capitol, but we were pushed back by the mob and police; and the photographers that tried to take pictures, some of them were arrested and they were generally manhandled. The commissioner of our state, over the public address system, said he appreciated the interest of the good white citizens that were there. "We thank you for coming out but we think that we have the situation in hand." So, at this most of them left and we proceeded back to our campus. This was on Sunday.

On the following Monday the Governor of Alabama called for a meeting of the school board to be held on Wednesday. The Governor recommended that twenty students be put on probation and that the nine agitators be expelled. In order to make it seem like there was outside agitation they got the out-of-state kids. Actually there were only two out-of-state kids, Bernard and a fellow from Chicago. The others they had listed as being out-of-state were raised in Alabama. Their parents had simply moved away. So that day we received notice that we had been expelled. That was March 4. And we held a mass meeting at which 1,500 of 2,400 students decided that if we would be expelled, they would walk out of school.

The next day, right in the middle of the examinations, the kids decided to sit down, and the executive committee of the student group that we had organized met. We decided that it would be best not to make all the kids suffer for the expulsion that had taken place. So we decided to let them take final examinations, after which we would continue our protest. Well, the kids were reluctant about taking them, but we finally persuaded them; in return for that the Governor let us take our final examinations also. Incidentally, one of the students involved in the expulsions of the nine was a senior and it was his last exam. But he won't receive a degree from Alabama, even though he finished the required work there.

By this time the kids were really in an uproar. Two days after, we held a mass demonstration on the campus. At this time—I left this out—we were greeted downtown by cowboys and police, who had these horses with the carbines and so forth. We decided to have a demonstration on the campus because we knew it wasn't safe off the campus any more. The placard-carrying kids were greeted by the same deputized white men and cowboys with machine guns, riot guns, shot guns, everything you can name. I believe they had more weapons than the United States Government.

So the kids were just walking around orderly and the police arrived to arrest them. And the only smart move the police department ever made was that they took the placards; therefore, the kids weren't just able to pick up the placards and stand out as they were arrested. But the kids gathered around and said, "Will you take me, I would like to go to jail." One of the instructors stood out to tell them not to resist, and when she stood out she was jailed also. And there was a male instructor who did that too, and they jailed him. So they had, I think, three patrol wagons full. These students were booked on disorderly conduct and they were found guilty. The cases have been appealed—all thirty-five of them. By this time, all the people that went with us, they kind of opened their eyes to what was happening. Things had generally cooled off till last Friday.

Now the nine of us who had been expelled had been continuously harassed by the police department; the Ku Klux Klan had been to our homes and tried to scare us off; police would pick us up in a car and charge us with vagrancy and they would keep us in jail most of the day. But we had the cases in court and that was enough. Dr. Nessmith of MacMurray College brought some kids and they stayed with us; we made a place for them to stay for the night.

The next noon we had a luncheon near the campus at a colored restaurant and the word got out that white people and niggers were eating together over on the campus. By the time we were served, the police came, and they just stood around for a while. Now we were in a private dining room; the public accommodations were on the right and we were over on the left. The mayor and the commissioner of the city came out and walked into this luncheon and they looked around. You had every law enforcement agency in Alabama there because people were eating their lunch.

Finally they decided that this was out of hand so they said, "We'll arrest them, but we're going to segregate them in arresting them." First the white boys were arrested and then the Negro boys, then the colored girls and then the white girls. And they took us to jail with no charges at all. This was last Friday, and they also arrested Dr. Nessmith's two-year-old daughter. I think she was out on two dollar bail. One of the ladies in the community offered to keep the little girl for the time, but she was colored and they didn't want any integration there, so they took her to the Welfare Office.

We stayed in jail for about six hours and they began to interrogate us one by one, and finally we were bonded, but still no charges. So they set the trial for the next day. We still didn't know what we were charged with or what laws we had broken.

In court, the prosecutor stated that we were guilty of inciting a riot, and that the colored people who gathered outside were going to attack the Negroes and whites that were eating together. Now you know if you see twenty-five or thirty police cars, you would think that the Al Capone gang had reassembled or something, and naturally you would want to see what was happening. That was the reason why people assembled. So they said that the people were there to attack us.

They found every one of us guilty and they gave us segregated fines. The white kids were fined fifty dollars apiece and we were fined one hundred and fifty dollars. And after they had fined all of us, that was the only time we had integration: they put us all in one room. We came out one by one and received our lectures.

So, you could see that we had our hands full and I would like to tell you that I would like you to keep up your demonstrations. It gives us morale. We know that somebody's with us and it won't be long before the evil forces of the South will crumble.

New University Thought 1 (Spring 1960): 16–18. Appended to this essay was a table recording the sit-ins and picket demonstrations held in the South up to April 9, 1960. Since that table was prepared, the editors added that demonstrations had taken place in Baltimore; Lexington, Kentucky; Bluefield, West Virginia; and Jackson, Mississippi. The table identified four institutions in Alabama, two in Arkansas, three in Florida (plus counter sit-ins in five other cities), six in Georgia, two in Louisiana, twenty-seven in North Carolina (including three white institutions), ten in South Carolina (in which three white women joined), five in Tennessee, four in Texas (one of which had white participants), and eight in Virginia. In addition there were at least seventy-three nonsouthern colleges and universities in which such demonstrations occurred.

9

"TO RID AMERICA OF RACIAL DISCRIMINATION"

by Ella J. Baker

One of the seeds of the civil rights movement of the sixties was a conference, held in April 1960, in the founding days of SNCC. This student leadership conference was held at Shaw University in Raleigh, North Carolina. Ella J. Baker, who had graduated from Shaw in the 1920s and had worked with Harlem youth in the 1930s and with the SCLC after the Second World War, urged youth to create their own organization—SNCC. In the publication of the Southern Conference Educational Fund, she described that Raleigh conference and emphasized her belief in the need for group rather than individual leadership.

RALEIGH, N.C.—The Student Leadership Conference made it crystal clear that current sit-ins and other demonstrations are concerned with something much bigger than a hamburger or even a giant-sized Coke.

Whatever may be the difference in approach to their goal, the Negro and white students, North and South, are seeking to rid America of the scourge of racial segregation and discrimination—not only at lunch counters, but in every aspect of life.

In reports, casual conversations, discussion groups, and speeches, the sense and the spirit of the following statement that appeared in the initial newsletter of the students at Barber-Scotia College, Concord, N.C., were re-echoed time and again:

> We want the world to know that we no longer accept the inferior position
> of second-class citizenship. We are willing to go to jail, be ridiculed, spat
> upon, and even suffer physical violence to obtain First Class Citizenship.

By and large, this feeling that they have a destined date with freedom was not limited to a drive for personal freedom, or even freedom for the Negro in the South. Repeatedly it was emphasized that the movement was concerned with the moral implications of racial discrimination for the "whole world" and the "Human Race."

This universality of approach was linked with a perceptive recognition that "it is important to keep the movement democratic and to avoid struggles for personal leadership."

It was further evident that desire for supportive cooperation from adult leaders and the adult community was also tempered by apprehension that adults might try to "capture" the student movement. The students showed willingness to be met on the basis of equality, but were intolerant of anything that smacked of manipulation or domination.

This inclination toward *group-centered leadership*, rather than toward a *leader-centered group pattern of organization*, was refreshing indeed to those of the older group who bear the scars of the battle, the frustrations, and the disillusionment that come when the prophetic leader turns out to have heavy feet of clay.

However hopeful might be the signs in the direction of group-centeredness, the fact that many schools and communities, especially in the South, have not provided adequate experience for young Negroes to assume initiative and think and act independently accentuated the need for guarding the student movement against well-meaning, but nevertheless unhealthy, overprotectiveness.

Here is an opportunity for adult and youth to work together and provide genuine leadership—the development of the individual to his highest potential for the benefit of the group.

Many adults and youth characterized the Raleigh meeting as the greatest or most significant conference of our period.

Whether it lives up to this high evaluation or not will, in a large measure, be determined by the extent to which there is more effective training in and understanding of non-violent principles and practices, in group dynamics, and in the re-direction into creative channels of the normal frustrations and hostilities that result from second-class citizenship.

Southern Patriot, June 1960.

10

A NATION-WIDE STUDENT CONFERENCE

by Several Speakers

A National Student Conference on the Sit-In Movement was held in Washington, D.C., April 22–23, 1960. Allard Lowenstein, president of the U.S. National Student Association (USNSA), 1950–51, was an instrumental organizer; other key figures were Albert Rozier, editor of the *Register*, a student paper of North Carolina A & T College; Bernard Lee, president of the Student Movement at Alabama State College in Montgomery; James Lawson, then southern regional secretary of the Fellowship of Reconciliation in Nashville; a representative of the Ceylon University Students Federation and several white individuals from Duke University and elsewhere.

The mimeographed "General Information" document (in the editor's possession) included portions of speeches by Al Rozier summing up relevant events in Greensboro, North Carolina; by Bernard Lee; and by the Reverend Wyatt Walker, who had been pastor of a Baptist church in New York City and in Petersburg, Virginia, and later was secretary of the Southern Christian Leadership Conference.

[A]

AL ROZIER

On February 1, four freshmen at North Carolina Agricultural and Technical College held the first sit-down at a chain variety store in downtown Greensboro. They entered the store at 4:30, were refused service and sat there till the store closed at 5:30.

They returned the next day for a longer period and from that day on the counters were always filled.

When the four freshmen realized the potential of the movement, they went to senior student leaders for direction.

On Wednesday, the presidents of the four Greensboro colleges, North Carolina A&T, Greensboro College, University of North Carolina Womens College and Bennett, met with the store managers. Later in the week they called in the student leaders and asked that they call off the demonstrations. The students refused and went out to continue demonstrating.

By Saturday of that week the lunch counters of Woolworths and Kress were crowded with about 200 students. That day both stores closed when a bomb threat was received.

On Sunday the demonstrations were called off for two weeks and discussions were held. Students met with a city councilman who said the mayor was forming an advisory committee. The committee worked for three weeks and compiled 2,300 letters on the question, 72.8% of which were in favor of integration. The city did not take any action as a result of the letters however, because they felt the thing had become a national issue and change in just Greensboro would not be very effective.

The students returned to their picketing. They were now picketing at about twelve stores.

Just before Easter, two stores, the Elmstreet Pharmacy and a variety store, began serving Negroes.

The group now feels it is important to concentrate on the smaller local stores.

[B]

BERNARD LEE

In his speech, Bernard Lee summarized the events in Montgomery, Alabama.

Mr. Lee sees the sit-ins as a second major stride for freedom in Montgomery. When Montgomery students learned of the North Carolina action, they felt their hour for dynamic action had come; they felt a keen sense of responsibility to act.

On February 24, thirty students met in the home of Rev. Ralph Abernathy and decided to hold their first sit-in at the Montgomery County Court House Snack Bar.

The next day thirty-five young men entered the Snack Bar and ordered coffee. They were refused service, but remained in the snack bar until a police officer announced that the snack bar was closing.

The Governor ordered an investigation of the sit-in, and the following week nine students were expelled from Alabama State College as ringleaders.

The demonstrations spread to the adult community which planned a march on the capital. They were met, however, by 400 armed policemen and 5,000 white citizens.

Bernard Lee also brought a message from the students of Montgomery; excerpts follow: "We have taken up the struggle for freedom without counting the costs...we are wrestling with a spirit of wickedness in high places.... We recognize our situation and nothing will deter us from the path we have decided to follow.... We expect to be thrown in jail on trumped up charges, but we shall continue to protest and fight for our rights in the courts of the land and push for integration in the schools.... We have the moral force of the universe on our side and we shall not fail."

[C]

REV. WYATT T. WALKER

Nonviolence, said Walker, is basically a religious and moral concept, and it is against this background that the southern sit-in movement has snowballed.

The choice of the nonviolent movement was no accident for several reasons:

1. It is dedicated to love and compassion.
2. It embraces the idea that its alternative is far too costly and is an incorrect answer. Hatred and violence lead to self-destruction as well as the destruction of the enemy. In a violent struggle one side has to be the victor and this is not the aim of the movement; they want to teach people to live together.
3. Anyone can join a nonviolent movement and have a sense of belonging. It is not limited to strong healthy males.
4. It does something wholesome for the opposition; it does not seek to destroy him but to win him.

11

"THE BEAUTY OF THE MOVEMENT"

by A. Keith Guy

The author of this letter, a former president of the Fisk Student Government, was fined and briefly jailed for participating in a 1960 demonstration in Nashville, Tennessee. The letter, undated, was addressed to Lawrence Landry, one of the editors of *New University Thought*.

Dear Lawrence,

The basic reason for my participation in the movement is a denial of personal freedom. Often we speak of America as being "the bastion of freedom," but how hollow these words are when American citizens are being denied their freedom because of color and the desire of merchants to make money. Is money, or color, more important than freedom? Of course it is not! But if some do not make personal sacrifices for freedom, what is to become of the precept?

When one is faced with the threat of bodily harm, imprisonment, or intimidation, the decision is not an easy one to make. Particularly so, when you have seen others injured. It gives me confidence though to see the number of those who are willing to undergo the hardships for what they believe to be right. And the beauty of the movement is, that it is nonviolent and for an ideal. Just think, fighting a reality with an ideal.

I am convinced we will win in the end, and that freedom will prove to be more important than color or profits. And because of this conviction I will use every legal and nonviolent means available to an American to eradicate the denial of personal freedom.

With this purpose in mind, and with help from you, and others who think as you do, the end is inevitable. The question though, is how much longer will we have to wait?

If I am not in jail in June, I should graduate, but just in case, "sacrifice that movie for attorney's fees."

Your friend,
Keith

New University Thought 1 (Spring 1960): 27. See "The Young Negro Rebels," by Charlotte Devree, in *Harper's*, October 1961.

12

THE NEGRO REVOLT AGAINST THE 'NEGRO LEADERS'

by Louis E. Lomax

The author was among African-American pioneers in breaking into 'white' periodicals and television. He was born in Georgia and was educated largely in the North, doing graduate work at American University.

As Pastor Kelly Miller Smith walked to the lectern to begin his Sunday sermon, he knew his parishioners wanted and needed more than just another spiritual message. The congregation—most of them middle-class Americans, many of them university students and faculty members—sat before him waiting, tense: for Nashville, like some thirty-odd other

Southern college towns, on that first Sunday in March of this year, was taut with racial tension in the wake of widespread student demonstrations against lunch-counter discrimination in department stores.

Among the worshipers in Pastor Smith's First Baptist Church were some of the eighty-five students from Fisk and from Tennessee Agricultural and Industrial University who had been arrested and charged with conspiracy to obstruct trade and commerce because they staged protests in several of Nashville's segregated eating places. Just two days before, Nashville police had invaded Mr. Smith's church—which also served as headquarters for the demonstrators—and arrested one of their number, James Lawson, Jr., a Negro senior theological student at predominantly white Vanderbilt University, on the same charge.

The adult members of the congregation were deeply troubled. They knew, as did Negroes all over America, that the spontaneous and uncorrelated student demonstrations were more than an attack on segregation: they were proof that the Negro leadership class, epitomized by the National Association for the Advancement of Colored People, was no longer the prime mover of the Negro's social revolt.

Each protest had a character of its own, tailored to the local goals it sought to achieve. Neither the advice nor the aid of recognized Negro leaders was sought until after the students had set the policy, engaged the enemy, and joined the issue. Despite the probability that the demonstrations would be met with violence, the students took direct action, something Negro leadership organizations consistently counseled against. By forcing these organizations not only to come to their aid but to do their bidding, these militant young people completely reversed the power flow within the Negro community.

"Father forgive them," Mr. Smith began, *"for they know not what they do."* And for the next half-hour, the Crucifixion of Christ carried this meaning as he spoke:

"The students sat at the lunch counters alone to eat and, when refused service, to wait and pray. And as they sat there on that southern Mount of Olives, the Roman soldiers, garbed in the uniforms of Nashville policemen and wielding night sticks, came and led the praying children away. As they walked down the streets, through a red light, and toward Golgotha, the segregationist mob shouted jeers, pushed and shoved them, and spat in their faces, but the suffering students never said a mumbling word. Once the martyr mounts the Cross, wears the crown of thorns, and feels the pierce of the sword in his side there is no turning back.

"And there is no turning back for those who follow in the martyr's steps," the minister continuted. *"All we can do is to hold fast to what we believe, suffer what we must suffer if we would win, and as we face our enemy let us say, 'Father, forgive them, for they know not what they do'."*

The New Gospel

This new gospel of the American Negro is rooted in the theology of desegregation; its major prophets are Christ, Thoreau, Gandhi, and Martin Luther King. But its missionaries are several thousand Negro students who—like Paul, Silas, and Peter of the early Christian era—are braving incalculable dangers and employing new techniques to spread the faith. It is not an easy faith, for it names the conservative Negro leadership class as sinners along with the segregationists. Yet, this new gospel is being preached by clergymen and laymen alike wherever Negroes gather. . . .

Negro leaders spent seventy-five years remodeling that structure, trying to make it more livable by removing such horrible reminders of the past as lynchings, denial of the ballot, restrictive covenants in housing, and inequalities of public facilities. Only after the intractable Deep South emasculated every move toward equalization did the Negro leadership class sue for school integration. Even then it was a segmented, room-by-room assault. But these student demonstrators have—in effect—put dynamite at the cornerstone of segregation and lit the fuse.

This revolt, swelling under ground for the past two decades, means the end of the traditional Negro leadership class. Local organization leaders were caught flat-footed by the demonstrations; the parade had moved off without them. In a series of almost frantic moves this spring, they lunged to the front and shouted loud, but they were scarcely more than a cheering section—leaders no more. The students completed their bold maneuver by jabbing the leadership class in its most vulnerable spot: the southern schoolteachers. Many of these, as the Norfolk *Journal and Guide* put it, "were ordered to stop the demonstrations or else!" Most Negro school administrators kept silent on the matter; a few of them, largely heads of private colleges, supported the students; while others—notably Dr. H. C. Trenholm of Alabama State College—were forced by white politicians to take action against the students. As a Negro reporter from New York, I talked with scores of southern Negro leaders and they admitted without exception that the local leadership class was in dire difficulty.

National leadership organizations fared only slightly better. The

NAACP rushed its national youth secretary, Herbert Wright, into the area to conduct "strategy and procedure" conferences for the students. Lester Granger, the executive director of the Urban League, issued a statement saying the demonstrations were "therapeutic for those engaged in them and a solemn warning to the nation at large"—this despite the fact that, in Mr. Granger's words, "the League does not function in the area of public demonstrations."

The NAACP does not always move with such swiftness when local groups, some of them laced with NAACP members, set off independent attacks on racial abuse. The Montgomery bus boycott is a classic case in point. But the impact of these new student demonstrations was such that the NAACP was forced to support the students or face a revolt by its southern rank and file. This does not impeach the NAACP's motives for entering the demonstrations—its motives and work have the greatest merit—but it does illustrate the reversal of the power flow within the Negro community.

"The demonstrations are not something we planned," NAACP public-relations director Henry Moon told me. "The students moved on their own. We didn't know what was going on until it happened. However, it should be kept in mind that many of the students involved are NAACP people."...

Many of us felt that the NAACP was too committed to legalism; not committed enough to direct action by local people. There was an endless parade in and out of the NAACP's national office of Negroes who felt that the desegregation fight should take on a broader base. But until the spring of 1958, four years after the school desegregation decision, not a single desegregation-minded Negro engaged in serious open debate with the NAACP. Even then, unfortunately, the debate came in terms of personalities rather than policy.

The decade of the fifties was an incredible era for the Negro leadership class, particularly for the NAACP. That the NAACP hung together at all is a monument to its vitality as well as to the effectiveness of its muffling curtain.

First off, by suing for school integration the NAACP immobilized the majority of the Negro leadership class. The entire structure of the Negro community was designed to function in a separate but equal America. Negro newspapers, in addition to being protest organs, were the social Bibles of Negro society. They had their "400" and a list of the year's best-dressed women. The Negro church was ofttimes more Negro than church.

Negro businesses depended upon the concept of a Negro community for survival (as late as 1958 Negro businessmen in Detroit criticized the NAACP for holding its annual convention at a "white" downtown hotel, which meant that the local Negro merchants failed to benefit from the gathering). The dilemma of the Negro teacher was even more agonizing. If Negroes really meant business about integration, then it was obvious that the Negro leadership class could remain leaders only by working to put themselves out of business.

The Bitterness Under the Glamour

To this one must add the internal problems of the NAACP itself. In 1948–49, Walter White, then the executive secretary of the NAACP, divorced his Negro wife and married Poppy Cannon, a white woman. This brought on an organizational crisis that might have resulted in ruin if the board of directors had not given Mr. White a year's leave of absence. Nobody expected Mr. White to return to his post and Roy Wilkins, who had been Mr. White's loyal assistant for almost twenty years, turned in an excellent performance as acting executive secretary. But the following spring Mr. White did return. Another organizational crisis was averted by making him secretary of external affairs and Mr. Wilkins secretary of internal affairs. Things remained that way until 1955, when Mr. White died. Nor was that the only separatist movement going on within the NAACP. Since 1939 the entity known to the public as the NAACP has actually been two organizations: the NAACP, headed by the late Walter White and now by Roy Wilkins, and the NAACP Legal Defense and Education Fund, headed by Thurgood Marshall.

The initial reason for the separation was to provide tax relief for contributors to the Legal Defense and Education Fund, which functions solely as a legal redress organization. The NAACP, on the other hand, maintains a lobby in Washington and so its contributors are not entitled to tax exemptions. For fifteen years, however, the two organizations maintained quarters in the same building and shared an interlocking directorate. In 1952 the Legal Defense and Education Fund moved to separate quarters and in 1955 the interlocking directorate was ended. The tax matter aside, the cleavage came about as a result of deep internal troubling, the details of which are still in the domain of "no comment." In the midst of all this, Mrs. Franklin D. Roosevelt left the NAACP board for reasons that have never been fully disclosed...

It was the tense drama of school integration that provided the bailing wire for a show of unity.

I was there and it was a moving and unforgettable experience to see Negro students at Clinton, Sturgis, Clay, and Little Rock dodge bricks as they raced to and from school under armed guard. It was a magnificent hour for these fortuitously elite youngsters, many of whom became international heroes. But few of us lost sight of the Negro masses in these cities. They were still called "Jim," "Mary," "Aunt Harriet," and "Uncle Job"; they had to buy clothes they were not allowed to try on; their homes were searched by police without warrants; their heads were bloodied, their jobs threatened if they dared protest. They darted in and out of drug and department stores where they dared not sit down. They were denied free access to the polls, and if they received a just day in court it was usually when all parties concerned were Negroes.

Despite the march of well-scrubbed, carefully selected Negro students into previously all-white schools, it was crystal clear that the fundamental question of the Negro's dignity as an individual had not been resolved. The glory was the NAACP's and nobody begrudged it. Yet, there was a widespread doubt that a nationally directed battle of attrition that took so long and cost so much to bring so little to so few would ever get to the heart of the issue.

There were many local heroes during the decade of the fifties: they all had a brief hour, were clasped to the breasts of national leadership organizations, but when their public-relations and fund-raising value slipped they fell into disuse.

Mrs. Daisy Bates, president of the Arkansas State NAACP and the undisputed moving spirit behind the integration of Little Rock's Central High School, affords an example of life behind the monolithic curtain.

The Spingarn Medal of 1958, voted annually by the NAACP to the person or persons who have contributed most to racial advancement during the previous year, was awarded to the Little Rock Nine. When the students received notice of the award and realized that it did not include Mrs. Bates—whose home had been bombed, her business destroyed— they rejected the citation. The powers-that-be at Twenty West Fortieth Street reversed themselves and Mrs. Bates was included in the award, which she and the students accepted with full smiles, amid thunderous ovations. The Negro press reported the Bates case in great detail and interpreted the incident as overt evidence of the covert pressure the NAACP had been exerting on local Negro leaders for some time.

Dr. King and Mr. Wilkins

The curtain had begun to lift; it had achieved a great good, for it had produced a façade of unity; yet it had cloaked some terrible wrongs, including the smothering of home-grown, local Negro leaders who, even then, sensed the restlessness of the masses. The Reverend Dr. Martin Luther King, Jr., was the lone successful exception, and even he came into international prominence mainly because the NAACP refused to help the Montgomery bus boycotters when they at first demanded something less than full integration.

Acting on pleas from Negroes in other southern communities, Dr. King organized the Southern Christian Leadership Council (the organization has undergone several name changes but this is the current one) to instigate nonviolent protests in southern cities. The NAACP has a most active program all through the South and a clash between the two organizations—that is to say, Dr. King and Mr. Wilkins—seemed inevitable. To end rumors of a power struggle between them, Dr. King flew to New York and made a public show of purchasing life memberships in the NAACP for himself and his Montgomery Improvement Association. Dr. King and Mr. Wilkins then embarked on a series of infrequent private talks that may go down in history as the Negro leadership class's great and final hour.

The King-Wilkins talks of 1957–58 undoubtedly covered the issue of just who would do what and where, but central in the discussion was the common knowledge that many NAACP members were disenchanted with Wilkins' leadership. The two men came out from the talks as one, each co-sponsoring the activities of the other's organization.

Dr. King and Mr. Wilkins joined also with A. Philip Randolph to sponsor the highly successful Washington Prayer Pilgrimage of 1957, during which Dr. King emerged, to quote editor James Hicks of the *Amsterdam News*, "as the number-one Negro leader." But the following year King and Wilkins ignored the sentiments of some five hundred Negro spokesmen, representing three hundred leadership organizations, at the Summit Meeting of Negro Leadership and give their reluctant endorsement to the Senate's watered-down civil-rights proposal. The Negro press reacted with shock.

The criticism was even worse when, a few months later, King, Wilkins, and Randolph met with President Eisenhower to explain why Negroes were displeased with the first civil-rights bill to be passed in eighty-three years. The *Afro-American*'s Louis Lautier wrote: "Ike charmed the Negro leaders and neither of them uttered a word of criticism."

Little Rock kept the NAACP in the foreground, while a near-fatal stiletto wound at the hands of a crazed Harlem woman—and internal difficulties with his own Montgomery Association—rendered Dr. King almost inactive for some eighteen months. But this year, Dr. King moved to Atlanta and began to give the lion's share of his time to the Southern Christian Leadership Council. Mr. Wilkins was on hand and the NAACP appeared as co-sponsor when the Council launched a South-wide voting drive on behalf of the Negro masses.

In one sense it was 1958 all over again. Congress was locked in a civil-rights debate that we all knew would culminate in some kind of legislation. Both Dr. King and Mr. Wilkins were on hand backstage as liberal Congressmen planned their moves. But in another, perhaps more significant, sense the early months of this year were unlike 1958. Negroes, particularly the youth, were restless; they were tired of compromises, piecemeal legislation, and token integration which, as Martin Luther King phrased it, "is a new form of discrimination covered up with certain niceties and complexities." A small but growing segment of the Negro population had joined a Muslim faith that preaches the superiority of the black man and the imminent destruction of the white man. Then there is the matter of Africa: hardly a week passes that that awakening giant's cries for "Free DOOM" don't ring out over the radio and television into the ears of American Negroes—ashamed, as they most certainly are, that they are still oppressed. The law, particularly in the South, was against them; but for the militant young people this was the time for all good Negroes to be in jail.

Meanwhile the Negro leadership class—itself often guilty of rank, class, and color discrimination—was continuing to operate under a concept that begged the question of the dignity of the Negro individual. The literature of Negro progress is littered with such terms as "the talented tenth," "the exceptional Negro," "the new Negro," "the break-through Negro," and in recent years "the accepted" and "the assimilated Negro." Sharing the outlook of the white liberals who finance them, and sincerely so, Negro leadership organizations have focused their attention, by and large, on matters that are of interest to the talented Negro rather than the Negro masses. By so doing the Negro leadership class ignored the basic problem of human dignity in favor of themselves and their white peers—a distinction which the segregationists refused to accept. Thus an impassable void has separated the leaders of both sides for the past decade; and the ordinary Negro has been in the no man's land between.

The lunch-counter demonstrations moved to the center of the void, and menaced both principals: the recalcitrant South, by striking closer to the heart of segregation than any other widespread local movements have ever struck before; the Negro leadership class by exposing its impotence.

The Negro leadership class, still torn by jealousy, dissension, and power struggles, rushed to the aid of the students and their mass supporters, and attempted to make complete recovery by "correlating" and "co-ordinating" the movements. But as one southern NAACP branch president said to me, "how can I correlate something when I don't know where and when it's going to happen?" . . .

The Genius Behind It

The genius of the demonstrations lies in their spirituality; in their ability to enlist every Negro, from the laborer to the leader, and inspire him to seek suffering as a badge of honor. By employing such valid symbols as singing, praying, reading Gandhi, quoting Thoreau, remembering Martin Luther King, preaching Christ, but most of all by suffering themselves—being hit by baseball bats, kicked, and sent to jail—the students set off an old-fashioned revival that has made integration an article of faith with the Negro masses who, like other masses, are apathetic toward voting and education.

Now the cook, the maid, the butler, and the chauffeur are on fire with the new faith. For the first time since slavery the South is facing a mass revolt against segregation. There is no total explanation for what has happened. All I know is that as I talked with the participants I realized that people were weary of the very fact of segregation. They were no longer content "to let the NAACP do it"; they wanted to get into the fight and they chose the market place, the great center of American egalitarianism, not because it had any overwhelming significance for them but because it was there—accessible and segregated. Tomorrow—and they all believe there will be a tomorrow—their target will be something else.

Few of the masses who have come to the support of these students realize that in attacking segregation under the banner of idealism they are fighting a battle they refused for five years to enter in the name of legalism. But there is a twinkle in the southern Negro's eye. One gets the feeling that he is proud, now that he has come to full stature and has struck out with one blow against both segregation and the stifling control of Negro leaders.

In all truth, the Negro masses have never been flattered by the presence of these leaders, many of whom—justifiably or not—they suspected were Judas goats. The Negro masses will name leaders and will give them power and responsibility. But there will never again be another class of white-oriented leaders such as the one that has prevailed since 1900.

What's Left?

For the Negro masses this is the laying down of a heavy burden. As the deep South is slowly learning, it faces a race of Negro *individuals*—any of whom, acting out of deep religious faith, may at any moment choose the most available evidence of segregation and stage a protest. And when he does the entire Negro community will close ranks about him.

If Negro leadership organizations accept this verdict of change gracefully they can find a continuing usefulness as a reservoir of trained personnel to aid the local Negro in pressure techniques and legal battles. Indeed, within four weeks after the lunch-counter demonstrations began, just such a pattern was established. I have investigated the mechanics of the demonstrations in twenty-six cities and in each instance I found that the students and their local supporters moved first on their own; CORE came in by invitation and provided classes in techniques of nonviolence; and the NAACP provided lawyers and bondsmen for those who were arrested. If Negro leadership organizations don't accept this state of affairs, they will be replaced, as they were in Montgomery.

Thurgood Marshall and the NAACP Legal Defense and Education Fund have already set an excellent pattern which other leadership organizations will do well to study. As a symbol, Mr. Marshall inspires local citizens to act; when they do act, and at their request, Marshall brings the skill of his organization to their defense. Thurgood Marshall's role as the inspiring servant of the masses accounts for much of what has been accomplished to date in and for the United States—including his appearance in London as counsel to the Kenya natives.

Negro leadership organizations know what the revolt means and are about reconciled to being servants rather than catalysts—at least I think so. I cannot say the same for the Negro leadership class as a whole. My month-long investigation unearthed a good deal of foot-dragging by moneyed Negroes in high places. They are not too pleased to see young Negro students sit down at the conference table with Southern white city officials. Some Negro college presidents are set to execute strange maneuvers. I would not be surprised, for example, if some of the student demonstrators who are studying under grants from foundations suddenly find their scholarships have been canceled on recommendation from their college presidents...for "poor scholarship." But nobody noticed their scholarship until they sat down at a previously all-white lunch counter...

Harper's, June 1960, pp. 41–48; published in part.

13

ALONG THE NAACP BATTLEFRONT

by the editors of The Crisis

Under the above title, the organ of the N.A.A.C.P. began its coverage of the sit-in movement and detailed supporting actions in the North sponsored by the organization. At a meeting of the board of directors, held on March 14, it was agreed "to support fully the protest demonstrations." Furthermore, "all organized units of the NAACP are advised that a racial self-defense policy on an expanded scale is in effect as of this date." In reporting picketing of the Kress and Woolworth stores on New York's Fifth Avenue by fifty staff members of the national office, the *Crisis* said this was done "to dramatize the NAACP's newly-expanded racial self-defense policy." The announcement of this significant shift and an account of supporting actions in dozens of cities appear below:

F. W. Woolworth, S. S. Kresge, S. H. Kress, and W. T. Grant stores publicly announced on March 15, 1960, that they would continue their policy of refusing to serve Negro customers at lunch counters in their stores in the southern states.

On March 15, the police forces of southern states arrested more than 500 Negro students who were protesting the lunch-counter policies of the chain stores.

Orangeburg, S.C., police used tear gas and fire hose on Negro students as the young people were walking peacefully along the streets *before* they had reached the retail business district.

Students numbering 350 were arrested in Orangeburg and held in a stockade. Others were arrested in Rock Hill and Columbia, S.C.

In Atlanta, Ga., 77 students protesting the lunch counter policies of the chain variety stores were arrested by police.

Gov. Ernest F. Hollings, Jr., of South Carolina, has stated that these protests against lunch counter policies will be crushed even though technically no law is being violated. Gov. S. Ernest Vandiver of Georgia has echoed the policy of Gov. Hollings.

Gov. John Patterson of Alabama is the original "get tough" southern governor. Protesting Negro students have been expelled from Alabama State College in Montgomery, the capital, and the chief of police has urged the governor to close down the college.

It is apparent that the full power of southern state governments, including special laws rushed through the legislatures, as well as state, local, and county police forces, is being used to support chain variety stores in their anti-Negro lunch counter policies, and that at the very height of this persecution the federal government, through the Congress of the United States, is steadfastly refusing to legislate adequate relief.

Thus, in their campaign for equality and human dignity, Negro Americans are forced to fall back upon their own resources, spiritual, economic, and political.

Therefore, under the provocations of March 15, cited above, and in accordance with the clearly expressed consensus of the NAACP Board of Directors at its meeting March 14 to support fully the protest demonstrations aimed at the humiliating policy of chain variety stores and to resist persecution connected therewith, all organized units of the NAACP are advised that a racial self-defense policy on an expanded scale is in effect as of the date of this issue of *The Crisis.*

NAACP Officers Picket Variety Stores

Led by 82-year-old president Arthur B. Spingarn and executive secretary Roy Wilkins, the national office staff of the Association picketed the S. H. Kress and the F. W. Woolworth variety stores on Fifth Avenue at 39th Street on March 30.

Fifty staff members braved drizzle and rain to dramatize the NAACP's newly expanded racial self-defense policy to New Yorkers.

This policy of "withholding patronage from all units of chain and variety stores in all sections of the country" which refuse lunch counter service to southern Negroes was announced by Mr. Wilkins on March 16.

Handbills distributed on the two picket lines cited the dual role of the marchers as NAACP staff members and American citizens "who believe in equal justice for all and who seek to preserve the good name of America as leader of the Free World."

National office staff members listed the following reasons for their action: "To demonstrate our full support of the southern Negro student protest against Jim Crowism in the South; and

"To focus public attention on the discriminatory policy of the chain in which this store is a link. And to rally support of all elements of the community in behalf of the gallant stand of southern youth for freedom."

Placards proclaimed the Association's support of the student demonstrations, branded segregation as immoral, and asked "why spend our money with chains whose southern stores refuse to serve Negroes at lunch counters?"

Responding to a memorandum from executive secretary Roy Wilkins calling for nationwide action in support of the southern students' "sit-in demonstrations" at lunch counters in the South, scores of local units of the Association have initiated picketing of Woolworth, Kress, Kresge and Grant variety stores in their respective communities.

NAACP-sponsored picket lines have been formed in front of these stores in cities across the nation from Boston to San Francisco. Already some branches are making plans for a sustained campaign of picketing. San Francisco and New Haven have plans for continuing their demonstrations.

In Baltimore, ministers, inspired by the church committee of the Baltimore NAACP branch, picketed the variety stores on April 9, the Saturday before Palm Sunday. This demonstration, according to Dr. Lillie M. Jackson, president of the branch "helped launch full-scale community support for the NAACP-sponsored racial self-defense program to withhold retail trade from stores that discriminate on a local basis and through their southern outlets."

Among cities, not previously announced, in which the NAACP has instituted picketing are Kansas City, Wichita, Topeka, Hutchinson, Ft. Scott, Wellington and Salina, Kansas; Washington, Omaha, Nebraska; Akron, Youngstown, Cleveland and Cincinnati, Ohio; St. Paul and Minneapolis, Minnesota; Chicago; Seattle, Washington; Portland, Oregon; St. Louis and Kansas City, Missouri.

Northern Colleges Support "Sit-ins"

In a variety of swiftly organized and inventive ways, great numbers of northern college students have indicated overwhelming support of the South's Negro student demonstrators.

Meanwhile, a number of NAACP college-chapter leaders in the South, who have spearheaded the drive against segregated facilities, took leave from front-line activities to speak in distant cities on behalf of their cause.

They addressed NAACP-sponsored rallies in Washington, New York, Columbus, Detroit, San Francisco, and Hartford, Connecticut, as fellow students in many of the North's foremost institutions marched, prayed, staged sympathy "sit-ins," picketed, and collected student defense funds.

At Oberlin College in Ohio students collected over $2,000 for defense of the Nashville students. On far-north campuses such as Wheaton College at Norton, Massachusetts, students trooped through nearby towns collecting student aid funds.

In Saratoga Springs, New York, about twenty Skidmore College faculty members joined two hundred college girls in a demonstration against lunch counter discrimination in the South.

Even medical students set aside their books and took up protest placards.

At New Haven, thirty-five Yale medical students, operating in four shifts, picketed three midtown chain stores. Meantime, Yale divinity students and faculty announced a "silent march" around the city's main square.

NAACP youth secretary Herbert Wright, who has coordinated many of the student activities in the South, said: "The increased activity by college students has brought new NAACP memberships and requests for formation of new college chapters in such schools as Vassar, Bennington, and Brandeis University."

While Vassar, at Poughkeepsie, New York, has no formal chapter, its student body led by a Negro undergraduate, Miss Marion Gray, staged widely publicized demonstrations at variety stores in that city. As if synchronized to act at the same time, college girls at Bennington and Smith Colleges launched similar protests.

In New York, three hundred NAACP student leaders from New York University, Columbia University, and the City College of New York paraded in front of a midtown Woolworth's store.

"Northern students must get involved," said Peter Steinberg, editor of the *City College Observation Post*, "They are neglecting their duty as students and citizens if they don't."

Meanwhile, in Washington, NAACP college chapters at Howard, Catholic, and American universities held a mass civil-rights rally in the capitol city's Lafayette Square on Saturday, March 26.

Student protest groups have been addressed by NAACP labor secretary Herbert Hill and NAACP program director James Farmer. Mr. Hill addressed students at Vassar College and met with students at the University of Connecticut on March 31. Mr. Farmer addressed a rally in San Francisco on April 1 when that city's NAACP branch also heard young Thomas Gaither, NAACP college chapter president, at Claflin College in Orangeburg, South Carolina.

On Sunday, March 21, Lloyd Williams, head of the NAACP South Carolina state youth conference and coordinator of student "sit-in demonstrations," addressed five hundred delegates at the New York State Christian Conference representing thirty-seven New York colleges.

Withholding Policy Catching On

There was considerable evidence in March that consumers in many cities are beginning to withhold patronage from chain-variety stores with units in the South that discriminate against Negro customers at lunch-counters.

The "withholding policy" was announced by NAACP executive secretary Roy Wilkins in a directive to all NAACP branches on March 16.

Up to this point NAACP units were only asked to support student demonstrators by sending wires to the store heads, picketing, and handing out literature.

"Almost every branch without exception has conducted meetings, launched picketing campaigns, and sent wires," Gloster B. Current, director of branches, said today.

The NAACP New England Regional Conference made Saturday, March 26, "New England NAACP Picket Day."

Mrs. Mary Johnson Lowe, president of the Bronx branch NAACP, reported the successful picketing of a Woolworth store in the Bronx community:

"During the four-and-one-half hours of picketing, the store was practically empty and we are pleased to report that we were greatly encouraged by the people on the street who displayed complete sympathy with our efforts and appreciated the public pronouncement of the fight of the Negro for equality in the North as well as the South."

Similar responses have come from such diverse cities, with NAACP branches, as Denver, Colorado; Danbury, Connecticut; Knoxville, Tennessee; and Dowagiac, Michigan.

In Salt Lake City, Utah, the membership took their message to the air waves, announced formation of picket lines, and urged listeners to write to the stores' home offices. Picketers gave out 2,500 leaflets in one day.

"I don't know when there has been such enthusiasm on the part of the branches for a specific cause," Mr. Current added.

The decision to urge withholding of patronage was made after F. W. Woolworth, S. S. Kresge, S. H. Kress, and W. T. Grant publicly announced on March 15 their intention to continue their policy of refusing to serve Negroes except on a segregated basis.

Mr. Current observed that it was "still too early to fully evaluate the effectiveness of the withholding patronage phase."

Crisis. July 1960, pp. 313–19. A detailed first hand account of the "sit-down" movement was written by Shirley Graham, "A Cup of Coffee, Please," in *Political Affairs*, June 1960, pp. 23–36.

14

A PLEA FOR STRAIGHT TALK
BETWEEN THE RACES

by Benjamin E. Mays

Dr. Mays held important positions in education and government. At the time of his presidency of Morehouse College in Atlanta, he published an essay in a leading magazine taking an advanced—and overly optimistic—position. Here he is in error when he writes that as of the 1940s "no Negro dared to advocate its [segregation's] abolition publicly"; still, his unequivocal demand for an end to Jim Crow and his optimism that the 1960s would see that achieved, demonstrate a widespread feeling as that decade began.

Many well-meaning intelligent people have argued since the May 17, 1954, decision of the United States Supreme Court outlawing segregation in public schools that communication between the races has broken down. They contend that, as a result, the racial situation in the South has grown worse. The plain truth is that, up to a few years ago, Negroes and white people in the South never had honest communication.

Honest communication is built on truth and integrity and upon respect of the one for the other. It is true that, for decades upon decades, Negroes and white people have talked to each other. But it was conversation between a "superior" and an "inferior," a "man" and a "boy," and conversation between "master" and "servant." In this relationship the truth could seldom, if ever, emerge.

For nearly a century the South made itself believe that Negroes and white people were really communicating. So convinced of this were the white southerners that they almost made the nation believe that they, and only they, knew the mind of the southern Negro. They were sure that the Negro was satisfied with segregation and with his subordinate role in American life. If only the Communists, the Yankees, and the NAACP would leave the Negro alone, they said, he would live happily forever within the confines of legal segregation. All the Negro wanted was equality within the segregation pattern.

The fallacy in this argument lies in the fact that it was based on falsehood from the beginning. White people got their information from two main sources: one source was their cooks, maids, and chauffeurs. These servants wanted to hold their jobs, and so they told their white employers what they wanted to hear—the Negro is happy with segregation. Most of the white people of the South—and the North, too, for that matter—have never known the cultured and trained Negro. The white South's other source of information was equally deceptive. Many Negro leaders led white southerners to believe that if the impossible doctrine of separate but equal could be attained—separate schools, but equal; separate jobs, but equal; separate hospitals and recreational facilities, but equal; separate transportation and separate eating establishments, but all equal—Negroes would be satisfied. Many of these Negro leaders courted the favor of the whites either because they were economically dependent upon them or feared that unfortunate economic and physical consequences would follow if they told white people the truth. If what is communicated is false, it can hardly be called communication...

We are now beginning to communicate without hypocrisy and without fear. The May 17, 1954, decision of the United States Supreme Court cleared the air for honesty between the races. The Negroes' contacts in wartime and through travel, and the uprising of suppressed peoples everywhere, have also helped to clear the air. Negroes do not wish to be branded as inferiors by being segregated, and they want to walk the earth as human beings with dignity. This idea was beautifully expressed by the Negro college students in Atlanta when they said, in "An Appeal for Human Rights": "We will use every legal and nonviolent means at our disposal to end segregation."

The demonstrations will continue, and the goals the students seek will be achieved. Their cause is just. Enlightened public opinion is sympathetic. Both political parties in their platforms approved the student's method of protest. The Negro students are determined to be free. Just before a thousand students of the six Atlanta Negro colleges marched through Atlanta to the Wheat Street Baptist Church, in defiance of state officials' threats and in celebration of the sixth anniversary of the Supreme Court decisions, they sang: "We will be free, We will be free, We will be free someday, Deep in our hearts, We will be free, We will be free someday." After they assembled in the Wheat Street Baptist Church, they sang: "That old Negro, He ain't what he used to be." For the first time since Emancipation, Negro youths are willing and proud to be arrested and serve time in jail for a cause they believe to be just.

Has communication broken down? The old hypocritical kind of communication between the races has broken down, and that is good. We can now build good human relations on truth, honesty, and sincerity.

Has progress in race relations been set back, as the conservatives claim? Not at all. I am convinced that as I travel throughout the South today I experience more friendly feeling toward me and receive more decent treatment than at any other time in my sixty years. I have never before felt so much like a free human being in the South as I do today.

Atlantic Monthly, December 1960, pp. 85–86; in L. H. Fishel and Benjamin Quarles, eds., *The Black American*, (Glenview, Ill.: 1970), pp. 507–509; published in part.

15

STRATEGY TO SURVIVE: JANUARY—MAY 1961

by James Meredith

The enigmatic James Meredith—an army veteran and native of Mississippi—captured national attention by his effort to enroll in the University of Mississippi. He did enroll after a fierce struggle; in October 1962, a racist mob left two men dead and nearly four hundred injured. With federal intervention, Meredith persevered and did graduate in 1963. Here he describes the first months of the episode.

How to engage in this war without becoming a casualty was of prime importance once the decision had been made to invade the enemy's most sacred and revered stronghold. Some precedents had occurred in recent Mississippi history, while James P. Coleman was governor. Clennon King (a teacher at the Negro Alcorn A & M College in Mississippi, who attempted to enroll at the University of Mississippi) had been hustled off the university campus in 1958 and taken to a mental institution and later driven from the state. Clyde Kennard (who tried to gain admission to Mississippi Southern University at Hattiesburg) had been taken from his interview with the president of that university in 1959 to a cell in a Mississippi jail, and then to the penitentiary where he would remain until shortly before his death.

In view of these facts of life in Mississippi, what would be the successful strategy to survive the ordeal? For a long time I had been impressed by a certain maxim which says, "The wise man learns by the mistakes of others, the average man learns by his own, and the fool never learns." King and Kennard must be witness to the fact that life is too uncertain in Mississippi for us to risk learning by our own mistakes.

The most obvious similarity in the fate of the Negroes who had challenged Mississippi's system had been their willingness to collaborate with the enemy. There is always that element of trust in the "good faith" of one or of a few of the men who make up the backbone of the system. I would not question the individual integrity per se of, say, the president of Mississippi Southern, but it would make no difference whether he was trustworthy or not, because under the system of "White Supremacy" it is not the individual that counts, only the system. The system always prevails.

Not once during the three years that I was in Mississippi did I have discourse with the enemy without the public as a witness. This included meeting with their "niggers" as well. There were many third- and fourth-person overtures contained in a rumor form. "I heard that Professor So-and-so told Reverend So-and-so that he heard that So-and-so had been told by the Citizens Council or the Sovereignty Commission to tell Meredith such-and-such." One fact that I prize highly, and it confirms my faith in the basic trustworthiness of all my people, is that no Negro ever approached me to make any deals for the "white folks." However, I must admit that I deliberately made myself unapproachable by anyone white or black.

The primary tactics that I chose to use were (1) to act secretly and quickly and (2) to capitalize on public concern and public opinion. The objective was to make myself more valuable alive than dead. This was the strategy that I followed during the entire period. . . .

The Scare Tactics

Fear is the natural reaction to violence and the threat of violence. Although the Negro community was constantly in a state of siege by the white community, the ultimate enforcement of the principles of "White Supremacy" among the Negroes was done indirectly by the whites. The direct aspects were carried out by the Negro community itself. The less frequent manifestations, such as a lynching, served mostly as symbolic acts to impress the Negro community. Usually when the white community wanted someone or something in the Negro community, it simply said, produce whatever it is we want or you will suffer. Although violence is a very definite part of Mississippi life, it is resorted to only occasionally. Some communities go for generations using only the threat of violence, and there has been no need for direct action. In fact, most whites are incapable of committing violence except under certain ritualistic conditions.

Kosciusko. The initial reaction to my application to the university was in Kosciusko and followed the time-tested formula for weeding out the attackers of the system. The first step was for the police to go around the Negro neighborhood, asking questions about me and my family. As a rule, this act has been enough to trigger off panic in the Negro community. One of the more intensified methods was to go to the homes of several of my parents' neighbors, often within sight of my parents' home, and pretend to look for them. The idea was to let the social pressure from the community and the neighborhood force the nonconformer to conform. The last resort of the white community, before taking direct action, is to call upon "its Negro leaders" to use their personal influence to bring about conformity.

I was well aware of these tactics and had previously briefed my parents, although they already knew even better than I what was to come. The last resort was to be the burden of the high school principal. It must have been a terribly painful experience for him. He was a member of the church in which I had been baptized, and every Sunday morning he and my mother went to the same church. The "powers-that-be" called on him to give my family what amounted to an ultimatum. The principal went to the home of my parents. The ultimatum was for my parents to tell me to withdraw or face the understood consequences. He suggested that my fate would be death if I continued, and my mother's answer was, "If someone has to die, who is my child more than anyone else's child to die?" The principal left in sorrow. . . .

My Relations with the Negro Community

Teachers and Administrators. By the time I had filed the application to the university, I had become more or less settled in my courses at Jackson State College. I had no intention of stopping my education there while attempting to gain admission to the university, and the relationships that I enjoyed with my instructors were important to me as a morale factor. Tacitly, and often openly, there was great support and even much enthusiasm, particularly among those whom I knew well.

It became apparent to me, however, that something was going on in the administration. I never knew what it was, however. I am sure that various attempts were made by the Mississippi power structure to pressure the administration into taking some type of action against me that would have prejudiced my case in one way or another. . . .

The In Group. The student group of intellectuals with whom I had been associated at the college were very much involved in this question of my going to the University of Mississippi. This was a tactical move and, in view of the overall objectives of our group, it was just one question among many to us.

An incident which will shed more light on the nature of this group occurred when the state of Mississippi sent a superpatriot to speak to the students at Jackson State College. The state had hired this ultra-anti-Communist and forced him upon us. I imagine all the schools, certainly all the Negro schools, must cooperate when "the man" recommends a certain speaker. It becomes simply a matter of making arrangements for the speech.

The dean of students was the victim, because he was chosen to host the superpatriot during his stay at the college. The president of the college, a very shrewd man, always somehow managed to stay away from these affairs. The speaker was accompanied by one of the famous (or infamous) Negro editors in the state. It was generally believed that this Negro's paper was being financed by the white Citizens Council. As a matter of fact, he had acknowledged that the council was making certain contributions to his paper.

The meeting was to be held in the science lecture theater. There was always a crowd at these meetings. The dormitory matrons would order all students out of the dormitories; since they could not all slip off the campus, naturally, they would have to go to the affair.

The In Group had done a thorough research job on this speaker. How they obtained all the material I have no idea. They had copies of his previous speeches and every conceivable bit of information regarding his other activities. The members of the group scattered themselves throughout the audience and obtained the most strategic seats.

The superpatriot made his speech without interruptions. He called former President Eisenhower "pink" and asserted that President Kennedy was the best and most willing helpmate that the Communist movement ever had. He maintained that Communists were behind all Negro movements and protests in America; he listed every Negro leader or outstanding personality as being in one way or another a willing or unwilling dupe of the Communists. He told about a plot that had been uncovered to overthrow the white government of Mississippi and install a black dictatorship.

During the question-and-answer period after the speech, the students, not so much discussing the speech they had just heard, asked about his previous speeches instead. He was completely inconsistent and attempted to answer the questions with qualifications; they would then recall a speech, give the date and place, and point out that he had said just the opposite. Without going to the trouble of chasing him and his Negro friend from the building and from the campus, as there were those prepared and willing to do, they simply made his visit ineffective by showing up the fallacies and inconsistencies of his position.

James Meredith, *Three Years in Mississippi* (Bloomington: Indiana University Press, 1966), pp. 78–91. On Meredith and Mississippi, see James W. Silver, *op. cit.*, pp. 114–20.

16

A PETITION TO THE HONORABLE JOHN F. KENNEDY

by W. E. B. Du Bois

Among the papers left by Du Bois was the text of a proposed petition which he drafted early in 1961, probably in February. This does not seem to have gone much further than his own study. In a short time he was to leave the United States to take up work as editor-in-chief of a projected Encyclopedia Africana, at the invitation of President Nkrumah of Ghana.

Dear Mr. President:

We come to you as Negro citizens conscious of our responsibility to add our contribution to the solution of the momentous problems confronting our country, conscious of our responsibility to ourselves, our children, and to all those who comprise our great nation.

You, Mr. President, have said that our country has lost prestige in the councils of the world. We believe that this is true and that there is a definite relationship between this fact and the attitude of government toward us, its Negro nationals. Some of us cast our vote impelled by the hope your words generated, and guided by the fact that we cannot live as formerly.

Obstacles and racial barriers have been raised that not only prevent our enjoyment of rights and privileges without which none can give their best to the growth and development of our country but are as well an impeachment of our democracy, destructive of national morality and injurious to our integrity as a people.

We petition you, Mr. President:

Arouse the nation from the self-denying lethargy into which it has been cast through acceptance of the un-American, subversive, and dehumanizing race relations. End the practice of gradualism. Use the Executive Order, the vast political powers which devolve upon you as Chief Executive decisively to change the policies of State and Federal governments in their relations with Negro citizens. Substitution of the doctrine of States' Rights for the Constitution in relations with Negro citizens must be stopped. American citizenship rights are paramount. Their priority must be respected. End segregation and Jim-Crow now.

Mr. President, use unsparingly the persuasive moral strength inherent in the office of President to end bias and prejudice in human relations. Use your great influence to bring respect for the inalienable rights of man. Mobilize science and the arts to render shattering blows to the myth of white superiority in every area of our cultural life.

Mr. President, order an end to discriminatory practices based on race, nationality, creed, or color in the realm of employment and job tenure, voting, housing, and education. These shameful features of our national life astound and shock the world. Their continued existence prevents the fulfillment of our obligations under the charter of the United Nations. It is impossible that they should not affect our prestige before the world.

Mr. President, the time is right for a new Emancipation Proclamation. President Abraham Lincoln showed the way. But the task was left unfinished. Our democracy must embrace all or it will embrace none.

Therefore, we petition you to:

1. Order an end to all practices and propagation of superiority based on race, nationality, creed, or color enforced by legal and police powers of the Federal government.

2. Appoint a Negro to a new Cabinet post to be known as Secretary of Civil Rights to safeguard the rights of the Negro against encroachments by any state agencies under the guise of "states' rights" or the fiction of racial superiority.

3. Call a national "End Segregation Conference" now to be attended by Negro and white leaders of labor, the Church, education, and culture to map out a moral code crusade against racist ideology.

4. Declare the Negro ghettoes that disgrace every metropolitan area distressed communities and formulate programs of relief and rehabilitation to eliminate the poverty, misery, illiteracy, and chronic ill health.

5. Cut off all grants of federal funds to colleges and universities which practice or propagate segregation or discrimination based on race, creed, or color.

6. Cancel all contracts with companies, corporations, or individuals which apply any form of segregation or discrimination in their employment practices.

7. Establish the right of Negro citizens in every state to vote for any candidate for the Federal office of President, Vice-President, presidential elector, member of Senate or House of Representatives, or in any special or primary election held solely or in fact for the purpose of selecting any such candidate.

8. Order an appropriate bi-racial Federal Committee or Commission on Housing to be established in every city and state

with a substantial non-white population to study racial problems in housing, receive and investigate complaints alleging discrimination.

9. Direct all Federal agencies to shape their policies and practices to make the maximum contribution to the achievement of this goal.

10. Direct that all the recommendations of the Civil Rights Commissions made to provide equality in housing and other sections of national life be immediately implemented and carried into action.

Yours is the hour of destiny, Mr. President. What we ask is within your power. We urge you to act now.

H. Aptheker, ed., *Against Racism: Unpublished Essays, Papers and Addresses, 1887–1963*, by W. E. B. Du Bois (Amherst: University of Massachusetts Press, 1985), pp. 318–19.

17

THE FEDERAL GOVERNMENT AND RACIST DISCRIMINATION

by the Leadership Conference on Civil Rights

An overall description of what the liberation movement faced as the 1960s dawned is offered in this examination of the role of the federal government in supporting racial discrimination. This was published in a sixty-one-page booklet emanating from the Leadership Conference on Civil Rights. Thirty-five "concurring organizations" supported this publication; included were leading Protestant, Catholic, and Jewish groups, eight international trade unions, four women's organizations, various antiracist groups, the National Urban League, and the NAACP.

The report was submitted to the president on August 29, 1961, by Roy Wilkins as chairman of the Leadership Conference and Arnold Aronson, its secretary.

Introduction

In the brief of the United States in *Shelley v. Kraemer* (1948) occurs this paragraph: "It is fundamental that no agency of government should participate in any action which will result in depriving any person of essential rights because of race or color or creed." That this assertion was grossly violated is demonstrated in this booklet, about half of which is reproduced here:

The Democratic Platform of 1960 had pledged executive action to achieve "equal employment opportunities throughout the federal establishment and on all government contracts." Such executive action also, the platform affirmed, should implement "the termination of racial segregation throughout federal services and institutions" and "an end to discrimination in federal housing programs, including federally-assisted housing."

Therefore:

Recommendations

1. To this end, the President, in accordance with his oath "to preserve, protect, and defend the Constitution," should by executive order promulgate a general Federal Civil Rights Code governing the operation of the *whole executive branch* of government. The Code should direct all departments and agencies of the Federal government to assure:

   a. nondiscrimination in the appointment, assignment, and promotion of all personnel, in all employment resulting from federal contracts, licenses, grants-in-aid, or loans: and in all job training, counselling, recruitment and referral programs, including apprenticeship, maintained, operated, or subsidized by the Federal Government.

   b. nondiscrimination in all institutions, facilities, and services maintained or operated directly by the Federal government, including parks, prisons, V.A. hospitals, restaurants, and restrooms in federal buildings, public housing, farm home and crop loans, and military services including reserve forces.

   c. nondiscrimination in all programs, services, and facilities, whether administered by state or local governments or by private institutions, which receive the benefit of any subsidy, loan, guarantee, or other form of federal assistance, including slum clearance, urban renewal and mortgage loan insurance programs, off-duty military training programs such as National Guard and ROTC, health, recreation and research services, airports, hospitals, libraries, schools, and colleges.

The Presidential Order should charge the head of each department and agency with responsibility for enforcing the Civil Rights Code. To this end, it should direct that a Civil Rights or Equal Opportunity Officer be designated whose sole function shall be the effective implementation of the declared national policy within the agency's areas of jurisdiction. In order to stress the importance attached to this function, the official so designated should be a person of high rank and stature, reporting and responsible directly to the agency head.

2. Although each department and agency should be held responsible for implementing the Civil Rights Code, the program will fail of its purpose if responsibility rests with the individual departments and agencies alone.

   Within every agency, to a greater or lesser degree, inertia, established procedures and traditions, the pressure of competing interests, and resistance will militate against full implementation of the nondiscrimination policy.

   In order to overcome these obstacles and to achieve an integrated national program of maximum effectiveness, the President should appoint one or more extra-agency committees to develop standards and procedures, to review and evaluate the programs of the agencies and to assist and coordinate their efforts.

   From the standpoint of administrative efficiency, it would seem advisable to establish either a single overall coordinating and supervisory committee, or to create two such committees, one on Equal Opportunity in Employment (with responsibility for all of the activities listed in 1a above) and another on Equal Opportunity in Facilities and Services (as indicated in 1b and 1c).

   In addition, it would seem advisable that a unit within the Bureau of the Budget be charged with responsibility for reviewing expenditures under all Federal grant and loan programs to assure compliance with the national nondiscrimination policy.

3. On the basis of experience with existing programs, three operating principles appear to be essential to effective implementation of the proposed Civil Rights Code:

   a. Under the procedures governing both the President's Committee on Government Contracts and the Committee on Government Employment Policy, responsibility for the investigation of complaints of discrimination is vested in the individual departments and agencies. Thus, an agency against which a complaint is filed is expected to investigate itself and the investigating officer is frequently called upon to pass judgment on his superiors. The training and competence of the investigator varies from agency to agency; the quality of the investigation varies accordingly. In some cases, an individual complaint is made the basis for an investigation of overall policy and practice; in others, a denial of discrimination is accepted as sufficient proof of compliance. The result has been inordinate delays in the processing of complaints (a full year is not at all uncommon) as well as uneven and, in many instances, inadequate investigations. Accordingly,

Such committee or committees as the President may establish to administer the executive civil rights program should be given clear responsibility, within their defined area of jurisdiction, for receiving, investigating, and processing complaints of discrimination in accordance with uniform standards and procedures.

b. Although procedures for the expeditious handling of all grievances are essential, complaints do not constitute a reliable index of the extent of discrimination nor do they provide an adequate base upon which to construct an effective compliance program.

Individuals who experience discrimination frequently fail to file complaints either because they fear reprisals or because they are unaware of their rights and of the channels for redress available to them.

Moreover, to construct a nondiscrimination program on individual cases is to permit the direction of the program to be determined not by the administering agency but by the random sequence of complaints. Such a program may be wholly unrelated to the areas of greatest discrimination or opportunity.

Reliance for the elimination of discrimination should rest less upon individual complaints than upon a systematic, self-initiated inspection program for testing compliance. Accordingly,

Such committee or committees as the President may establish to administer the program should be authorized on their own initiative to conduct surveys and inspections, to hold hearings, to seek to eliminate such discrimination as may be found through conference and conciliation, and, where such efforts prove unsuccessful, to issue cease and desist orders.

c. Remedial actions to correct violations of national policy are essential; deterrent actions to prevent such violations from occurring constitute an even more salutary approach to compliance. In many areas of federal activity the recipient of a government contract or grant is required to furnish evidence in advance of his willingness and ability to meet defined federal standards and procedures. The same approach should be applied to the civil rights program. Accordingly,

Prior to the approval of any contract, grant, loan, or other form of federal assistance, the recipient should be required to warrant and give evidence justifying certification that in the performance of the contract or in the administration of the funds his practices will conform to the standards of nondiscrimination demanded by the executive civil rights program. Should violations nevertheless occur, the administering agency should be authorized to terminate the contract or grant, to withhold future awards until compliance with its orders is obtained, and if necessary, to sue on the contractual warranty.

4. The goals of an effective civil rights program will not be realized by the exercise of legal restraints alone. There is an equally pressing need for a positive program to foster amicable relations among all the racial, religious, and ethnic groups in our society, based on mutual acceptance with respect for differences.

The Department of Agriculture provides a wide variety of technical and special services for the farmer. The Labor Department does the same for the trade unionist, the Department of Commerce for the businessman. No such service or assistance is available with respect to problems of intergroup relations, although the future well-being of our nation, and especially of our larger cities, may well depend upon our ability to learn to live together comfortably and harmoniously on the basis of equality.

A number of states and municipalities have established commissions for the accomplishment of these purposes. Federal grants to further the establishment and development of additional such agencies meeting defined Federal standards would be exceedingly helpful. But more important than funds is the need for the establishment of an Intergroup Relations or Community Relations Bureau (similar to the Children's Bureau) within the Federal government itself, as pledged in the platform.

The proposed bureau should concern itself with general and specific problems of intergroup relations and intergroup tension and should become a central clearing house for information, for research, and for technical assistance to other agencies—public and private—seeking to advance the goal of full equality.

It should conduct surveys, hold conferences, and disseminate educational materials regarding trends and developments affecting the status of intergroup relationships, as well as on methods and techniques for preventing or resolving intergroup conflicts. It should provide consultant services to state and municipal agencies to facilitate the harmonious desegregation of school, recreational or other facilities, to further the integration of migrants and immigrants and the like.

In short, the emphasis should be not so much on what the Federal government does directly as on how it can serve as a resource and catalyst for the extension and improvement of intergroup relations programs by other agencies of the community.

5. President Kennedy has expressed his belief that the Presidency "is the vital center of action in our whole scheme of government." Nowhere is this more true than in the area of civil rights. The importance of an early and comprehensive Civil Rights Code by Presidential order is underscored by the broad expansion of Federal supports to the economy which has been proposed in the President's economic message. Such an expansion, without the general safeguards advocated here, could involve the federal government

even more heavily than it is now in the active promotion of discriminatory enterprises.

In the final analysis, moreover, the success of the civil rights program will be determined by the attention and leadership which the President will give to it. Every agency of government can do much to eliminate discrimination. Every agency has a role to play in advancing the cause of equality. But every agency likewise has to contend with conflicting concerns, interests, pressures, and traditions. It is only as the President, either directly or through a designated representative, makes clear his continuing concern with these issues that civil rights will receive the priority attention it merits and requires. Accordingly,

In order to insure that the various departments, committees, commissions, and agency officers with civil rights responsibilities are working together effectively, the President, as he has done in areas of national security, science and technology, and of economic affairs, should appoint a special assistant responsible directly to him, for the development, coordination, and implementation of the national civil rights policy and program.

In each department of the federal government detailed proof of the existence of racial discrimination was offered in the remainder of this booklet: *Federal Supported Discrimination*; Leadership Conference on Civil Rights (New York, 1961). For the racism characteristic of the National Guard, see I. L. Newton, "The Negro and the National Guard" in *Phylon* (Spring, 1962): 18–28.

18

THE BLACK MUSLIMS IN AMERICA

by C. Eric Lincoln

The Black Muslims constitute a unique movement: a dynamic social protest that moves upon a religious vehicle. The Movement's main emphases are upon social action. Yet it is none the less essentially a religion—a religion of protest. . . .

It is within this frame of reference that the Black Muslim Movement must be evaluated.

The Edge of the Spectrum

The spectrum of Negro protest organizations covers a wide span, from the most reticent separatist groups to the most determined integrative movements. At what point on this span are the Black Muslims to be found?

On the surface, the Movement seems to be unequivocally separatist, with a restricted membership and an overwhelming dedication to group identification, racial solidarity, and mutual aid. But the membership is not restricted to Negroes; it is restricted to black men, who comprise all mankind except the white race. The Movement is thus highly integrative in intent. Yet whites and Negroes account for very nearly the entire population of America, so the Movement is clearly separatist in effect.

As a separatist group, the Muslims might be expected to show a strong awareness of group solidarity, backed by a generous program of mutual aid. And so they do. Like other Negro separatist groups, they might also be expected to pay only casual attention to racial tensions and the prospect of integration in America. The Muslims, however, are obsessed with this issue. They reject and detest the very idea of integration, but discussion of it dominates all their preachings and publications. In this focus of attention they seem to range themselves as an integrative group—turned inside out....

The Black Muslim Movement is functional for its membership, for the entire Negro community, and for the society as a whole in its insistence upon high standards of personal and group morality. It encourages thrift, cleanliness, honesty, sexual morality, diet control, and abstinence from intoxicating liquors, and it effectively reestablishes a center of authority in the home. Muslims are expected to hold steady jobs, to give a full day's work for their pay, and to respect all constituted authority. As a result, the Movement reduces adult and juvenile delinquency and strengthens its members' sense of independence and self-respect.

At a deeper level, the Movement provides outlets, short of physical violence, for the aggressive feelings roused in its members by the callous and hostile white society. Muslims tend to be Negroes for whom the pressures of racial prejudice and discrimination were intolerable, whose increasing resentment and hatred of the white man demanded release. Unable to rationalize their deprivations (as Negro intellectuals do) and unable to find relief in the Christian church or any secular institution, they might well have followed the downward paths open to the despairing everywhere—the paths of crime, drunkenness, dope addiction, prostitution, and wanton violence, directed indiscriminately against their oppressors or displayed senselessly against others of the oppressed. As Muslims, however, they find a "safe" outlet for their tensions in verbal attacks on the white man and in powerful demonstrations of group solidarity. Indeed, the Movement is most clearly functional in its regeneration of men and women who, having despaired of more creative possibilities, found themselves enslaved to destructive habits and lost to social usefulness.

The religious awakening which the Movement brings to its adherents is also functional for the entire society. Many Muslims had previously been affiliated with no religion; others had been Christians but found their needs unmet by the characteristic expressions of the contemporary church. On the whole, it is better for society for its dissatisfied elements to be associated with some religion rather than with none. (The specific religious doctrines of the Movement are, of course, irrelevant here. The organic unity of American society is not threatened by such articles of faith as the Muslims' respect for the Quran as the word of Allah or their belief in Fard as divine.)

In several important ways, the Muslims tend to strengthen the dignity and self-reliance of the Negro community. They are proving dramatically that a new, positive leadership cadre can emerge among American Negroes at the grass-roots level. The Muslim schools are emphasizing Negro history, Negro achievements, and the contributions of Negroes to the world's great cultures and to the development of the American nation. These facts are rarely taught in public schools, and the Muslims may be alone in trying to bring the Negro community to an awareness of its racial heritage. Again, the Muslims' "buy black" policy is creating some new opportunities for Negro business and professional men—opportunities which are almost universally denied them in the wider community.

The Black Muslims do not, of course, want the Negro community to share its new-found skills and creative energies with the despised white man. But their drive to make the Negro aware of his own potential is nevertheless functional. Despite the Muslims' appeal for separation, a Negro community awakened at last to dignity and self-reliance will be ready to insist upon its status as an equal partner in the American democratic enterprise.

Finally, the very existence of the Muslims—their extreme black nationalism and their astonishing growth and vitality—is functional to the extent that it forces the larger, Christian community to face the reality of racial tensions, to acknowledge its own malfeasance, and to begin a spiritual and moral reform. The Muslims' dramatic expression of racial solidarity may shock the white man into a realization that Negroes will no longer permit their just demands to be casually shrugged aside. Indeed, Muslim extremism may even rebound and actively assist the forces of integration. It may, for example, force a white reappraisal of other protest organizations, such as the NAACP, which are now widely resisted as "too pushy" or "radical." If these groups come to be seen as relatively conservative, if they gain increasing white support, and if the great surge of Negro protest is constructively channeled as a result, the Muslims will have proved integrative despite themselves. But this possibility hangs upon a slender thread—the hope that America will take the warning and act to save itself in time.

The Black Muslims' virulent attacks on the white man may prove to be a useful warning, but they are deeply dysfunctional in the most immediate sense. They threaten the security of the white majority and may lead those in power to tighten the barriers which already divide America. The attacks create guilt and defensiveness among both Negroes and whites, and offer to extremist elements on both sides a cover for antisocial behavior. Above all, the attacks promote a general increase in tension and mutual mistrust. Calm heads might see the Muslims as a timely warning; jittery and frightened men are more likely to lash back in an unreasoning and potentially explosive panic.

These attacks on the white man may also have tragic consequences for international relations. Americans tend to take for granted that the rising nations of Afro-Asia are Moslem, but few of us have a clear knowledge of even the major tenets of the Moslem faith. If the Black Muslims become accepted here as a legitimate Moslem sect, their doctrines—including their hatred of the white man—may well be mistaken for orthodox Moslem doctrines, at least by the rank and file. In that case, the true Moslem ideal of panracial brotherhood would either remain generally unknown or else be considered an all-too-familiar hypocrisy. Such a misunderstanding might contribute disastrously to the triggering of political tensions as the Western and Afro-Asian worlds meet.

Muslim attacks on Christianity, its clergy, and its believers are also immediately dysfunctional. The Muslims' refusal to distinguish the offenses of individuals from the principles of the Christian religion is inescapably divisive. The abuse of Negro women and the lynching of Negro men are not *Christian* acts. By identifying them as such, the Muslims are intensifying social discord and raising still higher the barriers to creative social interaction.

But these overt attacks on the white man and his prevailing religion are, at least, on the surface. They can be watched carefully and, to some extent, counteracted. A more insidious dysfunction is implicit in the very premise of the Movement and is furthered by every Muslim activity, even by those activities whose functional value must also command respect. This dysfunction is the deliberate attempt to break all contacts between the Negro and the white man in America.

Segregation is not, of course, a Muslim innovation. It was begun and enforced in America by the white man; the Muslims have added only a black seal of approval. But a deliberate policy of segregation is always dysfunctional, regardless of its source....

The Deeper Cause

The American Negro has chosen to be "American" rather than "black," and all his energies have been marshaled to achieve this goal. He does not want segregation or separation; he wants only to be an American citizen, with the rights and privileges of every other citizen. He is not shaken in his determination, even though he is receiving no significant support from any powerful factor of the white community. His prolonged and baffling failure to secure his rights does, however, leave him prey to frustration and anxiety; and this anxiety is compounded by the emergence of the "backward" Negroes of Africa into political independence. American Negroes are horrified to know that they may soon be the only victims of racial subordination left in the civilized world....

There is general agreement among American Negroes that the white man has failed to demonstrate any real capacity for genuine brotherhood and equal justice. There is a widespread belief that the white man will *never* of his own accord accept nonwhites as his equals in status and opportunity, in America or elsewhere. There is a surprisingly broad conviction that—as the Muslims insist—the white man has deliberately "written the Negro out of history," refusing to recognize the black man's contribution to the great Afro-Asian civilizations and, especially, to the development of America. The educated Negro is aware that little popular recognition is given to his forefathers in the stories of "the men who made America." Of this cultural snub, whether intentional or not, he is increasingly resentful. He has contributed to the making of America, first as a slave and then as a citizen, and he wants the recognition and unrestricted citizenship that are his due.

The Negro community is not willing to repudiate the Christian faith, as the Muslims demand. But there is a significant if silent reservoir of sympathy for the Muslims' racial doctrines. There is among American Negroes an increasing hostility for the white man—a hostility born of despair. The world around us is in cataclysm. It is hard to wait until tomorrow for what everyone else has today, especially in an atomic age, when tomorrow may never arrive. The Black Muslim Movement represents one attempt to break out of this bondage of discrimination and despair, which now threatens the peace and casts a dark shadow over the happiness and prosperity of all America. . . .

The Muslims are embarrassing to both the white and the Negro communities: they call attention to a situation so irrational and so ugly that neither side wants to face it squarely. It is, therefore, only to be expected that many people wish the Muslims would simply fold their tents and go away, and that they will try to hex them away by refusing to admit that they really exist.

But the Muslims do exist. They do attract the support of the masses and of a small but increasing number of intellectuals. And they will continue to expand as long as racial tension is permitted to flourish in America. True, the Movement in its present form may be crushed by an embarrassed and apprehensive citizenry, white or black. It can be stopped today—and it should be, if it seriously threatens the peace and security of the nation. But in shattering the Movement we shall not eliminate the tension and the need which created and catapulted it to its present momentum. Out of the ashes of the Black Muslims, another "black" specter will inevitably rise to challenge us, for we can destroy the Muslim organization but not the Negro's will to freedom. The essence of the Black Muslim Movement will endure—an extreme expression of the American Negro's rising dissatisfaction with the way things are, and his deepening conviction that this is not the way things have to be.

The meaning for America is clear. We must attack the disease, not its symptoms. We must confront the issue of racism and discrimination. When we have done so with the determination and moral conviction so brutal a problem deserves, there will be no Black Muslims. There will be no need for them. And America will be a better place for us all.

C. Eric Lincoln, *The Black Muslims in America* (1961, Boston: 1963, Beacon), pp. 246–55; originally a Ph.D. dissertation, Boston University. At the time of the publication of this work, Lincoln was professor of social philosophy at Clark College, Atlanta University.

19

EQUALITY NOW: THE PRESIDENT HAS THE POWER

by Martin Luther King, Jr.

The *Nation* started an annual report on "the state of the civil rights movement" early in 1961. Below is Dr. King's summary as of that date, commencing with the 1930s; analyzing the role of the federal government in that effort, he called it "pitifully insufficient in scope and limited in conception."

The new administration has the opportunity to be the first in one hundred years of American history to adopt a radically new approach to the question of civil rights. It must begin, however, with the firm conviction that the principle is no longer in doubt. The day is past for tolerating vicious and inhuman opposition on a subject which determines the lives of twenty million Americans. We are no longer discussing the wisdom of democracy over monarchism—and we would not permit hoodlum royalists to terrorize the streets of our major cities or the legislative halls of our states. We must decide that in a new era, there must be new thinking. If we fail to make this positive decision, an awakening world will conclude that we have become a fossil nation, morally and politically; and no floods of refrigerators, automobiles, or color television sets will rejuvenate our image.

The second element in a new approach is the recognition by the federal government that it has sufficient power at its disposal to guide us through the changes ahead. The intolerably slow pace of civil rights is due at least as much to the limits which the federal government has imposed on its own actions as it is to the actions of the segregationist opposition.

If we examine the total of all judicial, executive and legislative acts of the past three decades and balance them against the sum needed to achieve fundamental change, two startling conclusions are inescapable. The first is the hopeless inadequacy of measures adopted—pitifully insufficient in scope and limited in conception. The second conclusion is even more disturbing. Federal action has been not only inadequate; viewed as a whole, it has also been self-nullifying. In 1954, the Supreme Court declared school segregation to be unconstitutional. Yet, since then federal executive agencies and vast federal legislative programs have given millions of dollars yearly to educational institutions which continue to violate the Supreme Court decision.

Further, the federal government collects taxes from all citizens, Negro and white, which it is Constitutionally obligated to use for the benefits of all; yet, billions of these tax dollars have gone to support housing programs and hospital and airport construction in which discrimination is an open and notorious practice. Private firms which either totally exclude Negroes from the work force, or place them in discriminatory status, receive billions of dollars annually in government contracts. The federal government permits elections and seats representatives in its legislative chambers in disregard of the fact that millions of Negro citizens have no vote. It directly employs millions in its various agencies and departments, yet its employment practices, especially in southern states, are rife with discrimination.

These illustrations can be multiplied many times. The shocking fact is that while the government moves sluggishly, and in patchwork fashion, to achieve equal rights for all citizens, in the daily conduct of its own massive economic and social activities it participates directly and indirectly in the denial of these rights. We must face the tragic fact that the federal government is the nation's highest investor in segregation.

Therefore, a primary goal of a well-meaning administration should be a thorough examination of its own operations and the development of a rigorous program to wipe out immediately every vestige of federal support and sponsorship of discrimination. Such a program would serve not only to attack the problem centrally, where results can be produced, but collaterally to educate and influence the whole American populace, especially in the deep South of massive resistance. It would also be the first step in the evolution of federal leadership to guide the entire nation to its new democratic goals.

There is impressive precedent in recent history for massive governmental mobilization to create new conditions. As a consequence of economic crisis in the early thirties, the federal government, under the leadership of President Kennedy's party, undertook to change fundamental economic relationships. Every person in the nation was affected. In a bewilderingly brief period, wages were regulated at new levels, unemployment insurance created, relief agencies set up, public works planned and executed. Regulatory legislation covering banking, the stock market, and money market was immediately enacted. Laws protecting trade-union organization were brought into being and administrative agencies to interpret and enforce the labor laws were created. Along with this broad assault on the

Depression went an educational campaign to facilitate the changes in public psychology requisite to the acceptance of such formidable alternatives to old thought patterns. The nation which five years earlier viewed federal intervention on any level as collectivism or socialism, in amazingly swift transition, supported the new role of government as appropriate and justified.

These breathtaking, fundamental changes took place because a leadership emerged that was both determined and bold, that rejected inhibitions imposed by old traditions and habits. It utilized all agencies and organs of government in a massive drive to change a situation which imperiled the very existence of our society.

Viewed in this light, an administration with good will, sincerely desirous of eliminating discrimination from American life, could accomplish its goal by mobilizing the immense resources of the organs of government and throwing them into every area where the problem appears. There are at least three vital areas in which the president can work to bring about effective solutions.

First, there is the legislative area. The president could take the offensive, despite southern opposition, by fighting for a really far-reaching legislative program. With resolute presidential leadership, a majority in both houses could be persuaded to pass meaningful laws. A determined majority-party leadership possesses the means to carry the reluctant along—and to hasten the end of the political careers, or the privileges, of those who prove unyielding. The influence the president can exert upon Congress when, with crusading zeal, he summons support from the nation has been demonstrated more than once in the past.

An example of an area in which a vigorous president could significantly influence Congress is that of voter registration. The Civil Rights Commission has revealed that "many Negro American citizens find it difficult, and often impossible, to vote." It went on to assert that these voting denials are accomplished through the creation of legal impediments, administrative obstacles, and the fear of economic reprisal and physical harm. A truly decisive president would work passionately and unrelentingly to change these shameful conditions. He would take such a creative general proposal as that made by the Civil Rights Commission of 1959 on Federal Registrars to insure the right to vote, and would campaign "on the Hill" and across the nation until Congress acted. He would also have the courage to insist that, in compliance with the

Fourteenth Amendment, a state's representation in Congress be reduced in proportion to the number of citizens denied the right to vote because of race.

This approach would help us eliminate the defeatist psychology engendered by the alliance of dixiecrats and northern reactionaries in Congress. The same alliance, existing in even greater strength, failed in the past to stop legislation that altered patterns just as deeply embedded in American mores as racial discrimination. It is leadership and determination that counts—and these have been lacking of recent years.

A second area in which the president can make a significant contribution toward the elimination of racial discrimination is that of moral persuasion. The president is the embodiment of the democratic personality of the nation, both domestically and internationally. His own personal conduct influences and educates. If he were to make it known that he would not participate in any activities in which segregation exists, he would set a clear example for Americans everywhere, of every age, on a simple, easily understood level.

The calling of White House conferences of Negro and white leaders could be extremely useful. The president could serve the great purpose of opening the channels of communication between the races. Many white southerners who, for various reasons, fear to meet with Negro leaders in their own communities would participate unhesitatingly in a biracial conference called by the president.

It is appropriate to note here that, even in the hard-core South, a small but growing number of whites are breaking with the old order. These people believe in the morality as well as the constitutionality of integration. Their still, small voices often go unheard amid the louder shouts of defiance, but they are active in the field. They often face problems of ostracism and isolation as a result of their stand. Their isolation and difficulties would be lessened if they were among the invitees to the White House to participate in a conference on desegregation.

No effort to list the president's opportunities to use the prestige of his office to further civil rights could be adequate; from fireside chats to appearances at major events, the list is endless. All that is needed at the outset is a firm resolve to make the presidency a weapon for this democratic objective; the opportunities would then arise by themselves.

But beyond the legislative area and the employment of presidential prestige, a weapon of overwhelming significance lies in the executive itself. It is no exaggeration to say that the president could give segregation its death blow through a stroke of the pen. The power inherent in executive orders has never been exploited; its use in recent years has been microscopic in scope and timid in conception.

Historically, the executive has promulgated orders of extraordinary range and significance. The Emancipation Proclamation was an executive order. The integration of the armed forces grew out of President Truman's Executive Order 8891. Executive orders could require the immediate end to all discrimination in any housing accommodations financed with federal aid. Executive orders could prohibit any contractor dealing with any federal agency from practicing discrimination in employment by requiring (a) cancellation of existing contracts, (b) and/or barring violators from bidding, (c) and/or calling in of government loans of federal funds extended to violators, (d) and/or requiring renegotiation of payment to exact financial penalties where violations appear after performance of a contract. With such effective penalties, enforcement of fair employment practices would become self-imposed by those enjoying billions of dollars in contracts with federal agencies.

An executive order could also bring an immediate end to the discriminatory employment policies of federal agencies and departments. It is no secret that, despite statutes to the contrary, Negroes are almost totally excluded from skilled, clerical, and supervisory jobs in the federal government. A recent report of the President's Committee on Government Employment states: "That there is discrimination in federal employment is unquestionably true." A basic reason for this is that there have never been any sanctions imposed for violations of the law. In a real sense, a president can eliminate discrimination in federal employment, just as it was eliminated in the military services, by setting up adequately staffed committees with authority to punish those who violate official government policy from the inside.

We can easily see how an end to discriminatory practices in federal agencies would have tremendous value in changing attitudes and behavior patterns. If, for instance, the law enforcement personnel in the FBI were integrated, many persons who now defy federal law, might come under restraints from which they are presently free. If other law enforcement agencies under the Treasury Department, such as the Internal Revenue Service, the Bureau of Narcotics, the Alcohol Tax Unit, the Secret Service, and Customs had an adequate number of field agents, investigators, and administrators who were Negro, there would be a greater respect for Negroes as well as the assurance that prejudicial behavior in these agencies toward citizens would cease.

Another area in which an executive order can bring an end to a considerable amount of discrimination is that of health and hospitalization. Under the Hill-Burton Act, the federal government grants funds to the states for the construction of hospitals. Since this program began in 1948, more than one hundred million dollars a year has gone to the states in direct aid. The government also makes grants to the states for mental health, maternal, and child-care services, and for programs designed to control tuberculosis, cancer, and heart disease. In spite of this sizable federal support, it is a known fact that most of the federally financed and approved health and hospitalization programs in the South are operated on a segregated basis. In many instances, the southern Negroes are denied access to them altogether.

The president could wipe out these shameful conditions almost overnight by simply ordering his Secretary of Health, Education and Welfare not to approve grants to states whose plans authorize segregation or denial of service on the basis of race. This type of sanction would bring even the most recalcitrant southerners into line.

There is hardly any area in which executive leadership is needed more than in housing. Here the Negro confronts the most tragic expression of discrimination; he is consigned to ghettos and overcrowded conditions. And here the North is as guilty as the South.

Unfortunately, the federal government has participated directly and indirectly in the perpetuation of housing discrimination. Through the Federal Housing Administration (FHA), the Public Housing Administration (PHA), Urban Renewal Administration (URA), and the Veterans Administration Loan Program, the federal government makes possible most of the building programs in the United States. Since its creation in 1934, the FHA alone has insured more than thirty-three billion dollars in mortgages involving millions of homes. As a result of FHA programs, more than two million people presently live in more than two thousand low-rent housing projects in forty-four states and the District of Columbia. The URA, which was established in 1954 to help cities eliminate slum and blighted areas, has approved projects in more than 877 localities. The GI Bill of Rights authorizes the Veterans Administration to make loans outright to veterans for the construction of homes. This program has become so extensive that there have been years in which thirty percent of all new urban dwelling units were built with the help of VA loan guarantees.

While most of these housing programs have antidiscrimination clauses, they have done little to end segregated housing. It is a known fact that FHA continues to finance private developers who openly proclaim that none of their homes will be sold to Negroes. The urban renewal program has, in many instances, served to accentuate, even to initiate, segregated neighborhoods. (Since a large percentage of the people to be relocated are Negroes, they are more likely to be relocated in segregated areas.)

A president seriously concerned about this problem could direct the housing administrator to require all participants in federal housing programs to agree to a policy of "open occupancy." Such a policy could be enforced by (a) making it mandatory for all violators to be excluded from future participation in federally financed housing programs and (b) by including a provision in each contract giving the government the right to declare the entire mortgage debt due and payable upon breach of the agreement.

These are merely illustrations of acts possible of multiplication in many other fields.

Executive policy could reshape the practices and programs of other agencies and departments whose activities affect the welfare of millions. The Department of Health, Education and Welfare could be directed to coordinate its resources to give special aid in those areas of the country where assistance might change local attitudes. The department could give valuable assistance to local school boards without any additional legislative enactments.

The Department of Agriculture—which doubtless considers civil rights issues as remote from its purview—could fruitfully reappraise its present operations with a view to taking certain steps that require no new legislative powers. The department could be of tremendous assistance to Negro farmers who are now denied credit simply because of their desire to exercise their citizenship rights. To wipe out this kind of discrimination would be to transform the lives of hundreds of thousands of Negroes on the land. A department zealous to implement democratic ideals might become a source of security and help to struggling farmers rather than a symbol of hostility and discrimination on the federal level.

A Justice Department that is imbued with a will to create justice has vast potential. The employment of powerful court orders, enforced by sizable numbers of federal marshals, would restrain lawless elements now operating with inexcusable license. It should be remembered that in early American history it was the federal marshal who restored law in frontier communities when local authority broke down.

In the opinion of many authorities executive power, operating through the attorney general, opens many hitherto untried avenues for executive action in the field of school desegregation. There are existing laws under which the attorney general could go into court and become a force in the current school struggles. Atrophy is not alone a medical phenomenon; it has its counterpart in social and political life. Long years of ignoring this area of law and executive power have led, indeed, to atrophy; nothing is done, nothing is studied, though new situations arise constantly where existing laws could reasonably be utilized.

Space will not permit a spelling out of all the measures by which every federal body could contribute to the enforcement of civil rights. This is the task of a master plan. Nor is it necessary to detail a legislative program, nor to list still unused powers inherent in the judiciary. Justices J. Skelley Wright and W. A. Bootle in Louisiana and Georgia respectively have given examples of the ability of a single federal district judge to handle the unconstitutional maneuverings of state legislatures.

The purpose of this review is to emphasize that a recognition of the potentials of federal power is a primary necessity if the fight for full racial equality is to be won. With it, however, must go another indispensable factor—the recognition by the government of its moral obligation to solve the problem.

A recent visit to India revealed to me the vast opportunities open to a government determined to end discrimination. When it confronted the problem of centuries-old discrimination against the "untouchables," India began its thinking at a point that we have not yet reached. Probing its moral responsibilities, it concluded that the country must atone for the immense injustices imposed upon the untouchables. It therefore made provision not alone for equality, but for special treatment to enable the victims of discrimination to leap the gap from backwardness to competence. Thus, millions of rupees are set aside each year to provide scholarships, financial grants, and special employment opportunities for the untouchables. To the argument that this is a new form of discrimination inflicted upon the majority population, the Indian people respond by saying that this is their way of atoning for the injustices and indignities heaped in the past upon their seventy million untouchable brothers.

Although discrimination has not yet been eliminated in India, the atmosphere there differs sharply from that in our country. In India, it is a crime punishable by imprisonment to practice discrimination against an untouchable. But even without this coercion, so successfully has the government made the issue a matter of moral and ethical responsibility that no government figure or political leader on any level would dare defend discriminatory practices. One could wish that we here in the United States had reached this level of morality.

To coordinate the widespread activities on the civil rights front, the president should appoint a Secretary of Integration. The appointee should be of the highest qualifications, free from partisan political obligations, imbued with the conviction that the government of the most powerful nation on earth cannot lack the capacity to accomplish the rapid and complete solution to the problem of racial equality.

These proposals for federal action do not obviate the necessity for the people themselves to act, of course. An administration of good faith can be strengthened immeasurably by determined popular action. This is the great value of the nonviolent direct-action movement that has engulfed the South. On the one hand, it gives large numbers of people a method of securing moral ends through moral means. On the other hand, it gives support and stimulation to all those agencies which have the power to bring about meaningful change. Thousands of courageous students, sitting peacefully at lunch counters, can do more to arouse the administration to positive action than all of the verbal and written commentaries on governmental laxity put together.

When our government determines to ally itself with those of its citizens who are crusading for their freedom within our borders, and lends the might of its resources creatively and unhesitatingly to the struggle, the blight of discrimination will begin rapidly to fade.

History has thrust upon the present administration an indescribably important destiny—to complete a process of democratization which our nation has taken far too long to develop, but which is our most powerful weapon for earning world respect and emulation. How we deal with this crucial problem of racial discrimination will determine our moral health as individuals, our political health as a nation, our prestige as a leader of the free world. I can think of few better words for the guidance of the new administration than those which concluded the 1946 report of the President's Commission on Civil Rights: "The United States is not so strong, the final triumph of the democratic ideal not so inevitable that we can ignore what the world thinks of us or our record." These words are even more apt today than on the day they were written.

Nation, February 4, 1961, pp. 152–59; published in part.

20

LETTER FROM THE MAGNOLIA, MISSISSIPPI, JAIL

by Robert Moses

November 1, 1961

[To Tom Hayden]

We are smuggling this note from the drunk tank of the county jail in Magnolia, Mississippi. Twelve of us are here, sprawled out along the concrete bunker; Curtis Hayes, Hollis Watkins, Ike Lewis, and Robert Talbert, four veterans of the bunker, are sitting up talking— mostly about girls; Charles McDew ("Tell the story") is curled into the concrete and the wall; Harold Robinson, Stephen Ashley, James Wells, Lee Chester Vick, Leotus Eubanks, and Ivory Diggs lay cramped on the cold bunker; I'm sitting with smuggled pen and paper, thinking a little, writing a little; Myrtis Bennett and Janie Campbell are across the way wedded to a different icy cubicle.

Later on Hollis will lead out with a clear tenor into a freedom song; Talbert and Lewis will supply jokes; and McDew will discourse on the history of the black man and the Jew. McDew—a black by birth, a Jew by choice, and a revolutionary by necessity— has taken on the deep hates and deep loves which America, and the world, reserves for those who dare to stand in a strong sun and cast a sharp shadow.

In the words of Judge Brumfield, who sentenced us, we are "cold calculators" who design to disrupt the racial harmony (harmonious since 1619) of McComb into racial strife and rioting; we, he said, are the leaders who are causing young children to be led like sheep to the pen to be slaughtered (in a legal manner). "Robert," he was addressing me, "haven't some of the people from your school been able to go down and register without violence here in Pike county?"

I thought to myself that southerners are most exposed when they boast.

It's mealtime now: we have rice and gravy in a flat pan, dry bread and a "big town cake"; we lack eating and drinking utensils. Water comes from a faucet and goes into a hole.

This is Mississippi, the middle of the iceberg. Hollis is leading off with his tenor, "Michael, row the boat ashore, Alleluia; Christian brothers don't be slow, Alleluia; Mississippi's next to go, Alleluia." This is a tremor in the middle of the iceberg—from a stone that the builders rejected.

Tom Hayden, *Revolution in Mississippi* (Students for a Democratic Society, 1962) in J. Grant, ed., *Black Protest*, (Greenwood, Conn.: 1968), p. 303.

21

THE KENNEDY ADMINISTRATION IS WEAK

by Roy Wilkins

In March 1961, Wilkins wrote to Harris Wofford, at that time an assistant to President Kennedy, expressing dissatisfaction with the administration's weak action in regard to civil rights. This kind of pressure was of consequence in inducing Kennedy finally to support a significant Civil Rights bill.

Dear Mr. Wofford:

The Kennedy Administration has done with Negro citizens what it has done with a vast number of Americans; it has charmed them. It has intrigued them. Every seventy-two hours it has delighted them. On the Negro question it has smoothed Unguentine on a sting burn, even though, for a moment (or perhaps a year), it cannot do anything about a broken pelvis. It has patted a head even though it could not bind up a joint.

The point is not so much whether we have come out thus far with what we were due (we have not) but whether the lines have been set in such a way that we cannot later recall our proper share. It is plain why the civil rights legislative line was abandoned, but nothing was accomplished by the maneuver. It did not save the Minimum Wage Bill from gutting, and it will not save other legislation. The southerners and their northern satellites function whether a civil rights bill is proposed or not.

An Administration gets as much by whacking them as by wooing them. J.F.K. might as well have had a civil rights bill in the hopper; he might have won the Senate Rules fight (he could have) as he would have had a procedure open when he does decide to get behind a civil rights bill.

Roy Wilkins, with Tom Mathews, *Standing Fast: An Autobiography*, (New York: Viking, 1982), p. 283. At this writing, Harris Wofford is a U.S senator from Pennsylvania.

22

THE SOUTHERN BLACK PRESS RESPONDS TO THE FREEDOM RIDERS

by Benjamin F. Clark

In the spring and summer of 1961 the black press in the South responded to the freedom riders with caution at first—even, in one case, with disapproval. But as the effort continued, this press—with the exception of the Jackson, Mississippi, paper—warmly endorsed the effort. A recent doctoral dissertation documents this development.

Although the Freedom Riders encountered violence and arrest in almost every southern town and city, the rides continued until the Interstate Commerce Commission issued an order banning segregation in terminal facilities. This September 22, 1961 ruling implemented the Supreme Court decision and set new penalties for noncompliance.

True to its established tradition, the *Jackson Advocate* was opposed to the "Freedom Rides." It saw CORE as an organization determined to embarrass the United States government by exposing petty legal hypocrisy. *Advocate* editors believed CORE was using the struggle for civil rights and black first-class citizenship to support its real posture which was to expose the weaknesses of the United States and to arouse racial unrest. Thus, they urged blacks to refrain from joining CORE lest they jeopardize the civil rights progress already made.

In another editorial the *Advocate* wrote:

Those who have been observant of developments in American and World history during the past two decades will find it easy to recognize the fact that the come lately groups such as CORE and the Southern Christian non-violent resistance organizations have not contributed a single original thought or idea to the field of race relations in the South nor in the rest of the country. Every movement and technique endorsed and promoted by these groups being foreign and communist importations.

While the freedom riders received a reprimand from the *Advocate* which opposed the rides, they could look to the *New Orleans Louisiana Weekly* for consolation and encouragement. The *Louisiana Weekly* felt that freedom riders were doing a service to the nation because they were testing the moral fiber of this country. Deploring the violence that occurred, they called for federal intervention and beckoned their readers to participate because "It's our fight, too."

When Attorney General Robert Kennedy, the brother of the President, called for a "cooling off period" and a moratorium on all freedom rides, the *Weekly* revealed just how firmly it supported the cause. In a June 10 editorial, it asserted:

> All in all, Negro leaders were eminently correct in rejecting Attorney General Bob Kennedy's "cooling off" suggestion. For as they aptly replied, "We have been cooling off ninety-nine years and that's too long."
>
> To that reply might be added: full freedom is long overdue. It's time now to get hot, not cool. Now is the time to keep pouring it on.

In subsequent editorials, the *Louisiana Weekly* editors urged the "freedom riders" to continue and not turn back. The riders must continue, they argued,

> until the South replaces or is forced to replace outworn mores and customs with the American traditions of liberty and equality for all men, for if any race within a nation has not been granted all of the privileges that go along with full first class citizenship after ninety-eight years of "freedom" that race is in fact still in captivity.

In Tennessee, the *Memphis Tri-State Defender* had written very little about the "freedom rides" prior to May 20, 1961, when readers were provided with a lengthy, detailed account. In its first editorial devoted totally to the rides in July 1961, however, the paper urged the riders to continue. "Only one thing should bring the Freedom Riders to a halt," it exhorted, and that was "full attainment of their objectives." "We must bear the cross before earning the right to wear it and remember that nothing risked is nothing gained," it reminded its readers. The *Tri-State Defender* further suggested that if no southern blacks will volunteer, northerners and white ministers should be used to help increase the efficacy of the struggle.

"We are tired," they later warned, "of pleading on our knees and the day of praying and waiting for public opinion is over. We are exercising passive resistance and mass action...the old fogies out of step with the times have held us back and held the NAACP back."

The *Atlanta Daily World* was explicit in its position from the very beginning of the "Freedom Rides." On May 21, 1961, it editorialized in great detail:

> An interracial group called CORE came into the South last week. They were to travel from Washington to New Orleans testing the segregation practices. Everyone knows what happened now as a result of this planned test. The persons responsible for the violence were wrong and should be dealt with by the police and the courts. Even though the riders knew that they might be attacked, this action could have triggered a reaction that could have caused many innocent persons to suffer physical injury.
>
> Calm, quiet, intelligent approaches are the best way to solve complex problems of this sort. Fanatical emotionalism on the one part, only beget fanatical extremism as a reaction.
>
> The courts have decided the issue of interstate transportation and use of facilities. Dramatizing the lag between the legal rights and the social fact, it seems to us, only gives the communist adversary additional propaganda weapons to use in furthering their cause of capturing the undecided area of the world.

Unlike its parent paper in Atlanta, the *Birmingham World* never moved to the point of denouncing the "freedom rides," but seemingly silently approved them. To what extent the *Atlanta Daily World* influenced this silence is not known. However, the *Birmingham World* did speak out against the jailing of the riders and oddly enough, the editorial was published in the May 23 edition of the *Atlanta Daily World*. In this editorial the *Birmingham World* editors wrote:

> In Birmingham a few days ago, some freedom travelers were placed in jail for protective custody. If this were truly protective custody, why not take them to a hotel, why treat them as law breakers? Mob leaders were not arrested. Why were they not arrested for the protection of the good community?

Like the *New Orleans Louisiana Weekly* the *Dallas Express* did not like it at all when Attorney General Robert Kennedy asked freedom riders to postpone their demonstrations. In an editorial they wrote:

To Attorney General Kennedy's request that the "Freedom Riders" postpone their rights to travel freely in interstate commerce, they replied: had there not been a cooling off period following the Civil War, the Negro would be free today. Isn't ninety-nine years long enough to cool off, Mr. Attorney General?

Express editors announced their agreement with the reply of the "freedom riders" and added that this nation has a responsibility to protect the riders if it possesses any hopes of becoming a world leader. When President Kennedy requested funds for moon explorations, the *Express* was somewhat angry over the treatment of the "freedom riders." They responded to this request by writing, "It just does not make sense to Negroes to talk about spending billions upon billions of dollars to get to the moon when scores are in jail in Jackson for trying to get to Mississippi in peace."

As more and more freedom riders were arrested in Mississippi, the *Express* increased its criticism of the federal government. Blaming Washington for permitting Mississippi to do this, the *Express* charged that "the people in Washington are so busy trying to save the Cuban prisoners across the seas, that they have no time for the American prisoners here at home."

When the *Miami Times* learned of the beatings and arrests in Alabama, they wrote "actions by the Alabamians do a little hurt to the CORE folk, but do much more to the United States." *Times* editors felt that unchecked violence provided good propaganda for the Russians. "We must wait for further developments. The rioters may feel they have been of help to their city, but alas, they have been very unhelpful to their country," was the typical warning of the *Times* editor. Their support for the rides was implicit.

The *Raleigh Carolinian* editors urged readers to get behind CORE and support the freedom rides regardless of whether or not they agreed with the method because "they need your help." It repeated CORE's suggestion that "As American citizens, we must bear witness to this evil system by going and remaining in Mississippi jails until the moral weight of the universe is brought to a focus on Mississippi and the South." It endorsed CORE's suggestion that each church and community organization could recruit one freedom rider or contribute the cost of sending one freedom rider on a trip. If this could not be done, the paper urged its readers to write letters to the U.S. government, Mississippi officials, and to the people now in jail. Their editorial concluded with the statement, that

"You may not have much money, but you can afford the cost of a letter or a postcard."

The *Raleigh Carolinian* was moved to take an even stronger stand against bus discrimination when a member of its staff traveled to McRae, Georgia, and found facilities and restrooms for blacks, disgraceful and wholly unsanitary. It reported that

> In the Negro restaurant, which was across from a leaking restroom toilet, water from the defective room was standing in pools under the tables where Negroes were supposed to eat. Flies were as thick as beehives. How any passenger could have the appetite to eat in such a place is more than we can explain.... It is informative to note that for the second and third class facilities services in the segregated waiting rooms for Negroes, the Negro is asked to pay first-class prices.... If any...doubt the veracity of our statements we urge them to blacken their face and hands and ride a month through the South.

The Montgomery Bus Boycott and the freedom riders forced the middle aged editor-publishers of black newspapers to confront and evaluate direct action as a protest tactic. While several immediately endorsed the tactics, others displayed caution before giving solid endorsement to the boycott and the riders.

Benjamin F. Clark, *"The Editorial Reaction of Selected Southern Black Newspapers to the Civil Rights Movement, 1956–1968"* (Ph.D. diss., Howard University, 1989, pp. 130–37); footnotes omitted.

23

"MY SIGHT IS GONE, BUT MY VISION REMAINS"

by Henry Winston

Henry Winston, chairman of the Communist party, was sentenced to five years' imprisonment after conviction under the Smith Act. While in jail, due to inadequate care, Winston became blind. On June 30, 1961, after significant domestic and foreign protests, President Kennedy ordered Winston's release. On July 5, in an interview widely reported by the press and television, Winston made the following statement:

Upon my release by Presidential order on Friday, June 30, from the U.S.

Public Health Hospital at Staten Island after serving most of my time, I promised newspapermen answers to their questions later. I am glad to answer those questions today.

I am, of course, happy to be free and once more to be with my family and friends. My joy is marred, however, by the fact that my good comrade and friend, Gilbert Green, is still imprisoned in Leavenworth Prison, a victim, like myself and others, of a political frameup under the viciously undemocratic thought control law known as the Smith Act. He is due to be released July 29.

I want to thank publicly all those who fought so hard for my release—my family and my friends, and many, many others in various walks of life. I am deeply grateful to the many Negro leaders in the ministry and elsewhere, who spoke up for my freedom. I am deeply appreciative of the efforts of the Rev. Edler P. Hawkins, moderator of the Presbyterian Church, Roger Baldwin and Norman Thomas, who never permitted their political disagreement with me to stop their fight for justice and humanity.

My present plans call for some rest and then a lengthy visit with my mother and sisters who live in the Midwest.

Subsequently I plan to return to New York where I shall further retrain myself to activity under the handicap of blindness—a disability brought on by callous and criminal neglect of Federal officials. Had I been paroled in 1958, when I was eligible for parole, I would not have had to undergo surgery in 1960 and would not today be suffering from my affliction. Had prison officials and governmental authorities, even as late as 1959, heeded my complaints, I might not be blind today.

However, despite my handicap, I intend to resume my part in the fight for an America and a world of peace and security, free of poverty, disease, and race discrimination.

In prison I followed with special pride the accounts of the magnificent struggle of my people. I regard the Freedom Riders as heroes of our time who are making a contribution not only to the cause of Negro freedom but of democratic rights for all Americans.

I return from prison with the unshaken conviction that the people of our great land, Negro and white, need a Communist Party fighting for the unity of the people for peace, democracy, security, and socialism. I take my place in it again with deep pride. My sight is gone but my vision remains.

Political Affairs, August 1961, pp. 1–2.

24

HENRY WINSTON

by W. E. B. Du Bois

In September 1961 a banquet in honor of Henry Winston was held at the Hotel
Theresa in Harlem. One of the speakers was W. E. B. Du Bois; he said:

More than most men, Henry Winston has suffered for his determination to
think and act in accord with what he believed was right. In this day of the
coward and thief, the liar and murderer, it is a great honor to stand in the
presence of this man, and beholding his wounded body and undaunted
soul, to remember that great word of Emerson:

> Though love repine and reason chafe,
> There came a voice without reply
> 'Tis man's perdition to be safe
> When for the truth he ought to die.

W. E. B. Du Bois, *Unpublished Essays, op. cit.*, p. 320.

25

ON JOINING THE COMMUNIST PARTY

by W. E. B. Du Bois

Shortly after the U.S. Supreme Court upheld the constitutionality of the
McCarran Act—which outlawed the Communist party and provided imprisonment for its members—Dr. Du Bois, in his ninety-third year, applied for
membership in that party. His decision, in a letter addressed to Gus Hall as
general secretary of the party, briefly summarizes his path to socialism and
suggests a program which, he believes, should characterize the party.

On this first day of October, 1961, I am applying for admission to
membership in the Communist Party of the United States. I have been
long and slow in coming to this conclusion, but at last my mind is settled.

In college I heard the name of Karl Marx, but read none of his works, nor heard them explained. At the University of Berlin, I heard much of those thinkers who had definitively answered the theories of Marx, but again we did not study what Marx himself had said. Nevertheless, I attended meetings of the Socialist Party and considered myself a Socialist.

On my return to America, I taught and studied for sixteen years. I explored the theory of Socialism and studied the organized social life of American Negroes; but still I neither read nor heard much of Marxism. Then I came to New York as an official of the new NAACP and editor of the *Crisis* Magazine. The NAACP was capitalist oriented and expected support from rich philanthropists.

But it had a strong Socialist element in its leadership in persons like Mary Ovington, William English Walling, and Charles Edward Russell. Following their advice, I joined the Socialist Party in 1911. I knew then nothing of practical socialist politics and in the campaign of 1912, I found myself unwilling to vote the Socialist ticket, but advised Negroes to vote for Wilson. This was contrary to Socialist Party rules and consequently I resigned from the Socialist Party.

For the next twenty years I tried to develop a political way of life for myself and my people. I attacked the Democrats and Republicans for monopoly and disfranchisement of Negroes; I attacked the Socialists for trying to segregate the southern Negro members; I praised the racial attitudes of the Communists, but opposed their tactics in the case of the Scottsboro boys and their advocacy of a Negro state. At the same time I began to study Karl Marx and the Communists; I read *Das Kapital* and other Communist literature; I hailed the Russian Revolution of 1917, but was puzzled at the contradictory news from Russia.

Finally in 1926, I began a new effort: I visited Communist lands. I went to the Soviet Union in 1926, 1936, 1949, and 1959; I saw the nation develop. I visited East Germany, Czechoslovakia, and Poland. I spent ten weeks in China, traveling all over the land. Then, this summer, I rested a month in Rumania.

I was early convinced that Socialism was an excellent way of life, but I thought it might be reached by various methods. For Russia I was convinced she had chosen the only way open to her at the time. I saw Scandinavia choosing a different method, half-way between Socialism and Capitalism. In the United States I saw Consumers Cooperation as a path from Capitalism to Socialism, while England, France and Germany developed in the same direction in their own way. After the depression and the Second World War, I was disillusioned. The Progressive movement in the United States failed. The Cold War started. Capitalism called Communism a crime.

Today I have reached a firm conclusion:

Capitalism cannot reform itself; it is doomed to self-destruction. No universal selfishness can bring social good to all.

Communism—the effort to give all men what they need and to ask of each the best they can contribute—this is the only way of human life. It is a difficult and hard end to reach—it has and will make mistakes, but today it marches triumphantly on in education and science, in home and food, with increased freedom of thought and deliverance from dogma. In the end Communism will triumph. I want to help to bring that day.

The path of the American Communist Party is clear: It will provide the United States with a real Third Party and thus restore democracy to this land. It will call for:

1. Public ownership of natural resources and of all capital.
2. Public control of transportation and communications.
3. Abolition of poverty and limitation of personal income.
4. No exploitation of labor.
5. Social medicine, with hospitalization and care of the old.
6. Free education for all.
7. Training for jobs and jobs for all.
8. Discipline for growth and reform.
9. Freedom under law.
10. No dogmatic religion.

These aims are not crimes. They are practiced increasingly over the world. No nation can call itself free which does not allow its citizens to work for these ends.

Political Affairs, December, 1961, pp. 9–10.

26

THE STRUGGLE FOR THE LIBERATION OF THE BLACK LABORING MASSES IN THIS AGE OF A REVOLUTION OF HUMAN RIGHTS

by A. Philip Randolph

A. Philip Randolph, president of the Negro American Labor Council, gave the opening address at the council's Second Annual Convention, November 10–12, 1961, held in Chicago. A substantial portion follows:

In this mid-twentieth century black labor is one hundred years behind white labor. Black labor is behind white labor in the skilled crafts. They are behind in trade union organization. They are behind in workers' education. They are behind in employment opportunities.

Why? The answer is not because white labor is racially superior to black labor. Not because white labor is more productive than black labor.

In the race between black and white labor in American industry, black labor never had a chance. How could it be otherwise when Negro workers began as slaves while white workers began as free men, or virtually as free men?

In addition to a quarter of a thousand years of captivity in the labor system of chattel slavery, black labor, even after emancipation, has been a prisoner for a hundred years of a moneyless system of peonage, sharecropper-plantation-farm laborism, and a helpless and hopeless city-slum proletariat. . . .

No greater tragedy has befallen the working class anywhere in the modern world than that which plagues the working class in the South. Both white and black workers turned against their own class and gave aid to their enemy, the feudalistic-capitalist class, to subject them to sharper and sharper exploitation and oppression.

Verily, black and white workers did not fight each other because they hated each other, but they hated each other because they fought each other. They fought each other because they did not know each other. They did not know each other because they had no contact or communication with each other. They had no contact or communication with each other because they were afraid of each other. They were afraid of each other because each was propagandized into believing that each was seeking to take the jobs of the other.

By poisonous preachments by the press, pulpit, and politician, the wages of both black and white workers were kept low and working conditions bad, since trade union organization was practically nonexistent. And, even today, the South is virtually a "no man's land" for union labor.

There is no remedy for this plight of the South's labor forces except the unity of the black and white working class.

It is a matter of common knowledge that union organization campaigns, whether under the auspices of the old American Federation of Labor, or the younger Congress of Industrial Organizations, or the AFL-CIO, have wound up as miserable failures.

The reason is not only because the southern working class is divided upon a basis of race, but also because the AFL, the CIO, and the AFL-CIO never took cognizance of this fact. They never built their organization drives upon the principle of the solidarity of the working class. On the contrary, they accepted and proceeded to perpetuate this racial-labor more, the purpose of which was, and is, the perpetuation of segregation—the antithesis of trade union organization.

Thus, they sowed the winds of the division of the workers upon the basis of race, and now they are reaping the whirlwinds.

The leadership of the organized labor movement has at no time ever seriously challenged Jim Crow unionism in the South. White leaders of labor organizations, like white leaders of the Church, business, government, schools, and the press, marched together, under the banner of white supremacy, in the Ku Klux Klan, to put down and keep down by law or lawlessness, the Negro....

Thus, Negro workers are not yet fully free in the South. By the same token, white workers in the South are not yet fully free, because no white worker can ever become fully free as long as a black worker is in southern Bourbon bondage. And as long as white and black workers in the South are not fully free, the entire working class, North, East, South and West, is not and will not become fully free. There is no principle more obvious and universal than the indivisibility of the freedom of the workers regardless of race, color, religion, national origin, or ancestry, being based, as it were, upon the principle of least labor costs in a free market economy.

This is why the racial policies of the American Federation of Labor and

Congress of Industrial Organizations have so devastatingly weakened, morally, organizationally, and politically, the American labor movement before the Congress, the public, and the world.

One has only to note that while trade unions, such as the Amalgamated Clothing Workers, Ladies' Garment Workers, and United Textile Workers, are building up decent wage rates and sound rules governing working conditions in New York, Massachusetts, Pennsylvania, and Illinois, corporate capital, highly sensitive to the least threat to high rates of profits and interest upon investments, promptly takes flight into the land of non-union, low wage, low tax, race bias, mob law, and poor schools, namely, Dixie. Southern mayors, governors, and legislatures make special appeals in the northern press to industries to come South for nonunion, cheap labor.

But this antitrade union condition in the South is labor's fault. It is the direct result of the fact that neither the old AFL, nor the CIO, nor the AFL-CIO ever came to grips with the racial-labor problem in the South. Instead of meeting the racial-labor issue head on, organized labor has always adopted a policy of appeasement, compromise, and defeatism. The evidence exists in the fact that it has recognized and accepted:

(a) The Jim Crow union
(b) The color bar in union constitutions, rituals, or exclusionary racial policies by tacit consent
(c) Racially segregated seniority rosters and lines of job progression
(d) Racial sub-wage differential
(e) Indifferent recognition, if not acceptance, of the concept and practice of a "white man's job" and a "black man's job"
(f) Racial barriers against Negro participation in apprenticeship training programs
(g) Failure to demand Negro workers' participation in union democracy
(h) Racially segregated State conventions of the AFL-CIO in southern cities
(i) Racially segregated city central labor bodies of the AFL-CIO

Is there anyone so naive or cynical as to believe that these forms of race bias are not organizationally and economically disadvantageous to the black laboring masses? Not only has the long system of color caste condition in American industry thrust the Negro workers to the lowest rungs of the occupational hierarchy, but it tends to reinforce the accepted inferiority-hereditary position of black labor, which drastically limits their economic mobility and viability.

Although not unaware of the fact that racial discrimination in trade unions affiliated to the AFL-CIO has existed for almost a century, no profound concern is now manifest by the leadership about this dreadful evil.

Instead of becoming aroused and disturbed about the existence of race bias in unions that affect employment opportunities and the economic status of the Negro worker, AFL-CIO leadership waves aside criticism of the movement's racial policies, as pure exaggeration unworthy of dispassionate examination....

Keynote address, Negro American Labor Council, Chicago, November 10, 1961; in Joanne Grant, ed., *Black Protest* (Greenwich, Conn.: Fawcett, 1968), pp. 487–90; published in part.

27

THE ALBANY MOVEMENT

by James Forman

A key leader describes the founding of the "Albany Movement." Its efforts were basic to the creation of a force attacking racism which "for the first time since the sit-ins" united "all ages and all class backgrounds." Its immediate origin was a request by the mayor of Albany, Georgia, for a meeting to discuss developments in the city. The meeting, on November 17, 1961, resulted in no agreement. That evening, SNCC, the Federated Women's Clubs of Albany, and the Baptist Ministerial Alliance agreed to merge their efforts in what they called the Albany Movement. James Forman describes the events of the critical ensuing weeks:

On November 22, three persons representing the NAACP were arrested in the Trailways terminal. They were released on bond immediately after their arrest. However, Bertha Gober and Blanton Hall, SNCC volunteer workers, were arrested and declined bail.

In an interview with Bertha Gober she told this writer: "On November 22 about 5:;20 P.M. I went to the ticket window. I stood directly behind a white man that was purchasing his ticket. I stood there for five seconds when this uniformed officer said: 'You'll never get your ticket there.' I asked why. Still no answer. Then Detective Friend came up and introduced himself and said my appearance there 'was tending to create a disturbance.' He gave me a choice of going to the Negro waiting room or to be arrested. I informed him that I would not leave until I had purchased my ticket. He took me outside where Chief Pritchett was waiting. We then went to the station."

When asked why did she try to purchase her ticket at the so-called white window, Bertha replied: "I felt as a human being not of Albany but of the United States of America that I had a right to use all facilities. I felt it was necessary to show the people that human dignity must be obtained even if through suffering or maltreatment. . . . I'd do it again any-time. . . . After spending those two nights in jail for a worthy cause, I feel I have gained a feeling of decency and self-respect, a feeling of cleanliness that even the dirtiest walls of Albany's jail nor the actions of my institution cannot take away from me."

Not only were there policemen from the city of Albany at the bus station when Bertha and Blanton were arrested but the Dean of Students of Albany State College also appeared, attempting to convince them they should not transgress established conditions.

On Saturday morning Bertha received the following letter:

> I regret that your recent behavior as a student at Albany State College necessitates the following action.
>
> As a student of Albany State College, you are subject to the rules and regulations of the institution and the Board of Regents, the governing body of the University System of which the Albany State College is a unit.
>
> Please be informed that as a result of your being apprehended and arrested, charged with violation of the law on Wednesday November 22, 1961, you are hereby suspended indefinitely as a student at Albany State College.

We need not discuss the violations of the first amendment, but it must be clearly understood that Bertha checked out of Albany State to go home for Thanksgiving. The Supreme Court, moreover, has ruled that state institutions cannot dismiss students without a hearing. Yet Albany State College has not indicated to either Bertha or Blanton that their case will be reconsidered, despite a petition by the student body of Albany State or the requests of Albany citizens for a hearing.

On Monday morning, November 27, more than six hundred (600) people gathered around the City Hall for the trial of the arrested five. The police asked them to disperse. At this point Charles Jones led the group in prayer. Afterwards they marched around the city block while the trial was in process.

Sherrod interrupted courtroom procedures by sitting on the side of the court "reserved" for whites. A policeman tried to eject him bodily, but he was finally allowed to disturb the pattern of segregation.

On Tuesday November 28, 1961 Sherrod was arrested for trespassing on the campus of Albany State. He spent the night in jail. Although warrants had been taken out by the police for Jones and Reagan, they were never arrested. The next day William H. Dennis, Jr., President of Albany State, said the college withdrew the warrants on the advice of the State Board of Regents who preferred that the three SNCC "agitators" be prosecuted by the State Attorney General. All three were told further trespassing would result in such a warrant.

I came to Albany myself on December 10—by way of a Freedom Ride. We had decided to test the allegedly segregated seating policy of the Georgia Central Railroad, four blacks and five whites. When the conductor told the blacks in our group to move to the next coach, we refused and there was no further incident. But arriving in Albany, where about three hundred blacks were at the station to meet us, we went into the white waiting room and the police closed the doors behind us. Chief Laurie Pritchett then moved in and arrested eight of our group, although by that time some of us were no longer in the waiting room but just standing outside the station.

Chief Pritchett told the press, "We will not stand for these trouble-makers coming into our city for the sole purpose of disturbing the peace and quiet of the city of Albany." Pritchett appeared to be following the same policy used by the Jackson, Mississippi, police toward the Freedom Riders of 1961: Arrest quickly, quietly, and imprison. Move before white mobs can form, avoid brutal actions which can mobilize national support. Play it cool. "Peace and quiet," of course, meant maintaining segregation and oppression. There was no disturbance at the terminal, no one gathering, not even a traffic problem. As S.C. Searles, black editor of the *Southwest Georgian* commented, "The students had made the trip to Albany desegregated without incident. Things had gone so smoothly I think it infuriated the chief. There was a good feeling in the group. They wanted to stop this."

But the "good feeling" couldn't be stopped. The Albany Movement was in full swing. The next morning there was to be a prayer pilgrimage at City Hall during the trial of our group. My article tells what happened to the hundreds of people who came then, and of the events on the day following—an almost solid day of demonstrations:

As we went to trial Tuesday morning, the City dealt with the crowd of Negroes praying on the steps of City Hall by permitting them to pray for a few minutes and to walk around the block once. When the marchers appeared before the City Hall the second time, they were told they were under arrest and huddled into the alleyway between City Hall and an adjacent building. It started raining. People were excited. We could hear Sherrod: "We are going to stay in jail. We Shall Overcome!"

Although the trial took all day, the court refused to rule on it and adjourned until Wednesday at 9:00 A.M.

That Tuesday night at the mass meeting, it was decided a group would go to the City Hall and kneel during our trial, protesting it and the jailing of 267 persons that morning.

On Wednesday morning, the city had an attorney at the trial for the first time. He moved to continue the case until Thursday at 1:00 P.M. because of his prior involvement in another court. His request was granted. As we left the courthouse, we saw around eighty-five people kneeling on cold, wet concrete, singing and praying. Personally I felt it was the most pathetic sight I have ever witnessed, pathetic because it was in mid-century America with a so-called tradition of humanism. . . . Yet, it was moving to know that a community had developed an awareness of social justice to the point that young people, old people, rich people, and poor were able to unite to protest injustice, an awareness that made the community feel what affected one affected all.

Judge Abner Israel, who also tried us, found Slater King in contempt of court for leading the praying and singing Negroes while his court was in session. Sentenced to five days in jail, Slater King refused to appeal his sentence. On Monday, Mrs. Slater King had been arrested and also refused bond. The Kings' three children were at home under the supervision of a housekeeper. The determination of Slater, a prominent businessman in Albany, to join his wife in jail reflects the overcoming-of-the-fear-of-jail and the willingness of the Negro community in Albany to demonstrate to the power structure that no longer could it resist the demands of Negroes.

Around four o'clock Wednesday afternoon the Negro community was informed the Mayor was coming to Shiloh Baptist Church for a meeting. At four-thirty his so-called emissary appeared stating that the Mayor could not meet with them. The Negroes immediately left the church and marched around the courthouse. No one was arrested. However, after returning to the church, it was decided another group should proceed to the City Hall. Led by Bernice Johnson and Bobby Birch, two dynamic young leaders, the group left the church full of enthusiasm. Just as they reached the street on which City Hall is located a loud siren announced: "You are all under arrest." The people started singing "We Shall Overcome" and continued to cross the street, going directly to the alleyway where they were immediately jailed and shipped out of the county. The papers announced: 265 more arrested.

Despite the mass arrests, in a situation where federal law had clearly been violated, the Justice Department wasn't saying "boo." We wanted to force its hand, or at least expose its inaction, and planned a demonstration at the Trailways terminal, together with demonstrations at the library, parks, and train station for Thursday morning. And Chief Pritchett did it again: Ten blacks went into the terminal lunchroom, were served coffee, were arrested, and jailed. They were later released and escorted back to the terminal, but the other demonstrations had to be canceled.

That same day, the city dropped charges against me and seven others (the trial had continued from the day before). But we were rearrested in the courtroom on state charges of conspiring to breach the peace and unlawful assembly, and we went back to jail—this time for a week. By now some 560 people had been arrested and there were at least three hundred still in jail. The jails of Albany and of several nearby counties were jammed. National Guardsmen had been called up by Georgia's governor and telegrams were flowing into Attorney General Kennedy's office. At this point, the mayor of Albany contacted the Albany Movement and requested "a biracial meeting."

By noon the next day, Friday, the city had agreed in principle to desegregate bus and train facilities and to release those jailed. We were on the verge of winning our immediate objectives. More importantly, we had helped to create a movement in which—for the first time since the sit-ins—not only students, but also adults were actively participating in large numbers. Adults of all ages and class backgrounds. The older people of

Albany had demonstrated their willingness not merely to boycott, collect food, and provide other kinds of material support, but to march in the streets, confront the police, go to jail.

James Forman, *The Making of Black Revolutionaries* (Seattle: Open Hand Publishers, 1985), pp. 251–54.

28

ON VIETNAM, U.S. SHOULD REMEMBER FRANCE'S "HUMILIATING DEFEAT"

by Robert S. Browne

Robert Browne was assistant program officer of the U.S. foreign aid mission to Vietnam from 1958 to 1961. Thereafter, he chose to leave such employment and contributed a prophetic letter published in the *New York Times* on February 18, 1962. Browne played a significant role in later developments of the African-American struggle.

Your February 14 editorial exhorted the administration to be candid about the extent of United States military involvement in Vietnam. Alongside the editorial James Reston analyzed facets of the same problem. The tenor of both commentaries was that United States military involvement in Vietnam is already so extensive that there can be no turning back; that with luck a limited conflict may be possible, but that inasmuch as full-scale war may well be shaping up we should be psychologically prepared for it.

Although it is comforting to know that at least some eyes are open as we rush ourselves into this conflict, it is a bit alarming to reflect that the decision has apparently been irrevocably made to push for a military solution to the Vietnam problem with hardly a bow being made toward a peaceful solution there—and, what is equally startling, to push for this military victory with a deadly weight chained to our necks.

Are the *Times'* and Mr. Reston's silence on both these points to be interpreted as their acquiescence in what is evidently the Administration's belief that there is no other road open to us in Vietnam? I should hope not.

Toward Ending Rebellion

Unlike the struggles in Laos, Berlin, and the other cold-war battlefronts, the Vietnam rebellion has never enjoyed any serious examination of ways to resolve it short of war. The reasons for this make interesting speculation.

Certainly one of the first factors to come to mind is President Diem's persistent refusal to entertain consideration of any but a military solution—an obstinacy which is perhaps equaled only by his refusal to moderate in the least the authoritarian tactics by which he maintains his regime in power. Inevitably one wonders if the former stance is not inextricably entwined with the latter.

The *Times* has not feared to describe on several occasions the repressive nature of the South Vietnam Government and to suggest that a genuinely popularly based regime in that country offered the best hope for rallying the support of the Vietnamese people, without which the Viet Cong menace cannot be defeated. With this thinking, most Vietnamese and many knowledgeable foreigners are likely to agree.

The increasing severity of the Vietnam rebellion is intelligible only within the framework of widespread toleration and harboring of the rebels by the rural populace. Whether this acceptance is read as "growing sympathy with the rebels' cause" or merely as protest against existing authority, the lesson for America is much the same.

Increasing Commitments

Unfortunately President Diem has apparently hoodwinked American officials once again into increasing already excessive commitments to the maintenance in power of his corrupt regime. Despite the flurry of talk last fall about "basic reforms" as a condition for additional aid, there has been no indication that the regime has undergone any noticeable modification of its tactics and my Vietnamese friends write me that, if anything, the atmosphere is getting more oppressive than ever.

As we plunge into this conflict it might be well to recall that France, with its not inconsiderable military machine and supplemented by enormous quantities of United States equipment and support, was humiliatingly defeated at Dien Bien Phu (and on numerous other Vietnamese battlefields) by ill-equipped guerrilla warriors whose greatest asset was the cooperation which they won, whether by intimidation or by idealism, from the peasant population.

29

A PROPOSAL OF THE STUDENT NON-VIOLENT COORDINATING COMMITTEE

by James Forman

A leader of SNCC participated in a meeting in February 1962 to consider the Voter Education Project sponsored by the Southern Regional Council. Among those present was Roy Wilkins. When SNCC projected the idea of working in the rural South, Wilkins objected because he felt the effort should concentrate on the major cities in the Deep South. The proposal described below, however, was approved at this meeting:

We have developed in detail only the plans for Georgia; our intentions in the other states are only sketched. At this time we are prepared to move ahead in Georgia, Alabama, and Mississippi; the program in the other states must be delayed until we have adequate financial resources.

Georgia

In Georgia the Student Nonviolent Coordinating Committee proposes to work in two heavily populated Congressional Districts as the initial thrust of our efforts.

Several counties have been chosen as focal points. In the Third Congressional District, we will work the following:

1) Terrell County—Located in the southern part of the Third District, it touches upon the Second District. This places it in a central location where it serves as the symbol of oppression in southwest Georgia. It was here that the first court action under the Civil Rights Act of 1957 was brought. The county is presently under a court injunction against further discrimination in the registration process. Since Negroes comprise 67.7% of the total population, the county is a point of high focus for all of southwest Georgia.

2) Peach County—The presence of Fort Valley State College increases the potential for student activity in this county. It could serve as a training area for students for other counties. Negroes outnumber the white population by a two to one ratio, but out of the 8,000 Negroes in the county only 679 were registered in 1958. From Peach County, Houston, Macon, and Taylor Counties are easily accessible.

3) Marion County—This is the beachhead to the northeast. With 62.5% of the population Negro, only 3.8% of the registered voters are Negro. It could

serve as an example of the possibility of progress in the northeast.

4) Lee County—Lee will be the focal point for the southeast section of the District. We have had strong support already indicated for a summer voter registration program. Since 67.7% of the population is Negro, success here would have strong positive effect upon the neighboring counties.

In the Second Congressional District, four counties have also been chosen:

1) Dougherty County—Here lies the crossroads for people in the rural areas for miles around. It holds tremendous potential, since most of the students at Albany State College live in south Georgia. Negroes comprise 38.1% of the population in the county. A suit has been filed against the county and city officials for enforcing segregation in voting facilities, and has been upheld. The result of this has been that there is a greater awareness of the voter registration process as it relates to the destruction of segregation. It is the home of the only Negro lawyer in south Georgia, and thus has a helpful resource for legal difficulties. And finally, it is in Albany that we have persons willing to study and evaluate our gains in registration through statistical analysis.

The Student Nonviolent Coordinating Committee has been active in Dougherty County for many months, has a good knowledge of the county, and is well known to the inhabitants.

2) Early County—On the northwestern border is Early County, which has a Negro population of 9,300, 54.7% of the total population in 1958. It lies on the Alabama line and has a record of atrocities against Negroes, which may account for the recent Negro population shifts. Whites are also apparently leaving the county: in 1958 the 228 registered Negroes accounted for 4.7% of the registered population, while in 1960 the 214 accounted for 6.5%.

3) Baker County—This is another symbol in Georgia which must be shattered: "no hope for Baker County." People in this area have a strong motivation to register. Baker is one of the forty counties in Georgia where over 50% of the total population is Negro: the percentage in 1958 was 63.3%. At that time no Negro had been allowed to register. At present, there are nine Negroes registered, despite a Federal injunction against the discrimination practiced in the registration process. Baker is said to be worse in police brutality and judicial injustice than the well-known Terrell County. We feel that when Negroes register in Baker County the effect will be felt across the south of Georgia.

4) Worth County—While Negroes compose 50.8% of the population in the county, they represent only 4.8% of the registered population. We have many contacts in the county and can work here in voter registration.

In Georgia, the methods used to systematically exclude the Negro from citizenship participation through the ballot have had one goal: the obliteration of all motivation toward suffrage. Whatever the apparent procedure, purging or inflating of voter lists, economic warfare, police brutality, etc., all attempts to nullify the right to vote among Negroes have aimed at a psychological enslavement which has increased in effectiveness through the years.

The Student Nonviolent Coordinating Committee will use a similar approach to that of segregationists, but with opposite goals. We also intend to engage in a battle for men's minds. Interest in the pursuit of happiness exists in people under the most atrocious conditions of servitude. If we lift the veil of fear from the eyes of the people and provide in its place the motivation to become responsible citizens, the people will rally among themselves toward the achievement of this goal.

Our operations are based on the premise that we cannot and should not do the work ourselves; it is desirable to involve local citizens and groups as much as possible. They should and must want to do the footwork. The people—ministers, students, the man in the street, businessmen, house-wives—must be motivated to feel their responsibility for the entire task. Each is vital to the campaign. . . .

Mississippi

A large part of our total effort will be directed towards producing a larger electorate in one of the toughest southern states. To effectively register voters in Mississippi there must be a system whereby everyone who is working in the state can be brought together to work as one. This system is being promoted through the formation of the Mississippi Federated Voters League, an organization which has representation from all over the state and provides the best contact for the various people working in the field. The role that the Student Nonviolent Coordinating Committee plays in the League is as follows:

We help provide part of the leadership within the state organization and some funds to aid in its operation. We also help by providing part of the manpower needed to get out into the rural areas and teach the people. We have people serving as a liaison between the farms and the central office of the Voters League. We provide the "door knockers" and instructors for the registration schools.

We have people strategically located in each of the five Congressional

Districts within the state. We are prepared to place workers in Marshall County of the Second District; Bolivar County of the Third District; Hinds and Pike Counties of the Fourth District; Kemper County of the Fifth District; and Jefferson Davis County of the First District. The field workers will operate out of each of these counties and coordinate the registration activities in the surrounding counties. In this way we hope to establish a well-coordinated statewide organization which will provide the needed unified "community" effort needed to increase the electorate in Mississippi.

Alabama

Since the largest number of Negroes extends through the middle of Alabama we will concentrate on that area. We intend to have people stationed in Marengo and Clarke Counties in the extreme western section of the state; Dallas and Butler Counties in the central part of Alabama; and Bullock and Lee Counties in eastern Alabama. The idea here will be to establish a base in these counties and move through the rural areas and teach the people on a door-to-door basis.

South Carolina

This particular state has a situation which will easily adapt to the type of work we will be doing. In most of the areas where we would like to work, there is a sizeable city we can work out of in order to reach the people in the rural areas. We would like to work on a district-by-district basis and cover five of the six Congressional Districts in South Carolina. In the First District we would have people in Allendale and Colleton Counties; in the Second, in Orangeburg and Sumter Counties; in the Third, we would have people stationed at Newberry and Edgefield Counties; in the Fifth District, in Chester and Kershaw Counties; and in the Sixth District, Darlington and Georgetown Counties. In every District except the Fifth we will attempt to work in all of the counties surrounding the area in which we are based. The voter registration program has been carried out quite well in general along the coast, and we do not feel that we can do much in adding to the existing progress. This also holds true in Richmond County in the Second District. The ultimate success in effecting a meaningful change in the political structure of the state will come from breaking the strangle-hold that the rural areas have on the urban centers in the state's political makeup.

Conclusion

In order to increase registration in rural southern areas there can be only one approach. We are going to have to penetrate the rural areas, live with the people, develop their own leaders, and teach them the process of registration and effective use of the franchise. There will have to be workers travelling from county to county doing just that, making sure that the people are qualified and that registration is being carried on at a steady rate.

Although the traditional methods of increasing voter registration have concentrated upon the large, heavily populated urban centers, our work will be directed primarily toward the rural areas of the South with particular emphasis on areas that have large concentrations of Negro people. We intend to tap the potential power of the people in the black belt.

This original proposal also listed Louisiana as a work area, but SNCC was unable to extend the project into that state. Nor did it send workers into every single one of the Georgia counties listed. However, the Voter Education Project would become an important instrument that helped SNCC develop a number of its bases—particularly in Mississippi—within the next year and a half.

Our relationship with the Voter Education Project would always be strained, for the activities of those receiving subsistence from it were supposed to be confined solely to voter registration work and not direct action. Staff members felt that this regulation was too restricting. In November 1963, the staff in Mississippi would begin to run candidates in a mock election. This became the excuse for the Voter Education Project to withhold all funds in Mississippi. Walking the fine line of contradiction—our participation in an Establishment-sponsored project—would thus come to an end. Most of us knew in early 1962 that this had to happen, but we were ready and willing to walk the line as long as we could do so and without compromising basic principles or goals.

James Forman, *op. cit.*, pp. 266–69.

30

POLICE BRUTALITY: MISSISSIPPI

by Several Survivors

Affidavits on police brutality regularly encountered by the African-American people were assembled into a book, *Mississippi Black Paper*; two examples follow:

Hinds County

I am a resident of Jackson, Negro, 22 years of age.

On July 5, 1961, I was in the Trailways bus station in Jackson, Mississippi, trying to get a ticket to New Orleans. Jackson police came up, asked me to move from the white section. I refused and the police hit me three times on the back of the neck with night sticks. This was during the Freedom Rides sponsored by CORE. I was then taken to city jail and charged with breach of the peace; and was eventually taken to the state penitentiary on conviction of $200 and four months. I served 45 days in the penitentiary. While I was still in city jail I had to see a doctor because my neck was bleeding from the beating in the Trailways station. The police allowed a doctor into the jail to give me treatment.

On March 9, 1962 (approximately), I went to the county courthouse in Jackson (Hinds County) to attend a trial of Diane Nash. I went into the courtroom and I took a seat on the so-called white side. I was approached by the bailiff of the court, asking me to move to the Negro side. I refused. The presiding judge, Russell Moore, then asked me to move from the bench. He stopped the trial for this purpose. I asked him why. He gave no reason and just said: "Are you going to move?" Then he said I was under arrest for contempt of court. I was then taken to county jail by the bailiff of the court. On the 22nd I had my trial. I had no lawyer. I asked Judge Russell Moore to continue my trial so that I could obtain a lawyer. He said: "Motion denied." I made another motion that he step down from the bench and have another judge in his place so he could take the witness stand and testify why he had placed me under arrest. He said: "Motion denied," again. He then put the bailiff on the witness stand, who testified that I had come into the court to start trouble and that I had been sitting "on the wrong side of the courtroom."

Then I asked the bailiff some questions. I asked him if he had authority to tell everyone in the courtroom where to sit and he said yes. Then I asked him why did he ask me to move. He said that the seats in my area had been reserved for some witnesses in the court. I then asked whether a white minister who had been sitting next to me and had come down from the North to observe the trial had been a witness. The bailiff said no. I asked why not. He said he had the right to ask whoever he wanted to move. Then he said: "We didn't want you to sit there." I then asked: "In other words the courtroom is segregated?" And he replied, "Yes." I then testified in my behalf. I said that my arrest had been unconstitutional, and that if released that day I would go right back into the courtroom and sit anywhere I pleased. I was then sentenced to $100 fine and 30 days on the county farm.

The bailiff who had testified was the one who took me back upstairs. And on our way back to the elevator, I asked him how long he had been working for the court. He said: "None of your damn business." I then said: "You guys are pretty smart. First you segregate us, and then you testify against us in court and tell lies." At this point he got mad and called over three deputy sheriffs. He said: "Ride on up in the elevator with me. This nigger's trying to get tough." The deputies told me to put my hands up against the wall of the elevator. Then they started to beat me. They beat me with their fists until I fell to the floor. Then they began to kick me in the face and side. All four officers took part in the beating. When they put me in the cell, I was bleeding from my nose, above my eyes, and on the back of my neck. I asked for a doctor. The jailer refused to call one.

I was in the county jail for about a week and was then shifted to the county farm. I was singled out as a "troublemaker." I was the only prisoner there dressed in completely striped uniform, most prisoners being dressed in overalls and a T-shirt. I was told that if I was seen talking to anybody, the person that I talked to would be beaten. I was told that I must address all the guards as "Captain" and that if I didn't obey the guards' orders I would be punished.

I was assigned to the road gang, under a Captain _____. He asked me what I was in for. I said contempt of court. He said: "You're one of those god-damn Freedom Riders." I said I didn't know what that meant. He said: "Well, I'm going to have to whip your ass." Then he called four other prisoners and said: "Take this nigger to the woods, and we're going to whip his ass." They threw me on the ground and started pulling off my clothes. He took up a long hose pipe and hit me about fifteen times on the back, neck, buttocks, etc. Then he said, "Get up and put on your clothes." I asked him what he did that for. He said: "We always break in new people like that." Then I said: "I'm going to have to report you to the superintendent, and file a complaint with federal officers." Then he looked at the other prisoners and said: "Well, we got a smart nigger here." I laid back down and pulled off my clothes again and asked if he was going to beat me again. He said: "No, get up." When we got back to the county farm I asked to see the superintendent. He came in and asked me what I wanted. I told him what had happened. He asked me what I was going to do about it. I told him I wanted to file a complaint against the guard, and if he didn't do anything about it I would file a complaint against him. He asked me not to do that, and that if I did I would "catch hell." Then he left. He seemed both worried and mad. He pleaded with me not to file a complaint, but he shook and acted like he'd like to shoot me.

About a week later, the same guard asked me to move a three-hundred-pound log. I told him I wouldn't. He started to hit me with a big stick he picked up off the ground. He hit me fifteen or twenty times. I grabbed the stick out of his hand and threw it away and said that if he ever hit me again, "me and him was going to have it." He pulled out his gun and started backing up and shaking and saying: "Nigger, I ought to kill you." Then he put me in a truck and took me back to the county farm, and took me to the superintendent and told the superintendent that I had hit him. Then they put me in a car and brought me back to the county jail and threw me in solitary.

I was in solitary for 36 hours. The cell was 9 by 12, a "sweatbox." I was naked. The cell was a big steel vault in the ground, with no windows. They turned on heated air into the vault, and left it on all the time I was in the cell. Then they came back and took me back to the county farm. They started asking me questions, such as whether I was ready to "act right." I said, "If somebody treat me right." They said that everything would be okay.

Then they put me back on the same road gang. After about one week, the guard (Captain _____), pulled out a long hose pipe and started to beat me one day without provocation. He struck me about ten or fifteen times. I asked him why he had done that. He said: "You one of them smart-ass niggers. I don't like your ass." He took me back again to the county farm. I was put in a cell for about four days until I was released.

SIGNED: *Jesse Harris*

Coahoma County

I am a Negro, 21 years old.

On February 6, 1962, when I was 19, I was walking with a young man down a Clarksdale street when Clarksdale police officers _____ and _____ stopped us and accused me of having been involved in a theft. I was taken to jail by the officers and they forced me to unclothe and lie on my back. One of the officers beat me between my legs with a belt. A few minutes later, the other officer began to beat me across my naked breasts.

SIGNED: *Bessie Turner*

Mississippi Black Paper (New York: Random House) in Leon Friedman, ed., *The Civil Rights Reader* (New York: Walker and Co., 1967), pp. 197–200.

31

THE TRAVEL JOURNAL OF A BLACK WOMAN IN THE SOUTH

by Betty Rice Hughes

A black woman traveling alone in the South early in 1962, soon after the Freedom Riders had tested the new antiracist rulings, describes her experiences.

It was mostly curiosity that caused me to set out from Los Angeles on a tour of the South by bus last November, just twelve days after the Interstate Commerce Commission's order went into effect forbidding separation by races in interstate busses and terminals. My trip lasted six weeks and carried me through Oklahoma, Arkansas, Tennessee, the Carolinas, Florida, Georgia, Alabama, and part of Mississippi.

The purpose of my tour was twofold: I wanted to see at first hand how many southern states were complying with the ICC ruling; and I also wanted to see if a female Negro tourist traveling alone—unheralded and unprepared for —would receive a different reception from that which had greeted the Freedom Riders.

The trip began uneventfully. I traveled straight across the middle of Arkansas and saw no "White" or "Colored" signs on the rest rooms or waiting rooms. I was certainly not welcomed with open arms and I could sense the hostility brought on by my presence in some towns, but I was served without incident.

In Memphis I encountered the first separate waiting rooms. There were stares from other passengers when I went into the main waiting rooms, but nothing more. I was served in the restaurant. In Monteagle, Tennessee, I saw the first evidence that the "Colored" and "White" signs had recently been removed. After a while I began to look for the different methods used in covering over these signs. In no case were new ones installed. Above the doors of rest rooms the color designations were often painted out or covered with metal strips, leaving an off-centered "Men" and "Women." But there were still four rooms, their racial backgrounds identifiable by location and by the length of the covered-up area on the signs.

I realize now that my naïveté about southern customs was a protective cloak. Even when white people appeared to ignore me, my actions often drew stares from Negro passengers. I was subjected to my first real attempt at discrimination in Florence, South Carolina. I had transferred from Trailways to Greyhound. The bus was an express from New York City and was crowded with passengers going home for Thanksgiving. Florence was the first stop in South Carolina. I had not intended at first to go inside the terminal. I wasn't particularly hungry and I was a little short of money anyway. But a Negro girl sitting next to me, a native South Carolinian, said she wished she had a Coke and a hot dog and I thought I might as well join her. I asked her to go in with me, but she refused and asked me to bring her a sandwich.

There were no signs, so I went in the waiting room in front of me and on through to the restaurant just as I had been doing in other cities. As I walked into the restaurant the cashier looked up, turned red, and started pointing and yelling. "There's another one just across the waiting room!" Since she was looking everywhere but directly at me, I wasn't entirely sure at first that she was talking to me. I thought she might be talking to an elderly white man in front of me. (So did the poor old man, who turned and went out.)

Then I noticed a young Negro fellow who had been following me stop abruptly and leave the restaurant. There was no mistake about whom she meant. Stalling for time, I feigned innocence and asked her, "What's the difference? This one's fine, thank you." The cashier gave me a look that was anything but cordial but turned away from me to attend to her cash register. As soon as I moved toward the counter, a tall white counterman followed, and all the myths, half-truths, exaggerations, and facts concerning treatment of Negroes in the South swarmed through my mind. He kept repeating, "There's another one for you over there, through that door."

"What's the difference?" I asked him. "All I want is a sandwich."

"Just go on over to the other restaurant and you'll find out the difference," he said. He began to get redder and I got scared. "I don't want to stand here and argue. Just go on over to the other restaurant where you belong."

"I'm not arguing," I insisted, "but one's as good as another with me."

At this point he stalked off and I felt sure he was going to get the police or the White Citizens Council or the Ku Klux Klan—maybe all three. To my surprise, all he did was go back behind the lunch counter.

By now most of the white passengers were pointedly staring at their food. No one uttered a word and only a few even glanced at me. A customer got up from the counter and I sat down. I had no idea what was going to happen. I was sure I would not get service, but I did not intend to leave and give the counterman the satisfaction of saying that I went because of his threats. So I sat.

Just before the end of the lunch break, a waitress came over and took my order. My bravado had paid off. Nevertheless, when I returned to the bus I was no longer optimistic about what might lie ahead as we moved farther south, and I dreaded the next bus stop.

And yet at Charleston and Savannah, much farther south, I received service in restaurants and went into the main waiting rooms and rest rooms without incident. The other Negro passengers, who went to the waiting rooms formerly designated as "Colored," had started watching to see what I was going to do at the rest and lunch stops. Several of them asked me, "Are you riding for us?" I said in a sense I was. But no one offered to go into the main waiting area with me.

Throughout Florida all "Colored" and "White" signs had been removed, and at the terminals that had separate waiting rooms I received service along with the other passengers. My courage had returned somewhat, so once again I was not prepared for trouble. When I entered the main restaurant in Tallahassee, a white man yelled back to the kitchen, "Tell Roy to come here!" Roy came out of the kitchen with his dishwasher's apron on. We were both black. So Roy could serve me, the ICC ruling would be obeyed, and the management could save face. Very neat. I had read of this happening to other Negro travelers in the South but when I was faced with a real live instance I didn't know whether to laugh or cry. Roy came over, very nervous, and asked for my order. I smiled at him and said, "What are they doing? Making you the scapegoat?" No answer. So I put on a sober face and gave him my order.

My first stop in Alabama was at Dothan. I had been worrying about Alabama all night. When we got to the terminal, I saw no "White" or "Colored" signs, and when the other Negro passengers went into the once segregated waiting room I went into the main waiting room and then into the restaurant. As I sat down I noticed the ICC ruling against discrimination on the wall and I must say it made me feel much better. The waitress took my order while a Negro cook stared through the service door from the kitchen. After she had brought my coffee, I heard the waitress say to a white woman sitting at the counter, "I know how you feel. I don't like it either but there ain't nothing we can do about it." The white woman got up and walked out.

But after I had sat over my coffee about five minutes, the waitress came over, smiled at me, and asked me where I was from. She stayed and talked. How did I like the South? Where was I going? As I was paying my check, she called after me, "I hope you have a nice trip."

From Dothan I traveled northeast into Georgia. At the major stops in that state—Atlanta, Macon, Savannah—I saw the separate waiting rooms but no "White" or "Colored" signs in the terminals. I went into the main waiting rooms and adjoining rest rooms and ate in the main restaurants. But at the smaller towns where the interstate express busses do not stop, the signs were still up, and all along the highway I noticed that Negroes and whites were still using separate waiting rooms. Discrimination is still rigidly enforced for passengers traveling within the state of Georgia. Only the interstate Negro passengers would sit in the middle or to the front of the bus. All other Negro passengers moved as far back as they could even though posted at the bus entrance was a sign stating that according to the ICC ruling, passengers were to be seated without regard to race, color, creed, or national origin. In Georgia and also in Alabama I often saw white passengers stand up in the aisles for miles rather than sit down beside a Negro passenger. I also saw a Negro woman stand for two hours rather than take an empty seat beside a white passenger.

At Winfield, Alabama, a white man had been holding the door of the restaurant open for the bus passengers. But he took one look at me and slammed the door in my face. Nothing was said by the driver, by me, or by the bus passengers following. I just opened the door and went into the restaurant. As soon as I had sat down, the waitress was in front of me to take my order. I smiled to myself: this sort of hospitality was nearly as hard to bear as more direct forms of hostility. But I was given service.

Of all the towns I stopped in, I was most apprehensive about Anniston, Alabama. It had made international headlines six months previously when a bus carrying Freedom Riders had been burned. There were stares and an oppressive silence as I sat and drank my buttermilk. Negro passengers who had gone into the "Colored" waiting room would glance in at me. But I was served.

When the Greyhound express bus to Los Angeles reached Mississippi, it took what seemed to me a curious route. It certainly would have been faster to go from Alabama straight through the middle of Mississippi and then down to El Paso—the main transfer point for all southern routes. Instead, we took a sharp turn northward, went across the northeastern tip of Mississippi, and without making a rest stop ended back "up north" in Memphis before we turned back down to El Paso. In other words, interstate passengers going from east to the west by Greyhound bus over the southern route never set foot on Mississippi soil.

On the return trip through Arkansas and Texas, I was given service in all the restaurants. At Dallas there were separate waiting rooms, but both Negro and white passengers as well as Indians and Mexicans were in the main one. There were, however, no Negroes eating in the main cafeteria during the time I was there.

Frankly, I do not know whether the treatment I received was due to the fact that I was traveling in the wake of the Freedom Riders or whether it was because I was traveling alone and without publicity. It may have been a combination of both. I felt that the threat of violence was always there—particularly in South Carolina, Georgia, and Alabama—but somehow it never erupted.

My own feeling, as one who is naturally interested in the securing of full rights for all members of my race, is that the advances that have been won through group action may now be reinforced by individual action. I believe that what must happen next is for southern white people to get used to seeing Negroes in waiting rooms, rest rooms, and cafeterias. And it is just as necessary, it seems to me, for southern Negroes to get used to seeing other Negroes bypassing the segregated areas so that they may take courage and insist on the best facilities and service available for their money.

Reporter, April 1962, pp. 20–21.

32

SEPARATION OR INTEGRATION: A DEBATE

by Malcolm X and James Farmer

The liberal magazine *Dialogue*, May 1962 (3:14–28) presented in direct confrontation the views of Malcolm X, when he was a leader of the Black Muslims, and James Farmer, when he was a leader of SNCC. Both lived to alter their views, but at this time they were outstanding figures in the integrationist and nationalist-separatist movements.

MALCOLM X

In the name of Allah, the Beneficent, the Merciful, to whom all praise is due whom we forever thank for giving America's twenty million so-called Negroes, the most honorable Elijah Muhammad as our leader and our teacher and our guide.

I would point out at the beginning that I wasn't born Malcolm Little. Little is the name of the slave master who owned one of my grandparents during slavery, a white man, and the name Little was handed down to my grandfather, to my father, and on to me. But after hearing the teachings of the Honorable Elijah Muhammad and realizing that Little is an English name, and I'm not an Englishman, I gave the Englishman back his name; and since my own had been stripped from me, hidden from me, and I don't know it, I use X; and someday, as we are taught by the Honorable Elijah Muhammad, every black man, woman, and child in America will get back the same name, the same language, and the same culture that he had before he was kidnapped and brought to this country and stripped of these things.

I would like to point out in a recent column by James Reston on the editorial page of the *New York Times*, December 15, 1961, writing from London, Mr. Reston, after interviewing several leading European statesmen, pointed out that the people of Europe or the statesmen in Europe, don't feel that America or Europe have anything to worry about in Russia; that the people in Europe foresee the time when Russia, Europe, and America will have to unite together to ward off the threat of China and the non-white world. And if this same statement was made by a Muslim, or by the honorable Elijah Muhammad, it would be classified as racist; but Reston who is one of the leading correspondents in this country and writing for one of the most respected newspapers, points out that the holocaust that the West is facing is not something from Russia, but threats of the combined forces of the dark world against the white world.

Why do I mention this? Primarily because the most crucial problem facing the white world today is the race problem. And the most crucial problem facing white America today is the race problem. Mr. Farmer pointed out beautifully and quoted one writer actually as saying that the holocaust that America is facing is primarily still based upon race. This doesn't mean that when people point these things out that they are racist; this means that they are facing the facts of life that we are confronted with today. And one need only to look at the world troubles in its international context, national context, or local context, and one will always see the race problem right there, a problem that it is almost impossible to duck around.

It so happens that you and I were born at a time of great change, when changes are taking place. And if we can't react intelligently to these changes, then we are going to be destroyed. When you look into the United Nations set-up, the way it is, we see that there is a change of power taking place, a change of position, a change of influence, a change of control. Wherein, in the past, white people used to exercise unlimited control and authority over dark mankind, today they are losing their ability to dictate unilateral terms to dark mankind. Whereas, yesterday dark nations had no voice in their own affairs, today the voice that they exercise in their own affairs is increasing, which means in essence that the voice of the white man or the white world is becoming more quiet every day, and the voice of the nonwhite world is becoming more loud every day. These are the facts of life and these are the changes that you and I, this generation, have to face up to on an international level, a national level, or a local level before we can get a solution to the problems that confront not only the white man, but problems that confront also the black man, or the nonwhite man.

When we look at the United Nations and see how these dark nations get their independence—they can out-vote the western block or what is known as the white world—and to the point where up until last year the

U.N. was controlled by the white powers, or Western powers, mainly Christian powers, and the secretaryship used to be in the hands of a white European Christian; but now when we look at the general structure of the United Nations we see a man from Asia, from Burma, who is occupying the position of Secretary, who is a Buddhist, by the way, and we find the man who is occupying the seat of President is a Moslem from Africa, namely Tunisia. Just in recent times all of these changes are taking place, and the white man has got to be able to face up to them, and the black man has to be able to face up to them, before we can get our problem solved, on an international level, a national level, as well as on the local level.

In terms of black and white, what this means is that the unlimited power and prestige of the white world is decreasing, while the power and prestige of the nonwhite world is increasing. And just as our African and Asian brothers wanted to have their own land, wanted to have their own country, wanted to exercise control over themselves and govern themselves—they didn't want to be governed by whites or Europeans or outsiders, they wanted control over something among the black masses here in America. I think it would be mighty naive on the part of the white man to see dark mankind all over the world stretching out to get a country of his own, a land of his own, an industry of his own, a society of his own, even a flag of his own, it would be mighty naive on the part of the white man to think that same feeling that is sweeping through the dark world is not going to leap 9000 miles across the ocean and come into the black people here in this country, who have been begging you for four hundred years for something that they have yet to get.

In the areas of Asia and Africa where the whites gave freedom to the nonwhites a transition took place, of friendliness and hospitality. In the areas where the nonwhites had to exercise violence, today there is hostility between them and the white man. In this, we learn that the only way to solve a problem that is unjust, if you are wrong, is to take immediate action to correct it. But when the people against whom these actions have been directed have to take matters in their own hands, this creates hostility, and lack of friendliness and good relations between the two.

I emphasize these things to point up the fact that we are living in an era of great change; when dark mankind wants freedom, justice, and equality. It is not a case of wanting integration or separation, it is a case of wanting freedom, justice, and equality.

Now if certain groups think that through integration they are going to get freedom, justice, equality, and human dignity, then well and good, we will go along with the integrationists. But if integration is not going to return human dignity to dark mankind, then integration is not the solution to the problem. And oft times we make the mistake of confusing the objective with the means by which the objective is to be obtained. It is not integration that Negroes in America want, it is human dignity. They want to be recognized as human beings. And if integration is going to bring us recognition as human beings, then we will integrate. But if integration is not going to bring us recognition as human beings, then integration "out the window," and we have to find another means or method and try that to get our objectives reached.

The same hand that has been writing on the wall in Africa and Asia is also writing on the wall right here in America. The same rebellion, the same impatience, the same anger that exists in the hearts of the dark people in Africa and Asia is existing in the hearts and minds of twenty million black people in this country who have been just as thoroughly colonized as the people in Africa and Asia. Only the black man in America has been colonized mentally, his mind has been destroyed. And today, even though he goes to college, he comes out and still doesn't even know he is a black man; he is ashamed of what he is, because his culture has been destroyed, his identity has been destroyed, he has been made to hate his black skin, he has been made to hate the texture of his hair, he has been made to hate the features that God gave him. Because the honorable Elijah Muhammad is coming along today and teaching us the truth about black people to make us love ourselves instead of realizing that it is you who taught us to hate ourselves and our own kind, you accuse the honorable Elijah Muhammad of being a hate teacher and accuse him of being a racist. He is only trying to undo the white supremacy that you have indoctrinated the entire world with.

I might point out that it makes America look ridiculous to stand up in world conferences and refer to herself as the leader of the free world. Here is a country, Uncle Sam, standing up and pointing a finger at the Portuguese, and at the French, and other colonizers, and there are twenty million black people in this country who are still confined to second-class citizenship, twenty million black people in this country who are still segregated and Jim-Crowed, as my friend Dr. Farmer has already pointed out. And despite the fact that twenty million black people here don't have freedom, justice, and equality, Adlai Stevenson has the nerve enough to stand up in the United Nations and point the finger at South Africa, and at Portugal and at some of these other countries. All we say is that South

Africa preaches what it practices and practices what it preaches; America preaches one thing and practices another. And we don't want to integrate with hypocrites who preach one thing and practice another.

The good point in all of this is that there is an awakening going on among whites in America today, and this awakening is manifested in this way: two years ago you didn't know that there were black people in this country who didn't want to integrate with you; two years ago the white public had been brainwashed into thinking that every black man in this country wanted to force his way into your community, force his way into your schools, or force his way into your factories; two years ago you thought that all you would have to do is give us a little token integration and the race problem would be solved. Why? Because the people in the black community who didn't want integration were never given a voice, were never given a platform, were never given an opportunity to shout out the fact that integration would never solve the problem. And it has only been during the past year that the white public has begun to realize that the problem will never be solved unless a solution is devised acceptable to the black masses, as well as the black bourgeoisie—the upper class or middle class Negro. And when the whites began to realize that these integration-minded Negroes were in the minority, rather than in the majority, then they began to offer an open forum and give those who want separation an opportunity to speak their mind too.

We who are black in the black belt, or black community, or black neighborhood can easily see that our people who settle for integration are usually the middle-class so-called Negroes, who are in the minority. Why? Because they have confidence in the white man; they have absolute confidence that you will change. They believe that they can change you, they believe that there is still hope in the American dream. But what to them is an American dream to us is an American nightmare, and we don't think that it is possible for the American white man in sincerity to take the action necessary to correct the unjust conditions that twenty million black people here are made to suffer morning, noon, and night. And because we don't have any hope or confidence or faith in the American white man's ability to bring about a change in the injustices that exist, instead of asking or seeking to integrate into the American society we want to face the facts of the problem the way they are, and separate ourselves. And in separating ourselves this doesn't mean that we are anti-white or anti-American, or anti-anything. We feel, that if integration all these years hasn't solved the problem yet, then we want to try something new, something different and something that is in accord with the conditions as they actually exist.

The honorable Elijah Muhammad teaches us that there are over 725 million Moslems or Muslims on this earth. I use both words interchangeably. I use the word Moslem for those who can't undergo the change, and I use the word Muslim for those who can. He teaches us that the world of Islam stretches from the China Seas to the shores of West Africa and that the twenty million black people in this country are the lost-found members of the nation of Islam. He teaches us that before we were kidnapped by your grandfathers and brought to this country and put in chains, our religion was Islam, our culture was Islamic, we came from the Muslim world, we were kidnapped and brought here out of the Muslim world. And after being brought here we were stripped of our language, stripped of our ability to speak our mother tongue, and it's a crime today to have to admit that there are twenty million black people in this country who not only can't speak their mother tongue, but don't even know they ever had one. This points up the crime of how thoroughly and completely the black man in America has been robbed by the white man of his culture, of his identity, of his soul, of his self. And because he has been robbed of his self, he is trying to accept your self. Because he doesn't know what belongs to him, he is trying to lay clam to what belongs to you. You have brain-washed him and made him a monster. He is black on the outside, but you have made him white on the inside. Now he has a white heart and a white brain, and he's breathing down your throat and down your neck because he thinks he's a white man the same as you are. He thinks that he should have your house, that he should have your factory, he thinks that he should even have your school, and most of them even think that they should have your woman, and most of them are after your woman.

The honorable Elijah Muhammad teaches us that the black people in America, the so-called Negroes, are the people who are referred to in the Bible as the lost sheep, who are to be returned to their own in the last days. He says that we are also referred to in the Bible, symbolically, as the lost tribe. He teaches us in our religion, that we are those people whom the Bible refers to who would be lost until the end of time. Lost in a house that is not theirs, lost in a land that is not theirs; lost in a country that is not theirs, and who will be found in the last days by the Messiah who will awaken them and enlighten them, and teach them that which they had been stripped of, and then this would give them the desire to come together among their own kind and go back among their own kind.

And this, basically, is why we who are followers of the honorable Elijah Muhammad don't accept integration; we feel that we are living at the end of time, by this, we feel that we are living at the end of the world. Not the end of the earth, but the end of the world. He teaches us that there are many worlds. The planet is an earth, and there is only one earth, but there are many worlds on this earth, the Eastern World and the Western World. There is a dark world and a white world. There is the world of Christianity, and the world of Islam. All of these are worlds and he teaches us that when the book speaks of the end of time, it doesn't mean the end of the earth, but it means the end of time for certain segments of people, or a certain world that is on this earth. Today, we who are here in America who have awakened to the knowledge of ourselves; we believe that there is no God but Allah, and we believe that the religion of Islam is Allah's religion, and we believe that it is Allah's intention to spread his religion throughout the entire earth. We believe that the earth will become all Muslim, all Islam, and because we are in a Christian country we believe that this Christian country will have to accept Allah as God, accept the religion of Islam as God's religion, or otherwise God will come in and wipe it out. And we don't want to be wiped out with the American white man, we don't want to integrate with him, we want to separate from him.

The method by which the honorable Elijah Muhammad is straightening out our problem is not teaching us to force ourselves into your society, or force ourselves even into your political, economic, or any phase of your society, but he teaches us that the best way to solve this problem is for complete separation. He says that since the black man here in America is actually the property that was stolen from the East by the American white man, since you have awakened today and realized that this is what we are, we should be separated from you, and your government should ship us back from where we came from, not at our expense, because we didn't pay to come here. We were brought here in chains. So the honorable Elijah Muhammad and the Muslims who follow him, we want to go back to our own people. We want to be returned to our own people.

But in teaching this among our people and the masses of black people in this country, we discover that the American government is the foremost agency in opposing any move by any large number of black people to leave here and go back among our own kind. The honorable Elijah Muhammad's words and work is harassed daily by the F.B.I. and every other government agency which use various tactics to make the so-called

Negroes in every community think that we are all about to be rounded up, and they will be rounded up too if they will listen to Mr. Muhammad; but what the American government has failed to realize, the best way to open up a black man's head today and make him listen to another black man is to speak against that black man. But when you begin to pat a black man on the back, no black man in his right mind will trust that black man any longer. And it is because of this hostility on the part of the government toward our leaving here that the honorable Elijah Muhammad says then, if the American white man or the American government doesn't want us to leave, and the government has proven its inability to bring about integration or give us freedom, justice, and equality on a basis, equally mixed up with white people, then what are we going to do? If the government doesn't want us to go back among our own people, or to our own people, and at the same time the government has proven its inability to give us justice, the honorable Elijah Muhammad says if you don't want us to go and we can't stay here and live in peace together, then the best solution is separation. And this is what he means when he says that some of the territory here should be set aside, and let our people go off to ourselves and try and solve our own problem.

Some of you may say, Well, why should you give us part of this country? The honorable Elijah Muhammad says that for four hundred years we contributed our slave labor to make the country what it is. If you were to take the individual salary or allowances of each person in this audience it would amount to nothing individually, but when you take it collectively all in one pot you have a heavy load. Just the weekly wage. And if you realize that from anybody who could collect all of the wages from the persons in this audience right here for one month, why they would be so wealthy they couldn't walk. And if you see that, then you can imagine the result of millions of black people working for nothing for 310 years. And that is the contribution that we made to America. Not Jackie Robinson, not Marian Anderson, not George Washington Carver, that's not our contribution; our contribution to American society is 310 years of free slave labor for which we have not been paid one dime. We who are Muslims, followers of the honorable Elijah Muhammad, don't think that an integrated cup of coffee is sufficient payment for 310 years of slave labor.

JAMES FARMER
When the Freedom Riders left from Montgomery, Alabama, to ride

into the conscience of America and into Jackson, Mississippi, there were many persons who said to us, "Don't go into Mississippi, go anyplace you like, go to the Union of South Africa, but stay out of Mississippi." They said, "What you found in Alabama will be nothing compared to what you will meet in Mississippi." I remember being a told a story by one minister who urged us not to go. He said, "Once upon a time there was a Negro who had lived in Mississippi, lived for a long time running from county to county. Finally he left the state, and left it pretty fast, as Dick Gregory would put it, not by Greyhound, but by bloodhound, and he went to Illinois to live, in Chicago. And unable to find a job there, after several weeks of walking the street unemployed, he sat down and asked God what he should do. God said, "Go back to Mississippi." He said, "Lord you surely don't mean it, you're jesting. You don't mean for me to go back to Mississippi. There is segregation there!" The Lord said, "Go back to Mississippi." The man looked up and said, "Very well, Lord, if you insist, I will do it, I will go. But will you go with me?" The Lord said "As far as Cincinnati."

The Freedom Riders felt that they should go all the way because there is something wrong with our nation and we wanted to try to set it right. As one of the nation's scholars [W. E. B. Du Bois] wrote at the turn of the century, "The problem of the twentieth century will be the problem of the color-line, of the relations between the lighter and the darker peoples of the earth, Asia and Africa, in America, and in the islands of the sea." What prophetic words, indeed. We have seen the struggle for freedom all over the world. We have seen it in Asia; we have seen it in the island of the sea; we have seen it in Africa, and we are seeing it in America now. I think the racist theories of Count DeGobineau, Lothrop Stoddard, and the others have set the pattern for a racism that exists within our country. There are theories that are held today, not only by those men and their followers and successors, but by Ross Barnett, John Patterson devotees and followers of the Klan and the White Citizens Councils, and Lincoln Rockwell of the American Nazi Party.

These vicious racist theories hold that Negroes are inferior and whites are superior innately. Ordained by God, so to speak. No more vicious theory has existed in the history of mankind. I would suggest to you that no theory has provided as much human misery throughout the centuries as the theory of races—The theories that say some people are innately inferior and that others are innately superior. Although we have some of those theories in our country, we also have a creed of freedom and of democracy. As Pearl Buck put it, "Many Americans suffer from a split personality. One side of that personality is believing in democracy and freedom, as much as it is possible for a man so to believe. The other side of this personality is refusing just as doggedly, to practice that democracy and that freedom in which he believes." That was the split personality. Gunnar Myrdal, in his book, *The American Dilemma*, indicated that this was basically a moral problem, and that we have this credo which Americans hold to, of freedom, and democracy, and equality, but still we refuse to practice it. Gunnar Myrdal indicated that this is sorely troubling the American conscience.

All of us are a part of this system, *all* a part of it. We have all developed certain prejudices, I have mine, you have yours. It seems to me that it is extremely dangerous when any individual claims to be without prejudice, when he really does have it. I'm prejudiced against women drivers. I think they are a menace to civilization, and the sooner they are removed from the highways, the safer we will all be, but I know that's nothing but a prejudice. I have seen women drivers who are better drivers than I am, but does that destroy my prejudice? No. What I do then, is to separate her from the group of women drivers and say, "Why she is an exception." Or maybe I say she is driving very well because she feels guilty. She knows that other women in the past have had accidents, and so she drives cautiously.

I remember several years ago when I was a youth, attending a church youth conference, and a young fellow from Mississippi and I became very good friends. The last day of the conference as we walked along the road he put his arm on my shoulder and said, "Jim, I have no race prejudice." "No," said I. "Absolutely not," said he. I raised my eyebrows. "As a matter of fact," he went on, "I was thirteen years old before I knew I was any better than a Negro." Well sometimes a supposed absence of racial prejudice runs quite along those lines. Now prejudice is a damaging thing to Negroes. We have suffered under it tremendously. It damages the lives of little children. I remember when I first came into contact with segregation; it was when I was a child in Mississippi when my mother took me downtown, and on the way back this hot July day I wanted to stop and get a coke, and she told me I couldn't get a coke, I had to wait until I got home. "Well why can't I, there's a little boy going in," said I, "I bet he's going to get a coke." He was. "Well, why can't I go?" "Because he's white," she said, "and you're colored." It's not important what happened to me, the fact is that the same thing over and over again happens to every mother's child whose skin happens to be dark.

If the damage that is done to Negroes is obvious, the damage that is done to whites in America is equally obvious, for they're prejudiced. I lived in Texas a large part of my life; remember driving through the state, and after dusk had fallen being followed by cars of whites who forced me off the road and said to me, "Don't you know that your kind is not supposed to be in this town after sundown." I wondered what was happening to these people; how their minds were being twisted, as mine and others like me had had our minds twisted by this double-edged sword of prejudice. It is a disease indeed. It is an American disease. It is an American dilemma.

The damage to Negroes is psychological, it is also economic. Negroes occupying the bottom of the economic ladder, the poorest jobs, the lowest paying jobs. Last to be hired, and first to be fired, so that today the percentage of unemployed Negroes is twice as high as that of whites. There has been political damage as well. In the South we find that comparatively few Negroes are registered to vote. Many are apathetic even when they could register. The percentage who are registered in the North is almost equally as low. As a result, comparatively few Negroes are elected to political office. This, the damage to the Negroes, as a result of the disease of segregation has been psychological, economic, social, and political. I would suggest to you that the same damages have occurred to whites. Psychological damages are obvious. Economic—the nation itself suffers economically, as a result of denying the right of full development to one-tenth of its population. Skills, talents, and abilities, are crushed in their cradle, are not allowed to develop. Snuffed out. Thus, the nation's economy has suffered. People who could be producing are instead walking the streets. People who could be producing in better jobs and producing more are kept in the lower jobs, sweeping the floors and serving other persons. The whole nation has been damaged by segregation. Now, all of us share the guilt too. I myself am guilty. I am guilty because I spent half of my life in the South. During those years I participated in segregation, cooperated with it, and supported it.

We are all intricately involved in the system of segregation. We have not yet extricated ourselves. Negroes are involved, and guilty, and share the blame to the extent they themselves have, by their deeds and their acts allowed segregation to go on for so long. I do not believe that guilt is a par of my genes or your genes. It hinges upon the deeds that you have done. If you have supported segregation, then you are guilty. If you continue to support it, then your guilt is multiplied. But that is your guilt, that is mine. We share the guilt for the disease of segregation, and its continued existence. All too long, Negro Americans have put up with the system of segregation, North and South. Incidentally, it is not a southern problem, it is a northern one as well. Segregation exists in housing and in jobs, and in schools. We have put up with it, have done nothing about it.

The day before the Freedom Riders left Washington, D.C. to ride into the South, I visited my father who was in the hospital on what proved to be his deathbed. I told him I was going on a freedom ride into the South. He wanted to know what it was and I told him. "Where are you going?" he asked, and I told him. He said, "Well, I'm glad that you're going, son, and I hope you survive. I realize you may not return, but," said he, "I'm glad you're going because when I was a child in South Carolina and Georgia, we didn't like segregation either, but we thought that's the way things always had to be and the way they always would be, so we put up with it, took part in it, decided to exist and to stay alive. I am glad," said he, "that there are lots of people today who are no longer willing to put up with the evil of segregation, but want to do something about it and know that something can be done." How right he was indeed.

The masses of Negroes are through putting up with segregation; they are tired of it. They are tired of being pushed around in a democracy which fails to practice what it preaches. The Negro students of the South who have read the Constitution, and studied it, have read the amendments to the Constitution, and know the rights that are supposed to be theirs— they are coming to the point where they themselves want to do something about achieving these rights, not depend on somebody else. The time has passed when we can look for pie in the sky, when we can depend upon someone else on high to solve the problem for us. The Negro students want to solve the problem themselves. Masses of older Negroes want to join them in that. We can't wait for the law. The Supreme Court decision in 1954 banning segregated schools has had almost eight years of existence, yet, less than eight percent of the Negro kids are in integrated schools. That is far too slow. Now the people themselves want to get involved, and they are. I was talking with one of the student leaders of the South only last week; he said, "I myself desegregated a lunch counter, not somebody else, not some big man, some powerful man, but me, little me. I walked the picket line and I sat in and the walls of segregation toppled.

Now all people can eat there." One young prize fighter was a cell-mate of mine in the prisons of Mississippi as a freedom rider; he had won his last fight and had a promising career. I saw him three weeks ago, and asked him, "How are you coming along?" He said, "Not very well, I lost the last fight and I am through with the prize ring. I have no more interest in it. The only fight I want now," said he, "is the freedom fight. Because I, a little man, can become involved in it, and can help to win freedom." So that's what's happening; you see, we are going to do something about freedom now, we are not waiting for other people to do it. The student sit-ins have shown it; we are winning. As a result of one year of the student sit-ins, the lunch counters were desegregated in more than 150 cities. The walls are tumbling down.

Who will say that lunch counters, which are scattered all over the country, are not important? Are we not to travel? Picket lines and boycotts brought Woolworth's to its knees. In its annual report of last year, Woolworth's indicated that profits had dropped and one reason for the drop was the nationwide boycott in which many northern students, including Cornellians, participated. The picketing and the nationwide demonstrations are the reason that the walls came down in the South, because people were in motion with their own bodies marching with picket signs, sitting in, boycotting, withholding their patronage. In Savannah, Georgia, there was a boycott, in which ninety-nine percent of the Negroes participated. They stayed out of the stores. They registered to vote. The store owners then got together and said, "We want to sit down and talk; gentlemen, you have proved your point. You have proved that you can control Negroes' purchasing power and that you can control their votes. We need no more proof, we are ready to hire the people that you send." Negroes are hired in those stores now as a result of this community-wide campaign. In Lexington, Kentucky, the theatres were opened up by CORE as a result of picketing and boycotting. Some of the theatres refused to admit Negroes, others would let Negroes sit up in the balcony. They boycotted that one, picketed the others. In a short period of time, the theatre owners sat down to negotiate. All of the theatres there are open now. Using the same technique, they provided scores of jobs in department stores, grocery stores, and more recently as city bus drivers.

Then came the freedom rides. Three hundred twenty-five people were jailed in Jackson, Mississippi, others beaten, fighting for freedom nonviolently. They brought down many many barriers. They helped to create desegregation in cities throughout the South. The ICC order was forthcoming as a result of the freedom rides and a more recent Supreme Court ruling. CORE sent test teams throughout the South after the ICC order went into effect. The test teams found that in hundreds of cities throughout the South, where terminals had been previously segregated, they now were desegregated and Negroes were using them. Mississippi is an exception, except for two cities; Louisiana is an exception, except for one pocket of the state; but by and large the Rides were successful. And then on Route 40. How many Negroes and interracial groups have driven Route 40 to Washington or to New York and carried their sandwiches, knowing that they could not eat between Wilmington and Baltimore. The freedom rides there, and some Cornell students participated in those freedom rides, brought down the barriers in more than half of those restaurants and each weekend, rides are taking place aimed at the others. By Easter we will have our Easter dinner in any place we choose on Route 40. At least fifty-three out of the eighty are now desegregated. In voter registration projects, we have registered 17,000 Negroes in South Carolina, previously unregistered. The politicians, segregationists, it's true, now call up our leaders and say, "I would like to talk to you because I don't believe in segregation as much as my opponent," or, "We would like to sit down and talk," or, "Can you come by my house and let's talk about his thing." Because they are realizing that now they have to be responsible to the votes of Negroes as well as the handful of whites, these are the things that are being done by people themselves in motion. Not waiting for someone else to do it, not looking forward to pie in the sky at some later date, not expecting a power on high to solve the problem for them; but working to solve it themselves and winning.

What are our objectives; segregation, separation? Absolutely not! The disease and the evils that we have pointed to in our American culture have grown out of segregation and its partner, prejudice. We are for integration, which is the repudiation of the evil of segregation. It is a rejection of the racist theories of DeGobineau, Lothrop Stoddard, and all the others. It matters not whether they say that whites are superior to Negroes and Negroes are inferior, or if they reverse the coin and say the Negroes are superior and whites are inferior. The theory is just as wrong, just as much a defiance of history. We reject those theories. We are working for the right of Negroes to enter all fields of activity in American life. To enter business if they choose, to enter the professions, to enter the sciences, to enter the arts, to enter the academic world. To be workers, to be laborers if they choose. Our objective is to have each individual accepted on the basis of his individual merit and not on the basis of his color. On the basis of what he is worth himself.

This has given a new pride to a large number of people. A pride to the people in Mississippi, who themselves saw others, white and Negro, joining them in the fight for freedom; forty-one local citizens went into the jails of Mississippi joining the freedom riders. They have come out now and they have started their own nonviolent Jackson movement for Freedom. They are sitting in. They are picketing, they are boycotting, and it is working. In Macomb, Mississippi, local citizens are now seeking to register to vote, some of them registering. In Huntsville, Alabama, as a result of CORE's campaign there (and we are now under injunction), for the past six weeks local Negro citizens have been sitting in every day at lunch counters. One of the white CORE leaders there in Huntsville was taken out of his house at gun point, undressed and sprayed with mustard oil. That's the kind of treatment they have faced, but they will not give up because they know they are right and they see the effects of their efforts; they see it in the crumbling walls in interstate transportation and in other public facilities.

We are seeking an open society, an open society of freedom where people will be accepted for what they are worth, will be able to contribute fully to the total culture and the total life of the nation.

Now we know the disease, we know what is wrong with America, we know now that the CORE position is in trying to right it. We must do it in interracial groups because we do not think it is possible to fight against caste in a vehicle which in itself is a representative of caste. We know that the students are still sitting in, they are still fighting for freedom. What we want Mr. X, the representative of the Black Muslims and Elijah Muhammad, to tell us today, is what his program is, what he proposes to do about killing this disease. We know the disease, physician, what is your cure? What is your program and how do you hope to bring it into effect? How will you achieve it? It is not enough to tell us that it may be a program of a black state. The Communists had such a program in the thirties and part of the forties, and they dropped it before the fifties as being impractical. So we are not only interested in the terminology. We need to have it spelled out, if we are being asked to follow it, to believe in it, what does it mean? Is it a separate Negro society in each city? As a Harlem, a South Side Chicago? Is it a separate state in one part of the country? Is it a separate nation in Africa, or elsewhere? Then we need to know how is it to be achieved. I assume that before a large part of land could be granted to Negroes or to Jews or to anybody else in the country it would have to be approved by the Senate of the United States.

You must tell us, Mr. X, if you seriously think that the Senate of the United States which has refused or failed for all these years to pass a strong Civil Rights Bill, you must tell us if you really think that this Senate is going to give us, to give you, a black state. I am sure that Senator Eastland would so vote, but the land that he would give us would probably be in the bottom of the sea. After seeing Alabama and Mississippi, if the power were mine, I would give you those states, but the power is not mine. I do not vote in the Senate. Tell us how you expect to achieve this separate black state.

Now it is not enough for us to know that you believe in black business, all of us believe that all Americans who wish to go into business, should go into business. We must know, we need to know, if we are to appraise your program, the kind of businesses, how they are to be established; will we have a General Motors, a General Electric? Will I be able to manufacture a Farmer Special? Where I am going to get the capital from? You must tell us if we are going to have a separate interstate bus line to take the place of Greyhound and Trailways. You must tell us how this separate interstate bus line is going to operate throughout the country if all of us are confined within one separate state.

You must tell us these things, Mr. X, spell them out. You must tell us also what the relationship will be between the black businesses which you would develop and the total American economy. Will it be a competition? Will it be a rival economy, a dual economy or will there be cooperation between these two economies?

Our program is clear. We are going to achieve our goals of integration by nonviolent direct action on an interracial level with whites and Negroes jointly cooperating to wipe out a disease which has afflicted and crippled all of them, white and black alike. The proof of the pudding is the eating. We have seen barriers fall as the result of using these techniques. We ask you, Mr. X, what is your program?

Rebuttal

JAMES FARMER

I think that Mr. X's views are utterly impractical and that his so-called "black state" cannot be achieved. There is no chance of getting it unless it is to be given to us by Allah. We have waited for a long time for God to give us other things and we have found that the God in which most of us happen to believe helps those who help themselves. So we would like you to tell us, Mr. X, just what steps you plan to go through to get this black state. Is it one that is going to be gotten by violence, by force? Is it going to be given to us by the Federal government? Once a state is allocated, then are the white people who happen to live there to be moved out forcibly, or Negroes who don't want to go to your black state going to be moved in forcibly? And what does this do to their liberty and freedom?

Now Mr. X suggests that we Negroes or so-called Negroes, as he puts it, ought to go back where we came from. You know, this is a very interesting idea. I think the solution to many of the problems, including the economic problem of our country, would be for all of us to go back where we came from and leave the country to the American Indians. As a matter of fact, maybe the American Indian can go back to Asia, where I understand the anthropologists tell us he came from, and I don't know who preceded him there. But if we search back far enough I am sure that we can find some people to people or populate this nation. Now the overwhelming number of Negroes in this country consider it to be their country; their country more than Africa: I was in Africa three years ago, and while I admire and respect what is being done there, while there is certainly a definite sense of identification, and sympathy with what is going on there, the fact is that the cultures are so very different. Mr. X, I am sure that you have much more in common with me or with several people whom I see sitting here than you do with the Africans, than you do with Tom Mboya. Most of them could not understand you, or you they, because they speak Swahili or some other language and you would have to learn those languages.

I tell you that we are Americans. This is our country as much as it is white American. Negroes came as slaves, most of us did. Many white people came as indentured servants; indentured servants are not free. Don't forget it wasn't all of you who were on that ship, The Mayflower.

Now separation of course has been proposed as the answer to the problem, rather than integration. I am pleased however that Malcolm, oh pardon me, Mr. X, indicated that if integration works, and if it provides dignity, then we are for integration. Apparently he is almost agreeing with us there. He is sort of saying as King Agrippa said to St. Paul, "Almost Thou Persuadest Me." I hope that he will be able to come forth and make the additional step and join me at the integrationist side of this table. In saying that separation really is the answer and the most effective solution to this problem, he draws a distinction between separation and segregation, saying that segregation is forced ghettoism while separation is voluntary ghettoism. Well now, I would like to ask Mr. X whether it would be voluntary for Negroes to be segregated as long as we allow discrimination in housing throughout our country to exist. If you live in a black state and cannot get a house elsewhere, then are you voluntarily separated, or are you forcibly segregated?

Now Mr. X suggests that actually the Negroes in this country want the white man's women. Now this is a view, of course, which is quite familiar to you; I've heard it before, there are some Negroes who are married to white people, and I, just before I came up, was looking over a back issue of the paper of the Muslims and saw in there an indication that I myself have a white wife. And it was suggested that therefore I have betrayed my people in marrying a white woman. Well you know I happen to have a great deal of faith in the virtues and abilities and capacities of Negroes. Not only Negroes, but all of the people too. In fact, I have so much faith in the virtues of Negroes that I do not even think those virtues are so frail that they will be corrupted by contact with other people.

Mr. X also indicated that Negroes imitate whites. It is true, we do, he is right. We fix our hair and try to straighten it; I don't do mine. I haven't had a conk in my life. I think they call it a process now, etc. But this is a part of the culture of course. After the black culture was taken away from us, we had to adapt the culture that was here, adopt it, and adapt to it. But it is also true that white people try to imitate Negroes with their jazz, with their hair curlers, you know, and their man-tans. I think, Mr. X, that perhaps the grass is always greener on the other side of the fence. Now when we create integration, perhaps it won't be so necessary for us to resort to these devices.

The black bourgeoisie—is it only the middle class that wants integration? Were the sit-in students black bourgeoisie? They didn't fit into the definition in E. Franklin Frazier's book on the black bourgeoisie. Quite to the contrary, these students were lower class people. Many of them were workers working to stay in school. In the Freedom Rides, were they black bourgeoisie? No, we didn't have exceptions there, we had some people who were unemployed. These are not the black bourgeoisie who want integration. Quite to the contrary, very frequently, the middle class developed a vested interest in the maintenance of segregation. Because if they have a store, and if segregation is eliminated, then I'll be in open competition with the white stores. And thus it is most often true as Frazier pointed out in his book, that the middle class tends to be opposed to desegregation. Now I would wonder also in the building of black businesses if we are not going to be building another black bourgeoisie? If Negroes may not perhaps be giving up one master for another, a white one for a black one? Are we going to build a new Negro middle class, and say that no matter how tyrannical it may prove to be it is my own and therefore, I like it?

Now we of course know that the Negro is sick, the white man is sick, we know that psychologically we have been twisted by all of these things; but still, Mr. X, you have not told us what the solution is except that it is separation, in your view. You have not spelled it out. Well, now, this sickness, as I tried to indicate in my first presentation, springs from segregation. It is segregation that produces prejudice, as much as prejudice produces segregation. In Detroit, at the time of the race riot, the only rioting, the only fighting, was in the all-Negro and all-white sections of the city, where separation was complete. In those several sections of the city where Negroes and whites lived together, next door to each other, there was no fighting because there the people were neighbors or friends. Now you propose separation as the solution to this problem, as the cure to the disease. Here we have a patient that is suffering from a disease caused by mosquitoes, and the physician proposes as a cure that the man go down and lie in a damp swamp and play with wiggletails.

MALCOLM X

I hadn't thought, or intended anyway, to get personal with Mr. Farmer in mentioning his white wife; I thought that perhaps it would probably have been better left unsaid, but it's better for him to say than for me to say it, because then you would think I was picking on him. I think you will find if you were to have gone into Harlem a few years back you would have found on the juke boxes, records by Belafonte, Eartha Kitt, Pearl Bailey, all of these persons were very popular singers in the so-called Negro community a few years back. But since Belafonte divorced Marguerite and married a white woman it doesn't mean that Harlem is antiwhite, but you can't find Belafonte's records there; or maybe he just hasn't produced a hit. All of these entertainers who have become involved in intermarriage, and I mean Lena Horne, Eartha Kitt, Sammy Davis, Belafonte, they have a large white following, but you can't go into any Negro community across the nation and find records by these artists that are hits in the so-called Negro community. Because, subconsciously, today the so-called Negro withdraws himself from the entertainers who have crossed the line. And if the masses of black people won't let a Negro who is involved in an intermarriage play music for him, he can't speak for him.

The only way you can solve the race problem as it exists, is to take into consideration the feelings of the masses, not the minority; the majority not the minority. And it is proof that the masses of white people don't want Negroes forcing their way into their neighborhood and the masses of black people don't think it's any solution for us to force ourselves into the white neighborhood, so the only ones who want integration are the Negro minority, as I say, the bourgeoisie and the white minority, the so-called white liberals. And that same white liberal who professes to want integration whenever the Negro moves to his neighborhood, he is the first one to move out. And I was talking with one today who said he was a liberal and I asked him where did he live, and he lived in an allwhite neighborhood and probably might for the rest of his life. This is conjecture, but I think it stands true. The Civil War was fought one hundred years ago, supposedly to solve this problem. After the Civil War was fought, the problem still existed. Along behind that, the thirteenth and fourteenth Amendments were brought about in the Constitution supposedly to solve the problem; after the Amendments, the problem was still right here with us.

Most Negroes think that the Civil War was fought to make them citizens; they think that it was fought to free them from slavery because the real purpose of the Civil War is clothed in hypocrisy. The real purpose of the Amendments is clothed in hypocrisy. The real purpose behind the Supreme Court desegregation decision was clothed in hypocrisy. And any time integrationists, NAACP, CORE, Urban League, or what you have, will stand up and tell me to spell out how we are going to bring about separation, and here they are integrationists, a philosophy which is supposed to have the support of the Senate, Congress, President, and the Supreme Court, and still with all of that support and hypocritical agreeing, eight years after the desegregation decision, you still don't have what the court decided on.

So we think this, that when whites talk integration they are being hypocrites, and we think that the Negroes who accept token integration are also being hypocrites, because they are the only ones who benefit from it, the handful of hand-picked high-class, middle-class Uncle Tom Negroes. They are hand-picked by whites and turned loose in a white community and they're satisfied. But if all of the black people went into the white community, over night you would have a race war. If four or five little black students going to school in New Orleans bring about the riots that we saw down there, what do you think would happen if all of the black people tried to go to any school that they want, you would have a race war. So our approach to it, those of us who follow the honorable Elijah Muhammad, we feel that it is more sensible than running around here waiting for the whites to allow us inside their attic or inside their basement.

Every Negro group that we find in the Negro community that is integrated is controlled by the whites who belong to it, or it is led by the whites who belong to it. NAACP has had a white president for fifty-three years, it has been in existence fifty-three years; Roy Wilkins is the Executive Secretary, but Spingarn, a white man has been the president for the past twenty-three years, and before him, his brother, another white man was president. They have never had a black president. Urban League, another so-called Negro organization, doesn't have a black president, it has a white president. Now this doesn't mean that that's racism, it only means that the same organizations that are accusing you of practicing discrimination, when it comes to the leadership they're practicing discrimination themselves.

The honorable Elijah Muhammad says, and points out to us that in this book ("Anti-Slavery") written by a professor from the University of Michigan, Dwight Lowell Dumond, a person who is an authority on the race question or slave question, his findings were used by Thurgood Marshall in winning the Supreme Court desegregation decision. And in the preface of this book, it says that second-class citizenship is only a modified form of slavery. Now I'll tell you why I'm dwelling on this, everything that you have devised yourself to solve the race problem has been hypocrisy, because the scientists who delved into it teach us or tell us that second-class citizenship is only a modified form of slavery, which means the Civil War didn't end slavery and the Amendments didn't end slavery. They didn't do it because we still have to wrestle the Supreme Court and the Congress and the Senate to correct the hypocrisy that's been practiced against us by whites for the past umteen years.

And because this was done, the American white man today subconsciously still regards that black man as something below himself. And you will never get the American white man to accept the so-called Negro as an integrated part of his society until the image of the Negro the white man has is changed, and until the image that the Negro has of himself is also changed.

See M. Parenti, "The Black Muslims: From Revolution to Institution." *Social Research* 31:(1964) 175–94.

33

THE TUSKEGEE VOTING STORY

by Charles G. Gomillion

The leader of the struggle for the ballot in Macon County, Alabama, describes its history:

The story of voting in Tuskegee, Alabama, is a long and complex one, but only selected aspects will be told here. In recent years, the story consists mainly of the political beliefs, aspirations, and activities of the members and supporters of the Tuskegee Civic Association, a civic education organization in Macon County.

Tuskegee, a town of approximately 6,000 citizens, is the county seat of Macon County in east central Alabama, about forty-four miles southwest of Columbus, Georgia, and approximately thirty-eight miles east of Montgomery, the capitol of Alabama, sometimes known as "The Cradle of the Confederacy." In 1960, the total population of the county was 26,717, of which 22,287 (83.4%) were Negroes. In 1950, Macon County had a higher percentage of Negroes in its population than any other county in the nation. In the town of Tuskegee in 1961, following the restoration of the city limits which existed prior to the gerrymander in 1957, Negroes outnumbered whites about three to one.

Macon County is somewhat atypical of counties in the rural South in that a higher percentage of gainfully employed Negroes is found in the professions and clerical occupations than is true in other rural counties. Most of these professional and clerical workers are employed by Tuskegee Institute, the United States Veterans Administration Hospital, and the Macon County Public School System. The percentage of Negroes with annual incomes above $5,000 is higher than is true of other counties in the state. The percentage engaged in business and in manufacturing is low. Because a high percentage of the gainfully occupied rural Negroes is engaged in cotton farming, the median income of the total Negro population in the county is low.

Negroes have been voting in Macon County since the Reconstruction Era, but until 1950 the numbers and percentages had been small. Just prior to 1881, when Tuskegee Institute was founded, Negro voters in Macon County promised to support a white candidate for the Alabama Legislature if he would seek an appropriation for the establishment in the county of a normal school for the "training of Negro teachers." The candidate was elected, the appropriation was made, and Tuskegee Institute was founded. Although Negroes continued to vote during the last years of the nineteenth century, the provisions of the Alabama Constitutional Convention (1901) virtually disfranchised most Negroes. In 1930, there were only thirty Negro voters in the county. During the decade following, stimulated by the Roosevelt New Deal, a few Macon County Negroes began to encourage their fellow citizens to become more civic-minded and politically active. By 1940, the number of Negro voters had risen to seventy-five. Most of the leadership in this ten-year effort was provided by persons in the Tuskegee Men's Club, composed of approximately thirty men who were interested in community welfare.

Race relations in Macon County and in the Tuskegee Community throughout the years following the emancipation of the slaves had been quite similar to those existing in the majority of southern communities. There was segregation of the races, followed or accompanied by discrimination on account of race or color. This resulted in superordinate status for whites and a subordinate status for Negroes, and differential civic opportunities favoring the whites. The nature of race relations in Macon County is revealed somewhat in a statement by a white public official who said to a white citizen from a northern state in 1940 that "Sometimes some of the rural Negroes and some of the colored professors at the Institute think that we don't treat them fairly, but in general we manage to keep them pacified." Briefly put, the relationship between the races has been characterized by domination and exploitation by one group and submission by the other.

During the 1930s there arose in the county a small group of Negroes who believed that "political democracy is government of the people, for the people, and by the people," that "voting intelligently is a civic responsibility," that "the ballot is the citizen's best self-help tool," and that one "who is without the ballot is politically disarmed." There was the further belief that through intelligent political actions Negroes would be able to improve their other civic opportunities.

Accordingly, in 1941, this group succeeded in reorganizing the Tuskegee Men's Club into the Tuskegee Civic Association, and admitted women to membership. The specified objectives of the Association are (1) intelligent study and interpretation of local and national civic and political issues and trends, (2) collection and dissemination of useful civic and political data, and (3) intelligent and courageous civic and political action.

The officers of the TCA have considered their major responsibility to be that of the civic education of all citizens in the community, Negro and white, and facilitation of intelligent civic action on the part of an increasing number of Negro citizens. Civic education meetings have been held regularly, weekly for three years, and semi-monthly at the present time. As a result, the number of Negroes manifesting interest in political affairs has been steadily increasing. As the political interest and action increased, the resistance of the members of the County Boards of Registrars increased.

Varied techniques have been employed to limit or prevent the participation of Negroes in local politics, the most obvious of which have been the following:

1. Requiring Negroes and whites to register in separate rooms and in separate parts of the Macon County Courthouse.
2. Registrars frequently reporting for work late and leaving early, thus reducing the number of hours available to Negro applicants.
3. Permitting only two Negro applicants in the registration room at the same time.
4. Requiring Negro applicants to read and transcribe articles from the Constitution of the United States, in addition to filling out the voter-registration questionnaire.
5. Conversing with applicants as they write, which disturbs them, and stimulates making errors.
6. Permitting a Negro voter to vouch for *only two* applicants per year.
7. Preventing some Negroes from vouching for any applicant.
8. Failing to issue certificates of registration to Negroes immediately upon the successful completion of the requirements for registration.
9. Failing to inform unsuccessful applicants of their failures to fulfill the requirements for registration.
10. Failing to work on many registration days.
11. Resigning from the Board in order not to register Negroes.

12. Refusing to appoint any Negro to serve on city or county government committees or agencies.
13. Enacting legislation which permits Board of Registrars to use twelve of their working days for clerical work only, and in even years to use up to twenty additional days in the precincts away from the courthouse.
14. Gerrymandering the city of Tuskegee in such a manner as to eliminate from residence in the city 400 of its 410 Negro voters. (Not a single white voter was removed from the city.)

Between 1940 and 1942, the political conflict between white and Negro citizens was almost continuous. Negroes worked in a variety of ways to increase the number of Negroes registered to vote. They complained about the discriminatory behavior of the Boards of Registrars. Open letters were published in daily and weekly newspapers; letters and petitions were sent to Governors and to other members of the State Board which appointed the County Board of Registrars; letters and telegrams were sent to selected members of the United States Congress, and to the U.S. Attorney General; legal suits against Boards of Registrars were threatened or filed. In 1943, a threat to sue resulted in the Board's repealing its rule that only white voters could vouch for Negro applicants to register. In 1945, William P. Mitchell sued the Board for a certificate of registration which he declared was due him. The case was carried to the U.S. Supreme Court, and was the Fifth U.S. Circuit Court of Appeals, on its way back to the Supreme Court, in 1947, when Mitchell was informed by public officials that he had been legally a registered voter "since January 29, 1943." According to a public official, Mitchell "just had not been notified."

In spite of the numerous difficulties experienced by Negroes in their efforts to become voters, there was a two-year period (1949–50) during which one Board of Registrars certified as voters approximately seven hundred applicants. This success was followed by greater resistance. Another suit was filed in 1953. In 1954, Mrs. Jessie P. Guzman, a Negro, was a candidate for membership on the County Board of Education. Although more than five hundred votes were cast for her, she was not elected. This event seemed to have intensified the fear and the belief on the part of whites that Negroes were trying "to take over" the governments of Tuskegee and Macon County.

As the number of Negro voters approached one thousand, bills were introduced in the Alabama Legislature (1957) to gerrymander Tuskegee and to abolish Macon County. On July 13, 1957, Senate Bill No. 291

became law without the signature of Governor Folsom, thus gerrymandering Tuskegee so as to put outside of the city limits approximately 3,500 of five thousand Negro residents, and approximately 400 of the 410 Negro voters.

The reaction of Negro citizens was immediately aggressive. When their pleas to local and state officials were not honored, Negroes publicized their plight through national news media. They urged Congress to enact the Civil Rights Bill, and they drafted a bill providing for Federal Registrars, which was submitted to a Congressional Committee. When local white merchants refused to speak out against the proposed gerrymander, many Negro citizens withdrew their patronage from them. (During a period of two years, twenty-six businesses operated by whites ceased to operate in the community. One moved to another town.) The Alabama Attorney General retaliated by securing a temporary injunction against the TCA and its "followers," and on January 21–22, 1958, sought in court to prove that the TCA was violating Alabama's Antiboycott statute. On June 21, 1958, the judge ruled that the Attorney General had not proved his charges and dissolved the injunction.

On August 4, 1958, twelve Negroes filed suit in a Federal Court, seeking to enjoin local and state officials from enforcing the gerrymandering legislation. The case was taken to the U.S. Supreme Court, which sent it back to the District Court for trial. On February 17, 1961, Federal Judge Frank M. Johnson enjoined Alabama public officials from enforcing the act, and ordered restored the boundaries of Tuskegee which existed at the time of the gerrymander. The four hundred Negro voters were again residents within the boundaries of Tuskegee, but they had missed the September, 1960, Municipal election.

In 1959, following numerous complaints of Macon County Negroes to the U.S. Department of Justice, the Department filed a suit against the Macon County Board of Registrars, charging it with discriminating against Negroes applying to register. On February 20–23, 1961, Judge Frank M. Johnson heard witnesses in the case, and on March 17, 1961, ordered Alabama officials to cease their discrimination practices against Negroes.

The following listing reveals the increase in the number of Negroes registered to vote in Macon County between 1954 and 1962, inclusive:

1954–857; 1956–953; 1958–1,030; 1960–1,095; 1962–2,434. In the county, there are approximately 3,200 white voters, but in the town of Tuskegee, as of 1962, Negro voters exceed white voters.

The civic education program of the TCA has been relatively successful. Many local Negro citizens are well-informed on local and state politics, and some of them seriously study political issues and the records of public officials and of candidates for public office. Members of the TCA are very active in the Alabama State Coordinating Committee on Registration and Voting, are helping to organize civic or political clubs in other counties, and are serving as consultants. During the past five years, Tuskegee Negroes have used to advantage the Civil Rights Acts of 1957 and 1960, the U.S. Civil Rights Commission, and personnel in the U.S. Department of Justice. The struggle for the ballot in Tuskegee and Macon County is almost won; the major task now is to educate for its intelligent use.

Freedomways, 2 (Summer 1962): 231–36.

34

"ENTIRE EQUALITY MUST AND WILL BE"

by Ralph J. Bunche

Ralph Bunche, a former professor at Howard University, had a distinguished career as assistant general secretary of the United Nations. For significant diplomatic work in the Near East he was awarded, in 1950, the Nobel Peace Prize. On July 6, 1962, he addressed the Annual Meeting of the NAACP, in Atlanta.

I need scarcely mention the painfully obvious fact that school integration proceeds far too slowly. What has happened thus far in most places is only a token and a small token at that. Instead of all deliberate speed there has been a disgracefully deliberate dragging of feet. But this is a foolish tactic, for school integration in Georgia and Alabama and Mississippi and everywhere else is bound to come. Who then is losing from this procrastination against the law? Negro children, of course. But the community and nation even more, in the blow to morality and in the inevitable corrosion of respect for law which follows from organized contempt for it even by public officials sworn to uphold it.

Impatience, I do not doubt, has been a prime motivation in the heroic actions of Negro youth—and some white youth too—in the sit-down, bus boycott, freedom ride, campus strikes and demonstrations, and other protest activities of recent years—activities in which I have rejoiced because they marked a new awakening for the Negro and a courage in support of bold action; because they demonstrated conclusively that the Negro could no longer be intimidated and could, and readily would, laugh at and ridicule the Klansmen and their silly trappings and the futile threats of the white citizen councils alike.

Such demonstrations were not only timely, they were long overdue. Actions of this kind have accelerated the pace of progress in the achievement of social justice by dramatizing the struggle for the nation and all the world to see; they afford a convincing demonstration of the determination of the Negro to carry on the struggle for equality with ever more insistence, and the Negro's—and particularly the young Negro's—readiness to make costly sacrifices in that struggle.

I feel rather strongly that not enough has been done to honor those young people who, with such spontaneity and courage, rose to man the breastworks, so to speak, and to encourage youth to enroll in the continuing struggle in ever greater numbers. These many and largely anonymous young men and women are heroes, as genuine as any on battlefields. Their deeds must be kept fresh in our minds.

It is axiomatic in the process of social progress that the more the progress the more people will demand that it be quickened. This is a classical pattern in the development of the peoples of colonies toward emergence into independence and nationhood. It is equally true with regard to a minority ethnic group such as the American Negro. How long could anyone expect American Negro youth to be studying in schools and colleges about the glorious fruits of American democracy and be content with only the peelings? How long could it be expected that Negro youth would tolerate the absurd situations wherein their presence and money were sought after at sales counters in stores but they were unwelcome and their money refused at lunch counters and restaurants in those same stores? How could it be supposed that Negro youth would long stand for the indignity of the back seat in public transportation?

How could anyone in his senses expect young Negroes of this day and age, many of whom are called upon to give a couple of the best years of their lives to Uncle Sam's military service, to have their dignity as human beings assaulted at every turn and not defend it?

When I was age fourteen, my sister and I lost our parents and we were thereafter reared by our maternal grandmother. She was a tiny little woman physically, but a giant spiritually. She taught me many things, but the most important, I am sure, was the admonition to defend one's dignity at all costs. If you let anyone deprive you of your dignity, she would tell us, you lose your self-respect and there is then no moral strength left in you and you are less than a man. That counsel I will never forget and never ignore.

This, of course, is what the Negro is demanding—the complete right to human dignity, to self-respect, to be a man in full. We all know that this is possible only in a society in which there is entire equality, and this there must and will be....

I have no mandate to speak on behalf of anyone but myself. But I know what I, who have been for fifty-seven years an American of Negro ancestry, want and how I feel. I do not doubt that my wants and feelings are fairly representative of those of most of my race. I want to be a man on the same basis and level as any white citizen—I want to be as free as the whitest citizen. I want to exercise, and in full, the same rights as the white American. I want to be eligible for employment exclusively on the basis of my skills and employability, and for housing solely on my capacity to pay. I want to have the same privileges, the same treatment in public places as every other person. But this should not be read by anyone to mean that I want to be white; or that I am "pushy," seeking to go where I am not wanted. Far from it. I am as proud of my origin, ancestors, and race as anyone could be. Indeed, I resent nothing more than a racial slur or stigma. I want to go and to do only where and what all Americans are entitled to go and to do.

This I think is what every American Negro feels. It may be expressed in polite eloquence by some; in bitterness or even outright belligerence by others; it may cause some just to break out and start to knock things around. But in each case the emotion is sound and urgent and American.

I believe I could readily understand and accept this if I were not a Negro; if I were white. I can never really understand why the white man, whether from south or north, seems to find it difficult to do so. I am not sure that he does: it is possible that deep down in his heart he knows that the Negro cause is right and just. That, I think, may explain why there is so much less of racial tension in southern and northern communities today than there was a quarter century ago, despite the fact that the Negro is bolder and more demanding and that the walls of segregation have been often breached; why race riots do not occur; why Ku Klux Klansmen now just meekly hand out leaflets. I cannot understand how anyone claiming to be a good American can condone the denial of these elementals of democracy to any other American. How can anyone be so manifestly against the very essence of Americanism—not to mention fairness and decency—and at the same time purport to be fighting communism while thus giving to the Communists the strongest weapon they have against us? Negro citizens may be pardoned for expecting their white fellow citizens to be at least consistent.

The logic and the evidence are all against the race-baiting bitterenders. It is so obvious that no one can miss it that the South, as it has reluctantly lowered some of its racial bars, is better off—politically, economically, and culturally—than it has ever been. The greatest resource of any community, state, or nation is its people, and it is recklessly shortsighted to waste that resource, as the South, and to only lesser extent the North, has been doing for so long. Depriving the Negro worker of fair employment costs the nation dearly in lost man-hours, production, consumption, and taxes.

I suppose I speak with an unavoidable bias, but I feel that if I were a white citizen in the South today, I would look at my black or brown brother and say to myself: what responsibility do I share for the crime that has been perpetrated not alone against this individual, but against the community and the nation? What have I contributed to the humiliation and degradation of this fellow American who except for a sheer accident of birth could be me or my brother? What can I do to rectify an injustice to the individual and a loss to the nation?

This being youth night, I really should close on a word especially for youth, although I do not care very much for distinctions among people, even on the basis of age. White or black, old or young, the real test comes in what you have done or can do. In a competitive world you must rise to meet the competition. That means preparation. It also means building up confidence on the basis of demonstrated performance. In connection with preparation, the school drop-out figures for Negro youth are alarming.

It is an exciting and inspiring world to be in. And, although there are great dangers in it, much tension and cause for worry, it affords vast opportunity—greater, I think, for youth, black as well as white, than has ever been known.

Harvey Wish, ed., *The Negro Since Emancipation* (Englewood Cliffs, N.J.: Prentice-Hall, 1964), pp. 138–41.

35

"THE DAY I BECAME A MAN"

by Charles McLaurin

A vivid description of the vital role and great courage of black women in the movement to democratize the South is this description of an incident in Mississippi. The author was among the young SNCC activists.

I will always remember August 22, 1962, as the day I became a man. It was on this day that I was to test myself for courage and the ability to move in the face of fear and danger such as I had never faced before. About 7:00 A.M. that morning, I had been around to the homes of people who had given me their names as persons willing to go to the courthouse and attempt to register to vote. I was very disappointed; I had only been able to find three of the ten. The others because of fear had left home rather than say no to me. Since I was going down to the courthouse for my first time, I, too, was afraid; not of dying and not of the man per se, but of the powers of the sheriff's department, the police, the courts; these are the powers and the forces which keep Negroes in their so-called places.... About 8:00 A.M., I had only three people to go to the courthouse; this was the day I learned that the numbers were not important. I learned that a faithful few was better than an uncertain ten. These three old ladies whose ages ranged from 65–85, knew the white man and his ways; they knew him because they had lived, worked, and raised families on his plantations, and on this day, they would come face-to-face with his sons and daughters to say, 'We must be Free; Now!'

We pulled up in front of the courthouse and as I opened the door to get out I got a feeling in my stomach that made me feel weak. At this point I was no longer in command, the three old ladies were leading me, I was following them. They got out of the car and went up the walk to the courthouse as if this was the long walk that lead to the Golden Gate of Heaven, their heads held high. I watched from a short distance behind them; the pride with which they walked. The strong convictions that they held. I watched as they walked up the steps into the building. I stepped outside the door and waited, thinking how it was that these ladies who have been victimized by white faces all of their lives would suddenly walk up to the man and say, I want to vote. This did something to me. It told me something. It was like a voice speaking to me, as I stood there alone, in a strange place and unknown land. This voice told me that although these old ladies knew the risk involved in their being there they were still willing to try. It said you are the light, let it shine and the people will know you, and they will follow you, if you show the way they will go, with or without you.

From the records of SNCC, quoted in a paper by Vicki Crawford of the University of Massachusetts, given November 5, 1992, at a meeting of the Southern Historical Association. The author sent the paper to the editor and kindly offered permission to quote therefrom.

36

A CHALLENGE TO ARTISTS

by Lorraine Hansberry

Lorraine Hansberry (1930–65) achieved remarkable success by the age of twenty-seven with *A Raisin in the Sun* which opened on Broadway in March 1959 and ran for nineteen months; it was made into a motion picture, having among its original cast Sidney Poitier, Ruby Dee, and Claudia McNeil. In April 1962 she was diagnosed as having cancer—this will help explain the opening words in the speech that follows. The occasion was a meeting protesting the House Un-American Activities Committee, held at Carnegie Hall in New York City, on October 27, 1962.

I am afraid that I haven't made a speech for a very long time, and there is a significance in that fact, which is part of what I should like to talk about this evening.

A week or so ago I was at my typewriter working on a scene in a play of mine in which one character, a German novelist, is trying to explain to another character, an American intellectual, something about what led the greater portion of the German intelligentsia to acquiesce to Nazism. He says this: "They [the Nazis] permitted us to feel, in return for our silence, that we were nonparticipants—merely irrelevant if inwardly agonized observers who had nothing whatsoever to do with that which was being committed in our names."

Just as I put the period after that sentence, my own telephone rang and I was confronted with the voice of Dr. Otto Nathan, asking this particular American writer if she would be of this decade and this nation and appear at this rally this evening and join a very necessary denunciation of a lingering *American* kind of travesty.

It is the sort of moment of truth that dramatists dearly love to put on the stage but find as uncomfortable as everyone else in life. To make it short, however, I am here.

I mean to say that one can become detached in this world of ours; we can get to a place where we read only the theater or photography or music pages of our newspapers. And then we wake up one day and find that the better people of our nation are still where they were when we last noted them: in the courts defending *our* Constitutional rights for us.

This makes me feel that it might be interesting to talk about where are our artists in the contemporary struggles. Some of them, of course, are being heard and felt. Some of the more serious actresses such as Shelley Winters and Julie Harris and a very thoughtful comedian such as Steve Allen have associated themselves with some aspect of the peace movement and Sidney Poitier and Harry Belafonte have made significant contributions to the Negro struggle. But the vast majority—where are they?

Well, I am afraid that they are primarily where the ruling powers have always wished the artist to be and to stay: in their studios. They are consumed, in the main, with what they consider to be larger issues—such as "the meaning of life," et cetera....I personally consider that part of this detachment is the direct and indirect result of many years of things like the House Committee and concurrent years of McCarthyism in all its forms. I mean to suggest that the climate of fear, which we were once told, as I was coming along, by wise men, would bear a bitter harvest in the culture of our civilization, has in fact come to pass. In the contemporary arts, the rejection of this particular world is no longer a mere grotesque threat, but a fact.

Among my contemporaries and colleagues in the arts the search for the roots of war, the exploitation of man, of poverty and of despair itself, is sought in any arena other than the one which has shaped these artists. Having discovered that the world is incoherent, they have—some of them—also come to the conclusion that it is also unreal and, in any case, beyond the corrective powers of human energy. Having determined that life is in fact an absurdity, they have not yet decided that the task of the thoughtful is to try and help impose purposefulness on that absurdity. They don't yet agree, by and large, that simply being against life as it is is not enough; that simply *not* being a "rhinoceros" is not enough. That, moreover, replacing phony utopianisms of one kind with vulgar and cheap little philosophies of accommodation is also not enough. In a word, they do not yet agree that it is perhaps the task, I should think certainly the joy, of the artist to chisel out some expression of what life can conceivably be.

The fact is that this unwitting capitulation really does aim to be a revolt; really does aim to indict—*something*. Really does aim to be partisan in saying no to a world which it generally characterizes as a "brothel." I am thinking now, mainly, of course, of writers of my generation. It is they, upon whom we must depend so heavily for the refinement and articulation of the aspiration of man, who do not yet agree that if the world is a brothel, then someone has built the edifice; and that if it was the hand of man, then the hand of man can reconstruct it—that whatever man renders, creates, imagines, he can render afresh, re-create and even more gloriously re-imagine. But, I must repeat, that anyone who can even think so these days is held to be an example of unparalleled simple-mindedness.

Why? For this is what is cogent to our meeting tonight; the writers that I am presently thinking of come mainly from my generation. That is to say that they come from a generation which was betrayed in the late forties and fifties by the domination of McCarthyism. We were ceaselessly told, after all, to be everything which mutilates youth: to be silent, to be ignorant, to be without unsanctioned opinions, to be compliant and, above all else, obedient to all the ideas which are in fact the dregs of an age. We were taught that agitational activity in behalf of changing this world was nothing but an expression, among other things, of our "neurotic compulsions" about our own self-dissatisfactions because our mothers dominated our fathers or some such as that. We were told in an age of celebrated liberations of repressions that the repression of the *urge* to protest against war was surely the only *respectable* repression left in the universe.

As for those who went directly into science or industry it was all even less oblique than any of that. If you went to the wrong debates on campus, signed the wrong petitions, you simply didn't get the job you wanted and you were forewarned of this early in your college career.

And, of course, things are a little different than in my parents' times— I mean, with regard to the candor with which young people have been made to think in terms of money. It is the only single purpose which has been put before them. That which Shakespeare offered as a curse, "Put money in thy purse," is now a boast. What makes me think of that in connection with what we are speaking of tonight? Well, I hope that I am wise enough to determine the nature of a circle. If, after all, the ambition in life is merely to be rich, then all which might threaten that possibility is much to be avoided, is it not? This means, therefore, not incurring the disfavor of employers. It means that one will not protest war if one expects to draw one's livelihood from, say, the aircraft industry if one is an engineer. Or, in the arts, how can one write plays which have either implicit or explicit in them a quality of the detestation of commerciality, if in fact one is beholden to the commerciality of the professional theater? How can one protest the criminal persecution of political dissenters if one has already discovered at nineteen that to do so is to risk a profession? If all one's morality is wedded to the opportunist, the expedient in life, how can one have the deepest, most profound moral outrage about the fact of the condition of the Negro people in the United States? Particularly, thinking of expediency, when one has it dinned into one's ears day after day that the only reason why, perhaps, that troublesome and provocative group of people must some day be permitted to buy a cup of coffee or rent an apartment or get a job—is *not* because of the recognition of the universal humanity of the human race, but because it happens to be extremely expedient international politics to now *think* of granting these things!

As I stand here I know perfectly well that such institutions as the House Committee, and all the other little committees, have dragged on their particular obscene theatrics for all these years not to expose "Communists" or do anything really in connection with the "security" of the United States, but merely to create an atmosphere where, in the first place, I should be afraid to come here tonight at all and, secondly, to absolutely guarantee that I will not say what I am going to say, which is this:

I think that my government is wrong. I would like to see them turn back our ships from the Caribbean. The Cuban people, to my mind, and I speak only for myself, have chosen their destiny and I cannot believe that it is the place of the descendants of those who did not ask the monarchists of the eighteenth century for permission to make the United States a republic, to interfere with the twentieth-century choice of another sovereign people.

I will go further, speaking as a Negro in America, and impose a little of what Negroes say all the time to each other on what I am saying to you. And that is that it would be a great thing if they would not only turn back the ships from the Caribbean but turn to the affairs of our country that need righting. For one thing, empty the legislative and judicial chambers of the victims of political persecution so we know why that lamp is burning out there in the Brooklyn waters. And, while they are at it, go on and help fulfill the American dream and empty the southern jails of the genuine heroes, practically the last vestige of dignity that we have to boast about at this moment in our history; those students whose imprisonment for trying to insure what is already on the book is our national disgrace at this moment.

And I would go so far—perhaps with an over sense of drama, but I don't think so—to say that maybe without waiting for another two men to die, that we send those troops to finish the Reconstruction in Alabama, Georgia, Mississippi, and every place else where the fact of our federal flag flying creates the false notion that what happened at the end of the Civil War was the defeat of the slavocracy at the political as well as the military level. And I say this not merely in behalf of the black and oppressed but, for a change—and more and more thoughtful Negroes must begin to make this point—also for the white and disinherited of the South, those poor whites who, by the millions, have been made the tragic and befuddled instruments of their own oppression at the hand of the most sinister political apparatus in our country. I think perhaps that if our government would do that it would not have to compete in any wishful way for the respect of the new black and brown nations of the world.

Finally, I think that all of us who are thinking such things, who wish to exercise these rights that we are here defending tonight, must really exercise them. Speaking to my fellow artists in particular, I think that we must paint them, sing them, write about them. All these matters which are not currently fashionable. Otherwise, I think, as I have put into the mouth of my German novelist, we are indulging in a luxurious complicity—and no other thing.

I personally agree with those who say that from here on in, if we are to survive, we, the people—still an excellent phrase—we the people of the world must oblige the heads of all governments to become responsible to us. I personally do not feel that it matters if it be the government of China presently engaging in incomprehensible and insane antics at the border of India or my President, John F. Kennedy, dismissing what he knows to be in the hearts of the American people and engaging in overt provocation with our sister people to the South. I think that it is imperative to say "No" to all of it—"No" to war of any kind, anywhere. And I think, therefore, and it is my reason for being here tonight, that it is imperative to remove from the American fabric any and all such institutions or agencies as the House

Committee on Un-American Activities which are designed expressly to keep us from saying "No!"

Freedomways 3 (Winter 1963): 31–35.

37

NOT *PROGRESS* BUT *FREEDOM*

by Loren Miller

Under the title "Farewell to Liberals: A Negro View," the *Nation*, October 20, 1962 (pp. 235–38), published this challenging essay. The author was a vice president of the NAACP and a civil rights attorney in Los Angeles.

Liberals who were shocked or surprised at James Baldwin's recent statement that Negroes "twenty years younger than I don't believe in liberals at all" haven't been doing their homework. Discontent with the liberal position in the area of race relations has been building up for the past several years. Of course there are liberals and liberals, ranging from Left to Right; still, there does exist a set of beliefs and attitudes, not easily defined but readily identified, constituting the liberal outlook on the race question. Simply stated, it contemplates the ultimate elimination of all racial distinctions in every phase of American life through an orderly, step-by-step process adjusted to resistance and aimed at overcoming such resistance. In the field of constitutional law, the classic liberal position, exemplified in the Supreme Court's "all deliberate speed" formula of the school-segregation cases, requires and rationalizes Negro accommodation to, and acquiescence in, disabilities imposed because of race and in violation of the fundamental law.

On his part, the Negro has to put up with such practices, but he cannot admit that they have constitutional sanction; to do so would be to give away his case and knuckle under to the revisionist theory that the Civil War Amendments conferred less than complete equality under the law. The liberal sees "both sides" of the issue: the force of the Negro's constitutional argument and the existence of customs, sometimes jelled into law, that justify the gradualist approach. He is impatient with "extremists on both sides."

The Negro is outraged at being called an extremist. Since he takes the position that the Constitution confers complete equality on all citizens, he must rest his case on the proposition that there is only one side; his side, the constitutional side. That his attitude in that respect is firming up is evidenced by the fact that Negro spokesmen who once won applause by claiming that their activities made for progress in race relations are being elbowed aside by others whose catchword is Freedom Now. "We want our Freedom Here; we want it Now, not tomorrow; we want it All, not just a part of it," Martin Luther King tells receptive audiences. Whoever opposes, or even doubts, that doctrine is cast in the role of a foe, whether he calls himself conservative or liberal. The middle ground on which the traditional liberal has taken his stand is being cut from beneath him.

Every civil-rights victory adds to the Negro's intransigence; he becomes ever more impatient and demanding. To the extent that this attitude tends to precipitate racial conflict, a substantial number of liberals shy away. As they see it, their role is to ease, not heighten, racial tensions while they create a climate in which progress is possible. But the new militants don't want *progress*; they *demand* Freedom: "The courts take time and we want Freedom Now—Today," the Rev. Ralph Abernathy told cheering Georgians last month. Abernathy's cry, echoing King and the student leaders, underscores the strong trend away from dependence on legalistic methods and, equally important, implies rejection of the dogma that racial reforms must await a change in the hearts and minds of men— the so-called educational approach that once numbered many adherents.

The swing away from major reliance on legal methodology and the educational approach poses new problems for liberals. It was easy and comfortable to wait for the filing of civil-rights cases or proposals for anti-discriminatory legislation and then lend support to those causes, or an even greater mark of liberalism to initiate them. However, the persistence of discriminatory practices in the wake of the NAACP's sweeping court victories which have destroyed the legal base of the southern segregation system, and in the face of an upsurge of civil-rights legislation in the North has shaken the faith of the Negro in the efficacy of the law. It is significant that King abjures his followers to disobey "unjust laws" and ironic that some segregationists, harried by the direct actionists, now argue that racial issues should be left to the courts. The plea for civil disobedience flies in the face of liberal doctrine of respect for the law; direct action in the form of sit-ins or stand-ins is seen by many as raising grave questions as to infringements of personal and property rights.

The liberal dilemma does not spring solely from doubts as to the

advisability of direct action or the disobedience doctrine. The hard core of
the difficulty lies in the circumstance that in the eighty years since the
failure of Reconstruction, racial discrimination has become deeply rooted
and thoroughly institutionalized in governmental agencies (local, state
and federal), in the civil service and in churches, labor unions, political
parties, professional organizations, schools, trade associations, service
groups, and in that vast array of voluntary organizations which play such a
vital role in our society. Racial discrimination can't be uprooted unless
governmental agencies are administered with that purpose in mind and
unless voluntary organizations exert constant and consistent pressure to
that end on local, state, and federal governments, and at the same time
accord Negroes all of the privileges and benefits that accrue from
membership in such organizations. Those requirements aren't being met.
Negroes are dismayed as they observe that liberals, even when they are in
apparent control, not only do not rally their organizations for an effective
role in the fight against discrimination, but even tolerate a measure of
racial discrimination in their own jurisdictions.

Again, the liberal is restrained by his historical choice of seeing "both
sides" of the issue. He understands the justice of the Negro's claim, but he
argues that as a responsible administrator, he must reckon with deep-
seated resistance to quick change and with the breakdown that might
follow precipitate disruption of institutionalized practices. He may vacil-
late, as the President has done in the case of the Executive housing order,
in an attempt to coax a consensus favorable to a change in policy. In any
event, he is not, he says, as free as the Negro thinks; he must gauge the
situation and settle for progress in the face of Negro clamor for immediate
action.

Take the case of a liberal administrator of a government agency. He may
owe his eminence to a political victory insured by a four- or five-to-one
vote cast by urban Negroes. He now finds himself head of an agency
mired in civil service and hobbled by a heritage of discriminatory
practices. His underlings are apt to be wedded to that past; they helped
frame the rules. He is a new broom that can hardly sweep at all, let alone
sweep clean. Ordinarily, he appoints a few Negroes and institutes such
reforms as will not call down upon his head the wrath of Congress, the
state legislature, or the Chamber of Commerce. Not personal cowardice
makes him fear that wrath, but concern lest the opposition—through a
crippling withdrawal of funds from his agency, perhaps—might make *all*
reform impossible.

He may have done the best he could, but he hasn't endeared himself to Negroes, who contrast performance to pre-election speeches and campaign promises.

Civil service is a trap for unwary Negroes who enter it and find themselves frozen in its lower reaches. The United States Civil Rights Commission has found that, just as in private industry, there are "Negro" jobs and "white" jobs with Negroes at the bottom of the civil-service heap. The liberal who comes to head a civil service-staffed department of government is caught in a web of rules and regulations deliberately designed, in some instances, to institutionalize racial discrimination, or having that effect. Again there may be token appointments and token promotions, but the establishment yields slowly. The Negro looks for results and what he sees often makes him take the cynical position that the liberal differs no whit from his conservative predecessor.

Or take the situation in the AFL-CIO, where discrimination is rife in craft unions. The federation professes an inability to compel constituent unions to abandon time-honored racial practices. That is bad enough. What is worse is the stance of liberal-led industrial unions. The Steelworkers maintain Jim Crow locals in the South, where union halls double in brass as meeting places for White Citizens Councils. It is an open secret that Negroes have next to nothing to say in the policy-making bodies of unions, craft or industrial, on local, state, or national levels. When the Pullman Porters' A. Philip Randolph, the only Negro member of the AFL-CIO Executive Board, urged reforms in federation, George Meany, described in labor circles as a liberal, shouted at him, "Who the hell gave you the right to speak for Negroes?" and accused him of attacking the labor movement. The Executive Board, at Meany's urging, then censured Randolph for anti-union activities—without a dissent from such liberals as Walter Reuther or David Dubinsky. Randolph's answer was the formation of a *Negro* labor council; he was denounced again by labor leaders of all shades of opinion on the ground that he was fathering "Jim Crow in reverse." Yet for many years, the AFL-CIO has thrown its official weight behind state and federal fair housing, fair employment, and other civil-rights legislation and has assisted in tests of segregatory laws.

An examination of the practices of other voluntary organizations, including churches, would produce a similar yield of institutionalized discriminatory practices. In almost every case in which the leadership of such organizations is classified as liberal, there has been announced public support of civil-rights objectives. Everybody seems to want everybody else to practice what he preaches and nobody seems to be able, or willing, to practice what everybody else preaches.

It is very easy to charge hypocrisy in the situation, but what is really at play here is a cleavage between the burgeoning Freedom Now thinking of the Negro and the old progress concept to which liberals still cling. That conflict flares into the open when liberals exercise the prerogative, long held by them, of speaking *for* the Negro, and of espousing views which the Negro is abandoning. The liberal custom of speaking for the Negro is rooted in history; there was a time when the Negro needed spokesmen. Inevitably, a measure of paternalism and a father-knows-best attitude developed. But as the Negro becomes more articulate and discerning, he insists on voicing his own aspirations, particularly in the light of what he regards as the shortcomings of liberal leadership.

When the Negro insists on speaking for himself, the rebuffed liberal may shout as Meany did at Randolph that the dissenters are agitators or trouble makers (another replication, in a liberal context, of a familiar Southern cliché). Others take the tack popularized by John Fischer in *Harper's* and, transforming themselves into spokesmen for all whites, issue stern warnings that discrimination will prevail until all Negroes conform to middle-class standards of morality—a cozy variant of the theme that all Negroes are chargeable with the sins of every Negro. Negroes aren't dismayed at the opposition to their taking matters into their own hands. Detroit Negroes, led by unionists revolted against the UAW's mayoralty endorsement in that city and turned the tide against the union's choice; the NAACP and the AFL-CIO are increasingly at odds over the treatment of Negroes in the labor movement; Roy Wilkins defended bloc voting by Negroes in his Atlanta keynote speech. Muslims are drawing substantial urban support by proposing to have done with all "white devils."

There is a growing cynicism about the current stress being laid on absolute fairness in public and private employment and in political appointments—beginning as of today. The Negro wants a little more than that. One hundred years of racial discrimination have produced a wide gap between him and white Americans. The Negro wants that gap closed in political appointments, in civil service, in schools, and in private industry. He sees no way to close it unless he gets preferential treatment. Logic favors his position, but such a proposal runs into opposition from those who argue, correctly, that preferential treatment cannot be extended to a Negro without impinging on the personal rights of the white person over whom he will be preferred.

In truth, the impasse between liberals and Negroes is the end-product of a long historical process in which Americans of African, or partially African, descent have been treated as Negroes rather than as individuals, in legal lore as well as in popular concept. But constitutional protections run to persons—individuals—rather than to groups; American idealism exalts the individual and insists that group identification is an irrelevance. The liberal's historic concern is with individual rights and he seeks to apply that formula in the area of race relations. The Negro, whose ultimate ideal is the attainment of the right to be treated as an individual without reference to his racial identification, sees his immediate problem as that of raising the status of the group to which he has been consigned by popular attitude and action and by laws which permit a racial classification. The liberal sees progress in the admission of a few select Negro children to a hitherto white school; the Negro wants all Negro children admitted and spurns the concession as mere tokenism.

The Negro's quarrel with liberal leadership does not portend his subscription to conservative or radical philosophies of race relations. Indeed, the Negro revolt, as Louis Lomax has pointed out, is a rebellion against white leadership, whether that leadership is asserted directly or filtered down through Negroes who accept it. There is a certain irony in the fact that liberals are the targets of Negro displeasure precisely because of their long association in the quest for equality. It is the ally, not the enemy, who gets the blame when the alliance fails to gain its objectives. Rejection of liberal leadership does not mean that Negroes do not want, and expect, continued liberal aid. But they want it on their own terms and they are too sophisticated to believe that liberals can resign a battle involving fundamental equalitarian issues out of pique at the rejection of their leadership.

It is against this background, and to some extent because of it, that the young Negro militants "don't believe in liberals at all." Profoundly influenced by the overthrow of white colonialism in Asia and Africa, they not only want Freedom Now, but insist on substituting a grand strategy for the liberal tactics of fighting one civil-rights battle at a time. They are determined to plot the strategy and dictate the tactics of the campaign. The details of the grand strategy haven't been blueprinted as yet, but in bold outline it calls for direct action by way of sit-ins, stand-ins, kneel-ins, boycotts, freedom rides, civil disobedience, and as-yet-unheard-of techniques as the occasion demands, with resort to legal action when expedient—all under Negro leadership, all calculated to produce immediate results. Heavy stress is being laid on voter registration in the Deep South and it is significant that student leaders make no bones about the fact that *Negro* voting is seen as a device to elect *Negroes* to public office. The very choice of weapons, incidentally, requires action by Negroes. Only Negroes can desegregate a cafe or a hotel or an airport by a sit-in, or a beach by a wade-in, or a church by a kneel-in, or withdraw Negro patronage through a boycott.

It would not be accurate to say that the direct actionists speak for all Negroes under all circumstances. It is fair to say that their philosophy is ascendant, that their influence is becoming pervasive and that their voices are heard with increasing respect and diminishing dissent in Negro communities. Those voices are harsh and strident, and jarring to the liberal ear. Their message is plain: To liberals a fond farewell, with thanks for services rendered, until you are ready to re-enlist as foot soldiers and subordinates in a Negro-led, Negro-officered army under the banner of Freedom Now.

38

A LETTER TO MY NEPHEW

by James Baldwin

After Richard Wright, the African-American author with the greatest impact on the United States was James Baldwin. By 1962 he had already published two books of essays, *Notes of a Native Son* and *Nobody Knows My Name*, and three novels, *Another Country, Giovanni's Room,* and *Go Tell It on the Mountain.* In a remarkable issue of the *Progressive*, December 1962, he joined Adlai Stevenson, Archibald MacLeish, Lillian Smith, John Hope Franklin, A. Philip Randolph, C. Vann Woodward, Martin Luther King, Jr., and others in "A Century of Struggle," marking the hundredth anniversary of the Emancipation Proclamation:

Dear James:

I have begun this letter five times and torn it up five times. I keep seeing your face, which is also the face of your father and my brother. I have known both of you all your lives and have carried your daddy in my arms and on my shoulders, kissed him and spanked him and watched him learn to walk. I don't know if you have known anybody from that far back, if you have loved anybody that long, first as an infant, then as a child, then as a man. You gain a strange perspective on time and human pain and effort.

Other people cannot see what I see whenever I look into your father's face, for behind your father's face as it is today are all those other faces which were his. Let him laugh and I see a cellar your father does not remember and a house he does not remember and I hear in his present laughter his laughter as a child. Let him curse and I remember his falling down the cellar steps and howling and I remember with pain his tears which my hand or your grandmother's hand so easily wiped away, but no one's hand can wipe away those tears he sheds invisibly today which one hears in his laughter and in his speech and in his songs.

I know what the world has done to my brother and how narrowly he has survived it and I know, which is much worse, and this is the crime of which I accuse my country and my countrymen and for which neither I nor time nor history will ever forgive them, that they have destroyed and are destroying hundreds of thousands of lives and do not know it and do not want to know it. One can be—indeed, one must strive to become—tough and philosophical concerning destruction and death, for this is what most of mankind has been best at since we have heard of war; remember, I said most of mankind, but it is not permissible that the authors of devastation should also be innocent. It is the innocence which constitutes the crime.

Now, my dear namesake, these innocent and well meaning people, your countrymen, have caused you to be born under conditions not far removed from those described for us by Charles Dickens in the London of more than a hundred years ago. I hear the chorus of the innocents screaming, "No, this is not true. How bitter you are," but I am writing this letter to you to try to tell you something about how to handle them, for most of them do not yet really know that you exist. I know the conditions under which you were born for I was there. Your countrymen were not there and haven't made it yet. Your grandmother was also there and no one has ever accused her of being bitter. I suggest that the innocent check with her. She isn't hard to find. Your countrymen don't know that she exists either, though she has been working for them all their lives.

Well, you were born; here you came, something like fifteen years ago, and though your father and mother and grandmother, looking about the streets through which they were carrying you, staring at the walls into which they brought you, had every reason to be heavy-hearted, yet they were not, for here you were, big James, named for me. You were a big baby. I was not. Here you were to be loved. To be loved, baby, hard at once and forever to strengthen you against the loveless world. Remember that. I know how black it looks today for you. It looked black that day too. Yes, we were trembling. We have not stopped trembling yet, but if we had not loved each other, none of us would have survived, and now you must survive because we love you and for the sake of your children and your children's children.

This innocent country set you down in a ghetto in which, in fact, it intended that you should perish. Let me spell out precisely what I mean by that for the heart of the matter is here and the crux of my dispute with my country. You were born where you were born and faced the future that you faced because you were black and for no other reason. The limits to your ambition were thus expected to be settled. You were born into a society which spelled out with brutal clarity and in as many ways as possible that you were a worthless human being. You were not expected to aspire to excellence. You were expected to make peace with mediocrity. Wherever you have turned, James, in your short time on this earth, you have been told where you could go and what you could do and how you could do it, where you could live and whom you could marry.

I know your countrymen do not agree with me here and I hear them saying, "You exaggerate." They do not know Harlem and I do. So do you. Take no one's word for anything, including mine, but trust your experience. Know whence you came. If you know whence you came, there is really no limit to where you can go. The details and symbols of your life have been deliberately constructed to make you believe what white people say about you. Please try to remember that what they believe, as well as what they do and cause you to endure, does not testify to your inferiority, but to their inhumanity and fear.

Please try to be clear, dear James, through the storm which rages about your youthful head today, about the reality which lies behind the words "acceptance" and "integration." There is no reason for you to try to become like white men and there is no basis whatever for their impertinent assumption that they must accept you. The really terrible thing, old buddy, is that you must accept them, and I mean that very seriously. You must accept them and accept them with love, for these innocent people have no other hope. They are in effect still trapped in a history which they do not understand and until they understand it, they cannot be released from it. They have had to believe for many years, and for innumerable reasons, that black men are inferior to white men.

Many of them indeed know better, but as you will discover, people find it very difficult to act on what they know. To act is to be committed and to be committed is to be in danger. In this case the danger in the minds and hearts of most white Americans is the loss of their identity. Try to imagine how you would feel if you woke up one morning to find the sun shivering and all the stars aflame. You would be frightened because it is out of the order of nature. Any upheaval in the universe is terrifying because it so profoundly attacks one's sense of one's own reality. Well, the black man has functioned in the white man's world as a fixed star, as an immovable pillar, and as he moves out of his place, heaven and earth are shaken to their foundations.

You don't be afraid. I said it was intended that you should perish in the ghetto, perish by never being allowed to go beyond and behind the white man's definition, by never being allowed to spell your proper name. You have, and many of us have, defeated this intention and by a terrible law, a terrible paradox, those innocents who believed that your imprisonment made them safe are losing their grasp of reality. But these men are your brothers, your lost younger brothers, and if the word "integration" means anything, this is what it means, that we with love shall force our brothers to see themselves as they are, to cease fleeing from reality and begin to change it, for this is your home, my friend. Do not be driven from it. Great men have done great things here and will again and we can make America what America must become.

It will be hard, James, but you come from sturdy peasant stock, men who picked cotton, dammed rivers, built railroads, and in the teeth of the most terrifying odds, achieved an unassailable and monumental dignity. You come from a long line of great poets, some of the greatest poets since Homer. One of them said, "The very time I thought I was lost, my dungeon shook and my chains fell off."

You know and I know that the country is celebrating one hundred years of freedom one hundred years too early. We cannot be free until they are free. God bless you, James, and Godspeed.

Your uncle,
JAMES

39

ON THE ENCYCLOPAEDIA AFRICANA

by W. E. B. Du Bois

On December 18, 1962, Dr. Du Bois spoke at the opening plenary session of the conference devoted to the creation of the *Encyclopaedia Africana*. He was then in his ninety-fourth year; this is the final formal address of his illustrious career. The project—aborted by the coup in Ghana three years later—has not yet reached fruition. It is not unlikely that this dream will yet be realized.

I wish first to express my sincere thanks to those of you here who have accepted the invitation of our Secretariat to participate in this Conference and thus assist us in the preparatory work which we have undertaken for the creation of an Encyclopaedia Africana.

Had there been any doubts in your minds of the importance of African studies, I am sure the papers and discussions of the past week have dispelled them. The wide attendance to the First International Congress of Africanists attests the almost feverish interest throughout the world in the hitherto "Dark Continent." Remains, therefore, for me only to lay before you the importance of an Encyclopaedia Africana based in Africa and compiled by Africans.

You have noted from letters cited in our Information Report, the most gratifying endorsement from scholars in all sections of the world of the general aims of this work. Some of you, however, ask if an Encyclopaedia Africana at this time is not premature. Is this not a too-ambitious undertaking for African scholars to attempt? Is there enough scientifically proven information ready for publication? Our answer is that an Encyclopaedia Africana is long overdue. Yet, it is logical that such a work had to wait for independent Africans to carry it out. We know that there does exist much scientific knowledge of Africa which has never been brought together. We have the little known works of African scholars of the past in North Africa, in the Sudan, in Egypt. Al Azhar University and the Islamic University of Sankore made large collections; *Presence Africaine* has already brought to light much material written in the French language. We can, therefore, begin, remembering always that an encyclopaedia is never a finished or complete body of information. Research and study must be long and continuous. We can collect, organize, and publish knowledge as it emerges. The encyclopaedia must be seen as a living effort which will grow and change—which will expand through the years as more and more material is gathered from all parts of Africa.

It is true that scientific written records do not exist in most parts of this vast continent, but the time is now for beginning. The Encyclopaedia hopes to eliminate the artificial boundaries created on the continent by colonial masters. Designations such as "British Africa," "French Africa," "Black Africa," "Islamic Africa," too often serve to keep alive differences which in large part have been imposed on Africans by outsiders. The Encyclopaedia must have research units throughout West Africa, North Africa, East, Central, and South Africa which will gather and record information for these geographical sections of the continent. The Encyclopaedia is concerned with Africa as a whole.

It is true that there are not now enough trained African scholars available for this gigantic task. In the early stages we have need of the technical skills in research which have been highly developed in other parts of the world. We have already asked for and to a most gratifying degree been granted the unstinted cooperation and assistance of the leading institutes of African studies outside Africa. Many of you who have gathered here from distant lands can, and I believe will, make valuable contributions to this undertaking. And you can assist us in finding capable African men and women who can carry the responsibilities of this work in their own country and to their people. For it is African scholars themselves who will create the ultimate Encyclopaedia Africana.

My interest in this enterprise goes back to 1909 when I first attempted to launch an Encyclopaedia Africana while still teaching history at Atlanta University in Georgia, U.S.A. Though a number of distinguished scholars in the United States and various European countries consented to serve as sponsors, the more practical need of securing financial backing for the projected Encyclopaedia was not solved and the project had to be abandoned. Again, in 1931, a group of American scholars met at Howard University and agreed upon the necessity of preparing an Encyclopaedia of the Negro using this term in its broadest sense. There was much organizational work and research done in the preparation, but once again, the undertaking could not be carried through because money could not be secured. Educational foundations had doubts about a work of this kind being accomplished under the editorship of Negroes. We are deeply grateful to the President of Ghana and to the Government of this Independent African State for inviting us to undertake this important task here where the necessary funds for beginning this colossal work have been provided. After all, this is where the work should be done—in Africa, sponsored by Africans, for Africa. This Encyclopaedia will be carried through.

Much has happened in Africa in the last twenty years. Yet, something of what I wrote in the preparatory volume of the Encyclopaedia of the Negro which was published in 1945 will bear repeating now. I quote:

"Present thought and action are all too often guided by old and discarded theories of race and heredity, by misleading emphasis and silence of former histories. These conceptions are passed on to younger generations of students by current textbooks, popular histories, and even public discussion...our knowledge of Africa today is not, of course, entirely complete; there are many gaps where further information and more careful study is needed; but this is the case in almost every branch of knowledge. Knowledge is never complete, and in few subjects does a time arrive when an encyclopaedia is demanded because no further information is expected. Indeed, the need for an Encyclopaedia is greatest when a stage is reached where there is a distinct opportunity to bring together and set down a clear and orderly statement of the facts already known and agreed upon, for the sake of establishing a base for further advance and further study."

For these reasons and under these circumstances it would seem that an Encyclopaedia Africana is of vital importance to Africa as a whole and to the world at large. I now have the pleasure of declaring opened this Conference for the Encyclopaedia Africana.

From a manuscript in the editor's possession.

40

THE FIRE NEXT TIME

James Baldwin

One of the most penetrating and influential authors of the post–World War II generation was James Baldwin. Following are selections from a widely read work:

The treatment accorded the Negro during the Second World War marks, for me, a turning point in the Negro's relation to America. To put it briefly, and somewhat too simply, a certain hope dies, a certain respect for white Americans faded. One began to pity them, or to hate them. You must put yourself in the skin of a man who is wearing the uniform of his country, is a candidate for death in its defense, and who is called a "nigger" by his comrades-in-arms and his officers; who is almost always given the hardest, ugliest, most menial work to do; who knows that the white G.I. has informed the Europeans that he is subhuman (so much for the American male's sexual security); who does not dance at the U.S.O. the night white soldiers dance there, and does not drink in the same bars white soldiers drink in; and who watches German prisoners of war being treated by Americans with more human dignity than he has ever received at their hands. And who, at the same time, as a human being, is far freer in a strange land than he has ever been at home. *Home*! The very word begins to have a despairing and diabolical ring. You must consider what happens to this citizen, after all he has endured, when he returns—home: search, in his shoes, for a job, for a place to live; ride, in his skin, on segregated buses; see, with his eyes, the signs saying "White" and "Colored," and especially the signs that say "White Ladies" and "Colored *Women*"; look into the eyes of his wife; look into the eyes of his son; listen, with his ears, to political speeches, North and South; imagine yourself being told to "wait." And all this is happening in the richest and freest country in the world, and in the middle of the twentieth century. The subtle and deadly change of heart that might occur in you would be involved with the realization that a civilization is not destroyed by wicked people; it is not necessary that people be wicked but only that they be spineless. I and two Negro acquaintances, all of us well past thirty, and looking it, were in the bar of Chicago's O'Hare Airport several months ago, and the bartender refused to serve us, because, he said, we looked too young. It took a vast amount of patience not to strangle him, and great insistence and some luck to get the manager, who defended his bartender on the ground that he was "new" and had not yet, presumably, learned how to distinguish between a Negro boy of twenty and a Negro "boy" of thirty-seven. Well, we were served, finally, of course, but by this time no amount of Scotch would have helped us. The bar was very crowded and our altercation had been extremely noisy; not one customer in the bar had done anything to help us. When it was over, and the three of us stood at the bar trembling with rage and frustration, and drinking—and trapped, now, in the airport, for we had deliberately come early in order to have a few drinks and to eat—a young white man standing near us asked if we were students. I suppose he thought that this was the only possible explanation for our putting up a fight. I told him that he hadn't wanted to talk to us earlier and we didn't want to talk to him now. The reply visibly hurt his feelings, and this, in turn, caused me to despise him. But when one of us, a Korean War veteran, told this young man that the fight we had been having in the bar had been his fight, too, the young man said, "I lost my conscience a long time ago," and turned and walked out. I know that one would rather not think so, but this young man is typical. So, on the basis of the evidence, had everyone else in the bar lost *his* conscience. A few years ago, I would have hated these people with all my heart. Now I pitied them, pitied them in order not to despise them. And this is not the happiest way to feel toward one's countrymen.

[Baldwin is a dinner guest at the home of Elijah Muhammad]

Elijah's intensity and the bitter isolation and disaffection of these young men and the despair of the streets outside had caused me to glimpse dimly what may now seem to be a fantasy, although, in an age so fantastical, I would hesitate to say precisely what a fantasy is. Let us say that the Muslims were to achieve the possession of the six or seven states that they claim are owed to Negroes by the United States as "back payment" for slave labor. Clearly, the United States would never surrender this territory, on any terms whatever, unless it found it impossible, for whatever reason, to hold it—unless, that is, the United States were to be reduced as a world power, exactly the way, and at the same degree of speed, that England has been forced to relinquish her Empire. (It is simply not true—and the state of her ex-colonies proves this—that England "always meant to go.") If the states were southern states—and the Muslims seem to favor this—then the borders of a hostile Latin America would be raised, in effect, to, say,

Maryland. Of the American borders on the sea, one would face toward a powerless Europe and the other toward an untrustworthy and non-white East, and on the North, after Canada, there would be only Alaska, which is a Russian border. The effect of this would be that the white people of the United States and Canada would find themselves marooned on a hostile continent, with the rest of the white world probably unwilling and certainly unable to come to their aid. All this is not, to my mind, the most imminent of possibilities, but if I were a Muslim, this is the possibility that I would find myself holding in the center of my mind, and driving toward. And if I were a Muslim, I would not hesitate to utilize—or, indeed, to exacerbate—the social and spiritual discontent that reigns here, for, at the very worst, I would merely have contributed to the destruction of a house I hated, and it would not matter if I perished, too. One has been perishing here so long!

And what were they thinking around the table? "I've come," said Elijah, "to give you something which can never be taken away from you." How solemn the table became then, and how great a light rose in the dark faces! This is the message that has spread through streets and tenements and prisons, through the narcotics wards, and past the filth and sadism of mental hospitals to a people from whom everything has been taken away, including, most crucially, their sense of their own worth. People cannot live without this sense; they will do anything whatever to regain it. This is why the most dangerous creation of any society is that man who has nothing to lose. You do not need ten such men—one will do. And Elijah, I should imagine, has had nothing to lose since the day he saw his father's blood rush out—rush down, and splash, so the legend has it, down through the leaves of a tree, on him. But neither did the other men around the table have anything to lose. "Return to your true religion," Elijah has written. "Throw off the chains of the slavemaster, the devil, and return to the fold. Stop drinking his alcohol, using his dope—protect your women—and forsake the filthy swine." I remembered my buddies of years ago, in the hallways, with their wine and their whiskey and their tears; in hallways still, frozen on the needle; and my brother saying to me once, "If Harlem didn't have so many churches and junkies, there'd be blood flowing in the streets." *Protect your women*: a difficult thing to do in a civilization sexually so pathetic that the white man's masculinity depends on a denial of the masculinity of the blacks. *Protect your women*: in a civilization that emasculates the male and abuses the female, and in which, moreover, the male is forced to depend on the female's bread-winning power. *Protect your women*: in the teeth of the white man's boast "We figure we're doing you folks a favor by pumping some white blood into your kids," and while facing the southern shotgun and the northern billy. Years ago, we used to say, "*Yes*, I'm black, goddammit, and I'm beautiful!"—in defiance, into the void. But now—now—African kings and heroes have come into the world, out of the past, the past that can now be put to the uses of power. And black has *become* a beautiful color—not because it is loved but because it is feared. And this urgency on the part of American Negroes is *not to be forgotten*! As they watch black men elsewhere rise, the promise held out, at last, that they may walk the earth with the authority with which white men walk, protected by the power that white men shall have no longer, is enough, and more than enough, to empty prisons and pull God down from Heaven. It has happened before, many times, before color was invented, and the hope of Heaven has always been a metaphor for the achievement of this particular state of grace. The song says, "I know my robe's going to fit me well. I tried it on at the gates of Hell."

It was time to leave, and we stood in the large living room, saying good night, with everything curiously and heavily unresolved. I could not help feeling that I had failed a test, in their eyes and in my own, or that I had failed to heed a warning. Elijah and I shook hands, and he asked me where I was going. Wherever it was, I would be driven there—"because, when we invite someone here," he said, "we take the responsibility of protecting him from the white devils until he gets wherever it is he's going." I was, in fact, going to have a drink with several white devils on the other side of town. I confess that for a fraction of a second I hesitated to give the address—the kind of address that in Chicago, as in all American cities, identified itself as a white address by virtue of its location. But I did give it, and Elijah and I walked out onto the steps, and one of the young men vanished to get the car. It was very strange to stand with Elijah for those few moments, facing those vivid, violent, so problematical streets. I felt very close to him, and really wished to be able to love and honor him as a witness, an ally, and a father. I felt that I knew something of his pain and his fury, and, yes, even his beauty. Yet precisely because of the reality and the nature of those streets—because of what he conceived as his responsibility and what I took to be mine—we would always be strangers and possibly, one day, enemies. The car arrived—a gleaming, metallic, grossly American blue—and Elijah and I shook hands and said good night once more. He walked into his mansion and shut the door. . . .

Now, there is simply no possibility of real change in the Negro's situation without the most radical and far-reaching changes in the American political and social structure. And it is clear that white Americans are not simply unwilling to effect these changes; they are, in the main, so slothful have they become, unable even to envision them. It must be added that the Negro himself no longer believes in the good faith of white Americans—if, indeed, he ever could have. What the Negro *has* discovered, and on an international level, is that power to intimidate which he has always had privately but hitherto could manipulate only privately—for private ends often, for limited ends always. And therefore when the country speaks of a "new" Negro, which it has been doing every hour on the hour for decades, it is not really referring to a change in the Negro, which, in any case, it is quite incapable of assessing, but only to a new difficulty in keeping him in his place, to the fact that it encounters him (again! again!) barring yet another door to its spiritual and social ease. This is probably, hard and odd as it may sound, the most important thing that one human being can do for another—it is certainly *one* of the most important things; hence the torment and necessity of love—and this is the enormous contribution that the Negro has made to this otherwise shapeless and undiscovered country. Consequently, white Americans are in nothing more deluded than in supposing that Negroes could ever have imagined that white people would "give" them anything. It is rare indeed that people give. Most people guard and keep; they suppose that it is they themselves and they identify with themselves that they are guarding and keeping, whereas what they are actually guarding and keeping is their system of reality and what they assume themselves to be. One can give nothing whatever without giving oneself—that is to say, risking oneself. If one cannot risk oneself, then one is simply incapable of giving. And, after all, one can give freedom only by setting someone free. This, in the case of the Negro, the American republic has never become sufficiently mature to do. White Americans have contented themselves with gestures that are now described as "tokenism." For hard example, white Americans congratulate themselves on the 1954 Supreme Court decision outlawing segregation in the schools; they suppose, in spite of the mountain of evidence that has since accumulated to the contrary, that this was proof of a change of heart—or, as they like to say, progress. Perhaps.

It all depends on how one reads the word "progress." Most of the Negroes I know do not believe that this immense concession would ever have been made if it had not been for the competition of the Cold War, and the fact that Africa was clearly liberating herself and therefore had, for political reasons, to be wooed by the descendants of her former masters. Had it been a matter of love or justice, the 1954 decision would surely have occurred sooner; were it not for the realities of power in this difficult era, it might very well not have occurred yet. This seems an extremely harsh way of stating the case—ungrateful, as it were—but the evidence that supports this way of stating it is not easily refuted. I myself do not think that it can be refuted at all. In any event, the sloppy and fatuous nature of American good will can never be relied upon to deal with hard problems. These have been dealt with, when they have been dealt with at all, out of necessity—and in political terms, anyway, necessity means concessions made in order to stay on top. I think this is a fact, which it serves no purpose to deny, *but, whether it is a fact or not, this is what the black population of the world, including black Americans, really believe.* The word "independence" in Africa and the word "integration" here are almost equally meaningless; that is, Europe has not yet left Africa, and the black men here are not yet free. And both of these last statements are undeniable facts, related facts, containing the gravest implications for us all. The Negroes of this country may never be able to rise to power, but they are very well placed indeed to precipitate chaos and ring down the curtain on the American dream...

This past, the Negro's past, of rope, fire, torture, castration, infanticide, rape; death and humiliation; fear by day and night, fear as deep as the marrow of the bone; doubt that he was worthy of life, since everyone around him denied it; sorrow for his women, for his kinfolk, for his children, who needed his protection, and whom he could not protect; rage, hatred, and murder, hatred for white men so deep that it often turned against him and his own, and made all love, all trust, all joy impossible— this past, this endless struggle to achieve and reveal and confirm a human identity, human authority, yet contains, for all its horror, something very beautiful. I do not mean to be sentimental about suffering—enough is certainly as good as a feast—but people who cannot suffer can never grow up, can never discover who they are. That man who is forced each day to snatch his manhood, his identity, out of the fire of human cruelty that rages to destroy it knows, if he survives his effort, and even if he does not survive it, something about himself and human life that no school on earth—and, indeed, no church—can teach. He achieves his own authority, and that is unshakable. This is because, in order to save his life, he is forced to look beneath appearances, to take nothing for granted, to hear the meaning behind the words. If one is continually surviving the worst that life can bring, one eventually ceases to be controlled by a fear of what life can bring; whatever it brings must be borne. And at this level of experience one's bitterness begins to be palatable, and hatred becomes too heavy a sack to carry. The apprehension of life here so briefly and inadequately sketched has been the experience of generations of Negroes, and it helps to explain how they have endured and how they have been able to produce children of kindergarten age who can walk through mobs to get to school. It demands great force and great cunning continually to assault the mighty and indifferent fortress of white supremacy, as Negroes in this country have done so long. It demands great spiritual resilience not to hate the hater whose foot is on your neck, and an even greater miracle of perception and charity not to teach your child to hate. The Negro boys and girls who are facing mobs today come out of a long line of improbable aristocrats—the only genuine aristocrats this country has produced. I say "this country" because their frame of reference was totally American. They were hewing out of the mountain of white supremacy the stone of their individuality. I have great respect for that unsung army of black men and women who trudged down back lanes and entered back doors, saying "Yes, sir" and "No, Ma'am" in order to acquire a new roof for the schoolhouse, new books, a new chemistry lab, more beds for the dormitories, more dormitories. They did not like saying "Yes, sir" and "No, Ma'am," but the country was in no hurry to educate Negroes, these black men and women knew that the job had to be done, and they put their pride in their pockets in order to do it. It is very hard to believe that they were in any way inferior to the white men and women who opened those back doors. It is very hard to believe that those men and women, raising their children, eating their greens, crying their curses, weeping their tears, singing their songs, making their love, as the sun rose, as the sun set, were in any way inferior to the white men and women who crept over to share these splendors after the sun went down. But we must avoid the European error; we must not suppose that, because the situation, the ways, the perceptions of black people so radically differed from those of whites, they were racially superior. I am proud of these people not because of their color but because of their intelligence and their spiritual force and their beauty. The country should be proud of them, too, but, alas, not many people in this country even know of their existence. And the reason for this ignorance is that a knowledge of the role these people played—and play—in American life would reveal more about America to Americans than Americans wish to know. . . .

James Baldwin, *The Fire Next Time* (New York: Dial Press, 1963), pp. 68–70; 89–93; 99–102; 112–15.

41

TEN DEMANDS IN NASHVILLE

by Black Citizens

Nashville, Tennessee, with a considerable African-American population and the seat of Fisk University with hundreds of increasingly militant students, was the locale for the following demands in 1963 meetings with Mayor Beverly Briley:

(1) That no segregation or racial discrimination be practiced anywhere in or by the government of metropolitan Nashville itself. This would include hiring and appointing personnel purely on basis of qualifications, with no consideration whatsoever being given to racial identity. That all institutions and establishments operated by the local government cease practices of racial exclusiveness, and that parks, swimming pools, and other recreational facilities be opened to all citizens.

(2) That the operators of restaurants, drug stores, religious establishments such as the YMCA and YWCA and the Church-sponsored hospitals and other establishments and businesses be made aware of the fact that the leaders of local government feel strongly that the practice of racial discrimination in accommodations and employment be promptly ended as such practices are not in the best interest of the city as a whole nor any of our citizens.

(3) That the new metropolitan government forbid law enforcement officers from arresting persons when their only real offense is that they have an unfulfilled desire for full and complete freedom as American citizens. Further, we urge that Negro law enforcement personnel be used in the entire metropolitan area whether that area be Negro or not and that they receive regular promotions as do other officials.

(4) We want the enactment and enforcement of laws which will serve as a deterrent to the violent forces in the community which would intimidate those who dream and labor for justice, equality and freedom.

(5) That operators of hotels and motels in the metropolitan area be made aware of the fact that metropolitan Nashville would profit by an increased number of conventions if their facilities were open to all persons and that city officials are intensely interested in this economic dividend as well as the moral implications of the practice of exclusiveness.
(6) That the services of no person whose salary is paid by the taxes of all the citizens be used to prosecute those whose only real offense is that they work for the cause of freedom.
(7) That metropolitan officials set into motion machinery which will condemn and prohibit housing discrimination and will defend the right of any citizen to build or buy in any area he may choose.
(8) That metropolitan officials work diligently for the enactment of public accommodations and fair employment laws.
(9) That metropolitan officials call upon established human relations groups and knowledgeable individuals to assist in whatever manner possible in helping to immediately erase the color line from the affairs of Nashville.
(10) That a human relations commission as a part of the structure of the metropolitan government be established. Such a commission to be a permanent part of the government with full-time concern for the problems in the area of human relations.

James E. Jackson, *The Bold, Bad '60s* (New York: International Publishers, 1992), pp. 61–62. This book consists of the reportage by the author on the scene at the time.

42

WHAT WE WANT

by Elijah Muhammad

Elijah Poole, from Georgia, chose the above name. Appearing first in Detroit, the Black Muslim movement had followers by the 1960s in almost every major city. In 1963 the movement's official newspaper, *Mr. Muhammad Speaks,* presented the protest portion of that effort:

1. We want freedom. We want a full and complete freedom.
2. We want justice. Equal justice under the law. We want justice applied equally to all, regardless of creed or class or color.
3. We want equality of opportunity. We want equal membership in society with the best in civilized society.
4. We want our people in America whose parents or grandparents were

descendants from slaves, to be allowed to establish a separate state or territory of their own....

5. We want freedom for all Believers of Islam now held in federal prisons. We want freedom for all black men and women now under death sentence in innumerable prisons in the North as well as the South.
   We want every black man and woman to have the freedom to accept or reject being separated from the slave master's children and establish a land of their own....

6. We want an immediate end to the police brutality and mob attacks against the so-called Negro throughout the United States.

7. As long as we are not allowed to establish a state or territory of our own, we demand not only equal justice under the laws of the United States, but equal employment opportunities—NOW!...

8. We want the government of the United States to exempt our people from ALL taxation as long as we are deprived of equal justice under the laws of the land.

9. We want equal education—but separate schools up to sixteen for boys and eighteen for girls on the condition that the girls be sent to women's colleges and universities. We want all black children educated, taught without hindrance or suppression.

10. We believe that intermarriage or race mixing should be prohibited. We want the religion of Islam taught without hindrance or suppression.

These are some of the things that we, the Muslims, want for our people in North America.

C. Eric Lincoln, "The Black Muslims As A Protest Movement," in Arnold M. Rose, ed., *Assuring Freedom To The Free* (Detroit: Wayne State University Press, 1964), pp. 222–40.

43

HARLEM RENT STRIKE RALLY

Speeches by James Baldwin and John Lewis

On January 12, 1963, a Harlem rent-strike rally was held in a gymnasium on 117th Street; it was attended by about six hundred local people. Speakers included James Baldwin and John Lewis.

James Baldwin

I don't have anything to say to you that you don't already know. I was born in Harlem. There were nine of us in a series of horrible apartments. I remember one apartment on 134th Street above the river. [He stops to adjust sound.]

I am only here really as a witness. I was born in Harlem hospital in 1924. That means I was raised in the depression days. Our father—there were nine of us—as far as I know he never made more than $27.50 a week all the years I was growing up. Many times he didn't work at all. My sisters and brothers and I slept five and six to a bed, catercorner.

I know about the rats and the plaster and the roaches and the lack of heat. I know how hard it is to find the landlord even to complain. I know the intent of the ghetto is to create so many obstacles to getting through a single day that by the time you are thirty you have had it.

It is done deliberately because black people have always played a certain role. Our role has been to corroborate the white man's vision of himself. He can't be what he says and thinks he is unless we are what he thinks we are. In order to keep us where he thinks we should be he has the most brutal set of laws and "customs" in the South. And a very effective economic system in the North designed to keep us at the bottom of the labor barrel for all our life.

It isn't only the landlord you have to fight. It is also the insurance companies. I'm sure you know something about that.... In spite of all the policemen walking in Harlem my brother has been robbed four times in the last six months. And nothing is done about it. One doesn't even call the police anymore. It isn't worth it. This is what we are trying to fight against.

It is a more complex situation in the North. It's hard to find the landlord. It's hard to know where the enemy is. I know where he is. He's in the bank. He's in the bank! Harlem is a very lucrative place for a great many people. You don't have to repair the houses and the people have to pay the rent. A great many people live on it, not all of them white.

This is a revolution. It is going to be harder and harder and harder because the revolution has got to revise the entire system in order for us, as Negroes, to live and in order for the country to survive. It connects with the condition of black and dark people all over the world. One must be bold enough to see and say this....

It is important to remember that once we get the vote in the South the

Democratic Party, as we know it, and the Republican Party, as we know it, and the South, as we know it, and the country, as we know it, will be different. Now a great many people in power know this, obviously, and are determined with everything that they have in their hands to prevent such a transformation. And that is why the country at the moment is really, spiritually speaking, at the edge of civil war. It is important not to lose our courage or compromise. Don't believe anyone who says to relax and they will take care of it for us. It is important for us to take care of it ourselves and prepare ourselves for a very long and terrible battle which we can't afford to lose.

When one talks about the power structure, whites say they are not responsible and say: "We have Negro friends and maids and have not hurt a Negro in our lives." As far as it goes it is true. When the train passes 125th Street over the Park Avenue railroad station they're on their way to Connecticut and all they see is the few housing projects they put up to keep us there and they are very proud of it. There is a contradiction between the lives white people live and the lives we live.

The landlords, the city, and the state *are* responsible. Things *can* be corrected but only if we force them to act. They will never do it otherwise. In the South, for example, we see some changes have been made. I'm not being cheerful about this. I'm not a liberal. . . . But we know the situation in the South was precipitated by the Negro people in the streets. If not, the situation would be exactly what it was 50–60 and a hundred hears ago. It is because the people couldn't wait for Mr. Charley to give them their freedom.

John Lewis

I must say to all of you here who are involved in the struggle, that this is indeed a great privilege to be here. I got out of jail in Atlanta at 1:30 this morning. A group of us were arrested last night because we were involved in some protests in public accommodation. People from SNCC, SCLC, NAACP . . . went to jail last night but I had made a commitment to be here today, so on this one occasion I said I want to be bailed out of jail to make it and here I am.

Those of us who live and work in the Deep South have been following the struggle here in Harlem with great interest. This represents something very new and meaningful not only to the state of New York but to the whole nation. Some of us have been saying all along that when the masses get moving in Harlem, the masses in the whole nation will move.

I think 1964 is the year for us to move and you are moving. At the present time, and I think I am right here, this community is the only community in this nation at the present time that is mobilized and prepared to move. We must say not only to this community but to other communities all over this nation—South and North—like Chicago, and Detroit, Cleveland, Buffalo, Birmingham, Atlanta, Nashville, and all of these large ghetto communities, that we are not going to pay our rent for what we don't get.

NO MORE

I had a feeling that there would come a time like this in the life of the people. I think it is here in Harlem now that in a real sense the cup runneth over. You are really saying in so many words: "I am not going to take it any longer." You are saying it not only to the city of New York but to a lot of us in the Deep South.

We must rise up and use new means to complete this revolution. In all the ghettoes our people are paying rent for nothing. They have no lights in some places, no hot water, they have rats. If all over this nation, if during the next two weeks and February there is born a general rent-strike you will see something very beautiful. You will make 1963 look very petty and 1964 will be the year of the civil-rights revolution. It is not just going to come from city hall or Albany or not even from Washington, D.C., but from the people like you. And all of us are going to have to not only refuse to pay our rent but we might be called upon to get in the streets and go to city hall and maybe move out in the summer months because there are too many rats on the inside, and block up some of these city streets.

The time is now for oppressed people throughout this nation and this world to stop playing. We wanted to be free by 1963. We are not free yet. We keep saying let's fight here and there. If we really want to be free, to put an end to this very system, I think each of you must continue doing what you now are, but intensifying the struggle, not only through Harlem but throughout this nation.

In the South we are not free. We must say to the people in Harlem who want to live in a decent home, in Chicago who want a decent meal, none of us are free until all of us are truly and really free. We say in a real sense that it takes the force, the power of our own bodies. In SNCC where people are working in Alabama, they talk about putting their bodies on the line. As someone suggested we don't have money but we have bodies. We don't have a lot of money but we have bodies. If we get together as bodies and move together in a great mass, we would turn this nation upside down.

WILL TO STRUGGLE

Not one thing is going to be given to us. We are going to have to struggle for it. As the great Frederick Douglass said, there can be no progress without struggle. We must be willing to struggle here in Harlem and throughout every village and hamlet and city of this nation until all the people can say we are really free. If we don't do this then our revolution will come to an end before we gain independence and freedom.

I call upon everyone to do everything possible in your power to carry the revolution further. We in SNCC support and salute your efforts. Today in the cities like Knoxville, Atlanta, New Orleans, people are thinking about the same thing. Maybe during the month of February we will get something going. Thank you very much.

John O. Killens and Fred Halstead, eds., *Harlem Stirs* (New York: Marzani and Munsell, 1966), pp. 62–64.

44

"THOSE WHO WANT TO BE FREE"

by Robert P. Moses

Robert Moses, a product of Harlem, studied at Harvard, on a scholarship, where he earned a master's degree. He began his adult life teaching mathematics on the high school level in New York City. His first experience in the black liberation movement involved a trip to Virginia, where he participated in very early sit-in demonstrations. Soon, while still teaching, he became a rank-and-file worker in SCLC, and later a full-time SCLC worker. He led the voter-registration drive in McComb, Mississippi. That drive involved teaching black volunteers how to complete a twenty-one-question registration application and how to explain the 285 sections of the Mississippi Constitution. It was Moses who, in the summer of 1961, brought black people—heroes all—to the country courthouse located in a town named Liberty. Moses was arrested and suffered a severe beating. At about this time, Herbert Lee, an Amite County farmer, had also been helping people register; on September 25, 1961, he was shot dead.

Moses persevered in the struggle in Mississippi for many months and was arrested numerous times. By early 1963, Moses was director of SNCC's voter registration project.

A letter to unstated recipients was dated Greenville, Mississippi, February 27, 1963.

The food drive you organized and publicized with the help of Dick Gregory and others has resulted in and served as the immediate catalyst for opening new dimensions in the voter registration movement in Mississippi.

Wherever food has been sent it has given the opportunity, depending directly upon the amount of food, for:

1. Contact with hundreds or thousands of Negroes.
2. Development of a core of workers who come to help process the applications, packaging and distribution of the food, and stay to help on the voter registration drive.
3. An image in the Negro community of providing direct aid, not just "agitation."

The food is identified in the minds of everyone as food for those who want to be free, and the minimum requirement for freedom is identified as registration to vote.

The voting drives I've experienced in Mississippi have proceeded by steppes instead of slopes and we have been on a deep plateau all winter, shaking off the effects of the violence of August and September and the eruption that was Meredith at Ole Miss.

We know this plateau by now; we have had to crawl over it in McComb city, Amite and Walthall Counties, Hattiesburg, Greenwood and Ruleville. You dig into yourself and the community to wage psychological warfare; you combat your own fears about beatings, shootings, and possible mob violence; you stymy, by your mere physical presence, the anxious fear of the Negro community, seeded across town and blown from paneled pine and white sunken sink to windy kitchen floors and rusty old stoves, that maybe you *did* come only to boil and bubble and then burst, out of sight and sound; you organize, pound by pound, small bands of people who gradually focus in the eyes of Negro and whites as people "tied up in that mess"; you create a small striking force capable of moving out when the time comes, which it must, whether we help it or not.

When a thousand people stand in line for a few cans of food, then it is possible to tell a thousand people that they are poor, that they are trapped in poverty, they *they* must move if they are to escape. In Leflore County there are 14,400 non-white workers, 12,060 make less than $1,500 a year and 7,200 of these make less than $500 a year. After more than six hundred lined up to receive food in Greenwood on Wednesday, 20 Feb., and Sam's subsequent arrest and weekend in prison on Thurs. 21 Feb., over one hundred people overflowed city hall on Mon. 25 Feb. to protest at his trial, over 250 gathered at a mass meeting that same night and on Tues. by 10:30 A.M., I had counted over fifty people standing in silent line in the county courthouse; they say over two hundred stood in line across the day.

This is a new dimension for a voting program in Mississippi; Negroes have been herded to the polls before by white people, but have never stood en masse in protest at the seat of power in the iceberg of Mississippi politics. Negroes who couldn't read and write stood in line to tell the registrar they still wanted to vote, that they didn't have a chance to go to school when they were small and anyway Mr. John Jones can't read and write either and *he* votes.

We don't know this plateau at all. We were relieved at the absence of immediate violence at the courthouse, but who knows what's to come next.

The weather breaks in mid-April and I hope you will be able to continue to send food until then.

Joanne Grant, ed., *op. cit.*, pp. 299–301.

45

THE BIRMINGHAM MANIFESTO

by F. L. Shuttlesworth and N. H. Smith

On April 3, 1963—the initial day of the nonviolent campaign in Birmingham—the following "Manifesto" was issued. It was widely circulated in the city and in much of the African-American press. It was signed by the Reverend F. L. Shuttlesworth, and the Reverend N. H. Smith, president and secretary, respectively, of the Alabama Christian Movement for Human Rights.

The patience of an oppressed people cannot endure forever. The Negro citizens of Birmingham for the last several years have hoped in vain for some evidence of good faith resolution of our just grievances.

Birmingham is part of the United States and we are *bona fide* citizens. Yet the history of Birmingham reveals that very little of the democratic process touches the life of the Negro in Birmingham. We have been segregated racially, exploited economically, and dominated politically. Under the leadership of the Alabama Christian Movement for Human Rights, we sought relief by petition for the repeal of city ordinances requiring segregation and the institution of a merit hiring policy in city employment. We were rebuffed. We then turned to the system of the courts. We weathered set-back after set-back, with all of its costliness, finally winning the terminal, bus, parks, and airport cases. The bus decision has been implemented begrudgingly and the parks decision prompted the closing of all municipally-owned recreational facilities with the exception of the zoo and Legion Field. The airport case has been a slightly better experience with the experience of hotel accommodations and the subtle discrimination that continues in the limousine service.

We have always been a peaceful people, bearing our oppression with super-human effort. Yet we have been the victims of repeated violence, not only that inflicted by the hoodlum element but also that inflicted by the blatant misuse of police power. Our memories are seared with painful mob experience of Mother's Day 1961 during the Freedom Rides. For years, while our homes and churches were being bombed, we heard nothing but the rantings and ravings of racist city officials.

The Negro protest for equality and justice has been a voice crying in the wilderness. Most of Birmingham has remained silent, probably out of fear. In the meanwhile, our city has acquired the dubious reputation of being the worst big city in race relations in the United States. Last fall, for a flickering moment, it appeared that sincere community leaders from religion, business, and industry discerned the inevitable confrontation in race relations approaching. Their concern for the city's image and commonweal of all its citizens did not run deep enough. Solemn promises were made, pending a postponement of direct action, that we would be joined in a suit seeking the relief of segregation ordinances. Some merchants agreed to desegregate their rest-rooms as a good-faith start, some actually complying, only to retreat shortly thereafter. We hold in our hands now, broken faith and broken promises.

We believe in the American Dream of democracy, in the Jeffersonian doctrine that "all men are created equal and are endowed by their Creator with certain inalienable rights, among these being life, liberty, and the pursuit of happiness."

Twice since September we have deferred our direct action thrust in order that a change in city government would not be made in the hysteria of community crisis. We act today in full concert with our Hebraic-

Christian tradition, the law of morality, and the Constitution of our nation. The absence of justice and progress in Birmingham demands that we make a moral witness to give our community a chance to survive. We demonstrate our faith that we believe that The Beloved Community can come to Birmingham.

We appeal to the citizenry of Birmingham, Negro and white, to join us in this witness for decency, morality, self-respect, and human dignity. Your individual and corporate support can hasten the day of "liberty and justice for all." This is Birmingham's moment of truth in which every citizen can play his part in her larger destiny.

Freedomways 4 (Winter 1964): 20–21.

46

IMPRISONED CHILDREN "SERVE THEIR TIME"

by New York Times *Correspondents*

Two reports give firsthand accounts of the views of black youngsters jailed for "rioting against racial segregation" as the *New York Times* declared.

BIRMINGHAM, ALA., May 8—Anita Woods said today: "My mother told me I had to serve my time."

Anita is a twelve-year-old Negro girl, one of the thousand or more juveniles arrested here on Monday for rioting against racial segregation.

She is at the Jefferson County Detention Home, along with about 110 other girls, none older than thirteen.

Anita Woods spoke with a reporter in a locked room she shares with twenty other Negro girls, all arrested for parading without a permit, a violation of Section 1159 of the General City Code.

The room was hot and steamy; downstairs, the main corridor and offices of the detention home were coolly air-conditioned.

"Do you want to go home?" the girls were asked.

"Yes!" they chorused.

"But I'd do it again," Anita Woods said. "I'll keep on marching till I get freedom."

"What is freedom?" a reporter asked.

"It's equal rights," another girl shouted. "I want to go to any school and any store downtown and sit in the movies." She giggled. "And sit around in a cafeteria."

They were asked why their parents had not come to get them, since, in a change of policy, Juvenile Court Judge Talbot Ellis had decided to permit parents to call for their children in exchange for signing an appearance bond, instead of the $500 cash bond that was previously required.

It was then that Anita Woods announced what her mother had told her.

Dale G. Oltman, the chief probation officer of the juvenile court, a soft-spoken former Nebraskan, said the detention home normally accommodated sixty-two youngsters. With the present population of 110 or so, it was like having guests drop in unexpectedly, he said. The home is doing its best to feed and bed the children, he said, "but, of course, it's not like home."

Some of the inmates slept in blankets on the floor, he said.

The youngest person arrested in the riots was a seven-year-old girl. She was picked up by her parents yesterday.

Boys between thirteen and eighteen were being held in the Jefferson County Jail and the Bossenter Jail. Girls from thirteen to eighteen were in the 4-H Club building at the State Fairgrounds. There were 594 girls there just after the arrests Monday. Only two hundred were there today. Girls arrested last Monday outnumbered boys by almost two to one.

BIRMINGHAM, ALA., May 8 (A.P.)—Here, in a juvenile court judge's office, many sides of the Birmingham story emerged today.

Judge Talbot Ellis sat behind his desk. He has crisp gray hair, a clean-cut profile. He speaks in a low, kindly voice.

On the other side of the desk was a fifteen-year-old Negro boy, Grosbeck Preer Parham. He is big for his age. He was arrested five days ago for participating in the integration demonstrations here.

A sign in the desk bore the motto: "Prayer changes everything."

Behind Judge Talbot was the boy's mother, Mrs. Aileen Parham.

The conversation among the three went like this:

JUDGE: Grosbeck, I'm going to let you go. Your mother must have been mighty worried when she couldn't find you. Why did you tell the officer you were seventeen? That's why they put you in jail instead of bringing you here.

BOY: I said I was fifteen.

JUDGE: Well, anyway, I'm letting you go.

JUDGE: Now, Grosbeck, you know violence in the streets is not the answer to this. Just the other day, Attorney General Kennedy said this problem 'won't be solved in the streets.' And I often think of what one of the founding fathers said: 'There is no freedom without restraint.' Now, I want you to go home and go back to school. Will you do that?

There was no answer. The boy stared at the judge, unblinking.

JUDGE: Are you mad at me, son?

BOY: Can I say something?

JUDGE: Anything you like.

BOY: Well, you can say that about freedom because you've got your freedom. The Constitution says we're all equal but Negroes aren't equal.

JUDGE: But you people have made great gains and they still are. It takes time.

BOY: We've been waiting over one hundred years.

The judge told him about attending legal conferences, working there with Negro judges and attorneys.

JUDGE: Now, we were all equal there, not because the Constitution says so, but because we are equal in our profession.

MOTHER: May I say something? I don't approve of street violence either. But after a civil rights meeting we did try to get in touch with city officials and they wouldn't see us. And I know this, judge—these younger people are not going to take what we took. I have another son in Oberlin [College], and he'll never want to come back here."

She described her experiences as a shopper in downtown Birmingham and said, "If I'm going to spend my money in the stores, I think I should have the right to sit down and eat a sandwich in them."

JUDGE: Mrs. Parham, what do you think of Booker T. Washington?

MOTHER: I think he was a fine man. But his day is past. The younger people won't take what we did.

BOY: Does Birmingham have a health board? Are they concerned about what happens to Negroes in jail?

The judge nodded affirmatively.

BOY: We were picked up at 2:30 and we didn't get anything to eat all day. The next morning we wouldn't have gotten anything either if we hadn't gotten together and beat on the bars and yelled.

A juvenile court officer asked, "Would your mother have had food for over one hundred people if they had all come at once to your home?"

BOY: Maybe not. But you should have seen the slop they fed us. It wasn't fit for a human being to eat.

JUDGE: Well, I expect we could talk all day about these things. I want you to go now and I still hope you'll go back to school.

MOTHER: Thank you, Judge.

BOY (under his breath): Thanks for nothing.

47

A NEW SOLIDARITY IN STRUGGLE FOR HUMAN DIGNITY

by Robert C. Weaver

In June 1963 the Center for the Study of Democratic Institutions sponsored a symposium in Chicago on "Challenges to Democracy." The result was published by the center as one of its occasional papers. The publication was opened by the text of a speech by Vice President Lyndon Johnson. It was followed by the paper given at the symposium by Robert C. Weaver, whose long career as a Washington office holder began under Franklin Delano Roosevelt, serving as an assistant to Harold Ickes. Some thirty years later he was administrator of the U.S. Housing and Home Finance Agency in Washington. His paper, given here in part, reflects the approach of a successful African-American liberal.

What are the responsibilities of Negro leadership? Certainly the first is to keep pressing for the status of first-class citizenship for all—an inevitable goal of those who accept the values of this nation. Another is to encourage and help Negroes to prepare for the opportunities that are now and will be open to them.

The ultimate responsibilities of Negro leaders, however, are to show results and to maintain a following. This means that they cannot be so "responsible" that they forget the trials and tribulations of those less fortunate or less recognized. They cannot stress progress—the emphasis that is so palatable to the majority group—without, at the same time, delineating the unsolved business of democracy. They cannot provide models that will have any meaning for their followers unless they can bring about social changes that will facilitate the emergence of these models from the *typical* environment of the Negro community.

Negro leadership must also face up to the deficiencies that plague the Negro community. Although crime, poverty, illegitimacy, and hopelessness can all be explained, in large measure, in terms of the history and current status of the Negro in America, they do exist. We need no longer be self-conscious in admitting these unpleasant facts, for we know enough about human behavior now to recognize that antisocial activities are not innate in any people.

For many successful older colored Americans, middle-class status—the American standard—has been difficult to attain. Restricted for the most part to racial ghettos, they have made great efforts to protect their children from falling back into the dominant values of that environment, values that are probably more repugnant to them than to most Americans. This is understandable in terms of their origins. They have come largely from lower-middle-class families, where industry, good conduct, family ties, and a willingness to postpone immediate rewards for future success are stressed; their standards of conduct have been those of success-oriented middle-class Americans.

It is not that these Negroes fail to feel shame about the muggings or the illegitimate births among other Negroes. Many of them, in fact, feel too much shame and either repudiate the "culprits" in terms of scathing condemnation or try to escape from the problem lest it endanger their own none too secure status. Few Negroes are immune from the toll of upward mobility. Their struggles have usually been difficult, and the maintenance of status exacts a heavy toll. As long as this is true, they will have less energy to devote to the problems of the Negro subculture.

But these attitudes are shifting. Younger middle-class Negroes are more secure, and so place less stress upon the quest for respectability. It is significant that the sit-ins and Freedom Marches in the South have been planned and executed by Negro college students most of whom come from middle-class families. Middle-class Negroes have long led the fight for civil rights, and today its youthful members are not hesitating to resort to direct action. In so doing they are forging a new solidarity in the struggle for human dignity.

There are today, as there always have been, thousands of dedicated colored Americans who do not make the headlines but are successful in raising the horizons of Negroes. Teachers, social workers, political leaders, ministers, doctors, and an assortment of other indigenous leaders at the local level are familiar with the environmental factors that dull or destroy motivation. They are involved with the total Negro community. They demonstrate—rather than verbalize—a concern for the problems of Negro youth. They are trying to reach these young people, not by coddling them or by providing excuses for failure, but by identifying themselves with them and helping to develop their potentialities. Both genuine affection and sufficient toughness to encourage the development of self-reliance are in these local leaders.

When these people—white as well as black—suggest thrift, good deportment, greater emphasis upon education and training, as proper goals to seek, they do it pragmatically. It is not a matter of proselytizing but of identifying those values and patterns of behavior which will help young people to move upward in contemporary American society. This practical, sophisticated approach also enables them to identify the deviations from dominant standards that can be left undisturbed because they are not inconsistent with a productive and healthy life in modern urban communities. The adjustment of values and concepts need only be minimal for eventual full social participation.

However, if emphasis upon self-betterment is employed indiscriminately by Negro leaders, it is seized upon by white supremacists and their apologists to support the assertion that Negroes—and they mean all Negroes—are not ready for full citizenship. Thus, because of the nature of our society, Negro leadership must continue to stress *rights* if it is to receive a hearing for programs of self-improvement. Black Muslims, who identify the white man as the devil, emphasize—with a remarkable degree of success—morality, industry, and good conduct. But the Negro leader who refuses to repudiate his own Americanism or that of his followers can do so effectively only as he does clearly repudiate identification with the white supremacists. This he indicates, of course, when he champions equal rights, just as the Black Muslims indicate it by directing hate toward all white people.

Most Negroes in leadership roles have made clear that they and those who follow them are a part of America. They have striven for realization of the American dream. But they cannot succeed alone. Sophisticated whites realize that the status of Negroes in our society depends not only on what the Negro himself does to achieve his goals and to prepare himself for opportunities but, even more, on what all America does to expand these opportunities. The quality and character of future Negro leadership will be determined by how effective those leaders who relate to the *total* society can be in satisfying the yearnings for human dignity that lie in the hearts of all Americans.

"The Negro as an American," a paper published in 1963 by the Center for the Study of Democratic Institutions, pp. 6–8.

48

THE FUNERAL OF MEDGAR W. EVERS

by James E. Jackson

One of the many martyrs in the black freedom struggle was Medgar W. Evers, field secretary of the NAACP for Mississippi. Early in the morning of June 12, 1963, he was murdered by a bullet in the back. In the afternoon of June 15 his funeral was held in Jackson. Behind the white hearse carrying his body marched a fourth of the black population of the city. An eyewitness report of this event follows:

Over four thousand of his friends, neighbors, and fighters in the cause had crowded into every available space of the gymnasium-like hall of the Negro Masonic Temple Building on Lynch Street, in Jackson, Mississippi, by 10:15 A.M. for the funeral service for Medgar W. Evers, leader of the Mississippi Negroes' freedom fight who was slain by an assassin's bullet on June 12th. The service had been scheduled for 11:30 A.M., last Saturday, June 15th.

On the platform facing the silent and reverent audience of mourners sat Roy Wilkins, the executive secretary of the NAACP; Dr. Ralph J. Bunche, Under-Secretary of the United Nations; Congressman Charles Diggs of Michigan; George Biddle, President of Tougaloo College; Clarence Mitchell, legislative secretary of the NAACP, and several Jackson clergymen. Seated in the center of the first row in the audience was the widow of the martyred leader, Mrs. Myralie Evers with two of her three children—Darrell Kenyatta, nine, and Rena Denise, eight, Medgar's brother Charles Evers and other members of the family. To the left of the family group, near the front of the audience, the Rev. Martin Luther King, Rev. Abernathy, Rev. Lawrence, and Rev. Wyatt Tee Walker were seated with a full delegation from the leadership of the Southern Christian Leadership Conference. Other delegations were present—from CORE, headed by its executive officer James Farmer; from the veterans' organization (AVC). Some fifty prominent personalities from throughout the country could be identified in the vast crowd, including Dick Gregory, the celebrated "message comedian," Roy Reuther of the United Automobile Workers; and Daisy Bates, heroine of the Battle of Little Rock.

An associate of Medgar Evers in earlier struggles in Mount Bayou and elsewhere in Mississippi, Dr. T.R.M. Howard, was the first speaker to pay a secular tribute to the foully murdered leader.

Dr. Howard invoked the Biblical quotation that "without the shedding of blood there can be no remission of sins" to serve warning on the minions of the law in Mississippi to stop murdering and torturing its Negro citizens. "For over a hundred years now, we have been turning first one and then the other cheek. Our neck has gotten tired of turning now!" he said to the accompaniment of a great roar of shouted approvals from the mourners, "We aren't going to absorb many more of their blows," he said. Dr. Howard likened Evers to the sainted John Brown and said he would live in history alongside the name of the old martyr of the anti-slavery struggle.

Roy Wilkins' funeral oration articulated the anger, and the unextinguishable and not to be denied resolve of the twenty million Negro Americans to secure now their full and uncircumscribed rights. He identified the segregation system and the ruling powers in the nation who have for so long failed to act to end it as the forces behind the madman who fired the assassination shot.

Roy Wilkins declared that: "The lurking assassin at midnight June 11-12 pulled the trigger, but in all wars the men who do the shooting are trained and indoctrinated and keyed to action. The southern political system put him behind that rifle; the lily-white southern governments, local and state; the senators, governors, state legislators, mayors, judges, sheriffs, chiefs of police, commissioners, etc. Not content with mere disfranchisement, the office holders have used unbridled political power to fabricate a maze of laws, customs, and economic practices which has imprisoned the Negro.

"Speaking of the public school decision of 1954 of the United States Supreme Court, Senator James O. Eastland told a 1955 Senatobia, Mississippi, audience: 'You are obligated to disobey such a Court.'

"In far-away Washington, the southern system has its outposts in the Congress of the United States and by their deals and maneuvers they helped put the man behind the deadly rifle on Guynes Street this week. The killer must have felt that he had, if not an immunity, then certainly a protection for whatever he chose to do, no matter how dastardly.

"The opposition has been reduced to clubs, guns, hoses, dogs, garbage trucks, and hog wire compounds. But obviously, nothing can stop the drive for freedom. It will not cease here or elsewhere. After a hundred years of waiting and suffering, we are determined, in Baldwin's language, 'not upon a bigger cage, but upon no cage at all.' "

Wilkins' speech concluded the funeral services which lasted less than an hour. Then the great crowd of mourners calmly flowed through the single exit of the big hall on Lynch Street. There, joined by several thousand other Negroes and some two score of white crusaders against racist persecution, a funeral cortege shaped up. With his stoic, infinitely brave, and undauntable widow in line and alone, a few paces behind the white hearse bearing the remains of Medgar Evers, a vast army of freedom fighter veterans fell in formation, four abreast to wend their way in a twenty-block-long column throughout the length of Jackson, in a mile and a half silent march.

The march, which began on the street which bears the name of John R. Lynch, the Negro statesman who was Speaker of the House in the Mississippi State Assembly during the Reconstruction years, ended at the Negro business district.

Roy Wilkins and the Rev. Martin Luther King, Dick Gregory and other famous names in the freedom struggle of America's Negroes composed the front ranks of the marchers.

I was there and marched in the front ranks of the contingent of uniformed Elks. The temperature was 103 degrees but I saw no one fall out of rank in the long walk under a merciless sun.

Only for the occasion of this sacred tribute to the dead had the Mayor lifted his edict against "Negroes congregating, demonstrating, or indulging in any public manifestations whatsoever." And the terms of this march were that it had to be totally silent, along the specified police-patrolled route, and promptly ended, with the crowd dispersed by 2:00 P.M. that day.

But in the aftermath of this moving silent processional, a spontaneous demonstration of revolutionary explosiveness occurred. An event from which the racist police regime of Jackson is not likely to recover. I saw frail-bodied schoolgirls, with blazing honey-brown faces, and with hands bare of weapons charge fearlessly into a phalanx of helmeted police with raised riot guns. I saw Angels storming into the defenders of the bastions of Hell—Mississippi, that is. . . .

All business establishments along the route of march were closed or shuttered. All cross traffic had come to a stop. As the silent cortege moved through the "white" part of town in measured step, I watched, as I walked, the faces of the white citizens who sat in their cars at the intersections, who formed clusters in the windows of stores and dwellings on either side of the concrete-surfaced street along which we marched, or who gathered in little clusters at the corners and in front of taverns.

But for the most part, the faces I saw bore a grim and troubled countenance. One could identify the expressions of fear, of hate, of bewilderment and startled disbelief.

Also, I could see etched in the faces of some, lines of compassion and sorrow, and there were heads inclined downward at an angle of shame and embarrassment. The white onlookers for the most part were as silent and apparently reflective as were the close-ranked columns of Negro marchers.

Nor were the Negroes marching alone. For integrated in their ranks was a small representation, a score or more of those millions of white Americans who are increasingly coming to see their own identity with the Negro's struggle for justice.

The Mayor had imposed brutal conditions for the funeral procession. Among the stipulations was one prohibiting any singing or shouting of slogans. Two blocks from the terminal point of the mile and a half processional, subdued voices began to raise a song in protest which rolled gently along the whole length of the marching column. It was the modern version of the old spiritual from the days of slavery—"We Shall Overcome, Some Day." The steel-helmeted, jack-booted police, with their heavy pistols slung low on their hips, pounded their clubs in their hands and shifted nervously from foot to foot but made no move to interfere. After all, the march had reached its end, the 2:00 witching hour was only minutes away and the "off the streets" curfew would soon be back in force.

The funeral march was over. Thousands of mourners milled about the Collins Funeral Home on North Farish Street which held the remains of Medgar Evers. Somehow there was comfort in the confraternity of the crowd of one's friends, colleagues, kinsmen.

No one was in a mood to rush away to the chores of a Saturday evening household. Especially when one carries within oneself the iron weight of knowledge that "the law" commands that you, a Negro, must get off of the streets and into your own house.

Then it was that I heard it. The soft soprano voice rising above the sounds of the throng, caroling the words to the tune that has become a kind of anthem of the freedom matchers, "Oh Freedom; Oh, Oh Freedom! Before I be a slave, I'll be buried in my grave...."

The song was coming from the half-opened mouth of a little slip of a girl maybe five feet tall but not quite a hundred pounds, whose skin had the soft brown color of honey; whose eyes now flashed wide and brown pupiled, then closed tight in the prayerful ecstasy of the resolution of the words of her song. She kept the beat of her song by patting the fingers of one hand into the palm of the other.

The people opened a circle of space for her. And into the circle came first one then another young woman of her own late teen or early 20s age group.

As the volume of song rose, the circle enlarged and in the circle had now come several young men to join the chorus. Those in the outer ring of the circle were now joining in the singing and vigorously clapping out the beat. Soon the singing crowd had fully covered the street from sidewalk to sidewalk.

Hundreds of voices were now raised full and loud in the familiar freedom songs and the little slip of a girl was the mover and shaker of them all. She never gave a verbal command but she converted that crowd into a well disciplined chorus, commanding them through the gestures of a master-pantomimist: a roll of the eye, a pout of the lips, a smile, a shrug of the shoulders, an exaggerated pat of the foot. Suddenly she raised both hands aloft, and the crowd now hundreds deep, fell instantly silent. She cocked her head to the side, rolled her eyes toward her colleagues and with a half-secretive but all-knowing smile, began a new song.

The words I heard were: "This little light of mine, it is going to shine; oh, it is going to shine."

A roar of identifying applause came from the crowd and a thousand voices joined in the chorus of "This little light of mine. . . . " The verses were improvised by volunteer soloists taking the initiative in rounds, and all came in on the chorus.

At this point a police car bearing the chief himself edged into the crowd who opened a passageway. The young people who constituted the inner ring of the crowd pointed their fingers like so many searchlights at the police as they fairly shouted their verses which called for freedom and the clean-out of segregation.

Someone ad-libbed a verse that said "we want the killers of Evers" and the little girl in the center of the ring gracefully arched her thin arm and pointing finger in the direction of Capital Street. Capital Street crosses Farish at the top of a rise. It demarcates the division between the two worlds, it separates the "colored" part of town from the "white." There at the crest of the knoll where Farish Street climbs up to Capital was the phalanx of the blue steel-helmeted police with riot guns at the ready.

The rhythmic pace of "This little light of mine" beat faster and firmer. Now hundreds of arching arms pointed to the police at the top of the incline.

A voice in the crowd said: "What are we waiting for?" And the little slip of a girl answered back: "Well, all right, then!" She made a half turn and stepped toward the top of the hill, with a kind of dance step that was neither walking nor running.

The other young men and women in the crowed formed an eight-abreast line behind her, and, before you could sing out, "This little light of mine" there were some six hundred youth and grown people and old people marching toward the top of the hill, and the shouted chant of "FREEDOM! FREEDOM!" filled the canyon of Farish Street.

As the singing and chanting crowd, with that daring youth guard in its van, approached the line of police, a squad of six motorcycles raced down the hill into the crowd. But the surging mass of demonstrators never broke their pace, they opened channels for the motorcycles and kept forging ahead.

I could hear the screams of the sirens, and the frantic clang of fire-engine bells. Canvas-covered army transports roared into view. They were followed by the tinny clatter of the garbage trucks which Jackson's police use as an inventive piece of cruelty to haul demonstrators to the concentration camp-style prison.

With the first ranks of the demonstrators only a half block from the crest of the hill, the police, now reinforced by two hundred State Troopers, charged down upon them, indiscriminately battering and slashing the front ranks with the butts of their rifles and submachine guns. Along the sidewalks came two columns of police with drawn pistols and flaying clubs.

I saw a middle-aged woman belabored by a club-wielding policeman until she fell unconscious to the ground. He then grabbed her by the hair and dragged her to the nearest garbage truck where he hoisted her to his shoulders and dumped her in as though he were handling a sack of potatoes.

I saw the wife of a paraplegic veteran of the Korean War beaten to the ground, then battered by the clubs of three policemen before being bodily lifted and thrown into a garbage truck. Her only offense had been that she had not pushed her wheelchair-ridden husband fast enough in the direction that the police had demanded.

The Negro demonstrators retreated before the wild charge of the police, who were cursing like maniacs and letting out frenzied Confederate army "Rebel yells."

The dogs arrived and were given full freedom of the length of their leashes. One opened a long gash on the leg of a woman whose dress had been already half-torn from her body and who was leaning against a door sill, trying to wipe the blood and dust from her eyes, when the dog lunged upon her.

A distance of several yards had opened between the police phalanx and the demonstrators when, from the roofs and the sides of the buildings came volley after volley of "Coke" bottles and rocks that shattered on the pavement, or caromed off of the steel helmets of the police barbarians. Some dropped their rifles as they fled for cover. Others cursed and some screamed in pain.

But now, from the bottom of Farish Street came a second phalanx of police. The demonstrators retreated into nearby houses and some stores and blended into the sidewalk crowds.

The police grappled with, and beat, and dragged scores of people off the porches, out of windows, off of the sidewalks, until the garbage trucks had their cargoes, and the canvas-covered army transport vehicles were crowded.

The heroic demonstrators were transported to the newly improvised concentration camp which has been pressed into service; the jails have been long since filled with the victims of the rampant racist reign of terror here.

I saw this concentration camp at Jackson. The hundreds of Negro youth and white adults, men and women, are kept in the corrugated quonset exhibition pens used to house livestock during state and county fairs.

The sun, beating down on the metal buildings, built up an oven-like temperature inside. The only toilet facilities are slit trenches which accommodated the needs of the cattle. There are two hose pipes, to provide all the water for any purpose, accessible to the prisoners who now number over nine hundred, the youngest being less than eight years old.

Each quonset building is surrounded by barbed "pig wire."

One wouldn't know that such barbarities are going on at the Fair Grounds, for at a distance the eye is drawn to a huge carousel-like building with candy stripe painted surface and rolling tree-terraced grounds.

The radio reported that only twenty-seven people were "officially" arrested on this day; the others were detained without charges, then released. Another seventeen were admitted for hospitalization for gaping wounds and internal injuries sustained from police weapons.

James E. Jackson, *The Bold, Bad '60's* (New York: International Publishers, 1992), pp. 67–74. This was originally published in the *Worker*, June 1963. James E. Jackson for over fifty years was active in the black liberation movement. At this time he was editor of the *Worker*.

49

BIRMINGHAM: THE MOMENT OF TRUTH

by Bayard Rustin

Bayard Rustin, a courageous civil rights leader since the 1940s, was formerly executive secretary of the War Resisters League. At this time he was executive director of the A. Philip Randolph Institute. He considered himself a "democratic socialist." Entitled "The Meaning of Birmingham," this essay originally appeared in *Liberation,* June 1963 (Vol. 8, No. 4). It reflects the great optimism characteristic of the early 1960s.

Since the signing of the Emancipation Proclamation in 1863, the struggle for justice by Afro-Americans has been carried out by many dedicated individuals and militant organizations. Their ultimate aim, sometimes stated, often not, has always been total freedom. Many forms of strategy and tactics have been used. Many partial victories have been won. Yet the gradual and token "progress" that many white liberals pointed to with pride served only to anger the black man and further frustrate him. That frustration has now given way to an open and publicly declared war on segregation and racial discrimination throughout the nation. The aim is simple. It is directed at all white Americans—the President of the United States, his brother, Robert, the trade-union movement, the power elite, and every living white soul the Negro meets. The war cry is "unconditional surrender—end *all* Jim Crow now." Not next week, not tomorrow—but *now.*

This is not to say that many have not felt this way for decades. The slave revolts, the occasional resorts to violence in recent times, the costly fifty-year struggle that the National Association for the Advancement of Colored People has carried on in the courts, the thousands arrested throughout the South since the Montgomery bus boycott—all reveal an historic impatience and a thirst for freedom. What is new springs from the white resistance in Birmingham, with its fire hoses, its dogs, its blatant disregard for black men as people, and from the Afro-American's response to such treatment in "the year of our Lord" 1963.

For the black people of this nation, Birmingham became the moment of truth. The struggle from now on will be fought in a different context. Therefore, to understand the mood, tactics, and totality of the black people's relentless war on Jim Crow, we must grasp fully what is taking place in this southern industrial city.

For the first time, every black man, woman, and child, regardless of station, has been brought into the struggle. Unlike the period of the Montgomery boycott, when the Southern Christian Leadership Conference had to be organized to stimulate similar action elsewhere, the response to Birmingham has been immediate and spontaneous. City after city has come into the fight, from Jackson, Mississippi, to Chesterton, Maryland. The militancy has spread to Philadelphia, where the "city fathers" and the trade-union movement have been forced to make reluctant concessions. It has reached the old and established freedom organizations. For example, Roy Wilkins, executive secretary of the NAACP, who only a year ago, from a platform in Jackson, Mississippi, criticized the direct-action methods of the Freedom Riders, was arrested recently for leading a picket line in that very city, after hundreds of NAACP members had been arrested in a direct-action struggle.

Before Birmingham, the great struggles had been waged for specific, limited goals. The Freedom Riders sought to establish the right to eat while traveling; the sit-ins sought to win the right to eat in local restaurants; the Meredith case centered on a single Negro's right to enter a state university. The Montgomery boycott, although it involved fifty thousand people in a year-long sacrificial struggle, was limited to attaining the right to ride the city buses with dignity and respect. The black people now reject token, limited, or gradual approaches.

The package deal is the new demand. The black community is not prepared to engage in a series of costly battles—first for jobs, then decent housing, then integrated schools, etc., etc. The fact that there is a power elite which makes the decisions is now clearly understood. The Negro has learned that, through economic and mass pressures, this elite can be made to submit step by step. Now he demands unconditional surrender.

It is significant that in city after city where the spirit of Birmingham has spread, the Negroes are demanding fundamental social, political, and economic changes. One can predict with confidence that in the future the scope of these demands will be widened, not narrowed, and that if they are not met in the North as well as in the South, a very dangerous situation will develop. Federal troops may well become a familiar sight in the North as well as the South, since the black community is determined to move vigorously and fearlessly and relentlessly ahead.

Gandhi used to say that the absence of fear was the prime ingredient of nonviolence: "To be afraid is to be a slave." A. J. Muste frequently says that to be afraid is to behave as if the truth were not true. It was the loss of all fear that produced the moment of truth in Birmingham: children as young as six paraded calmly when dogs, fire hoses, and police billies were used against them. Women were knocked down to the ground and beaten mercilessly. Thousands of teen-agers stood by at churches throughout the whole county, waiting their turn to face the clubs of Bull Connor's police, who are known to be among the most brutal in the nation. Property was bombed. Day after day the brutality and arrests went on. And always, in the churches, hundreds of well-disciplined children eagerly awaited their turns.

While these youngsters, unlike Meredith, had the advantage of operating in groups, and while Meredith's ordeal must have been the most difficult borne by any freedom fighter short of death—the children of Birmingham, like no other person or group, inspired and shamed all Afro-Americans, and pulled them into a united struggle.

E. Franklin Frazier wrote in the past of the Negro bourgeoisie. He told of the efforts of the Negro upper classes to ape white people, of the exploitation of Negroes by wealthy members of their own race and the absence of identity among Negroes. But had Frazier been alive to see Birmingham he would have discovered that the black community was welded into a classless revolt. A. G. Gaston, the Negro millionaire who with some ministers and other upper-class elements had publicly stated that the time was not ripe for such a broad protest, finally accommodated himself, as did the others, to the mass pressure from below and joined the struggle. Gaston owns much property, including a funeral parlor and the motel that eventually became the headquarters for the Birmingham campaign. The bombing of his motel was one cause of the outbreak of rioting on the part of elements that had not come into the nonviolent struggle.

On the basis of the behavior of the black business community in the cities where protests have emerged since Birmingham, one can confidently predict that future struggles will find the Negro bourgeoisie playing a major role in social change and nonviolence. They know that unless they join in the struggle they will lose the business of their fellow Negroes, who are in no mood to tolerate Uncle Tom-ism.

Black people have waited a hundred years for the government to help them win their rights. President after President has made commitments before election and failed to use the executive power he possesses after election. Congress today, dominated by southern Democrats, cannot pass any meaningful civil-rights legislation. The Supreme Court, from 1954 to 1963, took a gradualist approach, thereby putting its stamp of approval on "with all deliberate speed," which spells tokenism.

So the black people have looked elsewhere for allies, hoping to discover some major power group within American society which would join them not only in the struggle for Negro rights, but also in the struggle for a more democratic America. The trade-union movement and the churches have issued radical pronouncements but in fact have done precious little and on occasion have even blocked progress. Thus the black population has concluded that the future lies in casting not just a ballot, what Thoreau called "a piece of paper merely," but the *total* vote—the human person against injustice.

This is not to say that black people are not deeply appreciative of those few independent radicals, liberals, and church people who have offered time, money and even their lives. They have nothing but admiration for people like Jim Peck, who was brutally beaten in Mississippi and Alabama during the Freedom Rides, Barbara Deming, who was arrested in Birmingham, Eric Weinberger, who fasted for a month in Alabama jails, and William Moore, the slain postman. One can be thankful that the number of such *individuals* is increasing. However, social change of such magnitude requires that major power groups in our society participate as meaningful allies.

The use of the "black body" against injustice is necessary as a means of creating social disruption and dislocation precisely because the accepted democratic channels have been denied the Negro.

In practice, it works like this: having urged the social institutions to desegregate to no avail, having pleaded for justice to no avail, the black people see that the white community would rather yield to the threats of the segregationist (in the name of law and order) than change the social system. And so Negroes conclude that they must upset the social equilibrium more drastically than the opposition can. They place their bodies against an unjust law by sitting in a restaurant, or a library, playing in a park or swimming in a pool. The segregationists, frequently joined by the police, attack. Arrest and brutality follow. But the black people keep coming, wave after wave. The jails fill. The black population boycotts the stores. Businessmen begin to lose money.

At this point the white community splits into two groups. On one side are the political and law-enforcement agencies, supported by the arch-segregationists, who fearfully resort to indiscriminate violence as a stop-gap measure. Then the more enlightened section of the community, including many business leaders, begin to act for the first time. They sense not only the rightness of the Negroes' demands but their inevitability. They realize that police violence may bring both a violent response from unorganized elements of the black population and increased economic reprisals. Thus the business community, previously having sided with the forces of reaction, at first quietly and then openly sue for discussion and negotiation with the Negro community, an approach they had earlier dismissed when it was proposed by Negro leaders.

This method of massive nonviolence has many dangers. The greatest threat is that violence, which has been smoldering beneath the surface for generations, will inevitably manifest itself. But the creative genius of people in action is the only safeguard in this period and it can be trusted to bring about, ultimately, a better community, precisely because the tactic of mass action is accompanied by nonviolent resistance. The protesters pledge themselves to refrain from violence in word and deed, thereby confining whatever inevitable violence there may be in the situation to an irreducible minimum.

The genius of this method and philosophy lies in its ability to destroy an old unjust institution and simultaneously create a new one. For finally the white community is forced to choose between closing down the schools, restaurants, parks, buses, etc, and integrating them. Faced for the first time with a choice that can impose discomfort, inconvenience, and economic turmoil on the white community—that community discovers that it would prefer integrated institutions to no public institutions at all.

It is therefore clear that we can now expect, following Birmingham, a more sympathetic ear from the power structure, in both the North *and* the South.

Loss of money to retail stores throughout the country, the reluctance of many industries to move to Little Rock during the school integration struggle, the fear of capitalists to invest in Mississippi and Alabama now, and the disrupting of the economy in Birmingham have caused big businesses, including steel, to take a second look at the "Negro problem."

The nation gives Robert Kennedy credit for the fact that the real rulers of Birmingham sat down with representatives of the black revolution. But knowledgeable people realize that it was the withdrawal of black purchasing power in a city which is almost half black, and the militant, unconditional surrender policies of the nonviolent struggle that turned the tide.

Again, Birmingham is a turning point in that all significant elements of the power structure have now acknowledged that the white community must recognize the true nature of the black revolution and its economic consequences.

Therefore, in city after city, following Birmingham, the real powers have moved to convince the politicians that they should negotiate. Chain store, moving picture, hotel, and restaurant executives have recently sought out representatives of the black community to ask for negotiations leading to nationwide desegregation. This is new. It is a consequence of the handwriting they see on the wall. They see it in police brutality and the bombed-out homes and business establishments. They see it in the eyes of Birmingham's children.

The tragedy is that the trade-union movement, the children and educational institutions which lay claim to freedom and justice, reveal that they have learned nothing from the Battle of Birmingham. This is especially sad since the great battle lies ahead. And this battle the black population is now prepared to wage. This is going to be the battle for jobs.

Negroes are finally beginning to realize that the age of automation and industrialization presents them with peculiar problems. There is less and less of a market where the unskilled can sell his labor. Inadequate, segregated schools increase the problem. The negative attitude of the trade unions compounds it further. The Cold War economy, geared to armaments production (perhaps the most automated of all industries) is throwing millions out of work, but the minority groups are being hit hardest. For every white person unemployed, there are close to three Negroes without jobs.

In general, the unemployed, whether white or black, are not yet prepared to take radical action to demand jobs now. However, unemployed black people are prepared to move in conjunction with the rest of the black community and its many white supporters, within the context of the broad civil-rights upheaval. Since their most immediate ends are economic, their banner will be "Dignity of work with equal pay and equal opportunity." This agitation on the part of Negroes for jobs is bound to stimulate unemployed white workers to increased militancy. There will be sit-downs and other dislocating tactics. Nonviolent resistance will have to be directed against local and federal governments, the labor unions, against the A.F.L.-C.I.O. hierarchy, and any construction plant or industry that refuses to grant jobs. Such mass disturbances will probably soon take place in the major industrial centers of the country and it is likely that they will be more vigorous in the North than they have been in the South. And they will have incalculable effects on the economic structure.

The great lesson of Birmingham is at once dangerous and creative; black people have moved to that level where they cannot be contained. They are not prepared to wait for courts, elections, votes, government officials, or even Negro leaders. As James Baldwin said in an interview published in the *New York Times* for June 3rd: "No man can claim to speak for the Negro people today. There is no one with whom the power structure can negotiate a deal that will bind the Negro people. There is, therefore, no possibility of a bargain." The black people *themselves* are united and determined to destroy all unjust laws and discriminatory practices, and they want total freedom, including equal economic opportunity and the right to marry whom they damned well please. They know that at a time when the Kennedy brothers were fighting hard to maintain an aura of leadership and control of the civil-rights movement, the children of Birmingham, using methods of nonviolent resistance, restored the leadership to the black community. This was, as reported in the June 6th issue of *Jet,* a "terrible licking" for the federal government. If *kids* can revitalize the civil rights movement in Birmingham, the least we can do is to act like men and women and fight now to provide them with a decent future.

The mood is one of anger and confidence of total victory. The victories to date have given added prestige to the method of nonviolent resistance. One can only hope that the white community will realize that the black community means what it says: *freedom now.*

50

THE POLICE TERROR IN BIRMINGHAM

by Len Holt

A vivid firsthand account of the struggles in Birmingham in the spring of 1963 was written by the black attorney Len Holt. His book *An Act of Conscience* also offers an account of the fierce confrontations in Danville, Virginia, earlier that spring. Holt was described by a participant in Mississippi encounters later in the sixties as "a brilliant and fearless young lawyer who is one of the few black lawyers handling civil rights cases" in that state. The account went on, concerning Holt: "He is greatly admired for his courtroom style, which is proud, abrasive, and uncompromising toward expressions of racism from officers of the Mississippi courts."

Coming from the airport May 6, we drove past the post office and onto Fifth Ave. toward the A. G. Gaston Motel, integration headquarters. Then we saw why the downtown area was "cop-less." On the roofs of the three and four story buildings surrounding Kelly-Ingram Park were clusters of policemen with short-wave radios over their shoulders. At the four intersections surrounding the park were dozens of white-helmeted officers.

With the Birmingham police were reinforcements from such nearby cities as Bessemer, Fairfield, and Leeds. Also on hand were deputy sheriffs of Jefferson County and a sprinkling of State Troopers. The officers seemed fearful. This fear was expressed in marathon chatter and forced joviality as they waited for the ordeal that was to come: another massive demonstration.

Pressing on each cop were the eyes of four thousand Negro spectators—women, men, boys, girls, and mothers with babies. They were on the porches, lawns, cars, and streets surrounding the park. They didn't talk much, just looked . . . and waited.

Frequently both the policemen and Negro spectators turned toward the 16th St. Baptist Church. From the more than two thousand persons inside the church, and three hundred pressing toward its doors on the outside— mostly grammar and high school students—came the loud songs of Freedom: "We Shall Overcome," "Ain't Gonna Let Nobody Turn Me Round."

The temperature hit 90 degrees. Everybody was sweating. "Freedom! Freedom!" A roar arose from the church. The cops, almost as one, faced the church. Some unleashed clubs from their belts. The faces of those I could see had turned crimson. Jeremiah X, Muslim minister from Atlanta standing near me, commented: "At any moment those cops expect three hundred years of hate to spew forth from that church."

"Y'all niggers go on back. We ain't letting no more get on those steps," a police captain ordered as I approached the church. I turned away. The time was 1:10 P.M. Four fire engines arrived at the intersections and set themselves up for "business." Each disgorged its high-pressure hoses, and nozzle mounts were set up in the street. I was to learn the reason for the mounts later, when I watched the powerful water stripping bark off trees and tearing bricks from the walls as the firemen knocked Negroes down.

Before I could get back to the motel the demonstrations began; sixty demonstrators were on their way, marching two abreast, each with a sign bearing an integration slogan. Dick Gregory, the nightclub comedian, was leading the group.

At a signal, forty policemen converged, sticks in hand. Up drove yellow school buses.

"Do you have a permit to parade?" asked the police captain.

"No," replied Gregory.

"No what?" asked the captain in what seemed to be a reminder to Gregory that he had not used a "sir."

"No. No. A thousand times No," Gregory replied.

The captain said, "I hereby place you all under arrest for parading without a permit, disturbing the peace, and violating the injunction of the Circuit Court of Jefferson County."

Bedlam broke loose. The young demonstrators began shouting a freedom song. They broke into a fast step that seemed to be a hybrid of the turkey-trot and the twist as they sang to the tune of "The Old Grey Mare":

> "I ain't scared of your jail
> cause I want my freedom!
> ...want my freedom!"

And for the next two hours this scene was repeated over and over as group after group of students strutted out of the church to the cheers of the spectators, the freedom chants of those being carried away in buses, and a continuous banging on the floors and the sides of the buses—a cacophony of freedom.

That day, the dogs were kept out of sight. The Birmingham riot tank was on the side street. The fire hoses were kept shut. The police clubs did not flail. The thousands of spectators also kept calm. The police savagery of the preceding week was contained.

Back at the Gaston Motel, there was a joyous air. Leaders in the organizational work, such as Dorothy Cotten, James Bevel, and Bernard Lee of the Southern Christian Leadership Conference; Isaac Wright, CORE field secretary; and James Forman, William Porter, William Ricks, Eric Rainey, and students of the Student Non-Violent Coordinating Committee joined others in the motel parking lot in a parade and song fest.

Victory was suggested by the absence of the dogs, the lack of violence. Added to this was the news that a judge had continued the cases of forty persons because "there was no room at the inn" for those sentenced. The threat of the Movement to fill the jails had been realized in Birmingham.

Rejoicing was short-lived. At 6 P.M. word got back to the motel that the one thousand students arrested earlier had neither been housed nor fed. With Jim Forman of SNCC I drove to the jail. There were youths throwing candy bars over the fence to the students; spectators had passed the hat to purchase the candy. While we were there it began to rain. The students got soaked. The spectators, too, got wet. There was no shelter for the kids. The cops and their dog got into the squad car. They stayed dry.

Forman begged the cops to put the kids inside, in the halls, in the basement of the jail, anywhere. Nothing was done. A new day had not yet come to Birmingham.

That night the weather turned cool. We learned that the students were still in the jail yard, unsheltered and unfed. The same message got to the others in the Negro Community. An estimated five hundred cars and 1,200 people drove to the jail with blankets and food. The police responded by bringing up dogs and fire hoses. The food and blankets were given to the kids. The crowd waited until all of the children were finally taken inside.

Later that night Forman and Dorothy Cotten of the Southern Christian Leadership Conference met with the student leaders. In the planning emphasis was placed on the need for speed and mobility. Heretofore the demonstrators seldom got downtown, or if they did, never in a large group. It was decided that instead of starting the demonstrations every day at 1 P.M., when the fire hoses were in place and the police were all on duty, an element of surprise would be introduced. The next demonstration would begin earlier. Picket signs would be taken downtown to prearranged spots in cars where the students could pick them up.

That night five of us slept in a motel room designed for two. We were crowded, but so were the two thousand students crammed seventy-five or more in cells for eight in the city jail. Our room was hot that night, but not so hot as the unventilated sweat boxes in which Cynthia Cook, fifteen, and other girls were placed as punishment by the jail personnel when they refused to say "sir." Those on the outside were tired, but not so tired as the hundreds who had been forced to make marathon walks because they sang "We Shall Overcome" in jail. And there were beatings for many.

At 6 A.M. Tuesday SNCC and CORE fellows hurried to the schools to get out the students. Before ten—and before the police lines and firehoses were in place—six hundred students had been to the church and been given assignments downtown. Cars were dispatched with picket signs. The clock struck noon. The students struck. Almost simultaneously, eight department stores were picketed.

I was standing near a police motorcycle, and could hear the pandemonium at police headquarters. Police not due to report until after 12:30 were being called frantically. Policemen speeded, sirens screaming, from Kelly-Ingram Park to downtown. Inside the 16th St. Baptist Church the folk laughed and sang "We Shall Overcome."

Over the police radio I heard Bull Connor's voice. He was mad. He had been betrayed. Never before had the students demonstrated before 1 P.M. I suspect the merchants were mad. And the kids downtown, all six hundred of them, sang "We Shall Overcome." And they did overcome. No arrests were made. When the police finally got to the area, they merely ripped up the signs and told the youngsters to go home. The jails were full.

For the students, "home" was back to the 16th St. Baptist Church. There they were reassigned to go to Woolworth's and six other department stores, sit on the floor, and not move unless arrested. Since the jails were full, the cops still weren't arresting. A policeman went to the church to tell somebody from the Movement to ask the students to leave. When the announcement was made in the church, two thousand persons went downtown. These thousands were joined by two thousand spectators and made a wild, hilarious parade through downtown Birmingham, singing "We Shall Overcome."

Then the nearly four thousand persons returned to the church from the "victory march." And while the throngs joyously sang inside, preparations were being made outside. The cars with dogs drove up. About three hundred police officers surrounded the church and park area. Fire hoses were set up.

For a few minutes I left the area of the church and went to a nearby office. When I emerged I saw three thousand Negroes encircled in the Kelly-Ingram Park by policemen swinging clubs. The hoses were in action with the pressure wide open. On one side the students were confronted by clubs, on the other, by powerful streams of water. The firemen used the hoses to knock down the students. As the streams hit trees, the bark was ripped off. Bricks were torn loose from the walls.

The hoses were directed at everyone with a black skin, demonstrators and nondemonstrators. A stream of water slammed the Rev. Fred Shuttlesworth against the church wall, causing internal injuries. Mrs. Colia LaFayette, 25-year-old SNCC field secretary from Selma, Alabama, was knocked down and two hoses were brought to bear on her to wash her along the sidewalk. A youth ran toward the firemen screaming oaths to direct their attention from the sprawling woman.

Meanwhile, over the police address system inside the church, I could hear a speaker admonishing the people to be nonviolent.... "We want to redeem the souls of people like Bull Connor."

I wondered how long it would be before some Negro lost his restraint. It had almost happened Monday, the day before, when cops flung a Negro woman to the ground and two of them had put their knees in her breast and twisted her arm. This was done in the presence of the woman's nineteen-year-old son and thousands of Negro spectators. Four two hundred-pound Negro men barely managed to restrain the son.

The terrible Tuesday, May 7, ended finally. There was much talk about an impending "settlement." This news discouraged all but the most cursory plans for the next day. Everyone realized the influx of state troopers would make downtown demonstrations difficult.

A strange thing about the demonstrations up until Wednesday was that all of the brutality had been police brutality. Where were the thugs who with razor blades, a few years previously, had cut off the penis of a Negro? Where were the men who stabbed Mrs. Ruby Shuttlesworth when she attempted to enroll her child in the white high school? Where were the whites who repeatedly bombed Birmingham churches and synagogues?

On Wednesday, after almost five weeks of protesting, the non-uniformed racists had not spoken. On May 12th, Mother's Day, they spoke... and the cup of nonviolence of Birmingham Negroes overflowed.

America learned that the patience of one hundred years is not inexhaustible. It is exhausted.

National Guardian, May 16, 1963. Holt's *Act of Conscience* was published in Boston, by Beacon Press, 1965. The description of him used above is from Michael Thelwell, *Duties, Pleasures and Conflicts* (Amherst: University of Massachusetts Press, 1987), p. 75.

51

LETTER FROM BIRMINGHAM CITY JAIL

by Martin Luther King, Jr.

On April 10, 1963, Judge Jenkins in Birmingham issued an injunction forbidding the SCLC as an organization and King, Fred Shuttlesworth, and Ralph Abernathy, as individuals, to participate in further demonstrations. It was by deliberately violating this court order that King was jailed and placed in solitary confinement. While thus confined, King penned this historic Birmingham letter in response to the "Appeal for Law and Order and Common Sense" that eight white clergymen of Birmingham had made public earlier that year. King's letter was headed: "Birmingham City Jail April 16, 1963":

My dear Fellow Clergymen,

While confined here in the Birmingham City Jail, I came across your recent statement calling our present activities "unwise and untimely." Seldom, if ever, do I pause to answer criticism of my work and ideas. If I sought to answer all of the criticisms that cross my desk, my secretaries would be engaged in little else in the course of the day and I would have no time for constructive work. But since I feel that you are men of genuine goodwill and your criticisms are sincerely set forth, I would like to answer your statement in what I hope will be patient and reasonable terms.

I think I should give the reason for my being in Birmingham, since you have been influenced by the argument of "outsiders coming in." I have the honor of serving as president of the Southern Christian Leadership Conference, an organization operating in every southern state with headquarters in Atlanta, Georgia. We have some eighty-five affiliate organizations all across the South—one being the Alabama Christian Movement for Human Rights. Whenever necessary and possible we share staff, educational, and financial resources with our affiliates. Several months ago our local affiliate here in Birmingham invited us to be on call to engage in a nonviolent direct action program if such were deemed necessary. We readily consented and when the hour came we lived up to our promises. So I am here, along with several members of my staff, because we were invited here. I am here because I have basic organizational ties here. Beyond this, I am in Birmingham because injustice is here. Just as the eighth century prophets left their little villages and carried their "thus saith the Lord" far beyond the boundaries of their home town, and just as the Apostle Paul left his little village of Tarsus and carried the gospel of Jesus Christ to practically every hamlet and city of the Graeco-Roman world, I too am compelled to carry the gospel of freedom beyond my particular home town. Like Paul, I must constantly respond to the Macedonian call for aid.

Moreover, I am cognizant of the interrelatedness of all communities and states. I cannot sit idly by in Atlanta and not be concerned about what happens in Birmingham. Injustice anywhere is a threat to justice everywhere. We are caught in an inescapable network of mutuality tied in a single garment of destiny. Whatever affects one directly affects all indirectly. Never again can we afford to live with the narrow, provincial "outside agitator" idea. Anyone who lives inside the United States can never be considered an outsider anywhere in this country.

You deplore the demonstrations that are presently taking place in Birmingham. But I am sorry that your statement did not express a similar concern for the conditions that brought the demonstrations into being. I am sure that each of you would want to go beyond the superficial social analyst who looks merely at effects, and does not grapple with underlying causes. I would not hesitate to say that it is unfortunate that so-called demonstrations are taking place in Birmingham at this time, but I would say in more emphatic terms that it is even more unfortunate that the white power structure of this city left the Negro community with no other alternative.

In any nonviolent campaign there are four basic steps: (1) collection of the facts to determine whether injustices are alive; (2) negotiations; (3) self-purification; and (4) direct action. We have gone through all of these steps in Birmingham. There can be no gainsaying of the fact that racial injustice engulfs this community. Birmingham is probably the most thoroughly segregated city in the United States. Its ugly record of police brutality is known in every section of this country. Its unjust treatment of Negroes in the courts is a notorious reality. There have been more unsolved bombings of Negro homes and churches in Birmingham than any city in this nation. These are the hard, brutal, and unbelievable facts. On the basis of these conditions Negro leaders sought to negotiate with the city fathers. But the political leaders consistently refused to engage in good faith negotiation.

Then came the opportunity last September to talk with some of the leaders of the economic community. In these negotiating sessions certain promises were made by the merchants—such as the promise to remove the humiliating racial signs from the stores. On the basis of these promises Rev. Shuttlesworth and the leaders of the Alabama Christian Movement for Human Rights agreed to call a moratorium on any type of demonstrations. As the weeks and months unfolded we realized that we were the victims of a broken promise. The signs remained. As in so many experiences of the past we were confronted with blasted hopes, and the dark shadow of a deep disappointment settled upon us. So we had no alternative except that of preparing for direct action, whereby we would present our very bodies as a means of laying our case before the conscience of the local and national community. We were not unmindful of the difficulties involved. So we decided to go through a process of self-purification. We started having workshops on nonviolence and repeatedly asked ourselves the questions, "Are you able to accept blows without retaliating?" "Are you able to endure the ordeals of jail?"

We decided to set our direct action program around the Easter season, realizing that with the exception of Christmas, this was the largest shopping period of the year. Knowing that a strong economic withdrawal program would be the by-product of direct action, we felt that this was the best time to bring pressure on the merchants for the needed changes. Then it occurred to us that the March election was ahead, and so we speedily decided to postpone action until after election day. When we discovered that Mr. Connor was in the run-off, we decided again to postpone action so that the demonstrations could not be used to cloud the issues. At this time we agreed to begin our nonviolent witness the day after the run-off. This reveals that we did not move irresponsibly into direct action. We too wanted to see Mr. Connor defeated; so we went through postponement after postponement to aid in this community need. After this we felt that direct action could be delayed no longer.

You may well ask, "Why direct action? Why sit-ins, marches, etc.? Isn't negotiation a better path?" You are exactly right in your call for negotiation. Indeed, this is the purpose of direct action. Nonviolent direct action seeks to create such a crisis and establish such creative tension that a community that has constantly refused to negotiate is forced to confront the issue. It seeks so to dramatize the issue that it can no longer be ignored. I just referred to the creation of tension as a part of the work of the nonviolent resister. This may sound rather shocking. But I must confess that I am not afraid of the word tension. I have earnestly worked and preached against violent tension, but there is a type of constructive nonviolent tension that is necessary for growth. Just as Socrates felt that it was necessary to create a tension in the mind so that individuals could rise from the bondage of myths and half-truths to the unfettered realm of creative analysis and objective appraisal, we must see the need of having nonviolent gadflies to create the kind of tension in society that will help men rise from the dark depths of prejudice and racism to the majestic heights of understanding and brotherhood. So the purpose of the direct action is to create a situation so crisis-packed that it will inevitably open the door to negotiation. We, therefore, concur with you in your call for negotiation. Too long has our beloved Southland been bogged down in the tragic attempt to live in monologue rather than dialogue.

One of the basic points in your statement is that our acts are untimely. Some have asked, "Why didn't you give the new administration time to act?" The only answer that I can give to this inquiry is that the new administration must be prodded about us, much as the outgoing one before it acts. We will be sadly mistaken if we feel that the election of Mr. Boutwell will bring the millennium to Birmingham. While Mr. Boutwell is much more articulate and gentle than Mr. Connor, they are both segregationists dedicated to the task of maintaining the status quo. The hope I see in Mr.

Boutwell is that he will be reasonable enough to see the futility of massive resistance to desegregation. But he will not see this without pressure from the devotees of civil rights. My friends, I must say to you that we have not made a single gain in civil rights without determined legal and nonviolent pressure. History is the long and tragic story of the fact that privileged groups seldom give up their privileges voluntarily. Individuals may see the moral light and voluntarily give up their unjust posture; but as Reinhold Niebuhr has reminded us, groups are more immoral than individuals.

We know through painful experience that freedom is never voluntarily given by the oppressor; it must be demanded by the oppressed. Frankly I have never yet engaged in a direct action movement that was "well timed," according to the timetable of those who have not suffered unduly from the disease of segregation. For years now I have heard the word "Wait!" It rings in the ear of every Negro with a piercing familiarity. This "wait" has almost always meant "never." It has been a tranquilizing thalidomide, relieving the emotional stress for a moment, only to give birth to an ill-formed infant of frustration. We must come to see with the distinguished jurist of yesterday that "justice too long delayed is justice denied." We have waited for more than three hundred and forty years for our constitutional and God-given rights. The nations of Asia and Africa are moving with jet-like speed toward the goal of political independence, and we still creep at horse and buggy pace toward the gaining of a cup of coffee at a lunch counter.

I guess it is easy for those who have never felt the stinging darts of segregation to say wait. But when you have seen vicious mobs lynch your mothers and fathers at will and drown your sisters and brothers at whim; when you have seen hate filled policemen curse, kick, brutalize, and even kill your black brothers and sisters with impunity; when you see the vast majority of your twenty million Negro brothers smothering in an air-tight cage of poverty in the midst of an affluent society; when you suddenly find your tongue twisted and your speech stammering as you seek to explain to your six-year-old daughter why she can't go to the public amusement park that has just been advertised on television, and see tears welling up in her little eyes when she is told that Funtown is closed to colored children, and see the depressing clouds of inferiority begin to form in her little mental sky, and see her begin to distort her little personality by unconsciously developing a bitterness toward white people; when you have to concoct an answer for a five-year old son asking in agonizing pathos: "Daddy, why do white people treat colored people so mean?"; when you take a cross country drive and find it necessary to sleep night after night in the uncomfortable corners of your automobile because no motel will accept you; when you are humiliated day in and day out by nagging signs reading "white" men and "colored"; when your first name becomes "nigger" and your middle name becomes "boy" (however old you are) and your last name becomes "John," and when your wife and mother are never given the respected title "Mrs."; when you are harried by day and haunted by night by the fact that you are a Negro, living constantly at tip-toe stance never quite knowing what to expect next, and plagued with inner fears and outer resentments; when you are forever fighting a degenerating sense of "nobodiness";—then you will understand why we find it difficult to wait. There comes a time when the cup of endurance runs over, and men are no longer willing to be plunged into an abyss of injustice where they experience the bleakness of corroding despair. I hope, sirs, you can understand our legitimate and unavoidable impatience.

You express a great deal of anxiety over our willingness to break laws. This is certainly a legitimate concern. Since we so diligently urge people to obey the Supreme Court's decision of 1954 outlawing segregation in the public schools, it is rather strange and paradoxical to find us consciously breaking laws. One may well ask, "How can you advocate breaking some laws and obeying others?" The answer is found in the fact that there are two types of laws: There are *just* laws and there are *unjust* laws. I would be the first to advocate obeying just laws. One has not only a legal but moral responsibility to obey just laws. Conversely, one has a moral responsibility to disobey unjust laws. I would agree with Saint Augustine that "An unjust law is no law at all."

Now what is the difference between the two? How does one determine when a law is just or unjust? A just law is a man-made code that squares with the moral law or the law of God. An unjust law is a code that is out of harmony with the moral law. To put it in the terms of Saint Thomas Aquinas, an unjust law is a human law that is not rooted in eternal and natural law. Any law that uplifts human personality is just. Any law that degrades human personality is unjust. All segregation statutes are unjust because segregation distorts the soul and damages the personality. It gives the segregator a false sense of superiority and the segregated a false sense of inferiority. To use the words of Martin Buber, the great Jewish philosopher, segregation substitutes an "I-it" relationship for the "I-thou" relationship, and ends up relegating persons to the status of things. So segregation is not only politically, economically, and sociologically unsound, but it is morally wrong and sinful. Paul Tillich has said that sin is separation. Isn't segregation an existential expression of man's tragic separation, an expression of his awful estrangement, his terrible sinfulness? So I can urge men to obey the 1954 decision of the Supreme Court because it is morally right, and I can urge them to disobey segregation ordinances because they are morally wrong.

Let us turn to a more concrete example of just and unjust laws. An unjust law is a code that a majority inflicts on a minority that is not binding on itself. This is *difference* made legal. On the other hand a just law is a code that a majority compels a minority to follow that it is willing to follow itself. This is *sameness* made legal.

Let me give another explanation. An unjust law is a code inflicted upon a minority which that minority had no part in enacting or creating because they did not have the unhampered right to vote. Who can say the legislature of Alabama which set up the segregation laws was democratically elected? Throughout the state of Alabama all types of conniving methods are used to prevent Negroes from becoming registered voters and there are some counties without a single Negro registered to vote despite the fact that the Negro constitutes a majority of the population. Can any law set up in such a state be considered democratically structured?

These are just a few examples of unjust and just laws. There are some instances when a law is just on its face but unjust in its application. For instance, I was arrested Friday on a charge of parading without a permit. Now there is nothing wrong with an ordinance which requires a permit for a parade, but when the ordinance is used to preserve segregation and to deny citizens the First Amendment privilege of peaceful assembly and peaceful protest, then it becomes unjust.

I hope you can see the distinction I am trying to point out. In no sense do I advocate evading or defying the law as the rabid segregationist would do. This would lead to anarchy. One who breaks an unjust law must do it *openly, lovingly* (not hatefully as the white mothers did in New Orleans when they were seen on television screaming "nigger, nigger, nigger") and with a willingness to accept the penalty. I submit that an individual who breaks a law that conscience tells him is unjust, and willingly accepts the penalty by staying in jail to arouse the conscience of the community over its injustice, is in reality expressing the very highest respect for law.

Of course there is nothing new about this kind of civil disobedience. It was seen sublimely in the refusal of Shadrach, Meshach, and Abednego to obey the laws of Nebuchadnezzar because a higher moral law was involved. It was practiced superbly by the early Christians who were willing to face hungry lions and the excruciating pain of chopping blocks, before submitting to certain unjust laws of the Roman Empire. To a degree academic freedom is a reality today because Socrates practiced civil disobedience.

We can never forget that everything Hitler did in Germany was "legal" and everything the Hungarian freedom fighters did in Hungary was "illegal." It was "illegal" to aid and comfort a Jew in Hitler's Germany. But I am sure that, if I had lived in Germany during that time, I would have aided and comforted my Jewish brothers even though it was illegal. If I lived in a communist country today where certain principles dear to the Christian faith are suppressed, I believe I would openly advocate disobeying these anti-religious laws.

I must make two honest confessions to you, my Christian and Jewish brothers. First, I must confess that over the last few years I have been gravely disappointed with the white moderate. I have almost reached the regrettable conclusion that the Negroes' great stumbling block in the stride toward freedom is not the White Citizens' "Counciler" or the Ku Klux Klanner, but the white moderate who is more devoted to "order" than to justice; who prefers a negative peace which is the absence of tension to a positive peace which is the presence of justice; who constantly says, "I agree with you in the goal you seek, but I can't agree with your methods of direct action"; who paternalistically feels that he can set the time-table for another man's freedom; who lives by the myth of time and who constantly advises the Negro to wait until a "more convenient season." Shallow understanding from people of good will is more frustrating than absolute misunderstanding from people of ill will. Lukewarm acceptance is much more bewildering than outright rejection.

I had hoped that the white moderate would understand that law and order exist for the purpose of establishing justice, and that when they fail to do this they become the dangerously structured dams that block the flow of social progress. I had hoped that the white moderate would understand that the present tension in the South is merely a necessary phase of the transition from an obnoxious negative peace, where the Negro passively accepted his unjust plight, to a substance-filled positive peace, where all men will respect the dignity and worth of human personality. Actually, we who engage in nonviolent direct action are not the creators of tension. We merely bring to the surface the hidden tension that is already alive. We bring it out in the open where it can be seen and dealt with. Like a boil that can never be cured as long as it is covered up but must be opened with all its pus-flowing ugliness to the natural medicines of air and light, injustice must likewise be exposed, with all of the tension its exposing creates, to the light of human conscience and the air of national opinion before it can be cured.

In your statement you asserted that our actions, even though peaceful, must be condemned because they precipitate violence. But can this assertion be logically made? Isn't this like condemning the robbed man because his possession of money precipitated the evil act of robbery? Isn't this like condemning Socrates because his unswerving commitment to truth and his philosophical delvings precipitated the misguided popular mind to make him drink the hemlock? Isn't this like condemning Jesus because His unique God consciousness and never-ceasing devotion to His will precipitated the evil act of crucifixion? We must come to see, as federal courts have consistently affirmed, that it is immoral to urge an individual to withdraw his efforts to gain his basic constitutional rights because the quest precipitates violence. Society must protect the robbed and punish the robber.

I had also hoped that the white moderate would reject the myth of time. I received a letter this morning from a white brother in Texas which said: "All Christians know that the colored people will receive equal rights eventually, but is it possible that you are in too great of a religious hurry? It has taken Christianity almost two thousand years to accomplish what it has. The teachings of Christ take time to come to earth." All that is said here grows out of a tragic misconception of time. It is the strangely irrational notion that there is something in the very flow of time that will inevitably cure all ills. Actually time is neutral. It can be used either destructively or constructively. I am coming to feel that the people of ill will have used time much more effectively than the people of good will. We will have to repent in this generation not merely for the vitriolic words and actions of the bad people, but for the appalling silence of the good people. We must come to see that human progress never rolls in on wheels of inevitability. It comes through the tireless efforts and persistent work of men willing to be co-workers with God, and without this hard work time itself becomes an ally of the forces of social stagnation.

We must use time creatively, and forever realize that the time is always ripe to do right. Now is the time to make real the promise of democracy, and transform our pending national elegy into a creative psalm of brotherhood. Now is the time to lift our national policy from the quicksand of racial injustice to the solid rock of human dignity.

You spoke of our activity in Birmingham as extreme. At first I was rather disappointed that fellow clergymen would see my nonviolent efforts as those of the extremist. I started thinking about the fact that I stand in the middle of two opposing forces in the Negro community. One is a force of complacency made up of Negroes who, as a result of long years of oppression, have been so completely drained of self-respect and a sense of "somebodiness" that they have adjusted to segregation, and of a few Negroes in the middle class who, because of a degree of academic and economic security, and because at points they profit by segregation, have unconsciously become insensitive to the problems of the masses. The other force is one of bitterness and hatred and comes perilously close to advocating violence. It is expressed in the various black nationalist groups that are springing up over the nation, the largest and best known being Elijah Muhammad's Muslim movement. This movement is nourished by the contemporary frustration over the continued existence of racial discrimination. It is made up of people who have lost faith in America, who have absolutely repudiated

Christianity, and who have concluded that the white man is an incurable "devil." I have tried to stand between these two forces saying we need not follow the "do-nothingism" of the complacent or the hatred and despair of the black nationalist. There is the more excellent way of love and nonviolent protest. I'm grateful to God that, through the Negro church, the dimension of nonviolence entered our struggle. If this philosophy had not emerged I am convinced that by now many streets of the South would be flowing with floods of blood. And I am further convinced that if our white brothers dismiss us as "rabble rousers" and "outside agitators"— those of us who are working through the channels of nonviolent direct action—and refuse to support our nonviolent efforts, millions of Negroes, out of frustration and despair, will seek solace and security in black nationalist ideologies, a development that will lead inevitably to a frightening racial nightmare.

Oppressed people cannot remain oppressed forever. The urge for freedom will eventually come. This is what has happened to the American Negro. Something within has reminded him of his birthright of freedom; something without has reminded him that he can gain it. Consciously and unconsciously, he has been swept in by what the Germans call the *Zeitgeist,* and with his black brothers of Africa, and his brown and yellow brothers of Asia, South America, and the Caribbean, he is moving with a sense of cosmic urgency toward the promised land of racial justice. Recognizing this vital urge that has engulfed the Negro community, one should readily understand public demonstrations. The Negro has many pent-up resentments and latent frustrations. He has to get them out. So let him march sometime; let him have his prayer pilgrimages to the city hall; understand why he must have sit-ins and freedom rides. If his repressed emotions do not come out in these nonviolent ways, they will come out in ominous expressions of violence. This is not a threat; it is a fact of history. So I have not said to my people, "Get rid of your discontent." But I have tried to say that this normal and healthy discontent can be channeled through the creative outlet of nonviolent direct action. Now this approach is being dismissed as extremist. I must admit that I was initially disappointed in being so categorized.

But as I continued to think about the matter I gradually gained a bit of satisfaction from being considered an extremist. Was not Jesus an extremist in love? "Love your enemies, bless them that curse you, pray for them that despitefully use you." Was not Amos an extremist for justice—"Let justice roll down like waters and righteousness like a mighty stream." Was not Paul an extremist for the gospel of Jesus Christ—"I bear in my body the marks of the Lord Jesus." Was not Martin Luther an extremist—"Here I stand; I can do none other so help me God." Was not John Bunyan an extremist—"I will stay in jail to the end of my days before I make a butchery of my conscience." Was not Abraham Lincoln an extremist—"This nation cannot survive half slave and half free." Was not Thomas Jefferson an extremist—"We hold these truths to be self-evident; that all men are created equal." So the question is not whether we will be extremist but what kind of extremist will we be. Will we be extremists for hate or will we be extremists for love? Will we be extremists for the preservation of injustice—or will we be extremists for the cause of justice? In that dramatic scene on Calvary's hill three men were crucified. We must never forget that all three were crucified for the same crime—the crime of extremism. Two were extremists for immorality, and thus fell below their environment. The other, Jesus Christ, was an extremist for love, truth, and goodness, and thereby rose above His environment. So, after all, maybe the South, the nation, and the world are in dire need of creative extremists.

I had hoped that the white moderate would see this. Maybe I was too optimistic. Maybe I expected too much. I guess I should have realized that few members of a race that has oppressed another race can understand or appreciate the deep groans and passionate yearnings of those that have been oppressed, and still fewer have the vision to see that injustice must be rooted out by strong, persistent, and determined action. I am thankful, however, that some of our white brothers have grasped the meaning of this social revolution and committed themselves to it. They are still all too small in quantity, but they are big in quality. Some like Ralph McGill, Lillian Smith, Harry Golden, and James Dabbs have written about our struggle in eloquent, prophetic, and understanding terms. Others have marched with us down nameless streets of the South. They have languished in filthy, roach-infested jails, suffering the abuse and brutality of angry policemen who see them as "dirty nigger lovers." They, unlike so many of their moderate brothers and sisters, have recognized the urgency of the moment and sensed the need for powerful "action" antidotes to combat the disease of segregation.

Let me rush on to mention my other disappointment. I have been so greatly disappointed with the white Church and its leadership. Of course there are some notable exceptions. I am not unmindful of the fact that each of you has taken some significant stands on this issue. I commend you, Rev. Stallings, for your Christian stand on this past Sunday, in welcoming Negroes to your worship service on a non-segregated basis. I commend the Catholic leaders of this state for integrating Springhill College several years ago.

But despite these notable exceptions I must honestly reiterate that I have been disappointed with the Church. I do not say that as one of those negative critics who can always find something wrong with the Church. I say it as a minister of the gospel, who loves the Church; who was nurtured in its bosom; who has been sustained by its spiritual blessings and who will remain true to it as long as the cord of life shall lengthen.

I had the strange feeling when I was suddenly catapulted into the leadership of the bus protest in Montgomery several years ago that we would have the support of the white Church. I felt that the white ministers, priests, and rabbis of the South would be some of our strongest allies. Instead, some have been outright opponents, refusing to understand the freedom movement and misrepresenting its leaders; all too many others have been more cautious than courageous and have remained silent behind the anesthetizing security of stained glass windows.

In spite of my shattered dreams of the past, I came to Birmingham with the hope that the white religious leadership of this community would see the justice of our cause and, with deep moral concern, serve as the channel through which our just grievances could get to the power structure. I had hoped that each of you would understand. But again I have been disappointed.

I have heard numerous religious leaders of the South call upon their worshipers to comply with a desegregation decision because it is the law, but I have longed to hear white ministers say follow this decree because integration is morally right and the Negro is your brother. In the midst of blatant injustices inflicted upon the Negro, I have watched white churches stand on the sideline and merely mouth pious irrelevancies and sanctimonious trivialities. In the midst of a mighty struggle to rid our nation of racial and economic injustice, I have heard so many ministers say, "Those are social issues with which the Gospel has no real concern," and I have watched so many churches commit themselves to a completely other-worldly religion which made a strange distinction between body and soul, the sacred and the secular.

So here we are moving toward the exit of the twentieth century with a religious community largely adjusted to the status quo, standing as a tail light behind other community agencies rather than a headlight leading men to higher levels of justice.

I have travelled the length and breadth of Alabama, Mississippi, and all the other southern states. On sweltering summer days and crisp autumn mornings I have looked at her beautiful churches with their spires pointing heavenward. I have beheld the impressive outlay of her massive religious education buildings. Over and over again I have found myself asking: "Who worships here? Who is their God? Where were their voices when the lips of Governor Barnett dripped with words of interposition and nullification? Where were they when Governor Wallace gave the clarion call for defiance and hatred? Where were their voices of support when tired, bruised, and weary Negro men and women decided to rise from the dark dungeons of complacency to the bright hills of creative protest?"

Yes, these questions are still in my mind. In deep disappointment, I have wept over the laxity of the Church. But be assured that my tears have been tears of love. There can be no deep disappointment where there is not deep love. Yes, I love the Church; I love her sacred walls. How could I do otherwise? I am in the rather unique position of being the son, the grandson, and the great grandson of preachers. Yes, I see the Church as the body of Christ. But, oh! How we have blemished and scarred that body through social neglect and fear of being nonconformist.

There was a time when the Church was very powerful. It was during that period when the early Christians rejoiced when they were deemed worthy to suffer for what they believed. In those days the Church was not merely a thermometer that recorded the ideas and principles of popular opinion; it was a thermostat that transformed the mores of society. Wherever the early Christians entered a town the power structure got disturbed and immediately sought to convict them for being "disturbers of the peace" and "outside agitators." But they went on with the conviction that they were a "colony of heaven" and had to obey God rather than man. They were small in number but big in commitment. They were too God-intoxicated to be "astronomically intimidated." They brought an end to such ancient evils as infanticide and gladiatorial contest.

Things are different now. The contemporary Church is so often a weak, ineffectual voice with an uncertain sound. It is so often the arch-supporter of the status quo. Far from being disturbed by the presence of the Church, the power structure of the average community is consoled by the Church's silent and often vocal sanction of things as they are.

But the judgment of God is upon the Church as never before. If the Church of today does not recapture the sacrificial spirit of the early Church, it will lose its authentic ring, forfeit the loyalty of millions, and be dismissed as an irrelevant social club with no meaning for the twentieth century. I am meeting young people every day whose disappointment with the Church has risen to outright disgust.

Maybe again I have been too optimistic. Is organized religion too inextricably bound to the status quo to save our nation and the world? Maybe I must turn my faith to the inner spiritual Church, the church within the Church, as the true *ecclesia* and the hope of the world. But again I am thankful to God that some noble souls from the ranks of organized religion have been broken loose from the paralyzing chains of conformity and joined us as active partners in the struggle for freedom. They have left their secure congregations and walked the streets of Albany, Georgia, with us. They have gone through the highways of the South on torturous rides for freedom. Yes, they have gone to jail with us. Some have been kicked out of their churches and lost the support of their bishops and fellow ministers. But they have gone with the faith that right defeated is stronger than evil triumphant. These men have been the leaven in the lump of the race. Their witness has been the spiritual salt that has preserved the true meaning of the Gospel in these troubled times. They have carved a tunnel of hope through the dark mountain of disappointment.

I hope the Church as a whole will meet the challenge of this decisive hour. But even if the Church does not come to the aid of justice, I have no despair about the future. I have no fear about the outcome of our struggle in Birmingham, even if our motives are presently misunderstood. We will reach the goal of freedom in Birmingham and all over the nation, because the goal of America is freedom. Abused and scorned though we may be, our destiny is tied up with the destiny of America. Before the pilgrims landed at Plymouth, we were here. Before the pen of Jefferson etched across the pages of history the majestic words of the Declaration of Independence, we were here. For more than two centuries our foreparents labored in this country without wages; they made cotton "king"; and they built the homes of their masters in the midst of brutal injustice and shameful humiliation—and yet out of a bottomless vitality they continued to thrive and develop. If the inexpressible cruelties of slavery could not stop us, the opposition we now face will surely fail. We will win our freedom because the sacred heritage of our nation and the eternal will of God are embodied in our echoing demands.

I must close now. But before closing I am impelled to mention one other point in your statement that troubled me profoundly. You warmly commended the Birmingham police force for keeping "order" and "preventing violence." I don't believe you would have so warmly commended the police force if you had seen its angry violent dogs literally biting six unarmed, nonviolent Negroes. I don't believe you would so quickly commend the policemen if you would observe their ugly and inhuman treatment of Negroes here in the city jail; if you would watch them push and curse old Negro women and young Negro girls; if you would see them slap and kick old Negro men and young Negro boys; if you will observe them, as they did on two occasions, refuse to give us food because we wanted to sing our grace together. I'm sorry that I can't join you in your praise for the police department.

It is true that they have been rather disciplined in their public handling of the demonstrators. In this sense they have been rather publicly "nonviolent." But for what purpose? To preserve the evil system of segregation. Over the last few years I have consistently preached that nonviolence demands that the means we use must be as pure as the ends we seek. So I have tried to make it clear that it is wrong to use immoral means to attain moral ends. But now I must affirm that it is just as wrong, or even more so, to use moral means to preserve immoral ends. Maybe Mr. Connor and his policemen have been rather publicly nonviolent, as Chief Prichett was in Albany, Georgia, but they have used the moral means of nonviolence to maintain the immoral end of flagrant racial injustice. T. S. Eliot has said that there is no greater treason than to do the right deed for the wrong reason.

I wish you had commended the Negro sit-inners and demonstrators of Birmingham for their sublime courage, their willingness to suffer, and their amazing discipline in the midst of the most inhuman provocation. One day the South will recognize its real heroes. They will be the James Merediths, courageously and with a majestic sense of purpose, facing jeering and hostile mobs and the agonizing loneliness that characterizes the life of the pioneer. They will be old, oppressed, battered Negro women, symbolized in a seventy-two year old woman of Montgomery, Alabama, who rose up with a sense of dignity and with her people decided not to ride the segregated buses, and responded to one who inquired about her tiredness with ungrammatical profundity: "My feets is tired, but my soul is rested." They will be young high school and college students, young ministers of the gospel and a host of the elders, courageously and nonviolently sitting in at lunch counters and willingly going to jail for conscience sake. One day the South will know that when these disinherited children of God sat down at lunch counters they were in reality standing up for the best in the American dream and the most sacred values in our Judeo-Christian heritage, and thus carrying our whole nation back to great wells of democracy which were dug deep by the founding fathers in the formulation of the Constitution and the Declaration of Independence.

Never before have I written a letter this long (or should I say a book?). I'm afraid that it is much too long to take your precious time. I can assure you that it would have been much shorter if I had been writing from a comfortable desk, but what else is there to do when you are alone for days in the dull monotony of a narrow jail cell other than write long letters, think strange thoughts, and pray long prayers?

If I have said anything in this letter that is an overstatement of the truth and is indicative of an unreasonable impatience, I beg you to forgive me. If I have said anything in this letter that is an understatement of the truth and is indicative of my having a patience that makes me patient with anything less than brotherhood, I beg God to forgive me.

I hope this letter finds you strong in the faith. I also hope that circumstances will soon make it possible for me to meet each of you, not as an integrationist or a civil rights leader, but as a fellow clergyman and a Christian brother. Let us all hope that the dark clouds of racial prejudice will soon pass away and the deep fog of misunderstanding will be lifted from our fear-drenched communities and in some not too distant tomorrow the radiant stars of love and brotherhood will shine over our great nation with all of their scintillating beauty.

Yours for the cause of Peace and Brotherhood
MARTIN LUTHER KING, JR.

Martin Luther King, Jr., *Letter from Birmingham City Jail* (Philadelphia: American Friends Service Committee, 1963)

52

"HARLEM IS A CONDITION OF LIFE"

by the Editors of Freedomways

The summer 1963 issue of *Freedomways* was entitled "Harlem: A Community in Transition." This enlarged number opened with a brief statement:

Harlem is something else than a particular ethnic community of Manhattan's upper east side; Harlem is a condition of life for the overwhelming number of the two-thirds of America's twenty million Negroes who live in its cities.

Harlem is a community of New York but Harlem is a euphemism for those most deprived areas in every city of the country which are assigned to Negroes in the United States.

Negro citizens live in the Harlems of her cities not out of choice but from the absence of choice.

Poverty more than the distinctiveness of color hold Negro Americans fast in the Harlems of America and set them apart from their fellow Americans.

The massive deprivation and poverty of those who live in the Harlems of America are, ironically, a direct and indirect source of fabulous riches which flow into the coffers of those who command the economic and political power structure of our nation.

Harlem has grievances. Harlem is angry. Harlem is determined on a course of mass direct action to obtain redress of her grievances. The Harlems of the North and West are joining the new democratic revolution which was born of the Southern Negroes' desegregation battles.

Freedomways 3 (Summer, 1963): 261–62.

53

NOTES FROM SOUTHERN DIARIES

by Various Authors

The following short pieces are from manuscripts, letters, or field diaries of the young leaders in the Student Nonviolent Coordinating Committee (SNCC) with headquarters in Atlanta, Georgia.

Gadsden, Alabama

Demonstrations began in Gadsden on June 10, 1963. There were five hundred people in the streets downtown demonstrating for their freedom. We demonstrated for two weeks and only two persons were arrested: Handy McNair and myself. We were arrested following a protest at the county court house but were released the next morning. When we were jailed, one of the officers stepped on my face and kicked me about seven or eight times.

After two weeks of demonstrations we learned that the sheriff had sent for the state troopers. On the day the troopers were supposed to have arrived we went downtown and closed the lunch counters again and picketed in front of the theatres. About fifty people were arrested. We walked to the court house to protest the arrests and sat down in the middle of the street. At that time three hundred people were arrested and by the time the state troopers arrived that evening there were six hundred people on the court house lawn praying for the release of their people from the jail. Women had babies in their arms and there were many young children sitting on the lawn. The state troopers sneaked up on the people and began beating them as they prayed. There was a lady standing with her baby in her arms on the court house steps and the troopers knocked her down and pushed the baby from her hands. Some were knocked down two and three times. There were so many people arrested that the jails were filled. The men were sent to Camp Gadsden, others were sent to the city and county jails. We stayed in jail for fourteen days and were released on bond. When our trial came up the judge postponed the trial indefinitely.

On July 11 about twenty-eight of us demonstrated again and were arrested for "vagrancy." We stayed in jail six days and were released. After being released from jail this time, we set our sights for another demonstration on August 3, 1963 which we called D-Day. We began going into the communities talking to everyone about getting out on this date. The police followed us everywhere we went. We always carried our tooth brushes with us to be prepared in case we were arrested. On D-Day there were close to 2,300 people ready to demonstrate. We went downtown and picketed again.

That evening we had another demonstration. About 1,200 people were arrested and in order to make room in the jails, some youths were released as juveniles. There were about six hundred and fifty people still in jail after some were released. This was the largest mass jailing of any civil rights demonstration up to that time, north or south. The beatings by troopers and police continue. There is need for federal intervention by the President and Attorney General.

ERIC RAINEY,
Field Secretary

Danville, Virginia

In the alley between the court house and the jail, Reverend H. G. McGhee was on his knees praying for an end to beatings and jailings. Behind him were sixty-five fellow demonstrators. Mayor Stinson, standing nearby, told Police Chief Bull McCain, "All right, go get 'em." Police and newly-deputized firemen, bus drivers, cabbies, garbage men, and water meter readers barricaded the alley and turned on high pressure hoses. While demonstrators staggered from the force of the water, the "posse" attacked them with riot sticks, black-jacks, and sawed-off baseball bats. Some forty-eight people were hospitalized for injuries that night. Some had broken noses, open head wounds, broken limbs, and lacerated breasts. Prior to the march all demonstrators had turned in all pencils, nail files, and anything resembling a weapon, and they had committed themselves to nonviolence.

Danville is in central Virginia seven miles from the North Carolina border. It is the home of Dan River Mills, Inc., the makers of Dan River cottons; and the largest single-unit textile mill in the world. The city is literally run by the mill, which employs twenty five percent of the work force. One-third of the total population is Negro but only nine hundred of the ten thousand mill workers are Negro.

For six weeks last summer, I helped picket, register voters, write news releases, and plan demonstrations. My nights were spent at mass meetings, informal examples of democracy in action. Only once did a Danville white person walk with us. One day a boy of ten with no shoes on asked if he could join the picket line. We said yes, and he picketed with us for about an hour. When police stopped him, he told them he was thirteen so (as he later explained) they wouldn't say, "Go home, little kid." We took him to the office and he called his mother. She was frightened and asked him to come home before the police or some youngsters roughed him up. He started to cry and said, "But mommy, they can only hurt you on the outside, not on the inside." He didn't come back.

Louie Nasper
Field Worker

Jackson, Mississippi

The last two weeks of September and the month of October 1963 were spent organizing and campaigning for a mock election in which Negroes throughout the state of Mississippi were asked to participate. SNCC, in cooperation with other civil rights organizations, canvassed the entire state in an effort to bring the issue of the importance of political power to the Negro community. In many ways, both Negroes in various communities and SNCC field workers, were harassed and intimidated by the local police in an effort to discourage political activities of any kind. The following is an example of one of the methods that local police, under the direction of local political power structures, seek to make sure that workers are discouraged from taking part in political activity.

Charles Cobb and I arrived at the Jackson, Mississippi office (Henry-for-Governor Campaign Headquarters) at approximately 7 P.M. to talk with Bob Moses (Mississippi SNCC leader) about the possibility of getting more manpower and a better means of transportation in and around the counties we were assigned to canvass. We had spent the entire day canvassing in Issaquena and Sharkey Counties. Moses decided that he would rent some cars to supplement the need to be more mobile in the counties. He asked us to wait around and go with him to the airport to pick up a couple of rented cars later that night. Around 11:15, Cobb, Jessie Harris, and I met with Moses in the office and left for the airport. We got into a 1963 Oldsmobile that Moses had rented earlier. We were to pick up two 1963 Ford Galaxies and leave the Oldsmobile for Moses. (He was taking a plane flight and would return in a few hours.)

We pulled into the parking space reserved for rented cars at the Jackson Municipal Airport. A green Valiant police car was parked with the motor running just a few cars away. As we got out of the car, a policeman came over and checked out the license on our car and told Bob Moses to "come here." The rest of us walked inside the terminal building where Moses joined us in a couple of minutes. Moses reported that the cop asked him if the Olds was rented. Bob then gave Jessie Harris one set of keys for the two rented cars (Fords) and myself the other set. Then he discovered that he only had papers for one Ford. Bob tried to call the office several times but the line either went dead or someone answered and said it was the wrong number. Finally we got a line through and someone from the office was to bring out the papers for the other Ford.

The policeman who had previously questioned Bob was now wandering around the terminal watching him board his plane. We returned downstairs to wait for the other papers. The policeman told us we would have to leave the airport or be arrested for *vagrancy*. Although we explained that we were waiting for someone, he threatened to arrest us again.

We all got into the white rented Ford for which I had papers and was driving. The policeman also got into his car and followed us out of the airport onto the highway. While we were on the highway the green Valiant police car passed us and two other police cars, both white, started following us. About a half mile from the Jackson City limits, one of the police cars flagged me off the road. One of the policemen got out of the car and told me to pull over to the gas station across the highway. All of us were ordered out of the car and searched. I gave the police my license.

There were four policemen. They told us to put our hands up. During this time, the policemen started a series of verbal harassments and intimidations. They threw in a couple of threatening gestures for good measure. Their language was abusive and vile:... "Nigger, where you from...Boy! what's your name?...Goddamned nigger twenty years old, ain't old enough to register himself, come down here to get other niggers to register...If you stay down here long enough, you gonna make a mistake...Just like your mother paddled your behind, I'm going to have to paddle yours...Goddamned NAACP Communist trouble maker, ain't you, Boy?..."

After about twenty minutes of that and other forms of routine Mississippi cop interrogation, one of the policemen told me I was under arrest for having illegal plates on the car. I got into the back of one of the police cars while one of the policemen got in the front of the other car. The other three fellows were still standing in front of the gas station with their hands up. A policeman got into the front of the car in which I was sitting and turned around and looked at me as we were driving off. It seemed as though the harassment was to begin again.

"...Nigger, what's your mamma's name?" I didn't answer. "Boy, if you feel so God damned sorry for these black son of a bitches, why don't you take them all up north with you?...Nigger, if I had your god damned ass over in Branden I'd kill you. Before you goddamned black Communist sonofabitches started coming down here, everything was all right. Niggers down here don't need to vote—ain't supposed to vote."

All during this period of time I was just sitting, only answering questions which seemed half-way reasonable and that I felt were in his jurisdiction to ask. Finally, he told me that if the federal government ever sent troops down to Jackson, he would "kill every nigger he met. Boy, don't you know that whites are better than niggers?" I told him no. He unbuckled his holster, pulled out his gun, and swung it at me. It caught me across the knuckles of my right hand.

"God damned black bastards think they're going to be taking over around here. Well, you and the other god damned Moses' niggers around here ain't gonna git nuthin' but a bullet in the haid!" With that, he swung his gun at me again and caught me on the other hand. "Black son of a bitch, I'm gonna kill you, nigger. God damn it, I'm gonna kill you!" He was almost hysterical as he lifted his gun and put it just inches from my face. He cocked the hammer and for a couple of seconds I felt it was just about all over. Just about the same time he was cocking the hammer, one of the other three policemen who were outside with the fellows, came in and told the other cop, "You just can't kill that nigger, heah."

They both just stared at me for what seemed like an eternity. I noticed that the other policemen were in the car and the fellows I was with had gotten back into the Ford. Finally, the cop who had arrested me threw my license in my face. "Don't let me catch your ass here in Rankin County agin, nigger, evah agin, or Ah'll kill you."

I got back into the driver's seat of my car and tried to calm my nerves which felt like they were about to explode. I explained to the fellows what happened. It was already after two o'clock. Moses had taken off at 12:32, so we had been out on the highway for nearly two hours.

As I drove back to the office, I reflected over the incident just narrated. There was simply nothing to do except to chalk it up as something to be expected, especially when you're trying to bring the vote to the black man in Mississippi.

IVANHOE DONALDSON
Field Worker

Freedomways 4 (Winter, 1964): 137–42. The italicized headnote is from the original.

54

"AN OUTCRY FOR JUSTICE"

by A. Philip Randolph

On August 26, 1963, two days before the March on Washington, the National Press Club provided a reception for Randolph. At that time, he told the journalists:

Demonstrations are the hallmark of every revolution since the birth of civilization. . . . These are the outbursts . . . the manifestations of deep convictions about the evils that people suffer. While they sometimes take the form of some irrational upsurge of emotionalism, they come from the fact that the people are the victims of long-accumulated wrongs and deprivations. Therefore, these are an outcry for justice, for freedom. And there is no way . . . to stem these demonstrations until the cause is removed; and the cause is a racial bias, the cause is exploitation and oppression, the cause is second-class citizenship in a first-class nation. This is the cause for the march on Washington. This is the reason for the civil rights revolution. . . . The civil rights revolution is not trying to tear down a democratic government, it is not trying to overthrow a government, because a civil rights revolution is a bourgeois revolution. It is concerned with what it says—civil rights—and civil rights certainly will not upset our economic structure. . . . Therefore, we are seeking to implement our human rights. . . . No individual and no State has the right to take from me my life, my liberty, and my right to the pursuit of happiness. These are natural rights.

Jervis Anderson, *A. Philip Randolph* (New York: Harcourt, Brace, Jovanovich, 1972), p. 328.

55

ON THE MARCH ON WASHINGTON

by Bayard Rustin and Malcolm X

"The night before the march," Bayard Rustin said, "I came out of a strategy meeting of the Big Ten leaders at the Hilton and I saw Malcolm standing outside holding a press conference. He was denouncing the march. 'This is nothing but a circus, it's nothing but a picnic.' I said, 'Now Malcolm, be careful—there are going to be a half-million people here tomorrow, and you don't want to tell *them* this is nothing but a picnic.' He looked at me, and there was a twinkle in his eye. He said, 'What I tell them is one thing. What I tell the press is something else.' Later on, I saw him talking to some of the marchers. I said, 'Why don't you tell them this is just a picnic?' He was being affable. He just smiled, and again there was a twinkle.

"But afterward I saw him again, and he said, 'You know, this dream of King's is going to be a nightmare before it's over.' There was no twinkle in his eye this time. I think he did feel a sense that there would be a hard period ahead. And I said, 'You're probably right.'"

Peter Goldman, *The Death and Life of Malcolm X* (Urbana: University of Illinois Press, c. 1973); 2nd ed., 1979, p. 107.

56

"A MASSIVE MORAL REVOLUTION"

by A. Philip Randolph

Randolph was the first speaker at the historic gathering of over a quarter of a million people in Washington on August 28. This was the last major speech of his public life. After his brief remarks, Randolph referred to Martin Luther King, Jr., as "the man who personifies the moral leadership of the civil rights revolution."

... Let the nation and the world know the meaning of our numbers. We are not a pressure group, we are not an organization or a group of organizations, we are not a mob. We are the advance guard of a massive moral revolution for jobs and freedom.... But this civil rights revolution is not confined to the Negro, nor is it confined to civil rights, for our white allies know that they cannot be free while we are not, and we know we have no future in a society in which six million black and white people are unemployed and millions live in poverty.... We want a free democratic society dedicated to the political, economic, and social advancement of man along moral lines.... We know that real freedom will require many changes in the nation's political and social philosophies and institutions. For one thing, we must destroy the notion that Mrs. Murphy's property rights include the right to humiliate me because of the color of my skin. The sanctity of private property takes second place to the sanctity of the human personality. It falls to the Negro to reassert this priority of values, because our ancestors were transformed from human personalities into private property. It falls to us to demand full employment and to put automation at the service of human needs, not at the service of profits.... All who deplore our militancy, who exhort patience in the name of false peace, are in fact supporting segregation and exploitation. They would have social peace at the expense of social and racial justice. They are more concerned with easing racial tensions than enforcing racial democracy.

Jervis Anderson, *op. cit.*, pp. 328–29.

57

THE MARCH ON WASHINGTON

by Roy Wilkins

A brief description of the historic March occurs in Roy Wilkins's autobiography. He notes that he reported the death in Ghana of W. E. B. Du Bois, who early in the twentieth century had called for an end to Jim Crow. Mr. Wilkins speaks of Du Bois's "self-exile" in Ghana; this is inaccurate, as Du Bois had planned working on an *Encyclopaedia Africana* sixty years earlier, and when an independent Ghana offered him the facilities to realize that dream, he went to Ghana.

I can still see all those faces staring up toward the Lincoln Memorial, and I well remember the words Randolph spoke that day. He said, "Let the nation know the meaning of our numbers. We are not a pressure group, not an organization or a group of organizations. We are not a mob. We are the advance guard of a massive moral revolution for jobs and freedom." On this day word came that W. E. B. Du Bois had died in self-exile in Ghana, and in my speech I said, "Now, regardless of the fact that in his later years Dr. Du Bois chose another path, it is incontrovertible that at the dawn of the twentieth century his was the voice that was calling to you to gather here today in this cause." Then Dr. King enunciated his magnificent dream of integration, to close out the afternoon. No one who heard him speak that day will ever forget him.

Roy Wilkins with Tom Mathews, *Standing Fast: The Autobiography* (New York: Viking, 1982), p. 293.

58

A SERIOUS REVOLUTION

by John Lewis

John Lewis, then SNCC national chairman, spoke briefly at the historic march on Washington for "jobs and freedom." The text submitted by Lewis was censored as being excessively militant; the original remarks that he had planned to make and the speech as delivered follow:

Original Text

We march today for jobs and freedom, but we have nothing to be proud of. For hundreds and thousands of our brothers are not here. They have no money for their transportation, for they are receiving starvation wages ...or no wages, at all.

In good conscience, we cannot support, wholeheartedly, the administration's civil rights bill, for it is too little, and too late. There's not one thing in the bill that will protect our people from police brutality.

This bill will not protect young children and old women from police dogs and fire hoses, for engaging in peaceful demonstrations. This bill will not protect the citizens in Danville, Virginia, who must live in constant fear in a police state. This bill will not protect the hundreds of people who have been arrested on trumped-up charges. What about the three young men in Americus, Georgia, who face the death penalty for engaging in peaceful protest?

The voting section of this bill will not help thousands of black citizens who want to vote. It will not help the citizens of Mississippi, of Alabama, and Georgia, who are qualified to vote, but lack a sixth grade education. "One man, one vote," is the African cry. It is ours, too. (It must be ours.)

People have been forced to leave their homes because they dared to exercise their right to register to vote. What is in the bill that will protect the homeless and starving people of this nation? What is there in this bill to insure the equality of a maid who earns $5 a week in the home of a family whose income is $100,000 a year?

For the first time in one hundred years this nation is being awakened to the fact that segregation is evil and that it must be destroyed in all forms. Your presence today proves that you have been aroused to the point of action.

We are now involved in a serious revolution. This nation is still a place of cheap political leaders who build their careers on immoral compromises and ally themselves with open forms of political, economic, and social exploitation. What political leader here can stand up and say "My party is the party of principles"? The party of Kennedy is also the party of Eastland. The party of Javits is also the party of Goldwater. Where is *our* party?

In some parts of the South we work in the fields from sun-up to sundown for $12 a week. In Albany, Georgia, nine of our leaders have been indicted not by Dixiecrats but by the Federal Government for peaceful protest. But what did the Federal Government do when Albany's Deputy Sheriff beat Attorney C. B. King and left him half-dead? What did the Federal Government do when local police officials kicked and assaulted the pregnant wife of Slater King, and she lost her baby?

It seems to me that the Albany indictment is part of a conspiracy on the part of the Federal Government and local politicians in the interest of expediency.

I want to know, which side is the Federal Government on?

The revolution is at hand, and we must free ourselves of the chains of political and economic slavery. The nonviolent revolution is saying, "We will not wait for the courts to act, for we have been waiting for hundreds of years. We will not wait for the President, the Justice Department, nor Congress, but we will take matters into our own hands and create a source of power, outside of any national structure that could and would assure us a victory." To those who have said, "Be Patient and Wait," we must say that, "Patience is a dirty and nasty word." We cannot be patient, we do not want to be free gradually, we want our freedom, and we want it now. We cannot depend on any political party, for both the Democrats and the Republicans have betrayed the basic principles of the Declaration of Independence.

We all recognize the fact that if any radical social, political, and economic changes are to take place in our society, the people, the masses, must bring them about. In the struggle we must seek more than more civil rights; we must work for the community of love, peace, and true brotherhood. Our minds, souls, and hearts cannot rest until freedom and justice exist for *all the people*.

The revolution is a serious one. Mr. Kennedy is trying to take the revolution out of the street and put it into the courts. Listen, Mr. Kennedy, Listen Mr. Congressman, listen fellow citizens, the black masses are on the march for jobs and freedom, and we must say to the politicians that there won't be a "cooling-off" period.

All of us must get in the revolution. Get in and stay in the streets of every city, every village, and every hamlet of this nation, until true Freedom comes, until the revolution is complete. In the Delta of Mississippi, in southwest Georgia, in Alabama, Harlem, Chicago, Detroit, Philadelphia and all over this nation. The black masses are on the march!

We won't stop now. All of the forces of Eastland, Barnett, Wallace, and Thurmond won't stop this revolution. The time will come when we will not confine our marching to Washington. We will march through the South through the Heart of Dixie, the way Sherman did. We shall pursue our own "scorched earth" policy and burn Jim Crow to the ground—nonviolently. We shall fragment the South into a thousand pieces and put them back together in the image of democracy. We will make the action of the past few months look petty. And I say to you, WAKE UP AMERICA!!!

John Lewis, "Text of Speech to Be Delivered at Lincoln Memorial: Original," August 28, 1963 (Atlanta, Student Nonviolent Coordinating Committee), mimeo. Reprinted in Staughton Lynd, ed., *Nonviolence in America: A Documentary History* (Indianapolis: Bobbs-Merrill, 1968), pp. 482–85.

The Speech as Delivered by John Lewis

We march today for jobs and freedom, but we have nothing to be proud of. For hundreds and thousands of our brothers are not here. They have no money for their transportation, for they are receiving starvation wages . . . or no wages at all. While we stand here, there are sharecroppers in the Delta of Mississippi who are out in the fields working for less than three dollars a day for twelve hours of work. While we stand here, there are students in jail on trumped-up charges. Our brother, James Farmer, along with many others is also in jail. We come here today with a great sense of misgiving.

It is true that we support the present civil rights bill in the Congress. We support it with great reservations, however. Unless Title Three is put in this bill, there is nothing to protect young children and old women from police dogs and fire hoses, their penalties for engaging in peaceful demonstrations. In its present form this bill will not protect the citizens of Danville, Virginia, who must live in constant fear in a police state. It will not protect the hundreds of people who have been arrested on phony charges. What about the three young men—SNCC field secretaries—in Americus, Georgia who face the death penalty for engaging in peaceful protest?

As it stands now the voting section of this bill will not help thousands of black people who want to vote. It will not help the citizens of Mississippi, of Alabama and Georgia who are qualified to vote but lack a sixth grade education. "One man, one vote," is the African cry. It is ours, too. It must be ours. Let us tell the Congress: One man, one vote.

We must have legislation that will protect the Mississippi sharecropper who is put off his farm because he dares to register to vote. We need a bill that will provide for the homeless and starving people of this nation. We need a bill that will ensure the equality of a maid who earns $5 a week in the home of a family whose income is $100,000 a year. We must have a good FEPC bill.

Let us not forget that we are involved in a serious social revolution. By and large, American politics is dominated by politicians who build their careers on immoral compromises and ally themselves with open forms of political, economic, and social exploitation. There are exceptions, of course. We salute those. But what political leader can stand up and say, "My party is the party of principles?" The party of Javits is also the party of Goldwater. Where is *our* party? Where is the political party that will make it unnecessary to have Marches on Washington?

Where is the political party that will protect the citizens of Albany, Georgia? Do you know that in Albany, Georgia, nine of our leaders have been indicted not by Dixiecrats but by the Federal Government for peaceful protest? But what did the Federal Government do when Albany's Deputy Sheriff beat Attorney C. B. King and let him go half dead? What did the Federal Government do when local officials kicked and assaulted the pregnant wife of Slater King, and she lost her baby?

To those who have said, be patient and wait, we must say that we cannot be patient, we do not want to be free gradually. We want our freedom and we want it *now!* We are tired of being beaten by policemen. We do not want to go to jail if that is what we must pay for love, brotherhood, and peace.

All of us must get in this great social revolution sweeping our nation. Get in and stay in the streets of every city, every village, and every hamlet of this nation, until true Freedom comes, until the unfinished revolution of 1776 is complete. In the Delta of Mississippi, in southwest Georgia, in Alabama, Harlem, Chicago, Detroit, Philadelphia, and all over this nation—the black masses are on the march. You must go home from this March and help us to get our Freedom.

We will not stop now. All of the forces of Eastland, Barnett, Wallace, and Thurmond will not stop this revolution. If we do not get meaningful legislation out of this Congress, the time will come when we will not confine our marching to Washington. We will march through the South— through the streets of Jackson, Danville, Cambridge, Nashville, and Birmingham—with the dignity and spirit we have shown here today. By the force of our demands, our determination, and our numbers, we shall splinter the segregated South into a thousand pieces and put them back together in the image of God and democracy. Wake up, America!

In James Forman, *op. cit.,* pp. 336–37.

59

I HAVE A DREAM

by Martin Luther King, Jr.

The leaders of the March on Washington, August 28, 1963, affirmed that its purpose was to prevail upon the U.S. government "to grant and guarantee complete equality in citizenship to the Negro minority of our population." The organizers "called upon all, black and white, to resist provocations to disorder and violence." They ended: "Let's win at Washington." The signers of this call were ten men: three white religious leaders—Protestant, Catholic, and Jewish; six black men—James Farmer of CORE, Martin Luther King, Jr., of the Southern Christian Leadership Conference, John Lewis, of SNCC, A. Philip Randolph, of the Negro American Labor Council, Roy Wilkins of the NAACP, Whitney Young, Jr., of the National Urban League; and Walter Reuther, of the UAW and the Industrial Union Department, AFL-CIO. The highlight of this historic event was the inspired speech by Reverend King.

Over 250,000 people participated in this March.

I am happy to join with you today in what will go down in history as the greatest demonstration for freedom in the history of our nation.

Five score years ago, a great American, in whose symbolic shadow we stand today, signed the Emancipation Proclamation. This momentous decree came as the great beacon light of hope for millions of Negro slaves who had been seared in the flames of withering injustice. It came as the joyous daybreak to end the long night of their captivity.

But one hundred years later the Negro still is not free. One hundred years later, the life of the Negro is still badly crippled by the manacles of segregation and the chains of discrimination. One hundred years later, the Negro lives on a lonely island of poverty in the midst of a vast ocean of material prosperity. One hundred years later, the Negro is still languished in the corners of American society and finds himself an exile in his own land. So we have come here today to dramatize the shameful condition.

In a sense we've come to our Nation's Capital to cash a check. When the architects of our republic wrote the magnificent words of the Constitution and the Declaration of Independence, they were signing a promissory note to which every American was to fall heir. This note was a promise that all men, yes, black men as well as white men, should be guaranteed the unalienable rights of life, liberty, and the pursuit of happiness.

It is obvious today that America has defaulted on this promissory note insofar as her citizens of color are concerned. Instead of honoring this sacred obligation, America has given the Negro people a bad check, a check which has come back marked "Insufficient Funds." But we refuse to believe the bank of justice is bankrupt. We refuse to believe that there are insufficient funds in the great vaults of opportunity of this nation. So we have come to cash this check, a check that will give us upon demand, the riches of freedom and the security of justice. We have also come to this hallowed spot to remind America of the fierce urgency of now.

This is no time to engage in the luxury of cooling off or to take the tranquilizing drug of gradualism. Now is the time to make real the promises of democracy. Now is the time to rise from the dark and desolate valley of segregation to the sunlit path of racial justice. Now is the time to lift our nation from the quicksands of racial injustice to the solid rock of brotherhood. Now is the time to make justice a reality for all of God's children.

It would be fatal for the nation to overlook the urgency of the moment. This sweltering summer of the Negro's legitimate discontent will not pass until there is an invigorating autumn of freedom and equality. Nineteen sixty-three is not an end but a beginning. Those who hoped that the Negro needed to blow off steam and will now be content will have a rude awakening if the nation returns to business as usual. There will be neither rest nor tranquility in America until the Negro is guaranteed his citizenship rights. The whirlwinds of revolt will continue to shake the foundations of our nation until the bright day of justice emerges.

But there is something I must say to my people who stand on the warm threshold which leads them to the palace of justice. In the process of gaining our rightful place we must not be guilty of wrongful deeds. Let us not seek to satisfy our thirst for freedom by drinking from the cup of bitterness and hatred. We must forever conduct our struggle on the high plane of dignity and discipline. We must not allow our creative protest to degenerate into physical violence. Again and again we must rise to the majestic heights of meeting physical force with soul force.

The marvelous new militancy which has engulfed the Negro community must not lead us to a distrust of all white people, for many of our white brothers, as evidenced by their presence here today, have come to realize that their destiny is tied up with our destiny. They have come to realize that their freedom is inextricably bound to our freedom. We cannot walk alone.

And as we walk we must make the pledge that we shall always march ahead. We cannot turn back. There are those who are asking the devotees of civil rights: "When will you be satisfied?" We can never be satisfied as long as our bodies, heavy with the fatigue of travel, cannot gain lodging in the motels of the highways and the hotels of the cities. We cannot be satisfied as long as the Negro's basic mobility is from a smaller ghetto to a larger one. We can never be satisfied as long as our children are stripped of their selfhood and robbed of their dignity by signs stating: "For Whites Only." We cannot be satisfied as long as the Negro in Mississippi cannot vote and the Negro in New York believes he has nothing for which to vote. No, no, we are not satisfied and we will not be satisfied until justice rolls down like the waters and righteousness like a mighty stream.

I am not unmindful that some of you have come here out of great trials and tribulations, some of you have come fresh from narrow jail cells, some of you have come from areas where your quest for freedom left you battered by the storms of persecution and staggered by the winds of police brutality. You have been the veterans of creative suffering. Continue to work with the faith that unearned suffering is redemptive.

Go back to Mississippi, go back to Alabama, go back to South Carolina, go back to Georgia, go back to Louisiana, go back to the slums and ghettos of our northern cities, knowing that somehow this situation can and will be changed. Let us not wallow in the valley of despair.

I say to you today, my friends, even though we face the difficulties of today and tomorrow, I still have a dream. It is a dream deeply rooted in the American dream. I have a dream that one day this nation will rise up and live out the true meaning of its creed: "We hold these truths to be self-evident that all men are created equal."

I have a dream that one day on the red hills of Georgia the sons of former slaves and the sons of former slaveowners will be able to sit down together at the table of brotherhood.

I have a dream that one day even the State of Mississippi, a state sweltering with the heat of injustice, sweltering with the heat of oppression, will be transformed into an oasis of freedom and justice. I have a dream that my four little children will one day live in a nation where they will not be judged by the color of their skin but by the content of their character. I have a dream today.

I have a dream that one day down in Alabama with its vicious racists, with its Governor having his lips dripping with the words of interposition and nullification—one day right there in Alabama, little black boys and black girls will be able to join hands with little white boys and white girls as sisters and brothers.

I have a dream today.

I have a dream that one day every valley shall be exalted, every hill and mountain shall be made low, the rough places will be made plain and the crooked places will be made straight, and the glory of the Lord shall be revealed, and all flesh shall see it together.

This is our hope. This is the faith that I go back to the South with. With this faith we will be able to hew out of the mountain of despair a stone of hope. With this faith we will be able to transform the jangling discords of our nation into a beautiful symphony of brotherhood. With this faith we will be able to work together, to pray together, to struggle together, to go to jail together, to stand up for freedom together, knowing that we will be free one day.

This will be the day when all of God's children will be able to sing with new meaning:

> My country 'tis of thee,
> Sweet land of liberty,
> Of thee I sing:
> Land where my fathers died,
> Land of the pilgrims' pride,
> From every mountain-side
> Let Freedom ring.

And if America is to be a great nation, this must become true. So, let freedom ring from the prodigious hill tops of New Hampshire. Let freedom ring from the mighty mountains of New York. Let freedom ring from the heightening Alleghenies of Pennsylvania. Let freedom ring from the snowcapped Rockies of Colorado. Let freedom ring from the curvaceous slopes of California. But not only that, let freedom ring from Stone Mountain of Georgia.

Let freedom ring from Lookout Mountain of Tennessee.

Let freedom ring from every hill and molehill of Mississippi. From every mountainside, let freedom ring. And when we allow freedom to ring, when we let it ring from every village, from every hamlet, from every state and every city, we will be able to speed up that day when all of God's children, black men and white men, Jews and Gentiles, Protestants and Catholics, will be able to join hands and sing in the words of the old Negro spiritual: "Free at last! free at last! thank God almighty, we are free at last!"

The NAACP published in New York in 1963 *Speeches by the Leaders: The March on Washington for Jobs and Freedom, August 28, 1963.* Via radio and television the event and, especially, King's speech was heard and seen by tens of millions; the speech has been reprinted perhaps as often as Lincoln's Gettysburg Address or George Washington's Farewell.

60

EULOGY FOR THE MARTYRED CHILDREN

by Martin Luther King, Jr.

The worst single day of violence against the movement for liberation came on September 13, 1963. On that day fifteen sticks of dynamite were detonated at the Sixteenth Street Baptist Church in Birmingham. The church had been a staging center for the struggle. The explosion that Sunday morning killed four girls—one ten years old, one eleven, and two fourteen; dozens of children were injured. Later that day, in Birmingham, a policeman shot a black boy in the back with a shotgun, and another thirteen-year-old black child was killed while riding his bicycle.

    Dr. King spoke at the funeral of the four girls:

This afternoon we gather in the quiet of this sanctuary to pay our last tribute of respect to these beautiful children of God. They entered the stage of history just a few years ago, and in the brief years that they were privileged to act on this mortal stage, they played their parts exceedingly well. Now the curtain falls; they move through the exit; the drama of their earthly life comes to a close. They are now committed back to that eternity from which they came.

    These children—unoffending; innocent and beautiful—were the victims of one of the most vicious, heinous crimes ever perpetrated against humanity.

    Yet they died nobly. They are the martyred heroines of a holy crusade for freedom and human dignity. So they have something to say to us in their death. They have something to say to every minister of the gospel who has remained silent behind the safe security of stained-glass windows. They have something to say to every politician who has fed his constituents the stale bread of hatred and the spoiled meat of racism. They have something to say to a federal government that has compromised with the undemocratic practices of southern dixiecrats and the blatant hypocrisy of right-wing northern Republicans. They have something to say to every Negro who passively accepts the evil system of segregation, and stands on the sidelines in the midst of a mighty struggle for justice. They say to each of us, black and white alike, that we must substitute courage for caution. They say to us that we must be concerned not merely about *WHO* murdered them, but about the system, the way of life and the philosophy which *PRODUCED* the murderers. Their death says to us that we must work passionately and unrelentingly to make the American dream a reality.

So they did not die in vain. God still has a way of wringing good out of evil. History has proven over and over again that unmerited suffering is redemptive. The innocent blood of these little girls may well serve as the redemptive force that will bring new light to this dark city. The holy Scripture says, "A little child shall lead them." The death of these little children may lead our whole Southland from the low road of man's inhumanity to man to the high road of peace and brotherhood. These tragic deaths may lead our nation to substitute an aristocracy of character for an aristocracy of color. The spilt blood of these innocent girls may cause the whole citizenry of Birmingham to transform the negative extremes of a dark past into the positive extremes of a bright future. Indeed, this tragic event may cause the white South to come to terms with its conscience.

So in spite of the darkness of this hour we must not despair. We must not become bitter; nor must we harbor the desire to retaliate with violence. We must not lose faith in our white brothers. Somehow we must believe that the most misguided among them can learn to respect the dignity and worth of all human personality.

May I now say a word to you, the members of the bereaved families. It is almost impossible to say anything that can console you at this difficult hour and remove the deep clouds of disappointment which are floating in your mental skies. But I hope you can find a little consolation from the universality of this experience. Death comes to every individual. There is an amazing democracy about death. It is not aristocracy for some of the people, but a democracy for all of the people. Kings die and beggars die; death comes to the innocent and it comes to the guilty. Death is the irreducible common denominator of all men.

I hope you can find some consolation from Christianity's affirmation that death is not the end. Death is not a period that ends the great sentence of life, but a comma that punctuates it to more lofty significance. Death is not a blind alley that leads the human race into a state of nothingness, but an open door which leads man into life eternal. Let this daring faith, this great invincible surmise, be your sustaining power during these trying days.

At times, life is hard, as hard as crucible steel. It has its bleak and painful moments. Like the ever-flowing waters of a river, life has its moments of drought and its moments of flood. Like the ever-changing cycle of the seasons, life has the soothing warmth of the summers and the piercing chill of its winters. But through it all, God walks with us. Never forget that God is able to lift you from fatigue of despair to the buoyancy of hope, and transform dark and desolate valleys into sunlit paths of inner peace.

Your children did not live long, but they lived well. The quantity of their lives was disturbingly small, but the quality of their lives was magnificently big. Where they died and what they were doing when death came will remain a marvelous tribute to each of you and an eternal epitaph to each of them. They died not in a den or dive nor were they hearing and telling filthy jokes at the time of their death. They died within the sacred walls of the church after discussing a principle as eternal as love.

Shakespeare had Horatio utter some beautiful words over the dead body of Hamlet. I paraphrase these words today as I stand over the last remains of these lovely girls.

"Good-night sweet princesses; may the flight of angels take thee to thy eternal rest."

Epilogue: The doors of the Sixteenth Street Baptist Church reopened on Sunday, June 7, 1964.

The "reentry" sermon was preached by a white clergyman, the Reverend H. O. Hester, secretary of the Department of Missions, Alabama Baptist Convention.

Offprint in Library of the Center for Non-Violent Social Change, Atlanta, in J. M. Washington, ed., *The Essential Writings and Speeches of Martin Luther King, Jr.*, (San Francisco: Harper, 1986), pp. 221–23.

61

BEDFORD-STUYVESANT: A LAND OF SUPERLATIVES

by Milton A. Galamison

The Reverend Dr. Galamison was pastor of the Siloam Presbyterian Church in Brooklyn and president of the Parents' Workshop for Equality in New York City Schools. This description of the ghetto in Brooklyn, New York may be taken as illuminating all the ghettos of the nation.

Brooklyn's Bedford-Stuyvesant area is a land of superlatives. Compared with other communities of the world's largest borough it claims the most residents, the most teenagers, the most overcrowding, the most churches, the greatest religious diversity, and the highest rent per square foot of living space. The area under discussion also houses the greatest economic need, the greatest number of public assistance cases, the highest rate of infant mortality, the highest incidence of tuberculosis, a disproportionate crime and delinquency rate, and more exploitation than conceivable in an area so geographically limited. In countless ways the Bedford-Stuyvesant area defies statistical norms. It is the residential area of least desirability on the totem pole of cultural status-seeking.

Most articles on "The Box," as the area is sometimes called, have been insensitive and unfair. To gratify a perverted public fancy for sensationalism, to confirm prejudices, writers have consistently projected a distorted image of an abused but heroic people. They burlesque the brokenness and ignore the creativity. They dramatize the juggled crime statistics and neglect the impressive well-spring of spiritual and religious life. They catalogue the shiftless and overlook the teeming thousands who daily crowd the transportation facilities enroute to gainful employment. While intent that nonresident readers should suffer no pangs of guilt for the plight of "The Box," those who write commentary on Bedford-Stuyvesant forget that no area could be so deprived unless there were forces outside far more evil than the forces within. In short, articles that most seek to defame and incriminate the people of the area have been the most serious indictments of the people not of this area. Efforts to present the Negro as an isolated monstrosity, however literary, do not negate the reality of the political, social, economic, and historic context in which the ghetto Negro has been created. They do not absolve guilt. They confirm it.

This is not a community of slum-dwellers. It is more so a haven for corrupt, absentee landlords and real estate speculators. This is not a community of shiftless husbands. It is a world of wounded men historically deprived of the right to equal employment. This is not a vast neighborhood of negligent mothers. It is a congregation of homemakers without homes and toilers without rest. Nor are our children justly depicted by delinquency statistics. They are condemned at the outset by an unequal, ethnocentric educational structure which few survive. Feeling with all other human beings the need for success, they seek to gratify this need in less creative endeavors. They have not failed so much as they have been failed. The Bedford-Stuyvesant area is not a front-page anomaly. It is a land of ghettoized human beings: men denied creative work, women denied creative living space and children denied a qualifying education. Few who write about or read of the area could manage half as well under similar circumstances.

Button, Button, Who's Got the Button?

The gigantic question mark, then, does not hover over the residents of the area. The basic question is whose condition is blessed at the expense of this blightedness? In what community will we find the sinners who destroy the families of men for the sake of their ambition and the minds of children for the gratification of their greed?

As the Bedford-Stuyvesant area is a land of superlatives, it is also a land of dead-end streets. Here Dante might well have posted the sign hung over the threshold of the entrance to his Hell, "ABANDON HOPE ALL YE WHO ENTER HERE." The usual routes by which people achieve redemption are few and elusive in this community. Education would be one such avenue, politics another.

There are two school systems in New York City. One is for the whites and for the sprinkling of Negroes who manage by design or grace to matriculate. The second school system is for the ghetto children and the disparity is grotesque. Unlike the conventional school system, the racial school system functions by a one-word policy called "IFISM." In essence it is a conditioned pedagogy for, according to the philosophy of the professional participants, the children involved could learn "IF." They could learn if they were not from the South. They could learn if they had a different set of parents. They could learn if they enjoyed higher income homes or if they just weren't on public assistance. They could learn if they didn't come from a broken home or perhaps if the home, even though broken, had a library. These are obviously conditions which the child cannot change. It is also apparent that if these kinds of conditions are set up as an obstacle to learning, conditions impossible to fulfill, they will preclude both teaching and learning. The supreme and thoroughly possible condition has yet to be stated, that the children might learn if they are properly taught.

Like the community generally, the schools have their share of superlatives: the most over-crowding, the most part-time sessions, the most inexperienced and substitute teachers, the most out-of-license instruction, the most nonresident staff members and the most teachers lowest on the salary scale. The curriculum, like the low expectation attitude, is predicated on "Ifism." Since one is never quite sure what the curriculum is, it will suffice to say that it leaves the majority of children woefully unprepared to compete academically and vocationally with success aspirants from other communities. The fruit of the system is perceptible on the high school level where the mortality rate among Negroes is frightening and in the free institutions of higher learning, such as Brooklyn College, where Negroes, who most need the free education, have long since been squeezed out by the competition and are infinitesimal in number. . . .

Can I Sell You the Brooklyn Bridge?

It should be reported that an effort was made several years ago to limit the rapidly-multiplying number of liquor stores in the Negro quarter. To this end a survey was made by two qualified experts and at the expense of eight hundred dollars. The study confirmed our wildest speculations that there existed in the Bedford-Stuyvesant area more than three times the number of liquor establishments found in a comparably-sized community. Armed with this statistical picture I appealed to the area's Neighborhood Council, an echelon group composed of the presidents of the various neighborhood block associations. The response was instant, wrathful indignation and they unanimously agreed on a three-point program. First, they would underwrite the cost of the survey; secondly, they would organize a delegation to Albany to protest the heinous condition; thirdly, they would demand a moratorium on the issuance of new liquor licenses and on the transfer of existing liquor licenses into the community. The crusade to defend the community against creeping saturation was of short duration. Not many days after the eventful meeting I received a letter from the president of the association. His type is of more importance than his name, his disease more significant than his identity. The letter said in essence that the executive council of the association had found it necessary to invalidate the action of the meeting on the grounds that to prevent the opening of new liquor establishments would be tantamount to creating a monopoly for those businesses already in existence. I was stunned! The voice was the voice of Jacob, but the hands were the hands of Esau. It was not hard for even a disillusioned clergyman to conclude what had happened here. But, then, no people could be kept in this kind of predicament were not their best efforts constantly undermined and betrayed by those in whom they place their trust.

In studying another aspect of the retail liquor store business, more recently, we estimated from available facts that more than half a million dollars is gleaned annually for sales commissions alone. Of this startling sum, less than five percent accrues to Negro salesmen. The Dorian Gray portrait of the scarred economic soul of the community becomes ominously clearer.

Idle in the Market Place

The same dismal and disproportionate statistics that apply to Negro unemployment through the nation would apply here. A survey was conducted in the not-too-distant past to determine the number of business establishments in the quarter that did not employ Negro help. There were few such establishments in the district studied and most of those without representative employees offered satisfactory reasons for the omission. One pharmacy, for example, had the union confirm its effort to locate an available Negro pharmacist. None could be found. Another union supported a local shoemaker's explanation that no skilled Negro was available. A third store consisted of three separate concessions operated by three different families. There was almost no evidence of a flagrant refusal to employ Negroes.

The ministers did become greatly exercised over the failure of neighborhood merchants to support non-profit community agencies, such as the YMCA, and, to rectify the situation, organized a Ministers' Movement. The merchants were operating without any sense of responsibility to the area civic and benevolent causes. They were taking everything out and giving nothing back. The Merchant's Association was practically defunct. Repeated appeals on behalf of the most deserving charitable efforts achieved no response.

In the wake of this apathy the ministers and their people picketed the merchants during April and May of 1962. The demonstrations brought an instant and enthusiastic response. A series of joint meetings followed during which machinery was set up to prevent a recrudescence of the historic neglect and, while much remains to be done, there now exists a cooperative effort in a new direction. The ministers, meanwhile, have set their sights on larger, city-wide and national industries and efforts will be made to involve the people in selective buying campaigns wherever discrimination rears its ugly head.

The most blatant violation of fair employment practices was uncovered in the local plant of a prominent dairy company by an aspiring political group. This plant, located deep in the heart of "The Box," employed less than five Negroes among its more than two hundred workers. In fact, the only black face in evidence on the site was a worker with thirty-five years seniority who had been upgraded to the grand responsibility of guiding trailer trucks to the loading platform. With the help of an advertising executive of a Negro magazine, conferences were set up with the personnel representatives of the company. Since it has never been their policy to discriminate against Negroes the request for a new policy was not in order. It was all a big mistake. But they did agree to make a deliberate effort to compensate for the oversight and to provide even on-the-job training for Negroes. Within the past month I received a call from the personnel director asking for some twenty job applicants to function as salesmen on delivery routes.

The people are not idle. The storm is ever-brewing. Any evidence of injustice can precipitate a deluge of social action. Those who listen can hear the rumbling beyond the hills.

Deprivation Without Representation

If colonialism can be acceptably defined as "a territory distant from the people who govern it," the picture we have been painting here is that of a domestic colonialism. The delivery trucks and the merchants, the real estate speculators and the rent gougers, the business executives and the bank tellers, the school principals and the ethnomaniacal school teachers, the precinct captains, and the wine merchants all come from far-away places. The hospital in which I am born, the apartment in which I live, and the cemetery in which I am buried are owned and controlled by commuter circuit riders whose allegiance lies in another world which I cannot visit, not even in my dreams. The masters of my destiny are faceless foreigners who find my community a satisfactory place to make a living but not a very satisfactory place to live. If my people suffer injustice it is because it is impossible to deal justly with those we neither know nor understand. . . .

Even as I write there is before me a press release from the New York City Board of Education. It proudly announces that the new superintendent of schools has invited a number of civic organizations to sit with him for the purpose of discussing school desegregation. Conspicuously absent from the organizations listed are the two organizations that have done more than any others to revolutionize the racial policy of the school system, The Brooklyn Congress on Racial Equality and The Parents' Workshop For Equality in New York City Schools. The job of desegregation will be achieved with or without the roundtable discussions and their ensuing studies. But this release dramatizes so well what we have been trying to say here. We are caught in a sick chess game and the black people are the pawns. Wherever the militant Negro fights for an equal slice in America, he is swept under the rug by local whites and climbed on by the opportunists in his own race. The white majority continues to listen only to those Negroes, hand-picked, purchased and paid for who say what it wants to hear. There is manifest in this an arrogant refusal to listen and an unteachableness that can only lead to destruction.

Charles Dickens raised the question why Midas in his palace should care about Tom-all-alone in his slum-infested cellar. Then Dickens answered his own question. "There is not an atom of Tom's slime, not a cubic inch of any pestilential gas in which he lives, not one obscenity or degradation about him but shall work its retribution."

We have hope because we live in this kind of a universe. We have hope because this greatest darkness must be the darkness before the dawn. We dare hope because, whether or not we read the face of the clock, eternity keeps its own inscrutable timetable. We dare hope because only order can come from this chaos.

Were we to pray we would pray with one voice the prayer of Ezekiel for this Land of Superlatives: "COME FROM THE FOUR WINDS, O BREATH, AND BREATHE UPON THESE SLAIN, THAT THEY MAY LIVE."

Freedomways 3 (Summer, 1963): 413–23; published in part.

62

"NOW OR NEVER: ANGER MOUNTING"

by Lakhmond Robinson

As the African-American protest mounted, the *New York Times,* on August 12, 1963, in a front-page article by Lakhmond Robinson, which ran over into page 10, headlined: "New York's Racial Unrest: Negroes' Anger Mounting." A subhead continued: "Years of Resentment Find Outlet in Wave of Protests—'Now-or-Never' Feeling Is Sweeping Moderation Aside." The text in part follows:

Nailed over the door of the Church of God and True Holiness on Harlem's 135th Street is a freshly painted sign that reads:

"Protest Meeting Every Monday—8:30 P.M."

A Negro lawyer, waving his hand at the sign as he passed it the other day, declared:

"See that? See that? That thing expresses my sentiments exactly. Only I would change it to read 'Protest Meeting Every Monday, Tuesday, Wednesday, Thursday, Friday, Saturday, and Sunday'"

The sign and the lawyer's amendments to it are symbols of a rising discontent in the Negro districts of the metropolitan area.

The resentment among the 1,500,000 black residents in the city and its suburbs, long built-up, has found an outlet. Negroes and their supporters have taken to the streets in an assault on racial segregation and discrimination.

In scenes similar to those in Birmingham, Alabama; Jackson, Mississippi; and centers of racial strife, sit-ins, hunger strikes, selective buying campaigns, boycotts, and freedom marches have taken place.

Hundreds of praying, chanting demonstrators have been jailed. Scattered violence has broken out. Some say more violence is inevitable.

Suddenly, it seems, the Negro is mad at everybody.

The protest movement has arisen in a region that has more laws to protect the civil rights of Negroes and other citizens than any other place in America.

It has shaken many New Yorkers, who view their city and its environs as a racial melting pot—as the historic haven of the disadvantaged immigrant and the oppressed minority.

To shock New Yorkers—both white and black, some of whom have remained apathetic or supported minor separatist movements—is precisely the goal of the wave of mass demonstration for integration.

"Our aim is to force the people of this city to sit up and take notice of the injustices Negroes have suffered from for a hundred years!" a speaker at a Brooklyn rally shouted the other night.

"The mood of the Negro is one of impatience, anger, and insistence," asserts Percy E. Sutton, a Harlem lawyer who has participated in sit-ins, picketing, and civil rights rallies.

"He seeks a final break-through, a final toppling of the walls of segregation and discrimination. He has learned, much to his sorrow, that he can't get these things by promises—that he's got to go out and get his equality—that it won't come to him."

Victories Whet Appetite

Each victory in the movement sharpens the appetite of the demonstrators for another battle.

Mrs. Jean Booker was one of those in the picket line that forced the suspension of construction at the Harlem Hospital annex.

"Our people are incensed," she declared. "How long are they supposed to wait to get decent jobs and homes and schools? They've been revolting quietly for some time. Now it's out in the open."

Mrs. Alice Gill, a Queens housewife and former Government worker, insisted that: "Many Negroes have lost faith in the word of the white man. They took to the streets because they were tired of begging and asking."

Walter Foley, a post office employee, put it this way: "I think that this is the hundredth anniversary of the Emancipation Proclamation. It had a lot to do with the blowup. Many Negroes were shocked to discover that they've been kicked around for a hundred years. A hundred years has a frightening ring to it, they decided they weren't going to wait another hundred."

"Showdown Has Come"

"The showdown has come!" an ebony-skinned demonstrator, his arms extended toward the heavens, shouted on a Brooklyn street corner.

"It's now or never. The showdown is here and we're ready for it, Lord. Men, women, and children, we're ready for it."

The tide seems to have swept away the Negro communities. In recent weeks some speakers at civil rights rallies who have urged moderation and caution have been loudly booed.

A survey by the *Times* shows, however, that a significant portion of the Negro community lives on a plateau of apathy and indifference toward the battle.

The Negroes' impassive faces and indifferent responses to questions testify to the attitude that, for them, New York is a place where the poor, the unskilled, and the uneducated face an indefinite future in the slums.

Such a response came from a thin, shirtless man sitting on a stoop on 118th Street:

"Man, just lemme alone. I don't care about nothing. It's too hot to bother about all this noise about integration."

Many Unconvinced

But the protest movement is sweeping forward with an emotional force that is drawing an increasing number of the apathetic. Many continue to remain convinced, however, that the movement won't change their condition in any material way.

There is also another segment of the Negro community that is angry over the Negro's treatment at the hands of the white man—and it demands a change. But it insists on segregation—not integration—as the black man's salvation.

It is represented most vocally by the Black Muslims, a religious sect, and by various black nationalist and African nationalist organizations, most of them based in Harlem.

The separatist movements are thus far only minor, compared to the integrationist drive, which is carrying along most of the Negro community.

Some of the Negro's militancy on civil rights is spontaneous. Some of it has been fanned by organizations, two of which—the urban league and the National Association for the Advancement of Colored People—have spearheaded the battle for Negro rights for more than half a century.

The fires of racial friction in the South have helped spark the movement in New York, as have the flames of independence and nationalism in black Africa. So have the pressures of the cold war between the United States and the Soviet Union.

Pro-integration sentiment is running as strong on the treelined streets of the Negro middle-class districts as it is on the hot and crowded streets of Harlem and other slum areas.

This mood is reflected in such statements as one by Representative Adam Clayton Powell, Jr., Harlem's preacher-politician.

"What do we Negroes want? We want the same thing the white man wants, and we want it right now—this afternoon!"

It is reflected in the statement of Junius Brown, Negro factory worker:

"White folks ain't going to give you nothing. You've got to go out and take it. That what they did." . . .

"Our people are trapped," says Moses Brown, a laborer. "All they know is they got to get out of this trap somehow. They got to fight for it."

Civil rights laws, numerous as they are, have never been vigorously enforced by the city or the state, argues J. Raymond Jones, Harlem City Councilman.

Moreover, he says, some labor unions practicing discrimination have been virtually immune from the state and city laws on antidiscrimination because of their political power. This has been especially true, he asserts of the "aristocrats of the union movement—the craft unions."

Others close to the Negro community hold that United States competition with the Soviet Union has forced the Federal Government and state and city governments to take a more active role in championing the rights of minorities since World War II.

"It's put-up or shut-up time," one civil rights official says. "People in this country have got to come across or stop yakking about equality and freedom for the rest of the world."

"The Negro has got to take advantage of this atmosphere," another observed. "He's got to strike while the iron is hot. The final breakthrough to complete, final, and lasting equality must be won now—or the chance may never come again." . . .

The major civil rights organizations, including the NAACP, the Urban League, and CORE, aware that wildcat demonstrators could provoke bloodshed, have begun coordinating their activities to keep better control over them.

In addition, the nonviolent nature of the demonstrations acts as a safety valve.

Revolution Called Peaceful

"We're not fighting a military battle. We're not trying to overthrow the government. This is a peaceful revolution," explain the Urban League's national executive director Whitney Young, Jr.

Moreover, a steady procession of whites is joining the protest demonstrations, thus giving concrete expression of their sympathy for the Negro's cause.

The current explosion over civil rights is the biggest—and seems sure to become the most sustained—in the history of the metropolitan area.

Civil rights groups view it as possibly the last massive assault against "northern-style" discrimination and segregation in New York.

James Farmer, national director of the Congress of Racial Equality describes "an undercurrent of racism" in this and other northern cities.

"It must be brought into the open before we can deal with it," he says. The demonstrations he adds are spotlighting it and forcing it into the open.

This is one of the ways in which the rights groups have deliberately sought to stimulate the current movement.

"The demonstrations serve as an emotional release, a focal point of participation for the masses," observes Mr. Randolph, who is currently planning another march on Washington on August 28, some twenty years after he planned the first one. He said:

"The situation is so crucial that an outlet has to be provided for the common people to liberate themselves, to release pent-up frustrations that could explode into violence. These demonstrations give them this outlet."

What built up the pressures that have to be released by demonstrations?

Negroes insist that though the city and its suburban areas are covered by many civil rights laws banning discrimination and segregation in housing, schools, public accommodations, and other areas of public life, these laws have never been properly enforced.

They also point to the fact that the Negro slum districts are spreading rather than shrinking.

Population pressures add to the general unrest. New York City's Negro population jumped from 61,000—or less than 2 per cent of its total population in 1900—to 1,100,000 or about 15 per cent of the city's population in 1963. About 1,500,000 Negroes live in the metropolitan region, most of them jammed into slum districts.

Many Negroes have come to New York, as others have done, thinking that the streets were paved with gold. They found out otherwise.

"We came up here looking for the Promised Land and didn't find it," asserts a Negro truck driver. "If the boss don't discriminate against you the unions do. You live in a hole the landlords call an apartment and your children go to nothing schools."

"Despite some gains, despite all the laws protecting his rights, the Negro has been for generations overcrowded, underemployed, frustrated, and poor," declares Edward S. Lewis, executive director of the Urban League of Greater New York.

Social dynamite, he argues, is building up among high school students who are dropping out of school "at an alarming rate, partly because they have no hope of getting a break in life."

About 25,000 to 40,000 children drop out of the New York City public schools each year, according to school officials. Though no racial census is kept, at least half are Negroes.

"All these years Negroes in the North have been getting big promises and making little or no gains in jobs, education, and housing," insists Dr. Kenneth B. Clark, City College psychology professor, and a Negro.

"Now suddenly they realize they've been trampled on for a hundred years. In that time there's been as much backtracking on civil rights as there has been progress, and Negroes are fed up."

Strong resentment has also built up over housing discrimination and slum conditions, though the city and the state have the strongest laws in the country forbidding discrimination in both public and private housing. Moreover, many "housekeeping" laws and regulations are aimed at preventing the growth of slum conditions in multiple dwellings.

Here again, Negro civil rights officials, as well as Negroes on the street, say that a lot of lip service has been given to these laws, but that there has been little actual enforcement.

Hulan E. Jack, former Manhattan Borough President, warns of a "blowup" over housing conditions in the 14th Assembly District in Harlem, where he serves as Democratic district leader.

"You can feel the tension over these stinking housing conditions rising up like heat from the sidewalks," he remarked on a sultry night recently as he walked along 116th Street near Lenox Avenue.

"Rats are taking over some of these buildings," he exclaimed, waving his arms at the rows of tenements. "And you think people should accept this—that their children should have to live in this? Why, some people around here are ready to kill landlords."

Cold War Impact Felt

But unemployment, poor housing, and poor schools are not the only causes of the civil rights revolt in the metropolitan area.

The rise of the black nations of Africa and the pressures of the cold war have had a heavy impact on it, some observers contend.

"Negroes here see other black people who were subjugated only a few years ago presiding over their countries as prime ministers, presidents, and ambassadors," City Councilman Jones comments.

"All this hollering over integration don't mean nothing to me," a Negro laundry worker comments. "All them Negroes who are doing it hope to git something for themselves. All this stuff don't help people like me. I'm going to be working in a laundry all my life and there's no way to git out of it."

The despair and hopelessness of many Negroes is shown in other ways. Though there are some 400,000 Negroes packed into Harlem, the NAACP, foremost of the civil rights groups, has never had more than 25,000 members in the community.

Almost invariably, Negroes talked to in the *Times* survey insisted they did not seek separation from whites but wanted—as Maude Blair, a Greenwich Village maid, put it—"to live as Americans in America and as Christians in a Christian country."

The victories in the drive for integration increase the impetus for more demonstrations.

"If they could not see success in sight, if there were no hope," says Mr. Randolph, "there would be no demonstrations. People without hope don't fight. If we stopped they'd think we were contented."

When the criticism is made that some demonstrations are irrational and inconvenience many people, James Farmer of CORE replies:

"Well, the Negro has been inconvenienced for a hundred years. We feel these demonstrations are necessary to dramatize the need for corrective measures."

The Urban League's Mr. Young has proposed a program of preferential treatment for Negroes to enable them to catch up with whites in jobs, education, and housing.

Aware that his plan is controversial, Mr. Young argues that: "White people have had special preference all along, though they won't admit it. They've hired the white man, though the Negro might have been as qualified or better qualified. It's time we instituted a program of special treatment for Negroes as compensation for generations of denial, at least for a while."

As the summer wears on, the voices of protest rise higher.

The integrationist forces are stepping up their picketing, sit-ins, and rallies.

At the same time, thousands are attending similar rallies in Harlem and Brooklyn to hear the Black Muslims denounce the white man and demand separation of the races.

Many integrationists scoff at the program of the Muslims and the nationalists and contend that the increasing surge of the integration movement is cutting the ground out from under the segregation forces, white or black.

But some ardent integrationists back the right of the Muslims and others to preach and practice racial separation and their own brand of "racial purity" and to make plans for the establishment of a black Zion.

Ernest E. Johnson, a Harlem insurance man who has long supported integrationist causes, puts it this way:

"We've got to recognize that the Negro community is not monolithic—economically, socially, or politically. There is room for the leftists, the rightists, and the moderates. And there's a place for the Muslims and any other group that desires racial separation."

"The black man doesn't necessarily want integration," says James Lawson, head of the United African Nationalist Movement. "He wants justice and fair play."

But the overwhelming sentiment among Negroes interviewed is that integration means justice and fair play, and that is how the Negro's historic second-class status will be finally erased.

And for the present, the general Negro community continues to be swept along, at an ever-increasing tempo, on the wave of the integration movement.

A Negro lawyer received a call from his 12-year-old daughter the other day. "Daddy, daddy," she cried. "I've been picketing."

She had been picketing a decision by playground officials to close the area earlier than usual.

Thus has the protest movement spread like fire through the Negro community.

63

BIRMINGHAM: DELIBERATE MASS MURDER

by James E. Jackson

The reporter quoted the pastor's thirteen-year-old daughter Barbara Cross as saying:

"The lights fell down and all of a sudden there was a big boom and there was a lot of smoke.

"Little children were screaming and everything."

And four little children were blasted to death on a September Sunday when segregationist revenge-seekers lobbed a fifteen-stick packet of dynamite through the basement window of the 16th Street Baptist Church in Birmingham where eighty Negro children were in Sunday School classes.

Upstairs in the main auditorium, some four hundred parishioners were seated in their pews, and the Rev. John Cross was conducting the preliminaries to the opening of his service as he stood in the pulpit.

The bomb exploded at 10:22 A.M. The pastor was hurled from his pulpit by the force of the blast. A yawning hole opened in the wall of the church. Splintered timber, chunks of plaster, and fragments of stained glass windows showered down upon the worshippers who were scattered about the floor amidst upturned pews in eerie disarray.

In the basement, the horribly mangled bodies of the four little girls lay buried under the rubble. The head of little Denise McNair, who had taken the full blast of the explosive, was severed from her body, the rest of her was cut up in little pieces in the shambles of rubble that once was a Sunday School class.

Within moments, the area around the 16th Street Baptist Church—famed as the headquarters of the great protest demonstrations and marches against segregation during last May's struggle against former police Commander Bull Connor and his police dogs—swarmed with riot-gun-armed police and the whole city was shrill with the shriek of police car sirens. The guns of a police force which had failed to find a trace of a single one of the perpetrators of twenty-one bombings were levelled at the Negroes.

Within hours the police had added to the toll of the children who were killed this Sunday in Birmingham by racists turned murdering beasts.

Standing in the shadow of the church sanctuary, slight Johnny Robinson, age sixteen, was shot in the back and killed instantly by a uniformed policeman wielding a shotgun. And across town, thirteen-year-old Virgil Wade was gunned down while riding his bicycle at play.

In addition to the six young people who were killed, over a score of Sunday School children and adult worshippers were injured; some remained in the hospital gravely wounded. Almost simultaneously with the bombing of the church, as if in accord with a prearranged plan, fire bombs were exploded in several Negro business establishments and at residences of civil rights activists. The proprietor of a Negro establishment close by the church fumbled helplessly with his handkerchief in his hands as the tears streamed down his face, and said to a reporter words whose sentiments echo the innermost feelings of twenty million Negroes in America this day. He said: "My grandbaby was killed in there. You know how I feel? I feel like blowing the whole town up."

From the national headquarters of the National Association for the Advancement of Colored People, Roy Wilkins, its executive secretary, branded the killing of the Negro children of Birmingham as "a deliberate mass murder" encouraged by Gov. George C. Wallace of Alabama.

"If the Government will not furnish more than piecemeal and picayune aid," said Wilkins, "Negroes will marshal such resources as we possess and employ such methods as our desperation may dictate."

Hurrying to Birmingham from Atlanta, the Rev. Martin Luther King wired a telegram to President Kennedy which declared in part:

"I'm convinced that unless some immediate steps are taken by the Federal Government to restore a sense of confidence in the protection of life, limb, and property . . . we shall see in Birmingham and Alabama the worst racial holocaust the nation has ever seen."

From Unity House in Pennsylvania, where the Jewish Labor Committee's National Trade Union Council for Human Rights is in session, Charles Zimmerman, in a message to President Kennedy, said:

"It is imperative that the Federal Government act quickly and with full vigor to find the perpetrators of this fiendish deed. Every decent citizen in the land is sick to death of these acts of terrorism in our United States. They have got to be stopped, and only the National Government can do the job."

A week ago Governor Wallace was quoted as saying that "seven or eight funerals" were what was needed to solve the racial problems in Alabama. Last Thursday he criticized the work of the bomb gangs with the cynical comment that "of forty-seven bombings, no one had been killed."

John P. Roche, national chairman of Americans for Democratic Action, in a statement in the name of this progressive grouping in the Democratic Party, ridiculed the cynicism of Wallace in offering a reward for the bomb-killers' capture. He said:

"Governor Wallace has offered $5,000 as his blood money in the savage murder of four small Americans. In fact, Wallace is as guilty as if he himself planted the bomb.

"It was Wallace who gave the lead to those who, in their own varied fashions, imitate his defiance of the law. The $5,000 reward will not get him absolution from the terrible responsibility."

Dr. Robert W. Spike, executive director of the National Council of Churches Commission on Religion and Race, appealed in a call to white Christians in Birmingham to speak out against "the madness which has swept their city."

Declaring that the "lives of all Americans had been stained by these racist murders," the statement said that silence of Christian whites there had permitted this racist madness to take root and grow "and it has been encouraged and inflamed by the reckless and irresponsible statements of open defiance made by the Governor."

Benjamin J. Davis of the Communist Party declared in his telegram to Kennedy that the Negro people have received "a blow to their soul and they cry out that the murderers of their children be avenged and the segregation system that spawned such bestial racists be brought down once and for all."

James E. Jackson, *op. cit.*, pp. 33–35; on-the-scene report in the *Worker*, September 16, 1963.

64

THE NEGRO REVOLT

by Whitney M. Young, Jr.

The current demonstrations in the South by citizens seeking fundamental civil rights for the Negro may well be mild compared with the potential for violence in the cities of the North.

In teeming northern ghettos, hundreds of thousands of Negro citizens—unemployed, ill-housed, disillusioned—are nearing the breaking point. Disorders have already begun. Violence could erupt at any moment unless swift and realistic action is taken to prevent violence by eliminating its basic cause.

For 18.7 million American Negroes, already handicapped by discrimination in employment and inadequate training and now caught up in the quicksand of rapid technological change, the problem is immediate and desperate.

Federal action, however commendable, is still too little—and may well be too late. We believe the answer lies in effective action by responsible individuals and institutions—acting privately and in concert—who will undertake a massive program to close the intolerable economic, social, and educational gap that separates the vast majority of Negro citizens from other Americans.

After World War II, our country initiated a Marshall Plan to help the war-shattered countries of Western Europe function in full partnership with the United States. Our Negro citizens are asking for a similar chance to attain their rightful position as full partners of every other citizen of the United States.

This is a plea for a special effort, but it is *not* a plea for special privilege. The effects of generations of deprivation and denial have made it almost impossible for the American Negro to take advantage of any guarantee of equal opportunity. Unless he can do so, legal progress is an illusion; and the civil rights struggle will continue with unforeseeable consequences.

A Realistic Basis

In this sense, the National Urban League urges the responsible leadership of our country to undertake a domestic "Marshall Plan"—a special effort to help the Negro help himself and, by so doing, reach the point at which he can compete on a realistic basis of equality within the nation's complex economy.

The United States realized after the Second World War that it was in jeopardy so long as it had within its bloc nations that were unable to assume their full responsibilities. It must now realize that it is also in jeopardy so long as it has within its body politic a group of socially and economically handicapped citizens—often dependent, poorly educated and unable to assume the normal responsibilities of citizenship.

Without a genuine preventive effort, it is entirely possible that these conditions will become worse and that we may by default create a class of permanently dependent citizens unable to make a useful contribution to society.

This idea of temporary special help now being called for is not new to our society. We have generously—and with justification—given special consideration in employment, education, and welfare to Hungarian and Cuban refugees fleeing oppression. We have given preferential treatment to the G.I. after World War II—in the form of free education, reduced interest loans for homes and business, a ten-point advantage on civil-service examinations, and other benefits—because he had been out of the mainstream for four or five years. Even now we designate certain geographic areas as depressed and disaster centers, and their people entitled to special help because of joblessness and acts of God.

Another reason for a special effort arises from historic considerations. A great many of the intense needs and problems evident in so many Negro communities are the result of exclusion based on racial discrimination. Apart from historical equity, a massive compensatory effort may well be the only means of overcoming all present results of past neglect.

Despite progress in certain areas, a large segment of the Negro population continues to lag seriously behind other Americans. This is particularly evident among the youth, who face greater employment problems than other young workers.

In 1962, about one out of every four Negro teenagers in the labor force was unemployed, compared with about one out of every eight white teenagers. Since 1955, the jobless rate among Negro teenagers has risen faster than for white teenagers—up about sixty per cent among Negroes, compared with a thirty per cent rise for white teenagers. Negro girls have a much higher unemployment rate than any other group in the entire labor force.

Negro youth, both graduates of high school and dropouts, are primarily employed in low-paying service occupations. Even when Negro youth have high-school diplomas, their unemployment rate is about double that for white graduates.

Thus, for these children spawned in a cesspool of national indifference to their hopes and aspirations, the frequent admonition to "stay in school and get an education" sometimes, and understandably, falls on deaf ears.

As a result, more Negro youths drop out of high school than white youths, and fewer Negro high school graduates enter college. During one of the most recent school years, Negroes, who constitute something less than eleven per cent of the total population, supplied twenty-one per cent of the school dropouts but only seven per cent of the high school graduates.

Inadequate and Unequal

By themselves, these young people cannot change their situation. And unless this situation is changed drastically now, the nation may be the loser in ways not yet imagined. Without immediate help a larger proportion will join the ranks of those suffering from dependency and frustration, and they in turn will raise their offspring in their own stunted image.

This, of course, serves not only to underscore the importance of education to American life, but the importance of adequate and equal educational opportunity. The under-utilization of Negro ability begins in the classroom and reaches out into all other areas of work experience. In this respect, the opportunities afforded Negroes for vocational education, generally, have been both inadequate and unequal.

To correct these and many other problems, the Urban League believes that a "crash" attack is required. A cooperative and deliberate effort on the part of agencies, unions, business and industry, institutions and individuals, both public and private, could, if sustained for a realistic period of time, reverse the widespread social deterioration of Negro families and their children and help develop the tools and understanding for progress to full and equal citizenship....

We face a clear alternative of providing Negro youth with better education, training, and job opportunity, or of paying for higher welfare costs, crime rates, and human demoralization.

There is a place for sectional or regional difference in American life, especially when this difference serves to enrich the diversity of our cultural heritage. But this difference should never be permitted to obscure or to impede our national objective of guaranteeing equal opportunity for all our citizens.

In the opinion of the National Urban League, this kind of constructive action represents the only way in which significant progress can be made. The civil rights struggle has been characterized as the "Negro revolt."

This term may be appropriate in some respects. But it differs from many revolutions inasmuch as it is an attempt by an underprivileged element of society not to change the fabric of that society, but to "revolt" into partnership with it. It is a revolt with which every American should sympathize and become involved.

Before becoming executive director of the National Urban League, Whitney had been dean of the Atlanta University School of Social Work. The essay above appeared in a debate on "Preferential Hiring for Negroes" in the *American Child,* November, 1963, (45:5–8).

65

THE BLACK PRESS ON PRESIDENT KENNEDY'S ASSASSINATION

by Marion Butts

Illustrative was the essay by Marion Butts in the *Dallas Express,* December 14, 1963:

Dallas citizens must face up to the realization that because Dallas is a city where hate is bred, born, grows, and destroys the minds of its citizens, the President of the United States was murdered on its streets.

Like most American cities, Dallas has organized hate groups which preach racial hate, religious hate, ideological hate, etc.

Regardless of what direction hate is projected, taught, and cultivated, some individual's mind will become completely destroyed by the vicious poison of hate to the extent that he will destroy that which he hates.

Dallas is a city where people of African descent are denied the privilege to worship in certain churches because its membership is bred from the hotbed of racial hate. Dallas is a city where a leading newspaper points up the fact that hate exists, but says let time take care of the situation, legislation and agitation will do no good.

In Dallas, like other cities in America, some religious bodies deny their membership the privilege to visit worship services of other religious bodies.

Dallas is a city where the top leadership speaks out against acts of hate only when these acts are threatening the economy of the city.

With this kind of hotbed, where hate can breed, not only do we kill each other, our families, ourselves, but the President of the United States, who was a most honored and invited guest.

The sins of silent leadership, inaction, complacency, and hypocritical lip service have caught up with "Big Friendly" Dallas.

Benjamin F. Clark, *op. cit.*, pp. 219–20. Quotations from several other African-American newspapers are similar and are offered in this source.

66

"MORE RATS THAN PEOPLE"

by Jesse Gray and the New York Times

On the day before Christmas, 1963, Jesse Gray, a leader of Harlem protest movements, managed to get important news coverage of the appalling conditions in Harlem. He did this by asking the American Red Cross to declare Harlem a disaster area. On Christmas Day, the *New York Times* published an account of Harlem's reality. The headline read:

Harlem Leader Loses Plea for Disaster Assistance

The leader of the Harlem rent strike asked the American Red Cross yesterday to declare lower Harlem a disaster area. He said three hundred children and seven hundred adults were living in freezing cold apartments that had been without heat since December 1.

The protest leader, Jesse Gray, chairman of the Community Council on Housing and the Rent Strike Coordinating Committee, asked the Red Cross to move in with blankets, heaters, and coal. He said that 125 families faced Christmas without heat or hot water.

A spokesman for the New York Chapter of the American Red Cross explained that the city, state, or Federal Government would first have to declare a disaster area before the Red Cross could act.

Mr. Gray later appealed to the Department of Health and was told that the city was doing everything it could to halt violations. Landlords are required by law to provide enough heat so that room temperatures are at least 68 degrees between the hours of 6 A.M. and 10 P.M. when the outside temperature is 55 degrees or lower.

21 Summonses Ordered

Assistant Health Commissioner Jerome Trichter said thirty-five Harlem tenement buildings were inspected December 3 after complaints by the council. Twenty-one summonses were ordered in these buildings, Commissioner Trichter said, but the department was able to serve only fifteen. Owners of slum buildings are seldom easy to find. Commissioner Trichter said six landlords had not be located.

Eight summonses were served for no heat and thirteen for poor housing conditions. Of these cases, three have been disposed of with fines of $100, $50, and $30.

Last night Commissioner Trichter said the Health Department would send several public health nurses to the affected buildings today to see if anyone living there required medical attention.

At 15 East 117th Street, Mrs. Muriel Jackson and her five daughters were huddling around the gas stove of their third-floor tenement. There was no other heat. Mrs. Jackson, as a special holiday treat for the children, planned to keep the oven on all night.

It was colder in the hallway than in the slushy street outside. The stairwell was incredibly filthy. Like most tenement buildings, No. 15 has no lock on the front door. Narcotics addicts could wander in from the street, poke holes in the plaster, and cache their "fixes" inside. Addicts and derelicts use the hall as a toilet. The passage was littered with empty bottles and other debris.

Bath Water Heated on Stove

Mrs. Jackson's husband, Frank, a cutter in the garment industry, said he had to get up early in the morning and heat ten to fifteen gallons of water on the stove so the family could bathe. "I don't like my kids to be smelly when they go to school," he said.

On the fourth floor, Mrs. Doris Roper said she turned the oven on constantly, despite mounting gas bills, so her four children, aged one to four, could gather in the kitchen and keep warm. She had tacked newspapers around the hall door to keep out the dank air. Mrs. Roper said the building was infested with rodents, one of them large enough to make off with her rat trap. "I always think one day I'll see a life-sized one," laughed Miss Elise McGee at 54 West 118th Street. "You often see them walking in the hall. One day I had a couple of dollars on the table and rats chewed them up. There are more rats in this building than people. You close up one rathole and they just open up another."

"I'm here having tea and there they sit, looking me straight in the face," said Miss McGee's next door neighbor, Mrs. May Robinson.

Mrs. Robinson is house chairman for the rent strike called December 3 in which tenants refused to pay rent until housing violations were eliminated. Her radiators were tepid. She explained that the tenants had chipped in $75.88 for coal for the building.

67

"HAVING A BABY INSIDE ME IS THE ONLY TIME I FEEL ALIVE"

by a Black Woman Talking to Robert Coles

In a book published in 1964 a distinguished psychologist reported remarks made to him by an anonymous black woman who had recently arrived in Boston:

They came telling us not to have children, and not to have children, and sweep up, and all that. There isn't anything they don't want to do to you, or tell you to do. They tell you you're bad, and worse than others, and you're lazy, and you don't know how to get along like others do. Well, for so long they told us we couldn't ever go near anyone else, I suppose we should be grateful for being told we're not going to get near enough if we don't behave in the right way—which is the sermon I get all the time now.

Then they say we should look different, and eat different—use more of the protein. I tell them about the prices, but they reply about "planning"—planning, planning, that's all they tell you. The worst of it is that they try to get you to plan your kids, by the year; except they mean by the ten-year plan, one every ten years. The truth is, they don't want you to have any, if they could help it.

To me, having a baby inside me is the only time I'm really alive. I know I can make something, do something, no matter what color my skin is, and what names people call me. When the baby gets born I see him, and he's full of life, or she is; and I think to myself that it doesn't make any difference what happens later, at least now we've got a chance, or the baby does. You can see the little one grow and get larger and start doing things, and you feel there must be some hope, some chance that things will get better; because there it is, right before you, a real, live, growing baby. The children and their father feel it, too, just like I do. They feel the baby is a good sign, or at least he's *some* sign. If we didn't have that, what would be the difference from death? Even without children my life would still be bad—they're not going to give us what *they* have, the birth control people. They just want us to be a poor version of them, only without our children and our faith in God and our tasty fried food, or anything.

They'll tell you we are "neglectful"; we don't take proper care of the children. But that's a lie, because we do, until we can't any longer, because the time has come for the street to claim them, to take them away and teach them what a poor nigger's life is like. I don't care what anyone says: I take the best care of my children. I scream the ten commandments at them every day, until one by one they learn them by heart—and believe me they don't forget them. (You can ask my minister if I'm not telling the truth.) It's when they leave for school, and start seeing the streets and everything, that's when there's the change; and by the time they're ten or so, it's all I can do to say anything, because I don't even believe my own words, to be honest. I tell them, please to be good; but I know it's no use, not when they can't get a fair break, and there are the sheriffs down South and up there the policemen, ready to kick you for so much as breathing your feelings. So I turn my eyes on the little children, and keep on praying that one of them will grow up at the right second, when the schoolteachers have time to say hello and give him the lessons he needs, and when they get rid of the building here and let us have a place you can breathe in and not get bitten all the time, and when the men can find work—because *they* can't have children, and so they have to drink or get on drugs to find some happy moments, and some hope about things.

In Robert Coles, *Children of Crisis* (Boston: Little, Brown, 1964), in Gerda Lerner, ed., *Black Women in White America: A Documentary History* (New York: Random House, 1972), pp. 313–15.

68

WHAT IS WRONG?

by a Twelve-Year-Old Girl

In the Freedom School in Biloxi, Mississippi, a child submitted a poem to her
teacher:

> What is wrong with me everywhere I go
> No one seems to look at me.
> Sometimes I cry.
>
> I walk through woods and sit on a stone.
> I look at the stars and I sometimes wish.
>
> Probably if my wish ever comes true,
> Everyone will look at me.

Elizabeth Sutherland, ed., *Letters from Mississippi* (New York: McGraw-Hill, 1965),
p. 97. A good description of "The Mississippi Summer of 1964," by James Findlay (a
history teacher at the University of Rhode Island) is in the *Christian Century*, June
8–15, 1988, pp. 574–76.

69

LITERACY AND LIBERATION

by Septima P. Clark

Septima P. Clark was director, teacher training, Citizen Education Program of the
Southern Christian Leadership Conference. Women were central to the African-
American struggle; none was more consequential than Ms. Clark. Here she offers
a description of a seminal effort going back to the 1950s, culminating in the next
decade.

The teacher wrote "Citizen" on the blackboard. Then she wrote "Constitution" and "Amendment." The she turned to her class of thirty adult
students.

"What do these mean, students?" she asked. She received a variety of answers, and when the discussion died down, the teacher was able to make a generalization.

"This is the reason we know we are citizens: Because it's written in an amendment to the Constitution."

An elderly Negro minister from Arkansas took notes on a yellow legal pad. A machine operator from Atlanta raised his hand to ask another question.

This was an opening session in an unusual citizenship education program that is held once each month at Dorchester Center, McIntosh, Georgia for the purpose of helping adults help educate themselves.

In a five day course, those three words became the basis of a new education in citizenship for the Negroes and whites who attended the training session. Each participant left with a burning desire to start their own Citizenship Education schools among their own communities.

The program now being sponsored by the Southern Christian Leadership Conference has resulted in the training of more than eight hundred persons in the best methods to stimulate voter registration back in their home towns, their home towns comprising eleven southern states from eastern Texas to northern Virginia. The program was transferred to SCLC from The Highlander Folk School in Monteagle, Tennessee.

I learned of Highlander in 1952 but attended my first workshop in 1954. In 1955 I directed my first workshop and did door to door recruiting for the school. Unable to drive myself I found a driver for my car and made three trips from Johns Island, South Carolina to Monteagle, Tennessee. On each trip six islanders attended and were motivated. They became literate and are still working for liberation.

In 1954 in the South, segregation was the main barrier in the way of the realization of democracy and brotherhood. Highlander was an important place because Negroes and whites met on equal basis and discussed their problems together.

There was a series of workshops on Community Services and Segregation; Registration and Voting; and Community Development. Then it became evident that the South had a great number of functional illiterates who needed additional help to carry out their plans for coping with the problems confronting them. Problems such as the following: Six-year-old Negro boys and girls walking five miles on a muddy road in icy, wet weather to a dilapidated, cold, log cabin school house in most of the rural sections of the South. In cities like Charleston, South Carolina children of

LITERACY AND LIBERATION

that same tender age had to leave home while it was yet dark, 7:00 A.M., to attend an early morning session and vacate that classroom by 12:30 P.M. for another group in that same age bracket which would leave 5:30 P.M. for home (night time during the winter months). These children would pass white schools that had regular school hours and fewer children enrolled. The Negro parents accepted this for many years. They did not know what to do about it. They had to be trained.

Highlander had always believed in people and the people trusted its judgment and accepted its leadership. It was accepted by Negroes and whites of all religious faiths because it had always accepted them and made them feel at home. The staff at Highlander knew that the great need of the South was to develop more people to take leadership and responsibility for the causes in which they believed. It set out on a program designed to bring out leadership qualities in people from all walks of life.

Adults from all over the South, about forty at a time, went there for the specific purpose of discussing their problems. They lived together in rustic, pleasant, rural surroundings on the top of the Cumberland Plateau in a number of simple cabins around a lake, remote from business and other affairs that normally demand so much attention and energy. Though of different races and often of greatly contrasting economic or educational backgrounds, they rarely felt the tension that such differences can cause and if they did, as it occurred sometimes, it was never for long. They soon became conscious of the irrelevance of all such differences. Each person talked with people from communities with problems similar to those of his own. Each discussed both formally and informally the successes and difficulties he had had in his efforts to solve these problems in various ways.

The participants of the workshops included community leaders and civic minded adults affiliated with agencies and organizations. They had a common concern about problems but no one knew easy solutions. The issues then as now were among the most difficult faced by society. The highly practical discussions at the workshops challenged their thinking which in turn helped them to understand the difficulties and in most cases steps were suggested towards a solution. They found out that it was within their power to take the steps necessary to meet with members of school boards. In Charleston County they asked for new schools and buses to transport their children. They staged a boycott to get rid of double sessions. *They won!* The immense value of a willingness to take responsibility and to act becomes clear when one sees what others have done, apparently through this willingness alone.

Prior to the Supreme Court's decision of 1954 the Negro communities of the South would have been characterized as uncoordinated, made up of groups whose interests diverged or conflicted. Today one can say that the school integration issue has served to mobilize and unify the groups. The present psychological health of Negro leaders is good. Such a thing as an official ballot handed to Negro leaders in Alabama, on which is engraved a rooster crowing "white supremacy" will not weaken their determination nor courage to be free. They have amassed funds, sent men to the Justice Department, and took their gerrymandering cases to the courts. Today they are registering to vote. The registrars are not hiding in the bank vaults any more. Literacy means liberation. . . .

Negro maids and custodians in the Atlanta schools asked the Atlanta board of education for a raise in pay. It was such an audacious step for them to take that the superintendent of schools put an article in the November 9th, Atlanta *Constitution* entitled "Maids Ask City Schools for a Raise." The article further states that the maids said "discriminatory practice in promotions and holidays are noted." The maids and custodians have only three days during the Christmas season while other employees have two weeks.

They said, "We have had several meetings and stand firmly and united seeking to have these grievances dealt with. We have elected a chairman among us."

Maids receive $30 a week and custodians $234 to $288 a month. According to the standard today they said, custodians should receive a minimum salary of $350 a month and maids $200.

Copies of the letter were sent to the mayor and two members of the board of education, one of whom is a Negro.

Literacy means liberation.

Freedomways 4 (Winter 1964): 113–24. See her own brief account of her life in Bruno Lasker and Barbara Summers, eds. *I Dream A World* (New York: Stewart, Tabori and Chang, 1959), p. 164.

70

THE MOVEMENT, SO FAR

by Lerone Bennett, Jr.

The senior editor of the influential *Ebony* magazine offered, in 1964, an eloquent analysis of the nation's crisis.

The 1960–64 convulsion, to sum up, meets some of the basic tests of a classic upheaval: the direct intervention of the masses, for example, and the reliance on direct action which is, to the Freedom Movement, what Clausewitz called war: a continuation of politics by other means.

Tactics, strategy, objectives: all point to a petit revolution straining on the edge of an open confrontation. But the movement, so far, has not solved the two basic problems that would make it a real revolution: the organization of a sustained national resistance movement and the mobilization of the so-called underclass in the great concrete ghettos. For this reason and others, primarily the limitations of the Negro situation, it would be more accurate to call the upheaval a rebellion, a turning away from, a going out of—a becoming.

Semantics apart, the cataclysm in the streets is real enough, and it proceeds from revolutionary premises. The fundamental premise is that old forms and old ways are no longer adequate and that the social system, as organized, is incapable of solving, through normal channels, the urgent problem presented to it by history. The second major premise is allied to the first: that the social system, as organized, is part of the problem and cannot be appealed to or relied upon as an independent arbiter in power conflicts of which it is a part. The third major premise is that white Americans, generally speaking, lack the will, the courage, and the intelligence to voluntarily grant Negroes their civil rights and that they must be forced to do it by pressure.

Here are the minor premises:

1) That people do not discriminate for the fun of it, that the function of prejudice is to defend interests (social, economical, political, and psychological interests) and that appeals to the fair play of prejudiced people are prayers said to the wind.

2) That communities will change discriminatory patterns if they are forced to make a clear-cut choice between bias and another highly cherished value— economic gain, education, or civic peace.

3) That struggle and conflict are necessary for social change, that showdown situations are desirable because they throw the whole range of race relations into the arena of public discussion.

4) That the constitutional rights of live human beings are at stake and that these rights are neither ballotable nor negotiable; that negotiation, to be meaningful, must take place between equals acting in good faith and that the issues here are precisely equality and the good faith, if not the good sense, of white Americans.

5) That peace is the presence of community and not the absence of conflict; and that demonstrations against Jim Crow are attempts to establish peace and not breaches of the peace which, according to black rebels, has never existed anywhere and at anytime between black and white Americans.

We may or may not agree with these premises. It doesn't matter, really. For what we must realize now is that the burden of proof is on us. The face of the Commonwealth gives abundant testimony of the total failure of the politics of good intentions. What we must do now is to examine our own inarticulate promises and our own involvement or lack of involvement in a struggle that goes to the heart of our meaning as a people.

We stand now in a lull in the lurch of history. The barometer drops so low before a storm. No man wants a storm, but wishing will not sweep away the clouds. If we do not act, the storm will come—if not now, five years from now; if not then, ten years later. There has been, as we have seen, a Negro revolt in every decade of this century. Each revolt failed, only to emerge in the next decade on a higher level of development. It is not to our best interest for the current rebellion to fail. For one hesitates to speculate on the form and intensity a Negro revolt will take in the seventies and eighties when Negroes form a majority in many of our major cities.

We are heading now for a land no American has traversed. For perhaps the first time in our history, we have a thoroughly restive minority population on our hands. So far we have done our best to bring out the worst in urban Negroes who are strategically placed to cause social chaos. Negroes, for the most part, inhabit the inner cores of America's largest cities; and they hold the key to the future of the city and the future of American democracy. If we do not want a black Ireland here, if we do not want our cities divided into mutually hostile casbahs, if we do not want the Negro rebellion to become a real revolution, then we must dare to flesh out the words we profess.

This is an important moment in the history of the Commonwealth. There stretch out before us two roads and two roads only. America must now become America or something else, a Fourth Reich perhaps, or a Fourth Reich of the spirit. To put the matter bluntly, we must become what we say we are or give in to the secret dream that blights our hearts.

Let us not deceive ourselves. The problem before us now is not the Negro but ourselves; not civil rights but the city; not love but the creation of that America which could have been and should have been and never was.

71

"IS THIS AMERICA?"

by Fannie Lou Hamer

At the 1964 Democratic party convention delegates elected by the Mississippi Freedom Democratic party (MFDP) attempted to gain acceptance as that state's delegates. The attempt failed. One of those elected by the MFDP was Fannie Lou Hamer. At a hearing February 22, the credentials committee of the party heard testimony as to the seating of MFDP representatives. Fannie Lou Hamer testified:

Mr. Chairman, and the Credentials Committee, my name is Mrs. Fannie Lou Hamer, and I live at 626 East Lafayette Street, Ruleville, Mississippi, Sunflower County, the home of Senator James O. Eastland, and Senator Stennis.

It was the 31st of August in 1962 that eighteen of us traveled twenty-six miles to the county courthouse in Indianola to try to register to try to become first-class citizens. We was met in Indianola by Mississippi men, highway patrolmens, and they only allowed two of us in to take the literacy test at the time. After we had taken this test and started back to Ruleville, we was held up by the City Police and the State Highway Patrolmen and carried back to Indianola, where the bus driver was charged that day with driving a bus the wrong color.

After we paid the fine among us, we continued on to Ruleville, and Reverend Jeff Sunny carried me four miles in the rural area where I had worked as a timekeeper and sharecropper for eighteen years. I was met there by my children, who told me the plantation owner was angry because I had gone down to try to register. After they told me, my husband came, and said the plantation owner was raising cane because I had tried to register, and before he quit talking the plantation owner came, and said, "Fannie Lou, do you know—did Pap tell you what I said?"

I said, "Yes, sir."

He said, "I mean that," he said. "If you don't go down and withdraw your registration, you will have to leave," said, "Then if you go down and withdraw," he said. "You will—you might have to go because we are not ready for that in Mississippi."

And I addressed him and told him and said, "I didn't try to register for you. I tried to register for myself." I had to leave that same night.

On the 10th of September, 1962, sixteen bullets was fired into the home of Mr. and Mrs. Robert Tucker for me. That same night two girls were shot in Ruleville, Mississippi. Also Mr. Joe McDonald's house was shot in.

And in June, the 9th, 1963, I had attended a voter-registration workshop, was returning back to Mississippi. Ten of us was traveling by the Continental Trailway bus. When we got to Winona, Mississippi, which is Montgomery County, four of the people got off to use the washroom, and two of the people—to use the restaurant—two of the people wanted to use the washroom. The four people that had gone in to use the restaurant was ordered out. During this time I was on the bus. But when I looked through the window and saw they had rushed out, I got off of the bus to see what had happened, and one of the ladies said, "It was a state highway patrolman and a chief of police ordered us out."

I got back on the bus and one of the persons had used the washroom got back on the bus, too. As soon as I was seated on the bus, I saw when they began to get the four people in a highway patrolman's car. I stepped off the bus to see what was happening and somebody screamed from the car that the four workers was in and said, "Get that one there," and when I went to get in the car, when the man told me I was under arrest, he kicked me.

I was carried to the county jail, and put in the booking room. They left some of the people in the booking room and began to place us in cells. I was placed in a cell with a young woman called Miss Euvester Simpson. After I was placed in the cell I began to hear sounds of licks and screams. I could hear the sounds of licks and horrible screams, and I could hear somebody say, "Can you say, yes sir, nigger? Can you say yes, sir?"

And they would say other horrible names. She would say, "Yes, I can say yes, sir."

"So say it."

She says, "I don't know you well enough."

They beat her, I don't know how long, and after a while she began to pray, and asked God to have mercy on those people.

And it wasn't too long before three white men came to my cell. One of these men was a State Highway Patrolman and he asked me where I was from, and I told him Ruleville. He said, "We are going to check this." And they left my cell and it wasn't too long before they came back. He said, "You are from Ruleville all right," and he used a curse word, and he said, "We are going to make you wish you was dead."

I was carried out of that cell into another cell where they had two Negro prisoners. The State Highway Patrolman ordered the first Negro to take the blackjack. The first Negro prisoner ordered me, by orders from the State Highway Patrolman for me, to lay down on a buck bed on my face, and I laid on my face. The first Negro began to beat, and I was beat by the first Negro until he was exhausted, and I was holding my hands behind me at that time on my left side because I suffered from polio when I was six years old. After the first Negro had beat until he was exhausted, the State Highway Patrolman ordered the second Negro to take the blackjack.

The second Negro began to beat and I began to work my feet, and the State Highway Patrolman ordered the first Negro who had beat to set on my feet to keep me from working my feet. I began to scream and one white man got up and began to beat me in my head and tell me to hush. One white man—my dress had worked up high, he walked over and pulled my dress down—and he pulled my dress back, back up.

I was in jail when Medgar Evers was murdered.

There was a slight pause. Tears were welling in her eyes, but she went on. "All of this is on account we want to register, to become first-class citizens, and if the Freedom Democratic Party is not seated now, I question America, is this America, the land of the free and the home of the brave where we have to sleep with our telephones off the hooks because our lives be threatened daily because we want to live as decent human beings, in America?

"Thank you."

Someone took off her microphone. She dabbed at her eyes, picked up her purse, and left the witness table. Some of the seasoned politicians listening were in tears.

Kay Mills, *This Little Light of Mine: The Life of Fannie Lou Hamer* (N.Y.: Dutton, 1993), pp. 119–21. See Jerry De Muth, "I'm Tired of Being Sick and Tired," *Nation*, June 1, 1964, pp. 548–51.

72

MY TRIP TO MECCA

by Malcolm X

M. S. Handler of the *New York Times* (May 8, 1964), basing his report on information in a letter written to a friend from Saudi Arabia, affirmed that Malcolm X had declared "that for the first time in his life he had felt no racial antagonism toward whites nor had he sensed any antagonism on their part against him." Handler—quoting directly—continued this reportage in this letter from Mecca, dated April 25, Malcolm X went on:

"There are Muslims of all colors and ranks here in Mecca from all parts of this earth," he wrote.

"During the past seven days of this holy pilgrimage, while undergoing the rituals of the hajj [pilgrimage], I have eaten from the same plate, drank from the same glass, slept on the same bed or rug, while praying to the same God—not only with some of this earth's most powerful kings, cabinet members, potentates, and other forms of political and religious rulers—but also with fellow-Muslims whose skin was the whitest of white, whose eyes were the bluest of blue, and whose hair was the blondest of blond—yet it was the first time in my life that I didn't see them as 'white' men. I could look into their faces and see that these didn't regard themselves as 'white.'

"Their belief in the Oneness of God (Allah) had actually removed the 'white' from their minds, which automatically changed their attitude and behavior toward people of other colors. Their belief in the Oneness of God has actually made them so different from American whites, their outer physical characteristics played no part at all in my mind during all my close associations with them. . . . I have never before witnessed such sincere hospitality and the practice of true brotherhood as I have seen and experienced during this pilgrimage here in Arabia.

"In fact, what I have seen and experienced on this pilgrimage has forced me to 'rearrange' much of my own thought-pattern, and to toss aside some of my previous conclusions. . . ."

73

"OVERWHELMING SPIRIT OF TRUE BROTHERHOOD BY PEOPLE OF ALL COLORS AND RACES"

by Malcolm X

From April 13 to May 21, 1964, Malcolm X visited Egypt, Lebanon, Saudi Arabia, Nigeria, Ghana, Morocco, and Algeria. The absence of racism in these lands made a deep impression upon him. From Saudi Arabia, one week after he left New York, he wrote in a letter:

Never have I witnessed such sincere hospitality and the overwhelming spirit of true brotherhood as is practiced by people *of all colors and races* here in this ancient holy land, the home of Abraham, Muhammad, and all the other prophets of the Holy Scriptures. For the past week I have been utterly speechless and spellbound by the graciousness I see displayed all around me by people *of all colors.*

Last night, April 19, I was blessed to visit the holy City of Mecca, and complete the "Omra" part of my pilgrimage. Allah willing, I shall leave for Mina tomorrow, April 21, and be back in Mecca to say my prayers from Mt. Arafat on Tuesday, April 22. Mina is about twenty miles from Mecca.

Last night I made my seven circuits around the Kaaba, led by a young Mutawif named Muhammad. I drank water from the well of Zem Zem, and then ran back and forth seven times between the hills of Mt. Al-Safa and Al-Marwah.

There were tens of thousands of pilgrims from all over the world. They were *of all colors,* from blue-eyed blonds to black-skinned Africans, but were all participating in the same ritual, displaying a spirit of unity and brotherhood that my experiences in America had led me to believe could never exist between the white and nonwhite.

America needs to understand Islam, because this is the one religion that erases the race problem from its society. Throughout my travels in the Muslim world, I have met, talked to, and even eaten with, people who would have been considered "white" in America, but the religion of Islam in their hearts has removed the "white" from their minds. They practice sincere and true brotherhood with other people irrespective of their color.

Before America allows herself to be destroyed by the "cancer of racism" she should become better acquainted with the religious philosophy of Islam, a religion that has already molded people of all colors into one vast family, a nation or brotherhood of Islam that leaps over all "obstacles" and stretches itself into almost all the Eastern countries of this earth.

The whites as well as the nonwhites who accept true Islam become a changed people. I have eaten from the same plate with people whose eyes were the bluest of blue, whose hair was the blondest of blond, and whose skin was *the whitest* of white—all the way from Cairo to Jedda and even in the Holy City of Mecca itself—and I felt the same sincerity in the words and deeds of these "white" Muslims that I felt among the African Muslims of Nigeria, Sudan, and Ghana.

True Islam removes racism, because people of all colors and races who accept its religious principles and bow down to the one God, Allah, also automatically accept each other as brothers and sisters, regardless of differences in complexion.

You may be shocked by these words coming from me, but I have always been a man who tries to face facts, and to accept the reality of life as new experiences and knowledge unfold it. The experiences of this pilgrimage have taught me much, and each hour here in the Holy Land opens my eyes even more. If Islam can place the spirit of true brotherhood in the hearts of the "whites" whom I have met here in the Land of the Prophets, then surely it can also remove the "cancer of racism" from the heart of the white American, and perhaps in time to save America from imminent racial disaster, the same destruction brought upon Hitler by his racism that eventually destroyed the Germans themselves....

George Breitman, ed., *Malcolm X Speaks: Selected Speeches and Statements* (N.Y.: Grove Weidenfeld, 1990), pp. 65–66.

74

"ALL MEN AS BROTHERS"

by Malcolm X

M. S. Handler continues his reportage on Malcolm in a story in the *New York Times*, October 4, 1964, headlined: "Malcolm Rejects Racist Doctrine." Extensive quotations from a letter from Mecca to an unnamed friend in New York City, dated September 22, 1964, follow:

For 12 long years I lived within the narrow-minded confines of the 'straitjacket world' created by my strong belief that Elijah Muhammad was a messenger direct from God Himself, and my faith in what I now see to be a pseudoreligious philosophy that he preaches. But as his then most faithful disciple, I represented and defended him at all levels...and in most instances, even beyond the level of intellect and reason.

I shall never rest until I have undone the harm I did to so many well-meaning, innocent Negroes who through my own evangelistic zeal now believe in him even more fanatically and more blindly than I did. If Western society had not gone to such extremes to block out the knowledge of True Islam, there would not be such a religious 'vacuum' among American Negroes today into which any religious faker can bring all forms of distorted religious concoctions and represent it to our unsuspecting people as True Islam.

I declare emphatically that I am no longer in Elijah Muhammad's 'strait jacket,' and I don't intend to replace his with one woven by someone else. I am a Muslim in the most orthodox sense; my religion is Islam as it is believed in and practiced by the Muslims here in the Holy City of Mecca.

This religion recognizes all men as brothers. It accepts all human beings as equals before God, and as equal members in the Human Family of Mankind. I totally reject Elijah Muhammad's racist philosophy, which he has labeled "Islam" only to fool and misuse gullible people, as he fooled and misused me. But I blame only myself, and no one else for the fool that I was, and the harm that my evangelic foolishness in his behalf has done to others....

We must forget politics and propaganda and approach this as a Human Problem which all of us as human beings are obligated to correct. The well-meaning whites must become less vocal and more active against racism of their fellow whites...and Negro leaders must make their own people see that with equal rights also go equal responsibilities.

Their sincere submission to the Oneness of God, and their true acceptance of all nonwhites as equals makes the so-called "whites" also acceptable as equals into the brotherhood of Islam with the "nonwhites." Color ceases to be a determining factor of a man's worth or value once he becomes a Muslim. I hope I am making this part very clear, because it is now very clear to me.

If white Americans would accept the religion of Islam, if they would accept the Oneness of God (Allah), then they could also sincerely accept the Oneness of Man, and they would cease to measure others always in terms of their "differences in color"....

The American Negro should never be blamed for racial "animosities," because his are only reactions, or defense mechanisms which his subconscious intelligence has forced him to erect against the conscious racism practiced...by American whites.

But as America's insane obsession with racism leads her up the suicidal path, nearer and nearer to the precipice that leads to the bottomless pits below, I do believe that whites of the younger generation, in the colleges and universities, through their own young, less hampered intellect, will see the "handwriting on the wall" and turn for spiritual salvation to the religion of Islam and force the older generation of American whites to turn with them.

75

THE BATTLE OF SAN FRANCISCO

by John Pittman

The civil rights movement, while naturally centered in the South, was by no means confined there. A thorough examination of one northern struggle was written by a longtime resident of San Francisco who was one of the editors of the *People's World.*

On April 21, 1964, an organization called PACT (Plan of Action for Challenging Times) published a study of Negro employment conditions in the San Francisco-Oakland area. The study found that the San Francisco business community was below the statewide average in placing Negroes in responsible positions. Negroes were at the bottom of the statistics of professional, sales and managerial jobs. Only seven percent of employed Negroes were in higher paying jobs. There were only nine hundred Negro businessmen in the entire Bay Area, whereas if the percentage employed in business were the same as that of whites there would be six thousand Negroes in business.

In March,...the San Francisco Labor Council disclosed its findings concerning the city's poor. It discovered that forty-one percent of San

Francisco's population were living in conditions defined by Federal authorities as those of poverty and deprivation. Needless to say, included in this forty-one percent were the majority of San Francisco Negroes.

It was this economic aspect of Jim Crow which was most distinctive in San Francisco, and this is what most distressed the Negro community. The Jim Crow structure rested not on law, as in the South, but on the more subtle base of economic exploitation. No laws or other restrictions deprived Negroes of their right to vote or be elected to public office, to eat and sleep and be served in places of public accommodation, to live wherever they desired and to send their children to school with white children. The reality is, such laws would have been superfluous; the same ends were attained by confining Negroes in an economic straitjacket.

So it happened that Jim Crow grew insidiously and without the usual legalistic skullduggery that attended its institutionalization in the South. Poverty proved as cunning a thief of civil rights as the post-Reconstruction legislation of Atlanta and Birmingham. And when the 1960s ushered in a period of stock taking, San Francisco Negroes found themselves living in ghetto sections of the city, sending their children to predominantly all-Negro schools, barred from places of public accommodation by the highest prices in America, and almost entirely deprived of representation in the administration of city affairs.

This, then, is part of the background of why San Francisco became, as it seemed to the *Chronicle*, "the Western outpost of the Negro civil rights revolution." It is only a part of the background, for there is another side of the picture. Yet the thoughtful reader may marvel, in the light of this part, not that the Battle of San Francisco erupted when it did, but that it did not break out sooner and culminate in tragedy.

As the civil rights struggle developed, it became apparent that another part of San Francisco's background was making itself felt. It was this that produced the new things that emerged.

In the assaults on the various bastions of Jim Crow—the Sheraton-Palace Hotel, Cadillac Agency, Macy's, Bank of America, etc.—Negroes were certainly influenced by the same motivations that produced the sit-ins and Freedom Rides in the South. The bitter reality of deteriorating economic and social conditions generated bitter ideas. There was disillusionment with the promise of American democracy and skepticism as to its eventual realization. There was disbelief in the good faith of the white leaders of business and government. There was disgust and resentment at the failure of the craft unions to live up to their pretensions of equality and fraternity. There was disrespect for the law and legalism as a means of effecting needed social changes, and a disdain of the older Negro leaders and leadership organization that seemed resigned to gradualism and token gains for middle-class Negroes. And there was the sense of lagging behind the masses of other countries who, equally if not more deprived, were creating a better life for themselves through militant struggle. But besides the bitterness, there was inspiration. What the heroic Negro youth were doing in the South, in conditions of racist terrorism and police violence, set an example for the entire country.

Every serious popular movement, it is said, produces its spokesmen and champions. In this respect, the San Francisco Negro community was singularly fortunate. It produced a crop of new leaders of exceptional ability, courage, and dedication, three of whom, as it turned out, became the main targets of the Establishment's reprisals.

Yet, San Francisco was not unique in the possession of these two ingredients of effective mass action. Is there a Negro community anywhere in the United States without grievances and anger? And were not the 2,062 civil rights demonstrations which the Justice Department in 1963 counted in 315 cities of forty states abundant evidence of able leaders among the country's twenty million Negroes? It was another ingredient that gave the Battle of San Francisco its distinctive character and produced a tremor in the city's financial-political hierarchy. This was the readiness of a section of the white community to go to jail, if necessary, in the fight for equal opportunities for Negroes.

The spectacle of large numbers of white men and women on the picket lines and in the sit-ins and shop-ins was not one to instill glee in the city's ruling powers. "Commies," "beatniks," "crackpots"—these were some of the epithets that assailed the demonstrators' ears. Even one or two of the former Negro leaders, instead of rejoicing that whites should identify their own interest with those of Negroes, grumbled at the predominance of whites in the demonstrations. The employers' spokesmen, striking the pose of champions of "law and order," intoned about the absence of "responsible leadership," a thinly-veiled bid to the old pliable Negro leaders to challenge the new leaders. And since no civil rights demonstration can occur anywhere in the United States without being attributed to the Communists, so the several skirmishes in the Battle of San Francisco were said by Hearst's editors and other herring hucksters to have been conceived, plotted, and, of course, "ordered" by the Kremlin.

What further jolted the Establishment was the failure of these strategems. Negro leaders who wilted under the pressure and expressed agreement with the employers' viewpoint were cried down by the demonstrators. The leaders of the active participants rejected attempts to set them at loggerheads with the old leaders. Red-baiting was spotted for what it was and denounced. The police came and the paddy-wagon rolled. But one by one, the bastions of Jim Crow capitulated.

The catalogue of victories already won is impressive. To the actual agreements won in negotiations backed by the demonstrations must be added a number of gains secured by San Francisco Negroes which would have been highly improbable without the show of organized Negro-white militancy.

Not only the Sheraton-Palace management, but the Hotel Employers' Association of San Francisco signed an agreement to hire workers without reference to race or color.

Not only the Cadillac Agency, but the Motor Car Dealers Association members pledged that they would "undertake to increase the percentage of minority-group persons employed," and to set up training programs to help such persons qualify for jobs.

Twenty-nine stores in the suburban San Mateo area signed an agreement promising equal treatment in hiring and promotion to minority workers.

Lucky Stores, Safeway Stores, Macy's, J.C. Penney, thirty department stores, and 317 stores in the food industry, signed agreements.

The powerful Bank of America, biggest bank in the world, blustered and growled—but hurried to change its policies and hire minorities.

The San Francisco United Freedom Movement and its affiliates—NAACP, CORE, Urban League, Ad Hoc Committee Against Discrimination—have not yet made a complete tabulation of the jobs won for minority workers in the Battle to date. But the visible signs of progress have increased daily. In July it was learned that since the Sheraton-Palace sit-in more than two thousand jobs had been filled in the city's hotel industry by nonwhite workers, 947 by Negroes. That would mean that in this industry alone, a livelihood has been given to several thousand of the city's population. By September the visitor to San Francisco, birthplace of the United Nations Organization, could observe Negroes, Orientals, and Hispano-Americans at work in most of the city's department stores and supermarkets.

Besides the gain in jobs, the Establishment has deemed it wise to pay some attention to the Negro community's demand for a share in the administration of city affairs. Since the Sheraton-Palace demonstration, Negroes have been appointed to the Board of Supervisors, a "War on Poverty" Committee, a Human Rights Committee, and the inspectors groups in the police department. On September 11 the Chamber of Commerce sponsored a day-long conference of San Francisco businessmen on the provision of equal employment opportunity, as sound an indication as any of the impact of the civil rights demonstrations.

But although the main pillars of Jim Crow have been shaken, none of the new leaders of the civil rights movement have any illusions that they are anywhere near collapse. The Establishment showed its teeth in the midst of the demonstrations. Four hundred and four of the arrested demonstrators were bound over for trial on charges of trespassing, disturbing the peace, unlawful assembly, and refusal to disperse. On August 5 the trials ended after the conviction and sentencing of 202. The severest sentences, and the sharpest tongue-lashings from the judges, were meted out to three of the new Negro leaders—NAACP president Dr. Thomas Nathaniel Burbridge, CORE leader William Bradley, and Ad Hoc Committee leader Tracy Sims. The convictions and sentences will be fought through higher courts, of course, but the trials and their implications inflicted severe hardship on the demonstrators.

Besides, one of the main pillars of Jim Crow has now been reinforced. Notwithstanding their overwhelming repudiation of Goldwater's right-wing program, and despite their cosmopolitan make-up and traditions, a majority of San Francisco voters on November 3 joined similar majorities throughout California to adopt an initiative measure (4,147,837 for; 2,133,134 against) which cannot but adversely affect the freedom struggle.

Adoption of the initiative measure, "Proposition 14," amends the state constitution to bar governmental action curbing racial and national discrimination in the sale, lease, or rental of real property. Thus, it wipes off the books fair housing laws adopted earlier after their introduction by two Negro legislators—former Assemblyman Augustus Hawkins, now a Congressman, and Assemblyman Byron Rumford.

Backed by the state's most powerful vested landlord interests, the new amendment encourages bigots and unscrupulous real estate operators who have played no small role in the perpetuation of ghettos and slums. It may stimulate the growth of "gentlemen's agreements" and other conspiratorial arrangements among bigoted property owners and developers to restrict sales and rentals to "Caucasians only," despite court decisions outlawing restrictive covenants. For the law's delays are costly as well as notorious, and the expense and time required to test such secret understandings are strong deterrents to efforts to escape from the ghetto. Further, the new amendment is expected to inspire the racists of other states—as the Rev. Martin Luther King, Jr. and others remarked on the eve of the election—who are striving to buttress the socio-economic bases of racial and national inequality. For the ghettos of sub-standard housing, segregated schools, inflated rents and prices, and generally neglected and inferior public facilities to which the amended California construction now condemns Negroes, Chinese, Japanese, Filipinos, and Mexican minorities are a major obstacle to integration and the realization of de facto equality.

In some circles it is fashionable to depict these ghettos as "picturesque," and travel magazine writers have said they add to the "glamor" of America's most beautiful city. The ghetto inhabitants, however, are less romantic. "If you scratch the surface of Chinatown, it is a slum," Chinese-American banker J. K. Choy told the City Planning Commission on October 22, and restauranteur George Chow added: "I was born in a Chinatown tenement. I have a very personal acquaintance with rats and roaches."

The election results on this measure, therefore, give additional proof that the old ways die hard, and that racism and Jim Crow will not be driven from the field of battle without a sustained, protracted struggle. Indeed, during the height of the election campaign, far right and terrorist racist cliques were emboldened, both the Ku Klux Klan and the White Citizens Councils attempting recruiting drives in the San Francisco area. Much vicious racist propaganda was distributed, most of it "sugar-coated" with anti-Communism.

Yet, among Freedom Fighters are many who think the old racist legacy of this metropolis will be routed by the new. This is also the city of the General Strike of 1934, which imposed on the entire population a climate of liberalism that has not yet evaporated. Some of the trade unions still balk at lowering bars to minority craftsmen, but the legacy of labor's struggles was manifest in the multiracial composition of the sit-ins and shop-ins. If the new housing amendment was approved by 159,314 San Franciscans, suggesting that a majority of the citizens gave precedence to property rights over human rights, it is not insignificant that 134,611 San Franciscans indicated by their vote against the measure a more conscious commitment on racial issues. Besides, San Francisco elected another

Negro to the State Assembly and adopted a low-rent public housing construction measure which will benefit mainly the poor of minority groups.

Such developments sustain the spirit of the Freedom Fighters. They are signs of the sweeping, drastic changes on the American political horizon. For if a considerable number of this city's white people have already come to realize that the condition of equality of opportunity for whites is the equality of opportunity for non-whites, how much larger will this number become as the course of technological and economic development, of automation and unemployment, increasingly compels common action to satisfy common needs!

What is more, the Establishment launched a counteroffensive. Its real estate section has joined other realty interests in the state to invalidate a state law banning racial discrimination in the sale, renting, and leasing of housing. One effect of such an initiative, as adopted by the electorate in the November 3rd election, was to sanction the malpractices of real estate interests which have contributed so much to the development of ghettos.

Although San Francisco is not a stronghold of the Far Right, the John Birchers are active. The old dies hard, and Jim Crow will not be driven from the field of battle without a sustained struggle. But the struggles of the recent past showed that an influential number of this city's population have come to realize that the condition of equality of opportunity for whites is equality of opportunity for nonwhites.

Freedomways, 4 (Fall, 1964): 489–502; published in part. For a study of the black movement in San Francisco prior to the 1954 Supreme Court decision, see Albert S. Broussard, *Black San Francisco: The Struggle for Racial Equality in the West, 1900–1954* (Lawrence: University of Kansas Press, 1992).

76

DEFENDING THE FLAG IN GHANA

by Adger E. Player

An anti-U.S. demonstration in Ghana imperiled the flag before the U.S. embassy. An African-American soldier, defending the embassy, personally saw to it that no affront was offered the flag. This evoked the expected demagogy from the mainstream media in the United States.

The result was a letter written by the soldier Adger Emerson Player from the embassy in Accra, dated February 19, 1964, to Rep. Augustus F. Hawkins (D.) of

California. Congressman Hawkins published Player's letter, with his own commentary in the *Congressional Record:*

Mr. Speaker, I am pleased to insert into the *Congressional Record* a remarkable statement on the real meaning of patriotism as viewed by one American citizen whose valor we commend but the significance of which many will misinterpret.

On February 4, 1964, Mr. Adger Emerson Player, in a strife-torn situation at the American Embassy in Ghana, at great peril to himself and with much personal humiliation, prevented our American flag from being desecrated in an anti-American demonstration.

Normally, and perhaps with much personal gain, another but dissimilar person might have accepted and profited from such commendation as Mr. Player received merely by remaining silent.

This, Mr. Player did not do, as the following letter so dramatically indicates.

Webster defines patriotism in terms of love and devotion for one's country. Obviously we need not fear that where such patriotism prevails defense of our flag is safe.

But love and devotion are not abstract terms to be commended and then dismissed; they are interwoven into the practical and meaningful everyday activity of our national life: a father's interest in making a living for his family, a mother's concern as she looks into a baby's eyes and wonders about its future, a young boy or girl who seeks fulfillment after having been told ours is a land of equal opportunity—and people everywhere across this great country of ours who yearn for the practical realization of freedom, justice, security, and human dignity. These, indeed, are the qualities that insure real love and devotion for one's country.

I am confident that in our affluent American society such patriotism that flows through the veins of Adger Player and twenty million other Negro Americans will survive in spite of police dogs, fire hoses, and merciless bombings.

But let us not mistake on whose side the vitality of America lies. Not with those who with false symbols and bigotry spread hate, deny simple constitutional rights to others, and insult the inherent dignity of the individual. Rather, our strength lies on the side of those who with nonviolence and passionate devotion to our country's most noble purposes have set out to prove ours is a God of love, and brotherhood is achievable in our lifetime here in our motherland.

It is up to us in Congress where a civil rights program is pending to make sure that the American flag in Ghana was not again raised in vain, but in deeds as in symbol flies majestically over us all.

Mr. Player's letter follows:

February 19, 1964

Dear Sir: I have been the subject of much publicity since February 4, 1964. Although unaware of all the various interpretations of my action of raising the American Flag in Ghana, I am concerned that some quarters in the United States and abroad—not fully in sympathy with the aspirations of the American Negro—may be interpreting that action in a way detrimental to the increasingly vigorous struggle that we American Negroes are now waging for full equality of opportunity in the American society.

President Johnson wrote that I "have the gratitude of freemen everywhere who respect the principles and ideals for which our flag stands." The American dilemma is still the contradiction of racial bondage, injustice, and inequality as practiced by some Americans with the American principles of liberty, justice, and equality. I would like to set the record straight regarding what I consider the true meaning of my action.

My action was something that any American—black or white—would have done. However, my raising of the flag decreases in real significance when compared with the real acts of heroism and sacrifice by countless American Negroes who since August 1619 and continuing through today have lost their lives because they asserted their God-given rights as human beings and as Americans. I did only what American Negroes have been doing from the very beginning of the history of the United States—loyally defending the country that our ancestors made along with other Americans of all origins and races. This is our country in every respect. We have a perfect right to defend it. In addition, we must honor those Negro Americans of yesterday who sowed American and foreign soil with their lives so that generations of today and tomorrow may reap the rewards, benefits, duties, and responsibilities of free men and women. These—our ancestors—were real heroes and courageous American Negroes whose names have been hidden in America's history far too long.

I feel most Americans still have to experience that as Negroes and whites interact in work and pleasure, they discover that they have the same cultural and historical foundations and the same aspirations and ambitions for themselves and for their country. I feel most Americans still have to realize that Negro Americans are determined to obtain full equality of opportunity in every facet of life in the United States.

White Americans must allow the American dream of equality, freedom, and justice to live in their hearts and to be reflected in their everyday actions toward their black brothers. It will never be enough to pass civil rights laws and to speak in glowing terms about the patriotic deed of one American Negro. White Americans must demonstrate as much love for their black fellow Americans as they do for the red, white, and blue American flag. Yes, we—American Negroes—are loyal to the United States. This proven loyalty in no way diminished our firm resolve to be accepted as Americans in the fullest extent. We will share in the privileges, rights, and responsibilities as completely free American men and women.

I hope that all the words of praise for my deed in raising the American flag in Ghana will be translated now in the United States into respect and full acceptance of American Negroes. If this full respect and acceptance does not take place, then one must draw the sad conclusion—as many American Negroes and other people throughout the world will—that the American flag was raised once again in vain.

Congressional Record, March 3, 1964, appendix, 1040–41.

77

THE CHURCHES WILL FOLLOW

by Benjamin E. Mays

The president of Morehouse College in Atlanta expressed the optimism that largely prevailed even in the mid-1960s despite the noncompliance and violence that characterized the period.

The churches will follow the rest of society, and finally become desegregated. In using the term "follow" I do not mean to indict those world and national religious bodies that have practiced true Christian fellowship over a long span of years. Nor do I mean to say that *all* local churches are mere followers; for a long time many churches in the North and a few in the South have accepted all Christians irrespective of color or race.

I do mean to say, however, that on the local level the majority of our churches will practice open membership only when it is considered "safe" to do so. The leadership necessary for successful desegregation of communities has seldom come from white ministers and their congregations, and it is hardly likely to come from them in the future. In the main that leadership will come from men and women who represent other organizations, even though they may incidentally be members of churches.

Inevitably, When It Is 'Safe'

What's ahead for the churches? Open membership! But in most churches achievement of that goal will be a slow, agonizing process. Moves toward desegregation will be timid: the officers will be afraid, the minister will be cautious. But a desegregated church is inevitable because in time all other agencies in the community will have been desegregated or will be in the process of becoming so. And the church will have to follow in order to save face, to catch up with the procession....

Yes, I know: After a long time, here and there ministers *did* speak out. But their words were very carefully chosen so as not to attack the *institution* of segregation. How could they? Their own churches were tightly segregated; they could call only for communication between the races, for maintenance of the public schools, for obedience to law and the findings of the courts. In local communities ministers either were conspicuous by their silence on the implications of the court's decision, or spoke in terms of "moderation." They were afraid.

If the local churches had followed the Supreme Court, had moved in at once to support the 1954 decision on the basis of religion and morals, it could be that the turmoil and bitterness through which the nation has passed during the past ten years—and is still passing—would have been avoided, or at least greatly reduced. We might not have had Little Rock, Oxford, New Orleans. Even the sit-ins might have been unnecessary. Perhaps dishonest politicians would have been deprived of the chance to deceive the people into believing that the decision did not have to be obeyed. The southern states might not have been led to pass 379 bills in efforts to avoid compliance or to ensure that the decision was implemented at no more than a snail's pace. The December 1962 issue of *Southern School News* pointed out that nine years after the decision only four-tenths of one per cent of the Negro pupils in the deep South were attending schools with white children. At that rate it will take more than two thousand years before all the schools in that area are desegregated. It is particularly at this point—noncompliance—that the local churches have abdicated their moral leadership.

Be all this as it may, the local churches *will* follow, *will* desegregate. Whatever the reasons, segregation is now a sick old man, waiting for death to take him away so the people, Negro and white, can be free, so the ministers of Christ can be free to proclaim God's word, to expound and practice the fatherhood of God and the brotherhood of man—unafraid.

The churches will follow. Sports are widely integrated, restaurants are beginning to serve all comers, segregation on trains and buses is becoming a thing of the past, hotels in the North have opened their doors to any and all guests, several in the South—in Miami Beach, Louisville, Memphis, Dallas, Houston—are following suit, setting the pace for others. However slowly, schools, theaters, and golf courses are being desegregated, parks, and swimming pools are beginning to serve all the people, Negroes are increasingly finding it possible to exercise their right to vote.

The process of desegregation will continue; it cannot be stopped. So the churches will have no choice; they will follow. Powerful laymen, supporting their minister in his desire to live as well as preach the gospel, will free his hands. The guilt that besets the minister's conscience because he preaches what he cannot practice will be washed away, and there will be peace in his soul.

So None Need Be Afraid

What then? Within his heart every church member will feel better, for his conscience will no longer trouble him. Negroes will worship in and join white churches. White people will worship in and join Negro churches. How many? It doesn't matter! God's people will be free to worship God anywhere they choose. In the South it will become common for a Negro minister to be invited to preach to white Christians, just as it has been common through the years for white ministers to be invited to preach to Negroes. In an expansion of a situation that even now prevails in a few places, co-pastors, one Negro and one white, will serve one congregation—even in the South. White ministers will be called to serve predominantly Negro congregations, Negro ministers to serve white congregations—a practice that is followed in some cases today and will become increasingly the case after the false god segregation is dead.

In that day Negro and white Christians will worship together, sing together, pray together, share each other's joys and sorrows. And none shall be afraid. They will sing: "Walk together, children; don't get weary/ There is a great camp meeting in the promised land." We will then know that our greatest fears are fears of things that never happen. And God will bless us.

Christian Century, April 22, 1964, pp. 513–14; published in part.

78

ON BLACK NATIONALISM

by Malcolm X

In a phonograph record released after his death, in February 1965 but made in March or April 1964, Malcolm X stated his influential views as of that date. In the ensuing months he moved closer to a concept of unity of all deprived and oppressed peoples; his emphasis remained upon the need for worldwide unity of African-derived peoples.

The economic philosophy of black nationalism only means that our people need to be re-educated into the importance of controlling the economy of our community, controlling the economy of the community in which we live. And controlling the economy of the community in which we live means that we have to learn how to own and operate the businesses of our community and develop them into some type of industry that will enable us to create employment for the people of our community so that they won't have to constantly be involved in picketing and boycotting other people in other communities in order to get a job.

Also, in line with this economic philosophy of black nationalism, in order for us to control the economy of our own community, we have to learn the importance of spending our money in the community where we live. Anyone who knows the basic principles of economics must be aware of the fact that when you take the money out of the neighborhood in which you live and spend it in an integrated neighborhood—or rather, in your effort to integrate, you spend it in a neighborhood in which you don't live—the neighborhood in which you spend your money becomes wealthier and wealthier, and the neighborhood out of which you take your money becomes poorer and poorer. And this is one of the reasons why wherever you find Negroes, a slum condition usually develops, or we have to live in the ghetto—because all our wealth is spent elsewhere.

And even when we try to spend the money in the neighborhood where we live, usually, because we haven't learned the importance of owning and operating businesses, the businesses of our community are usually also controlled by outsiders, the stores are controlled by people who don't even live in our community. So even when we try and spend our money in the neighborhood where we live, we're spending it with someone who puts it in a basket and takes it out as soon as the sun goes down.

So the economic philosophy of black nationalism puts the burden upon the black man of learning how to control his own economy. . . .

Just as it took nationalism to bring about the independence of our brothers and sisters in Africa and Asia, the goal or the objective of the political, social, and economic philosophy of black nationalism is designed to bring about the complete independence of the black people in this country by making us become consciously involved in controlling our own community. Once we can control our own communities now, then perhaps we will later be able to control our own country, control our own nation, and govern ourselves and in some way have control over our own destiny. . . . This philosophy in itself will bring about the independent thinking of the black people in this country, and eventually lead to the complete physical independence of the black people in this country.

George Breitman, *The Last Year of Malcolm X: The Evolution of a Revolutionary,* (New York: Schocken Books, 1968), pp. 88–89. See Michael E. Dyson, "Malcolm X and the Revival of Black Nationalism," in *Tikkun,* March–April, 1993, pp. 45–48.

79

"A TEMPORARY CHANGE OF EMPHASIS"

by Roy Wilkins, Martin Luther King, Jr., Whitney M. Young, Jr., and A. Philip Randolph

The signing, on July 2, of the Civil Rights Act of 1964, the impending election campaign with Sen. Barry Goldwater the nominee of the Republican party, and the massive and militant demonstrations—often involving violence—by black communities in several cities, were decisive in explaining a meeting of national African-American leaders in New York City later in July.

The four signers of one of two public statements from that meeting were the chief officers of the NAACP, the Southern Christian Leadership Conference, the National Urban League, and the Negro American Labor Council. The text of this first statement, in its entirety, as well as the second statement follow. These were printed in the *New York Times* on July 30, 1964.

First Statement

We believe that developments since July 2, the date President Johnson signed the Civil Rights Act of 1964, warrant analysis by the organized civil rights groups and by all thoughtful unaffiliated civil rights advocates.

We call upon our members and supporters to utilize the months ahead to enlist voters, to expand the enforcement of the new Civil Rights Act, and to win new friends and new supporters for the civil rights cause, which is not alone our cause but the cause of America. Without the freedoms inherent in this cause, neither we nor our country will be free.

Our own estimate of the present situation is that it presents such a serious threat to the implementation of the Civil Rights Act and to subsequent expansion of civil rights gains that we recommend a voluntary, temporary alteration in strategy and procedure.

Change in Strategy

Now we propose a temporary change of emphasis and tactic, because we sincerely believe that the major energy of the civil rights forces should be used to encourage the Negro people, North and South, to register and to vote. The greatest need in this period is for political action.

We, therefore, propose and call upon our members voluntarily to observe a broad curtailment, if not total moratorium, of all mass marches, mass picketing, and mass demonstrations until after Election Day next November 3.

Such a move is not without precedent, since each of our organizations at one time or another, in one local struggle or another, has voluntarily agreed to call off demonstrations for varying periods of time in order to make progress toward a goal.

In our view the election contest which is shaping up is a more imperative reason for a moratorium on demonstrations than any local or state condition that has confronted our forces heretofore.

Goldwater 'Threat' Seen

We see the whole climate of liberal democracy in the United States, the climate in which government has been brought properly into the service and protection of the people, threatened.

The platform adopted under the Goldwater forces at the Republican Convention in San Francisco is a states' rights platform, chosen at the very time Mississippi was exhibiting to a shocked nation the callous repression, the violence and death which mark the operation of the states' rights theory in the human rights field.

The proponents of liberalizing the civil rights plank of the platform to include specific mention of the obligation of the Federal Government were hooted down.

The platform, as adopted, called for "maximum restraint" of Federal "intrusions into matters more productively left to the individual."

We believe racism has been injected into the campaign by the Goldwater forces. The Senator himself maintains his position that civil rights matters should be left to the states—clear enough language for any Negro American.

Second Statement

We wish to register our serious concern with the recent riots which have taken place in several urban areas. We would like to once again go on record as strongly opposing looting, vandalism, or any type of criminal activities, and urge the cooperation and support of local leaders toward the elimination of this type of activity, which damages both the community and the civil rights movement.

On the other hand we wish to draw a sharp distinction between the above-named activity and legitimate protest effort by denied and desperate citizens seeking relief.

In meeting these situations we call for more socially sensitive police action, for machinery for continuing communication and local civilian review.

We suggest that leadership must seek in these situations justice and equality as well as law and order. Responsible Negro leadership needs desperately responsive white leadership, as it relates to jobs, improved housing, and educational opportunities.

The established civil rights organization has by word, deed, and constitution consistently rejected the participation of extremist groups, such as Communists.

The second statement was signed by the above four persons plus James Farmer, national director of the Congress of Racial Equality (CORE). It was not signed by John Lewis, chairman of the Student Nonviolent Coordinating Committee (SNCC); this failure was explained in this way: "It is not the policy of SNCC to publicly discuss situations in individual Negro communities."

80

"WHAT DO THEY WANT?"

by Langston Hughes

One of the many uprisings of the 1960s shook Harlem in July 1964. Langston Hughes offered one of his inimitable comments on the "problem."

Opinion in Harlem is divided as to whether or not riots do any good. Some say *yes,* they achieve concrete results in community improvements. Others say *no,* they set the Negro race back fifty years. Those who disagree say, in effect, "But Negroes are always being set back fifty years by something or another, so what difference does a riot make?"

Old-timers who remember former riots in Harlem say, "White folks respect us more when they find out we mean business. When they only listen to our speeches or read our writing—if they ever do—they think we are just blowing off steam. But when rioters smash the plate glass windows of their stores, they know the steam has some force behind it. Then they say, 'Those Negroes are mad! What do they want?' And for a little while they will try to give you a little of what you want.

"After every riot in Harlem, the whites respect you more. After that big riot in 1935, the white-owned shops all along 125th Street that would not hire Negro clerks, began to hire at least one. We got a great many jobs out of that riot that we couldn't get before in our own community because the clerks, cashiers, and everything were all white."

The big riot in 1943, which grew out of a white policeman shooting a black soldier at 126th Street and 8th Avenue during a period of much police brutality in the area, produced remarkable changes in police attitudes in Harlem, and resulted in a number of additional Negro officers being added to the force.

Chocolate and vanilla teams of policemen appeared on uptown streets walking together. Squad cars became integrated. And a white policeman would often grant his Negro colleague the courtesy of making the arrest, if an arrest had to be made. And for a long time, after the '43 riots, seldom did Negro or white cops beat a culprit's head in public—as they frequently did before the riots. . . .

After the 1943 riots, one night on Lenox Avenue, I saw two white policemen attempting to push a young Negro into a squad car. The man refused to get in. Each time the police tried to force him, he would spread out his arms and legs or twist his body so that they could not get him through the door. With a crowd of Negroes all around, the white cops seemingly did not dare hit the Negro. But, to their fortune a colored policeman on foot arrived. He simply said, "Get in that car, fellow!" The Negro got in, and the car sped away with its prisoner.

Folks in the crowd said, "You see—since the riots, they sure do arrest you politely. Now his head won't be cracked, till they get him down to the precinct house." The riots of 1943 almost ended *public* police brutality on the streets of Harlem.

Out of our 1964 riot this week I do not know what concrete results will come but certainly its repercussions have already reached into high places. No less an authority than President Johnson has spoken from the capital saying grandiloquently, "Violence and lawlessness cannot, must not, and will not be tolerated." Some Harlemites interpret this to mean that there will be no more head-bustings on the part of the police, or shooting of adolescents, black, white, or Puerto Rican by men representing New York's Finest. "American citizens have a right to protection of life and limb," continued the President, "whether driving along a highway in Georgia, a road in Mississippi, or a street in New York City."

. . . Negroes have been asking for years that Georgia and Mississippi be made safe—and getting no results from federal or state governments. But now, after a weekend of rioting in Harlem, you see what the President says! The riots have already produced one good result. . . .

New York Post, July 23, 1964, p. 29. In William L. Katz, ed., *Eyewitness: The Negro in American History* (New York: Pitman Publishers, 1967), pp. 509–11.

81

"I AM SICK AND TIRED"

by Dave Dennis

The assistant director for the Mississippi Summer Project spoke for COFO (Council of Federated Organizations) in Laurel, Mississippi, on August 11, 1964, at the funeral of James Chaney (along with Michael Schwerner and Andrew Goodman, a martyr in the struggle):

I am not here to memorialize James Chaney, I am not here to pay tribute— I am too sick and tired. Do YOU hear me, I am S-I-C-K and T-I-R-E-D. I have attended too many memorials, too many funerals. This has got to stop. Mack Parker, Medgar Evers, Herbert Lee, Lewis Allen, Emmett Till, four little girls in Birmingham, a thirteen-year old boy in Birmingham, and the list goes on and on. I have attended these funerals and memorials and I am SICK and TIRED. But the trouble is that YOU are NOT sick and tired and for that reason YOU, yes YOU, are to blame, Everyone of your damn souls. And if you are going to let this continue now then you are to blame, yes YOU. Just as much as the monsters of hate who pulled the trigger or brought down the club; just as much to blame as the sheriff and the chief of police, as the governor in Jackson who said that he "did not have time" for Mrs. Schwerner when she went to see him, and just as much to blame as the President and Attorney General in Washington who wouldn't provide protection for Chaney, Goodman, and Schwerner when we told them that protection was necessary in Neshoba County . . . Yes, I am angry, I AM. And it's high time that you got angry too, angry enough to go up to the courthouse Monday and register—every one of you. Angry enough to take five and ten other people with you. Then and only then can these brutal killings be stopped. Remember it is your sons and your daughters who have been killed all these years and you have done nothing about it, and if you don't do nothing NOW baby, I say God Damn Your Souls. . . .

Elizabeth Sutherland, *op. cit.,* p. 191.

82

"THERE'S GOT TO BE A CHANGE"

by Fannie Lou Hamer

The day before the credential committee voted to defeat the effort of the Mississippi Freedom Democratic party (MFDP) to challenge the delegates from the Jim Crow official Democratic party, Nan Robertson of the *New York Times* (August 24, 1964, p. 12) reported her conversation with Fannie Lou Hamer:

Why should I leave Ruleville and why should I leave Mississippi? I go to the big city and with the kind of education they give us in Mississippi I got problems. I'd wind up in a soup line there. That's why I want to change things in Mississippi. You don't run away from problems—you just face them.

[Speaking of the delegates of the regular Democratic party she said:]

Maybe plenty people could hate them. I feel sorry for anybody that could let hate wrap them up. Hate will not only destroy us. It will destroy them.

Is this America? Do you think I came here to compromise and sit in a back seat at the convention? People from all the states are watching us now.

I'm not proud of being black more than being white. I'm proud of being black because of my heritage. The Negroes are the only race in America that had babies sold from their breasts and mothers sold from their families.

One day I know the struggle will change. There's got to be a change—not only for Mississippi, not only for the people in the United States, but people all over the world.

83

THE MISSISSIPPI FREEDOM DEMOCRATIC PARTY AND THE 1964 CONVENTION

by Charles M. Sherrod

Following with care the procedures of the Democratic party in Mississippi, sixty-eight delegates were elected by the Mississippi Freedom Democratic party (MFDP), to attend its National Convention, held in Atlantic City, New Jersey in

August. They failed in an effort to be recognized by the Convention as official delegates.

The story of this struggle is told by Charles Sherrod, one of the original members of SNCC and a leader in its efforts throughout the years of the embattled 1960s; he was one of the sixty-eight challenging the Democratic party.

It was a cool day in August beside the ocean. Atlantic City, New Jersey, was waiting for the Democratic National Convention to begin. In that Republican fortress history was about to be made. High on a billboard smiling out at the breakers was a picture of Barry Goldwater and an inscription "In your heart you know he's right." Later someone had written underneath, "Yes, extreme right." Goldwater had had his "moment," two weeks before on the other ocean. This was to be L.B.J.'s "moment," and we were to find out that this was also his convention...

No one could say that we were a renegade group. We had tried to work within the structure of the state Party. In fact, we were not only trying to be included in the state Party, but we also sought to insure that the state Party would remain loyal to the candidates of the National Democratic Party in November. . . .

No one could say that we had not tried. We had no alternative but to form a State Party that would include everyone.

So sixty-eight [Freedom Democratic Party] delegates from Mississippi—black, white, maids, ministers, carpenters, farmers, painters, mechanics, schoolteachers, the young, the old—they were ordinary people but each had an extraordinary story to tell. And they could tell the story! The Saturday before the convention began, they presented their case to the Credentials Committee, and through television, to the nation and to the world. No human being confronted with the truth of our testimony could remain indifferent to it. Many tears fell. Our position was valid and our cause was just.

But the word had been given. The Freedom Party was to be seated without voting rights as honored guests of the Convention. The [MFD] Party caucused and rejected the proposed "compromise." The slow and now frantic machinery of the administration was grinding against itself. President Johnson had given Senator Humphrey the specific task of dealing with us. They were desperately seeking ways to seat the regular Mississippi delegation without any show of disunity. The administration needed time!

Sunday evening, there was a somewhat secret meeting held at the Deauville Hotel, for all Negro delegates. The MFDP was not invited but was there. In a small, crowded, dark room with a long table and a blackboard, some of the most prominent Negro politicians in the country gave the "word," one by one. Then an old man seated in a soft chair struggled slowly to his feet. It was the black dean of politics, Congressman Charles Dawson of Chicago.

Unsteady in his voice, he said exactly what the other "leaders" had said: (1) We must nominate and elect Lyndon B. Johnson for President in November; (2) we must register thousands of Negroes to vote; and (3) we must follow leadership—adding, "we must respect womanhood"—and sat down.

With that a little woman, dark and strong, Mrs. Annie Devine from Canton, Mississippi, standing near the front, asked to be heard. The Congressman did not deny her. She began to speak.

"We have been treated like beasts in Mississippi. They shot us down like animals." She began to rock back and forth and her voice quivered. "We risk our lives coming up here...politics must be corrupt if it don't care none about people down there...these politicians sit in positions and forget the people put them there." She went on, crying between each sentence, but right after her witness, the meeting was adjourned.

...Here we were in a life-death grip, wrestling with the best political strategists in the country. We needed only eleven votes for a minority report from the Credentials Committee....

A compromise was suggested by [Congresswoman] Edith Green (D.-Ore.), a member of the Credentials Committee. It was acceptable to the Freedom Party and could have been the minority report: (1) Everyone would be subjected to a loyalty oath, both the Freedom Party and the Mississippi regular party; (2) Each delegate who took the oath would be seated and the votes would be divided proportionally. It was minimal; the Freedom Party would accept no less.

The administration countered with another compromise. It had five points. (1) The all-white Party would take the oath and be seated: (2) The Freedom Democratic Party would be welcomed as honored guests of the Convention; (3) Dr. Aaron Henry and Rev. Edwin King, Chairman and National Committeeman of the Freedom Democratic Party respectively, would be given delegate status in a special category of "delegates at large"; (4) The Democratic National Committee would obligate states by 1968 to select and certify delegates through a process without regard to race, creed, color, or national origin; and (5) The Chairman of the

National Democratic Committee would establish a special committee to aid the states in meeting standards set for the 1968 Convention....

The "word" had come down for the last time. We had begun to lose support in the Credentials Committee. This came mainly as a result of a squeeze play by the administration.

It was Tuesday morning when the Freedom Democratic Party delegation was hustled to its meeting place, the Union Temple Baptist Church. You could cut through the tension; it was so apparent. People were touchy and on edge. It had been a long fight; being up day and night, running after delegations, following leads, speaking, answering politely, always aggressive, always moving. Now, one of the most important decisions of the convention had to be made.

... The hot day dragged on; there were speeches and speeches and talk and talk—Dr. Martin Luther King, Bayard Rustin, Senator Wayne Morse, Edith Green, Jack Pratt, James Farmer, James Forman, Ella Baker, Bob Moses. Some wanted to accept the compromise and others did not. A few remained neutral and all voiced total support whatever the ultimate decision. But time had made the decision. The day was fast spent when discussion was opened to the delegation.

The administration had succeeded in baiting us into extended discussion and this was the end....

The [administration's] proposal was rejected by the Freedom Democratic Delegation; we had come through another crisis with our minds depressed and our hearts and hands unstained. Again we had not bowed to the "massa." We were asserting a moral declaration to this country that the political mind must be concerned with much more than the expedient; that there are real issues in this country's politics and "race" is one....

We could have accepted the compromise, called it a victory, and gone back to Mississippi, carried on the shoulders of millions of Negroes across the country as their champions. But we love the ideals of our country; they mean more than a moment of victory. We are what we are—hungry, beaten, unvictorious, jobless, homeless, but thankful to have the strength to fight. This is honesty, and we refuse to compromise here. It would have been a lie to accept that particular compromise. It would have said to blacks across the nation and the world that we share the power, and that is a lie! The "liberals" would have felt great relief for a job well done. The Democrats would have laughed again at the segregationist Republicans and smiled that their own "Negroes" were satisfied. That is a lie! We are a country of racists with a racist heritage, a racist economy, a racist language, a racist religion, a racist philosophy of living, and we need a naked confrontation with ourselves.

Clayborne Carson, et al., eds. *The Eyes on the Prize: Civil Rights Reader* (New York: Penguin Group, 1991), pp. 186–87.

84

THE SOUTHERN BLACK PRESS AND 1964 DEVELOPMENTS

by Benjamin F. Clark

Earlier pages, using Clark's 1984 dissertation, exemplified the response to the 1960 developments in southern black newspapers. The same source shows the response of such newspapers to the dramatic developments at the National Convention of the Democratic party in 1964, when the challenge for seats from representatives of the Mississippi Freedom Democratic Party captured national attention. The challenge was thwarted, but the embarrassment to the Democratic party had lasting impact. The response of the black press generally favored the antiracist effort, but this was not unanimous. The Jackson, Mississippi, *Advocate* reflected the fierce opposition in that state by those who ruled it to any advance in civil rights. But the dominant response of this press is exemplified below:

Because the Freedom Party held open elections, they claimed to be the legitimate party delegates. When the issue was debated before the Credentials Committee and on national television, Fannie Lou Hamer, a sharecropper's wife, captured national sympathy for their cause as she described how she was beaten for attempting to register. "Is this America the land of the free and the home of the brave where we are threatened daily because we want to live as decent human beings?" she asked. After the regular Mississippi delegation walked out of the convention the MFDP seized their seats and refused to leave. This incident provoked a mixed response from the black press. The *Richmond-Baltimore Afro-American* was totally on the side of the MFDP. Its editor wrote [September 5, 1964]:

There may be some question in different quarters as to whether or not the so-called regular Mississippi delegation to the 34th Democratic National Convention "walked out" or was "kicked out," but insofar as the Mississippi Freedom Democratic Party is concerned the members of the

FDP come out of the Mississippi mess ten feet tall, their heads high.

The truth is this is what the Freedom Party's complaint was about all the time. They contended, and correctly so, that the Mississippi regular delegation was an unlawful group because it had been chosen at meetings or elections which barred colored persons from participating. Notwithstanding Mississippi's almost fifty-fifty racial population, the regular delegation was lily-white and has always been lilywhite.

In the face of widespread publicity and longtime knowledge of Mississippi's suppression of the colored vote by violence, no stretch of imagination would allow any clear-thinking person to believe the regular Mississippi delegation had been selected legally.

It took courage and determination for the sixty-eight-member Freedom Party delegates, sixty-four colored and four white, to push the battle the way they did but the outcome was certainly worth the fight—All hail the Freedom Democratic Party.

The *Durham Carolinian Times* was equally as proud of the MFDP. It suggested that the testimony seen and heard on national television should certainly provoke federal action. It told readers [August 29, 1964]:

> We think the time has come for some action to be taken by the federal government to establish law and order in Mississippi and to protect the rights of its Negro citizens. For the federal government to sit idly by while one segment of the people of any state runs rough shod over the rights of others is tantamount to endorsement of such lawlessness and tyranny.
>
> What we suggest for Mississippi, we recommend for any other state of this nation in which such utter disregard for law and order exists or may arise.

The *Norfolk Journal and Guide* did not respond immediately to the confrontation between the regular Democratic delegates and the Freedom Democratic delegates. On September 5, however, it ran a syndicated column written by the noted baseball star, Jackie Robinson. In the editorial Robinson declared, "Every decent American, whatever his race, background, or shade of political conviction, owes a tremendous debt to those courageous and determined leaders of the Mississippi Freedom Democratic party who brought into the nation's living rooms the stark, naked definition of liberty." Robinson considered the situation in Mississippi to be "awful" and joined Fannie Lou Hamer in raising the question, "what kind of America is this?"

85

THE DEMOCRATIC PARTY'S BETRAYAL

by James Forman

In the 1964 convention of the Democratic party, a crucial question was seating delegates from Mississippi. Would the convention reject the delegates chosen by the Mississippi Freedom Democratic party, or would it seat the delegates from the official Mississippi Democratic party whose leaders were defying the U.S. Supreme Court and the rhetoric of Lyndon Johnson, the party which disfranchised most of the citizens of the state? A leader of SNCC describes the scene.

[Robert] Moses was singled out by the powers at Atlantic City as the person who could make the Freedom Democrats accept any compromise that the Credentials Committee worked out. But he wouldn't—he couldn't, for it was not his decision to make. The situation became critical for the traditional brokers between black people and the Democratic Party. It seemed that Walter Reuther and Roy Wilkins, the long-time supersalesmen of human stocks and bonds, no longer had control of the ticker tape. This convention wasn't going right, from their viewpoint. Three days had passed since the Credentials Committee opened its hearings on the question. It was taking too long to settle this little matter. Wilkins had told Mrs. Hamer, after her testimony, that she and the other people from Mississippi had made their point—they should go back home now and leave politicking to those who knew how to do it. That was an insult that Mrs. Hamer never forgot, but she didn't go home and neither did the others. Too bad for the brokers.

For three full days, poor, working-class people and one middle-class white preacher—Ed King, who had run as lieutenant governor with Aaron Henry in the Freedom Vote—brought the great convention to a standstill.

Meanwhile, the word had flashed through the liberal-labor circle that Lyndon Baines Johnson, the man most likely to be nominated as presidential candidate, had said, if Hubert Humphrey doesn't settle this thing, he can forget about the vice-presidential nomination. And so the squeeze was now put on, full force. Congressman Charles C. Diggs, Jr., of Michigan obtained from Moses, by using heavy pressure and distorting his intentions, the names of people on the Credentials Committee who had said they would sign their names to a minority report if the full

Credentials Committee did not vote to seat the Freedom Democrats. We do not know all the forms of the great squeeze, but we do know that a telephone call was made to one delegate from California by someone saying that her husband would lose his appointment as a federal judge if she voted for the minority position. She backed out, sorrowfully—she just couldn't go through with it. And we do know that Walter Reuther told Joseph Rauh that if there were a floor fight—another possible development, which we had real hope of seeing happen at one point—then he could forget about his job as general counsel of the UAW. We do know that Edith Green, congresswoman from Oregon, made a public statement later to the people from Mississippi that she never knew Johnson would stoop to some of the things he did.

Soon the squeeze began to be felt further down the line, closer to our own people. Bayard Rustin, considered a very good friend by Moses, Courtland Cox, and others at that time, had originally promised to help the Freedom Democrats. Now he began to work with "the greater coalition," as he saw it, and urged our people not to "wreck" the convention—we must allow Humphrey to become Vice President. Like the others, he thought that Humphrey's nomination would make it possible to bargain with the administration. The whole liberal-labor syndrome saw the possible election of Humphrey as their finest hour, the crowning glory to years of sellout, compromise, and so-called coalition. Humphrey was the shining knight of Americans for Democratic Action; he was the darling of some segments of the labor movement. No upstarts from Mississippi were going to destroy his chances. No "wild-eyed, idealistic bunch of kids" was going to say what's good for poor people in this country.

But the people of Mississippi had no faith in Humpty or Dumpty or any of those other smooth-talking jackals. They did have faith in us. They knew that none of those distinguished ladies and gentlemen had lain on the floor with them during the nights when the Klan rode by their houses firing guns. They knew that none of those fast-talking politicians had picked cotton with them to earn a meal, or lived on corn bread and grease and Kool Aid, or faced a sheriff like Jim Clark with murder in his eyes. They knew what party had sold them out before—the Democratic Party. And they knew the same party was trying to sell short their struggle again, sell short their years of waiting in lines trying to register to vote...their years of seeing neighbors shot at and many of them killed...their years of trying to make a living off the soil...their years of seeing children leave as soon as they were big enough, for the big city of Chicago, in hopes of eating a little better.

So they sat tight while the Credentials Committee and the other delegates squirmed—trying to find a bone to toss the people that would be accepted. On the boardwalk, our people sat and talked and walked— waiting for the word to charge the convention, if necessary. And the nation waited, too, and watched. At Atlantic City, in August of 1964, the whole Democratic Party was forced to deal with the black people of Mississippi.

It was Tuesday night, 8:30 P.M., and the convention was about to have its formal opening. As the chairman introduced George Lawrence, former governor of Pennsylvania, members of the Freedom Democratic Party entered the convention hall with passes obtained from sympathetic delegates. There they were, black Mississippians, led by Mrs. Fannie Lou Hamer, sitting in the seats of the Mississippi delegation. They had voted to reject the proposal adopted by the Credentials Committee—a proposal "giving" them a grand total of two seats as "delegates-at-large." This was not what they had come for, not by a long shot. So they came inside, all of them. This was their protest, their answer to Lyndon B. Johnson.

But Johnson's people had a trick bag for them. The word was passed in some delegations where we still had support that the Freedom Democrats had accepted the resolution of the Credentials Committee. I know this happened in the Michigan delegation, some members of which had been ready to fight Congressman Diggs and the administration. But when they got the false report that the MFDP had accepted the so-called compromise, they felt there was nothing they could do. The Credentials Committee report was adopted by the convention. Some people in SNCC and many in the MFDP were stunned—others were not.

James Forman, *The Making of Black Revolutionaries,* (Seattle: Open Hand Publishing, 1985), pp. 388–90. The reports in the *New York Times* by E. W. Kenworthy are especially revealing. See, for example, the page 1 account in the *Times,* August 23, 1964.

86

A PLEA FOR "MODERATION": ANNUAL ADDRESS, 1964

by Rev. J. H. Jackson

The Reverend Mr. Jackson was president of the National Baptist Church, which counted among its members a considerable proportion of the African-American adult population. At its Eighty-Fourth Annual Session, held in Detroit on

September 10, 1964, its president offered advice which urged moderation in the struggle against racism, eschewing mass activity and favoring continued reliance on persuasion and legal activity.

As Christians we are a part of our nation and a part of the struggle of America. America was brought into being to satisfy and to answer the human longing for freedom. There was the urge in man to be related to other men as men without a modifier or any kind of limitation or restriction. There was an awareness of a human kinship deeper than race, more profound than nationality, and more inclusive than any accepted religious creed. In addition to the quest for a new geographical spot there was a search for a new human relationship, a new freedom, and new opportunities. These basic urges inspired the early colonies to brave the dangers of a rough and unknown sea, and seek a land in which they could live as free men and aspire to the highest possible goals of life without the enslavement of the past or being the victims of the determinism of enforced circumstances. They wanted a chance to explore and to search out the meaning of life for themselves, and an opportunity to worship God according to the dictates of their conscience.

They soon became convinced that there was no such land, no such Utopia, but all they would find would be an opportunity to make such a land and such a country. They were convinced it could be made out of the desires that now possessed their souls and out of the thirst for liberty that dominated their lives.

America was born in a struggle and as a struggle for freedom, and for the opportunity to develop the highest resources of mankind. The Declaration of Independence and the Federal Constitution were the results of our fathers' attempts to put on paper the ideals that inspired the birth of the nation, and those principles by which and on which the nation was erected and sustained. There have been errors, mistakes, and gross sins committed against this American venture, but this high venture has not been repudiated or negated.

The Civil Rights Struggle

What is this struggle for civil rights? I answer, it is an effort of American citizens to get full equality of opportunity. It is the resolution and the determination that there shall be in these United States one class of citizens and that is first class citizens. This is a struggle to adopt in practice as well as theory the concept of man on which the Declaration of

Independence is based, and to fully implement the Federal Constitution, one of the greatest documents for human freedom since the writing of the Magna Carta. The civil rights struggle is a struggle for full freedom, justice, and equality before the law. It is a struggle to bring from paper the lofty ideals of America, and to apply them in practice to the lives and actions of all Americans. In reality it is America's struggle to be herself, to fulfill the highest promises of her being, and to build a social order after the pattern and dreams of our founding fathers and in the light of the wisdom of the ages.

The civil rights struggle then is not a struggle to negate the high and lofty philosophy of American freedom. It is not an attempt to convert the nation into an armed camp or to substitute panic and anarchy in the place of law and order. It is in no wise an attempt to negate or to amend downward the highest laws of this land proclaiming freedom and justice for all.

Why Then the Struggle?

This struggle for civil rights has remained for a hundred years because there are persons among us who are still the victims of the psychology of chattel slavery and are yet blinded to the verdict of history and indifferent to the logic of life, and in deep rebellion against the voice of God.

Some Suggestions to the American Negro

But we as a people must keep ever before us the true meaning of our struggle so that we will never be used as tools in the hands of those who love not the nation's cause but seek the nation's hurt and not our help. Hence there are some things that we must do.

1. In our struggle for civil rights we must remain always in the mainstream of American democracy. Our cause must never be divorced from the American cause, and our struggle must not be separated from the American struggle. We must stick to law and order, for as I have said in the past I say now, there are no problems in American life that cannot be solved through commitment to the highest laws of our land and in obedience to the American philosophy and way of life. In spite of criticisms and notwithstanding threats and open attacks, I have not retreated from this position and never will as long as America is the America of the Federal Constitution and a land of due process of law. We cannot win our battle through force and unreasonable intimidation. As a minority group we cannot win outside of the protection and power of the just laws of this land.

2. The methods that we employ in the present struggle must not lead us into open opposition to the laws of the land. In some cases, the technique of direct action and demonstrations have led to mob violence and to vandalism. At least some who have desired to practice these negative methods have used the technique of so-called direct action.

This year, after a long, hard, and laborious fight, the Congress of the United States passed the strongest civil rights bill in its history, and the president signed into law a document that said that segregation has no place in American life and destiny. The call is to all of us to accept these facts and build on them. We must not ignore the constructive laws of our land, we must not organize, condone, or support mobs that parade in the name of freedom. We must not turn aside from decency and the constructive American standards in our quest for freedom. In our haste let us not be haughty. In our determination we must not become detrimental, and in our demonstrations we cannot afford to damn the nation of which we are a vital part.

Direct Action in the Positive

We have heard much in recent months about direct action in terms of boycotts, pickets, sit-ins, and demonstrations of various kinds. In each case the purpose as stated is a lofty one; namely, the winning of civil rights and the achievement of the equality of opportunity. I repeat, these are worthy ends and desirable goals, but this kind of direct action is orientated against others, and for the most part, must be classified in the negative since they have been designed to stop, arrest, or hinder certain orderly procedures in the interest of civil rights. In some cases however, these actions have been against practices and laws considered to be both evil and unjust.

Today, I call for another type of direct action; that is, direct action in the positive which is orientated towards the Negro's ability, talent, genius, and capacity.

We must not play ourselves too cheap or postpone the day of greater things when the hour of fulfillment is already at hand. To the leaders of school boycotts who have called children to remain out of school in order to help correct the evils and errors of an imperfect system of education, are you willing now to use your influence to lead young people to desert the ranks of drop-outs and struggle now to make the best out of the education that is now available? The call to stay out of school does not appeal to the highest in students but to the ordinary and the easy. It requires less initiative to stay out of school than it does to attend school. It requires less mental alertness to refuse to study than it does to study. Is not some education better than no education? Of course we should get all the education possible and go as far up the ladder of intellectual attainments as our powers will allow us. We must strive for the very best opportunities, the best possible schools, and the best possible teachers, but if these are not available to us then let us make the best use of what we do have. Remember that the future is with the person who knows, thinks, understands, and who has character and soul, and who can produce, invest, create, and live in harmony with the highest and the best. Of course we adults must continue to correct all the evils which make education more difficult. We must strive for quality education and seek to make available all the resources possible for the education of the young, but our young people must keep their feet in the upward path of learning and their minds stayed on the quest for truth.

The progress of the race lies not in continued street demonstrations, and the liberation of an oppressed people shall not come by acts of revenge and retaliation but by the constructive use of all available opportunities and a creative expansion of the circumstances of the past into stepping stones to higher things.

Herbert J. Storing, ed., *What Country Have I? Political Writings by Black Americans* (New York: St. Martin's Press, 1970), pp. 134–43, published in part.

87

TRY TO LIVE THERE JUST ONE DAY

by Fannie Lee Chaney

Mrs. Chaney was the mother of James Chaney; their home was in Meridian, Mississippi. He, together with two white young men from New York City— Andrew Goodman and Michael Schwerner—were active participants in the civil rights struggle in Chaney's native state. Sometime in the summer of 1964, after the three were released from jail for their efforts, they were murdered by an alerted white mob. Mrs. Chaney spoke at a memorial meeting held later that year in New York City.

I am here to tell you about Meridian, Mississippi. That's my home. I have been there all of my days. I know the white man; I know the black man.

The white man is not for the black man—we are just there. Everything to be done, to be said, the white man is going to do it; *he* is going to say it, right or wrong. We hadn't, from the time that I know of, been able to vote or register in Meridian. Now, since the civil-rights workers have been down in Mississippi working, they have allowed a lot of them to go to register. A lot of our people are scared, afraid. They are still backward. "I can't do that; I never have," they claimed. "I have been here too long. I will lose my job; I won't have any job." So, that is just the way it is. My son, James, when he went out with the civil-rights workers around the first of '64 felt it was something he wanted to do, and he enjoyed working in the civil-rights movement. He stayed in Canton, Mississippi, working on voter registration from February through March. When he came home he told me how he worked and lived those few weeks he was there; he said, "Mother, one half of the time, I was out behind houses or churches, waiting to get the opportunity to talk to people about what they needed and what they ought to do." He said, "Sometime they shunned me off and some would say, 'I want you all to stay away from here and leave me alone.'" But he would pick his chance and go back again. That is what I say about Mississippi right now. There is one more test I want to do there. I am working with the civil-rights movement, my whole family is, and my son, Ben, here, he is going to take his big brother's place.

He has been working for civil rights. Everything he can do, he does it. For his activities, he had been jailed twice before he was twelve years old. He told me when he was in jail he wasn't excited. He is not afraid; he would go to jail again! I am too, because we need and we've got to go to jail and we've got to get where the white man is. The white man has got Mississippi and we are just there working for the white man. He is the one getting rich. And when he gets rich, we can be outdoors or in old houses and he is going to knock on the door and get his rent money.

This is not something that has just now started, it has been going on before my time and I imagine before my parents' time. It is not just *now* the white man is doing this; it was borne from generation to generation. So, as I say, Ben is going to take his big brother's place, and I am with him and the rest of the family also. You all read about Mississippi—all parts of Mississippi—but I just wish it was so you could just come down there and be able to see; just try to live there just for one day, and you will know just how it is there.

Freedomways (Second Quarter, 1965), pp. 290–91.

88

THE ALBANY MOVEMENT: BIRTH AND EARLY HISTORY

by Slater King

A leader of the Albany Movement—a significant development in the liberation efforts in the South—describes its formation and early struggles. At the time of publication, Slater King was acting president of the movement and had recently been a candidate for mayor in this Georgia city.

The City Commission had a policy of denying all Negro requests. There was also the continuation of white men constantly invading the privacy of Albany State College, while the President of the College would not allow any action to be taken by the more militant faculty members and students against the guilty parties; the continued affronts and approaches made to Negro women attending Albany State College by whites bred discontent. There were windows broken out of ministers' homes because they dared request the only local daily, the Albany *Herald*, to discontinue its abusive treatment of Negroes in the news. The catalytic agents who helped to channel this discontent were two student field directors from the Student Nonviolent Coordinating Committee, Atlanta Office; these were Charles Sherrod and Cordell Reagon. They held mass meetings with the youth and finally some of this feeling of great discontent under the repressive system channeled over into the older people. The Albany Movement was founded because of the rivalry between some of the existing civil rights organizations, and it was a feeling that if all of the activities were put under the aegis of one head then the program could be carried on much more effectively. Therefore, on November 17, 1961, the Albany Movement was founded. Dr. W. G. Anderson was elected president, M. S. Paige, secretary, and I, Slater King, vice president.

The aim of the organization is to totally desegregate all city facilities and secure equal educational and economic opportunities for every citizen. In an attempt to effect the aims of the organization, the Albany Movement has petitioned, attempted to negotiate, and protested.

These protest demonstrations involved the whole of the Negro community and in the summer of 1962, they began anew, and approximately two thousand people had been jailed.

After the dust had settled, many people began evaluating the situation. The whites said that nothing had been gained and that the Negroes were now further behind than they had ever been. I think that the immediate reaction of most Negroes, right after the demonstrations, was the feeling of being let down. For most expected out of the great emotionalism and drama that was a part of the first stage of the demonstrations—that these few days of jailing would act as penance to force the whites to accord to Negroes the privileges that they had withheld so long. There are very few visible gains; the municipal buses agreed to desegregate after the Negroes refused to ride, but the city stubbornly refused to give any written assurances to the Albany Movement that it would not harass and intimidate Negro passengers, so the bus line withdrew and Albany now has no municipal transit system.

The library has been integrated. The city has struck down all of its statutes involving segregation (this was done to give the individual businesses a stronger legal basis for the maintenance of segregation). The public schools have been ordered to desegregate, by a court order, in September of 1964. Negroes gained the right to use the interstate bus station waiting rooms and restaurants without being harassed and intimidated by the local police.

These tangible gains (if they can be called gains) are negligible and hardly worth mentioning. The main gains that I see are those that have internally shaken the Negro community.

There is more of a sense of community and identity in the Negro community than ever before. Crime among Negroes has dropped considerably.

There has been a tremendous number of self-help organizations arising in the Negro community—such as, the teachers volunteering to teach night classes to the old and to those who were not able to receive education in the past; the Albany Movement has acted as the organization to see that to those Negroes who are without, charity is extended in the form of clothes and food. It has also attempted to see that for those Negroes who have good minds and have been unable, because of economic reasons, to secure an education, some way be found to help them scholastically to further their education. This has been done in attempting to propagate many of the policies of Dr. Du Bois, who felt that the Negro could never advance as long as he allowed his best minds to wither and atrophy.

Another gain is the breaking down of the snobbishness with which professional Negroes formerly looked at the Negro masses. Out of the downtown boycott, the existing Negro businesses have been strengthened and new ones have been added.

The Movement Educates the Masses

For two years the Movement has been the place where the Negroes have come for inspiration, to learn Negro history, and to further the strong feeling of identity, to know that they are not alone, to learn how politics work, and how they have been taken advantage of. They have heard speakers with opinions ranging from Dr. Lonnie X. Cross, representative of the Black Muslims to Dr. Martin Luther King, Jr., representing the integrationist. This has been a tremendous educative process for the masses.

In the liability ledger, I would state the following items:

In the Albany area, there are so many areas where Negroes need help and yet there are so few trained people to work.

I feel that we have not brought a wide enough spectrum of speakers before the people in our meetings; I feel that the socialist should have been represented by speakers such as Norman Thomas, the Communist by speakers such as Benjamin Davis, the Black Muslims by such speakers as Malcolm X and others.

I feel that the masses should be educated by being exposed to all of the political ideologies and let them decide what assets they wish to accept or reject in making a new and more workable system.

We have aroused emotions of the people and whetted their desire for freedom but we have not done the thorough organizational work which I think is essential to the success of any movement. You have to have emotion, but you also have to have discipline, well-thought-out plans that our best minds must help draft, and army-like discipline. Most civil rights movements, including ours, have lacked these.

In my opinion, we have attacked segregation too broadly. We have really attacked too many areas to do an effective job on any one of them. We must now put all of our energies behind one project at one time, and then move on to another; *e.g.,* in Savannah, Birmingham, and Albany, all three cities have had tremendous demonstrations. Savannah has desegregated its hotels, motels, and movie theaters. Birmingham and Albany desegregated little or none. The difference is that in Savannah, before beginning demonstrations, Mr. Hosea Williams, the chairman of the Chatham County Crusade for Voters, had thoroughly organized the Negroes in his total Congressional District and had a large disciplined political machine that moved instantaneously and with unity. Because of this concentration on the political area in Savannah, the Negroes had been the balance of power which had elected the sheriff and mayor.

This is no attempt to state a panacea, but to really be effective in our Movements across the country, we must unite these three ingredients: Protest, Political Mobilization, and Economic Unity.

I recently ran for mayor of the city of Albany. The masses of the Negroes were very enthusiastic towards the candidacy of a Negro for mayor. It was only among some of the older and professional Negroes that it was felt that we were moving too rapidly, that a Negro should not run for the highest office in the city. However, the candidacy accomplished the following:

It consolidated the Negro vote and formed one bloc unit where Negroes voted ninety per cent together on all of the candidates.

It brought an end to a few Negro ministers and businessmen being able to sell out the Negro vote for money.

The racists have a monopoly of the news, but through paid television appearances, we were able to tell the other half of the story. I stated the Negro demands unequivocally, which opened many eyes and gained some white supporters.

We created a new image for Negro boys and girls, a quickening interest in the political, and a desire to take part in the political sphere.

My candidacy further served as a vehicle to teach Negroes how politics work. Heretofore, the candidates have come into the Negro community to pay the Negroes to vote for them. Negroes must learn that they must support financially the candidate most interested in their welfare. *All expenses for my campaign were paid for out of the Albany Negro community.*

One of the items that we spoke against in the campaign was the lack of a Negro truant officer in Albany. Now, a trained truant officer, a college graduate, has been hired.

The massed and unified black voting power frightens many of the white politicians and will make them grant concessions according to the number and unanimity of that vote.

It has great increased voter registration among Negroes, and many are continuing to register.

The Federal Government Indicts the Victims!

At the beginning of the Movement, we felt that we were not alone and that the power of the federal government was with us in our efforts. Though this feeling was rapidly washed away, as many Negroes began to feel that the F.B.I. was as prejudiced as the local police, we still were shocked by the series of events that took place.

On April 8th, there was a trial in Albany, Georgia, of Ware vs. Johnson, involving a Negro, Charlie Ware, who charged that Baker County sheriff L. Warren Johnson shot and beat him.

On April 12th, a federal jury decided in favor of the sheriff. Carl Smith, a white grocer, whose store received ninety-nine percent Negro patronage, was a juror.

It is alleged by the Justice Department that at the Monday night meeting on April 15th, Dr. W. G. Anderson, President of the Albany Movement, mentioned Carl Smith in the course of his remarks.

Saturday, April 20th, some high school students set up a picket line at the Smith store. They demanded that Smith upgrade Negro employees to responsible positions, such as cashiers. All Negro employees at the store held menial jobs. Similar campaigns had been started against employers throughout Albany during the previous eighteen months.

No picket sign made reference to Smith's service on the jury. The line lasted about an hour, during which time, several pickets were arrested, effectively breaking the picket line. The line was never renewed.

Monday, April 22nd, Smith began to move out of the store, contending that he had been driven out of business by the boycott. It is alleged that his attorney, B. C. Gardner, member of the legal firm of Smith, Gardner, Kelley, and Wiggins (Asa Kelley is Albany's mayor), requested immediate investigation. The Justice Department conducted the most vigorous prosecution yet seen in the history of the civil rights movement.

On August 9th, nine Albany leaders were indicted. Anderson, Luther Woodall, and Robert Colbert were charged with conspiracy to injure a juror because of his assent to a verdict in clearing the sheriff in a federal case.

Mrs. Goldie Jackson, Rev. Samuel Wells, Thomas Chatmon, and Robert Thomas and I were charged with perjury before the grand jury. The charges state that they either denied having been at a lawyer's meeting during the week of July 29th or denied remembering having been there.

Joni Rabinowitz, a white field worker with the Student Nonviolent Coordinating Committee, working in the area of voter registration in Albany was charged with perjury because she said that she was not at the scene of the picketing.

I am now acting president of the Albany Movement. Mrs. Jackson is recording secretary and full time employee of the Movement. Rev. Wells is one of the most active voter registration workers and led a protest march last July. Chatmon works in the area of voter registration and was a recent candidate for city commissioner of the city of Albany. The youth, Robert Colbert, pleaded guilty in New York and was sentenced to eighteen months on a suspended sentence. Dr. Anderson and Luther Woodall were tried in Albany. There was a mistrial, and it is alleged that three jurors on the all-white jury voted for acquittal. *The Justice Department has announced that they will try the Anderson and Woodall cases again in Albany in April.*

In the other charges, all defendants were held guilty of perjury except Mrs. Elza (Goldie) Jackson, whose trial will come up the second Monday in January. The five of us who had been found guilty are Rev. Samuel B. Wells, Joni Rabinowitz, Robert Thomas, Thomas Chatmon, and myself.

As I write this, John L. S. Barnum, treasurer of the Sumter County Movement in neighboring Americus, Georgia, has also been charged on two counts of perjury by the grand jury there.

Disillusionment with the Federal Role

As one observes this, one wonders if these perjury cases are precedents that may be used to stifle civil rights leaders throughout the South.

This is very hard for us to understand, since the government has never taken any affirmative action resulting in relief in Albany where there have been clear violations of Negroes' civil rights. Examples of such cases are: *Walter Harris was shot down in cold blood on the streets of Albany by the police; Attorney C. B. King was caned over the head by Dougherty County Sheriff D. C. Campbell, and required many stitches; William (Bill) Hansen's jaw was broken and several ribs cracked; my wife, Marion, of Albany, was beaten and kicked by police, causing the death of our unborn child; over 100 cases of police brutality have been reported to the Justice Department. Out of all these cases reported, there have been no indictments.*

From my observations the majority of the black people of Albany are disillusioned, frightened, and bitter. The faith that they had in the mighty white federal government has dwindled. They now seem to feel that they are on their own.

It is reported that the sales of guns and rifles among whites and blacks is at an all-time high.

There are two growing forces. There is a white opposition that says, "never" and the ever-growing number of Negroes who say "NOW!"

When two determined forces meet, there can only be a great conflagration. If the government continues its policy of evasiveness and its constant attempts to appease the segregationists who are in high places all over the country, these two forces will meet in what I am afraid will be a bloody battleground. I surely do not want to see this, because I feel that it may spell more loss for the Negroes than for the whites, but unless the government takes decisive action, all of America can be hurt.

When Du Bois wrote *The Souls of Black Folk,* in reference to this area and Dougherty County, Georgia, he stated that it had implications for millions of black people. We, too, in Albany, sixty years later, feel that what has taken place here in the past, and what takes place in the future will have heavy implications for twenty million blacks in America.

Slater King, "The Bloody Battleground of Albany," *Freedomways* 4 (Winter 1964): 93–101; published in part.

89

FREEDOM—HERE AND NOW

by Gloria Richardson

Gloria Richardson was one of the most militant and effective leaders of the African-American revolt of the 1960s. She chaired the Cambridge, Maryland, "Nonviolent Action Committee," which produced hard-fought and meaningful reform. In the concluding section of this essay she pointed the way to more basic changes.

Today the revolt is now ready to go into a new phase. No longer are we primarily interested in public accommodations. The "bread and butter" issues have come to the fore. A one-point program will become more and more obsolete as months wear on. The attack now has to be directed toward the economic and political structure of a community if any real progress is to be made and if tokenism is to be eliminated. The leadership within the movement is moving toward this and the people are moving with them. Always there is this togetherness after confidence in one another has been established. If the leadership ever defaults I am sure that the people for whom we are fighting will continue their own battle. For example, in Cambridge we have become very sophisticated in the technique of the boycott. Without even calling for one, the majority of the community will spontaneously put a boycott into effect.

Important to Educate the Community

This brings me to another facet of the Negro revolt: it is incumbent on every civil rights worker to educate the community as well as to articulate its desires. This does not mean educate in terms of books or schools. Many so-called educated people today do not understand what we mean when we say the first step is to educate the people, and a serious mistake can be made here. Education in this context simply means that a community has to become familiar with what it wants to achieve, how it can be achieved and how to apply techniques so that they become second nature, a part of one's way of life. To learn and believe that they can overcome, to learn that the fight will be hard, that great sacrifices will be demanded but that it will *not* take another hundred years or even ten to gain the victory. To learn that what happens in Danville, Selma, Birmingham, Jackson, Albany happens to us too, in Cambridge, Baltimore, and Washington: to feel the rapport with other Negroes in other parts of the country and to become slowly and surely aware that as long as one of us has a segregationist breathing down our necks all of us are enslaved; that even though we have partial progress within our own locale, we will have to continue to stage sympathy demonstrations or acts of civil disobedience until discrimination and segregation are erased, everywhere.

There is another significant development taking place within the rights struggle. It is important and it is dangerous. Perhaps only those of us who are working in the field are really aware of it. It is that slowly and surely there is being born within the hearts and minds of Negroes today attitudes of violence. One can sense it. It is just beginning to be vocalized. Let us hope and pray that it does not find active expression. This can be directly traced to the fact that the federal government has failed to *act* with vigor to stop police brutality; to see and demand that Negroes be allowed to register and not be arrested for the attempt; that the FBI, that great "fact-finding unit" can somehow never find enough evidence of brutality if a Negro is the victim; that the Justice Department only enters with vigor when a white man is hurt. There are Negroes who are committed to violence even as those of us are to nonviolence. How long can the line be held? To some Negroes it must be proved that nonviolence can win, that you cannot fight evil with evil. They are not concerned with the philosophy of Gandhi. Just as we count our lives as nothing in the nonviolent fight they are ready to spend theirs in violence. After all, America trained them to kill and to be immune to death in order to win for an ideal—democracy. The white power structure ignores this because it is not concerned with the reality of masses of Negroes in action.

The Choice: Progress or Anarchy

The choice that Cambridge and the rest of the nation finally faces is between progress and anarchy, between witnessing change and experiencing destruction. The status quo is now intolerable to the majority of Negroes and may soon be intolerable to the majority of whites. People have called our movement the Negro Revolution. They are right. The changes for America that will flow from what Negroes throughout the country are doing shall be truly revolutionary. And we can only hope and work, and work some more, to make that revolution creative. One hundred years ago, in the midst of the Civil War, President Lincoln in his Second Inaugural Address said: "Fondly do we hope—fervently do we pray—that the cruel scourge of war may speedily pass away. Yet, if God wills that it continue until all the wealth piled up by the bondsman's 250 years of unrequited toil shall be sunk, and that every drop of blood drawn with the lash shall be paid by another drawn with the sword, as was said three thousand years ago, so shall it still be said: The judgments of the Lord are just and righteous altogether." These words were issued in the thick of battle and when the war died they were quickly forgotten, their meaning lost. But now the battle has resumed. Lincoln's words are again an immediate warning. No one, black or white, wants violence or bloodshed; all the Negroes of Cambridge and America desire are our rights as American citizens, to improve our own lives and the lives of our community.

And we *are* Americans and truly we do not believe that our community is in any way confused to race. If the white leaders understand this, and treat us as equals, and open their hearts and minds to the kinds of courage that will bring peace to all then this is good, but if they remain indifferent and insensitive to change then all of us, in Cambridge and throughout America, will have to sacrifice and risk our personal lives and future in a nonviolent battle that could turn into civil war. For now, Negroes throughout the nation owe it to themselves and to their country to have Freedom—all of it, *here* and *now!*

Freedomways 4 (Winter 1964): 32–34.

90

MEDICAL MISSION TO MISSISSIPPI

by V. McKinley Wiles, M.D.

A Harlem physician describes experiences in Mississippi in the summer of 1964; a brief note is added as to experiences in Alabama during the March 1965 beatings of demonstrators. One, the white Reverend James Reeb, had his skull smashed and died on March 11.

Much has been done to identify the American Negro with our African heritage, and rightly so. But not enough has been done yet to have the Negro in the North identify with his brothers and sisters in the South. What happens seems as distant to some as Malaysia or Vietnam.

We came away from Mississippi feeling that we had witnessed something that, if nourished and allowed to grow on an individual, state or national level, could provide the rebirth that America so sorely needs. Black and white together: What a commitment, and challenge and legacy!

As you may know, during the Mississippi Summer Project about one thousand civil rights workers came from north, east, and west. Significantly, eighty per cent were white and all of these lived in Negro homes and experienced a brotherhood and maximum security within the Negro community. Moreover, to the Mississippi Negro, here was tangible evidence that not all white people were against him; and that there were white people who were not afraid to risk life itself to demonstrate concern and encourage the Negro's demand for civil rights.

On the other side of the coin, the presence of these white outsiders dramatized the white Mississippian's dilemma. It was a strangely significant thing to see a score of white volunteers and perhaps one hundred fifty black Mississippians holding hands under the eyes of the police, singing, *"We shall overcome," "God is on our side,"* and *"Black and white together,"* as they rocked from side to side, blue eyes looking into brown eyes and absorbing the incredible truth that on both sides were black and white individuals whose faith, stronger even than family ties or race, made them pledge to each other their lives and sacred honor.

The Medical Committee for Human Rights was formed at the urgent request from the Council of Federated Organizations in June, 1964, to recruit physicians, nurses, dentists, and other health workers who believe in the aims of the civil rights movement and wish to take an active supporting role. These doctors and nurses were all volunteers, serving without remuneration, many of them paying their own transportation and serving one to three weeks in Mississippi. My wife, who is a nurse-educator, and I applied so that to us this important struggle would not be "a thing apart" but a real part of our lives. This was a serious decision and I requested the prayers of my church for the success of our tour.

I was assigned to lead a group of twelve from Newark airport to Jackson, Mississippi. We were briefed at MCHR headquarters on security. Instructions were to report by phone back to New York headquarters upon arrival in Jackson, where we were to be met by representatives of the Jackson office. Accommodations had been made for us at the Sun'n Sand Motel which had complied with the civil rights law. Our baggage was sent to our room, but before we could unpack or see the room, I rushed off to accompany Dr. Aaron Wells to the University of Mississippi Medical Center where he participated in the second autopsy of Michael Schwerner, one of the civil rights workers who was so brutally murdered.

Frankly I was quite shaken and stunned by the evasion of medical scientists to admit that the cause of death was *murder.* Also from those to whom I spoke, it was always that the "Communists" were behind a "plot" to discredit and smear the *fair name of Mississippi.* This line of "reasoning" exposes a most sensitive area of attack to civil rights public relations experts. Since the Second World War we have seen how critical world opinion has generated Federal action because of embarrassment over the race question. For this reason everything and every act of this vicious system of disfranchisement should be fed to the national and international mirror for reflection. . . .

The local Negro doctors were the backbone of the medical care program, offering assistance wherever requested. Both doctors and nurses gave emergency assistance. Efforts were made to establish relationships with the local health agencies, to assist in enlisting the Negro community to take advantage of their services. Group talks were made at Freedom Schools, on personal health, sanitation, venereal diseases, and sex.

Among adults, family planning and sex education were discussed. The eagerness for learning was evident at every session.

Surveys were begun regarding the public health programs relating to child care, prenatal and postnatal care, immunization services, and free venereal disease therapy not familiar to the Negro community either because of apathy or negligence of the power structure.

At each center we equipped first aid supplies boxes with vitamins, salt tablets, iron, aspirin, insect repellent, bandages, dressings, laxative, cough mixture, thermometer, alcohol, and peroxide.

After prayer we drove from Jackson to Hattiesburg, a distance of ninety miles. My white nurse crouched in the back seat, anxious not to attract attention. *In all my travels in Africa, never had I known fear, but, in Mississippi it was here in depth.* The emphasis was on the denial of civil rights. We received daily bulletins of beatings, arrests, jailings, and the burning of churches. Two people could be arrested for "unlawful assembly." One woman worker from New York was arrested for vagrancy and jailed until released on bond. The Negro community stayed quietly indoors whenever the police patrol cruised. Many homes of Negroes are bonded to release those arrested. But the spirit of resistance and determination to be free is admirable and worthy of the support of all of us.

[Members of the Medical Committee for Human Rights sent the following message to *Freedomways*. They were on duty in Selma, Alabama.]

On Sunday, March 7 [1965] following the bloody beating of many demonstrators, the Alabama State Police refused to permit ambulances to cross the now infamous bridge, to bring them first aid and transfer them to a hospital or first-aid station. It was only after repeated questioning, and finally begging, that we were permitted to go to their aid.

On March 9, two of our physicians were taken to the Dallas County Courthouse by the State Police and a Mr. Benton, a representative of the Alabama Board of Licensure. These two physicians were interrogated, photographed, and threatened with arrest and jail if they "so much as touched anyone" in an attempt to give first aid. This was stated under the guise of not having an Alabama medical license. Furthermore, these physicians were told that had they been present when Rev. James Reeb was brutally beaten, they would have been arrested if they had attempted to give any first aid whatsoever.

Freedomways 5 (Spring 1965): 314–17; published in part.

91

FROM PROTEST TO POLITICS: THE FUTURE OF THE CIVIL RIGHTS MOVEMENT

by Bayard Rustin

One of the most significant strategists of the struggle for full civil rights offered a summing up of its nature and prospects as of the mid-1960s.

I

The decade spanned by the 1954 Supreme Court decision on school desegregation and the Civil Rights Act of 1964 will undoubtedly be recorded as the period in which the legal foundations of racism in America were destroyed. To be sure, pockets of resistance remain; but it would be hard to quarrel with the assertion that the elaborate legal structure of segregation and discrimination, particularly in relation to public accommodations, has virtually collapsed. On the other hand, without making lights of the human sacrifices involved in the direct-action tactics (sit-ins, freedom rides, and the rest) that were so instrumental to this achievement, we must recognize that in desegregating public accommodations, we affected institutions which are relatively peripheral both to the American socio-economic order and to the fundamental conditions of life of the Negro people. In a highly industrialized, 20th-century civilization, we hit Jim Crow precisely where it was most anachronistic, dispensable, and vulnerable—in hotels, lunch counters, terminals, libraries, swimming pools, and the like. For in these forms, Jim Crow does impede the flow of commerce in the broadest sense: it is a nuisance in a society on the move (and on the make). Not surprisingly, therefore, it was the most mobility conscious and relatively liberated groups in the Negro community—lower-middle-class college students—who launched the attack that brought down this imposing but hollow structure.

The term "classical" appears especially apt for this phase of the civil rights movement. But in the few years that have passed since the first flush of sit-ins, several developments have taken place that have complicated matters enormously. One is the shifting focus of the movement in the South, symbolized by Birmingham; another is the spread of the revolution to the North; and the third, common to the other two, is the expansion of the movement's base in the Negro community. To attempt to disentangle these three strands is to do violence to reality. . . .

Birmingham remains the unmatched symbol of grass-roots protest involving all strata of the black community. It was also in this most industrialized of southern cities that the single-issue demands of the movement's classical stage gave way to the "package deal." No longer were Negroes satisfied with integrating lunch counters. They now sought advances in employment, housing, school integration, police protection, and so forth.

Thus, the movement in the South began to attack areas of discrimination which were not so remote from the northern experience as were Jim Crow lunch counters. At the same time, the interrelationship of these apparently distinct areas became increasingly evident. What is the value of winning access to public accommodations for those who lack money to use them? The minute the movement faced this question, it was compelled to expand its vision beyond race relations to economic relations, including the role of education in modern society. And what also became clear is that all these interrelated problems, by their very nature, are not soluble by private, voluntary efforts but require government action—or politics. Already southern demonstrators had recognized that the most effective way to strike at the police brutality they suffered from was by getting rid of the local sheriff—and that meant political action, which in turn meant, and still means, political action within the Democratic party where the only meaningful primary contests in the South are fought.

And so, in Mississippi, thanks largely to the leadership of Bob Moses, a turn toward political action has been taken. More than voter registration is involved here. A conscious bid for *political power* is being made, and in the course of that effort a tactical shift is being effected: direct-action techniques are being subordinated to a strategy calling for the building of community institutions or power bases. Clearly, the implications of this shift reach far beyond Mississippi. What began as a protest movement is being challenged to translate itself into a political movement. Is this the right course? And if it is, can the transformation be accomplished?

II

This matter of economic role brings us to the greater problem—the fact that we are moving into an era in which the natural functioning of the market does not by itself ensure every man with will and ambition a place in the productive process. The immigrant who came to this country during the late 19th and 20th centuries entered a society which was expanding territorially and/or economically. It was then possible to start at the bottom, as an unskilled or semi-skilled worker, and move up the ladder, acquiring new skills along the way. Especially was this true when industrial unionism was burgeoning, giving new dignity and higher wages to organized workers. Today the situation has changed. We are not expanding territorially, the western frontier is settled, labor organizing has leveled off, our rate of economic growth has been stagnant for a decade. And we are in the midst of a technological revolution which is altering the fundamental structure of the labor force, destroying unskilled and semi-skilled jobs—jobs in which Negroes are disproportionately concentrated. . . .

III

Let me sum up what I have thus far been trying to say: the civil rights movement is evolving from a protest movement into a full-fledged *social movement*—an evolution calling its very name into question. It is now concerned not merely with removing the barriers to full *opportunity* but with achieving the fact of *equality*. From sit-ins and freedom rides we have gone into rent strikes, boycotts, community organization, and political action. As a consequence of this natural evolution, the Negro today finds himself stymied by obstacles of far greater magnitude than the legal barriers he was attacking before: automation, urban decay, *de facto* school segregation. These are problems which, while conditioned by Jim Crow, do not vanish upon its demise. They are more deeply rooted in our socio-economic order; they are the result of the total society's failure to meet not only the Negro's needs, but human needs generally.

These propositions have won increasing recognition and acceptance, but with a curious twist. They have formed the common premise of two apparently contradictory lines of thought which simultaneously nourish and antagonize each other. On the one hand, there is the reasoning of the *New York Times* moderate who says that the problems are so enormous and complicated that Negro militancy is a futile irritation, and that the need is for "intelligent moderation." Thus, during the first New York school boycott, the *Times* editorialized that Negro demands, while abstractly just, would necessitate massive reforms, the funds for which could not realistically be anticipated; therefore the just demands were also foolish demands and would only antagonize white people. Moderates of this stripe are often correct in perceiving the difficulty or impossibility of racial progress in the context of present social and economic policies. But they accept the context as fixed. They ignore (or perhaps see all too well) the potentialities inherent in linking Negro demands to broader pressures for radical revision of existing policies. They apparently see nothing strange in the fact that in the last twenty-five years we have spent nearly a trillion dollars fighting or preparing for wars, yet throw up our hands before the need for overhauling our schools, clearing the slums, and really abolishing poverty. My quarrel with these moderates is that they do not even envision radical changes; their admonitions of moderation are, for all practical purposes, admonitions to the Negro to adjust to the status quo, and are therefore immoral....

Commentary, February 1965, pp. 25–31; published in part.

92

"I STILL WINCE"

by Roy Wilkins

Probably in 1965, Roy Wilkins received a letter from a young man; "what he had to tell me was typical of the spirit of those times. Looking at that letter now, I still wince."

"Dear Mr. Wilkins," he wrote. "You, Dr. M. L. King, and A. Philip Randolph and many others have done a marvelous and outstanding feat and I sincerely embrace you wholeheartedly for it, but there is a biblical connotation that I believe has pertinence to our revolution, that is, God replaced Moses when he couldn't communicate with his followers in the wilderness. He replaced him with Joshua, a young militant warrior, who led the children of Israel to the promised land. He was the same gentleman who made the sun stand still, destroyed the walls of Jericho. God Almighty knew he was a man, and indeed so was Malcolm X and most certainly is Stokely Carmichael."

Roy Wilkins, *op. cit.,* p. 314.

93

THE CRY OF THE GHETTO

compiled by Kenneth B. Clark

Dr. Clark, an outstanding psychologist—one of the experts consulted by the U.S. Supreme Court in arriving at its historic antisegregation decision—preceded his book published in 1965 with what he called Prologue:

A lot of times, when I'm working, I become as despondent as hell and I feel like crying. I'm not a man, none of us are men! I don't own anything. I'm not a man enough to own a store; none of us are.

—Man, age about 30

You know the average young person out here don't have a job, man, they don't have anything to do. They don't have any alternative, you know, but to go out there and try to make a living for themselves. Like when you come down to the Tombs down there, they're down there for robbing and breaking in. They want to know why you did it and where you live, but you have to live. You go down to the employment agency and you can't get a job. They have you waiting all day, but you can't get a job. They don't have a job for you. Yet you have to live. I'm ready to do anything anyone else is ready to do—because I want to live—I want to live. No one wants to die. I want to live.

—Drug addict, male, age 30

If a man qualifies, it should be first come, first serve. You understand what I mean? Regardless of whether we're black or white, we all have families! It should be first come, first serve. But that's not how they do you! If you're black, you're automatically turned down on a lot of jobs. They'll take your application, but no sooner than you walk out of the office, or wherever it is, they take the application and put it in the wastebasket, and tell you they'll let you know in a couple of weeks.

—Man, age about 24

No one with a mop can expect respect from a banker, or an attorney, or men who create jobs, and all you have is a mop. Are you crazy? Whoever heard of integration between a mop and a banker?

—Man, age about 38

The way the Man has us, he has us wanting to kill one another. Dog eat dog, amongst us! He has us, like we're so hungry up here, he has us up so tight! Like his rent is due, my rent is due. It's Friday. The Man wants sixty-five dollars. If you are three days over, or don't have the money; like that, he wants to give you a dispossess! Take you to court! The courts won't go along with you, they say get the money or get out! Yet they don't tell you how to get the money, you understand? They say get the money and pay the Man, but they don't say how to get it. Now, if you use illegal means to obey his ruling to try to get it—which he's not going to let you do—if you use illegal means to pay your bills according to his ruling—he will put you in jail.

—Man, age 31

They are raising the rents so high, like that, with a job, the menial jobs that we have or get, the money we will receive—we won't be able to pay the rent! So where we going to go? They are pushing us further, and further, and further—out of Harlem.

—Man, age 31

If you could get onto the ninth floor of the Tombs, you would see for yourself. They are lying there like dogs, vomiting and what not, over one another. It is awful. It smells like a pigpen up there. If you look, you'll see nothing but Spanish. And the black man. You'll seldom see a white man. When you do, he is from a very poor group. They are twenty years old, looking like they were forty.

—Drug addict, male, age about 37

I want to go to the veins.
You want to do what?
I want to go to the veins.
You want to go to the veins; you mean you want to get high?
Yeah.
Why do you want to get high, man?
To make me think.
You can't think without getting high?
No.

Discrimination is even in the school I attend right now. I know my teacher is very prejudiced because I have certain questions that have to be answered for my knowledge, but he will never answer. I told him one night, to his face, that if he didn't want to answer my questions just tell me and I would leave. There are always other teachers. He didn't say anything. He just looked at me and figured I was going to—so he said, "Well, maybe next time." There is no next time—this is the time and I'm not taking second best from any white man.

—Boy, age 17

Well, the gang, they look for trouble, and then if they can't find no trouble, find something they can do, find something they can play around. Go in the park, find a bum, hit him in the face, pee in his face, kick him down, then chase him, grab him, and throw him over the fence.

—Boy, age 15

The conditions here are the way they are because of white domination of this community, and when that changes, as is being attempted here, by these [black] nationalists, or by any other nationalist groups, or by the Muslims; when they can unite and change these conditions, change the white domination for black domination, the conditions will change.

—Man, age 28

Why in the hell—now this is more or less a colored neighborhood—why do we have so many white cops? As if we got to have somebody white standing over us. Not that I am prejudiced or anything, but I can't understand why we have to have so many white cops! Now if I go to a white neighborhood, I'm not going to see a lot of colored cops in no white neighborhood, standing guard over the white people. I'm not going to see that; and I know it, and I get sick and tired of seeing so many white cops, standing around.

—Woman, age 38

My wife was even robbed coming back from the store. They tried to snatch her pocketbook, and she came upstairs crying to me. What could I do? Where was the police? Where is the protection?

—Man, age about 50

The white cops, they have a damn sadistic nature. They are really a sadistic type of people and we, I mean me, myself, we don't need them here in Harlem. We don't need them! They don't do the neighborhood any good. They deteriorate the neighborhood. They start more violence than any other people start. They start violence, that's right. A bunch of us could be playing some music, or dancing, which we have as an outlet for ourselves. We can't dance in the house, we don't have clubs or things like that. So we're out on the sidewalk, right on the sidewalk; we might feel like dancing, or one might want to play something on his horn. Right away here comes a cop. "You're disturbing the peace!" No one has said anything, you understand; no one has made a complaint. Everyone is enjoying themselves. But here comes one cop, and he'll want to chase everyone. And gets mad. I mean, he gets mad! We aren't mad. He comes into the neighborhood, aggravated and mad.

—Man, age about 33

Last night, for instance, the officer stopped some fellows on 125th Street, Car No. _____, that was the number of the car, and because this fellow spoke so nicely for his protection and his rights, the officer said, "All right, everybody get off the street or inside!" Now, it's very hot. We don't have air-conditioned apartments in most of these houses up here, so where are we going if we get off the streets? We can't go back in the house because we almost suffocate. So we sit down on the curb, or stand on the sidewalk, or on the steps, things like that, till the wee hours of the morning, especially in the summer when it's too hot to go up. Now where are we going? But he came out with his nightstick and wants to beat people on the head, and wanted to—he arrested one fellow. The other fellow said, "Well, I'll move, but you don't have to talk to me like a dog." I think we should all get together—everybody—all get together and every time one draws back his stick to do something to us, or hits one of us on the head, take the stick and hit *him* on *his* head, so he'll know how it feels to be hit on the head, or kill him, if necessary. Yes, kill him, if necessary. That's how I feel. There is no other way to deal with this man. The only way you can deal with him is the way he has been dealing with us.

—Man, about 35

Everything is a big laugh in this dump unless you kill a cop. Then they don't laugh. I had a cop walk up to me a couple of days ago. You know what he said? "Move over." They have the street blocked up and he's going to tell me you can go around them. I said, "Hell if I do." He said, "What did you say?" I said, "Hell if I do." He said, "I'll slap your black ass." I told him, "That's one day you'll know if you're living or dying." He just looked at me. I said, "Why don't you say it? You want to say nigger so bad."

—Man, age 21

The flag here in America is for the white man. The blue is for justice; the fifty white stars you see in the blue are for the fifty white states; and the white you see in it is the White House. It represents white folks. The red in it is the white man's blood—he doesn't even respect your blood, that's why he will lynch you, hang you, barbecue you, and fry you.

—Man, age about 35

A stereotyped Negro you see him in the movies or on TV, walking down the levee with a watermelon in his hand, his shiny teeth, and his straw hat on his head. That's the one you see on television, yassuh, yassuh, and the showboys come in Stepin Fetchit, because that's what every Negro is associated with. To me, the middle-class Negro and the upper-class Negro is one that's trying to get away from that stereotype. They're the ones trying to get away.

—Man, age 18

I don't see why we've got to always look up to the white man's life. That's what we've been exposed to, you know. Be like the white man. I think we have to have criteria of our own. They had "Amos and Andy" on radio, they were done by white men. You hear the fellows saying, "Oh, I'm going to get me a white broad." We should form our own criteria. We should try and have some more people like Martin Luther King, like James Baldwin. We can send some draftsmen to school, some engineers; people can come back and build a city for Negroes to live in, or you know, not just for Negroes but for Negroes and anyone else who wants to live there. Why do we always have to get up—come up to the white man's level? We struggle like the devil to get up there, and we hardly ever do it. Why can't we form our own level?

—Girl, age 15

I have been uncomfortable being a Negro. I came from the South— Kentucky, on the Ohio River line—and I have had white people spit on me in my Sunday suit.

—Woman

The main thing is to know just where he comes from, knowing about his race. The main thing. He will then disregard every time he turns on the television that he sees a white face. That won't mean anything to him; it will be just another program because he will know that the conditions of the way of this world are based on only the white man's psychology, that makes these things. It won't be because this man is better fitted than he is on the television; it is because he dominates, he capitalizes, he corrupts.

—Man, age 35

First stop wearing the white man's clothes. Dress in your ancestral clothes. Learn your history and your heritage. This is part of my culture and I'm proud. Wear your clothes! Put on your *abdaba,* your *dashiki* and your *fella.* You can do it.

—Woman, age about 45

The Honorable Elijah Mohammed teaches, but the only thing is, some of our people still don't take that old blue-eyed, hook-nosed picture of Christ off their wall—take it down and step on it. These people have been exploiting us for years.

—Man, age about 35

Hear me now, hear me. Thy kingdom come, thy will be done, on earth as it is in Heaven. The kingdom is ours, black man's kingdom. We want our own God, our own paradise, our own joys on this earth, and if we are not getting that, then something must be wrong somewhere, so with all of your Gospel and all your preaching, if you cannot benefit the children, it has no value.

—Man, age about 50

Churches don't mean us no good. We've been having churches all our lives under the same conditions, and look at the condition we're still in. The church must not have meant anything. See, when you go to church you don't learn how to read and write, and count, at church. You learn that in school. See what I mean? So what good the churches doing us? They are not doing us any good! You could build some factories or something in Harlem and give our people some work near home. That would do us more good than a church.

—Man, age about 45

The preacher is a hustler. He creates a system for people to believe in that makes faggots, homosexuals, and lesbians out of the population of the black people, and this is exactly what Whitey wants him to do. If you keep the damn preachers out of it, we'd solve our whole problem, just like the NAACP and the CORE over here in Brooklyn now; they don't want no part of the medicine, so that's it. But I'm a U-Pad member of the National

Black Nationalists, and that's all I have to say. I don't go with this. His members that are here can believe him, they can fall behind or whatsoever. The only thing he wants—you never see a rabbi ride in a Cadillac, you never see a Jew rabbi, a charity rabbi, ride in nothing. They walk—They're doing a big enough job in the church, we don't need any leaders out here. In fact, we need to get rid of preachers like this because they are the very first ones who are going to sell us down the creek like he has done, like ministers have been doing over and over again. And incidentally, there was a big crook over in Brooklyn who sold everybody out on the picket line.

—Man, age 35

We don't want any bloodshed if we can help it, but if there has to be a little bloodletting, well and good. But this is only the beginning—what happened here today. Our next big step is the Harlem Police Department—we want black captains and we're going to have them. I've been fighting for dozens of years here in Harlem, where the so-called leaders play—Uncle Tom—play politics and let the people starve. You have district leaders here that draw a big fat salary. You can't hardly walk the street for trash. You have captains here—district captains and what not—all kinds of leaders here in Harlem. You never see them until election.

—Woman, age about 30

I think there's a great lack of offensive direction and most of the adults have, more or less, succumbed to the situation and have decided, what the hell can I do? This is the attitude; that we can do nothing, so leave it alone. People think you're always going to be under pressure from the white man and he owns and runs everything, and we are so dependent on him that there's nothing I can do. This is the general impression I've gotten from most of the adults in Harlem.

—Girl, age 15

It's got to get better. It can't get worse—it's got to get better, and they'll open up. They have to open up because they will find themselves going down all over the world, not only here. It's not just us picketing that forced them to do this; all over the world people are talking about American imperialism, and it's forcing them to do all these things. Because whether I walk the line or not, whoever walks the line that has a black face is walking the line for me. Whether they are walking in Alabama, Arizona,

Mississippi, or wherever they're walking. And there isn't anything for the Man to do but begin giving us an equal chance if he wants to save himself, because he's going down and we're the only ones that are holding him up.

—Man, age about 45

All right, so you get into the school and you get your rights, but in the whole scope of the black man in America, how can you accomplish anything by doing this? Yes, all right, you are accepted into Woolworths; you fought and got your heads beat in. But what do your children think of you? Do you have any economic or political power? The people like you who're going into Greenwood, Mississippi, say, where the people are living—you are all dependent. It's unthinkable. The people have nothing. At this point they are living on things that are being sent to them from New York, Chicago, and other places in the United States. Do you know how much money we spend on foreign aid while here in the United States we people are starving?

—Man, age 18, and girl, age 15

When the time comes, it is going to be too late. Everything will explode because the people they live under tension now; they going to a point where they can't stand it no more. When they get to that point.... They want us to go to Africa, they say.

That would be the best thing they would want in the world because then they could get all of us together. All they would have to do is drop one bomb and we're dead.

—Men, ages 30 to 35

I would like to see the day when my people have dignity and pride in themselves as black people. And when this comes about, when they realize that we are capable of all things, and can do anything under the sun that a man can do, then all these things will come about—equality, great people, presidents—everything.

—Man, age 19

I would like to be the first Negro president.

—Boy, age about 17

Kenneth B. Clark, *Dark Ghetto: Dilemmas of Social Power* (New York: Harper & Row, 1965), pp. 1–10.

94

THE PROTEST AGAINST HOUSING SEGREGATION

by Loren Miller

At the time of the publication of this essay, Loren Miller was a municipal judge in Los Angeles. He had been a trustee of the National Urban League and in 1965 was a vice president of the NAACP. As an attorney he had been prominent in suits involving housing segregation before California State courts and the U.S. Supreme Court. A summing up of suggested remedies concludes this careful study.

Housing discrimination became an issue in the 1960 presidential campaign, and John F. Kennedy promised to end it in all federal agencies with a stroke of the pen. He did not stroke the pen until November 20, 1962, and then he stroked it with a light touch. His executive order forbade discrimination in the sale or rental of housing—and related facilities—owned or operated by the federal government or "provided in whole or in part with the aid of loans, advances, grants, or contributions" made after that date. The major defect of the Order is that it falls so far short of federal possibilities. The nation's banks and savings and loan associations, commanding assets of some $400 billion, are subject to control and regulation as members of the federal banking system. They represent the major source of home financing, but the only restraint put on their lending policies proscribes discrimination when they engage in FHA or VA transactions. They remain free to discriminate in conventional loans or to finance discriminatory builders. The result is that only about twenty-five per cent of the new housing market is covered by the Order.

The presidental Order is premised on the belief that governmental abstention from direct participation in discriminatory practices of the housing market, combined with an active campaign to encourage builders and developers to abandon those practices, meets today's needs. Negroes think much more is required. Ghettos were created by governmental action in catering to popular prejudice through a compound of judicial action, direct sanction, and approval and use of credit devices to pamper and stimulate a demand for, and enforce racial restrictions on the use of, urban land during that critical half-century when Negro in-migration was at floodtide. The Black Belts are here now; they cannot be disestablished through means that would have prevented their establishment and growth.

State fair housing laws are very important, but the South is not going to enact them, and there is a rising tide of resistance in the North. Voluntary fair housing councils have sprung up in and around every large city and do effective jobs in agitating for and implementing nondiscriminatory laws and decrees, but are impotent in the absence of legal safeguards. As the Negro sees it, the federal government must take the lead if anything effective is to be done in respect to halting the growth of Black Belts. He believes, correctly, that governmental involvement in housing will increase and that, as it increases, what government does will become increasingly crucial in determining occupancy patterns. Therefore, he reasons, the federal government must do more than abstain from aiding discrimination. It must devise affirmative methods of integration. He hopes government will become as vigilant and decisive on his side as it was in assisting residential segregation for almost thirty years.

An affirmative policy would comprehend a quick expansion of the presidential Order to cover *all* housing constructed through loans by banks and lending institutions subject to federal control and supervision. Urban renewal and urban redevelopment plans would be approved only when they contain built-in assurances that they will not compound residential segregation and, where possible, will further integration. The Housing and Home Finance Agency would require builders and developers to seek out and attract Negroes by posting proper notices of nondiscrimination as a condition of a loan from an affected lending institution, just as employers with government contracts are required to post notices that they are "equal opportunity" employers. The Agency itself would use its facilities to keep the public constantly advised that all housing constructed under loans from the affected lending institutions is open to purchase and rental without discrimination. Plans would be devised by the Agency to encourage and utilize voluntary fair housing groups and councils. In sum, the federal housing agencies would shift emphasis from their present role as mere policing agencies to undertaking leadership for nondiscrimination in housing and related industry. This is a tall order which will arouse opposition, but the need is great. The problem at hand cannot be dealt with effectively by official timidity or pious good wishes.

Last summer's outbreaks in Harlem and other ghettos are warning signals. Housing reforms, no matter how drastic, will not still all Negro discontent, nor will they lead to a quick halt of the expansion of our central city Black Belts. But a beginning must be made, and a beginning of the kind described will help dispel the mood of frustration and despair that lies back of the discontent now boiling over into riots and disturbances. Our central cities are becoming Negro cities spawning segregation in public facilities and turning political campaigns into racial contests. They are pregnant with the promise of ever-increasing and ever more bitter conflict. Government must, of course, quell disorder and conflict as is so often and so insistently urged. It is even more important to isolate and remove the causes of disorder and conflict. Residential segregation in the American city is one of the prime causes. Government which did its shameful, and successful, best to stimulate and effectuate that segregation must find ways of undoing that monumental wrong.

Annals of the American Academy of Political and Social Science 357 (January 1965): 74–79; published in part.

95

MALCOLM KNEW HE WAS A "MARKED MAN"

by Theodore Jones

Three days before he was killed, Malcolm gave an interview to a black reporter. He told him:

"I live like a man who's already dead," Malcolm said last Thursday in a two-hour interview in the Harlem office of the Organization for Afro-American Unity.

"I'm a marked man ... it doesn't frighten me for myself as long as I felt they would not hurt my family. . . .

"No one can get out [of the Black Muslim movement] without trouble and this thing with me will be resolved by death and violence. . . . I was the spokesman for the Black Muslims. I believed in Elijah Muhammad more strongly than Christians do in Jesus. I believed in him so strongly that my mind, my body, my voice functioned 100 per cent for him and the movement. My belief led others to believe.

"Now I'm out and there's the fear that if my image isn't shattered, the Muslims in the movement will leave. Then, they know I know a lot. As long as I was in the movement, anything he did was to me by divine guidance. . . .

"But I didn't want to harm anyone or the movement when I got out, but I had learned to disbelieve and Mr. Muhammad knew that. . . .

"I know brothers in the movement who were given orders to kill me. I've had highly-placed people within tell me 'be careful, Malcolm.' . . .

"The press gave the impression that I'm jiving about this thing. They ignored the evidence and the actual attempts. . . .

"I won't deny I don't know where I'm at. . . . But by the same token how many of us put the finger down on one point and say I'm here. . . .

"I feel like a man who has been asleep somewhat and under someone else's control. I feel what I'm thinking and saying now is for myself. Before it was for and by the guidance of Elijah Muhammad. Now I think with my own mind."

New York Times, February 22, 1965. There is a probing essay, "Many Malcolms," by Gerald Early, in the *Boston Globe*, December 7, 1992; I am obliged to Professor Early for sending me a copy of this study. See also Early's study of Malcolm in *Harper's*, December 1992. In the *American Historical Review* of April 1993, there are insightful essays on Malcolm as portrayed in the film on him directed by Spike Lee. See Nell Irvin Painter (98: 432–39) and Gerald Horne (98: 440–50).

96

OUR SHINING BLACK PRINCE

by Ossie Davis

On February 27, 1965, the noted actor delivered this eulogy of Malcolm X at the Faith Temple Church in Harlem.

Here—at this final hour, in this quiet place—Harlem has come to bid farewell to one of its brightest hopes—extinguished now, and gone from us forever.

For Harlem is where he worked and where he struggled and fought— his home of homes, where his heart was, and where his people are—and it is, therefore, most fitting that we meet once again—in Harlem—to share these last moments with him.

For Harlem has ever been gracious to those who have loved her, have fought for her, and have defended her honor even to the death. It is not in the memory of man that this beleaguered, unfortunate, but nonetheless proud community has found a braver, more gallant young champion than this Afro-American who lies before us—unconquered still.

I say the word again, as he would want me to: Afro-American—Afro-American Malcolm, who was a master, was most meticulous in his use of words. Nobody knew better than he the power words have over the minds of men. Malcolm had stopped being a "Negro" years ago.

It had become too small, too puny, too weak a word for him. Malcolm was bigger than that. Malcolm had become an Afro-American and he wanted—so desperately—that we, that all his people, would become Afro-Americans too.

There are those who will consider it their duty, as friends of the Negro people, to tell us to revile him, to flee, even from the presence of his memory, to save ourselves by writing him out of the history of our turbulent times.

Many will ask what Harlem finds to honor in this stormy, controversial, and bold young captain—and we will smile.

Many will say turn away—away from this man, for he is not a man but a demon, a monster, a subverter, and an enemy of the black man—and we will smile.

They will say that he is of hate—a fanatic, a racist—who can only bring evil to the cause for which you struggle!

And we will answer and say unto them: Did you ever talk to Brother Malcolm? Did you ever touch him, or have him smile at you? Did you ever really listen to him? Did he ever do a mean thing? Was he ever himself associated with violence or any public disturbance? For if you did you would know him. And if you knew him you would know why we must honor him: Malcolm was our manhood, our living, black manhood! This was his meaning to his people. And, in honoring him, we honor the best in ourselves.

Last year, from Africa, he wrote these words to a friend: "My journey," he says, "is almost ended, and I have a much broader scope than when I started out, which I believe will add new life and dimension to our struggle for freedom and honor and dignity in the States. I am writing these things so that you will know for a fact the tremendous sympathy and support we have among the African States for our Human Rights struggle. The main thing is that we keep a United Front wherein our most valuable time and energy will not be wasted fighting each other."

However much we may have differed with him—or with each other about him and his value as a man—let his going from us serve only to bring us together, now. Consigning these mortal remains to earth, the common mother of all, secure in the knowledge that what we place in the ground is no more now a man—but a seed—which, after the winter of our discontent, will come forth again to meet us. And we will know him then for what he was and is—a Prince—our own black shining Prince!—who didn't hesitate to die, because he loved us so.

In John Henrik Clarke, ed., *Malcolm X: The Man and His Times* (New York: Macmillan, 1969), pp. xi–xii.

97

THE URBAN LEAGUE AND ITS STRATEGY

by Whitney M. Young, Jr.

Young had been dean of the Atlanta University School of Social Work. In October 1961, he became director of the National Urban League. This essay offers a summary of the League's history and projects a kind of "domestic Marshall Plan" to overcome the fearful deprivation endured by the black population.

Basic League Action Programs

Although League method does not call for sit-ins and freedom rides, a recognized and vital part of the struggle for human rights, we join in demonstrations which are focused on the general situation such as the 1963 March on Washington. We helped to organize the March, sharing the aims and responsibilities of the civil rights groups that participated in it.

The Urban League considers itself an action agency. Our action programs are designed to motivate youth to stay in school to get the best possible education; to expand the housing supply for the Negro population; to eliminate racial barriers in the employment and promotion of qualified Negroes; to strengthen Negro family life; and to stimulate self-help among Negro citizens in solving their problems.

It becomes clear then that the strategy of the Urban League is twofold: (1) to help wipe out the last vestiges and barriers of discrimination and (2) to assist Negro citizens to rise through self-qualification until they can achieve the status of first-class citizenship not only in name but in fact. By working interracially, by obtaining the help of both the white and Negro community, by creating an atmosphere and climate of co-operation, and by emphasizing that it is in the best interest of all to work together, the Urban League hopes to effect changes which would not otherwise be possible.

The Urban League Programs

How does the League seek to achieve its objectives? First, by defining the problem (facts and figures can form a powerful picket line, too); second, by motivating youth; third, by finding jobs and increasing employment; fourth, by working to improve housing conditions; fifth, by stimulating adequate health and welfare services for Negroes. The League's strategies to cause change in these areas are manyfold.

A Domestic Marshall Plan

Last year, the National Urban League called for a massive, crash effort on the part of all governmental bodies, private institutions, foundations, and settlement houses—in short, by the entire fabric of American society—to make compensatory effort for a brief period in time to help Negro citizens qualify themselves for the new opportunities opening before them.

A nation which invested $17 billion to restore war-ravaged Europe after the Second World War should be able to create a domestic Marshall Plan which will enable Negro citizens to compete in the free enterprise marketplace. Ironically, critics of the Urban League's program—those who deplored "special compensation," even for a brief, ten-year period—have ignored or refused to admit that special effort was exerted for Hungarian and Cuban refugees and that their rise in this nation today as a whole far exceeds that of Negro citizens.

Fortunately there is growing evidence today that the League's Marshall Plan appeal has not fallen on deaf ears. Across the nation, a domestic Marshall Plan, under many varying names and titles, including the "War on Poverty," is coming into being. To date, the remedies proposed have been far short of the needs. Much more must be done, and soon.

There is abundance in this nation sufficient to meet the critical human needs of all our citizens, but we must have the courage and the vision to invest in all our people, in our cities, in our educational and vocational plants, colleges, and institutions if the great masses of Negro citizens, locked into pockets of poverty in urban slums and rural shanties, are to be elevated to a condition of dignity and equal opportunity to function effectively in the free marketplace.

The Annals of the American Academy 137 (January 1965): 103–107; published in part.

98

"DON'T YOU REALIZE I'M A NEGRO?"

by James Forman

GWEN PATTON: On May 28, George Wallace was to speak at the Macon Academy graduation exercises—that's a private white school. The newspapers said that the public was invited and we felt we had a right to go to that meeting. It was in the Armory. Wendy and his brother tried to get in, but couldn't. They came back to the office and we got more people. About a dozen of us went—there was a lot of tension there.

We almost got through but the whites lined up at the door and stopped us. They said we didn't have "invitations." There was a boy there who said, "I've just come from Vietnam fighting for freedom in this country and I can't even come into a National Guard Armory." Tears just ran down his face—and he was supposed to have been one of the outstanding men at the front. Somehow he recuperated himself. Then this whole thing about war, about killing the enemy, came to his mind. He drew a knife and said he was going to kill every white man in there and every white person he had seen. He didn't do anything, but we talked about the whole system— the war and what happened to people coming home from the war. How do they expect us to be nonviolent? We're supposed to kill the enemy over there and then coexist with the enemy here. It's ridiculous.

The rejection of nonviolence in violent America is not so recent a development in the current movement as some people think. For the Tuskegee students in the summer of 1965, the necessity of being prepared to defend oneself against white violence was an acknowledged fact. SNCC's position there, as elsewhere in the South, had always been that local residents had the right to defend themselves and their homes. In mass demonstrations, however, the tactic of nonviolence still prevailed in Tuskegee—though its days were numbered.

Meanwhile, the students continued their desegregation efforts.

BILL HALL: On May 31, we went to integrate the swimming pool. There are two city swimming pools; one is considered Negro and the other white. Sammy was one of the people who spearheaded the drive to integrate the white pool, which we did. The white kids jumped out, and we swam all day.

JIMMY ROGERS: We had been going swimming there for two days, when one day a man approached the pool with a shoe box. He said to the policeman who was standing on the outside, "Should I?" Sammy and Wendy heard him and they asked him, should he what? The man walked away and went up onto the balcony above the pool. Then he turned the box over and a baby alligator fell into the pool.

BILL HALL: The white personnel did nothing about that alligator in the water. One of the students from Tuskegee got it out.

The following day, the whites decided to sprinkle glass on the diving board. They were fine particles so that you couldn't see them; as the students would dive off the board, they would cut their feet. So they stopped going to the board. Then the whites threw acid and manure in the swimming pool, and this was the straw that broke the camel's back. They had to drain the pool, and they wouldn't refill it.

After a while, Sammy and other TIAL students raised the question about the city pool. "Okay, it's cleared out now. Why don't you open it up again?" The Mayor and several people on the City Council responded that the town's water level was low and they couldn't afford to refill it. More time passed, and we raised the question again. One excuse led to another. A few of the Negro councilmen were trying to arrange for Negro students to use the pool on certain days and white students on others. Sammy and the rest could not accept that and continued to press for reopening. They realized that Allen Parker, who is not only the chairman of the City Council but also the president of the Alabama Exchange Bank, could be made a focus of attack. They began to pressure Parker, to picket his bank.

James Allen Parker apparently held the keys to the city.

WENDY PARIS: Parker really screwed the whole county. He controlled all the Negroes. I guess that's why we didn't get anywhere picketing the bank.

Meanwhile, the whites were bringing strong counter-pressure to bear on Sammy Younge and his family.

MRS. YOUNGE: Right after they swam in that pool, the telephone rang and the white Superintendent of the school where I was teaching said, "Mrs. Younge, I'd like to have a conference with you." First time in my life anybody in the Superintendent's office wanted to talk to me about anything. So I went in and he said, "What I have to say won't take long. I'm going to tell you what you got to do and then you get up and go out of here and do it." That made me angry and I made up my mind right then that he would hear me out too. There hadn't been any communication before, now there was going to be some.

Then he told me that he had been informed that my son was the leader of the civil-rights group. He told me all he had tried to do to get the integrated school going, and said that this group was undoing everything he had done—with all the inroads the Negroes were making, the whites would refuse to send their children. I told him, "I'm not your problem— your own race is your problem. Why is it that the burden of integration always has to be on the shoulders of the Negro? You need to go out and do some work among your own race."

"Well, I have to have cooperation," he said. Then he went on about Sammy, and I asked, "Just what does this have to do with my being an effective teacher? You think that just because my son dared to swim in a pool that I paid to put water in—and I have been paying for years—that this makes me a less effective teacher?"

"Oh, I'm not saying that."

"Well, just what are you saying?" I was trying to get him, but he was too smart.

"I'm just saying that we need cooperation."

"Cooperation from whom?" I asked him. "I think Negroes have cooperated long enough, don't you?"

Then he got angry. He called the people who went to swim "a big bunch of nasty, dirty men." He said half of the white teachers at Tuskegee Institute weren't anything but perverts. Then he intimated that Sammy was mentally ill. Finally, he said that if I didn't take some action to cooperate, I would be ostracized and criticized. I said, "Mr. Wilson, being criticized doesn't bother me. Those that want to believe lies will believe them. As far as being ostracized is concerned, don't you realize I'm a Negro?"

James Forman, *Sammy Younge, Jr., The First Black Student to Die in the Black Liberation Movement* (New York: Grove, 1969), pp. 140–45.

99

VISITING AFRICA AND LIVING IN MISSISSIPPI

by Fannie Lou Hamer

After Fannie Lou Hamer visited Africa in 1965, she was interviewed by J.H. O'Dell, a contributing editor of *Freedomways*. Extracts follow:

Our foreparents were mostly brought from West Africa, the same place that we visited in Africa. We were brought to America and our foreparents were sold; white people bought them; white people changed their names...and actually...here, my maiden name is supposed to be Townsend; but really, what is my maiden name...? What is my name? This white man who is saying "it takes time." For three hundred and more years they have had "time," and now it is time for them to listen. We have been listening year after year to them and what have we got? We are not even allowed to *think* for ourselves. "I know what is best for you," but they *don't* know what is best for us! It is time now to let them know what they owe us, and they owe us a great deal. Not only have we paid the price with our names in ink, but we have also paid in blood. And they can't say that black people can't be intelligent, because going back to Africa, in Guinea, there are almost four million people there and what he, President Touré, is doing to educate the people: as long as the French people had it they weren't doing a thing that is being done now. I met one child there eleven years old, speaking three languages. He could speak English, French, and Malinke. Speaking my language actually better than I could. And this hypocrisy—they tell us here in America. People should go there and see. It would bring tears in your eyes to make you think of all those years, the type of brainwashing that this man will use in America to keep us separated from our own people. When I got on that plane, it was *loaded* with *white* people going to Africa for the Peace Corps. I got there and met a lot of them, and actually they had more peace there in Guinea than I have here. I talked to some of them. I told them before they would be able to clean up somebody else's house you would have to clean up yours; before they can tell somebody else how to run their country, why don't they do something here. This problem is not only in Mississippi. During the time I was in the Convention in Atlantic City, I didn't get any threats from Mississippi. The threatening letters were from Philadelphia, Chicago, and other big cities.

The only thing I really feel is necessary is that the black people, not only in Mississippi, will have to actually upset this applecart. What I mean by that is, so many things are under the cover that will have to be swept out and shown to this whole world, not just in America. There is so much hypocrisy in America. This thing they say of "the land of the free and the home of the brave" is all on paper. It doesn't mean anything to us. The only way we can make this thing a reality in America is to do all we can to destroy this system and bring this thing out to the light that has been under the cover all these years. That's why I believe in Christianity because the Scriptures said: "The things that have been done in the dark will be known on the house tops."

Now many things are beginning to come out and it was truly a reality to me when I went to Africa, to Guinea. The little things that had been taught to me about the African people, that they were "heathens," "savages," and they were just downright stupid people. But when I got to Guinea, we were greeted by the Government of Guinea, which is *Black People*—and we stayed at a place that was the government building, because we were the guests of the Government. You don't know what that meant to me when I got to Guinea on the twelfth of September. The President of Guinea, Sekou Touré, came to see us on the thirteenth. Now you know, I don't know how you can compare this by me being able to see a President of a country, when I have just been there two days; and here I have been in America, born in America, and I am forty-six years pleading with the President for the last two to three years to just give us a chance— and this President in Guinea recognized us enough to talk to us. . . .

We can do things if we only get the chance in America. It is there within us. We can do things if we only get the chance. I see so many ways America uses to rob Negroes and it is sinful and America can't keep holding on, and doing these things. I saw in Chicago, on the street where I was visiting my sister-in-law, this "Urban Renewal" and it means one thing: "Negro removal." But they want to tear the homes down and put a parking lot there. Where are those people going? Where will they go? And as soon as Negroes take to the street demonstrating, one hears people say, "they shouldn't have done it." The *world* is looking at America and it is really beginning to show up for what it is really like. "Go Tell It on the Mountain." We can no longer ignore this, that America is not "the land of the free and the home of the brave."

Freedomways Spring, 1965; 5:231–42.

100

"CRISIS IN RIGHTS"

by A. Philip Randolph and Martin Luther King, Jr.

On May 29, 1965, the *New York Times* reported the opening of a three-day meeting in Yonkers, New York, of the five-year-old Negro American Labor Council. A. Philip Randolph, its president, opened his remarks by declaring that with the passage of the Civil Rights Act in 1964, some had concluded that "the struggle for equal rights had been won." Not so, said Randolph, to the one hundred delegates coming from throughout the country. He continued:

There is a tendency of the civil rights revolution to lapse into a state of relaxation, as shown by a loss in membership and a deficit financial condition of civil rights organizations....

The civil rights revolution though indispensable to endow Negroes with full first-class citizenship and with political potentiality to help shape and direct the course of the American government, is wholly inadequate successfully to grapple with the basic economic and social problems of black Americans.

In the struggle of Negroes to solve the problem of unemployment, they must fashion a new weapon with which to fight. That weapon must consist of the alliance of the Negro and labor and the black poor and white poor. This is an alliance which has a natural basis because Negro nor labor is fully free.

At a church meeting later that same day, Dr. King stressed that without equalizing incomes the struggle was incomplete. He said:

"Call it what you may, call it democracy, or call it democratic socialism—but there must be a better distribution of wealth within this country for all of God's children."

101

THE WAR IN VIETNAM MUST BE STOPPED

by Martin Luther King, Jr.

At a rally sponsored by the Virginia branch of the Southern Christian Leadership Conference, held in Petersburg, July 3, Dr. King said:

I'm not going to sit by and see war escalated without saying anything about it. The war in Vietnam must be stopped. It must be a negotiated settlement. We must even negotiate with the Vietcong.

We're not going to defeat Communism with bombs and guns and gases. We can never accept Communism. We must work this out in the framework of our democracy.

New York Times, July 3, 1965, p. 6. See "The Vietnam War and the Civil Rights Movement," by Herbert Shapiro, in *Journal of Ethnic Studies* 16 (1988): 117–41.

102

"KEEP MY MOUTH SHUT"

by Wesley R. Brazier

The pattern of police maltreatment of black people, often quite regardless of class position, is illuminated in this testimony from "a taxpayer" who is "paying" the policeman's salary.

Police maltreatment does exist in Los Angeles. I have personally been maltreated for minor moving violations on several occasions. I have had the presence of mind to bite my tongue and keep my mouth shut, but you can believe that I boiled inside and felt defenseless.

QUESTION: Could you tell us a few of the several occasions when you have been maltreated?

THE WITNESS: Yes. I can also cite the one that, to me, was even worse in my case, and that was with my wife. And I discussed this one with Deputy Chief Simon, and he went through the record, but my wife couldn't remember the date, so we couldn't find the police officer.

But she was on the way to school at Crenshaw and Vernon, right near the Great Western Savings and Loan. She was making a left turn. She was right behind the police officer on the motorcycle, and as he took off she did too, with the green light, and he went up ahead and stopped another car and then stopped her.

Then she asked the officer, "Why have you stopped me?"

And he said, "You ran the red light."

She said, "Well, officer, I could not have. I was right behind you. You didn't run it and I followed you."

He said, "I said you did. Now, if you want to make something of it, get out of the car and we can settle it right now."

Now, he is a six-foot-two, two-hundred-pound officer, and my little wife is five-feet-two.

Now, had I been there and he said that, you can imagine how I would have felt. I mean, I am defenseless. He is wearing a badge and a pistol and he is a bully.

I have been stopped on numerous occasions, running a light, or failing to yield the right of way on a left turn, and I have said, "Officer, I must admit that I violated the law in running this light, my mind was on something else. Would you kindly give me my ticket so I may proceed to an appointment?"

"You are going to listen to what I got to tell you. Now, you know what you could have done? You could have killed somebody." I said, "Officer, I am aware of all this. Would you kindly write me my ticket? I don't need an educational lecture today."

"Oh, you are one of those smart so-and so's."

I said, "No, I am not———"

JUDGE BROADY: What is "smart so-and-so"?

THE WITNESS: Smart "nigger."

I said, "No, I am not trying to be smart. I merely asked you to give me my ticket."

"If you don't shut up, I will ———"

I said, "Officer, if you want to drive me down to the police station, I will go down with you. Give me my ticket or drive me down."

It has been this kind of harassment that I have received where I say it is not so much police brutality as it is police maltreatment, which can incite one into a state where, to defend himself, or to be a man, he doesn't care. And you are going to face more and more of this. The Negro is tired now of being looked down upon and, believe me, he is going to rebel. And when he does, he is going to tackle that policeman.

We have had cases where two women just beat a policeman to death. Two women. Now, they are just sick and tired of this maltreatment.

If we could get Chief Parker to recognize that when criticisms are heaped upon the police department it is not being heaped upon him, and I have said this to the Chief on numerous occasions, that "You are guilty of supporting them by saying that Los Angeles' finest can do no wrong. You have got sadists. You have got egotists. You have got everything on your police department."

And there are not tests developed yet that can pull out the ideal person to be a policeman.

So, I say there is considerable maltreatment. And it is against the Negro, regardless of what his station in life may be. I surely don't go out seeking trouble with the police officers. But, I do feel that I am a taxpayer and I am paying his salary and I think he should learn to respect and talk to me as a taxpayer and as one who is paying his salary.

Report of the Governor's Commission on the Los Angeles Riot (Sacramento, 1966), II, 32–33); in Joseph Boskin, ed., *Urban Violence in the Twentieth Century* (Beverly Hills, Calif: Glencoe Press, 1976), pp. 92–119.

103

THE WATTS UPRISING

by Roy Wilkins

The passion of Watts, the rage, the fires, the crackle of gunfire, the looting all took whites by surprise. I was not surprised in the slightest. We had had early warnings the year before in Harlem and elsewhere. Even so, California had blithely passed a statewide proposition rejecting fair housing, an injury that could only make California Negroes feel hopelessly penned in their ghettos. The chief of police in Los Angeles was the sort of fellow who could call Negroes "monkeys in a zoo." Mayor Sam Yorty was a law-and-order man—law for the white folks and plenty of orders for everyone else. Given this background the riot was no surprise, but I was not prepared for the sheer scale of the violence: night after night of bloody spasms that turned fifty square miles of the city into a war zone.

I remember watching the carnage on television, praying for it to stop, to burn itself out. As the fires died down, I picked up *Newsweek* and found that one of its reporters had captured the desperate new mood. Standing outside a ravaged store, a young teenager said ruthlessly, "You jes' take an' run, an' you burn when they ain't nothin' to take. You burn whitey, man. You burn his tail up so he know what it's all about."

I don't know which was worse—the grief I felt or the anger. There was no real philosophy, no law, not even any easily comprehensible sociology behind the riot. It was fury flashing up and striking out. Those were frightening days. The country was on the edge of a very destructive time, with eruptions of violence on one side and a real threat of repression on the other.

There was no mystery to what was going on. In the civil rights movement, we had reached into the worst corners of oppression in the South; we had held the country to its principles and conscience and obtained the 1964 Civil Rights Act and the 1965 Voting Rights Act; but we had not even touched the misery and desperation of the urban ghettos outside the South. Nor had we come any nearer to correcting the economic sources of the race crisis. The day President Johnson signed the Voting Rights Act, it looked as if we were bringing to an end all the years of oppression. The truth was that we were just beginning a new ordeal.

Roy Wilkins, *op. cit*, pp. 312–13.

104

WATTS BURNS WITH RAGE

by James E. Jackson

At the time of the publication of this eyewitness account its author was editor of the *Worker*.

After you have read all about the riot in Los Angeles, that is, you will have to weigh all of the thousands of words of the newsmen's "battle scene" stories against one solid statistic: the head count of the dead. The uncontestable fact is that of the thirty-six people who died in the six days of wrath, thirty-three were NEGROES.

In addition to the sum and the division of the dead, other statistics have been dutifully compiled. There were nine hundred persons hospitalized for injuries, and almost all of them were Negroes. Negroes arrested in the Watts area of Los Angeles were jammed into every available space in the city jails—of the over four thousand people who were arrested in the area, all were Negroes.

The papers reported in some detail how the National Guardsmen operated in "the field" while another eight thousand in reserve awaited their turn. An AP man wrote that on Sunday morning "about 4:30 A.M., a woman motorist approached a National Guard blockade at 59th Street and Vermont Avenue. When she failed to stop on command, guardsmen opened fire with a machine gun. A policeman who helped carry her to an ambulance said, 'Her legs were almost cut off.' She was identified as Mrs. Lerner Cooke, 47, a Negro."

A staff man for the New York *Herald Tribune* told of the team work between Lt. Richard Bogard's police from the Venice district and Col. Tom Haykin's 1st Battalion, 100th Infantry, 40th Armored Division of the National Guard. The combined force occupied the firehouse on 103rd St. (Watts) as their command post.

"The Guardsmen hit two men they figured were snipers. Maybe they were; maybe they were just curious," the reporter wrote. They were dragged into the firehouse and propped against the wall. One resisted as a doctor probed in the hole in his shoulder for the bullet lodged there.

"'Choke him till he blacks out,' a policeman said and somebody choked one of the suspects till he blacked out. He revived in a minute, coughing blood, and the fight was out of him." Again the reporter told how—

"The National Guardsmen shot into the blackness and a Negro came out, hands up, blood streaming down his face, soaking his clothes red. He was wounded, but he was alive.

"Earlier, one National Guardsman had fired a perfect shot. He hit a man in the middle of the forehead, the shot had ripped off the back of the man's head. He was dead upstairs in the firehouse. 'It was a beautiful shot,' a detective said. 'We've killed two here so far, wounded a lot of others,' someone said."

Who were the white victims of the riot? There was a sheriff's deputy, Ronald E. Ludlow, 27—and another white man died of a wound that could have come from a police riot gun; also a white fireman died when a wall of a burning building fell upon him.

Most of the thirty-three Negroes who were killed were gunned to death by police wielding riot guns. The National Guardsmen, of course, also machine-gunned a woman driving in her car. Then there was the four-year-old Negro "looter and rioter," Bruce Brown, who was shot to death in his front yard. His riotous three-year-old brother was wounded by the spray of police bullets and Guardsmen's .30 caliber machine-gun fire, but at last reports he was still alive.

Not so with eighteen-year-old Charles Shortridge, who was all set to enter Los Angeles City College in September; he lay there dead, as his uncle stared unbelievingly at the huge punched-out places the riot-gun shells had left in his nephew's head, neck and cheek.

They say it was a "race war," "an insurrection," etc. But how come it turns out that thirty-three Negroes were killed to one white deputy sheriff?

This was no "race riot." This was an elemental scream of outrage from a violated people entombed in a prison house of social deprivation and economic impoverishment.

No man has a right to expect that those whom the men of power and privilege, the capitalist ruling circle, have rendered reliefless in their wretchedness will forever slumber silently in the lower depths where they have been consigned by this society of bourgeois and billionaire.

Only those ignorant of history, only those blinded to the sight of injustice and the daily degradation of the Negro detainees of the slums of this country's great cities, ringed all about as they are by towering walls of white supremacy, hatred, and exclusion; only simpletons can assume that prisoners will not generate out of the fury of their circumstance the fire with which to ignite their cages. And so they set fire to their prisons, those unattended, denied, abused, and degraded ones. They burned their prisons as did the desperate ones who followed Spartacus. Like the ragged ones who marched and sang with Villon. Like the slave chain breakers who lived to hang with Nat Turner.

So they made other statistics—five hundred stores of absentee owners were set afire.

One of those who lost a store to the angry uprising of the downtrodden of Watts of Los Angeles (the City of the Angels it says in the Chamber of Commerce ads) was a certain Richard Gold. Mr. Gold has many stores, a chain of furniture stores, so he will simply write that burned one off of his income tax returns next year.

But the point is that Mr. Gold knows more about the time of day in the world we all live in than most of the men of his class and all of the Los Angeles city fathers. Said Mr. Gold:

"I cannot condemn these people. These people should not be shot down like dogs, white people who were as poor as they would burn and loot if they saw the chance. What's behind this is pentup anger over poverty and miserable housing."

Mr. Gold, the Watts businessman, is white and right on this score.

Watts is the city center of a Negro population which numbers some 523,000 in the whole of metropolitan Los Angeles. Watts is indeed the most poverty-ridden area of lush, plush, tinseled, and glittering Los Angeles. Into its 150 blocks are jammed 67,000 Negroes. They pay high rents for twenty-five-year-old houses. They shop in neighborhood enterprises that employ few of themselves.

There in Watts, income is lowest in all of Los Angeles, save the "skid row" district. Unemployment is several times higher in Watts than for the city as a whole. More than one-third of Watts Negroes are unemployed. Unemployment among its youth is almost twice as much. Close to sixty per cent of the Watts population depend on relief.

The *New York Times* on Sunday told it as it was when it said: "The fact is that the new Civil Rights Laws—and the related antipoverty program—have not yet greatly improved the lot of the Negroes in the teeming ghettos of the cities of the North."

The welkin sounds that came from Watts last weekend were loud and angry enough to have shaken the complacent into a wide-eyed confrontation of the reality of the challenge by the slum-confined millions who have come to the point where they were determined not to live longer in the same old way.

Billy Graham, the head of a Crusade for Christianity Movement, called the Watts' explosion a "dress rehearsal for revolution," and blessed the clubs and guns of the police for crushing it lest it spread to other cities, and "require the nation's armed might to quell it."

Fortunately, the frenetic fulminations of Billy Graham did not set the pattern for the commentary of notables in American life upon last week's social explosion in the Negro ghetto of Los Angeles. There were thoughtful observations and conclusions being suggested by many prominent personalities.

Senator Robert Kennedy, formerly Attorney General, scored the philistines who think the answer to Watts-like outbursts lies in applying more police muscle. He is quoted as saying,

"There is no point in telling Negroes to obey the law. To many Negroes, the law is the enemy. In Harlem, in Bedford-Stuyvesant (Brooklyn), it has almost always been used against them." He emphasized that "the only real hope for ending the violence is in speeding up social programs directed at the problems of slum Negroes."

Dr. Ralph J. Bunche, Under Secretary of the United Nations, in a statement to the press said:

"The ominous message of Watts is that city, state, and national authorities must quickly show the vision, the determination, and the courage to take those bold—and costly—steps necessary to begin the dispersal of every black ghetto in this land."

And he warned that continued social neglect and police abuse of the most oppressed and exploited Negroes, shoved as they are into ignored corners of the cities—"black ghettos"—are the tinder for future explosions "in every city in this country with substantial population."

Prof. Frank Hartung, sociologist of Southern Illinois University, asserted:

"It will be as difficult—but not more difficult—to eliminate this sort of violence as it is to eliminate poverty.... Major social reformation, going far beyond the passage of civil rights laws, will be required to eliminate the threat of future upheavals from the Negro slums." Herbert C. Ward, Machinists' District 727 business agent and chairman of the Communist Labor Committee, spoke for Negro labor leaders in the Los Angeles area in demanding the immediate removal of the Los Angeles police chief William H. Parker as the most universally hated symbol of the continuous and wanton police brutality and terror to which the Negro people are subjected. Furthermore, he called for: the immediate starting of slum clearance and new housing projects with public and private resources; the construction of a fully equipped hospital; the cooperation of all levels of government in an intensive program of placing unemployed and underemployed Negro young people in jobs or training for jobs at standard rates of pay.

Burt Lancaster, the Hollywood star, derided the hysterical reaction of some whites and their exclamation of alarm. Said Lancaster, "I'm just surprised it didn't happen sooner." And the screen writer, Abbey Mann, added, "I don't condone rioting, but anybody who doesn't understand it has no heart."

A man in Watts said the word over the television interview:

"We are never going back to letting anybody run over us anymore.

"We ain't going to just stand and look while they beat us.

"We ain't going hungry and ragged when they got more'n they can eat and wear either.

"Those fires lit something inside my soul too."

The challenge of the Watts explosion can be met only by a truly massive program to extend genuine material equality of opportunity to the Negro masses in particular and to those who dwell in poverty and social deprivation.

It means a vast increase in the investments in the War Against Poverty

Program, an increase that can only come about through a proportionate decrease in the expenditures in the criminal diversion of national resources and men to the dirty work the Johnson Administration is carrying out in Vietnam, where U.S. soldiers are busy killing people who have risen in behalf of freedom for themselves as did our forefathers in the Revolutionary War.

In Watts itself, what is called for is not only a total economic opportunity program for wiping out unemployment and for proper job training, but a program for the total reconstruction of the area. All the blight of slum conditions must be eliminated in accord with a plan speedily implemented. Housing, educational, and recreational facilities must be provided for in full measure.

In addition, Watts requires that Negroes, who are more than ninety per cent of the population, shall be predominant in the police department, fire fighting, and other city service jobs and functions for the area. Also, merchants doing business in the area must employ Negroes in their establishments in a just ratio.

With such an approach for Watts and for all the ghetto cities of the country, guarantees can be established against recurrences of such tragic outbursts of primitive protest and outrage at injustice.

As Rep. Augustus F. Hawkins, Los Angeles Negro Congressman, said, "The trouble is that nothing has ever been done to solve the long-range underlying problems."

Watts means that the time for stalling and demagogic promises and good will platitudes has run out. It has come down to this: Either wipe out the conditions that produce the slums; or the slums will wipe out the cities.

James E. Jackson, *The Bold, Bad '60s*, (New York; International Publishers, 1992) pp. 217–22.

105

SUPPORTING ARMED SELF-DEFENSE

by Charles R. Sims

The *National Guardian*, August 20, 1965, published this interview, conducted by William A. Price, of the president, Bogalusa, Louisiana, chapter of the Deacons for Defense and Justice. Given in part.

Q. Mr. Sims, why do you feel there is a need for the Deacons in the civil rights movement and in Bogalusa?

A. First of all, the reason why we had to organize the Deacons in the city of Bogalusa was the Negro people and civil rights workers didn't have no adequate police protection.

Q. Can you tell us what difference it may have made in Bogalusa to have the Deacons here?

A. Well, when the white power structure found out that they had mens, Negro mens that had made up their minds to stand up for their people and to give no ground, would not tolerate with no more police brutality, it had a tendency to keep the night-riders out of the neighborhood.

Q. You say the Deacons were formed because you were not given adequate police protection, does this mean that you consider the role of the Deacons to be a sort of separate police organ in behalf of the civil rights movement?

A. Well, I wouldn't say policemen, I would say a defense guard unit. We're not authorized to carry weapons.

Q. You say you're not authorized to carry weapons?

A. No we're not.

Q. Can you tell me how the Deacons view the use of weapons?

A. Self-protection.

Q. Do most Deacons, in their efforts to protect the civil rights movement, would they normally carry a gun or a pistol with them?

A. That's the only way you can protect anything, by having weapons for defense. If you carry weapons, you carry them at your own risk.

Q. Do the local authorities object to your carrying weapons?

A. Oh yeah, the local, the federal, the state, everybody object to us carrying weapons, they don't want us armed, but we had to arm ourselves because we got tired of the women, the children being harassed by the white night-riders.

Q. Have they done anything to try to get the weapons away from you?

A. Well, they threatened several times. The governor even said he was going to have all the weapons confiscated, all that the state troopers could find. But on the other hand, the governor forgot one thing—in an organization as large as the Deacons, we also have lawyers and we know about what the government can do. That would be unconstitutional for him just to walk up and start searching cars and taking people's stuff without cause.

Q. Has there been a court case to determine this?

A. No.

Q. The Second Amendment to the United States Constitution guarantees the right of the people to carry weapons, is that the way you feel about it, that the people have a right to carry weapons in their own self-defense?

A. I think a person should have the right to carry a weapon in self-defense, and I think the Louisiana state law says a man can carry a weapon in his car as long as it is not concealed. We found out in Bogalusa that that law meant for the white man, it didn't mean for the colored. Any time a colored man was caught with a weapon in his car, they jailed him for carrying a concealed weapon. So we carried them to court.

Q. It's your understanding then, that a person possessing a gun in his home, or carrying it in his car, that this is within your rights?

A. According to state law it is...

Q. Can you tell me what difference it has made with the white community, the fact that there are the Deacons here in Bogalusa and that they are prepared to use arms even if they may not?

A. For one thing that made a difference, there were a lot of night-riders riding through the neighborhood; we stopped them. We put them out and gave them fair warning. A couple of incidents happened when people were fired on. So the white man right away found out that a brand new Negro was born. We definitely couldn't swim and we was as close to the river as we could get so there was but one way to go.

Q. So you think there has been a difference in the attitude of the white people towards the civil rights movement in Bogalusa because you have been here to protect it?

A. Yes, I do believe that. I believe that if the Deacons had been organized in 1964, the three civil rights workers that was murdered in Philadelphia, Mississippi, might have been living today because we'd have been around to stop it...

Q. What has been the response to the existence of the Deacons from the civil rights movement, from the Congress of Racial Equality, other civil rights organizations or from unaffiliated whites that come in like we might come in?

A. They're most glad we have the Deacons organized. See, right now it's rather quiet. Two months ago a white civil rights worker or even a colored civil rights worker, he couldn't come into Bogalusa unless we brought him in. The whites would be on the road trying to stop cars. We've taken on the job of transportation in and out of Bogalusa, bringing people backwards and forwards, making sure that they get here safe. . . .

Q. Would you recommend that white persons interested in or working in the civil rights movement carry their own arms or guns when they travel in the South?

A. I will not recommend anyone to carry guns. I don't think that's my job to recommend people to carry weapons. When you carry a weapon, you have to have a made up mind to use it. I am president of the Deacons and not a legal advisor to everyone who passes through Bogalusa.

Q. Can you tell us anything about how you would operate in any particular kind of an emergency situation. Would you get a call by phone, or do you have a two-way radio set up? Suppose something was happening to somebody in an outlying district, how are you likely to know about it and how are you likely to respond to it?

A. The old saying that I've heard is that bad news travels fast. We have telephones, naturally, word of mouth, and we have some powerful walkie-talkies. We can receive a lot of different calls on the walkie-talkies that we can't transmit, but we can receive them. And that's what bugs the white man today, why was we able to be in so many places so quick. We was intercepting their calls.

Q. You were intercepting the calls of the white people?

A. Sure, the Ku Klux Klan, sometimes the police calls, all depends.

Q. You mean they have their own radios and you listen in to them?

A. Naturally. . . .

Q. The mere showing of a weapon, does that sometimes take care of a situation?

A. The showing of a weapon stops many things. Everybody want to live and nobody want to die. But here in Bogalusa, I'm one of the few peoples who is really known as a Deacon and anybody that I associate with, they just take for granted they are Deacons. I show up; then ten, twelve more mens show up, whether they Deacons or not, they branded, you know. That make the white man respect us even more, because nine out of ten he be right.

Q. There might be some people who feel that merely by your having weapons in your possession and being willing to use them, that this might create violence rather than stopping it. . . .

A. Well some peoples ought to take one other thing into consideration. I owned three or four weapons long before the civil rights movement. I went to jail, I think about three times for carrying concealed weapons ten years before the movement start. So, I mean, having a weapon's nothing new. What bugged the people was something else—when they found out what was the program of the Deacons. I do have a police record.

Q. If you say that the white man was not bugged until the Deacons were created, was it the organization of a group like the Deacons that made the difference rather than, say, you as an individual. . . .

A. No, not me as an individual. See, the southern white man is almost like Hitler in the South. He been dictating to the Negro people, "Boy, this," and "Uncle, that," and "Granma, go here," and people's been jumpin'. So he gets up one morning and discovers that "Boy," was a man, and that he can walk up and say something to "boy" and "boy" don't like what he say, he tell him to eat himself—you know? And then if he blow up, there's a good fight right there. So the man goes back home and sit down and try to figure out the Negro. Shortly after that we had several rallies. And I guess he received his answer—we told him a brand new Negro was born. The one he'd been pushin' around, he didn't exist anymore.

Q. Do you think people here in Bogalusa realize that now?

A. Oh, yes.

Q. Has it made a difference?

A. A great difference.

Q. Could you describe the difference?

A. First of all we don't have these people driving through this neighborhood throwing at people's houses, catching two or three fellows on the streets, jumping out their car, whipping them up 'cause these are Negroes and they are white. We don't be bothered because these paddies [whites] in the streets calling themselves collectors harassing the womens and going from door to door to see 'how that one is.' We don't have any of this. Because of the Deacons, we don't have any of this. We don't have much work to do now. But up until the middle of July we patrolled the streets twenty-four hours a day, and made sure we didn't have any of this. When we found this, we hadded 'em up and if they give us any resistance, we, you know, shook 'em up. . . .

Q. Now outside of Bogalusa, when there is some news about a Negro carrying a gun or about some kind of violence, and people don't know who the Deacons are and who may not be Deacons, they may feel that this is the Deacons at work. Have there been instances like that where there has been violence and the Deacons were blamed for it?

A. Yes, a lot of cases. Any time a Negro and a white man have any kind of round up and the Negro decide he going to fight him back, he's a Deacon. We had one case here where a Negro and a white man had a round and a little shootin' was done. He was named a Deacon. Now I can truthfully say he was not a Deacon. But the papers, the government, and everybody else say he was. So I laugh at the government to its face. I told them point blank; you do not know who Deacons is and quit gettin' on the air and telling peoples that people are Deacons just because they stood up to a white man....

Q. Could you say how many Deacons there are in Bogalusa and throughout the South?

A. No, but I'll tell you this, we have throughout the South at this time somewhere between fifty and sixty chapters.

Q. Roughly how many people in each chapter?

A. I won't tell you that.

Q. Could you tell us what areas they cover?

A. Alabama, Mississippi, Arkansas, Louisiana, Texas.

Q. Georgia?

A. No. We have Georgia and North Carolina in mind. As a matter of fact I was supposed to go to North Carolina and organize the people there, and in Florida, but I don't have time right now to do it.

Q. Have you been making trips outside of Louisiana to see these other groups, to help them organize?

A. No, I send mens. And the headquarters in Jonesboro sends mens out.

Q. The headquarters is in Jonesboro, Louisiana.

A. Yes.

Q. Is Jonesboro near Bogalusa?

A. No, it's about three hundred miles from here, way up north in Louisiana.

Q. Near the Arkansas border?

A. Shouldn't be too far.

Q. Could you tell us what views you might have on the civil rights tactic of nonviolence?

A. The nonviolent act is a good act—providing the policemens do their job. But in the southern states, not just Louisiana, but in the southern states, the police have never done their job when the white and the Negro are involved—unless the Negro's getting the best of the white man.

Q. How do you think the movement could best be advanced or get its aims the quickest if it didn't use nonviolence?

A. I believe nonviolence is the only way. Negotiations are going to be the main point in this fight.

Q. Would it be correct to put it this way, that you feel nonviolence is the correct way to get political and economic things done....

A. Sure.

Q. But that behind that, behind the nonviolence, the Deacons or organizations like the Deacons are necessary to protect the rights of this nonviolent movement?

A. That's right....

Q. Mr. Sims, just one last question, how long do you think the Deacons will be needed in the civil rights movement?

A. First of all, this is a long fight. In 1965 there will be a great change made. But after this change is made, the biggest fight is to keep it. My son, his son might have to fight this fight and that's one reason why we won't be able to disband the Deacons for a long time. How long, Heaven only knows. But it will be a long time.

106

PAST VICTORIES, FUTURE NEEDS: ALBANY, GEORGIA

by Slater King

The chairman of the Albany Movement summarizes past victories and projects future needs as of the middle of the 1960s.

In the struggle in Albany, we have often felt that we have been fighting against tremendously powerful forces not just in the state of Georgia, but also within the Federal Government itself as witnessed by the indictment and convictions of innocent Negro leaders in the Civil Rights struggle.

There have been a few rays of hope. A federal judge granted an injunction in June 1964 against the city of Albany prohibiting interference of our right to peacefully protest. So we have picketed and marched in protest of the killing of an innocent Negro by a white policeman and other injustices.

Most of the public facilities covered under the Civil Rights Bill have been desegregated. We have a few restaurants that have called themselves "private clubs" rather than integrate. We are testing these in Federal Court.

In all of the small and rural communities that surround Albany, the Negroes have been so "cowed" down and intimidated by hangings, being burned alive and all sorts of mayhem and torture, physical as well as psychological, until they will not even attempt to use the integrated facilities presumably made available to them through the recently enacted Civil Rights Bill. In one neighboring community where a few young Negroes have attempted to use the local previously "all white" theatre, police have stood in front of the theatre allowing whites to come and go but blocking the paths of Negroes attempting to enter. Their excuse is that they are keeping order. It is a definite axiom to say that in the majority, the police force and the machinery of the southern local and state enforcement agencies will be used not for the Negroes' protection but as a repressive instrument against them. The city of Albany hired six Negro policemen. There is a tremendous rapport between them and the Negroes of Albany. They have been very humane men who have restrained themselves greatly in the exercise of their police powers.

They have dramatically reduced the number of Negroes brought before the judge on Monday morning for cases involving drunkenness—fighting—and gambling. White policemen practiced quite a bit of brutality and killed quite a few Negroes. All of this has been cut out by the Negro officers.

We have begun to build political power by dramatically increasing the number of Negro voters and by turning out ninety per cent of that vote, a higher percentage than ever before. There is a certain irony in my being under a one year and one day *federal sentence* (presently under appeal in the Fifth Circuit Court of Appeals in New Orleans, Louisiana) and receiving an invitation to the President's inauguration last January.

We in Albany, Georgia feel a great sense of regard in the enactment of the Civil Rights Bill despite its many limitations. There were college students who were "sitting in" and conducting other demonstrations to protest segregation but we were the first community where there was the involvement of the total community protesting segregation. This caused thousands of blacks to be jailed (in 1961–62). After other communities, such as Birmingham and others followed our example, it was clear that this country would have to enact the Civil Rights Bill to stop the developments of embarrassing spectacles such as Albany and Birmingham, which were being viewed by an international audience.

It is pathetic that most of the Negroes who were arrested here for marching and sitting in and for the whole spectrum of Civil Rights activities will not enjoy the fruits of their labors because many aren't employed and many who are employed don't make enough to eat out or travel to enjoy these facilities that are now open to them. The people who will enjoy these new freedoms are the small group composing the "Black Bourgeoisie." Not only have most of them not helped financially or physically in the Civil Rights struggles, but many of them ridiculed those Negroes who did.

The Civil Rights Bill has helped in many ways in desegregating the restaurants, gas stations' rest rooms, and many other places. It will also help in opening a few jobs, but for the majority of these jobs the Negroes do not have the technical training necessary.

There are still thousands of Negroes here who are part of what is called the substrata of American society. The Civil Rights Bill will not help them. These black families have grown up generation after generation bordering on illiteracy. But most regrettable, they have lost all hope that America will help them. Today for these Negroes who form the substrata of American life, it looks more bleak and hopeless than ever. With the Civil Rights Bill passed, the lines in the battle are not as clearly demarcated as in the past. It is harder to get issues around which people will rally and yet the average Negro family finds that economically if anything it is *recessing* instead of *progressing*.

Injustices Continue

In Albany in March 1964, there were twenty-three Negroes at the Department of Labor office waiting for jobs. The manager of the office, who is paid by federal funds, had them arrested for vagrancy. They were then fined $23.00 by the judge or given thirty-day sentences to be served on the streets. Then some of their families got further into a financial bog by borrowing the money from "loan sharks" to have the men released while some served the thirty days' time. We wired the Secretary of Labor in Washington. The Department of Labor made a perfunctory check but no remedial action was ever taken. Then in March 1965, the same manager of the United States Employment Service threatened to have Negro employees removed forcibly from the offices and arrested if they did not agree to work for $1.00 per hour. The men felt that they should get a minimum of at least $1.25 per hour.

Do not these type actions make men think that they must use desperate means to alleviate their condition as it becomes more desperate?

In Albany we feel that we must continue to run Negro candidates for office in that it is extremely educative for the Negroes and whites and it spurs voter registration among Negroes more than anything else. SNCC and SCLC used this to launch a voter registration drive in the Second Congressional District. Attorney C. B. King ran for Congress and made a very impressive race. Thousands of new voters were added to the books. He received in excess of eight thousand votes and was number two in Albany, Bainbridge, Newton, Cordele, and other cities in the Second Congressional District. His television appearances helped to educate blacks *and* whites. However, all money for his campaign was raised in the Negro community. . . .

The city abolished *all* of the playgrounds, swimming pools, parks, rather than integrate them. Then they planned the ruse of having *all* of the "white" swimming pools open. These have been "allegedly" purchased by "private" investors. We are contesting this in Federal Court where the case is to come up in appeal soon, and we have been to jail for attempting to use these facilities. But as of now our children have *no public recreational facilities*.

Over two thousand of our children daily walk the streets of Albany as vagrants from school. The city does not care because it does not want our children to have an education. They have hired an incompetent Negro truant officer whom the Negro community is going to have to fight to have removed from his position.

As we looked at all of these ills that plague the Negro community, we felt that we needed a central place so that many forces in the Negro community could come together at regular intervals to communicate and to help drive out the "guilty mist" that plagues so much of our community; to let mothers honestly begin to discuss with one another their family difficulties and to see what could be done to rid themselves of these problems; to know that thousands in this community share their plight and their ills.

We wanted to incorporate a center where successful black businessmen would give certain hours of their time for free counseling: real estate brokers, people who know about finance, doctors, lawyers. We would get fathers to spend time with boys helping to supervise recreational facilities or crafts.

We have to begin a free day care center for those parents who could not pay for their children. This very modern day care center, under the direction of Mrs. Wendy Roberts, began April 1, 1965, which should help eliminate the many fire deaths that we have had each year.

To make the Negro church more relevant, to plan recreation for our kids who have none now, we incorporated the Dougherty County Resources Development Association, Inc. We have been granted a beginning sum from the United Presbyterian Church under its commission on Race and Religion. The sum is far less than we need so we are asking support from all of our friends in this great endeavor.

In conclusion I see as our main battle now an attempt to make a success of many rehabilitative programs in the Negro community covering the whole gamut of our lives. Much surgery has to be performed to remove the scars and defects left after three hundred years of mental and physical slavery.

The attempt will also be made to build strong political and economic power in the black community.

I do not think that there will be much integration here for some years to come. But as the Negro gains in his economic and political power, belief and pride in himself, he will no longer be thought of by the white majority as the "untouchable" in American life as the white man now regards him and for the first time there will be a possibility of meaningful integration.

Freedomways 5 (Summer, 1965): 417–23; published in part.

107

DESEGREGATING SCHOOLS: "ONE OF THE PROBLEMS"

by Unknown Black Parent in Deep South

The Southern Regional Council, headquartered in Atlanta, issued a pamphlet in September 1965 entitled "School Desegregation: Old Problems Under a New Law." As a frontispiece to this publication was reproduced a letter it received, dated September 9, 1965. The place of origin and signature were blacked out. It is reproduced below.

Sept 9–1965

We wont to than you for the information we recevied in Macon Ga. It has helped us to enroll 14 students in the all while school ******* hight school. We are having a lots of truble My life have all ready been threaled

My brother ****** house has been shoot in So we both will have to take the children out of school and move some where else so give me the best information on this looking to hear from you soon.

As of the close of 1965, African-American children constituted 6 percent of the pupils in public school districts in eleven southern states. In Alabama the figure was half of 1 percent; in Mississippi the figure was six-tenths of 1 percent. Nevertheless, the U.S. Office of Education stated as of that date that 95 percent of the school districts in the eleven southern states are listed as "in compliance" with the law (*Progressive*, February 1966, editorial).

108

THE THRESHOLD OF A NEW RECONSTRUCTION

by J. H. O'Dell

J. H. O'Dell had been an early staff member of the SCLC and a leader of the Danville, Virginia, movement. He was correctly characterized as an "old ally" of Martin Luther King's by David L. Lewis in his biography of the latter. In this essay, O'Dell, aware of a decline in the militancy of the early 1960s, calls for a deepening of the commitment and objectives of the movement. The concluding section of that analysis follows:

These are two interdependent principles and therefore could be viewed as two sides of a single principle; *i.e.*, genuinely representative government. The first of these is inherent in the 15th Amendment of the Constitution and in the newly enacted Voter Rights Act. However, the problem of vigorous, principled enforcement of these measures by a dilatory, undependable Federal government remains a very real and thorny problem for the Freedom Movement. The second of these, proportional representation, ultimately rests upon the first and vice-versa. Given the long history of racism which has characterized every area of U.S. life, no government (even one made of "good white friends") is adequately representative, unless the black population exercises a degree of power on all levels at least equal to their percentages in the local population.

We are not unmindful of the possibility that the public relations gesture towards "moderation" and "compliance" by the existing state system may, for a while, tend to have the effect of reinforcing the inclination of the black community to seek-out "white moderates" to be elected to governmental power. This has been our general political behavior over the past two decades of the civil rights era, and is not to be regarded as unusual, for a people still emerging from what is essentially a colonialist experience. We have suffered a certain loss of confidence in ourselves; a massive inferiority complex in relation to white people, part of the psychology created by the system of oppression. However, as we digest our American experience and, as a people, come to rediscover ourselves, this too will change, radically. . . .

Not the least formidable of the charges against southern government is that it has been the chief instrument for enforcing the segregation system for more than four generations. Nor can the Movement ignore the fact that the main segregationist political machines and the police power which supports them, still occupy the halls of State government, while the small towns like Greensboro and Haynesville, Alabama, Quincy, Florida, Allendale, South Carolina, etc. are everywhere still conducting a kind of hidden war against the Negro community and the Civil Rights Act. This is a well-organized campaign of terror and economic reprisals. These realities, and much more that has never been spoken of, are underscored by the freeing of Klansmen charged with murder in Alabama, Mississippi, and "moderate" Georgia, alike, as well as the growth in the State political influence of the right-wing New Conservatives of the Birch Society and the Goldwater-Republicans.

Southern government may still be defined as the power function of a regional oligarchy of segregationists presiding over an economy of exploitation, on behalf of a national power structure whose main bases are in the financial-industrial centers outside the South.

This reality dictates that the far-reaching job of political reconstruction in the South is a matter of nationwide active concern. However, the initiative for this concern and action has to come from the black community and its nationwide Freedom Movement, which unites Harlem with Mississippi and Watts in Los Angeles with Bogalusa and Chicago.

Adding "with all deliberate speed" a million more new black voters to the registration rolls in Mississippi, Alabama, and the other areas of the South, will transform the already significant quantitative growth of the Negro electorate into a qualitative new social force for the complete renovation of southern institutional life. It must be recognized that the mounting black vote is capable of supporting a far more progressive social ideology than now prevails in the country as a whole. To bring this potential to fruition depends decidedly upon the active role which the most exploited (and the still unheard from) sections of the black community play in shaping our political future. This means a kind of grass-roots organizing, and political education never quite achieved on a sustained basis during the Civil Rights era. Grass-roots organization, county by county, block by block, precinct by precinct, plantation by plantation. In this regard, the Movement in Mississippi with its Freedom Democratic Party and Freedom Labor Union (among the plantation workers) is among the finest examples to date. Whatever the style of activity or the techniques necessary our perspective should remain clear and that is getting into the seats of governmental power those men and women who went to jail for Freedom, or who have otherwise been identified with the Movement. . . .

What must be "overcome" is the very atmosphere in which the county courthouses, the city halls, sheriffs' offices, and the police stations are symbols of racist tyranny to black people. This is fundamentally a question of governmental power for the black community adequate to their needs. Without it no "civil rights" are as secure as the paper they are written on.

An inherent part of this political reconstruction is the formation of governmental organs with the power to clean up the prison system, review cases and secure justice for the uncounted numbers of prisoners innocent of any crime, but trapped by the state system. Many of these have been sent to jails under laws which the Negro population had no voice in making and at the whim of judges "elected" by means of our disfranchisement but who draw their salaries from our taxes.

In other cases the families of victims of police brutality should be indemnified and the guilty policemen or sheriffs brought to trial.

In general outline then, the struggle to implement the above measures will contribute towards providing a cohesiveness and a new sense of purpose, in harmony with the requirements of the present period in our developmental history as a Freedom Movement. Likewise, the achievement of such objectives will generally put our Movement in full stride with the present stage of development of the African revolutions. For the Afro-American, it is not a question of establishing a separate state or separate territory, but one of achieving representative governmental power in those areas wherein the black population has historically been a majority or a substantial minority. This is the next phase in our decolonization struggle.

Governmental power means to possess the leverage for the economic and social transformation of such areas, consistent with the material, cultural, and psychological well-being and security of the population inhabiting these areas. This may require, at a certain point, the reorganization of certain existing administrative state units and the establishment of new state or county boundaries in certain areas, in order to facilitate the rapid fulfillment of the above socioeconomic purposes. A reapportionment of state legislatures consistent with these objectives is, likewise, in order.

Further, the achievement of such objectives would have the overall effect of *aiding the country as a whole*, by transforming these areas which have historically been a cesspool of poverty, racist ideology, and pro-fascist, militaristic state organization. These are the operating factors and characteristics which have traditionally given the South its regional character, enriched the nation's economic royalists, and burdened the progressive forces of the nation with their greatest obstacle. The ascent to governmental power by the Negro community will be a landmark achievement, aiding the U.S. to develop in a progressive direction, based upon the implementation of whatever measures are necessary to correct its congenital deformity of racism.

Freedomways 5, (Fall 1965): 503–506; footnotes omitted. An insightful essay at the mid-sixties point is St. Clair Drake, "The Social and Economic Status of the Negro in the United States," in *Daedalus* 94 (1965).

109

NEXT STEP THE NORTH

by Martin Luther King, Jr.

The marvelous power of expression possessed by Martin Luther King, Jr., need not be argued. But among its splendid examples is the following exposition of the need for a massive confrontation of racism in the North.

The flames of Watts illuminated more than the western sky; they cast light on the imperfections in the Civil Rights movement and the tragic shallowness of white racial policy in the explosive ghettos.

Ten years ago in Montgomery, Alabama, seething resentment caused a total Negro community to unite to level a powerful system of injustice. The nation and the world were electrified by their new method of struggle—mass, nonviolent direct action. In the succeeding years the power of this method shook the nation from its somnolence and complacency, changed embedded customs, wrote historic legislation, and gave a whole generation vibrant ideals. In the decade the arena widened, the conflict intensified, and the stakes rose in importance, yet the method was undeviatingly nonviolent.

Yet on the tenth anniversary of nonviolence as a theory of social change, with its success acknowledged and applauded around the world, a segment of a Negro community united to protest injustice, but this time by means of violence.

The paradox is striking, but it can be understood: our movement has been essentially regional, not national—the confrontation of opposing forces met in climactic engagements only in the South. The issues and their solution were similarly regional and the changes affected only the areas of combat.

It is in the South that Negroes in this past decade experienced the birth of human dignity—eating in restaurants, studying in schools, traveling in public conveyances side by side with whites for the first time in a century. Every day southern Negroes perceive, and are reminded of, the fruits of their struggle. The changes are not only dramatic but are cumulative and dynamic, moving constantly toward broader application.

In the North, on the other hand, the Negro's repellent slum life was altered not for the better but for the worse. Oppression in the ghettos intensified. To the homes of ten years ago, squalid then, were added ten years of decay. School segregation did not abate but increased. Above all, unemployment for Negroes swelled and remained unaffected by general economic expansion. As the nation, Negro and white, trembled with outrage at police brutality in the South, police misconduct in the North was rationalized, tolerated, and usually denied.

The northern ghetto dweller lived in a schizophrenic social milieu. He supported and derived pride from southern struggles and accomplishment. Yet the civil rights revolution appeared to be draining energy from the North, energy that flowed south to transform life there while stagnation blanketed northern Negro communities. It was a decade of role reversal. The North, heretofore vital, atrophied, and the traditionally passive South burst with dynamic vibrancy.

If the struggle had been on a national front, the changes in the North would have been kaleidoscopic. To match the South in relative change, the North in the decade should have been well on its way to the dissolution of ghettos; unemployment due to discrimination should have disappeared;

tensions with the police should have been modified or eradicated by long-tested institutions, and interracial relationships should have been so commonplace that they should no longer have attracted comment or attention. In short, the North needed and was ready for profound progress and, relatively, the changes should have far surpassed those in the South. In fact, however, the North, at best, stood still as the South caught up.

Civil rights leaders had long thought that the North would benefit derivately from the southern struggle. They assumed that without massive upheavals certain systematic changes were inevitable as the whole nation reexamined and searched its conscience. This was a miscalculation. It was founded on the belief that opposition in the North was not intransigent; that it was flexible and was, if not fully, at least partially hospitable to corrective influences. We forgot what we knew daily in the South—freedom is not given, it is won by struggle.

In my travels in the North I was increasingly becoming disillusioned with the power structures there. I encountered the tragic and stubborn fact that in virtually no major city was there a mayor possessing statesmanship, understanding, or even strong compassion on the civil rights question. Many of them sat on platforms with all the imposing regalia of office to welcome me to their cities, and showered praise on the heroism of southern Negroes. Yet when the issues were joined concerning local conditions only the language was polite; the rejection was firm and unequivocal. All my experience indicated that hope of voluntary understanding was chimerical; there was blindness, obtuseness, and rigidity that would only be altered by a dynamic movement. Ironically, Mayor Ivan Allen of Atlanta and many other southern public officials, with all their conflicts, came much further in human relations than mayors of the major northern cities. Many political leaders in the South had only yesterday been implacable segregationists but found the inner resources to change their convictions. More than that, they had the courage and integrity to speak bluntly to their constituents and furnished the leadership for them to make necessary constructive changes.

Another inescapable contrast is in the role of national and local governments. The national administrations increasingly became more and more responsive to pressures from the South. As our movement, pursuing techniques of creative nonviolence, encountered savage and brutal responses, all branches of the federal government moved to face the challenge with increasing responsibility and firmness. Beyond this, a deeper human understanding of underlying causes became clearer to them and a true sense of identity and alliance emerged. In the North, in marked contrast, municipal and state laws were enacted without passion or evident conviction. Feeble and anemic enforcement amid political machinations made them all but ineffectual. It was worse then tokenism; it was trifling with life-and-death issues with unfeeling clumsiness and opportunism.

What was the culpability of Negro leaders? Southern Negro leaders remained substantially regional forces although inspirationally they emerged as national figures. Further, they projected solutions principally for southern conditions in framing proposals for national legislation. Finally, they took more from the North in support than they put into it. They found themselves overwhelmed with the responsibility of a movement of revolutionary dimensions and could not assume national command even had their leadership been desired. Northern Negro leaders were content to support the South and many did so devotedly. Others tended to coast with gradualism because the issues being sought in the South had long been solved in the North.

The key error of both Negro and white leadership was in expecting the ghettos to stand still and in underestimating the deterioration that increasingly embittered its life.

The white population is a stranger to the ghetto. Negroes are not only hemmed in in it; whites are shut out of it.

Unemployment and pitiful wages are at the bottom of ghetto misery. Life-sapping poverty roots negroes in the decayed tenements where rats and filth become inseparable parts of the structures. But dirt alone could not crush a people, especially those who are so widely employed in disposing of it. Unemployment and insecure employment more effectively undermine family life. Not only are the Negroes in general the first to be cast into the jobless army, but the Negro male precedes his wife in unemployment. As a consequence, he lives in a matriarchal society within the larger culture, which is patriarchal. The cruelest blow to his integrity as a man are laws which deprive a family of Aid to Dependent Children support if a male resides in the home. He is then forced to abandon his family so that they may survive. He is coerced into irresponsibility by his responsible love for his family. But even ensuring food on the table is insufficient to secure a constructive life for the children. They are herded into ghetto schools and pushed through grades of schooling without learning. Their after-school life is spent in neglected, filthy streets that abound in open crime. The most grievous charge against municipal police is not brutality, though it exists. Permissive crime in ghettos is the nightmare of the slum family. Permissive crime is the name for the organized crime that flourishes in the ghetto—designed, directed, and cultivated by white national crime syndicates operating numbers, narcotics, and prostitution rackets freely in the protected sanctuaries of the ghettos. Because no one, including the police, cares particularly about ghetto crime, it pervades every area of life. The Negro child who learns too little about books in his pathetic schools, learns too much about crime in the streets around him. Even when he and his family resist its corruption, its presence is a source of fear and of moral debilitation.

Against this caricature of the American standard of living is the immediate proximity of the affluent society. In the South there is something of shared poverty, Negro and white. In the North, white existence, only steps away, glitters with conspicuous consumption. Even television becomes incendiary when it beams pictures of affluent homes and multitudinous consumer products to an aching poor, living in wretched hovels.

In these terms Los Angeles could have expected riots because it is the luminous symbol of luxurious living for whites. Watts is closer to it, and yet farther from it, than any other Negro community in the country. The looting in Watts was a form of social protest very common through the ages as a dramatic and destructive gesture of the poor toward symbols of their needs.

Los Angeles could have expected the holocaust when its officials tied up federal aid in political manipulation; when the rate of Negro unemployment soared above the depression levels of the thirties; when the population density of Watts became the worst in the nation. Yet even these tormenting physical conditions are less than the full story. California in 1964 repealed its law forbidding racial discrimination in housing. It was the first major state in the country to take away gains Negroes had won at a time when progress was visible and substantial elsewhere, and especially in the South. California by this callous act voted for ghettos. The atrociousness of some deeds may be concealed by legal ritual, but their destructiveness is felt with bitter force by its victims. Victor Hugo understood this when he said, "If a soul is left in darkness, sins will be committed. The guilty one is not he who commits the sin, but he who causes the darkness."

Out of these many causes the Negro freedom movement will be altering its course in the period to come. Conditions in the North will come into focus and sharpened conflict will unfold.

The insistent question is whether that movement will be violent or nonviolent. It cannot be taken for granted that Negroes will adhere to nonviolence under any conditions. When there is rocklike intransigence or sophisticated manipulation that mocks the empty-handed petitioner, rage replaces reason. Nonviolence is a powerful demand for reason and justice. If it is rudely rebuked it is not transformed into resignation and passivity. Southern segregationists in many places yielded to it because they realized alternatives could be more destructive. Northern white leadership has relied too much on tokens, substitutes, and Negro patience. The end of this road is clearly in sight. The cohesive, potentially explosive Negro community in the North has a short fuse and a long train of abuses. Those who argue that it is hazardous to give warnings, lest the expression of apprehension head to violence, are in error. Violence has already been practiced too often, and always because remedies were postponed. It is now the task of responsible people to indicate where and why spontaneous combustion is accumulating.

The southern Negro created mass nonviolent direct action and made history with it and will go on to far greater gains, holding it firmly as his peaceful sword.

The North, on the other hand, has for several years been spontaneously testing violence. There are many who are arguing that positive gains have followed riots. They hold that in the complexities of urban life the tricks of sophisticated segregation cannot be defeated except by the power of violence. They are so close to white society but so alienated from it and consumed with revulsion toward its hypocrisies that they are disinterested in integration. Black nationalism is more fitted to their angry mood.

I do not believe this thinking will dominate the movement, however. I think it will fail, not because northern Negroes will settle for a no-win tranquillity and calm; it will fail because they can be convinced there is a more effective method and a more moral one—nonviolent direct action.

This method has never been utilized on a large or protracted scale in the North. But in the South it will mobilize Negroes for action more effectively than appeals to violence. Ultimately rioting has the serious defect that it can be terminated by greater force. The number available for violence is relatively small and can be countered. Conversely, nonviolence can mobilize numbers so huge there is no counterforce. Its power is such that it can be sustained by the will of its supporters not merely for days but even for extended periods.

If one hundred thousand Negroes march in a major city to a strategic location, they will make municipal operations difficult to conduct; they will exceed the capacity of even the most reckless mayor to use force against them; and they will repeat this action daily, if necessary. Without harming persons or property they can draw as much attention to their grievances as the outbreak at Watts, and they will have asserted their unwavering determination while retaining their dignity and discipline.

The critical task will be to convince Negroes driven to cynicism that nonviolence can win. Many municipal government leaders will have no more imagination than to scorn it and ridicule it. Nonetheless, though they will be serving the trend to violence, they will not influence the bulk of Negroes who, I am confident, will embrace nonviolence. In the South we are taunted, mocked, and abused beyond belief. A hundred political commentators interred nonviolence into a premature grave.

Yet in 1965 there is a new South, still far from democratic consistency or harmony, but equally distant from the plantation-overseer South. The northern Negro knows this because he helped to bring it into being. He has yet to use nonviolent direct action; he has not even examined its special tactical application in his different community. He may even be reluctant in his urban sophistication to embrace its moral simplicities. But his wisdom is not less than his southern brothers and a power that could break the savagery of southern segregation commands respect and induces emulation. The rushing history of change has been late to reach the North but it is now on a fixed northerly course. The urban slums need not be destroyed by flames; earnest people of good will can decree their end nonviolently—as atrocious relics of a persisting unjust past.

Saturday Review, November 13, 1965; in J. M. Washington, ed., cited work, pp. 189–94.

110

TRAVELING JIM CROW

Mahalia Jackson

Ms. Jackson was born in 1911 in New Orleans; at the age of sixteen, she went to Chicago, labored as a domestic servant, and sang in church. Her marvelous voice finally brought worldwide recognition. In her autobiography, published in 1966, she briefly describes problems of travel in the post–World War II world:

Until my singing made me famous, I'd lived so far inside the colored people's world that I didn't have to pay attention every day to the way some white people in this country act toward a person with a darker skin. I could go for long stretches and not be made angry or hurt by them....

A little while back I made a concert tour through the South from Virginia to Florida. There were lots of white people at those concerts and they sat side by side with colored folks because my instruction to the ushers is to say, "Come right in. Pick a seat and sit right down—anywhere." Because if you come to hear religious music, you're not supposed to feel any bigger than anybody else. Those white people—and a lot of them were ministers—applauded just as hard as anybody in the audience, and afterward some of them came around to tell me how much they had enjoyed the evening.

But the minute I left the concert hall I felt as if I had stepped back into the jungle. My accompanist, Mildred Falls, and I were traveling in my car, a Cadillac. My cousin, John Stevens, a young actor and drama teacher from Chicago, was doing the driving. From Virginia to Florida it was a nightmare. There was no place for us to eat or sleep on the main highways. Restaurants wouldn't serve us. Teen-age white girls who were serving as car hops would come bouncing out to the car and stop dead when they saw we were Negroes, spin around without a word and walk away. Some gasoline stations didn't want to sell us gas and oil. Some told us that no rest rooms were available. The looks of anger at the sight of us colored folks sitting in a nice car were frightening to see.

To turn off the main highway and find a place to eat and sleep in a colored neighborhood meant losing so much time that we finally were driving hundreds of extra miles each day to get to the next city in which I was to sing so that we could get a place to eat and sleep. It got so we were living on bags of fresh fruit during the day and driving half the night and I was so exhausted by the time I was supposed to sing I was almost dizzy.

When the white people came crowding around us after the concerts—ministers, teachers, educated people—I thanked them for their praise but I felt like saying, "How big does a person have to grow down in this part of the country before he's going to stand up and say, 'Let us stop treating other men and women and children with such cruelty just because they are born colored!'"

Mahalia Jackson, with E. M. Wylie, *Movin' On Up* (New York: Hawthorne Books, 1966), pp. 96–97; in Gerda Lerner, cited work, pp. 383–84.

111

THE KILLING OF AN AGITATOR

by James Forman, et al.

Sammy Younge had been killed by a single bullet in the back of the head, at approximately 11:45 P.M. on January 3, 1966. There was no question about who had killed him; the man admitted it soon afterward. The basic story of what had happened that night emerged from the reports of several witnesses.

GWEN PATTON: I've read five affidavits, and they all say basically the same thing about what happened. It seems that Sammy was at the gas station that evening when a group of Tuskegee students drove up into a sort of alley between the gas station and the bus depot. As far as they could gather, he was going in to buy a package of cigarettes and he also asked to use the restroom. The man at the station, a white man, pointed to the back. The bathroom for Negroes is there, the one for whites is inside. Sammy said—they heard him say this—"You haven't heard of the Civil Rights Act." Sammy wasn't going around to the back. Harsh words were exchanged and the man started waving his gun. He told Sammy to get off his property.

Sammy got in his car and moved it over near the bus station which is next to the gas station. There's a cab-stand there, too. They still had this exchange of words. At that point, the man waved the gun and then raised it. There were some golf clubs standing beside the bus station—they belonged to a passenger waiting for the late bus to Atlanta—and Sammy pulled one out. The man looked as though he was coming at Sammy. Sammy ran and the man fired. He missed.

Sammy ran onto the Greyhound bus standing there—the bus to Atlanta. He shouted, "Would you shoot me on this bus?" The bus driver got off and went to talk to the man, told him he'd better not do that. Sammy got off the bus and it pulled away. But those students were still there. Sammy was still running, trying to get back to his car. The man raised his gun again and shot. Sammy fell, hit in the head. There are some very strange things about all this. I can't see Sammy walking off the bus voluntarily without having had some type of satisfaction. Sammy would have torn that whole bus up rather than walk out there and face a bullet. I believe there must have been some type of exchange, that nobody's talked about, between the bus driver and the gas station man, which made

Sammy think there wouldn't be any trouble. Sammy wasn't afraid to go out and do something that needed to be done, but violence upset him a great deal and the consequences from violence really disturbed him. I can't see Sammy, twelve o'clock at night, aggravating or agitating somebody, like they say.

Others who knew Sammy well agreed on this point.

WENDY PARIS: People say that Sammy was standing there, cussing the man out. Saying, "You won't shoot me," and all that. But that wasn't the Sammy I knew. And he wasn't drunk. I know he wasn't drunk because I had seen him about forty minutes earlier and had put that sticker on his car. That's probably what did it.

ELDRIDGE BURNS: Call him nigger, send him to the back, he wasn't going. He was going to sit up there and tell you he wasn't a nigger. You treat him like a man. That night, Sammy was talking right back to the man. The thing must have just built up in him. He must have known that this was his night. He just told the guy, "You don't treat me this way." He probably cursed him.

But I know that when the stuff got rough, Sammy wasn't going to sit up there and argue. I just know. When he went to jail in Opelika that summer, he was nervous the whole time. I know Sammy was not sitting up there wolfing with that man when that man had a gun in his face. Sammy was gone. And the man had to shoot him in the back.

The question of what Sammy said that night at the station is, ultimately, irrelevant. He had been shot and killed in cold blood by a sixty-nine-year-old white man named Marvin Segrest because Sammy Younge was a black who refused to stay "in his place." Segrest even admitted firing at Sammy and was arrested shortly after the killing, then released on bail. Naturally, white Tuskegee would try to say that Segrest had a "right" to shoot Sammy. This old, familiar tactic was designed to justify outright murder of blacks by white racists and has sometimes even confused fellow blacks.

But it was not just the whites who had doomed Sammy Younge to death—and who now acted to protect his killer.

GWEN PATTON: Who is really the cause of Sammy's death? Whose hands are really bloody? The white people downtown knew that the TCA, which is the Negro leadership, didn't like Sammy. That gave them extra leeway to intimidate Sammy, Wendy, and Schutz. If the TCA had applied any pressure to the city fathers, nothing would have happened to Sammy. That's why, when the TCA went over to Mrs. Younge's house to express their sympathy, she said, "When my son needed your help and asked for your help, you weren't here. Now, he's dead."

ELDRIDGE BURNS: There's a Negro attendant down at that gas station. After the murder, they kept him constantly drunk and nobody understood why. He was always mumbling, "I saw it. I saw it." But then when some white people looked at him, he would say, "I didn't see it. I didn't see it." He saw, but if he tells, the white man's gonna kill him. He knows that, and he doesn't want to die.

GWEN PATTON: I want to know why those Negro students in the car couldn't have pulled Sammy in with them and taken him away. They drove off, man, and left him. They circled the block and came back—by then, of course, everything was quiet.

Sammy Younge was not the only casualty of January 3, 1966. A myth also died that night: the myth of the "model town." Beneath the surface of Tuskegee's calm "biracialism" lay white violence and black fear—racism in all its forms. Now the mask had been stripped off. Sammy Younge's work while alive, and the way he died were a message to Tuskegee: face reality and move on from there. As long as you live a lie, nothing will truly change. We will remain slaves, even if we call ourselves free.

The mask was off, but people still had to acknowledge the reality that had been revealed.

James Forman, *op. cit.*, pp. 192–96.

112

OPPOSING THE U.S. WAR IN VIETNAM

by the Student Non-Violent Coordinating Committee

On behalf of the Student Non-Violent Coordinating Committee, its chairman, John Lewis, issued the following statement at a press conference held on January 6, 1966, at Atlanta. Its full text, published below, was extracted and/or mentioned by the general press; it received considerable notice in the black press. Julian

Bond, the communications director of SNCC—and newly elected to the Georgia House of Representatives—endorsed this statement. His seat was therefore refused, but he did take his seat when the U.S. Supreme Court ruled his being barred was an affront to the Bill of Rights.

The Student Non-Violent Coordinating Committee assumes its right to dissent with United States foreign policy on any issue, and states its opposition to United States involvement in the war in Vietnam on these grounds:

We believe the United States government has been deceptive in its claims of concern for the freedom of the Vietnamese people, just as the government has been deceptive in claiming concern for the freedom of the colored people in such other countries as the Dominican Republic, the Congo, South Africa, Rhodesia, and in the United States itself.

We of the Student Non-Violent Coordinating Committee have been involved in the black people's struggle for liberation and self-determination in this country for the past five years. Our work, particularly in the South, taught us that the United States government has never guaranteed the freedom of oppressed citizens, and is not yet truly determined to end the rule of terror and oppression within its own borders.

We ourselves have often been victims of violence and confinement executed by U.S. government officials. We recall the numerous persons who have been murdered in the South because of their efforts to secure their civil and human rights, and whose murderers have been allowed to escape penalty for their crimes. The murder of Samuel Younge in Tuskegee, Alabama is no different from the murder of people in Vietnam, for both Younge and the Vietnamese sought and are seeking to secure the rights guaranteed them by law. In each case, the United States Government bears a great part of the responsibility for these deaths.

Samuel Younge was murdered because United States law is not being enforced. Vietnamese are being murdered because the United States is pursuing an aggressive policy in violation of international law. The United States is no respector of persons or law when such persons or laws run counter to its needs and desires. We recall the indifference, suspicion, and outright hostility with which our reports of violence have been met in the past by government officials. We know for the most part that elections in this country, in the North as well as the South, are not free. We have seen that the 1965 Voting Rights Act and the 1964 Civil Rights Act have not yet been implemented with full federal power and concern. We question then the ability and even the desire of the United States government to guarantee free elections abroad. We maintain that our country's cry of "preserve freedom in the world" is a hypocritical mask behind which it squashed liberation movements which are not bound and refuse to be bound by the expediency of the United States Cold War policy.

We are in sympathy with and support the men in this country who are unwilling to respond to the military draft which would compel them to contribute their lives to United States aggression in the name of the "freedom" we find so false in this country.

We recoil with horror at the inconsistency of this supposedly free society where responsibility to freedom is equated with responsibility to lend oneself to military aggression. We take note of the fact that sixteen percent of the draftees from this country are Negro, called on to stifle the liberation of Vietnam, to preserve a "democracy" which does not exist for them at home.

We ask: Where is the draft for the Freedom fight in the United States?

We therefore encourage those Americans who prefer to use their energy in building democratic forms within the country. We believe that work in the Civil Rights movement and other human relations organizations is a valid alternative, knowing full well that it may cost them their lives, as painfully as in Vietnam.

Freedomways 6 (Winter, 1966): 6–7.

113

CREATING THE BLACK PANTHER MOVEMENT

by John Hulett

What became known as the Black Panther party began in Lowndes County, Alabama, early in the 1960s. John Hulett, one of its founders—elected sheriff in 1970—describes the creation of this effort and its growth in a speech given in Los Angeles, May 22, 1966. This gathering was sponsored by a local group which had organized an anti–Vietnam War movement.

... Some time ago, we organized a political group of our own known as the Lowndes County Freedom Organization, whose emblem is the black panther.

We were criticized, we were called communists, we were called everything else, black nationalists and whatnot, because we did this. Any group which starts at a time like this to speak out for what is right—they are going to be ridiculed. The people of Lowndes County realized this. Today we are moving further....

Too long Negroes have been begging, especially in the South, for things they should be working for. So the people in Lowndes County decided to organize themselves—to go out and work for the things we wanted in life—not only for the people in Lowndes County, but for every county in the state of Alabama, in the southern states, and even in California.

You cannot become free in California while there are slaves in Lowndes County. And no person can be free while other people are still slaves, nobody.

In Lowndes County, there is a committee in the Democratic Party. This committee not only controls the courthouse, it controls the entire county. When they found out that the Negroes were going to run candidates in the primary of the Democratic Party on May 3, they assembled themselves together and began to talk about what they were going to do. Knowing this is one of the poorest counties in the nation, what they decided to do was change the registration fees in the county.

Two years ago, if a person wanted to run for sheriff, tax collector, or tax assessor, all he had to do was pay $50 and then he qualified to be the candidate. This year, the entrance fee is about $900. If a person wants to run, he has to pay $500 to run for office. In the primary, when they get through cheating and stealing, then the candidate is eliminated. So we decided that we wouldn't get into such a primary because we were tired of being tricked by southern whites. After forming our own political group today, we feel real strong. We feel that we are doing the right thing in Lowndes County.

We have listened to everybody who wanted to talk, we listened to them speak, but one thing we had to learn for ourselves. As a group of people, we must think for ourselves and act on our own accord. And this we have done.

Through the years, Negroes in the South have been going for the bones while whites have been going for the meat. The Negroes of Lowndes County today are tired of the bones—we are going to have some of the meat too.

At the present time, we have our own candidates which have been nominated by the Lowndes County Freedom Organization. And we fear that this might not be enough to avoid the tricks that are going to be used in Lowndes County against us....

In Lowndes County, the sheriff is the custodian of the courthouse. This is a liberal sheriff, too, who is "integrated," who walks around and pats you on the shoulder, who does not carry a gun. But at the same time, in the county where there are only eight hundred white men, there are 550 of them who walk around with a gun on them. They are deputies. This is true; it might sound like a fairy tale to most people, but this is true.

After talking to the sheriff about having the use of the courthouse lawn for our mass nominating meeting, not the courthouse but just the lawn, he refused to give the Negroes permission. We reminded him that last year in August, one of the biggest Klan rallies that has ever been held in the state of Alabama was held on this lawn of this courthouse. And he gave them permission. A few weeks ago an individual who was campaigning for governor—he got permission to use it. He used all types of loudspeakers and anything that he wanted.

But he would not permit Negroes to have the use of the courthouse. For one thing he realized that we would build a party—and if he could keep us from forming our own political group then we would always stand at the feet of the southern whites and of the Democratic Party. So we told him that we were going to have this meeting, we were going to have it here, on the courthouse lawn. And we wouldn't let anybody scare us off. We told him, we won't expect you to protect us, and if you don't, Negroes will protect themselves.

Then we asked him a second time to be sure he understood what we were saying. We repeated it to him the second time. And then we said to him, sheriff, if you come out against the people, then we are going to arrest you.

And he said, I will not give you permission to have this meeting here. I can't protect you from the community.

Then we reminded him that according to the law of the state of Alabama, that this mass meeting which was set up to nominate our candidates must be held in or around a voters' polling place. And if we decide to hold it a half a mile away from the courthouse, some individual would come up and protest our mass meeting. And our election would be thrown out.

So we wrote the Justice Department and told them what was going to happen in Lowndes County.

All of a sudden the Justice Department started coming in fast into the county. They said to me, John, what is going to happen next Tuesday at the courthouse?

I said, We are going to have our mass meeting. And he wanted to know where. And I said on the lawn of the courthouse.

He said, I thought the sheriff had told you you couldn't come there. And I said, Yes, but we are going to be there.

Then he wanted to know, if shooting takes place, what are we going to do. And I said, that we are going to stay out here and everybody die together.

And then he began to get worried, and I said, Don't worry. You're going to have to be here to see it out and there's no place to hide, so whatever happens, you can be a part of it.

And then he began to really panic. And he said, There's nothing I can do.

And I said, I'm not asking you to do anything. All I want you to know is we are going to have a mass meeting. If the sheriff cannot protect us, then we are going to protect ourselves. And I said to him, through the years in the South, Negroes have never had any protection, and today we aren't looking to anybody to protect us. We are going to protect ourselves.

That was on Saturday. On Sunday, at about two o'clock, we were having a meeting, and we decided among ourselves that we were going to start collecting petitions for our candidates to be sure that they got on the ballot. The state laws require at least twenty-five signatures of qualified electors and so we decided to get at least one hundred for fear somebody might come up and find fault. And we decided to still have our mass meeting and nominate our candidates.

About 2:30, here comes the Justice Department again, and he was really worried. And he said he wasn't satisfied. He said to me, John, I've done all I can do, and I don't know what else I can do, and now it looks like you'll have to call this meeting off at the courthouse.

And I said, we're going to have it.

He stayed around for a while and then got in his car and drove off, saying, I'll see you tomorrow, maybe. And we stayed at this meeting from 2:30 until about 11:30 that night. About 11:15, the Justice Department came walking up the aisle of the church and said to me, Listen. I've talked to the Attorney General of the state of Alabama, and he said that you can go ahead and have a mass meeting at the church and it will be legal.

Then we asked him, Do you have any papers that say that's true, that are signed by the Governor or the Attorney General? And he said no. And we said to him, Go back and get it legalized, and bring it back here to us and we will accept it.

And sure enough, on Monday at 3 o'clock, I went to the courthouse and there in the sheriff's office were the papers all legalized and fixed up, saying that we could go to the church to have our mass meeting.

To me, this showed strength. When people are together, they can do a lot of things, but when you are alone you cannot do anything. . . .

There are six hundred Negroes in the county who did not trust in themselves and who joined the Democratic Party. We warned the entire state of Alabama that running on the Democratic ticket could not do them any good, because this party is controlled by people like Wallace; and whoever won would have to do what these people said to do. . . .

Now, to me, the Democratic Party primaries and the Democratic Party is something like an integrated gambler who carries a card around in his pocket and every now and then he has to let somebody win to keep the game going. To me, this is what the Democratic Party means to the people in Alabama. It's a gambling game. And somebody's got to win to keep the game going every now and then. . . .

I would like to say here, and this is one thing I'm proud of, the people in Lowndes County stood together, and the six hundred people who voted in the Democratic primary have realized one thing, that they were tricked by the Democratic Party. And now they too are ready to join us with the Lowndes County Freedom Organization whose emblem is the black panther.

We have seven people who are running for office this year in our county; namely, the coroner, three members of the board of education—and if we win those three, we will control the board of education—tax collector, tax assessor, and the individual who carries a gun at his side, the sheriff.

Let me say this—that a lot of persons tonight asked me, Do you really think if you win that you will be able to take it all over, and live?

I say to the people here tonight—yes, we're going to do it. If we have to do like the present sheriff, if we have to deputize every man in Lowndes County twenty-one and over, to protect people, we're going to do it.

There was something in Alabama a few months ago they called fear. Negroes were afraid to move on their own, they waited until the man, the people whose place they lived on, told them they could get registered. They told many people, don't you move until I tell you to move and when I give an order, don't you go down and get registered.…

Then all the people were being evicted at the same time and even today in Lowndes County, there are at least seventy-five families that have been evicted, some now are living in tents while some are living in one-room houses—with eight or nine in a family. Others have split their families up and are living together with their relatives or their friends. But they are determined to stay in Lowndes County, until justice rolls down like water

Evicting the families wasn't all—there were other people who live on their own places who owe large debts, so they decided to foreclose on these debts to run Negroes off the place. People made threats—but we're going to stay there, we aren't going anywhere.

I would like to let the people here tonight know why we chose this black panther as our emblem. Many people have been asking this question for a long time. Our political group is open to whoever wants to come in, who would like to work with us. But we aren't begging anyone to come in. It's open, you come, at your own free will and accord.

But this black panther is a vicious animal as you know. He never bothers anything, but when you start pushing him, he moves backwards, backwards, and backwards into his corner, and then he comes out to destroy everything that's before him.

Negroes in Lowndes County have been pushed back through the years. We have been deprived of our rights to speak, to move, and to do whatever we want to do at all times. And now we are going to start moving. On November 8 of this year, we plan to take over the courthouse in Hayneville. And whatever it takes to do it, we're going to do it.

We've decided to stop begging. We've decided to stop asking for integration. Once we control the courthouse, once we control the board of education, we can build our school system where our boys and girls can get an education in Lowndes County. There are eighty-nine prominent families in this county who own ninety percent of the land. These people will be taxed. And we will collect these taxes. And if they don't pay them, we'll take their property and sell it to whoever wants to buy it. And we know there will be people who will buy land where at the present time they cannot buy it. This is what it's going to take.

We aren't asking any longer for protection—we won't need it—or for anyone to come from the outside to speak for us, because we're going to speak for ourselves now and from now on. And I think not only in

Lowndes County, not only in the state of Alabama, not only in the South, but in the North—I hope they too will start thinking for themselves. And that they will move and join us in this fight for freedom. . . .

Clayborne Carson et al., *op. cit.*, pp. 273–78.

114

THE BLACK PANTHER PARTY PLATFORM

by Huey Newton

Huey Newton, a foremost leader of the Black Panther party, wrote its program, which was adopted in 1966.

1. We want freedom. We want power to determine the destiny of our Black Community.
2. We want full employment for our people.
3. We want an end to the robbery by the capitalists of our Black Community.
4. We want decent housing, fit for shelter of human beings.
5. We want education for our people that exposes the true nature of this decadent American society. We want education that teaches us our true history and our role in present day society.
6. We want all black men to be exempt from military service.
7. We want an immediate end to POLICE BRUTALITY and MURDER of black people.
8. We want freedom for all black men held in federal, state, county, and city prisons and jails.
9. We want all black people when brought to trial to be tried in court by a jury of their peer group or people from their black communities, as defined by the Constitution of the United States.
10. We want land, bread, housing, education, clothing, justice, and peace. And as our major political objective, a United Nations–supervised plebiscite to be held throughout the black colony in which only black colonial subjects will be allowed to participate, for the purpose of determining the will of black people as to their national destiny.

Herbert H. Haines, *Black Radicals and the Civil Rights Mainstream* (Knoxville: University of Tennessee Press, 1988), p. 63.

115

"TIRED OF BEING WALKED OVER"

by Millie Thompson

Dr. King moved his energies to the North late in 1965 and concentrated on Chicago with an "end the slums" program. On January 26, 1966, Dr. King moved into what the *New York Times* (January 27, p. 13) called "a sparsely furnished flat in a West Side slum" in which "he will spend three or more days a week." He sought "to transplant his nonviolent movement to Northern cities."

A meeting was held that evening at which black "witnesses" told of abominable conditions. The "hearing" closed with these remarks by one of the witnesses:

"I get down and scrub all day. I'm tired of giving people my money. Just filled to the brim. Tired of being walked over. Tired of being mistreated. Thank God you came here, Rev. King. My house, just now the kitchen is falling in. I'm not going to pay no rent where there are rats and nobody going to throw me out."

116

"THE POOR PEOPLE OF MISSISSIPPI IS TIRED"

by Unita Blackwell and Others

The quotation comes from Ms. Blackwell, a leader of the movement early in 1966 to occupy an abandoned federal air base near Greenville. This story begins in May 1965 when tractor drivers and their families walked off a plantation in Washington County demanding increased pay. The strike spread. The bosses obtained injunctions; the strike was broken. A leader of this action was Isaac Foster.

Foster also was among the leaders of the effort early in 1966 of several hundred desperately poor black men and women, meeting in a church. They called themselves the Black Peoples Conference.

Action at that conference was precipitated by the discovery, at a nearby shanty, of the bodies of two black people who had frozen to death. On January 31, 1966, about seven hundred black people occupied the air base with its numerous buildings. They announced:

"We are here because we have no jobs. Many of us have been thrown off plantations where we worked for nothing all our lives. We don't want charity. We demand our rights to jobs, so that we can do something with our lives and build a future.... We are here because we don't have land. There are thousands of acres here that the government owns. We say we are supposed to be part of the government. We want the clear land and the unclear land and we'll clear the unclear land ourselves." In a telegram to President Johnson, they asked: "Whose side are you on—the poor people or the millionaires?"

They were forcibly evicted by scores of U.S. soldiers. At a press conference the next day, one of the leaders, Ida Mae Lawrence, said: "We ain't dumb, even if we are poor. We need jobs. We need food. We need houses. But even with the poverty program we ain't got nothing but needs." Another leader, Unita Blackwell, said: "We, the poor people of Mississippi is tired. We're tired of it so we're going to build ourselves, because we don't have a government that represents us."

Promises were made; the effort lasted several weeks. It was broken.

See the *New York Times*, February 1–3, 1966, and follow-up story in the *New York Times*, July 25, 1966. See also James C. Cobb, "Federal Farm and Welfare Policy and the Civil Rights Movement in the Mississippi Delta," *Journal of American History*, December 1990, pp. 912–36, and Leon Howell, *Freedom City: The Substance of Things Hoped For* (Richmond: John Knox Press, 1968).

117

"ACTION BEFORE IT IS TOO LATE"

by Martin Luther King, Jr.

In March 1966, President Johnson's Commission on Civil Disorders completed its report. Roy Wilkins served on that commission. Dr. King wrote to Mr. Wilkins soon after the report was made public:

The Commission's findings that white racism is the root cause of today's urban disorders is an important confession of a harsh truth. My only hope is that white America and our national government will heed your warnings and implement your recommendations. By ignoring them we will sink inevitably into a nightmarish racial doomsday. God grant that your excellent report will educate the nation and lead to action before it is too late.

Roy Wilkins, *op. cit.*, pp. 326–27.

118

THE POLITICS OF NECESSITY AND SURVIVAL
IN MISSISSIPPI

by Lawrence Guyot and Mike Thelwell

The authors of this extensive study were, respectively, the chairman of the
Mississippi Freedom Democratic party (MFDP) and one of the founders of the
MFDP who was director of its Washington office. Brief extracts from this
examination of Mississippi during the civil rights movement are given below:

There is nothing inherently unique in the idea and operation of the MFDP.
We are a political organization of people in Mississippi. Our purpose is
gaining and utilizing the greatest possible measure of political power and
influence in the interest of our constituency, *as that constituency expresses
its interests*. There is no radically dramatic mystique or visionary political
insight attendant on the MFDP's functioning—unless one considers as
new political insights the idea that Mississippi's Negroes can and must
gain political representation in proportion to their numbers, that the entire
community must be encouraged to participate in the decisions governing
their lives and that vote must be used as an instrument of social change.

   We are the political organization of a community, which, if it is quite
literally to survive, must win for itself those political rights which white
Americans take for granted. As we will show, the decisions taken, the
policies and programs pursued, and general strategy of the MFDP, to the
extent they are unique, derive not from a tendency toward abstract
political philosophy, but from a practical response to the primitive
conditions of political life in Mississippi, and the experiences that unless
we in Mississippi save ourselves politically, there is no source of salvation
in the country to which we can look.

   The movement for Negro rights in Mississippi indicates very bluntly
that we cannot look to the Office of the Presidency, the Democratic or
Republican Parties as presently constituted, the redemptive force of love,
public moral outrage, the northern liberal establishment, nor even to the
Congress with its "Great Society" legislation. We are not saying that these
institutions and groups are necessarily hostile or can be of no practical
assistance to the Mississippi Negro in his struggle for survival and
political freedom. This is not so. But it is true that the political and legal
rights of the Negroes of Mississippi, even when guaranteed by the

Constitution and enforced by civilized morality, will continue to be subject to the self-interests of these institutions unless reinforced by political power. This can be clearly illustrated by examining the historical record of Mississippi's illegal actions against its Negro population, and the national record of tolerance and indifference to these policies. And it is a fact (despite the much-vaunted "progress" in the area of civil rights), there has been no effective change, on any significant political or economic level, in the policy of tolerance on the part of those who hold national power, towards the systematized degradation of the black population in Mississippi by the State....

As 1966 opens, the economic interests in Mississippi have moved against the Delta population with a new ferocity. What appears to be the beginning of an organized wave of evictions has begun and some 250 families—about 2,200 human beings—have already moved or have been informed that there will be no work for them this spring. It has been estimated that between ten thousand and twelve thousand persons will lose their homes and livelihood this current season. These families are not eligible for social security, unemployment compensation, or any state or federal welfare program. The plantation owners are not required to give prior notice or compensation to those displaced. On one plantation in Bolivar County the owner gave notice to nearly one hundred workers by giving them $10 each and advising them to go to Florida. Many of the evictees are active in the MFDP and the Civil Rights Movement, but the evictions represent the bulk dismissal of unskilled workers on the large plantations. Only skilled workers—tractor drivers, cultivator and cotton picking machine operators—are being retained. This situation is aggravated by the actions of the Mississippi Economic Council, an association of planters and business men which has been campaigning for the rapid mechanization of cotton production as a means of spurring the Negro exodus, and by the fact that this year, the Federal acreage allotments for cotton production have been cut by thirty-five per cent.

The economic squeeze is undoubtedly the most effective and cruel of the State's weapons, but the full force of the "embattled minority" neurosis, that guides the actions of white rulers of Mississippi, was most fully reflected by the legislation introduced, and in many cases passed, in the legislative session in the spring of 1964.

When SNCC announced the plans for the Summer Project of 1964 a special session of the State Legislature was called and the legislative record shows clearly that Mississippi's attitudes towards the black population has remained remarkably free of change since the 1840s. Introduced and passed were: a bill outlawing economic boycotts; two bills outlawing the picketing of public buildings (courthouses are the scene of registration attempts). Both bills were almost identical but the second was to be used in the event the first was declared unconstitutional by the federal courts. A series of police oriented bills were introduced; these provided for extra deputies, for security and patrol personnel for public institutions, for placing the Safety Patrol at the disposal of the Governor and doubling its manpower, providing for a curfew which could be enforced at the discretion of local police authorities, providing for the sharing of municipal police forces during civil disturbances, providing for juveniles arrested for Civil Rights activities to be treated as adults, and finally a bill to prohibit the summer volunteers from entering the State.

On the question of education, bills were passed to prohibit the establishment of freedom schools and community centers and to revoke the charter of the integrated Tougaloo College. The pattern of the "Old Plan" of control by military force and restriction of educational opportunities can be clearly recognized in these legislative proposals.

Two pieces of legislation introduced in this session deserve special comment as they are symptomatic of a species of desperate hysteria which is completely unpredictable and therefore dangerous.

The first provided for the sterilization of persons convicted of a third felony. This was introduced by Rep. Fred Jones of Sunflower County in which there is a Negro majority. Jones was then a member of the Executive Committee of the Citizens' Council. While not specifically mentioning Negroes, the bill contained a clause placing the ordering of sterilization at the discretion of the all-white trustees of Parchman Penitentiary and since Negroes are more subject to criminal conviction in Mississippi courts, the intent of the proposal was clear.

A similar bill was introduced and *passed*, though with amendments. This bill provided for the sterilization of parents of the second illegitimate child, with the alternative of a prison sentence of from three to five years. In introducing this, Rep. Meeks of Webster County clearly indicated that it was intended towards the black population. After passing the House the bill went to the Senate where it passed with amendments deleting sterilization and making the birth of the second illegitimate child a misdemeanor rather than a felony and lessening the sentence. When it came back to the House for ratification, the proponents of sterilization argued for its inclusion, Rep. Ben Owen of Columbus saying, as reported by the *Delta Democratic Times* of May 21st, "This is the only way I know of to stop this rising black tide that threatens to engulf us." The bill finally passed as amended by the Senate.

Freedomways 6 (Spring 1966): 120–32. On the federal government and Mississippi at this time, see "The New Plantations," by Marvin Hoffman and John Mudd in the *Nation*, October 24, 1966, pp. 411–14.

119

"DESPAIR AND HATRED CONTINUE TO BREW"

by Bayard Rustin

The veteran of the civil rights struggle wrote a significant critique of the official report (the "McCone Report") as to the causes plus suggested remedies of events such as the Los Angeles outbreak in the summer of 1965.

The riots in the Watts section of Los Angeles last August continued for six days, during which 34 persons were killed, 1,032 were injured, and some 3,952 were arrested. Viewed by many of the rioters themselves as their "manifesto," the uprising of the Watts Negroes brought out in the open, as no other aspect of the Negro protest has done, the despair and hatred that continue to brew in the Northern ghettoes despite the civil rights legislation of recent years and the advent of the "War on Poverty." With national attention focused on Los Angeles, Governor [Edmund G.] Brown created a commission of prominent local citizens, headed by John A. McCone, to investigate the causes of the riots and to prescribe remedies against any such outbreaks in the future. Just as the violent confrontation on the burning streets of Watts told us much about the underlying realities of race and class relations in America—summed up best, perhaps, by the words of Los Angeles Police Chief William Parker, "We're on top and they're on the bottom"—so does the McCone Report, published under the title *Violence in the City—An End or a Beginning*, tell us much about the response of our political and economic institutions to the Watts "manifesto."

Like the much-discussed Moynihan Report, the McCone Report is a bold departure from the standard government paper on social problems. It goes beyond the mere recital of statistics to discuss, somewhat sympathetically, the real problems of the Watts community—problems like unemployment, inadequate schools, dilapidated housing—and it seems at first glance to be leading toward constructive programs. It never reaches them, however, for, again like the Moynihan Report, it is ambivalent about the basic reforms that are needed to solve these problems and therefore shies away from spelling them out too explicitly. Thus, while it calls for the creation of fifty thousand new jobs to compensate for the "spiral of failure" that it finds among the Watts Negroes, the McCone Report does not tell us how these jobs are to be created or obtained and instead recommends existing programs which have already shown themselves to be inadequate. The Moynihan Report, similarly, by emphasizing the breakdown of the Negro family, also steers clear of confronting the thorny issues of Negro unemployment as such....

If every policeman in every black ghetto behaved like an angel and were trained in the most progressive of police academies, the conflict would still exist. This is so because the ghetto is a place where Negroes do not want to be and are fighting to get out of. When someone with a billy club and a gun tells you to behave yourself amid these terrible circumstances, he becomes a zoo keeper, demanding of you, as one of "these monkeys" (to use Chief Parker's phrase), that you accept abhorrent conditions. He is brutalizing you by insisting that you tolerate what you cannot, and ought not, tolerate.

In its blithe ignorance of such feelings, the McCone Report offers as one of its principal suggestions that speakers be sent to Negro schools to teach the students that the police are their friends and that their interests are best served by respect for law and order. Such public relations gimmicks, of course, are futile—it is hardly a lack of contact with the police that creates the problem. Nor, as I have suggested, is it only a matter of prejudice. The fact is that when Negroes are deprived of work, they resort to selling numbers, women, or dope to earn a living; they must gamble and work in poolrooms. And when the policeman upholds the law, he is depriving them of their livelihood. A clever criminal in the Negro ghettoes is not unlike a clever "operator" in the white business world, and so long as Negroes are denied legitimate opportunities, no exhortations to obey the rules of the society and to regard the police as friends will have any effect.

The Watts manifesto is a response to realities that the McCone Report is barely beginning to grasp. Like the liberal consensus which it embodies and reflects, the Commission's imagination and political intelligence appear paralyzed by the hard facts of Negro deprivation it has unearthed, and it lacks the political will to demand that the vast resources of contemporary America be used to build a genuinely great society that will finally put an end to these deprivations. And what is most impractical and incredible of all is that we may very well teach impoverished, segregated, and ignored Negroes that the only way they can get the ear of America is to rise up in violence.

Bayard Rustin, "The Watts 'Manifesto' and the McCone Report," *Commentary*, March 1966, pp. 29–35; published in part. See Elizabeth Hardwick, "After Watts," in *New York Review of Books*, March 11, 1966.

120

"THE KIDS PLAY WITH RATS"

by Black People in Cleveland, Ohio

The Commission on Civil Rights was established by Congress in 1957. It was a result of the struggles attacking racism during the 1950s. It was charged with investigating denials of voting rights due to race, color, religion, or national origin; to examine any laws or practices which deny equal protection to all citizens; to appraise existing federal laws dealing with these matters; to serve as a clearinghouse of information relevant to its duties, and to investigate, especially, allegations of voting fraud in federal elections.

The commission conducted hearings—with sworn testimony—in Alabama, Arizona, the District of Columbia, Georgia, Illinois, Indiana, Louisiana, Massachusetts, Michigan, Mississippi, New Jersey, New York, Ohio, and Tennessee. Presidential orders began in 1960, relevant to the above subjects.

The record of the *Hearing Before the United States Commission on Civil Rights*, held in Cleveland, Ohio, April 1–7, 1966, contained sworn testimony from numerous witnesses on the subjects of housing, welfare and education, employment, and police community relations. It also contained fifty-three "exhibits" containing relevant findings (including photographs) in these areas. The volume containing all this was published in 1966 by the U.S. Government Printing Office and came to 888 pages. The testimony of one witness, reprinted below, is characteristic of all the testimony.

The members of the commission at this time were John A. Hanna, chairman, Eugene Patterson, Frankie M. Freeman, Erwin N. Griswold, the Reverend Theodore M. Hesburgh, and Robert S. Rankin. The staff director was William L.

Taylor; the general counsel (who did most of the questioning) was Howard A. Glickstein. Most of the witnesses were African-American men and women; in addition, a considerable number of white officials testified. Excerpts from the former follow:

Mrs. Hattie Mae Dugan is being questioned:

MR. GLICKSTEIN. Mrs. Dugan, have you taken any steps to complain about these conditions in your apartment?

MRS. DUGAN. Yes, I have. When I first moved into the building, I had an understanding that they would furnish me paint if I painted it myself.

MR. GLICKSTEIN. Did you paint it?

MRS. DUGAN. I received three gallons of paint a month after I moved in and a month and a half later I received one roller and I tried to paint but the thing fell apart. It had taken them two months to unstop the toilet, so during my complaints the building was changed to a different hand and then I called those people and complained about the ceiling, about the hallways. There still hasn't been anything done about that.

MR. GLICKSTEIN. Did you ever complain to city authorities?

MRS. DUGAN. We called the Board of Health two weeks ago Thursday and there hasn't anyone been out. I talked to Mr. Field Mason who is, I think, with Neighborhood Conference in the Hough area. I talked to him about it and there still hasn't been anything done.

MR. GLICKSTEIN. Mrs. Dugan, of the check for welfare that you receive each month, how much of this do you spend for food stamps?

MRS. DUGAN. I spend $28 for food stamps and receive $44.

MR. GLICKSTEIN. You were able to buy $44 worth of food for those stamps, is that right?

MRS. DUGAN. Yes.

MR. GLICKSTEIN. Are you able to buy such things as soap and detergents and clothes with your food stamps?

MRS. DUGAN. I am not able to buy any clothes, period. With my daughter going to school, I can only buy one box of washing powder a month.

MR. GLICKSTEIN. Can you use food stamps for washing powder?

MRS. DUGAN. No.

MR. GLICKSTEIN. You have to use cash for that?

MRS. DUGAN. You have to use cash. And then in cashing your check, you have to spend $2 or more in order to get your checks cashed because you can't cash them in a bank.

MR. GLICKSTEIN. And the stores require that you buy two dollars or more worth of goods before they will cash the checks for you?

MRS. DUGAN. Yes, they do.

MR. GLICKSTEIN. How are you able to make ends meet, Mrs. Dugan, on the payments that you receive?

MRS. DUGAN. On the payments that I receive, I owe out every month from $10 to $15 of my check in order to make ends meet. I have got a boy friend who will come by and give me a few dollars here and there, and this is the only way that I can survive.

MR. GLICKSTEIN. We understand, Mrs. Dugan, that you were arrested last summer in a demonstration at City Hall. Why were you demonstrating and what did you do at the time?

MRS. DUGAN. At the time that I was arrested, I had the understanding that it was supposed to have been maximum participation of the poor on the CEO Board.

MR. GLICKSTEIN. The CEO Board is what?

MRS. DUGAN. Council of Economic Opportunity, and during that particular time there was only one poor person on the Board and we of the Citizens Committee felt that it should have been more. We asked for eleven people and they [turned] "thumbs down" and they accepted five and, in turn, we placed rats on the steps.

MR. GLICKSTEIN. You did what, Mrs. Dugan?

MRS. DUGAN. We placed rats on the City Hall steps.

MR. GLICKSTEIN. And it was as a result of this demonstration that you were arrested?

MRS. DUGAN. Yes.

MR. GLICKSTEIN. Are rats a real problem in your neighborhood?

MRS. DUGAN. Yes, they are. I was living in one apartment, the rats got in the bed with me and my sister is still living in the same building and the rats are jumping up and down. The kids they play with rats like a child would play with a dog or something. They chase them around the house and things like this.

MR. GLICKSTEIN. What in your opinion can the residents in the neighborhood do to get rid of rats?

MRS. DUGAN. The tenants, if they have sufficient garbage cans, it would be nice. If they are taught how to wrap garbage, it would be nice. If the home owners would provide a place with the proper garbage cans that are covered, that would be nice.

MR. GLICKSTEIN. Do these rats tend to be found in empty lots near your building?

MRS. DUGAN. They are all over. They are not only in the empty lots, they are in the house, too.

MR. GLICKSTEIN. Mrs. Dugan, you mentioned that you had a daughter. Where does she go to school?

MRS. DUGAN. She is attending the Hough Elementary School.

MR. GLICKSTEIN. In your opinion, is your daughter receiving a good education in her school?

MRS. DUGAN. No, she isn't.

MR. GLICKSTEIN. Are there white children attending that school?

MRS. DUGAN. A very few.

MR. GLICKSTEIN. Very few?

MRS. DUGAN. Very few.

MR. GLICKSTEIN. What do you think is wrong with the school?

MRS. DUGAN. The school is out of date for one thing. We have got wooden floors. It is an old building and to me, my opinion is that the teacher has too many children in a classroom and she can't spend enough time with one individual child that is slower than the others.

MR. GLICKSTEIN. Would you mind speaking a little louder, Mrs. Dugan? Perhaps you could move closer to the microphone. Do you think your daughter would receive a better education if she attended a school in which there were a significant number of white children?

MRS. DUGAN. I don't think that the color has anything to do with it. If we had one Negro child to the rest of the class of white children—if the classroom is overcrowded, she still wouldn't receive a proper education.

MRS. GLICKSTEIN. Your principal concern is the size of the classrooms?

MRS. DUGAN. Chiefly.

MR. GLICKSTEIN. Mrs. Dugan, were you a candidate for your Neighborhood Poverty Council?

MRS. DUGAN. Yes, I was.

MR. GLICKSTEIN. When you were campaigning, did you find that people knew anything about the new poverty programs?

MRS. DUGAN. There were very few people in my neighborhood who knew anything about it, even understood anything about it. Quite a few people hadn't even heard about it even up to the day of the election. A lot of people was wondering and questioning me about what this election was all about and what was it for and what did it mean and what would it do for them.

MR. GLICKSTEIN. You were able to explain this to the people?

MRS. DUGAN. I tried the best I knew how.

MR. GLICKSTEIN. Mrs. Dugan, do you believe that there is adequate police protection in your neighborhood?

MRS. DUGAN. No, there isn't.

MR. GLICKSTEIN. Do the police respond to calls for assistance when they are called?

MRS. DUGAN. Well, if you call a policeman in my area, they might come out and then they may not. You have to wait from two to five hours and it is nothing but a conversation. They are not concerned about the people. In my area, there is a lot of things that are going on. You can't find a policeman when you want him. I walked one night from 93rd to 79th and, during that time, I had come in contact with a lot of different people and I didn't see a policeman at all. On my way back up from 79th, I saw one car and it was going up Crawford Road.

MR. GLICKSTEIN. Is your impression of the police protection in your neighborhood shared by your neighbors?

MRS. DUGAN. Yes, it is.

MR. GLICKSTEIN. Mrs. Dugan, have you attempted to find a job?

MRS. DUGAN. Yes, I have.

MR. GLICKSTEIN. Would you tell us about it, please?

MRS. DUGAN. The majority of the places that I went looking for a job, they asked me about work experience, how much work experience do I have. The only experience that I have is in a restaurant or a presser. I went to school to be a power sewer but I didn't—

MR. GLICKSTEIN. To be a power sewer?

MRS. DUGAN. Yes, I finished the course of required hours and I received a diploma and I carried it around to various jobs and in turn they asked me how much work experience did I have.

MRS. GLICKSTEIN. Do you feel that it is because of your lack of training that you have had difficulty getting a job?

MRS. DUGAN. I think that the problem is, if you don't have experience on the job, you can't get a job.

MR. GLICKSTEIN. Mrs. Dugan, what are your hopes for yourself and your daughter for the future?

MRS. DUGAN. In the future, one thing I am not intending to be on ADC. I would love to see my daughter finish school and if she so desires, I would love to see her go to college and not live like I have to live.

MR. GLICKSTEIN. Thank you, Mrs. Dugan, I have no further questions.

CHAIRMAN HANNAH. Mrs. Dugan, how long have you lived in Cleveland?

MRS. DUGAN. I have been back in Cleveland six years now.

CHAIRMAN HANNAH. How much education do you have?

MRS. DUGAN. I finished the ninth grade.

CHAIRMAN HANNAH. In Cleveland?

MRS. DUGAN. No, I didn't finish in Cleveland. I finished in Detroit, Michigan.

CHAIRMAN HANNAH. Detroit?

MRS. DUGAN. Yes, then I went to trade school for two years.

CHAIRMAN HANNAH. Mr. Patterson, do you have any questions?

VICE CHAIRMAN PATTERSON. Mrs. Dugan, you said you received training as a power sewer?

MRS. DUGAN. Yes.

VICE CHAIRMAN PATTERSON. This was operating a power sewing machine?

MRS. DUGAN. Yes, at Jane Addams.

VICE CHAIRMAN PATTERSON. Did you get this training from a private company or a government program?

MRS. DUGAN. Well, I had to pay $10 for the training.

VICE CHAIRMAN PATTERSON. I see. Have you investigated any government training programs that might be able to equip you to hold a job?

MRS. DUGAN. Now I have been transferred over to Title V and my understanding is that as of now, I will be placed on the job training under the Federal Government.

VICE CHAIRMAN PATTERSON. What kind of training, do you know?

MRS. DUGAN. They asked me what did I want to do. The first thing was to be an outreach worker. I wanted to finish school to get a better education.

VICE CHAIRMAN PATTERSON. What kind of work?

MRS. DUGAN. An outreach worker.

VICE CHAIRMAN PATTERSON. I see. Thank you very much.

COMMISSIONER HESBURGH. Mrs. Dugan, I was curious why you had to come to Cleveland. If it is a personal question, you don't have to answer if you don't want to. I was just curious.

MRS. DUGAN. Why did I come back to Cleveland?

COMMISSIONER HESBURGH. Oh, you were born here?

MRS. DUGAN. No, I wasn't born in Cleveland. I was born in West Virginia.

COMMISSIONER HESBURGH. Then you were in California?

MRS. DUGAN. Yes.

COMMISSIONER HESBURGH. And then you were in Detroit?

MRS. DUGAN. Yes, and back to California and Columbus and Cleveland and so forth. But the reason why I came back to Cleveland: I was living in California and I was a long way from my family. My parents lived in Cleveland, all of my relatives, my close relatives are here in Cleveland. When I came back, my mother was very ill, sick, and they had asked me to please come home and I came home.

COMMISSIONER HESBURGH. Is your mother still living here in Cleveland?

MRS. DUGAN. Yes, she's living here.

COMMISSIONER HESBURGH. Do you see her quite a bit?

MRS. DUGAN. I see her every day.

COMMISSIONER HESBURGH. That is good. One other thing I was curious about: who owns the building? I should tell you I was in your building yesterday. We knocked on your door and I guess your daughter didn't want to let us in because she didn't know who we were. I thought that was good judgment on her part.

MRS. DUGAN. I teach her these things because we have got a lot of things going on in that building. I tell her to keep the doors closed.

COMMISSIONER HESBURGH. What I found curious was, first of all, the front door was completely open. Anybody could walk in and out.

MRS. DUGAN. Well, the front door—I'm quite sure you came in the front door. Well, this door is open at all times around the clock. It used to be I had a part-time job and I would come in, I was even afraid to come in myself. There would be some teenagers standing out there drinking wine or something, throwing bricks and breaking windows, using foul language and things like this. I asked for the door to be locked but there hasn't been anything done about it.

COMMISSIONER HESBURGH. I could tell even on your door it looked as though the lock had been jimmied at one point. You could see the marks on the front door.

MRS. DUGAN. Well, I have got a dead lock on my door but someone else has a key to it. I bought the lock but someone else's key will fit. I am wondering how it will guard. I don't have a door knob.

COMMISSIONER HESBURGH. Who takes the rent from you? You say it costs sixty dollars a month rent.

MRS. DUGAN. It's different people take the rent. Everytime I pay rent, it is a different person coming.

COMMISSIONER HESBURGH. How do you know they represent the people who own the building?

MRS. DUGAN. I don't. They just come and say it is rent time and give me your money. I don't know. The custodian I have never paid him any rent. It's Rose and Company I paid rent to. There was a bank I paid rent to. The bank has two Rose and Companies I have paid rent to.

COMMISSIONER HESBURGH. You don't know really who owns that building?

MRS. DUGAN. Well, I received a letter from Ohio Association—Bank of Ohio Association, I believe it is.

COMMISSIONER HESBURGH. I think it would be interesting to find out who owns that building because—

MRS. DUGAN. Well, I have a little card in my purse if you want me to get it, that they gave me and said this is it. Then Thornton Realty is the last person who came out and talked to me.

COMMISSIONER HESBURGH. I wish we had the person who owned the building here as well as you because I have a few questions I have to ask him about renting this kind of building.

MRS. DUGAN. Well, I'll tell you when you start complaining about that particular building no one seems to want to own the building. When I first started to complain, I started with one realty company and I complained so long and loud they sent someone else out and then I complained to him and they sent someone else out and I complained to him and they sent someone else out. Now we complain—it's five of us are complaining now. There are only five of us living in the building now, there are only five complaining now, because when we called the Board of Health, the water was running in Apartment 8, the water was running from the toilet all the way through the three rooms. And so I told let us call the man and talk to him about it, so they sent someone else out and he is a different person. The only time anybody really wants the building is when it is time to pay rent and after then nobody wants the building.

COMMISSIONER HESBURGH. It is probably not the proper time but I would like to know who owns the building.

VOICE. The city owns the building.

MRS. DUGAN. We don't have anything on the walls to identify who owns the building. There is nothing on it.

COMMISSIONER HESBURGH. I don't think any human being ought to live in that building and I am sorry that you have to live there.

MRS. DUGAN. I am, too. There are quite a few of us living in there. We are trying to get out as quick as we can.

CHAIRMAN HANNAH. Dean Griswold?

Commissioner GRISWOLD. Mrs. Dugan, how many apartments are there in the building?

MRS. DUGAN. It's nine apartments in the building.

Commissioner GRISWOLD. Are they all occupied?

MRS. DUGAN. No.

Commissioner GRISWOLD. How many of them are occupied?

MRS. DUGAN. Five.

COMMISSIONER GRISWOLD. How are they occupied? By people who live there or by groups or what?

MRS. DUGAN. Well, if you—oh, God, well you got me up here and you want the truth? I will tell you there are more than five apartments being occupied. There are five residents living in the building—I hope this is all right—and then there are two more apartments being occupied. One is downstairs in the back which is an illegal place, one across the hall from me which is an illegal place, and there is one right down the hall from me that things are going on there that really—why did you ask me this?

COMMISSIONER GRISWOLD. Let me raise the suggestion that there are what are called after-hour clubs in the building, does that mean anything to you?

MRS. DUGAN. Yes, it do.

COMMISSIONER GRISWOLD. Can you tell me what is an after-hour club? Well, don't if you don't wish to. I am only trying to find out.

MRS. DUGAN. It is a place that—oh—it is a place that you sell whisky after the bars close and so far we have two in this building. And they are run by the custodian.

CHAIRMAN HANNAH. Any questions, Mr. Griswold?

COMMISSIONER GRISWOLD. No, thanks.

CHAIRMAN HANNAH. Mrs. Freeman?

COMMISSIONER FREEMAN. Mrs. Dugan, how long have you lived in this building?

MRS. DUGAN. Since the 17th of November.

COMMISSIONER FREEMAN. During the time that you have lived there, have you ever seen a representative of the city make an inspection of the premises?

MRS. DUGAN. Can I hear that again?

COMMISSIONER FREEMAN. Did anybody from the Department of Health or from the city make any kind of inspection of the premises?

MRS. DUGAN. No.

COMMISSIONER FREEMAN. You stated already that the landlord has not ever been to that building during the time that you have been there. Is that correct?

MRS. DUGAN. The landlord? I have seen one person from the bank, I have seen one person from a couple of realty companies—different realty people. Two different real estates have been out to collect the rent.

COMMISSIONER FREEMAN. You indicated that you would like to live in a better place. Have you ever made application for the low rent housing?

MRS. DUGAN. I don't like the projects, if that is what you are speaking about. I would love to live in a regular house. I don't really go for projects. I don't like to be cooped up and I don't like to know what the next neighbor is cooking, what they are saying, I don't like to be involved in their personal problems and I find that to me, my idea of living in a project, you would be involved in a lot of different things. It would mean that your daughter—my child would be involved in a lot of different things that I wouldn't want her to be. I would rather live in a house—maybe upstairs or downstairs.

CHAIRMAN HANNAH. Any question, Dr. Rankin?

COMMISSIONER RANKIN. I have two questions. Mrs. Dugan, you pay your rent on time, is that right, when it comes due?

MRS. DUGAN. I pay my rent seven days before it is due.

COMMISSIONER RANKIN. Seven days before it is due?

MRS. DUGAN. Yes, my rent is due on the 17th of the month. I pay my rent on the 10th of the month.

COMMISSIONER RANKIN. Do you happen to know if any of the people who live there ever get delinquent or get behind in their payments?

MRS. DUGAN. As far as I know, everyone has paid their rent.

COMMISSIONER RANKIN. In advance?

MRS. DUGAN. Yes.

COMMISSIONER RANKIN. My second question: you mentioned the collection of garbage. Is that just once a week?

MRS. DUGAN. It is once a week. They collect garbage on Monday morning if the custodian puts garbage out on the sidewalk. If he don't take the garbage cans out and put them on the sidewalk, it won't be collected.

COMMISSIONER RANKIN. You have gone for two weeks without collection of garbage?

MRS. DUGAN. We have gone longer than that without the collection of garbage because there was no one to put it out.

COMMISSIONER RANKIN. Thank you.

121

"BLACK POWER"

Statement by the National Committee of Negro Churchmen

This statement appeared as a full-page advertisement in the *New York Times* on July 3, 1966. It was signed by forty-seven ministers and bishops in fifteen states and the District of Columbia and by Dr. Anna A. Hedgeman of the Commission on Religion and Race, National Council of Churches, New York City.

We, an informal group of Negro churchmen in America, are deeply disturbed about the crisis brought upon our country by historic distortions of important human realities in the controversy about "black power." What we see shining through the variety of rhetoric is not anything new but the same old problem of power and race which has faced our beloved country since 1619.

We realize that neither the term "power" nor the term "Christian Conscience" are easy matters to talk about, and especially in the context of race relations in America. The fundamental distortion facing us in the controversy about "black power" is rooted in a gross imbalance of power and conscience between Negroes and white Americans. It is this distortion, mainly, which is responsible for the widespread, though often inarticulate, assumption that white people are justified in getting what they want through the use of power, but that Negro Americans must, either by nature or by circumstances, make their appeal only through conscience. As a result, the power of white men and the conscience of black men have both been corrupted. The power of white men is corrupted because it meets little meaningful resistance from Negroes to temper it and keep white men from aping God. The conscience of black men is corrupted because, having no power to implement the demands of conscience, the concern for justice becomes chaotic self-surrender. Powerlessness breeds a race of beggars. We are faced now with a situation where conscience-less power meets powerless conscience, threatening the very foundations of our nation.

Therefore, we are impelled by conscience to address at least four groups of people in areas where clarification of the controversy is of the most urgent necessity. We do not claim to present the final word. It is our hope, however, to communicate meanings from our experience regarding power and certain elements of conscience to help interpret more adequately the dilemma in which we are all involved.

I. To the Leaders of America: Power and Freedom

It is of critical importance that the leaders of this nation listen also to a voice which says that the principal source of the threat to our nation comes neither from the riots erupting in our big cities, nor from the disagreements among the leaders of the civil rights movement, nor even from mere raising of the cry for "black power." These events, we believe, are but the expression of the judgment of God upon our nation for its failure to use its abundant resources to serve the real well-being of people, at home and abroad.

We give our full support to all civil rights leaders as they seek for basically American goals, for we are not convinced that their mutual reinforcement of one another in the past is bound to end in the future. We would hope that the public power of our nation will be used to strengthen the civil rights movement and not to manipulate or further fracture it.

We deplore the overt violence of riots, but we believe it is more important to focus on the real sources of these eruptions. These sources may be abetted inside the ghetto, but their basic causes lie in the silent and covert violence which white middle-class America inflicts upon the victims of the inner city. The hidden, smooth, and often smiling decisions of American leaders which tie a white noose of suburbia around the necks, and which pin the backs of the masses of Negroes against the steaming ghetto walls—without jobs in a booming economy; with dilapidated and segregated educational systems in the full view of unenforced laws against it; in short: the failure of American leaders to use American power to create equal opportunity *in life* as well as in *law*—this is the real problem and not the anguished cry for "black power."

From the point of view of the Christian faith, there is nothing necessarily wrong with concern for power. At the heart of the Protestant reformation is the belief that ultimate power belongs to God alone and that men become most inhuman when concentrations of power lead to the conviction—overt or covert—that any nation, race, or organization can rival God in this regard. At issue in the relations between whites and Negroes in America is the problem of inequality of power. Out of this imbalance grows the disrespect of white men for the Negro personality and community and the disrespect of Negroes for themselves. This is a fundamental root of human injustice in America. In one sense, the concept of "black power" reminds us of the need for and the possibility of authentic democracy in America.

We do not agree with those who say that we must cease expressing concern for the acquisition of power lest we endanger the "gains" already made by the civil rights movement. The fact of the matter is, there have been few substantive gains since about 1950 in this area. The gap has constantly widened between the incomes of nonwhites relative to the whites. Since the Supreme Court decision of 1954, de facto segregation in every major city in our land has increased rather than decreased. Since the middle of the 1950s unemployment among Negroes has gone up rather than down while unemployment has decreased in the white community.

While there has been some progress in some areas for equality for Negroes, this progress has been limited mainly to middle-class Negroes who represent only a small minority of the larger Negro community.

These are the hard facts that we must all face together. Therefore, we must not take the position that we can continue in the same old paths.

When American leaders decide to serve the real welfare of people instead of war and destruction; when American leaders are forced to make the rebuilding of our cities first priority on the nation's agenda; when American leaders are forced by the American people to quit misusing and abusing American power; then will the cry for "black power" become inaudible, for the framework in which all power in America operates would include the power and experience of black men as well as those of white men. In that way, the fear of the power of each group would be removed. America is our beloved homeland. But, America is not God. Only God can do everything. America and the other nations of the world must decide which among a number of alternatives they will choose.

II. To White Churchmen: Power and Love

As black men who were long ago forced out of the white church to create and to wield "black power," we fail to understand the emotional quality of the outcry of some clergy against the use of the term today. It is not enough to answer that "integration" is the solution. For it is precisely the nature of the operation of power under some forms of integration which is being challenged. The Negro Church was created as a result of the refusal to submit to the indignities of a false kind of "integration" in which all power was in the hands of white people. A more equal sharing of power is precisely what is required as the precondition of authentic human interaction. We understand the growing demand of Negro and white youth for a more honest kind of integration; one which increases rather than decreases the capacity of the disinherited to participate with power in all of the structures of our common life. Without this capacity to *participate with power*—i.e., to have some organized political and economic strength to really influence people with whom one interacts— integration is not meaningful. For the issue is not one of racial balance but of honest interracial interaction.

For this kind of interaction to take place, all people need power, whether black or white. We regard as sheer hypocrisy or as a blind and dangerous illusion the view that opposes love to power. Love should be a controlling element in power, but what love opposes is precisely the misuse and abuse of power, not power itself. So long as white churchmen continue to moralize and misinterpret Christian love, so long will justice continue to be subverted in this land.

III. *To Negro Citizens: Power and Justice*

Both the anguished cry for "black power" and the confused emotional response to it can be understood if the whole controversy is put in the context of American history. Especially must we understand the irony involved in the pride of Americans regarding their ability to act as individuals on the one hand, and their tendency to act as members of ethnic groups on the other hand. In the tensions of this part of our history is revealed both the tragedy and the hope of human redemption in America.

America has asked its Negro citizens to fight for opportunity *as individuals* whereas at certain points in our history what we have needed most has been opportunity for the whole group, not just for selected and approved Negroes. Thus in 1863, the slaves were made legally free, as individuals, but the real question regarding personal and group power to maintain that freedom was pushed aside. Power at that time for a mainly rural people meant land and tools to work the land. In the words of Thaddeus Stevens, power meant: "40 acres and a mule." But this power was not made available to the slaves and we see the results today in the pushing of a landless peasantry off the farms into our cities where they come in search mainly of the power to be free. What they find are only the formalities of unenforced legal freedom. So we must ask, "what is the nature of the power which we seek and need today?" Power today is essentially organizational power. It is not a thing lying about in the streets to be fought over. It is a thing which, in some measure, already belongs to

Negroes and which must be developed by Negroes in relationship with the great resources of this nation.

Getting power necessarily involves reconciliation. We must first be reconciled to ourselves lest we fail to recognize the resources we already have and upon which we can build. We must be reconciled to ourselves as persons and to ourselves as an historical group. This means we must find our way to a new self image in which we can feel a normal sense of pride in self, including our variety of skin color and the manifold textures of our hair. As long as we are filled with hatred for ourselves we will be unable to respect others.

At the same time, if we are seriously concerned about power then we must build upon that which we already have. "Black power" is already present to some extent in the Negro church, in Negro fraternities and sororities, in our professional associations, and in the opportunities afforded to Negroes who make decisions in some of the integrated organizations of our society.

We understand the reasons by which these limited forms of "black power" have been rejected by some of our people. Too often the Negro church has stirred its members away from the reign of God in *this world* to a distorted and complacent view of *an other worldly* conception of God's power. We commit ourselves as churchmen to make more meaningful in the life of our institution our conviction that Jesus Christ reigns in the "here" and "now" as well as in the future he brings in upon us. We shall, therefore, use more of the resources of our churches in working for human justice in the places of social change and upheaval where our Master is already at work.

At the same time, we would urge that Negro social and professional organizations develop new roles for engaging the problem of equal opportunity and put less time into the frivolity of idle chatter and social waste.

We must not apologize for the existence of this form of group power, for we have been oppressed as a group, not as individuals. We will not find our way out of that oppression until both we and America accept the need for Negro Americans as well as for Jews, Italians, Poles, and white Anglo-Saxon Protestants, among others, to have and to wield group power.

However, if power is sought merely as an end in itself, it tends to turn upon those who seek it. Negroes need power in order to participate more effectively at all levels of the life of our nation. We are glad that none of those civil rights leaders who have asked for "black power" have suggested that it means a new form of isolationism or a foolish effort at domination. But we must be clear about why we need to be reconciled with the white majority. It is *not* because we are only one-tenth of the population in America; for we do not need to be reminded of the awesome power wielded by the ninety percent majority. We see and feel that power every day in the destructions heaped upon our families and upon the nation's cities. We do not need to be threatened by such cold and heartless statements. For we are men, not children, and we are growing out of our fear of that power, which can hardly hurt us any more in the future than it does in the present or has in the past. Moreover, those bare figures conceal the potential political strength which is ours if we organize properly in the big cities and establish effective alliances.

Neither must we rest our concern for reconciliation with our white brothers on the fear that failure to do so would damage gains already made by the Civil Rights movement. If those gains are in fact real, they will withstand the claims of our people for power and justice, not just for a few select Negroes here and there, but for the masses of our citizens. We must rather rest our concern for reconciliation on the firm ground that we and all other Americans *are* one. Our history and destiny are indissolubly linked. If the future is to belong to any of us, it must be prepared for all of us whatever our racial or religious background. For in the final analysis, we are *persons* and the power of all groups must be wielded to make visible our common humanity.

The future of America will belong to neither white nor black unless all Americans work together at the task of rebuilding our cities. We must organize not only among ourselves but with other groups in order that we can, together, gain power sufficient to change this nation's sense of what is *now* important and what must be done *now*. We must work with the remainder of the nation to organize whole cities for the task of making the rebuilding of our cities first priority in the use of our resources. This is more important than who gets to the moon first or the war in Vietnam.

To accomplish this task we cannot expend our energies in spastic or ill-tempered explosions without meaningful goals. We must move from the politics of philanthropy to the politics of metropolitan development for equal opportunity. We must relate all groups of the city together in new ways in order that the truth of our cities might be laid bare and in order that, together, we can lay claim to the great resources of our nation to make truth more human.

IV. To the Mass Media: Power and Truth

The ability or inability of all people in America to understand the upheavals of our day depends greatly on the way power and truth operate in the mass media. During the southern demonstrations for civil rights, you men of the communications industry performed an invaluable service for the entire country by revealing plainly to our ears and eyes the ugly truth of a brutalizing system of overt discrimination and segregation. Many of you were mauled and injured, and it took courage for you to stick with the task. You were instruments of change and not merely purveyors of unrelated facts. You were able to do this by dint of personal courage and by reason of the power of national news agencies which supported you.

Today, however, your task and ours is more difficult. The truth that needs revealing today is not so clear-cut in its outlines, nor is there a national consensus to help you form relevant points of view. Therefore, nothing is now more important than that you look for a variety of sources of truth in order that the limited perspectives of all of us might be corrected. Just as you related to a broad spectrum of people in Mississippi instead of relying only on police records and establishment figures, so must you operate in New York City, Chicago, and Cleveland.

The power to support you in this endeavor *is present* in our country. It must be searched out. We desire to use our limited influence to help relate you to the variety of experience in the Negro community so that limited controversies are not blown up into the final truth about us. The fate of this country is, to no small extent, dependent upon how you interpret the crises upon us, so that human truth is disclosed and human needs are met.

122

"WE HAVE TO GET BLACK POWER"

by Stokely Carmichael

On July 28, 1966, Stokely Carmichael, then chairman of SNCC, delivered the following speech in Chicago.

This is 1966 and it seems to me that it's "time out" for nice words. It's time black people got together. We have to say things nobody else in this country is willing to say and find the strength internally and from each other to say the things that need to be said. We have to understand the lies this country has spoken about black people and we have to set the record straight. No one else can do that but black people.

I remember when I was in school they used to say, "If you work real hard, if you sweat, if you are ambitious, then you will be successful." I'm here to tell you that if that was true, black people would own this country, because we sweat more than anybody else in this country. We have to say to this country that you have lied to us. We picked your cotton for $2.00 a day, we washed your dishes, we're the porters in your bank and in your building, we are the janitors and the elevator men. We worked hard and all we get is a little pay and a hard way to go from you. We have to talk not only about what's going on here but what this country is doing across the world. When we start getting the internal strength to tell them what should be told and to speak the truth as it should be spoken, let them pick the sides and let the chips fall where they may.

Now, about what black people have to do and what has been done to us by white people. If you are born in Lowndes County, Alabama, Swillingchit, Mississippi, or Harlem, New York and the color of your skin happens to be black you are going to catch it. The only reason we have to get together is the color of our skins. They oppress us because we are black and we are going to use that blackness to get out of the trick bag they put us in. Don't be ashamed of your color.

A few years ago, white people used to say, "Well, the reason they live in the ghetto is they are stupid, dumb, lazy, unambitious, apathetic, don't care, happy, contented," and the trouble was a whole lot of us believed that junk about ourselves. We were so busy trying to prove to white folks that we were everything they said we weren't that we got so busy being white we forgot what it was to be black. We are going to call our black brothers' hand....

We have to define how we are going to move, not how they say we can move. We have never been able to do that before. Everybody in this country jumps up and says, "I'm a friend of the civil rights movement. I'm a friend of the Negro." We haven't had the chance to say whether or not that man is stabbing us in the back or not. All those people who are calling us friends are nothing but traitorous enemies and we can take care of our enemies but God deliver us from our "friends." The only protection we are going to have is from each other. We have to build a strong base to let them know if they touch one black man driving his wife to the hospital in Los Angeles, or one black man walking down a highway in Mississippi, or if they take one black man who has a rebellion and put him in jail and start talking treason, we are going to disrupt this whole country...

Now, let's get to what the white press has been calling riots. In the first place don't get confused with the words they use like "antiwhite," "hate," "militant" and all that nonsense like "radical" and "riots." What's happening is rebellions not riots.... The extremists in this country are the white people who force us to live the way we live. We have to define our own ethic. We don't have to (and don't make any apologies about it) obey any law that we didn't have a part to make, especially if that law was made to keep us where we are. We have the right to break it.

We have to stop apologizing for each other. We must tell our black brothers and sisters who go to college, "Don't take any job for IBM or Wall Street because you aren't doing anything for us. You are helping this country perpetuate its lies about how democracy rises in this country." They have to come back to the community, where they belong and use their skills to help develop us. We have to tell the doctors, "You can't go to college and come back and charge us $5.00 and $10.00 a visit. You have to charge us 50¢ and be thankful you get that." We have to tell our lawyers not to charge us what they charge but to be happy to take a case and plead it free of charge. We have to define success and tell them the food Ralph Bunche eats doesn't feed our hungry stomachs. We have to tell Ralph Bunche the only reason he is up there is so when we yell they can pull him out. We have to do that, nobody else can do that for us.

We have to talk about wars and soldiers and just what that means. A mercenary is a hired killer and any black man serving in this man's army is a black mercenary, nothing else. A mercenary fights for a country for a price but does not enjoy the rights of the country for which he is fighting. A mercenary will go to Vietnam to fight for free elections for the Vietnamese but doesn't have free elections in Alabama, Mississippi, Georgia, Texas, Louisiana, South Carolina, and Washington, D.C. A mercenary goes to Vietnam and gets shot fighting for his country and they won't even bury him in his own home town. He's a mercenary, that's all. We must find the strength so that when they start grabbing us to fight their war we say, "Hell no."

We have to talk about nonviolence among us, so that we don't cut each other on Friday nights and don't destroy each other but move to a point where we appreciate and love each other. That's the nonviolence that has to be talked about. The psychology the man has used on us has turned us against each other. He says nothing about the cutting that goes on Friday night but talk about raising one finger-tip towards him and that's when he jumps up. We have to talk about nonviolence among us first.

We have to study black history but don't get fooled.... You have to know what Mr. X said from his own lips not the *Chicago Sun-Times*. That responsibility is ours. The Muslims call themselves Muslims but the press calls them black Muslims. We have to call them Muslims and go to their mosque to find out what they are talking about firsthand and then we can talk about getting together. Don't let that man get up there and tell you, "Oh, you know those Muslims preach nothing but hate. You shouldn't be messing with them." "Yah, I don't mess with them, yah, I know they bad." The man's name is the Honorable Elijah Muhammad and he represents a great section of the black community. Honor him.

We have to go out and find our young blacks who are cutting and shooting each other and tell them they are doing the cutting and shooting to the wrong people. We have to bring them together and spend the time if we are not just shucking and jiving. This is 1966 and my grandmother used to tell me, "The time is far spent." We have to move this year.

There is a psychological war going on in this country and it's whether or not black people are going to be able to use the terms they want about their movement without white people's blessing. We have to tell them we are going to use the term "Black Power" and we are going to define it because Black Power speaks to us. We can't let them project Black Power because they can only project it from white power and we know what white power has done to us. We have to organize ourselves to speak from a position of strength and stop begging people to look kindly upon us. We are going to build a movement in this country based on the color of our skins that is going to free us from our oppressors and we have to do that ourselves....

Everybody in this country is for "Freedom Now" but not everybody is for Black Power because we have got to get rid of some of the people who have white power. We have got to get us some Black Power. We don't control anything but what white people say we can control. We have to be able to smash any political machine in the country that's oppressing us and bring it to its knees. We have to be aware that if we keep growing and multiplying the way we do in ten years all the major cities are going to be ours. We have to know that in Newark, New Jersey, where we are sixty percent of the population, we went along with their stories about integrating and we got absorbed. All we have to show for it is three councilmen who are speaking for them and not for us. We have to organize ourselves to speak for each other. That's Black Power....

I want to show you what the man does to our minds. Do you remember watching Tarzan and how we used to yell for him to beat up the black, uncivilized, cannibal natives? Well, they are putting Tarzan back on TV this September and we ought to yell for the black people to beat the hell our of Tarzan and send him back to Europe.

Now I want to explain about this "Western Civilization" we are being upgraded into. The man got on radio and said, "Well, when they start rioting they are nothing else but savages," and we got mad but you know the man was right, because a savage throws a Molotov Cocktail, civilized man just drops a bomb, that's all. Civilized Lyndon is just dropping bombs and daring the people to touch the men who dropped the bombs on them. That's civilization.....

In Gilbert Osofsky, ed., *The Burden of Race* (New York: Harper & Row, 1967), pp. 631–36; published in part.

123

TO WIPE OUT SLUMS, GHETTOES, AND RACISM

by the Chicago Freedom Movement

In July 1966, a "Program of the Chicago Freedom Movement" was issued in mimeograph form. It represented a coalition of thirty-six religious and secular organizations. These formed, in Chicago, the Coordinating Council of Community Organizations (CCCO). It is this organization which invited Dr. King, as leader of the SCLC, to come to Chicago and help in the endeavor to cleanse the city of organized expressions of racism.

Introduction: The Problems of Racism, Ghettoes, and Slums

Racism, slums, and ghettoes have been the essentials of Negro existence in Chicago. While the city permitted its earlier ethnic groups to enter the mainstream of American life, it has locked the Negro into the lower rungs of the social and economic ladder. The Negro in Chicago has been systematically excluded from the major rewards of American life; he is restricted in the jobs he may hold, the schools he may attend, and the places where he may live. In the year 1966 the Negro is as far behind the white as he was in the year 1940.

Chicago today is a divided city—segregated in all areas of social and economic activity, in employment, in education, in housing, and in community organization. The Negro community is sectioned off from the larger metropolis into areas of the city that have been set aside for black ghettoes. Within these confines the Negro community is regulated from the outside like a colony—its potential economic resources under-developed, its more than one million inhabitants the daily victims of personal rebuffs, insults, and acts of prejudice, and its poorer citizens at the mercy of police, welfare workers, and minor government officials.

Racism in the large northern cities has not featured lynchings, denial of the vote, or other clear injustices that could easily be removed as is the case in the South. Yet, racism in Chicago has been a stark reality, visible in many dimensions. It is reflected in the existence of the massive overcrowded ghetto that grows each year. It is reflected in the crime-infested slums where the living standards of the Negro poor often do not cover the bare necessities of urban living. It is reflected in the exploitation of Negroes by the dominant white society in higher rents and prices, lower wages, and poorer schools.

Under the system of northern racism the Negro receives inferior and second-class status in every area of urban living. The Negro is concentrated in the low-paying and second-rate jobs. In housing, proportionately more Negroes live in substandard or deteriorating dwellings. In education, Negro schools have more inexperienced teachers, fewer classrooms, and less expenditures per pupil. In the maintenance of law and order Negroes are frequently the victims of police brutality and of stop and search methods of crime detection.

All Negroes in Chicago are confined to the ghetto and suffer second-class treatment regardless of their social or economic status. But the worst off are the Negro poor, locked into the slum which is the most deprived part of the ghetto. The forty per cent of the Negro population who make up a black urban peasantry in the slums are the hardest hit victims of discrimination and segregation. Their incomes often have to be supplemented by welfare payments dispensed under procedures that are ugly and paternalistic. They are frequently unemployed. They are forced to live in rat infested buildings or in the Chicago Housing Authority's cement reservations. Their children are all but ignored by the school system. In short they have been frozen out of American society by both race and poverty.

The subjugation of Negroes in Chicago has not been the result of long-established legal codes or customs, like those that existed in the South. Although Chicago has not for a century had any segregation laws or discrimination ordinances, the subordination of Negroes in the North has been almost as effective as if there had been such laws. Northern segregation resulting from policies, in particular the decision-making procedures, of the major economic and social institutions. The employment policies of business firms and government, and practices of realtors, and the operation of the Chicago School System have all reinforced one another to keep the Negroes separate and unequal. The system of racial separation resulting from their interaction have become so strongly imbedded in the city's life that present racial patterns are passed on from generation to generation.

In many instances, although these restrictive policies have now been formally abolished or concealed, the effects of their operations over several decades remains. Very often, Negroes are no longer excluded consciously and deliberately. In employment, personnel men need not discriminate so long as Chicago's inferior schools send their pupils into the labor market less prepared than white graduates. Realtors can justify their discrimination when white parents rightfully fear that integrated schools eventually deteriorate because the school system considers them less important than white schools. School administrators can efficiently segregate by following neighborhood school policies in allocating school facilities.

In the past, the Negro's efforts to improve his living conditions have concentrated on going through the well-defined channels of white authority. Negroes for years have been asking, begging, and pleading that white employers, board presidents, bankers, realtors, politicians, and government officials correct racial patterns and inequities. The major lesson that the Negro community has learned is that racial change through this process comes only gradually, usually too late, and only in small measures.

In this rapidly changing world where technological changes may displace the unskilled workers, where affluence makes it possible to spend millions in waging wars in far away places like Vietnam, and where the elimination of poverty and racism have become national goals, Negroes no longer have the patience to abide by the old, unsuccessful gradualism of the respectable defenders of the status quo.

The present powerlessness of Negroes hinders them from changing conditions themselves or even in developing effective coalitions with others, but the time has now come for Negroes to set up their own instruments that will direct pressure at the institutions that still adhere to racism policies. Negroes must form their own power base from which Negro aspirations and goals can be demanded, a base from which they can make a strong common fight with others that can share their problems or their aspirations. Chicago will become an open city only when Negroes develop power in proportion to their numbers.

The Chicago Freedom Movement

The Chicago Freedom Movement is a coalition of forces for the purpose of wiping out slums, ghettoes, and racism. Its core is formed by the unity of the Southern Christian Leadership Conference (SCLC) and the Coordinating Council of Community Organizations (CCCO). SCLC, operating under the leadership of Dr. Martin Luther King, Jr., was invited to Chicago by CCCO because of its dynamic work in the South. CCCO is a coalition of thirty-six Chicago civil-rights and Negro community organizations. Cooperating with the Chicago Freedom Movement are a number of religious organizations, social agencies, neighborhood groups, and individuals of good will.

Nonviolence is based on the truth that each human being has infinite dignity and worth. This truth, which is at the heart of our religious and democratic heritage, is denied by systems of discrimination and exploitation. The beginning of change in such systems of discrimination is for men to assert with simple dignity and humanity that they are men and human and that they will no longer be oppressed or oppressors. A just society is born when men cease to be accomplices in a system of degradation.

Then specific injustices and discriminations must be exposed by direct actions which reveal, without excuse or rationalization, the extent and nature of the problem. They bring into the open, as conflicts, social antagonisms that in the past had been hidden as subjugation or exploitation. The methodology of nonviolence keeps attention focused on the real issues of injustice and discrimination rather than on false issues which arise when conflict becomes violent.

The nonviolent movement seeks to create a community in which justice and equality provide the framework for all human relationships and are embodied in its institutions. The practice of justice is the evidence of a community based on respect for every person and of a society in which human values prevail over cash values. A genuine human community does not exist until all citizens are given an opportunity to participate to the fullest limits of their capacity. In this way each person contributes to the community's solution to its problems and fulfills himself as a member of the community.

The Chicago Freedom Movement commits itself to the struggle for freedom and justice in this metropolis and pledges our nonviolent movement to the building of the beloved community where men will live as brothers and no group or class or nation will raise its hand against another. . . .

In John H. Bracey, Jr., August Meier, Elliott Rudwick, eds., *The Afro-Americans: Selected Documents* (Boston: Allyn and Bacon, 1972), pp. 709–16. On Chicago at this time, see Paul Good, "Bossism, Racism and Dr. King", *Nation*, September 19, 1966, pp. 237–42.

124

"BRING POWER TO BOTH BLACK AND WHITE"

by Whitney M. Young, Jr.

The National Urban League met in Philadelphia from July 31 to August 4, 1966. From its offices the *New York Times* (August 5, 1966) quoted a statement which "deplored attention" being given to the black power controversy. That "diverted attention from the more meaningful debate around the real problems of poverty and discrimination." The *Times* then quoted Mr. Young, executive director of the League, who, on August 3, issued a statement which declared that the League had:

. . . carefully refrained from becoming involved in the fruitless dispute over the value of a slogan which has not even yet been carefully defined by its originators.

"Rather we will continue to devote ourselves to bettering the position of the Negro in the nation.

"We will continue through our unique structure to expand and develop positive programs of action which bring jobs to the unemployed, housing to the dispossessed, education to the deprived, and necessary voter education to the disfranchised.

"In the final analysis these are the things in our American system which bring power to both black and white citizens—and dignity and pride to all."

125

"TOO LONG HAVE WE ALLOWED WHITE PEOPLE..."

Position Paper of SNCC

In a May 1966 SNCC meeting near Nashville, James Forman resigned as executive secretary and John Lewis as chairman. The latter was replaced in that office by Stokely Carmichael.

The position adopted by SNCC as a result of these changes appeared in a lengthy statement, most of which was published in the *New York Times* on August 5.

In an attempt to find a solution to our dilemma, we propose that our organization (SNCC) should be black-staffed, black-controlled, and black-financed. We do not want to fall into a similar dilemma that other civil rights organizations have fallen. If we continue to rely upon white financial support we will find ourselves entwined in the tentacles of the white power complex that controls this country. It is also important that a black organization (devoid of cultism) be projected to our people so that it can be demonstrated that such organizations are viable.

More and more we see black people in this country being used as a tool of the white liberal establishment. Liberal whites have not begun to address themselves to the real problem of black people in this country; witness their bewilderment, fear, and anxiety when nationalism is mentioned concerning black people. An analysis of their (white liberal) reaction to the word alone (nationalism) reveals a very meaningful attitude of whites of any ideological persuasion toward blacks in this country. It means previous solutions to black problems in this country have been made in the interests of those whites dealing with these problems and not in the best interests of black people in this country. Whites can only subvert our true search and struggle for self-determination, self-identification, and liberation in this country. Re-evaluation of the white and black roles must now take place so that white no longer designate roles that black people play but rather black people define white people's roles....

It must be repeated that the whole myth of "Negro citizenship," perpetuated by the white elite, has confused the thinking of radical and progressive blacks and whites in this country. The broad masses of black people react to American society in the same manner as colonial peoples react to the West in Africa, and Latin America, and had the same relationship—that of the colonized toward the colonizer....

If we are to proceed toward true liberation, we must cut ourselves off from white people. We must form our own institutions, credit unions, co-ops, political parties, write our own histories.

To proceed further, let us make some comparisons between the Black Movement of the early 1900s and the movement of the 1960s—the NAACP with SNCC Whites subverted the Niagara movement [the forerunner of the NAACP] which, at the outset, was an all-black movement. The name of the new organization was also very revealing, in that it pre-supposed blacks have to be advanced to the level of whites. We are now aware that the NAACP has grown reactionary, is controlled by the black power structure itself, and stands as one of the main roadblocks to black freedom. SNCC, by allowing the whites to remain in the organization, can have its efforts subverted in the same manner—i.e., through having them play important roles such as community organizers, etc. Indigenous leadership cannot be built with whites in the positions they now hold.

These facts do not mean that whites cannot help. They can participate on a voluntary basis. We can contract work out to them, but in no way can they participate on a policy-making level.

The charge may be made that we are "racists," but whites who are sensitive to our problems will realize that we must determine our own destiny.

See Stokely Carmichael, "What We Want," *New York Review of Books*, September 22, 1966, pp. 5–8; published in part.

126

MEET THE PRESS

A discussion—Carl Rowan, Martin Luther King, Jr., and Roy Wilkins

NBC television and radio broadcast, under the above title, on August 21, 1966, a discussion on the Civil Rights movement. Participating in this popular program—witnessed by millions—was a panel of questioners, consisting of four white people, all quite conservative (Lawrence Spivak, Rowland Evans, James J. Kilpatrick, and Richard Valeriani) and one black person, also conservative, Carl Rowan.

Being questioned were King, Wilkins, James Meredith, Stokely Carmichael, Floyd McKissick, and Whitney M. Young, Jr. The complete text of this program was placed in the *Congressional Record*, August 29, 1966 (Senate, 112:21095-21102) by Senator Harry F. Byrd, a Democrat of West Virginia. An excerpt follows:

SPIVAK. Dr. King, I'm sure you either heard or read President Johnson's speech yesterday when he warned that violence and discord would destroy Negroes' hopes for racial progress. Now isn't it time to stop demonstrations that create violence and discord?

KING. Well, I absolutely disagree with that and I hope the President didn't mean to equate nonviolent demonstrations with a riot, and I think it is time for this country to see the distinction between the two. There is a great distinction between individuals who are nonviolently engaged in pursuit of basic constitutional rights and who in the process face violence and face hatred perpetrated against them, and individuals who aggressively throw Molotov cocktails and engage in riots. So that there can be no equation or there can be no identity between riots and demonstrations. I think demonstrations must continue, but I think riots must end because they are socially disruptive. I think they are self-defeating, and I think they can destroy the many creative steps that we have made in a forward sense over the last few years.

ROWAN. Mr. Wilkins, despite the fact that you gentlemen sit here together there is a feeling around the country that there's a crisis of leadership in the Civil Rights movement. Do you agree that the movement toward Negro equality is jeopardized by what now seems to be a host of warring civil rights groups, each pursuing its own special interests?

WILKINS. No, Mr. Rowan, I don't think it's quite that serious. We tend to feel that unity should be exhibited at all times, no matter what kind of organizations or what kind of personalities or what kind of tactics are involved. I think we have to grow up to the idea that there will be differences of opinion and that these will manifest themselves from time to time. I don't see as yet any great split in the Civil Rights movement.

ROWAN. Well, I've noticed in the *New York Times,* Mr. Wilkins, a quotation from a so-called SNCC position paper saying we are now aware that the NAACP has grown reactionary, is controlled by the black power structure itself, and stands as one of the main roadblocks to black freedom. I note also that an NAACP official was referring to the Urban League as an Uncle Tom organization. Now this you don't think is serious division, or anything to be worried about?

WILKINS. No, no. I call your attention, first of all, to the fact that the SNCC person said that we were, the NAACP, was controlled by the black power structure.

ROWAN. I wondered if that was a typo.

WILKINS. No, it wasn't a typographical error. And for that we moved up on the scale because there was a time when the spokesman would have said that we were controlled by the white power structure. But the NAACP officials you referred to by calling the Urban League Uncle Tom was only a local official, an extremely individualistic one at that and in no sense can be said to represent the sentiment of the NAACP.

ROWAN. Well now I note, Mr. Wilkins, that your organization lost some fifteen thousand members between 1954 and 1965. Now you don't think the NAACP and the country are in trouble today because the NAACP put its faith in the law and court decisions but that when the crunch came the decisions were not enforced and the laws became just so much paper?

WILKINS. No, I do not think we're in trouble because we lost fifteen thousand members out of a half million; I don't consider that serious or beyond accounting for in the normal course of events. Nor do I believe that the adherence to law and order is a penalty that we suffer. I think we all have to come back to law and order.

127

"BLACK POWER" AND COALITION POLITICS

by Bayard Rustin

At the time of the writing of this essay, Rustin was executive director of the A. Philip Randolph Institute.

There are two Americas—black and white—and nothing has more clearly revealed the divisions between them than the debate currently raging around the slogan of "black power." Despite—or perhaps because of—the fact that this slogan lacks any clear definition, it has succeeded in galvanizing emotions on all sides, with many whites seeing it as the expression of a new racism and many Negroes taking it as a warning to white people that Negroes will no longer tolerate brutality and violence. But even within the Negro community itself, "black power" has touched off a major debate—the most bitter the community has experienced since the days of Booker T. Washington and W. E. B. Du Bois, and one which threatens to ravage the entire Civil Rights movement. Indeed, a serious split has already developed between advocates of "black power" like Floyd McKissick of CORE and Stokely Carmichael of SNCC on the one hand, and Dr. Martin Luther King of SCLC, Roy Wilkins of the NAACP and Whitney Young of the Urban League on the other.

There is no question, then, that great passions are involved in the debate over the idea of "black power"; nor, as we shall see, is there any question that these passions have their roots in the psychological and political frustrations of the Negro community. Nevertheless, I would contend that "black power" not only lacks any real value for the Civil Rights movement, but that its propagation is positively harmful. It diverts the movement from a meaningful debate over strategy and tactics, it isolates the Negro community, and it encourages the growth of anti-Negro forces.

In its simplest and most innocent guise, "black power" merely means the effort to elect Negroes to office in proportion to Negro strength within the population. There is, of course, nothing wrong with such an objective in itself, and nothing inherently radical in the idea of pursuing it. . . .

The relevant question, moreover, is not whether a politician is black or white, but what forces he represents. Manhattan has had a succession of Negro borough presidents, and yet the schools are increasingly segregated. Adam Clayton Powell and William Dawson have both been in Congress for many years; the former is responsible for a rider on school integration that never gets passed, and the latter is responsible for keeping the Negroes of Chicago tied to a mayor who had to see riots and death before he would put eight-dollar sprinklers on water hydrants in the summer. I am not for one minute arguing that Powell, Dawson, and Mrs. Motley should be impeached. What I am saying is that if a politician is elected because he is black and is deemed to be entitled to a "slice of the pie," he will behave in one way; if he is elected by a constituency pressing for social reform, he will, whether he is white or black, behave in another way.

Southern Negroes, despite exhortations from SNCC to organize themselves into a Black Panther party, are going to stay in the Democratic party—to them it is the party of progress, the New Deal, the New Frontier, and the Great Society—and they are right to stay. For SNCC's Black Panther perspective is simultaneously utopian and reactionary—the former for the by now obvious reason that one-tenth of the population cannot accomplish much by itself, the latter because such a party would remove Negroes from the main area of political struggle in this country (particularly in the one-party South, where the decisive battles are fought out in Democratic primaries), and would give priority to the issue of race precisely at a time when the fundamental questions facing the Negro and American society alike are economical and social. . . .

In some quarters, "black power" connotes not an effort to increase the number of Negroes in elective office but rather a repudiation of non-violence in favor of Negro "self-defense." Actually this is a false issue, since no one has ever argued that Negroes should not defend themselves as individuals from attack. Nonviolence has been advocated as a *tactic* for organized demonstrations in a society where Negroes are a minority and where the majority controls the police. Proponents of nonviolence do not, for example, deny that James Meredith has the right to carry a gun for protection when he visits his mother in Mississippi; what they question is the wisdom of his carrying a gun while participating in a demonstration.

There is, as well, a tactical side to the new emphasis on "self-defense" and the suggestion that nonviolence be abandoned. The reasoning here is that turning the other cheek is not the way to win respect, and that only if the Negro succeeds in frightening the white man will the white man begin taking him seriously. The trouble with this reasoning is that it fails to recognize that fear is more likely to bring hostility to the surface than respect; and far from prodding the "white power structure" into action, the new militant leadership, by raising the slogan of black power and lowering the banner of nonviolence, has obscured the moral issue facing this nation, and permitted the President and Vice President to lecture us about "racism in reverse" instead of proposing more meaningful programs for dealing with the problems of unemployment, housing, and education. . . .

The Vietnam war is also partly responsible for the growing disillusion with nonviolence among Negroes. The ghetto Negro does not in general ask whether the United States is right or wrong to be in Southeast Asia. He does, however, wonder why he is exhorted to nonviolence when the United States has been waging a fantastically brutal war, and it puzzles him to be told that he must turn the other cheek in our own South while we must fight for freedom in South Vietnam.

Thus, as in roughly similar circumstances in the past—circumstances, I repeat, which in the aggregate foster the belief that the ghetto is destined to last forever—Negroes are once again turning to nationalistic slogans, with "black power" affording the same emotional release as "Back to Africa" and "Buy Black" did in earlier periods of frustration and hopelessness. This is not only the case with the ordinary Negro in the ghetto; it is also the case with leaders like McKissick and Carmichael, neither of whom began as a nationalist or was at first cynical about the possibilities of integration. It took countless beatings and twenty-four jailings—that, and the absence of strong and continual support from the liberal community—to persuade Carmichael that his earlier faith in coalition politics was mistaken, that nothing was to be gained from working with whites, and that an alliance with the black nationalists was desirable. In the areas of the South where SNCC has been working so nobly, implementation of the Civil Rights Acts of 1964 and 1965 has been slow and ineffective. Negroes in many rural areas cannot walk into the courthouse and register to vote. Despite the voting-rights bill, they must file complaints and the Justice Department must be called to send federal registrars. Nor do children attend integrated schools as a matter of course. There, too, complaints must be filed and the Department of Health, Education and Welfare must be notified. Neither department has been doing an effective job of enforcing the bills. The feeling of isolation increases among SNCC workers as each legislative victory turns out to be only a token victory—significant on the national level, but not affecting the day-to-day lives of Negroes. Carmichael and his colleagues are wrong in refusing to support the 1966 bill, but one can understand why they feel as they do.

It is, in short, the growing conviction that the Negroes cannot win—a conviction with much grounding in experience—which accounts for the new popularity of "black power."...

We must see, therefore, in the current debate over "black power," a fantastic challenge to American society to live up to its proclaimed principles in the area of race by transforming itself so that all men may live equally and under justice. We must see to it that in rejecting "black power," we do not also reject the principle of Negro equality. Those people who would use the current debate and/or the riots to abandon the Civil Rights movement leave us no choice but to question their original motivation.

If anything, the next period will be more serious and difficult than the preceding ones. It is much easier to establish the Negro's right to sit at a Woolworth's counter than to fight for an integrated community. It takes very little imagination to understand that the Negro should have the right to vote, but it demands much creativity, patience, and political stamina to plan, develop, and implement programs and priorities. It is one thing to organize sentiment behind laws that do not disturb consensus politics, and quite another to win battles for the redistribution of wealth. Many people who marched in Selma are not prepared to support a bill for a $2.00 minimum wage, to say nothing of supporting a redefinition of work or a guaranteed annual income.

It is here that we who advocate coalitions and integration and who object to the "black power" concept have a massive job to do. We must see to it that the liberal-labor-civil rights coalition is maintained and, indeed, strengthened so that it can fight effectively for a Freedom Budget. We are responsible for the growth of the "black power" concept because we have not used our own power to insure the full implementation of the bills, whose passage we were strong enough to win, and we have not mounted the necessary campaign for winning a decent minimum wage and extended benefits. "Black power" is a slogan directed primarily against liberals by those who once counted liberals among their closest friends. It is up to the liberal movement to prove that coalition and integration are better alternatives.

Commentary, September 1966, pp. 35–40; published in part.

128

NONVIOLENCE: THE ONLY ROAD TO FREEDOM

by Martin Luther King, Jr.

In the face of several urban uprisings and a wave of intensely militant rhetoric, the SCLC, through King, held to its basic strategy. In a leading African-American monthly he wrote late in 1966:

The year 1966 brought with it the first public challenge to the philosophy and strategy of nonviolence from within the ranks of the Civil Rights movement. Resolutions of self-defense and Black Power sounded forth from our friends and brothers. At the same time riots erupted in several major cities. Inevitably a link was made between the two phenomena though movement leadership continued to deny any implications of violence in the concept of Black Power.

The nation's press heralded these incidents as an end of the Negro's reliance on nonviolence as a means of achieving freedom. Articles appeared on "The Plot to get Whitey," and, "Must Negroes fight back?" and one had the impression that a serious movement was underway to lead the Negro to freedom through the use of violence.

Indeed, there was much talk of violence. It was the same talk we have heard on the fringes of the nonviolent movement for the past ten years. It was the talk of fearful men, saying that they would not join the nonviolent movement because they would not remain nonviolent if attacked. Now the climate had shifted so that it was even more popular to talk of violence, but in spite of the talk of violence there emerged no action in this direction. . . . A mere check of statistics of casualties in the recent riots shows that the vast majority of persons killed in riots are Negroes. All the reports of sniping in Los Angeles's expressways did not produce a single casualty. The young demented white student at the University of Texas has shown what damage a sniper can do when he is serious. In fact, this one young man killed more people in one day than all the Negroes have killed in all the riots in all the cities since the Harlem riots of 1964. This must raise a serious question about the violent intent of the Negro, for certainly there are many ex-GIs within our ghettos, and no small percentage of those recent migrants from the South have demonstrated some proficiency hunting squirrels and rabbits.

I can only conclude that the Negro, even in his bitterest moments, is not intent on killing white men to be free. This does not mean that the Negro is a saint who abhors violence. Unfortunately, a check of the hospitals in any Negro community on any Saturday night will make you painfully aware of the violence within the Negro community. Hundreds of victims of shooting and cutting lie bleeding in the emergency rooms, but there is seldom if ever a white person who is the victim of Negro hostility.

I have talked with many persons in the ghettos of the North who argue eloquently for the use of violence. But I observed none of them in the mobs that rioted in Chicago. I have heard the street-corner preachers in

Harlem and in Chicago's Washington Park, but in spite of the bitterness preached and the hatred espoused, none of them has ever been able to start a riot. So far, only the police through their fears and prejudice have goaded our people to riot. And once the riot starts, only the police or the National Guard have been able to put an end to them. This demonstrates that these violent eruptions are unplanned, uncontrollable temper tantrums brought on by long-neglected poverty, humiliation, oppression, and exploitation. Violence as a strategy for social change in America is nonexistent. All the sound and fury seems but the posturing of cowards whose bold talk produces no action and signifies nothing.

I am convinced that for practical as well as moral reasons, nonviolence offers the only road to freedom for my people. In violent warfare, one must be prepared to face ruthlessly the fact that there will be casualties by the thousands. In Vietnam, the United States has evidently decided that it is willing to slaughter millions, sacrifice some two hundred thousand men and twenty billion dollars a year to secure the freedom of some fourteen million Vietnamese. This is to fight a war on Asian soil, where Asians are in the majority. Anyone leading a violent conflict must be willing to make a similar assessment regarding the possible casualties to a minority population confronting a well-armed, wealthy majority with a fanatical right wing that is capable of exterminating the entire black population and which would not hesitate such an attempt if the survival of white Western materialism were at stake.

Arguments that the American Negro is a part of a world which is two-thirds colored and that there will come a day when the oppressed people of color will rise together to throw off the yoke of white oppression are at least fifty years away from being relevant. There is no colored nation, including China, which now shows even the potential of leading a revolution of color in any international proportion. Ghana, Zambia, Tanzania, and Nigeria are fighting their own battles for survival against poverty, illiteracy, and the subversive influence of neocolonialism, so that they offer no hope to Angola, Southern Rhodesia, and South Africa, and much less to the American Negro.

The hard cold facts of racial life in the world today indicate that the hope of the people of color in the world may well rest on the American Negro and his ability to reform the structures of racist imperialism from within and thereby turn the technology and wealth of the West to the task of liberating the world from want.

This is no time for romantic illusions about freedom and empty philosophical debate. This is a time for action. What is needed is a strategy for change, a tactical program which will bring the Negro into the mainstream of American life as quickly as possible. So far, this has only been offered by the nonviolent movement.

Our record of achievement through nonviolent action is already remarkable. The dramatic social changes which have been made across the South are unmatched in the annals of history. Montgomery, Albany, Birmingham, and Selma have paved the way for untold progress. Even more remarkable is the fact that this progress occurred with a minimum of human sacrifice and loss of life.

Not a single person has been killed in a nonviolent demonstration. The bombings of the 16th Street Baptist Church occurred several months after demonstrations stopped. Rev. James Reeb, Mrs. Viola Liuzzo, and Jimmie Lee Jackson were all murdered at night following demonstrations. And fewer people have been killed in ten years of action across the South than were killed in three nights of rioting in Watts. No similar changes have occurred without infinitely more sufferings, whether it be Gandhi's drive for independence in India or any African nation's struggle for independence.

The Question of Self-Defense

There are many people who very honestly raise the question of self-defense. This must be placed in perspective. It goes without saying that people will protect their homes. This is a right guaranteed by the Constitution and respected even in the worst areas of the South. But the mere protection of one's home and person against assault by lawless night riders does not provide any positive approach to the fears and conditions which produce violence. There must be some program for establishing law. Our experience in places like Savannah and Macon, Georgia, has been that a drive which registers Negroes to vote can do more to provide protection of the law and respect for Negroes by even racist sheriffs than anything we have seen.

In a nonviolent demonstration, self-defense must be approached from quite another perspective. One must remember that the cause of the demonstration is some exploitation or form of oppression that has made it necessary for men of courage and good will to demonstrate against the evil. For example, a demonstration against the evil of *de facto* school segregation is based on the awareness that a child's mind is crippled daily by inadequate educational opportunity. The demonstrator agrees that it is better for him to suffer publicly for a short time to end the crippling evil of school segregation than to have generation after generation of children suffer in ignorance.

In such a demonstration, the point is made that schools are inadequate. This is the evil to which one seeks to point; anything else detracts from that point and interferes with confrontation of the primary evil against which one demonstrates. Of course, no one wants to suffer and be hurt. But it is more important to get at the cause than to be safe. It is better to shed a little blood from a blow on the head or a rock thrown by an angry mob than to have children by the thousands grow up reading at a fifth- or sixth-grade level.

It is always amusing to me when a Negro man says that he can't demonstrate with us because if someone hit him he would fight back. Here is a man whose children are being plagued by rats and roaches, whose wife is robbed daily at overpriced ghetto food stores, who himself is working for about two-thirds the pay of a white person doing a similar job and with similar skills, and in spite of all this daily suffering it takes someone spitting on him or calling him a nigger to make him want to fight.

Conditions are such for Negroes in America that all Negroes ought to be fighting aggressively. It is as ridiculous for a Negro to raise the question of self-defense in relation to nonviolence as it is for a soldier on the battlefield to say he is not going to take any risks. He is there because he believes that the freedom of his country is worth the risk of his life. The same is true of the nonviolent demonstrator. He sees the misery of his people so clearly that he volunteers to suffer in their behalf and put an end to their plight.

Furthermore, it is extremely dangerous to organize a movement around self-defense. The line between defensive violence and aggressive or retaliatory violence is a fine line indeed. When violence is tolerated even as a means of self-defense there is grave danger that in the fervor of emotion the main fight will be lost over the question of self-defense.

When my home was bombed in 1955 in Montgomery, many men wanted to retaliate, to place an armed guard on my home. But the issue there was not my life, but whether Negroes would achieve first-class treatment on the city's buses. Had we become distracted by the question of my safety we would have lost the moral offensive and sunk to the level of our oppressors.

I must continue my faith or it is too great a burden to bear and violence, even in self-defense, creates more problems than it solves. Only a refusal to hate or kill can put an end to the chain of violence in the world and lead us toward a community where men can live together without fear. Our goal is to create a beloved community and this will require a qualitative change in our souls as well as a quantitative change in our lives.

Strategy for Change

The American racial revolution has been a revolution to "get in" rather than to overthrow. We want a share in the American economy, the housing market, the educational system, and the social opportunities. This goal itself indicates that a social change in America must be nonviolent.

If one is in search of a better job, it does not help to burn down the factory. If one needs more adequate education, shooting the principal will not help, or if housing is the goal, only building and construction will produce that end. To destroy anything, person or property, can't bring us closer to the goal that we seek.

The nonviolent strategy has been to dramatize the evils of our society in such a way that pressure is brought to bear against those evils by the forces of good will in the community and change is produced.

The student sit-ins of 1960 are a classic illustration of this method. Students were denied the right to eat at a lunch counter, so they deliberately sat down to protest their denial. They were arrested, but this made their parents mad and so they began to close their charge accounts. The students continued to sit-in, and this further embarrassed the city, scared away many white shoppers, and soon produced an economic threat to the business life of the city. Amid this type of pressure, it is not hard to get people to agree to change.

So far, we have had the Constitution backing most of the demands for change, and this has made our work easier, since we could be sure that the federal courts would usually back up our demonstrations legally. Now we are approaching areas where the voice of the Constitution is not clear. We have left the realm of constitutional rights and we are entering the area of human rights.

The Constitution assured the right to vote, but there is no such assurance of the right to adequate housing, or the right to an adequate income. And yet, in a nation which has a gross national product of 750 billion dollars a year, it is morally right to insist that every person has a decent house, an adequate education, and enough money to provide basic necessities for one's family. Achievement of these goals will be a lot more difficult and require much more discipline, understanding, organization, and sacrifice.

It so happens that Negroes live in the central city of the major cities of the United States. These cities control the electoral votes of the large states of our nation. This means that though we are only ten percent of the nation's population, we are located in such a key position geographically—the cities of the North and black belts of the South—that we are able to lead a political and moral coalition which can direct the course of the nation. Our position depends upon a lot more than political power, however. It depends upon our ability to marshall moral power as well. As soon as we lose the moral offensive, we are left with only our ten percent of the power of the nation. This is hardly enough to produce any meaningful changes, even within our own communities, for the lines of power control the economy as well and once the flow of money is cut off, progress ceases.

The past three years have demonstrated the power of a committed, morally sound minority to lead the nation. It was the coalition molded through the Birmingham movement which allied the forces of the churches, labor, and the academic communities of the nation behind the liberal issues of our time. All of the liberal legislation of the past session of Congress can be credited to this coalition. Even the presence of a vital peace movement and the campus protest against the war in Vietnam can be traced back to the nonviolent action movement led by the Negro. Prior to Birmingham, our campuses were still in a state of shock over the McCarthy era and Congress was caught in the perennial deadlock of southern Democrats and midwestern Republicans. Negroes put the country on the move against the enemies of poverty, slums, and inadequate education.

Techniques of the Future

When Negroes marched, so did the nation. The power of the nonviolent march is indeed a mystery. It is always surprising that a few hundred Negroes marching can produce such a reaction across the nation. When marches are carefully organized around well-defined issues, they represent the power which Victor Hugo phrased as the most powerful force in the world, "an idea whose time has come." Marching feet announce that time has come for a given idea. When the idea is a sound one, the cause a just one, and the demonstration a righteous one, change will be forthcoming. But if any of these conditions are not present, the power for change is missing also. A thousand people demonstrating for the right to use heroin would have little effect. By the same token, a group of ten thousand marching in anger against a police station and cussing out the chief of police will do very little to bring respect, dignity, and unbiased law enforcement. Such a demonstration would only produce fear and bring about an addition of forces to the station and more oppressive methods by the police.

Marches must continue in the future, and they must be the kind of marches that bring about the desired result. But the march is not a "one shot" victory-producing method. One march is seldom successful, and as my good friend Kenneth Clark points out in *Dark Ghetto*, it can serve merely to let off steam and siphon off the energy which is necessary to produce change. However, when marching is seen as a part of a program to dramatize an evil, to mobilize the forces of good will, and to generate pressure and power for change, marches will continue to be effective.

Our experience is that marches must continue over a period of thirty to forty-five days to produce any meaningful results. They must also be of sufficient size to produce some inconvenience to the forces in power or they go unnoticed. In other words, they must demand the attention of the press, for it is the press which interprets the issue to the community at large and thereby sets in motion the machinery for change.

Along with the march as a weapon for change in our nonviolent arsenal must be listed the boycott. Basic to the philosophy of nonviolence is the refusal to cooperate with evil. There is nothing quite so effective as a refusal to cooperate economically with the forces and institutions which perpetuate evil in our communities.

In the past six months simply by refusing to purchase products from companies which do not hire Negroes in meaningful numbers and in all job categories, the Ministers of Chicago under SCLC's Operation Breadbasket have increased the income of the Negro community by more than two million dollars annually. In Atlanta the Negroes' earning power has been increased by more than twenty million dollars annually over the past three years through a carefully disciplined program of selective buying and negotiations by the Negro minister. This is nonviolence at its peak of power, when it cuts into the profit margin of a business in order to bring about a more just distribution of jobs and opportunities for Negro wage earners and consumers.

But again, the boycott must be sustained over a period of several weeks and months to assure results. This means continuous education of the community in order that support can be maintained. People will work together and sacrifice if they understand clearly why and how this sacrifice will bring about change. We can never assume that anyone understands. It is our job to keep people informed and aware.

Our most powerful nonviolent weapon is, as would be expected, also our most demanding, that is organization. To produce change, people must be organized to work together in units of power. These units might be political, as in the case of voters' leagues and political parties; they may be economic units such as groups of tenants who join forces to form a tenant union or to organize a rent strike; or they may be laboring units of persons who are seeking employment and wage increases.

More and more, the Civil Rights movement will become engaged in the task of organizing people into permanent groups to protect their own interests and to produce change in their behalf. This is a tedious task which may take years, but the results are more permanent and meaningful.

In the future we will be called upon to organize the unemployed, to unionize the businesses within the ghetto, to bring tenants together into collective bargaining units, and establish cooperatives for purposes of building viable financial institutions within the ghetto that can be controlled by Negroes themselves.

There is no easy way to create a world where men and women can live together, where each has his own job and house and where all children receive as much education as their minds can absorb. But if such a world is created in our lifetime, it will be done in the United States by Negroes and white people of good will. It will be accomplished by persons who have the courage to put an end to suffering by willingly suffering themselves rather than inflict suffering upon others. It will be done by rejecting the racism, materialism, and violence that has characterized Western civilization and especially by working toward a world of brotherhood, cooperation, and peace.

Ebony, October 1966, pp 27–30.

129

RACISM AND THE ELECTIONS:
THE AMERICAN DILEMMA, 1966

by The National Committee of Negro Churchmen

On November 6, 1966, a full-page advertisement appeared in the *New York Times* under the above headline in bold type. The statement it contains was made on November 3 at the Statue of Liberty by the National Committee of Negro Churchmen. Appended to this advertisement were the names of 175 clergymen and one woman, Dr. Anna A. Hedgeman, of the Commission on Religion and Race, National Council of Churches, in New York City, and Robert W. Mance, M.D., secretary of finance, the A.M.E. Church in Washington. The signers came from every section of the country, with those from New York State predominating.

A few days ago the eightiethth anniversary of the Statue of Liberty was celebrated here on Liberty Island. On November 8, a so-called "white backlash" will confront the American people with a fateful choice in the elections across the country. We, an informal group of Negro churchmen, assembled from the four corners of this land, gather here today in order to highlight the critical moral issues which confront the American people in those elections—issues symbolized here in the Statue of Liberty.

Our purpose here is neither to beg nor to borrow, but to state the determination of black men in America to exact from this nation not one whit less than our full manhood rights. We will not be cowed nor intimidated in the land of our birth. We intend that the truth of this country, as experienced by black men, will be heard. We shall state this truth from the perspective of the Christian faith and in the light of our experience with the Lord of us all, in the bleakness of this racially idolatrous land.

The inscription inside the Statue of Liberty, entitled "The New Colossus," refers to America as the "Mother of Exiles." It concludes with these moving words:

"Keep ancient land, your storied pomp!"
  Cries she
With silent lips. "Give me your tired, your
  poor,
Your huddled masses yearning to breathe free.
The wretched refuse of your teeming shore.
Send these, the homeless, tempest-tost to me
I lift my lamp beside the Golden Door!"

This poem focuses on the linked problems of identity and power which have been so tragically played out on the stage of this nation's history. "Mother of Exiles" and "The New Colossus"—these symbols capture both the variety of groups and experience out of which this nation has been hammered and the fervent hope of many early Americans that in this land the world would see a new and more human use of power, dedicated to the proposition that all men are created equal.

We remind Americans that in our beginnings we were all exiles, strangers sojourning in an unfamiliar land. Even the first black men who set foot on these shores came, as did most white men, in the role of pilgrims, not as slaves. Sharing common aspirations and hopes for a land where freedom could take root and live, for the briefest of moments black men and white men found each other in a community of trust and mutual acceptance.

However, if America became a "Mother of Exiles" for white men she became at the same time a cruel system of bondage and inhumanity to black men. Far from finding here a maternal acceptance, her black sons were thrust into the depth of despair, at times so hopeless that it wrung from their lips the sorrow song: "Sometimes I feel like a motherless child." What anguish is keener, what rejection more complete, or what alienation more poignant than this experience which called forth the metaphor, "motherless child"?

But that is only part of our story. For somewhere in the depth of their experience within this great land, those same black men and women found a ground of faith and hope on which to stand. Never accepting on the inside the identity forced upon them by a brutalizing white power, they also sang—even prior to emancipation—"Before I'll be a slave, I'll be buried in my grave and go home to my Lord and be free." A faith of this quality and integrity remains alive today.

There is, to be sure, a continuing dilemma of "crisis and commitment" in our country. But, it is not the quarrels among the civil rights leaders, nor is it the debate about Black Power, nor is it the controversy surrounding the riots in our cities. The crisis is what it has always been since shortly after the first black Americans set foot upon these shores. It is not a crisis rooted in the Negro community. It is a "crisis of commitment" among white Americans who have consistently taken two steps forward toward becoming mature men on race and one and a half steps backward at the same time. The power of "The New Colossus" has never been fully committed to eliminating this monstrous racism from the life of the American people.

Look at the record of fitful and mincing steps forward and of cowardly steps away from the goal of racial justice. The slaves were freed in 1863, but the nation refused to give them land to make that emancipation meaningful. Simultaneously, the nation was giving away millions of acres in the midwest and west—a gift marked "for whites only." Thus an economic floor was placed under the new peasants from Europe but America's oldest peasantry was provided only an abstract freedom. In the words of Frederick Douglass, emancipation made the slaves "free to hunger; free to the winter and rains of heaven...free without roofs to cover them or bread to eat or land to cultivate.... We gave them freedom and famine at the same time. The marvel is that they still live."

We should, therefore, be neither shocked nor surprised that our slums today confront us with the bitter fruits of that ancient theft. Is it conceivable that the shrill cry "Burn, Baby, Burn" in Watts, Los Angeles, and across this country, could ever be invented by men with reasonable chances to make a living, to live in a decent neighborhood, to get an adequate education for their children? Is it conceivable that men with reasonable prospects for life, liberty, and the pursuit of happiness for themselves and for their children could ever put the torch to their own main streets? The answer is obvious. These are the anguished, desperate acts of men, women, and children who have been taught to hate themselves and who have been herded and confined like cattle in rat-infested slums.

Frederick Douglass is indeed correct when he suggests that "the marvel is that Negroes are still alive" not to mention sane. Look at the record. We submit that to pass a Civil Rights Bill as this nation did in 1875 and then refuse to enforce it; to pass another Civil Rights Bill (weaker this time) in 1964 and then refuse to enforce it; to begin an antipoverty program with insufficient funds in the first place and then to put the lion's share of this minuscule budget into Head Start programs when unemployment among Negro men continues to skyrocket; to declare segregation in our schools unconstitutional as the Supreme Court did in 1954, and then refuse to end it forthwith; to set up guidelines for desegregating hospitals and then refuse to appropriate monies for the enforcement of these guidelines; to insist on civil rights legislation aimed at the South and then to defeat the first piece of such legislation relevant to areas outside the South; to preach "law and order" into the anguish of Negro slums in full view of the contributions of policemen to that anguish and then to insist that policemen be their own judges; to hear suburban politicians declaim against open occupancy in one breath and in the very next breath insist that they are not racists: these are the ironies which stare us in the face and make it all but impossible to talk about how much "progress" has been made. The fact of the matter is if black Americans are not accorded basic human and constitutional rights which white Americans gain immediately upon their entry into citizenship, then there really are no substantive gains of which to speak.

Therefore, we will not be intimidated by the so-called "white backlash," for white America has been "backlashing" on the fundamental human and constitutional rights of Negro Americans since the eighteenth century. The election of racists in November will merely be a continuation of this pattern.

But: Let us try to be very clear about one thing, America. Black Americans are determined to have all of their full human and constitutional rights. We will not cease to agitate this issue with every means available to men of faith and dignity until justice is done.

We are dealing at bottom with a question of relationship between black and white, between rich and poor, ultimately between believers in different gods. We support all of our civil rights leaders for we believe that they all have important insights to share with us on this critical question. For our part, we submit that our basic goal in this struggle is to make it possible for all persons and groups to participate with power at all levels of our society. Integration is not an aesthetic goal designed to add token bits of color to institutions controlled entirely by whites. Integration is a political goal with the objective of making it possible for Negroes and other Americans to express the vitality of their personal and group life in institutions which fundamentally belong to all Americans.

If the tremendous power of this nation—this "New Colossus"—begins to move "with conquering limbs astride from land to land," then we are bound to forget the tired, the poor, the "huddled masses yearning to be free." America is rich and powerful. But America is neither infinitely rich nor omnipotent. Even America must make choices.

We submit that the resolution of the crisis which is upon us requires a change in the nation's priorities. The welfare and dignity of all Americans is more important than the priorities being given to military expansion, space exploration, or the production of supersonic jet airliners.

To this end, we of the Negro church call for a massive mobilization of the resources in the Negro community in order to give leadership in the fulfillment not only of our own destiny but in order to help produce a more sane white America.

We further call upon white churchmen to join us by endeavoring to mobilize the resources of the white community in completing with us the task at hand.

Finally, we say to the American people, white and black, there is no turning back of the clock of time. America cannot be America by electing "white backlash" candidates in the November elections.

Again we say: America is at the crossroad. Either we become the democracy we can become, or we tread the path to self-destruction.

130

ON BECOMING A MUSLIM

by Muhammad Ali

The religious principles of Muhammad Ali forbade him from participating in war. When, during the U.S.–Vietnam War, Ali was classified as 1-A and ordered to duty, he refused. His world heavyweight championship was taken from him, costing him millions of dollars, but he held to his beliefs. From the proceedings in 1966 and 1967 before the U.S. Court of Appeals, for the Fifth Circuit (No. 24, 991), extracts follow from the appeal filed on his behalf by seven attorneys, black and white.

A. Well, my name is Muhammad Ali, and my slave name was Cassius Marcellus Clay, Jr., and my home address is now at 4610 Northwest 15th Court, in Miami, Florida.

Q. And where do you spend most of your time?

A. I spend most of my time at my business office and with my leader, Honorable Elijah Muhammad, at his house in Chicago, Illinois.

Q. Now, tell Judge Grauman—we have heard about your being raised up as a Baptist—how it was that you got acquainted with the faith of the Nation of Islam?

A. Well, it's true I was raised as a Baptist and during the time that I was a Baptist I never understood the teachings of the Christian—

Q. (Interrupting) I wonder if you would be good enough to talk a little louder?

A. It's true that I was raised as a Baptist and while being raised as a Baptist I never understood the teachings of the Christian preacher, and I never understood why that Heaven was in the sky and I never understood why Hell was under the ground and I never understood why the so-called Negroes had to turn their cheeks and have to take all the punishment while everyone else defends themselves and fought back.

I never understood why our people were the first fired and the last hired.

I never understood why when I went to the Olympics in Rome, Italy, and won the Gold Medal for great America and come back to Kentucky and I couldn't go in a downtown restaurant, and I always wondered why everything in it was white.

I always wondered these things and I am saying this to tell you why I accepted the religion of Islam the minute I heard it then while in 1961 I was walking down the streets of Miami, Florida, a Muslim walks up to me and asked me would I like to come to Muhammad's Mosque and listen to the teachings of Islam and listen to why we are the lost people and listen to why—what my true religion was before we were made slaves and this sounded interesting and, by me being a person of common sense, I went to the Mosque to listen and immediately, on entering the Mosque—I would say the first half hour after being there, I immediately wanted to know what could I do to become a member, and I started to say that the minister of the Mosque was preaching on the subject of why are we called Negroes. He said that the Chinese are named after China and Cubans are named after Cuba and Russians are named after Russia and Hiwaiians [*sic*] are named after Hiwaii [*sic*] and Mexicans are named after Mexico and Indians are named after India.

So, he said, what country is named Negroes and he said why are we called Negroes, and this made sense to me and I had to check into it.

I asked questions and he gave me good answers and he also said that we do not have our own names and all intelligent people on earth are named after their people of their land and their ancestors. He said the Chinese have names such as Chang-Chong, and Cubans have names such as Mr. Castro, and Russians have names such as Mr. Kruschev [sic], and Africans have names such as Lmumba. [sic] We call ourselves Culpepper, Mr. Tree, Mr. Bird, Mr. Clay, Mr. Washington, and he said these were names of our slave masters, and by me being an intelligent man and the Lord blessing me with five senses, I have to accept it because there have been write-ups in the Louisville papers where my father and me were named after a great white slave father named Cassius Marcellus Clay.

So, I had to accept this, and he also told us that the proper name of God is Allah and that the Honorable Elijah Muhammad was taught by Allah for three and one half years to teach the so-called Negroes the true knowledge of his God, the true knowledge of his religion, true knowledge of his names and his future and not to force himself on whites and not to beg whites to come to clean up the rats, but to clean up our own neighborhoods, respect our women, do something for ourselves, quit smoking, quit drinking, and obey the laws of the land and respect those in authority.

Immediately, I had to check and see who is Elijah Muhammad because Elijah Muhammad teached and I asked all the press who he is and they said that he was a self-styled leader and I had to find out what self-styled meant and I found out that everything that he teached then he had to style it his self.

So, common sense just told me that a man can't stand here in the middle of America preaching the things that he's preaching and no government, no lawyers, no doctors, no theologists, nobody would challenge him or as much as even mention his name in public.

So, after finding out who he was, and I had to convince myself that he was a divine man from God because I knew that I would have to give up a lot and now that I have accepted the religion of Islam, I turned down at least one million, eight hundred thousand in novies [sic].

I have turned down a two million bout in Chicago with Ernie Terrell, and I have—I just put up fifty thousand cash yesterday to alimony fees on my wife only because she would not wear the proper dresses and be a Muslim.

All of this is why I am a Muslim and I really sincerely believe it and as my father and mother have said, I'll die right now in this courtroom, because I know this is the truth I'm talking.

Q. Now, you first got acquainted with the Muslims, the Muslim belief in Miami?

A. Yes, sir.

Q. Is that right?

A. Yes, sir.

Q. Now, who took you under wing, or who influenced or guided or directed you while you were in your initial stages of training in the Muslim faith?

A. Well, I would say the true person that really guided me and directed me while I was at the Mosque that was the minister at that time, his name was Ishmael X., and Sam Saxon here, my driver and helper, he was with me a lot when he would—I'd go to the restaurants and I would order bacon and ham and he would tell me about how the hog is an unclean animal and how the Lord created the hog as a scavenger and that we shouldn't eat it and that it affects our arteries, sometimes high blood pressure, some times low and he convinced me to quit eating hog and he always stuck with me and chased me out of the night clubs and I would be in there with women and drinks and all and he would get me out of night clubs and take me to the temple when I didn't want to go and he was one of the persons mainly instrumental in keeping a check on me as far as my young menbership [sic] was concerned.

Q. After what period of time were you able to be on your own?

A. Well, I was able to—I remember talking about it with the Honorable Elijah Muhammad and he said that we are all human and none of us are able really to be on our own.

Q. I understand, but where you didn't need the guidance or the constant surveillance or watching by Mr. Saxon?

A. That was about three weeks before the Sonny Liston fight when I became officially registered and put my name on the Lamb's Book of Life.

Q. Now, would you explain to Judge Grauman how it is and why it is that you have accepted the name Muhammad Ali?

A. Well, after, as I said, after hearing the teachings of the Honorable Elijah Muhammad and hearing the history of the so-called Negro and how we were given slave names and the fact that we do have names of our masters, and the Honorable Elijah Muhammad tells us that we were declared free a hundred hears [sic] ago by Abraham Lincoln and we were not free in name as well as fact, so therefore, we who come into the knowledge of ourselves and understand who the Honorable Elijah Muhammad is, it's an honor and a pleasure to receive an "X", which means that such as an ex-convict, or Joe Louis was an ex-champion, and it means we were ex-Christians, the "X" meaning we are no longer a product of the old Christian ways that we were.

So, therefore, we take the name of "X" and it's a great honor and pleasure and blessing to receive a holy name whether it's Robert or Corene or whether it's Robert Shabazz, or any last name, but I was blessed to have two holy names and I had to accept them and the Honorable Elijah Muhammad named me on radio about one month after my fight with Sonny Liston, and at the time I did not know that he would name me. I just heard on the air that would I accept the name and immediately, I did, and I would like to explain that the names of Muhammad Ali are two attributes of Allah. Muhammad means one who is worthy of all praises and one most praiseworthy, such as the supreme being, and Ali, means most high and ever since I have accepted the name of Muhammad Ali. . . .

Conclusion

Perhaps the appellant himself, in his own words said it best.

"The 1-A classification was the result of hysteria generated by the pressures of the press on the local board and an injustice was done me under the blinding fear that to do me justice would be misunderstood as partiality. However, the board was determined beyond any and all reasons, facts presented or reasonable cause to tell the waiting press I was still class 1-A. All this push to make me 1-A triggered a whole national mess which and wherein I became embroiled in and made the target of politicians and super flag-wavers, causing my last fight a fortune in losses of revenue to me and the governments in taxes. I should be in Class—III A.

s/ Muhammad Ali   Slave Name s/ Cassius M. Clay"

Extracts from transcript of testimony taken at Special Hearing Concerning Selective Service Classification of Cassius M. Clay, Jr., aka Muhammad Ali before Hon. Lawrence Grauman, August 23, 1966. The conclusion is from a letter to the Louisville Board, April 16, 1967. Manuscript in editor's possession.

131

ON THE VIETNAM WAR

by Muhammad Ali

"No, I am not going 10,000 miles to help murder and kill and burn other people simply to help continue the domination of white slavemasters over the dark people the world over. This is the day and age when such evil injustice must come to an end."

Freedomways 7 (Spring 1967): Cover.

132

"I RAISED MY HAND, AS HIGH AS I COULD"

by Fannie Lou Hamer

The legendary grass-roots leader of the southern movement for human dignity, Fannie Lou Hamer, told of her life in a taped interview by two leaders of SNCC— Julius Lester and Maria Varela. This was done in 1967.

I was born October sixth, nineteen and seventeen in Montgomery County, Mississippi. My parents moved to Sunflower County when I was two years old, to a plantation about four and a half miles from here, Mr. E. W. Brandon's plantation.

...My parents were sharecroppers and they had a big family. Twenty children. Fourteen boys and six girls. I'm the twentieth child. All of us worked in the fields, of course, but we never did get anything out of sharecropping....

My life has been almost like my mother's was, because I married a man who sharecropped. We didn't have it easy and the only way we could ever make it through the winter was because Pap had a little juke joint and we made liquor. That was the only way we made it. I married in 1944 and stayed on the plantation until 1962 when I went down to the courthouse in Indianola to register to vote. That happened because I went to a mass meeting one night.

Until then I'd never heard of no mass meeting and I didn't know that a

Negro could register and vote. Bob Moses, Reggie Robinson, Jim Bevel, and James Forman were some of the SNCC workers who ran that meeting. When they asked for those to raise their hands who'd go down to the courthouse the next day, I raised mine. Had it up as high as I could get it. I guess if I'd had any sense I'd a-been a little scared, but what was the point of being scared? The only thing they could do to me was kill me and it seemed like they'd been trying to do that a little bit at a time ever since I could remember.

Well, there was eighteen of us who went down to the courthouse that day and all of us were arrested. Police said the bus was painted the wrong color—said it was too yellow. After I got bailed out I went back to the plantation where Pap and I had lived for eighteen years. My oldest girl met me and told me that Mr. Marlow, the plantation owner, was mad and raising sand. He had heard that I had tried to register. That night he called on us and said, "We're not going to have this in Mississippi and you will have to withdraw. I am looking for your answer, yea or nay?" I just looked. He said, "I will give you until tomorrow morning. And if you don't withdraw you will have to leave. If you do go withdraw, it's only how I feel, you might still have to leave." So I left that same night. Pap had to stay on till work on the plantation was through. Ten days later they fired into Mrs. Tucker's house where I was staying. They also shot two girls at Mr. Sissel's.

That was a rough winter. I hadn't a chance to do any canning before I got kicked off, so didn't have hardly anything. I always can more than my family can use 'cause there's always people who don't have enough. That winter was bad, though. Pap couldn't get a job nowhere 'cause everybody knew he was my husband. We made it on through, though, and since then I just been trying to work and get our people organized.

I reckon the most horrible experience I've had was in June of 1963. I was arrested along with several others in Winona, Mississippi. That's in Montgomery County, the county where I was born. I was carried to a cell and locked up with Euvester Simpson. I began to hear the sound of licks, and I could hear people screaming. . . .

After then, the State Highway patrolmen came and carried me out of the cell into another cell where there were two Negro prisoners. The patrolman gave the first Negro a long blackjack that was heavy. It was loaded with something and they had me lay down on the bunk with my face down, and I was beat. I was beat by the first Negro till he gave out.

Then the patrolman ordered the other man to take the blackjack and he began to beat....

After I got out of jail, half dead, I found out that Medgar Evers had been shot down in his own yard....

I've worked on voter registration here ever since I went to that first mass meeting. In 1964 we registered 63,000 black people from Mississippi into the Freedom Democratic Party. We formed our own party because the whites wouldn't even let us register. We decided to challenge the white Mississippi Democratic Party at the National Convention. We followed all the laws that the white people themselves made. We tried to attend the precinct meetings and they locked the doors on us or moved the meetings and that's against the laws they made for their ownselves. So we were the ones that held the real precinct meetings. At all of these meetings across the state we elected our representatives to go to the National Democratic Convention in Atlantic City. But we learned the hard way that even though we had all the law and all the righteousness on our side—that white man is not going to give up his power to us.

We have to build our own power. We have to win every single political office we can, where we have a majority of black people.... The question for black people is not, when is the white man going to give us our rights, or when is he going to give us good education for our children, or when is he going to give us jobs—if the white man gives you anything—just remember when he get ready he will take it right back. We have to take for ourselves.

Clayborne Carson et al., eds., *op. cit.,* pp. 176–79.

133

BATTLING RACISM IN NORTHERN CALIFORNIA

by John Pittman

A longtime resident of San Francisco and a journalist associated with the *People's World,* a radical weekly published there, reports on the struggle against racism in California's Bay Area.

A number of incidents occurred during 1966 in the San Francisco–Oakland metropolitan area which the police and daily press were pleased to call "race riots."

In East Oakland last August 29, according to Negro residents, after an altercation between policemen and Negro youths, police riot squads descended on the area and instituted a reign of terror. For three days and nights, policemen in steel helmets and armed with shotguns and rifles abused and insulted Negroes of all ages. Approximately fifty Negro teenagers and older youth were arrested.

Again in East Oakland last October 18, Negro residents report that after a fight between police and brothers of a Negro girl they had roughed up, several score Negroes began roaming the streets, throwing bottles and bricks and breaking store-fronts. Again the police swarmed on the area in force. Fifty-two Negroes were arrested on charges of arson, possession of weapons, and disturbing the peace.

Similar incidents occurred in other localities of this area, according to the testimony of Negro residents. In Alameda last June, police harassed teenagers in a group of approximately seventy-five Negroes staging a "tent-in" in the city's public park to protest their eviction from a "temporary" housing project built during World War II. In Marin City last April, scores of Negro youth battled police in protest against continuous harassment. In East Palo Alto, Menlo Park, and Belle Haven, gangs of Negro teenagers and older youths during September and October broke windows and ruined store-fronts in defiance of police harassment.

The San Francisco events of last September 27–29, however, received most attention overseas and throughout the United States. A white policeman patrolling the Hunters Point ghetto in this "cradle of the United Nations Organization" shot in the back and killed a Negro teenager fleeing from what the policeman suspected was a stolen car. Negroes gathered in angry groups and retaliated by throwing rocks and bottles, breaking windows and store-fronts, and fighting police with bricks and Molotov cocktails. About 550 police, steel-helmeted with shotguns and rifles, sealed off two widely separated ghettos. Two thousand National Guardsmen were ordered into the area by Governor Edmund Brown at the request of Mayor John Shelley. At one point, police directed a fusillade at a Negro community center, shooting a number of Negroes. In the three days of disturbances 129 persons, mostly Negroes, were injured, 359 Negroes were arrested, and property damage was estimated at $110,000. But the policeman who killed the Negro teenager, after being suspended for a few days, was reinstated with full pay and the congratulations of his brother officers at a mass police demonstration at City Hall.

There has been, of course, an orgy of opinion and speculation concerning the ultimate causes of these incidents. But certain aspects deserve more scrutiny than they have received so far.

It is notable, first, that from start to finish and in all essential respects they conformed to a national pattern, displaying several features in common with scores of similar events during 1966, including most of those in thirty-eight major U.S. cities.

The incidents occurred mainly on the inside or on the periphery of the Negro ghetto, and the injured and arrested were predominantly residents of the ghetto.

They were preceded by years, even decades, of official neglect and callousness toward the gradual deterioration of living conditions and opportunity for the ghetto residents, accompanied by ever-increasing police surveillance and harassment.

They were set off by police action against residents of the ghetto and, except for destruction of property owned by nonresidents in or contiguous to the ghetto, they developed as conflict not between Negroes and the white community, but between Negroes and the authorities, especially the policing authorities.

Such observations, of course, are neither new nor unusual for any Negro who lives or has ever lived in the ghetto. Nor would they seem unusual to anyone sufficiently interested to review the history of so-called "race riots." With a few exceptions, every "race riot" in this country has taken place inside or on the periphery of the ghetto, has been incited by action of police and/or white racists, and has inflicted the bulk of casualties—the killed, wounded, and arrested, and the property destroyed or damaged—on Negroes. Seldom have Negroes, since the period of slave uprisings, carried the conflict into the white community.

This point deserves emphasis. It has not been mentioned in comment about the incidents here. An entire mythology has been fabricated around such incidents, of which the term "white backlash" is a current specimen. In this case, as in the others, we find the truth stood on its head, as if the Negro prostrate under the jackboot of oppression wields the lash, while the wearer of the jackboot merely flicks it back in response to the Negro's aggressiveness. . . .

There is something else the San Francisco–Oakland events have in common with similar occurrences around the country: Negroes, especially Negro youth, are becoming convinced that the owner of the jackboot has no conscience. They know he isn't either deaf or mute. They know he hears the Negro begging him to ease up on the pressure, because he is quicker than you can say "Please, boss!" to promise immediate, total, and permanent relief—that is to say, full and unrestricted equal opportunity, just as he has promised the Indians throughout the centuries.

A man who hopes and believes he will live in a house doesn't burn it down. Likewise, Negroes would hardly have resorted to bricks and bottled gasoline had they felt any real hope and belief in the promises of the enforcers of law and order. The fact is, they had valid reasons to believe the so-called Establishment would do nothing for them. . . .

What is pertinent to this inquiry is the fact that there has never been a time in the life of a single ghetto in this area when voices of anger and discontent were silent. Long before the incidents of 1966, appeals from the ghettos received widespread publicity. Some even found an echo in the statements of public officials and of community and public organizations.

A 1953 Community Chest survey of the neighborhood which includes Hunters Point found the area "one of special need . . . sadly neglected in special services," ranking first in the city in the number of children seventeen and below, and populated by workers who "support many children on a low income, and there may be an increasing concentration of families on public assistance." That finding was announced thirteen years ago.

As for police harassment of the ghetto, the police enjoy a sacrosanct status everywhere in the U.S., and it takes uncommon public figures with the guts to criticize them. Yet, Negro spokesmen in every ghetto in this area have repeatedly protested abuse by police. According to its 1961 report, the United States Commission on Civil Rights found that "police brutality by state and local officers presents a serious and continuing problem in many parts of the United States. Both whites and Negroes are the victims, but Negroes are the victims of such brutality far more, proportionately, than any other group in American society." That was reported five years ago. . . .

No, it's not that The Man doesn't hear. He can't claim ignorance of the facts. He knows the facts, otherwise he would not try to hide his responsibility for them behind rationalizations. Yet the usual thing is for the public official or city bigwig to assert his ignorance of conditions in the ghetto and in the next breath ask if, after all, Negroes don't choose to live there, or whether they could afford to live anywhere else.

Of course it is neither Negro choice nor Negro poverty that accounts for the growth and permanence of the ghetto: it is *racism*. Professor Karl E. Tauber of the University of Wisconsin recently surveyed the persistent trends in residential segregation in 207 U.S cities. He found (*Scientific American,* August 1965) that "regardless of income, most Negroes live in Negro neighborhoods and most whites live in white neighborhoods," and that Negroes can hardly be said to have any freedom of choice in the matter since in this racist society any Negro moving into a white neighborhood faces humiliation, ostracism, hostility, and even injury to person and property. . . .

It required thirteen years of strenuous campaigns before the state legislature, by-passing the electorate, finally enacted in 1959 a Fair Employment Practices law. When in 1946 it was submitted on the ballot, 1,682,000 people voted against it, only 675,000 for it. In 1953 the FEPC bill never got out of the state assembly committee; it passed the assembly in 1955 but was killed in a senate committee by a vote of 5–2; in 1958 it was tabled in the same senate committee by a vote of 4–2. The opposition to it came from the biggest employers in California finance, industry, and agriculture. And the coordinator of the whole operation against this measure was the Federated Employers of San Francisco. . . .

The 1964 demonstrations for jobs for minorities in the city's hotels and auto agencies were carried out at considerable sacrifice and risk for the participants. But they broke the ice which had frozen minority workers out of these and other places of employment in the area. True, it was not the kind of breakthrough the participants had hoped for. In November 1966, in establishments of members of the Motor Car Dealers Association, of 2,133 service and office employees, 168, or 7.9 per cent were Negroes, and another 253, or 11.9 per cent were members of other minority groups; in the hotel industry, there were twenty-one Negroes of 291 doormen, thirteen Negro waiters of 520, eleven Negro bartenders of 179, two Negro waitresses of 268, and 601 Negro maids of 1,181.

For these nominal gains in employment, participants in the demonstrations that won them deserved honor and awards. But the Establishment exacted a cruel price. The entire California judiciary was turned into a holy inquisition of law and order. More than two hundred demonstrators were sentenced to jail and served time. It was particularly significant that the Establishment "threw the book" at the Negro leader whose integrity, courage, and judgment had won the respect of both the Negro and white communities—Dr. Thomas Burbridge, a professor of pharmacology at the

University of California medical center. Burbridge's appeal of his sentence of nine months was rejected by both the California court of appeals and the California supreme court.

The impression seems to be general and widespread in white America that once a law against discrimination is adopted—presto! equality steps forth full-grown from the womb of society.

But equality of opportunity depends not only on clearing the road of racist and discriminatory barriers, a task just barely begun. It depends also on an equal start. In this country today there are twenty-three state FEP laws, thirty-five municipal FEP ordinances, a federal FEP, nineteen state fair housing laws, forty-nine municipal fair housing ordinances, and a federal fair housing executive order. Yet segregation, and discrimination still exist in all aspects of American life and in all areas—including those with the laws—of the United States.

Three hundred years of slavery and another century of disfranchise-ment, segregation, and discrimination have not prepared Negroes for an equal start in this intensely competitive, highly complex, industrialized society. To give Negroes an equal start means to compensate them for those four centuries during which they were unable to acquire the education, skills, and experience possessed by the white majority. It means to give them a special treatment, just as the veterans of two world wars were given special treatment to compensate them for time and opportunities lost.

This is the logic of the proposals for a massive domestic "Marshall Plan" which have come from many of the most prominent Negro spokesmen. The cost of such a plan has been put at approximately what the federal government spends for military purposes in two years. *A San Francisco Negro spokesman has remarked, for instance, that what the government spends annually only for the napalm it is using to give "freedom" to the Vietnamese would provide jobs and modern, up-to-date, open occupancy housing for all the Negroes in this metropolitan area.*

Essentially, this demand of America's twenty million Negroes for an equal start is a demand for practical democracy, for filling in the ever-growing gulf between promise and performance. It is a renovating and revitalizing initiative in behalf of the so-called American Dream. It deserves the gratitude and support of all Americans who want the American Dream to be realized. However, the initiative is lost on the bulk of the white population, and white liberals here as elsewhere find it easier to proselytize in the ghetto than to go into the white communities and educate the backward whites.

Who Are the Allies, What is the Future?

It would be false optimism to say that anything will be gained in the period ahead except through difficult and protracted struggles. Nor can the fight for equality and democracy be waged in isolation from other issues; it is inextricably bound up with the U.S. intervention in Southeast Asia. With the Johnson Administration already spending $25 billion a year on that war, the so-called war on poverty as well as other needed programs have been vitiated. Inflation caused by the war has cheapened the consumer's dollar and hiked his taxes, and the American economy is in deeper trouble than the economists care to admit. Moreover, the war itself, with its venality, corruption, and inhuman extermination of relatively defenseless colored nations, is a fountainhead of racism and a stimulant of every type of brutality and depravity.

The prospect is not in the least improved with Ronald Reagan and his backers in the seat of state power. A story is making the rounds of the ghettos that Reagan received all of eight votes in Watts and the rest of Watts is still out looking for the people who gave him those. The Birchers are already crowing over their contribution to Reagan's election, and an increase in the activity of racist organizations and sects of kooks seems indicated. Even before his inauguration Reagan trained his guns on the poor and waved the nuclear bomb at North Vietnam. . . .

Certainly the hotel sit-ins and auto row demonstrations of 1964 showed that not all white people are "white devils," as Elijah Muhammad would have us believe. In those struggles "Whitey" by the hundreds put his job, liberty, or college career on the line for equal opportunities for Negroes and other minorities. In the long campaign for a San Francisco FEP ordinance, some of the most eloquent advocacy came from the Catholic hierarchy, Jewish organizations, and associations of white women. Even several businessmen identified with the "power elite" presented arguments and statistics countering those offered by the big employers.

Another expression of support of Negro aspirations by large numbers of white Californians took the form of election victories of Negro candidates. This was shown most clearly last November 7, in mixed neighborhoods where Negroes ran against white candidates. Assemblyman Willie Brown, Negro civil rights attorney, won re-election in a San Francisco district which includes a heavy concentration of wealthy, middle class, and working class white workers. His opponent, incidentally, had a platform plank for "law enforcement legislation" which seemed to be aimed at people involved in the Hunters Point incident, whereas Brown's law firm handled the cases of many persons arrested there. John J. Miller, Negro president of the Berkeley board of education, won the 17th Assembly seat in a district with a large white population. William Byron Rumford, who vacated the 17th Assembly seat to run for the state Senate, lost the race, but received 150,968 of the 313,000 ballots cast. Obviously, despite his having given his name to the state's most controversial fair housing law, many thousands of white voters preferred that Rumford should represent them....

It is incontrovertible, for instance, that neither the FEP nor fair housing laws could have been adopted without the support of sections of California's trade unions. There is also no question but that the International Longshoremen's and Warehousemen's Union, while still bedeviled by instances of racial bigotry in its own ranks, has pioneered in the struggle for a Negro-labor coalition and continues to throw its not inconsiderable weight in support of equal opportunities for minorities.

These instances of whites uniting with Negroes to defend common interests will surely be multiplied in the period ahead. But for many residents of the ghetto, such reassurance is not enough. Their number, moreover, is growing rapidly, especially among the youth. They have lost all confidence not only in the promises of the local officials and "power elite," but in the system itself. They no longer believe the American Dream will be or can be realized in a society organized as it is today. So long as the present "power structure" remains, the jackboot will remain on their neck. Increasingly, they will identify their cause with that of all of America's poor, and their main grievance is the failure of the white poor to identify with them.

This development of the ghetto's consciousness is put in a nutshell by Thomas Fleming, the militant city editor of the weekly San Francisco *Sun-Reporter*. In his column of October 14, commenting on the "riots," Fleming wrote: "Negroes have learned, as the American Indian learned before him, that promises from the affluent society are made only to be broken. The two thousand promised jobs had dwindled to perhaps one hundred in a very few days, and of that one hundred none of them offered had wages within the minimum national average. Negroes will have to learn the hard way that their fight is a class fight which involves poor people all over the nation. It could be that Negroes already know this, but do the other poor have the same realization?"

Yes, it could be that Negroes, or at least many of them, already know this. Fleming's surmise stands on solid ground. Besides the incidents of ghetto defiance of the police, other developments show the influence of this current in Negro thought. A number of neighborhood newspapers addressed to the poor have sprung up in the ghettos since the incidents. A number of militant youth have stepped forward as spokesmen and leaders. Several organizations of the poor have begun to function.

The new thinking is evidently a product of the 1960–66 struggles for jobs, fair housing, integrated schools, and an end to police harassment. It represents a lesson learned "the hard way." But the way ahead may be harder. It seems inevitable that in the coming struggles in this six-county metropolitan area for equality and an end to Jim Crow, more and more Negroes will become convinced that a radically different organization of society is needed to realize the American Dream for all the people.

Freedomways 7 (Winter 1967): 42–53; published in part.

134

BLACK POWER AND THE AMERICAN CHRIST

by Vincent Harding

Dr. Harding was active from the start of the freedom effort in the South and later was chairman of the history department at Spelman College; in 1968 he became chairman of the Martin Luther King, Jr., Memorial Center in Atlanta. Lately he has been on the faculty of the Iliff School of Theology at the University of Denver. Notable among his several books is *There Is a River* (New York, 1981).

The mood among many social-action-oriented Christians today suggests that it is only a line thin as a razor blade that divides sentimental yearning over the civil rights activities of the past from present bitter recrimination against "Black Power." As is so often the case with reminiscences, the nostalgia may grow more out of a sense of frustration and powerlessness than out of any true appreciation of the meaning of the past. This at least is the impression one gets from those seemingly endless gatherings of old "true believers" which usually produce both the nostalgia and the recriminations. Generally the cast of characters at such meetings consists of well-dressed, well-fed Negroes and whites whose accents almost blend into a single voice as they recall the days "when we were all together, fighting for the same cause." The stories evoke again the heady atmosphere, mixed of smugness and self-sacrifice, that surrounded us in those heroic times when nonviolence was our watchword and integration our heavenly city. One can almost hear the strains of "our song" as men and women remember how they solemnly swayed in the aisles or around the charred remains of a church or in the dirty southern jails. Those were the days when Martin Luther King was the true prophet and when we were certain that the civil rights movement was God's message to the churches—and part of our smugness grew out of the fact that *we* knew it while all the rest of God's frozen people were asleep.

A Veil Between Then and Now

But as the reminiscences continue a veil seems to descend between then and now. The tellers of the old tales label the veil Black Power, and pronounce ritual curses on Stokely Carmichael and Floyd McKissick and their followers....

Perhaps the first and central discovery is also the most obvious: there is a strong and causative link between Black Power and American Christianity. Indeed one may say with confidence that whatever its other sources, the ideology of blackness surely grows out of the deep ambivalence of American Negroes to the Christ we have encountered here. This ambivalence is not new. It was ours from the beginning. For we first met the American Christ on slave ships....

If the American Christ and his followers have indeed helped to mold the Black Power movement, then might it not be that the God whom many of us insist on keeping alive is not only alive but just? May he not be attempting to break through to us with at least as much urgency as we once sensed at the height of the good old "We Shall Overcome" days? Perhaps he is writing on the wall, saying that we Christians, black and white, must choose between death with the American Christ and life with the Suffering Servant of God. Who dares deny that God may have chosen once again the black sufferers for a new assault on the hard shell of indifference and fear that encases so many Americans?...

Glad to Be Black

For a growing edge of bold young black people all that is past. They fling out their declaration: "No white Christ shall shame us again. We are glad to be black. We rejoice in the darkness of our skin, we celebrate the natural texture of our hair, we extol the rhythm and vigor of our songs and shouts and dances. And if your American Christ doesn't like that, you know what you can do with him." That is Black Power: a repudiation of the American culture-religion that helped to create it and a quest for a religious reality more faithful to our own experience. . . .

The seekers of Black Power, seeing their poorest, most miserable people deserted by the white American Christians, have come to stand with the forlorn in these very places of abandonment. Now they speak of black unity, and the old Christian buildings are filled with Negroes young and old studying African history. The new leaders in the ghettos tell them: "Whites now talk about joining forces, but who has ever wanted to join forces with you? They only want to use you—especially those white American Christian liars. They love you in theory only. They love only your middle-class incarnations. But they are afraid of you—you who are black and poor and filled with rage and despair. They talk about 'progress' for the Negro, but they don't mean *you*." . . .

Groveling No More

As black men they have long seen into the heart of American darkness. They have no patriotic illusions about this nation's benevolent intentions toward the oppressed nonwhite people of the world, no matter how often the name and compassion of divinity are invoked. With eyes cleared by pain they discern the arrogance beneath the pious protestations. The American Christ leads the Hiroshima-bound bomber, blesses the Marines on their way to another in the long series of Latin American invasions, and blasphemously calls it peace when America destroys an entire Asian peninsula. And as black men they know from their own hard experience that these things can happen because this nation, led by an elder of the church, is determined to have its way in the world at any cost—to others. How often have the white-robed elders led the mob thirsting for the black man's blood! . . .

If judgment stands sure it is not for Stokely Carmichael alone but for all of us. It is we Christians who made the universal Christ into an American mascot, a puppet blessing every mad American act, from the extermination of the original possessors of this land to the massacre of the Vietnamese on their own soil—even, perhaps, to the bombing of the Chinese mainland in the name of peace.

If judgment stands sure it is not primarily upon SNCC that it will fall, but upon those who have kidnaped the compassionate Jesus—the Jesus who shared all he had, even his life, with the poor—and made him into a profit-oriented, individualistic, pietistic cat who belongs to his own narrowly-defined kind and begrudges the poor their humilitating subsistence budgets. These Christians are the ones who have taken away our Lord and buried him in a place unknown.

We shall not escape by way of nostalgia or recrimination. For if he whom we call the Christ is indeed the Suffering Servant of God and man, what excuse can there be for those who have turned him into a crossless puppet, running away from suffering with his flaxen locks flapping in the wind?

If God is yet alive we cannot afford time to reminisce about the good old days of the civil rights movement when everybody knew the words of the songs. The time of singing may be past. It may be that America must now stand under profound and damning judgment for having turned the redeeming lover of all men into a white, middle-class burner of children and destroyer of the revolutions of the oppressed.

Chance for Redemption

This may be God's message for the church—through Black Power. It is a message for all who claim to love the Lord of the church. If this reading is accurate, our tears over the demise of the civil rights movement may really be tears over the smashing of an image we created or the withdrawal of a sign we were no longer heeding. Therefore if we weep, let it not be for the sins of SNCC and CORE but for our own unfaithfulness and for our country's blasphemy. And let us begin to pray that time may be granted us to turn from blond dolls to the living, revolutionary Lord who proclaimed that the first shall be last and the last, first.

If this message can break the grip of self-pity and nostalgia on us, the power of blackness may yet become the power of light and resurrection for us all. Has it not been said that God moves in mysterious ways his wonders to perform? I can conceive of nothing more wonderful and mysterious than that the blackness of my captive people should become a gift of light for this undeserving nation—even a source of hope for a world that lives daily under the threat of white America's arrogant and bloody power. Is that too much to hope for? Or is the time for hoping now past? We may soon discover whether we have been watching a wall or a curtain—or both.

Christian Century, January 4, 1967; published in part.

135

WE ARE A POLITICAL UNIT

by James Forman

In a January 1967 meeting of SNCC, Forman succinctly outlined its past role and suggested that new conditions required a new orientation—toward organized political activity. Here is his account of this development and his proposal for future activity.

Throughout my history with the Student Non-Violent Coordinating Committee, there have been various discussions about the importance of an education program for the members of the organization. At some time or another, this person or that one has assumed the responsibility for working on this program or aspects of it. It goes without saying that each day we work, we engage in various forms of political education. However, there still has not been a systematic attempt to educate ourselves; to train new members; to instill a sense of the history of the organization, its objectives, success and failures; to discuss and analyze many events occurring in the world.

I assume some responsibility for the failure to implement this internal education program. It was a mistake always to give in to the demands of the moment and not insist in a more active manner that we create and implement a program for the intellectual and political development of our staff. My present evaluation stems from observing and participating in the effects of the failure to do this, from my own development, and from accepting the criticism of many who have been crippled by the lack of an internal education program. Without question, every time we allowed a new member to join our staff without undergoing some indoctrination program, we were contributing to misunderstanding, suspicion, ill-will, wasted effort, and time lost....

Today, 1967, six years after the student movement started in February

1960, we are at Rock Bottom. There is nowhere to go but up or under. We have finally emerged, from my point of view, from many obstacles and can realistically assess what in fact has been true for more than two years: namely, that the massive attack on public accommodations and voter registration has been successful and we have played no small part in that success. With the passage of the 1965 Civil Rights Bill, the entire character of this organization changed. Some of us saw this, but we were unable to convince the organization of this shift and of the absolute need to revamp our programs. One of the reasons for this failure stemmed from the lack of an internal education program. As has been true throughout our history, we have been backed up against many walls, and changes have been forced upon us.

Today, we must face the reality that we have been successful, no matter what may have been all the shortcomings, and we must quickly revamp our entire style of operation—or there is no other way for us to go but out, nothing to do but destroy our effectiveness through lack of direction, lack of confidence in the future, a sense of failure, fatigue, despair, frustration, and bad health. These conditions in turn lead to internal bickering, feuding, factional fighting, inertia, inability to work, loss of morale, hanging-on, resignation, walking-out, . . .

By facing our success and evaluating that, I am saying that the framework within which the organization worked is no longer valid.

The question is no longer the right to vote, but the nature of the politics in which we should engage. The question is no longer segregation in public accommodations, but addressing ourselves to certain rock-bottom problems in the society. For instance, should we as an organization actively work to do something about inadequate housing, inferior education, the inequities of welfare, unemployment, insufficient medical attention, the malignment nature of America's racist foreign policy (stemming, of course, from a racist country and the exploitative wars in which we are asked to fight and to support).

At our December 1966 meeting at Peg Leg Bates's, we decided many things, but we also recognized that the nature of our struggle had changed. We did this in voting to create Freedom Organizations in the country. We voted that these Freedom Organizations would be all-inclusive political parties; namely, that these political parties would have within their structure a housing, a welfare, an educational, a cultural, an economic, and a youth division. We did this in full realization that politics in this country is usually election day campaigning. We wanted to help create political units that would speak in the name of the unit about day-to-day needs of the people we hope to organize.

We voted to do this, given our entire history of protest, voter registration efforts, and organizing people into political units. However, within our own organization we face the problem of who is going to do this work. We not only face that problem but we face many others given the nature of our history and again the nature of ourselves, the people in the organization. Therefore, it becomes crystal clear that the need for a political education program within the STUDENT NON-VIOLENT COORDINAT-ING COMMITTEE is a must. There are some basic questions in any internal education program that must be raised and answered and agreed upon by the members of a political unit. If there can be no agreement on certain fundamentals, or at least continuous discussion while one works, then SNCC as a political unit cannot survive.

We are in fact a political unit although we do not call ourselves that. We still cling to the rhetoric that we are a group of organizers. If we are successful in the development of the Freedom Organizations, we will inevitably become a political cadre within a political party. Whether we can assume our responsibilities and help move forward the struggle of black people—and thereby all people as we have done in the past, this is another question. It is quite possible that we cannot. It is also possible that we may not be able to overcome the inertia, the stagnant state in which we find ourselves.

James Forman, *op. cit.*, pp. 478–79.

136

A TIME TO BREAK SILENCE

by Martin Luther King, Jr.

On April 4, 1967, King delivered one of his most penetrating speeches. It affirmed the basic connection between the U.S. war in Vietnam and the presence of institutionalized racism in the United States. Hence, to deliver blows against U.S. intervention in Vietnam was to strengthen the struggle against Jim Crow at home.

... Some of us who have already begun to break the silence of the night have found that the calling to speak is often a vocation of agony, but we must speak. We must speak with all the humility that is appropriate to our limited vision, but we must speak. And we must rejoice as well, for surely this is the first time in our nation's history that a significant number of its religious leaders have chosen to move beyond the prophesying of smooth patriotism to the high grounds of a firm dissent based upon the mandates of conscience and the reading of history. Perhaps a new spirit is rising among us. If it is, let us trace its movements well and pray that our own inner being may be sensitive to its guidance, for we are deeply in need of a new way beyond the darkness that seems so close around us.

Over the past two years, as I have moved to break the betrayal of my own silences and to speak from the burnings of my own heart, as I have called for radical departures from the destruction of Vietnam, many persons have questioned me about the wisdom of my path. At the heart of their concerns this query has often loomed large and loud: Why are *you* speaking about the war, Dr. King? Why are *you* joining the voices of dissent? Peace and civil rights don't mix, they say. Aren't you hurting the cause of your people, they ask? And when I hear them, though I often understand the source of their concern, I am nevertheless greatly saddened, for such questions mean that the inquirers have not really known me, my commitment or my calling. Indeed, their questions suggest that they do not know the world in which they live.

In the light of such tragic misunderstanding, I deem it of signal importance to try to state clearly, and I trust concisely, why I believe that the path from Dexter Avenue Baptist Church—the church in Montgomery, Alabama where I began my pastorate—leads clearly to this sanctuary tonight.

I come to this platform tonight to make a passionate plea to my beloved nation. This speech is not addressed to Hanoi or to the National Liberation Front. It is not addressed to China or to Russia.

Nor is it an attempt to overlook the ambiguity of the total situation and the need for a collective solution to the tragedy of Vietnam. Neither is it an attempt to make North Vietnam or the National Liberation Front paragons of virtue, nor to overlook the role they can play in a successful resolution of the problem. While they both may have justifiable reason to be suspicious of the good faith of the United States, life and history give eloquent testimony to the fact that conflicts are never resolved without trustful give and take on both sides.

Tonight, however, I wish not to speak with Hanoi and the NLF, but rather to my fellow Americans who, with me, bear the greatest responsibility in ending a conflict that has exacted a heavy price on both continents.

Since I am a preacher by trade, I suppose it is not surprising that I have seven major reasons for bringing Vietnam into the field of my moral vision. There is at the outset a very obvious and almost facile connection between the war in Vietnam and the struggle I, and others, have been waging in America. A few years ago there was a shining moment in that struggle. It seemed as if there was a real promise of hope for the poor—both black and white—through the Poverty Program. There were experiments, hopes, new beginnings. Then came the build-up in Vietnam and I watched the program broken and eviscerated as if it were some idle political plaything of a society gone mad on war, and I knew that America would never invest the necessary funds or energies in rehabilitation of its poor so long as adventures like Vietnam continued to draw men and skills and money like some demonic destructive suction tube. So I was increasingly compelled to see the war as an enemy of the poor and to attack it as such.

Perhaps the more tragic recognition of reality took place when it became clear to me that the war was doing far more than devastating the hopes of the poor at home. It was sending their sons and their brothers and their husbands to fight and to die in extraordinarily high proportions relative to the rest of the population. We were taking the black young men who had been crippled by our society and sending them eight thousand miles away to guarantee liberties in Southeast Asia which they had not found in Southwest Georgia and East Harlem. So we have been repeatedly faced with the cruel irony of watching Negro and white boys on TV screens as they kill and die together for a nation that has been unable to seat them together in the same schools. So we watch them in brutal solidarity burning the huts of a poor village, but we realize that they would never live on the same block in Detroit. I could not be silent in the face of such cruel manipulation of the poor.

My third reason moves to an even deeper level of awareness, for it grows out of my experience in the ghettos of the North over the last three years—especially the last three summers. As I have walked among the desperate, rejected, and angry young men I have told them that Molotov cocktails and rifles would not solve their problems. I have tried to offer them my deepest compassion while maintaining my conviction that social change comes most meaningfully through nonviolent action. But they asked—and rightly so—what about Vietnam? They asked if our own nation wasn't using massive doses of violence to solve its problems, to bring about the changes it wanted. Their questions hit home, and I knew that I could never again raise my voice against the violence of the oppressed in the ghettos without having first spoken clearly to the greatest purveyor of violence in the world today—my own government. For the sake of those boys, for the sake of this government, for the sake of the hundreds of thousands trembling under our violence, I cannot be silent.

For those who ask the question, "Aren't you a Civil Rights leader?" and thereby mean to exclude me from the movement for peace, I have this further answer. In 1957 when a group of us formed the Southern Christian Leadership Conference, we chose as our motto: "To save the soul of America." We were convinced that we could not limit our vision to certain rights for black people, but instead affirmed the conviction that America would never be free or saved from itself unless the descendants of its slaves were loosed completely from the shackles they still wear. In a way we were agreeing with Langston Hughes, that black bard of Harlem, who had written earlier:

> O, yes,
> I say it plain,
> America never was America to me,
> And yet I swear this oath—
> America will be!

Now, it should be incandescently clear that no one who has any concern for the integrity and life of America today can ignore the present war. If America's soul becomes totally poisoned, part of the autopsy must read Vietnam. It can never be saved so long as it destroys the deepest hopes of men the world over. So it is that those of us who are yet determined that America *will* be are led down the path of protest and dissent, working for the health of our land.

As if the weight of such a commitment to the life and health of America were not enough, another burden of responsibility was placed upon me in 1964; and I cannot forget that the Nobel Prize for Peace was also a commission—a commission to work harder than I had ever worked before for "the brotherhood of man." This is a calling that takes me beyond national allegiances, but even if it were not present I would yet have to live with the meaning of my commitment to the ministry of Jesus Christ. To me the relationship of this ministry to the making of peace is so obvious that I sometimes marvel at those who ask me why I am speaking against the war. Could it be that they do not know that the good news was meant for all men—for Communist and capitalist, for their children and ours, for black and for white, for revolutionary and conservative? Have they forgotten that my ministry is in obedience to the one who loved his enemies so fully that he died for them? What then can I say to the "Viet Cong" or to Castro or to Mao as a faithful minister of this one? Can I threaten them with death or must I not share with them my life?

Finally, as I try to delineate for you and for myself the road that leads from Montgomery to this place I would have offered all that was most valid if I simply said that I must be true to my conviction that I share with all men the calling to be a son of the Living God. Beyond the calling of race or nation or creed is this vocation of sonship and brotherhood, and because I believe that the Father is deeply concerned especially for his suffering and helpless and outcast children, I come tonight to speak for them.

This I believe to be the privilege and the burden of all of us who deem ourselves bound by allegiances and loyalties which are broader and deeper than nationalism and which go beyond our nation's self-defined goals and positions. We are called to speak for the weak, for the voiceless, for victims of our nation and for those it calls enemy, for no document from human hands can make these humans any less our brothers.

Strange Liberators

And as I ponder the madness of Vietnam and search within myself for ways to understand and respond to compassion my mind goes constantly to the people of that peninsula. I speak now not of the soldiers of each side, not of the junta in Saigon, but simply of the people who have been living under the curse of war for almost three continuous decades now. I think of them too because it is clear to me that there will be no meaningful solution there until some attempt is made to know them and hear their broken cries.

They must see Americans as strange liberators. The Vietnamese people proclaimed their own independence in 1945 after a combined French and Japanese occupation, and before the Communist revolution in China. They were led by Ho Chi Minh. Even though they quoted the American Declaration of Independence in their own document of freedom, we refused to recognize them. Instead, we decided to support France in its re-conquest of her former colony. . . .

After the French were defeated it looked as if independence and land reform would come again through the Geneva agreements. But instead there came the United States, determined that Ho should not unify the temporarily divided nation, and the peasants watched again as we supported one of the most vicious modern dictators—our chosen man, Premier Diem. The peasants watched and cringed as Diem ruthlessly routed out all opposition, supported their extortionist landlords, and refused even to discuss reunification with the North. The peasants watched as all this was presided over by U.S. influence and then by increasing numbers of U.S. troops who came to help quell the insurgency that Diem's methods had aroused. When Diem was overthrown they may have been happy, but the long line of military dictatorships seemed to offer no real change—especially in terms of their need for land and peace.

The only change came from America as we increased our troop commitments in support of governments which were singularly corrupt, inept, and without popular support. All the while the people read our leaflets and received regular promises of peace and democracy—and land reform. Now they languish under our bombs and consider us—not their fellow Vietnamese—the real enemy. They move sadly and apathetically as we herd them off the land of their fathers into concentration camps where minimal social needs are rarely met. They know they must move or be destroyed by our bombs. So they go—primarily women and children and the aged.

They watch as we poison their water, as we kill a million acres of their crops. They must weep as the bulldozers roar through their areas preparing to destroy the precious trees. They wander into the hospitals, with at least twenty casualties from American firepower for one "Viet-cong"-inflicted injury. So far we may have killed a million of them—mostly children. They wander into the towns and see thousands of the children, homeless, without clothes, running in packs on the streets like animals. They see the children degraded by our soldiers as they beg for food. They see the children selling their sisters to our soldiers, soliciting for their mothers.

What do the peasants think as we ally ourselves with the landlords and as we refuse to put any action into our many words concerning land reform? What do they think as we test out our latest weapons on them, just as the Germans tested out new medicine and new tortures in the concentration camps of Europe? Where are the roots of the independent Vietnam we claim to be building? Is it among these voiceless ones?

We have destroyed their two most cherished institutions: the family and the village. We have destroyed their land and their crops. We have cooperated in the crushing of the nation's only non-Communist revolutionary political force—the unified Buddhist church. We have supported the enemies of the peasants of Saigon. We have corrupted their women and children and killed their men. What liberators!...

At this point I should make it clear that while I have tried in these last few minutes to give a voice to the voiceless on Vietnam and to understand the arguments of those who are called enemy, I am as deeply concerned about our own troops there as anything else. For it occurs to me that what we are submitting them to in Vietnam is not simply the brutalizing process that goes on in any war where armies face each other and seek to destroy. We are adding cynicism to the process of death, for they must know after a short period there that none of the things we claim to be fighting for are really involved. Before long they must know that their government has sent them into a struggle among Vietnamese, and the more sophisticated surely realize that we are on the side of the wealthy and the secure while we create a hell for the poor.

Somehow this madness must cease. We must stop now. I speak as a child of God and brother to the suffering poor of Vietnam. I speak for those whose land is being laid waste, whose homes are being destroyed, whose culture is being subverted. I speak for the poor of America who are paying the double price of smashed hopes at home and death and corruption in Vietnam. I speak as a citizen of the world, for the world as it stands aghast at the path we have taken. I speak as an American to the leaders of my own nation. The great initiative in this war is ours. The initiative to stop it must be ours.

This is the message of the great Buddhist leaders of Vietnam. Recently one of them wrote these words: *Each day the war goes on the hatred increases in the heart of the Vietnamese and in the hearts of those of humanitarian instinct. The Americans are forcing even their friends into becoming their enemies. It is curious that the Americans, who calculate so carefully on the possibilities of military victory, do not realize that in the process they are incurring deep psychological and political defeat. The image of America will never again be the image of revolution, freedom, and democracy, but the image of violence and militarism.*

If we continue there will be no doubt in my mind and in the mind of the world that we have no honorable intentions in Vietnam. It will become clear that our minimal expectation is to occupy it as an American colony and men will not refrain from thinking that our maximum hope is to goad China into a war so that we may bomb her nuclear installations. If we do not stop our war against the people of Vietnam immediately the world will be left with no other alternative than to see this as some horribly clumsy and deadly game we have decided to play.

The world now demands a maturity of America that we may not be able to achieve. It demands that we admit that we have been wrong from the beginning of our adventure in Vietnam, that we have been detrimental to the life of the Vietnamese people. The situation is one in which we must be ready to turn sharply from our present ways.

In order to atone for our sins and errors in Vietnam, we should take the initiative in bringing a halt to this tragic war. I would like to suggest five concrete things that our government should do immediately to begin the long and difficult process of extricating ourselves from this nightmarish conflict:

1. End all bombing in North and South Vietnam.
2. Declare a unilateral cease-fire in the hope that such action will create the atmosphere for negotiation.
3. Take immediate steps to prevent other battlegrounds in Southeast Asia by curtailing our military build-up in Thailand and our interference in Laos.
4. Realistically accept the fact that the National Liberation Front has substantial support in South Vietnam and must thereby play a role in any meaningful negotiations and in any future Vietnam government.
5. Set a date that we will remove all foreign troops from Vietnam in accordance with the 1954 Geneva Agreement.

Part of our ongoing commitment might well express itself in an offer to grant asylum to any Vietnamese who fears for his life under a new regime which included the Liberation Front. Then we must make what reparations we can for the damage we have done. We must provide the medical aid that is badly needed, making it available in this country if necessary. . . .

There is something seductively tempting about stopping there and sending us all off on what in some circles has become a popular crusade against the war in Vietnam. I say we must enter the struggle, but I wish to go on now to say something even more disturbing. The war in Vietnam is but a symptom of a far deeper malady within the American spirit, and if we ignore this sobering reality we will find ourselves organizing clergy and laymen-concerned committees for the next generation. They will be concerned about Guatemala and Peru. They will be concerned about

Thailand and Cambodia. They will be concerned about Mozambique and South Africa. We will be marching for these and a dozen other names and attending rallies without end unless there is a significant and profound change in American life and policy. Such thoughts take us beyond Vietnam, but not beyond our calling as sons of the living God. . . .

I am convinced that if we are to get on the right side of the world revolution, we as a nation must undergo a radical revolution of values. We must rapidly begin the shift from a "thing-oriented" society to a "person-oriented" society. When machines and computers, profit motives and property rights are considered more important than people, the giant triplets of racism, materialism, and militarism are incapable of being conquered.

A true revolution of values will soon cause us to question the fairness and justice of many of our past and present policies. On the one hand we are called to play the Good Samaritan on life's roadside; but that will be only an initial act. One day we must come to see that the whole Jericho Road must be transformed so that men and women will not be constantly beaten and robbed as they make their journey on Life's highway. True compassion is more than flinging a coin to a beggar; it is not haphazard and superficial. It comes to see that an edifice which produces beggars needs restructuring. A true revolution of values will soon look uneasily on the glaring contrast of poverty and wealth. With righteous indignation, it will look across the seas and see individual capitalists of the West investing huge sums of money in Asia, Africa, and South America, only to take the profits out with no concern for the social betterment of the countries, and say: "This is not just." It will look at our alliance with the landed gentry of Latin America and say: "This is not just." The Western arrogance of feeling that it has everything to teach others and nothing to learn from them is not just. A true revolution of values will lay hands on the world order and say of war: "This way of settling differences is not just." This business of burning human beings with napalm, of filling our nation's homes with orphans and widows, of injecting poisonous drugs of hate into the veins of peoples normally humane, of sending men home from dark and bloody battlefields physically handicapped and psychologically deranged, cannot be reconciled with wisdom, justice, and love. A nation that continues year after year to spend more money on military defense than on programs of social uplift is approaching spiritual death. . . .

These are revolutionary times. All over the globe men are revolting against old systems of exploitation and oppression and out of the wombs of a frail world new systems of justice and equality are being born. The shirtless and barefoot people of the land are rising up as never before. "The people who sat in darkness have seen a great light." We in the West must support these revolutions. It is a sad fact that, because of comfort, complacency, a morbid fear of Communism, and our proneness to adjust to injustice, the Western nations that initiated so much of the revolutionary spirit of the modern world have now become the arch anti-revolutionaries. This has driven many to feel that only Marxism has the revolutionary spirit. Therefore, Communism is a judgment against our failure to make democracy real and follow through on the revolutions that we initiated. Our only hope today lies in our ability to recapture the revolutionary spirit and go out into a sometimes hostile world declaring eternal hostility to poverty, racism, and militarism. With this powerful commitment we shall boldly challenge the status quo and unjust mores and thereby speed the day when "every valley shall be exalted, and every mountain and hill shall be made low, and the crooked shall be made straight and the rough places plain." ...

We are now faced with the fact that tomorrow is today. We are confronted with the fierce urgency of now. In this unfolding conundrum of life and history there is such a thing as being too late. Procrastination is still the thief of time. Life often leaves us standing bare, naked and dejected with a lost opportunity. The "tide in the affairs of men" does not remain at the flood; it ebbs. We may cry out desperately for time to pause in her passage, but time is deaf to every plea and rushes on. Over the bleached bones and jumbled residue of numerous civilizations are written the pathetic words: "Too late." There is an invisible book of life that faithfully records our vigilance or our neglect. "The moving finger writes, and having writ moves on. . . . " We still have a choice today; non-violent coexistence or violent co-annihilation.

We must move past indecision to action. We must find new ways to speak for peace in Vietnam and justice throughout the developing world— a world that borders on our doors. If we do not act we shall surely be dragged down the long dark and shameful corridors of time reserved for those who possess power without compassion, might without morality, and strength without sight.

Now let us begin. Now let us rededicate ourselves to the long and bitter—but beautiful—struggle for a new world. This is the calling of the sons of God, and our brothers wait eagerly for our response. Shall we say the odds are too great? Shall we tell them the struggle is too hard? Will our message be that the forces of American life militate against their arrival as full men, and we send our deepest regrets? Or will there be another message, of longing, of hope, of solidarity with their yearnings, of commitment to their cause, whatever the cost? The choice is ours, and though we might prefer it otherwise we *must* choose in this crucial moment of human history.

As that noble bard of yesterday, James Russell Lowell, eloquently stated:

> Once to every man and nation,
> Comes the moment to decide
> In the strife of truth and falsehood
> For the good or evil side;
> Some great cause God's new Messiah
> Offering each the gloom or blight
> And the choice goes by forever
> Twixt that darkness and that light.
>
> Though the cause of evil prosper
> Yet 'tis truth alone is strong
> Though her portion be the scaffold
> And upon the throne be wrong
> Yet that scaffold sways the future
> And behind the dim unknown
> Standeth God within the shadow
> Keeping watch above his own.

Freedomways 7 (Spring 1967): 103–17. For an incisive analysis of the criticism of King for "meddling" due to this attack on U.S. policy in Vietnam, see John D. Maguire in *Christianity and Crisis*, May 1, 1967.

137

CIVIL DISOBEDIENCE MAY BE NECESSARY

by Martin Luther King, Jr.

The *New York Times*, on April 2, 1967, devoted much of three pages to an interview it conducted with Dr. King. The major portion of that interview carried a headline, on page 76—over from page 1—"Dr. King Says Civil Disobedience May Be Necessary If U. S. Continues To Intensify War." This follows, in part:

In a real sense, the Great Society has been shot down on the battlefields of Vietnam. I feel it is necessary to take a stand against it or at least arouse the conscience of the nation against it so that at least we can move more and more toward a negotiated settlement of that terrible conflict.

There is another reason why I feel compelled at this time to take a stand against the war and that is that the constant escalation of the war in Vietnam can lead to a grand war with China and to a kind of full world war that could mean the annihilation of the human race.

And I think those of us who are concerned about the survival of mankind, those of us who feel and know that mankind should survive must take a stand against this war because it is more than just a local conflict on Asian soil. It is a conflict that in a real sense affects the whole world and makes possible, at least brings into being the possibility of, the destruction of all mankind, so because of my concern for mankind and the survival of mankind, I feel the need to take a stand.

The other reason is I have preached nonviolence in the movement in our country, and I think it is very consistent for me to follow a nonviolent approach in international affairs. It would be very inconsistent for me to teach and preach nonviolence in this situation and then applaud violence when thousands and thousands of people, both adults and children, are being maimed and mutilated and many killed in this war, so that I still feel and live by the principle, "Thou shalt not kill."

And it is out of this moral commitment to dignity and the worth of human personality that I feel it is necessary to stand up against the war in Vietnam.

I would hope that the people of this country standing up against the war are standing up against it because they love America and because they want to see our great nation really stand up as the moral example of the world.

The fact is we have alienated ourselves from so much of the world and have become morally and politically isolated as the result of our involvement in the war in Vietnam.

Peace Demonstrations

Q. Do you think civil rights organizations as such should join in peace demonstrations?

A. I would certainly say that individuals in the civil rights movement should join in peace demonstrations. I have to make a distinction at this point because of my own involvement, and that is I made a decision to become involved as an individual, as a clergyman, as one who is greatly concerned about peace.

SCLC as an organization has not yet become actively involved in the peace movement. There are many individuals in SCLC who are involved, but organizationally SCLC has backed me in all the decisions I have made and all the stands I have taken without becoming a peace organization.

Now this may be the way it will have to continue, but civil rights organizations will continue engaging in purely civil rights activities, leaving the way open for persons on staffs and persons on boards, and what have you, and the membership can, as individuals, feel free to participate.

I do feel that organizationally we are limited in terms of resources and energies in what we can do, and this means we probably will have to continue to give our prime time and work to civil rights activities through the civil rights organizations. But I as an individual will continue to stand up on the issue of peace and against the war in Vietnam.

Q. Dr. King, I understand you have been away for some time writing a new book and contemplating where to go from here. Did you reach any conclusions on where the civil rights movement is headed?

A. Well, I reached several conclusions which will be stated in the book. One of the things I tried to state in the first chapter is that for more than a decade we worked mainly to remove the stigma and humiliation of legal segregation. We have made some significant victories in this area. Many people in the nation, whites, joined in taking a stand against this kind of humiliation of the Negro.

But what we are faced with now is the fact that the struggle must be and actually is at this point a struggle for genuine equality. The struggle over the last ten or twelve years has been a struggle for decency, a struggle to get rid of extremist behavior towards Negroes, and I think we are moving into a period which is much more difficult because it is dealing with hard economic problems which will cost the nation something to solve.

It did not cost the nation anything to integrate lunch counters or public accommodations. It did not cost the nation anything to guarantee the right to vote. The problem is now in order—to end the long night of poverty and economic insecurity—it would mean billions of dollars. In order to end slums it would mean billions of dollars. In order to get rid of bad education, education devoid of poverty, it means lifting the educational level of the whole public school system, which would mean billions of dollars.

This, I feel, is much more difficult than the period we have gone through. There will be more resistance because it means the privileged groups will have to give up some of their billions. And I think the so-called white backlash is expressed right here.

It is a reaction to the demands that are presently being made by Negroes now demanding genuine equality, and not just integration of the lunch counters but an adequate wage; not just integration of the classrooms, but a decent sanitary house in which to live. It is much easier to integrate a restaurant than it is to demand an annual income. I think the growing debate is recognition of this difficulty.

The next conclusion I reached is that the great need in the Negro community and the civil rights movement is to organize the Negro community for the amassing of real political and economic power. The question now is not merely developing programs because we have put many programs on paper.

What is needed now is the undergirding power to bring about enough pressure so that these programs can become a reality, that they can become concretized in our everyday lives; not only under the legislative process but under all the processes necessary to make them real. This just means the hard job of organizing tenants, organizing welfare recipients, organizing the unemployed and the underemployed.

It is for this reason that I am recommending to the Southern Christian Leadership Conference that we begin to train more field organizers so that we can really go out and organize those people and thereby move into the area of political action. I think the Negro can improve his economic resources much more if these resources are pooled, and I intend to do much more in this area so that we can make an economic thrust.

Q. Dr. King, you have been called to the White House on many occasions to confer with the President about civil rights matters. Has your opposition to the war altered your relations in any way with President Johnson?

A. Not as far as I am concerned. I go to the White House when he invites me. I have followed a policy of being very honest with the President when he has consulted me about civil rights.

I have made it very clear to him why I have taken a stand against the war in Vietnam. I had a long talk with him on the telephone not too many months ago about this and made it clear to him I would be standing up against it even more. I am not centering this on President Johnson. I think there is collective guilt....

138

CALIFORNIA'S BAY AREA

Sworn Testimony

The same personnel identified in the previous document (of April 1966) held hearings on May 1–3, 1967, in San Francisco and May 4–6 in Oakland, California. The result was issued by the Government Printing Office in 1967 in a volume totaling 1,090 pages. Again the majority of the over one hundred witnesses were African-American people. Forty-two "exhibits" were also included. These ranged from real estate organizations to local trade unions to a report from the "Spanish Speaking Community of the San Francisco Bay Area." Included also were statements from some private corporations—as the Lockheed Company—and from a few government agencies, such as the Richmond City Council.

Testimony of Mr. Earl Williams, San Francisco, California, and Mr. Walter Robinson, San Francisco, California

MR. GLICKSTEIN. Will each of you please state your names and addresses for the record?

MR. WILLIAMS. My name is Earl Williams. I stay at 23 Waxman Way in the public housing project.

MR. ROBINSON. My name is Walter Robinson. I reside at 69 A Mirabel Street.

MR. GLICKSTEIN. Would you each please tell us what your occupation is?

MR. WILLIAMS. Community organizer for the EOC.

MR. GLICKSTEIN. "EOC" stands for Economic Opportunity Council, and it is a poverty program?

MR. WILLIAMS. Yes.

MR. ROBINSON. I am also a community organizer for the EOC.

MR. GLICKSTEIN. Mr. Robinson, would describe the relationship between the people living in the projects and the people living on Potrero Hill in private housing?

MR. ROBINSON. Well, at the risk of refuting the statements or the attitudes of some of the previous speakers, I would have to say that the relationship is almost nonexistent. I think you have two separate communities on Potrero Hill, the resident and the homeowners and the project dwellers.

MR. GLICKSTEIN. Are there problems of mutual concern to all persons living on the Hill?

MR. ROBINSON. Yes, I think there are problems of mutual concern because I think what is happening in the public housing area will certainly affect the private area.

MR. GLICKSTEIN. Have any attempts been made to form a spirit of cooperation in solving some of the problems.

MR. ROBINSON. Yes, some attempts have been made to form a spirit of cooperation in solving some of the problems.

MR. GLICKSTEIN. How successful have these attempts been?

MR. ROBINSON. I am afraid they haven't been very successful. For example, recently, not too long ago, there was a project. As you probably know, the public housing sector is very much isolated from any kinds of services. There are no medical facilities, no shopping centers, no drug stores. It is an area that is completely isolated and the transportation in this area is very, very bad.

The public housing residents had expressed a need and a great desire to have some kind of medical facilities on the Hill and some doctors have been willing to come in and to buy a private house and establish a medical clinic.

At this time we discovered that two of the organizations, the two organizations that have appeared here today, were very much opposed to this idea. It seems that their main area of concern was with the rezoning and not the human need, and we were very, very disappointed that they took this attitude.

MR. GLICKSTEIN. The project would have required rezoning of some sort?

MR. ROBINSON. Yes.

MR. GLICKSTEIN. What do most of the people in the project believe should be done when the temporary housing is torn down? What do they believe should be done with that land?

MR. ROBINSON. Well, they have overwhelmingly expressed a need, first of all, for a kind of multi-service center. They dislike very much having to go up the Hill for each and every little thing they have to buy and having to rely on public transportation.

Approximately a month or a month and a half ago a little four-week-old baby died in my arms. There are two doctors on the Hill and they are there by appointment only and the nearest place they can get medical attention is at the San Francisco Public General Hospital, and again transportation is very, very bad.

MR. GLICKSTEIN. What do you mean by multi-service center?

MR. ROBINSON. A place where there would be medical and dental facilities available for the residents, a place where they could buy medicines, a shopping center or a recreation area, barber shop, many of the services that you generally find within a community that are totally and completely lacking in the project area.

MR. GLICKSTEIN. And you would favor replacing the temporary war housing with this multi-service center?

MR. ROBINSON. Yes. Also there is a need for additional housing. The private housing market in San Francisco is dwindling all the time, and it is doubly hard for black people to find adequate or decent housing in the city of San Francisco.

It has been my personal experience that I have gone looking for housing, after having made initial contact over the telephone and having arrived and talked to the landlord, either the house was no longer available or the price had gone up some twenty or thirty percent, and it works a tremendous hardship on people who are black people who are seeking private housing in the city.

MR. GLICKSTEIN. Do you favor more public housing or some of the 221 (d) (3) housing?

MR. ROBINSON. Well, I am not in favor of additional public housing, but we have to face a reality here. The middle-class among black people is not growing. It is diminishing, and as I understand this 221 (d) (3) housing is designed primarily for middle-class people, for near-middle-class people.

MR. GLICKSTEIN. So you think that there is a greater need for public housing which would be available?

MR. ROBINSON. I am afraid so.

MR. GLICKSTEIN. Now, you mentioned that some of the projects that people in the public housing project are interested in haven't been supported by other people on the Hill. Are there other issues that the people in the project are interested in besides the multi-service center?

MR. ROBINSON. Yes, they are interested in the conditions of public housing. This has been one of their main concerns. They feel that the houses that they are living in now are overpriced and not commensurate with the services or the lack of services. They have been in opposition to many of the policies and abuses of the San Francisco Housing Authority.

MR. GLICKSTEIN. Have the residents of the project received any support from other people on the Hill in these endeavors?

MR. ROBINSON. I think the only support that they have received has been in the latest request for an unused building, an unoccupied building, to be used as a kind of community center.

MR. GLICKSTEIN. How would you appraise the attitudes of the persons in the project toward the white majority on the Hill?

MR. ROBINSON. Well, first of all, I think that the attitude is one of mounting frustration and perhaps bitterness. They see themselves as isolated people who have to go it alone because the other people aren't really concerned about them. Their problems are uniquely their own and they feel that they are the ones that are going to have to solve their problem.

MR. GLICKSTEIN. What effect has the poverty program had on meeting the needs of the people in the project?

MR. ROBINSON. Well, it is very difficult to evaluate the effects of the poverty program on the needs of the people. I would say that on the real needs of the people the poverty program has been rather ineffectual, but I think it has served—

MR. GLICKSTEIN. When you say "real needs" do you mean on jobs, housing?

MR. ROBINSON. Yes, on jobs, housing, but I think it has given a voice to the people and has attempted with some degree of success of getting people together and having them talk about their own problems and devise possible solutions to meeting some of them.

MR. GLICKSTEIN. Mr. Williams, in your work as a community organizer, do you see a trend toward black nationalism among the young people in the project?

MR. WILLIAMS. No, I don't see a trend toward the black nationalism but I see a trend toward black unity.

MR. GLICKSTEIN. Black unity. How would you define that?

MR. WILLIAMS. In other words, we are not sitting back any more and waiting on other people to dictate our lives. We are trying to organize ourselves where we have something to say about our own lives, and we are not going to sit back and let other organizations dictate to us how they think our lives should be run.

MR. GLICKSTEIN. Has this trend picked up in recent years?

MR. WILLIAMS. Quite a bit, picked up quite a bit this year.

MR. GLICKSTEIN. What do you think is the reason for the trend?

MR. WILLIAMS. Well, I think—for a long time I have been living on Potrero Hill, for nine years. I think for a long time every time something was done on the Hill it has been done by the Boosters and the Merchants, and they don't really know what the people are like in the projects. They go by what they hear, like this lady brought up this morning about they have five hundred members and two blacks. If they have them, they must have gotten them this morning.

MR. GLICKSTEIN. Do you think that this trend toward black unity is accompanied by feelings of hostility?

MR. WILLIAMS. Well, you wouldn't know, but most people would know that we have had hostility all our lives, and the situation on Potrero Hill isn't helping it any.

MR. GLICKSTEIN. Do you think that the city and the persons that hold economic power in this community are aware of the feeling of the people on the Hill?

MR. WILLIAMS. Of course they are, but they are scared to say it.

MR. GLICKSTEIN. They are scared to say it?

MR. WILLIAMS. Yes.

MR. GLICKSTEIN. Do you think that this trend toward black unity that you mentioned, do you think that can solve the problems and satisfy the needs of the people?

MR. WILLIAMS. I think it is the only way to solve the problems. When you get together and do something for yourself, and you know what you want done, not what someone thinks you should have, or how much of this you should have, or we don't think this should be this way. These people don't have the right to sit up here and say what they don't think should be on Potrero Hill. I don't care if they have been living there seventy years. They don't have this right.

MR. GLICKSTEIN. Do you think that there should be greater efforts on the Hill to try to increase communication between all the people that live on the Hill instead of trends toward separation?

MR. WILLIAMS. Well, I think the only effort we are getting right now as far as creating communication is coming from the homeowners and residents. Like the lady said a little while ago, that they invite everyone to their meetings, and like I say, I have been living there nine years and I never received an invitation to go to a Booster Merchants meeting yet.

MR. GLICKSTEIN. Do you think that it would be good to make an effort to improve communications?

MR. WILLIAMS. It would be good, you know, but, like I stated, I don't know how good it would be for them, for the simple reason we are not going to be dictated to any more.

MR. GLICKSTEIN. But you would be receptive to greater efforts of communication and greater attempts for all the people on the Hill to try to work out their problems?

MR. WILLIAMS. That is correct. We have tried that, and we have been trying ever since I have been there, but it is not working because you still have the selected few that is going to say what is going on, and that is the way it is supposed to be, and it is not going to be that way anymore.

MR. GLICKSTEIN. I have no further questions, Mr. Chairman.

VICE CHAIRMAN PATTERSON. Father Hesburgh?

COMMISSIONER HESBURGH. I am just wondering, in the best of all worlds, which I have to keep thinking about all the time, you don't have a good conversation unless you have a strong voice on each side. Would you agree with that, Mr. Williams?

MR. WILLIAMS. Beg pardon?

COMMISSIONER HESBURGH. You have to have a strong voice on each side of a good conversation?

MR. WILLIAMS. Well, I wouldn't say you had to have a strong voice, but I would say a strong determination.

COMMISSIONER HESBURGH. What I am thinking of is, if I read your remarks correctly, you don't want to have this conversation between whites and blacks as between superiors and inferiors. You want to have it as equal Americans. Right?

MR. WILLIAMS. That's right.

COMMISSIONER HESBURGH. So what you are doing to create a Negro community, or a black unity, as you say, could have a very positive value if coming out of it you would then be in a position to talk with a certain amount of idea, force, and vitality to the white community on the Hill. Correct?

MR. WILLIAMS. I think I would.

COMMISSIONER HESBURGH. And I get the impression, and again this is just a personal impression, but I get the impression at times looking at this around the country that people are afraid that the black unity will be a thing in itself and will create a deeper ghetto than has existed in the past. I think it would be more promising if we could look at it as a creation of a self-identity in the community and a self-consciousness even, and even a self-pride. So then, in turn, you could have a real conversation, not a phony conversation, which has so characterized past conversations. Would you agree with that?

MR. WILLIAMS. Yes.

COMMISSIONER HESBURGH. Mr. Robinson, I was curious of what your background was. Where are you from originally?

MR. WILLIAMS. Where am I from originally? I am from the Midwest, Chicago.

COMMISSIONER HESBURGH. I thought I got a little of that home accent there. I was just curious. Have you been here long in California?

MR. WILLIAMS. Yes.

COMMISSIONER HESBURGH. Mr. Robinson, if you really had the say completely, I mean if we could get rid of all of the structure, the establishment, the clubs and everything else, and you were to say we are going to start now and make a program for Potrero Hill in its totality with all its segments, how would you go about that?

MR. ROBINSON. Would you please repeat that?

COMMISSIONER HESBURGH. Sure. What I am thinking of, we have heard from some of the white residents on Potrero Hill. We have heard from some of the black residents on Potrero Hill. I am wondering, looking to the future, if you could say now, "This to me is an ideal of the way we would move forward on Potrero Hill to create one community that is interested in each other and one community that would be for the good of the total neighborhood there," how would you go about that? Would it be a federation of all existing forces? Would it be one single organization to which many people belonged, or how would you approach it, really?

I realize it is a difficult question I am asking you, but I am looking for a plan rather than just separate reactions off of a vacuum.

MR. ROBINSON. I would prefer to think that in any ideal situation that people of different ethnic or racial or religious backgrounds would regard the community as their community. Therefore, any problem of any resident in that community would affect every other community person.

So I would envision this kind of attitude within the community that would seek to act on the needs of individuals for the good of the community and to act jointly for the interests of the community.

COMMISSIONER HESBURGH. So what you are saying is we have to begin a conversation on the Hill between all of the parties to the Hill that live there, that are interested in it and have a stake in the neighborhood there, and to get them talking about real problems that affect everyone.

For example, this multi-service center could be everybody's center. It wouldn't have to be a black center or a white center. I think if you wind up with two of them, you again divide the community.

MR. ROBINSON. As we envision it, the service center would be open for all residents. The only thing is right now there is a greater need for this type of service for the people dwelling in the projects, because of economic reasons and because of their location.

Most of the people on the other side of the Hill, I should imagine, have their private doctors. They have their own automobiles and in cases of emergencies they can readily go to seek medical attention.

COMMISSIONER HESBURGH. But this multi-service center could be a way of uniting the community if it were, somewhat, closer to the public housing, but at the same time available to others?

MR. ROBINSON. Yes.

COMMISSIONER HESBURGH. Thank you, Mr. Robinson.

VICE CHAIRMAN PATTERSON. Mrs. Freeman?

COMMISSIONER FREEMAN. Mr. Robinson and Mr. Williams, I believe there are about four thousand residents in the low-rent housing developments there. Is that about right?

MR. ROBINSON. I think it is slightly higher than that, Mrs. Freeman.

COMMISSIONER FREEMAN. And about how many of them are black?

MR. ROBINSON. About 5,500 or 6,000.

COMMISSIONER FREEMAN. This multi-service center that you are talking about could be provided by the San Francisco Housing Authority, could it not?

MR. ROBINSON. It has been done in other cities and I see no reason why it couldn't be provided by public housing authority in this city.

COMMISSIONER FREEMAN. I would like to know if the organization that you are talking about has made this presentation or request of the San Francisco Housing Authority.

MR. WILLIAMS. May I say something about the San Francisco Housing Authority? We can't even get them to keep our places clean, let's don't try to get them to give us something else. So I don't think they would come across with it, because we have had rats and roaches we have been crying about for the last five or six years, and they haven't even got rid of those, and that is much cheaper than a multi-service center.

MR. ROBINSON. Along these lines, if I might add, I think that it is a fairly well publicized fact that many residents in the Potrero Hill Projects are on a rent strike.

Now, they were forced to this position after repeated frustrations and meeting with the Housing Authority, trying to get very minor things changed, such as Mr. Williams mentioned, the extermination of rats and roaches, paint jobs, et cetera, and we have gotten very little cooperation from the Housing Authority. So we don't think it is feasible to even approach them on something as big as this at this time.

COMMISSIONER FREEMAN. Who owns the Wisconsin Temporary Housing Project?

MR. ROBINSON. The city, I believe.

COMMISSIONER FREEMAN. I had the opportunity to tour that area on Saturday, and it seemed to me that among those temporary housing buildings that there were a lot of vacancies. There seems to be some use that could be made, rehabilitation, or what have you, to provide the kind of facility that you are talking about. To what extent is that feasible?

MR. ROBINSON. Well, actually, I think we have another location at 1095 Wisconsin Street which is in better condition and would probably serve a better purpose than any of the temporary housing over in the Wisconsin Project site.

COMMISSIONER FREEMAN. Who owns that land?

MR. ROBINSON. The city.

COMMISSIONER FREEMAN. So that the city could provide the services?

MR. ROBINSON. Yes.

COMMISSIONER FREEMAN. The city could provide the multi-service center. I would like to know what has been done to get the city to do it.

MR. WILLIAMS. Everything except holding a gun on them. In other words, like he mentioned a few moments ago about the rent strike, anyone who has been in this area can see the shape that it is in. The shape that the houses are in, and the whole—just the whole everyday life of the people that is living in the housing projects is bad. The mayor can see this, the board of supervisors can see this, but they will not speak out on this because they might not be elected in November.

So this is the type of city government that we have here in San Francisco, a bunch of big sissies.

COMMISSIONER FREEMAN. What plans does the organization have to remedy the situation?

MR. ROBINSON. Well, recently we have had meetings with architects to study the site and to advice us on the feasibilities of our desires for this particular area. So we have started to move in this direction. Once again, that is.

VICE CHAIRMAN PATTERSON. Dr. Rankin?

COMMISSIONER RANKIN. Mr. Robinson, if it is economically feasible to have a multi-service center, you would think stores like a drug store would make money if located on the Hill? Is that correct?

MR. ROBINSON. Well, we are not that concerned about economics, Mr. Rankin. We are more concerned about need.

COMMISSIONER RANKIN. I know you are, but a store would be more concerned about being located—I am trying to find out if the zoning ordinance is keeping stores from locating there, or is it just that they feel that no money could be made by a store at that location?

MR. ROBINSON. There are businesses in the area, two small grocery stores in the area.

COMMISSIONER RANKIN. But no supermarket or anything like that?

MR. ROBINSON. No, nothing of that sort.

COMMISSIONER RANKIN. Now, do you think that would be a good location for a supermarket?

MR. ROBINSON. I think they could make money there, yes.

COMMISSIONER RANKIN. And it is not prohibited—the locating of a supermarket there is not prohibited by zoning ordinance at the present time. Is that correct?

MR. ROBINSON. I don't know what the zoning ordinance is in relation to this particular site. I know that a very short distance from there we were frustrated in our attempts to get housing rezoned in order to establish a medical clinic.

COMMISSIONER RANKIN. Well, I will agree with you it looks like a good location for a multi-service center there. I agree with you on that, and I just wonder why somebody hasn't really latched onto the opportunity.

MR. WILLIAMS. Too many groups.

VICE CHAIRMAN PATTERSON. Mr. Taylor?

MR. TAYLOR. Mr. Robinson, what are the public services that the community is lacking? I think you mentioned transportation as one. I would appreciate a little bit more detail on that and any other services the community needs.

MR. ROBINSON. I could see that there would be a need for a social welfare office, an employment office in an area where you have some twenty-five or thirty percent of eligible males unemployed. I should imagine that in a clinic that there should be—yes, a clinic, I imagine, you should certainly classify that as a public service. You are aware that the transportation is bad.

MR. TAYLOR. How difficult is it right now for residents to get to shopping, to the most convenient shopping place or downtown? Do the buses run frequently?

MR. ROBINSON. The buses run very infrequently and the nearest shopping center, as I know, is down in the Mission, which means that you have to come completely off the Hill and go quite a number of blocks to get into shopping areas, and most residents do have to rely on public transportation.

VICE CHAIRMAN PATTERSON. Mr. Williams, if you could achieve this black unity of which you speak, how would you apply it? How would you get things done as a result of having black unity?

MR. WILLIAMS. I think November is the answer to that. You know, as far as the voting is concerned.

VICE CHAIRMAN PATTERSON. You are speaking then primarily in terms of voting?

MR. WILLIAMS. That is correct. I notice that our assemblymen and the board of supervisors and the mayor and all of them, they are quite interested in votes in November, and since they don't want to do nothing for the poor people now, I don't think the poor people should vote for them in November, and I think if two thousand to three thousand adults was to change their votes, it wouldn't make that much of a difference but it might if they were all cast the same way and in the same direction for someone who they thought was going to try to help them achieve some of the goals that they would like to have in their community.

MR. ROBINSON. I would just like to comment on that, and Mr. Williams and I have discussed this at length. We would like to be able to proceed along the established democratic lines for change if this is possible, but if this is not possible, then we will have to do whatever is necessary to make these changes.

VICE CHAIRMAN PATTERSON. Does this remind you in any way, Mr. Robinson, of the way some of my own home people in the South, whites, used to talk.

MR. ROBINSON. The way they used to talk?

VICE CHAIRMAN PATTERSON. Yes, sir.

MR. ROBINSON. I am not altogether sure how people in your home town used to talk, Mr. Patterson. Could you be a bit more explicit in your question?

VICE CHAIRMAN PATTERSON. Perhaps venturing outside the democratic process on occasion. This, what I am saying, has led the South, the white South, into a long period of folly, and my question to you is, are you sure that this couldn't work the other way?

MR. ROBINSON. I am sorry. I don't wish to belabor it, but I don't fully understand what you are saying.

VICE CHAIRMAN PATTERSON. I am stating a proposition in asking the question. I am saying as a southerner, I think that when the whites in my home region for a long period of time went outside the democratic process to achieve their wishes, this led them into many follies, and I wonder if this might not lead the Negro in the same direction.

MR. ROBINSON. I think that the black people in this country have been trying for the past four hundred or so years to achieve their goals within the democratic process, and I think there is a lot of disagreement as to how well they have succeeded.

VICE CHAIRMAN PATTERSON. Thank you. Any further questions? You are excused. Thank you very much. Would you call the next witness, Mr. Glickstein?

Hearings Before the U.S. Commission on Civil Rights; Hearings held in San Francisco, May 1–3, 1967, and Oakland, May 4–6, 1967, pp. 39–56. The subsequent hundreds of pages reflect the same reality.

139

HIGHER EDUCATION AND THE NEGRO

by Benjamin E. Mays

The Centennial Address at Howard University was delivered in June 1967 by the president of Morehouse College. Noteworthy was the insistence that "desegregation is not integration"; no, integration "means to organically unite, to form a perfect unity." "If we aren't careful," Dr. Mays continued, "we will live another century dangling between desegregation and integration, with all the discrimination inherent therein." One generation has passed; what now of this warning?

Although we have done fairly well in desegregating America, the job has not been finished. Segregation in housing is widespread. One Negro can still chase a thousand white persons by moving into a white residential area, and two can put ten thousand to flight. And in opposition to open occupancy, the North and the South speak the same language! They joined hands to defeat an open-occupancy bill. The next difficult hurdle to overcome is that of adequate employment. More Negroes will find good paying jobs, whereas more and more Negroes will find themselves at the bottom of the economic ladder or unemployed altogether—despite a desegregated society. Thirteen years after the May 17, 1954, decision of the United States Supreme Court, the South, and the North for that matter, is dragging its feet on desegregating the public schools. Recently, the conservative Republicans of the North and the conservative Democrats of the South joined hands in a measure to slow up desegregation of the schools and to place more control of federal money for education in the hands of the states, which means more opportunity for discrimination based on race. The South has allies in the North and can now rely upon many Northern Republicans and some Northern Democrats to do for it what in previous years it had to do for itself.

We use the word *desegregation* because it is not integration. When the courts opened public schools and universities, golf courses and swimming pools, abolished segregation on dining cars, in interstate travel, and on buses, and abolished the white primary, they were not integrating the facilities. They were desegregating them; when sit-ins, boycotts, and picketing opened restaurants, hotels and motels, this, to, was desegregation—not integration. This is also true when a church votes to drop the color bar. The church is desegregating, not integrating. Desegregation means the absence of segregation.

To integrate means to unite together to form a "more complete, harmonious, or coordinated entity." It means to organically unify, to form a more perfect entity.

In an integrated society, fellowship, comradeship, and neighborliness have no limits or boundaries based on nationality, race, or color. Association will be formed mainly in the realm of spiritual, mental, and cultural values. There will be no laws against interracial marriages, and custom will recognize the right of every man and every woman to marry whomever he or she pleases. Integration is largely spiritual. It is even possible for a married couple to live in the same housing bearing and rearing children, fussing and feuding, without ever becoming thoroughly integrated, without ever being unified in their purposes and outlook on life.

As Howard University closes out her first century and enters the second, the university, in the area of human relations, will be challenged on two fronts: First, to do its part to implement the civil-rights legislation already enacted into law. After passage of the Civil Rights Act of 1875 and its repeal in 1883 and after the Hayes-Tilden Compromise in 1877, the federal government felt that it had done enough for Negroes and retreated from the field of protecting Negro rights. Then followed an era of peonage, complete segregation, and lynching. The climax to the retreat came in 1896, when the Supreme Court made segregation legal. The federal government did not return in full blast to the civil-rights struggle until after the middle of the twentieth century. The North grew weary, felt it had done enough by freeing the enslaved persons and by adding to the Constitution the Thirteenth, Fourteenth, and Fifteenth Amendments. Colored Americans must earn the right to complete citizenship, whereas others get it at birth.

I am most unhappy over what I see going on on Capitol Hill today. There seems to be a feeling now that the Supreme Court has slapped down segregation and the Congress has enacted into law many of the Court's decisions, that the federal government has done enough: let the Negro now make it on his own, sink or swim, live or die. As long as we think in terms of black versus white and not in terms of Americans, regardless of the degree of desegregation, racism is a monster to be feared. A partially desegregated or a wholly desegregated society may, therefore, become normal. Herein lies the danger. After the Hayes-Tilden Compromise and the repeal of the Civil Rights Act of 1875, the North largely withdrew from the field of civil rights. Today, the conservative North and the conservative South are joining hands to slow down the process of desegregating America.

According to the Southern Educational Reporting Service, thirteen years after May 17, 1954, the average number of Negroes attending desegregated schools in the eleven Southern states represents 15.9 percent. At this rate, it will take eighty years to complete the job. Housing could remain largely segregated and the economic gulf between Negroes and other Americans could become wider and wider. The Howard leadership must make itself heavily felt in this new area, just as it provided the leadership to break the back of legal segregation.

The second challenge to Howard University in its second century will be to fight discrimination in the interim between desegregation and integration, and to train students who are so competent in their chosen fields and so skilled in their jobs that discrimination will become increasingly difficult. There is a time to demonstrate, to sit in, and to protest; and the irresponsible may precipitate riots; but there has *never* been and there *never* will be a substitute for academic excellence, and none for possession skills that the community needs. I know the conditions that produce riots and I know that it often takes riots to arouse the conscience of the community to do something about an intolerable situation; but I also know that demonstrations and riots alone have never produced skills in engineering nor competence in surgery. As John Dewey and James Hayden Tufts say in their book entitled *Ethics*: "The freedom of an agent who is merely released from direct external obstruction is formal and empty. If he is without resources or personal skills, without control of the tools of achievement, he must inevitably lend himself to carrying out the directions and ideas of others." We can be like this in a desegregated society.

Finally, let me warn you that we must not be swept off our feet by the glamour of a desegregated society. By all means, enjoy the swankiest hotels, eat in the finest restaurants, live on the boulevard, ride anywhere, worship anyplace, work anyplace, get high-paying jobs, send more men to Congress, get more judgeships—but remember that we can do all these things and not be a part of the policy-making bodies that shape education, industry, and government. We can do all these things and still be grossly discriminated against when there is no sign of segregation in sight. This kind of discrimination which we will meet in the interim between desegregation and integration will be subtle and will be administered not by the Maddoxes, the Wallaces, and the Barnetts, but by our liberal friends in Congress, in education, and in industry. If we aren't careful, we will live another century dangling between desegregation and integration, with all the discrimination inherent therein.

I am going to assume that Howard University in its second century will become one of America's top universities and that Congress will appropriate sums to enable the university to compete with the best in the nation. I am going to assume that Howard will turn out more and more graduates who will be ambassadors to foreign countries, not only to little countries as now, but ambassadors to the great power nations. I shall assume that Howard will send more men to Congress, train more judges, produce abler men in medicine and religion, turn out men who will be cabinet members and governors, and produce a President of the United States—provided we can break through the interim of discrimination that will exist between desegregation and integration and produce a society where this great nation of ours, born in revolution and blood, conceived in liberty, and dedicated to the proposition that all men are created free and equal, will truly become the lighthouse of freedom where none will be denied because his skin is black and none favored because his eyes are blue; where the nation is militarily strong but at peace; economically secure but just; learned but wise; where the poorest will have a job and bread enough to spare; and where the richest will understand the meaning of empathy.

But even this will not be enough. Howard University fought against racism in the latter part of its first century mainly in the courts. In the future, Howard will be challenged to create and design programs to close the gap between the college and university men and the dropouts and the unskilled, those who live in the ghettos and slums, poorly housed, ill-clad, living on substandard salaries or no salaries at all. Howard will be challenged to take the gown to the town and the slums, and bring the town and the slums to the university campus. This will take a will, a creativity, and an imagination which we may not now have, but it must be done if Howard University is to serve all classes of people in the decades ahead. Howard in the second century should never forget the words of Eugene Debs, who said in essence: "As long as there is a lower class, I am in it. As long as there is a criminal element, I am of it. And, as long as there is a man in jail, I am not free." Howard in the second century should train its graduates to know that we are all a part of mankind and that no man is good enough, no man is strong enough, and no man is wise enough to think that he is better than another man and thus justified in setting himself apart from the man farthest down; for if one man has more intellect than another, is richer than another, it may be luck or fate. We are all what we are largely by accident or God's grace. No one chooses his parents and no one chooses the circumstance under which he is born. I have seen a brilliant mind and a dull mind born into the same family. I have seen beauty and ugliness in the same family. The boy born in the slums has no choice, and the man born in the midst of splendor and wealth has no choice. The man in splendor and wealth has no right to look down on the one from the slums or the ghetto because he too might have been born in the slums. This is what John Donne is trying to tell us when he says: "No man is an island, entire of itself; every man is a piece of the continent; a part of the main; if a clod be washed away by the sea, Europe is the less, as well as if a promontory were...; any man's death diminishes me, because I am involved in mankind; and therefore never send to know for whom the bell tolls; it tolls for thee."

As Howard University becomes more famous in the decades ahead and as her graduates reach for the stars and grasp after the moon in politics, economics, education, and industry, may they also reach down and use their skills to bring a better life to the poor and justice to all mankind. It is my prayer and my prophecy that Howard's second century will be more glorious than the first.

Nathan Wright, Jr., ed., *What Black Educators Are Saying* (San Francisco: Leswick Press, 1970) pp. 104–13; published in part.

140

"NO RESPECT FOR THE PEOPLE HERE"

by Residents of Buffalo, New York

Buffalo was the site of one of the numerous racial outbreaks in the spring and summer of 1967. The police commissioner had said he was "willing to bet that we would never have a riot here"—where some one hundred thousand black people live. Of the fifteen hundred policemen in the city, the commissioner affirmed there were "about twenty" who were black and that it was "impossible to recruit more." Some black people were quoted in the *New York Times:*

"They're bigoted," said Assemblyman Arthur Eve, speaking of the police. "They live in the suburbs and have no idea of what goes on in the Negro areas, nor any respect for the people living there."

The Rev. James T. Hemphill insists that police relations were so bad that unless they improve they will turn the entire Negro community against the police.

Said Bruce Cosby, a youth of about eighteen: "White people don't know what it's like to have a policeman always beating you on the head."

Leroy Coles, director of Buffalo's Urban league, said he once was told by a policeman to stop interfering with police work when he tried to tell a Negro youth not to resist. He said he was apprehensive that the youth would probably be beaten into submission. "He was," Mr. Coles said.

"One of the biggest complaints," said Cordell Morehead, a NAACP Youth Council member, "is that the police will push you off the street corners and off the sidewalks if you stand there."

One admitted riot leader said of this, "And where else are you going to stand? You were probably pushed out of school and you can't get a job so you stand on the streets just hoping some money will come by or that you can get into something—something, something."

New York Times, July 11, 1967, p. 10. This outbreak lasted two days and resulted in sixty-eight wounded, including twenty-six from shotgun pellets, and 182 arrests, mostly on minor charges.

141

UPRISINGS IN NEWARK AND DETROIT

by the Editors of Freedomways

A significant force in thwarting the full realization and potential of the civil rights movement was the jailing, wounding, and killing of black leaders and rank and filers. In the summer of 1967 so-called race riots—actually insurrections— occurred in several cities. Those in Newark and Plainfield, New Jersey, and in Detroit brought this editorial response from the militant editors of *Freedomways:*

They called it a riot, the events in Newark on July 12th and during the six days that followed. But the identity of the corpses, the wounded and the jailed describes what occurred in different terms: in four days, twenty-six Negroes were shot dead and six others were dying among the twelve hundred wounded and only one white policeman had died. Also 1,275 Negroes were arrested but no white men. No, it was not a riot. Newark was the scene of yet another massacre of the poorest of black Americans. White mobsters in the uniforms of city and state policemen and National Guardsmen acting on the orders of racists, who occupy the seats of authority in the city and state governments, carried out a deadly pogrom, an urban lynching designed to terrorize and cower the slum-dwellers who are pounding at the barriers that enclose them.

The Newark massacre which was marked by the shooting to death of a four-year-old Negro girl and the pumping of thirty-nine bullets into the already lifeless corpse of an eleven-year-old black boy, was followed by the punitive expedition of the state police and National Guard against the Negro community of Plainfield, New Jersey.

Under the guise of a search for the case of missing rifles, New Jersey Governor Hughes suppressed constitutional liberties and soldiers were ordered to surround the Negro section while a house to house search was made. The white racist guardsmen broke down doors with their rifle butts, kicked open drawers, and menaced old people and little children with drawn revolvers and bayoneted rifles.

At this writing, with the summer only half over, policemen or National

Guardsmen have smashed into Negro communities to put down with fascist-styled violence, with guns blazing, the militant demonstrations of Negroes for jobs and dignity, against the continuation of the war in Vietnam, and for programs to rehouse the people.

Newark's Negroes vented their wrath at the at-hand symbols of their torment, deprivation, and denial of justice and equality. Some police cars and certain stores of leeches and slum-lord parasites of the ghettos went up in flames. At the same time, Congress was voting against the enactment of a rat-control bill designed to help eliminate millions of rats which infest the slums and often prey upon infants in their cribs.

Congress in these same days enacted by an overwhelming vote an anti-riot bill for imposing stringent criminal penalties upon anyone crossing state lines for purposes of inciting "disturbances." This bill, the so-called "Stokely Bill" for Stokely Carmichael of the Student Nonviolent Coordinating Committee, is designed to deprive the freedom struggle of a national leadership.

Newark and Plainfield, New Jersey, point to the need for united action of all the diverse elements who make up the freedom movement to make demands upon local, state, and national governments to put an end to the police terror that reigns over the Negro communities from one end of the country to the other. To the struggle to realize a truly adequate program of government spending to secure genuine economic, educational, medical, recreational, and housing equality; to the ongoing struggle to secure enfranchisement, representation in government in all branches and at all levels, there must be launched a movement to stop police brutality and to put an end to the use of National Guardsmen against the movement of our people to secure their rights. Among other things, such an anti-police brutality program should call for: placing the Negro community out of bounds to white police and uniformed National Guardsmen; establishing Civilian Review and Citizens Inspection Boards in all urban and rural area where Negroes are a factor in the population, and abolishing the National Guard which is under the command of reactionaries and Ku Klux Klan racists.

Detroit

The suppression of Negroes in Newark has neither cowed nor contained the spreading battles for freedom. In Detroit, black men and women mounted and carried through the struggle but *the new thing* was the participation of some whites in the uprising. It was not a black against white "race riot" but rather a class confrontation which impoverished Negroes led against the wealthy merchants, landlords, and police.

The fire damage in Detroit has been estimated at one billion dollars but the cost in human blood was dearer yet: forty lives were lost, some two thousand were wounded, some 3,500 were arrested. The flames of Detroit should serve to light up a great truth: It's that time, America. Grant Negroes freedom and equality or invite catastrophe!

Freedomways 7 (Summer 1967): 197–98.

142

DEVELOPING AFRICAN-AMERICAN NATIONALIST FEELINGS: THE NEWARK CONFERENCE OF 1967

the Delegates' Resolution

In 1967 there were violent outbreaks in the ghettos of 150 cities. In terms of casualties, the worst was that in Cleveland, where forty-three people died, of whom thirty-three were African-Americans. Second to that was the uprising in Newark—whose 500,000 population included about 260,000 black people. There the dead numbered twenty-three, of whom one was white.

In the latter part of the summer of this bloody year, a Conference on Black Power was held in Newark; there were seven hundred delegates, including the nationalist-minded Ron Karenga; H. Rap Brown, then president of SNCC; Horace Sheffield, of the United Auto Workers; Owen Brooks, of the civil rights division of the National Council of Chuches; Floyd B. McKissick, chairman of CORE; and Jesse Jackson, then of the SCLC. Women were notable by their absence.

This meeting, after extended debate, issued a resolution that follows:

Whereas the black people in America have been systematically oppressed by their white fellow countrymen

Whereas there is little prospect that this oppression can be terminated, peacefully or otherwise, within the foreseeable future

Whereas the black people do not wish to be absorbed into the larger white community

Whereas the black people in America find that their interests are in contradiction with those of white America

Whereas the black people in America are psychologically handicapped by virtue of their having no national homeland

Whereas the physical, moral, ethical, and esthetic standards of white

American society are not those of black society and indeed do violence to the self-image of the black man

Whereas black people were among the earliest immigrants to America, having been ruthlessly separated from their fatherland, and have made a major contribution to America's development, most of this contribution having been uncompensated, and

Recognizing that efforts are already well advanced for the convening of a Constitutional Convention for the prupose of revising the Constitution of the U. S. for the first time since America's inception, then

Be it resolved that the Black Power Conference initiate a national dialogue on the desirability of partitioning the U.S. into two separate and independent nations, one to be a homeland for white and the other to be a homeland for black Americans.

143

HUEY MUST BE SET FREE!

by the Black Panther

The sixth number of the *Black Panther*, demanding the freeing of the leader of the Black Panther party, expressed its unequivocal position. The party was hounded by state authorities; its leaders were wounded and killed and jailed. For three or four years it was a significant force; ruling-class violence, terror, and propaganda forced its demise.

Huey Newton, Minister of Defense of the Black Panther Party for Self-Defense, lies in the hospital at San Quentin State Prison, with a gunshot wound in his stomach, inflicted by an Oakland cop. An Oakland cop is dead and buried and a second cop lies somewhere in some hospital with three bullet wounds in his body. Huey has been charged with the murder of the first cop and the shooting of the second.

The shooting occurred in the heart of Oakland's black ghetto. Huey is a black man, a resident of Oakland's black ghetto, and the two cops were white and lived in the white suburbs. On the night that the shooting occurred, there were four hundred years of oppression of black people by white people focused and manifested in the incident. We are at that crossroads in history where black people are determined to bring down the final curtain on the drama of their struggle to free themselves from the boot of the white man that is on their collective neck. Huey Newton knew that the chief instrument of oppression of black people in America is the police departments of the cities. Through murder, brutality, and the terror of their image, the police of America have kept black people intimidated, locked in mortal fear, and paralyzed in their bid for freedom. He knew that the power of the police over black people has to be broken if we are to be liberated from our bondage. These gestapo dogs are not holy, they are not angels, and there is no more mystery surrounding them. They are brutal beasts who have been gunning down black people and getting away with it. They call this "justifiable homicide" carried out by an officer of the law in the line of duty. Black people understand that this is very true— but not in the way that the lying mass media would have people believe.

The "duty" that these wretched jackals are carrying out is to keep the niggers in check; the peace that they are charged with keeping is the peace of the power structure, the peace of the Bank of America and General Motors. To perform their duty, they must necessarily disturb the peace of black people. In fact, black people have had no peace since the first day they set foot on this bloody Babylonian soil called America. Peace is what black people seek, what they are determined to have. Peace is what is being withheld from black people.

Huey Newton is a child of Malcolm X. Malcolm said that we will get our freedom by any means necessary, and twenty million black people heard his voice and concur in his message. Huey Newton heard Malcolm's voice and understood his message. Twenty million black people heard Malcolm's message and that same twenty million feel exactly the same way about it as Huey Newton feels.

Twenty million black people say that the cops are down wrong from the get-go and that Huey Newton is right. Twenty million black people say that Huey is not guilty of any crime, that he is now being held as a political prisoner, and they want him set free. We know that white people, the majority of them, neither understand this nor do they believe that black people really mean this. Some white people understand this, know it to be true and just, and they back black people up in their just demands for liberation and an end to the terror.

Huey Newton's case is the showdown case. It marks the end of history. We cannot go a step beyond this point. Here we must draw the line. We say that we have had enough of black men and women being shot down like dogs in the street. We say that we have had enough of cops being set free with a verdict of justifiable homicide. We say that black people in

America have the right to self-defense. Huey Newton has laid his life on the line so that twenty million black people can find out just where they are at and so that we can find out just where white America is at.

We have reached the point in history where we must claim that a black man, confronted by a bloodthirsty cop who is out to take his life out of hatred for the black race, has a right to defend himself—even if this means picking up a gun and blowing that cop away, make no mistake about it: that is where we are at today. A cop is nothing but a man in a uniform. Through their propaganda and brainwashing of the people they have us believing that there is something supernatural or special about a cop. A cop is a human being just like anybody else, he came into the world just like anybody else, and he can leave this world just like anybody else.

Every week, from every corner of America, we hear the reports of how some cop has shot and killed some black man, woman, or child. We are sick and tired of hearing such news and we don't want to hear any more. The only way that it can be from now on is that there will be no more reports about more dead cops shot down by black men. There can be no two ways about it, there can no longer be a double standard, one for black people and one for white people, one for cops with guns and one for black men with guns. Either human life is sacred or it is not. If human life is sacred then we must demand that black life also be considered sacred.

On the very same day that the shooting incident involving Huey occurred, a 70-year-old black man in Palo Alto had his head blown off by a cop, from behind, and he was unarmed. Yet there has been no outcry about that. There has hardly been a peep about it. Was this 70-year-old black man's life sacred?

The racist dog Oakland cops say that this dead cop is the first one who has been killed "in the line of duty" in twenty years. Yet that same Oakland police force has shot and killed scores of black men and women in that same period. What about them? Don't they count? Who is keeping the statistics about them? And what are we supposed to do about that? Are we supposed to just sit back calmly and add another digit to the statistics every time another black person is killed by an Oakland cop? We know that this is what they want us to do—but we are here to say that those days are gone! Does everybody understand that? THOSE DAYS ARE GONE! THE DAY WHEN A COP CAN SHOOT A BLACK MAN, WOMAN, OR CHILD DOWN IN COLD BLOOD AND HAVE IT RULED JUSTIFIABLE HOMICIDE IS GONE FOREVER. FROM NOW ON WE SAY: ONE MAN, ONE LIFE!

Undoubtedly, the Oakland cops would be tickled pink if instead of having a dead cop and a live Huey on their hands, they had a dead Huey and a live cop. Black people all over America and around the world, and some white people in America and around the world, are glad for once to have a dead cop and a live Huey. But we go further and say that we want Huey to stay alive—we go even further and say that we want Huey set free.

Editorial, *Black Panther,* November 23, 1967.

144

A CHRISTMAS SERMON ON PEACE

by Martin Luther King, Jr.

This sermon was delivered at King's Ebenezer Baptist Church in Atlanta; it was broadcast, December 24, 1967, on the Canadian Broadcasting System. King's reference to his death became an insistent note in his speeches until it befell him a few months later.

Peace on Earth. . . .

This Christmas season finds us a rather bewildered human race. We have neither peace within nor peace without. Everywhere paralyzing fears harrow people by day and haunt them by night. Our world is sick with war; everywhere we turn we see its ominous possibilities. And yet, my friends, the Christmas hope for peace and good will toward all men can no longer be dismissed as a kind of pious dream of some utopian. If we don't have good will toward men in this world, we will destroy ourselves by the misuse of our own instruments and our own power. Wisdom born of experience should tell us that war is obsolete. There may have been a time when war served as a negative good by preventing the spread and growth of an evil force, but the very destructive power of modern weapons of warfare eliminates even the possibility that war may any longer serve as a negative good. And so, if we assume that life is worth living, if we assume that mankind has a right to survive, then we must find an alternative to war—and so let us this morning explore the conditions for peace. Let us this morning think anew on the meaning of that Christmas hope: "Peace on Earth, Good Will toward Men." And as we explore these conditions, I would like to suggest that modern man really go all out to study the meaning of nonviolence, its philosophy and its strategy.

We have experimented with the meaning of nonviolence in our struggle for racial justice in the United States, but now the time has come for man to experiment with nonviolence in all areas of human conflict, and that means nonviolence on an international scale.

Now let me suggest first that if we are to have peace on earth, our loyalties must become ecumenical rather than sectional. Our loyalties must transcend our race, our tribe, our class, and our nation; and this means we must develop a world perspective. No individual can live alone; no nation can live alone, and as long as we try, the more we are going to have war in this world. Now the judgment of God is upon us, and we must either learn to live together as brothers or we are all going to perish together as fools.

Yes, as nations and individuals, we are interdependent. I have spoken to you before of our visit to India some years ago. It was a marvelous experience; but I say to you this morning that there were those depressing moments. How can one avoid being depressed when one sees with one's own eyes evidences of millions of people going to bed hungry at night? How can one avoid being depressed when one sees with one's own eyes thousands of people sleeping on the sidewalks at night? More than a million people sleep on the sidewalks of Bombay every night; more than half a million sleep on the sidewalks of Calcutta every night. They have no houses to go into. They have no beds to sleep in. As I beheld these conditions, something within me cried out: "Can we in America stand idly by and not be concerned?" And an answer came: "Oh, no!" And I started thinking about the fact that right here in our country we spend millions of dollars every day to store surplus food; and I said to myself: "I know where we can store that food free of charge—in the wrinkled stomachs of the millions of God's children in Asia, Africa, Latin America, and even in our own nation, who go to bed hungry at night."

It really boils down to this: that all life is interrelated. We are all caught in an inescapable network of mutuality, tied into a single garment of destiny. Whatever affects one directly, affects all indirectly. We are made to live together because of the interrelated structure of reality. . . .

Now let me say, secondly, that if we are to have peace in the world, men and nations must embrace the nonviolent affirmation that ends and means must cohere. One of the great philosophical debates of history has been over the whole question of means and ends. And there have always been those who argued that the end justifies the means, that the means really aren't important. The important thing is to get to the end, you see.

So, if you're seeking to develop a just society, they say, the important thing is to get there, and the means are really unimportant; any means will do so long as they get you there—they may be violent, they may be untruthful means; they may even be unjust means to a just end. There have been those who have argued this throughout history. But we will never have peace in the world until men everywhere recognize that ends are not cut off from means, because the means represent the ideal in the making, and the end in process, and ultimately you can't reach good ends through evil means, because the means represent the seed and the end represents the tree.

It's one of the strangest things that all the great military geniuses of the world have talked about peace. The conquerors of old who came killing in pursuit of peace, Alexander, Julius Caesar, Charlemagne, and Napoleon, were akin in seeking a peaceful world order. If you will read *Mein Kampf* closely enough, you will discover that Hitler contended that everything he did in Germany was for peace. And the leaders of the world today talk eloquently about peace. Every time we drop our bombs in North Vietnam, President Johnson talks eloquently about peace. What is the problem? They are talking about peace as a distant goal, as an end we seek, but one day we must come to see that peace is not merely a distant goal we seek, but that it is a means by which we arrive at that goal. We must pursue peaceful ends through peaceful means. All of this is saying that, in the final analysis, means and ends must cohere because the end is preexistent in the means, and ultimately destructive means cannot bring about constructive ends. . . .

Every now and then I guess we all think realistically about that day when we will be victimized with what is life's final common denominator—that something we call death. We all think about it. And every now and then I think about my own death, and I think about my own funeral. And I don't think of it in a morbid sense. Every now and then I ask myself, "What is it that I would want said?" And I leave the word to you this morning.

If any of you are around when I have to meet my day, I don't want a long funeral. And if you get somebody to deliver the eulogy, tell them not to talk too long. Every now and then I wonder what I want them to say. Tell them not to mention that I have a Nobel Peace Prize, that isn't important.

Tell them not to mention that I have three or four hundred other awards, that's not important. Tell him not to mention where I went to school.

I'd like somebody to mention that day, that Martin Luther King, Jr., tried to give his life serving others. I'd like for somebody to say that day, that Martin Luther King, Jr., tried to love somebody. I want you to say that day, that I tried to be right on the war question. I want you to be able to say that day, that I did try to feed the hungry. I want you to be able to say that day, that I did try, in my life, to clothe those who were naked. I want you to say, on that day, that I did try, in my life, to visit those who were in prison. I want you to say that I tried to love and serve humanity.

Yes, if you want to say that I was a drum major, say that I was a drum major for justice; say that I was a drum major for peace; I was a drum major for righteousness. And all of the other shallow things will not matter. I won't have any money to leave behind. I won't have the fine and luxurious things of life to leave behind. But I just want to leave a committed life behind.

And that's all I want to say . . . if I can help somebody as I pass along, if I can cheer somebody with a word or song, if I can show somebody he's traveling wrong, then my living will not be in vain. If I can do my duty as a Christian ought, if I can bring salvation to a world once wrought, if I can spread the message as the master taught, then my living will not be in vain.

Yes, Jesus, I want to be on your right side or your left side, not for any selfish reason. I want to be on your right or your best side, not in terms of some political kingdom or ambition, but I just want to be there in love and in justice and in truth and in commitment to others, so that we can make of this old world a new world.

The Essential Writings and Speeches of Martin Luther King, Jr. (San Francisco: HarperCollins, 1991), pp. 253–55; 266–67.

145

WHERE DO WE GO FROM HERE?

Martin Luther King, Jr.

This was the last address by Dr. King as president of the Southern Christian Leadership Conference; it was delivered in 1967. Note its radical questioning of capitalism.

Now, in order to answer the question, "Where do we go from here?" which is our theme, we must first honestly recognize where we are now. When the Constitution was written, a strange formula to determine taxes and representation declared that the Negro was sixty percent of a person. Today another curious formula seems to declare that he is fifty percent of a person. Of the good things in life, the Negro has approximately one half those of whites. Of the bad things of life, he has twice those of whites. Thus half of all Negroes live in substandard housing. And Negroes have half the income of whites. When we view the negative experiences of life, the Negro has a double share. There are twice as many unemployed. The rate of infant mortality among Negroes is double that of whites and there are twice as many Negroes dying in Vietnam as whites in proportion to their size in the population.

In other spheres, the figures are equally alarming. In elementary schools, Negroes lag one to three years behind whites, and their segregated schools receive substantially less money per student than the white schools. One-twentieth as many Negroes as whites attend college. Of employed Negroes, seventy-five percent hold menial jobs.

This is where we are. Where do we go from here? First, we must massively assert our dignity and worth. We must stand up amidst a system that still oppresses us and develop an unassailable and majestic sense of values. We must no longer be ashamed of being black. The job of arousing manhood within a people that have been taught for so many centuries that they are nobody is not easy.

Even semantics have conspired to make that which is black seem ugly and degrading. In Roget's *Thesaurus* there are 120 synonyms for blackness and at least sixty of them are offensive, as for example, blot, soot, grim, devil, and foul. And there are some 134 synonyms for whiteness and all are favorable, expressed in such words as purity, cleanliness, chastity, and innocence. A white lie is better than a black lie. The most degenerate member of a family is a "black sheep." Ossie Davis has suggested that maybe the English language should be reconstructed so that teachers will not be forced to teach the Negro child sixty ways to despise himself, and thereby perpetuate his false sense of inferiority, and the white child 134 ways to adore himself, and thereby perpetuate his false sense of superiority.

The tendency to ignore the Negro's contribution to American life and to strip him of his personhood is as old as the earliest history books and as contemporary as the morning's newspaper. To upset this cultural homicide, the Negro must rise up with an affirmation of his own Olympian manhood. Any movement for the Negro's freedom that overlooks this necessity is only waiting to be buried. As long as the mind is enslaved, the body can never be free. Psychological freedom, a firm sense of self-esteem, is the most powerful weapon against the long night of physical slavery. No Lincolnian emancipation proclamation or Johnsonian civil rights bill can totally bring this kind of freedom. The Negro will only be free when he reaches down to the inner depths of his own being and signs with the pen and ink of assertive manhood his own emancipation proclamation. And, with a spirit straining toward true self-esteem, the Negro must boldly throw off the manacles of self-abnegation and say to himself and to the world, "I am somebody. I am a person. I am a man with dignity and honor. I have a rich and noble history. How painful and exploited that history has been. Yes, I was a slave through my foreparents and I am not ashamed of that. I'm ashamed of the people who were so sinful to make me a slave." Yes, we must stand up and say, "I'm black and I'm beautiful," and this self-affirmation is the black man's need, made compelling by the white man's crimes against him.

Another basic challenge is to discover how to organize our strength in terms of economic and political power. No one can deny that the Negro is in dire need of this kind of legitimate power. Indeed, one of the great problems that the Negro confronts is his lack of power. From old plantations of the South to newer ghettos of the North, the Negro has been confined to a life of voicelessness and powerlessness. Stripped of the right to make decisions concerning his life and destiny he has been subject to the authoritarian and sometimes whimsical decisions of this white power structure. The plantation and ghetto were created by those who had power, both to confine those who had no power and to perpetuate their powerlessness. The problem of transforming the ghetto, therefore, is a problem of power—confrontation of the forces of power demanding change and the forces of power dedicated to the preserving of the status quo. Now power properly understood is nothing but the ability to achieve purpose. It is the strength required to bring about social, political, and economic change. Walter Reuther defined power one day. He said, "Power is the ability of a labor union like the UAW to make the most powerful corporation in the world, General Motors, say, 'Yes' when it wants to say 'No.' That's power."

Now a lot of us are preachers, and all of us have our moral convictions and concerns, and so often have problems with power. There is nothing wrong with power if power is used correctly. You see, what happened is that some of our philosophers got off base. And one of the great problems of history is that the concepts of love and power have usually been contrasted as opposites—polar opposites—so that love is identified with a resignation of power, and power with a denial of love.

It was this misinterpretation that caused Nietzsche, who was a philosopher of the will to power, to reject the Christian concept of love. It was this same misinterpretation which induced Christian theologians to reject the Nietzschean philosophy of the will to power in the name of the Christian idea of love. Now, we've got to get this thing right. What is needed is a realization that power without love is reckless and abusive, and love without power is sentimental and anemic. Power at its best is love implementing the demands of justice, and justice at its best is power correcting everything that stands against love. And this is what we must see as we move on. What has happened is that we have had it wrong and confused in our own country, and this has led Negro Americans in the past to seek their goals through power devoid of love and conscience.

This is leading a few extremists today to advocate for Negroes the same destructive and conscienceless power that they have justly abhorred in whites. It is precisely this collision of immoral power with powerless morality which constitutes the major crisis of our times.

We must develop a program that will drive the nation to a guaranteed annual income. Now, early in this century this proposal would have been greeted with ridicule and denunciation, as destructive of initiative and responsibility. At that time economic status was considered the measure of the individual's ability and talents. And, in the thinking of that day, the absence of worldly goods indicated a want of industrious habits and moral fiber. We've come a long way in our understanding of human motivation and of the blind operation of our economic system. Now we realize that dislocations in the market operations of our economy and the prevalence of discrimination thrust people into idleness and bind them in constant or frequent unemployment against their will. Today the poor are less often dismissed, I hope, from our consciences by being branded as inferior or incompetent. We also know that no matter how dynamically the economy develops and expands, it does not eliminate all poverty.

The problem indicates that our emphasis must be twofold. We must create full employment or we must create incomes. People must be made consumers by one method or the other. Once they are placed in this position we need to be concerned that the potential of the individual is not wasted. New forms of work that enhance the social good will have to be devised for those for whom traditional jobs are not available. In 1879 Henry George anticipated this state of affairs when he wrote *Progress and Poverty*:

The fact is that the work which improves the condition of mankind, the work which extends knowledge and increases power and enriches literature and elevates thought, is not done to secure a living. It is not the work of slaves driven to their tasks either by the task, by the taskmaster, or by animal necessity. It is the work of men who somehow find a form of work that brings a security for its own sake and a state of society where want is abolished.

Work of this sort could be enormously increased, and we are likely to find that the problems of housing and education, instead of preceding the elimination of poverty, will themselves be affected if poverty is first abolished. The poor transformed into purchasers will do a great deal on their own to alter housing decay. Negroes who have a double disability will have a greater effect on discrimination when they have the additional weapon of cash to use in their struggle.

Beyond these advantages, a host of positive psychological changes inevitably will result from widespread economic security. The dignity of the individual will flourish when the decisions concerning his life are in his own hands, when he has the means to seek self-improvement. Personal conflicts among husbands, wives, and children will diminish when the unjust measurement of human worth on the scale of dollars is eliminated.

Now our country can do this. John Kenneth Galbraith said that a guaranteed annual income could be done for about twenty billion dollars a year. And I say to you today, that if our nation can spend thirty-five billion dollars a year to fight an unjust, evil war in Vietnam, and twenty billion dollars to put a man on the moon, it can spend billions of dollars to put God's children on their own two feet right here on earth.

Now, let me say briefly that we must reaffirm our commitment to nonviolence. I want to stress this. The futility of violence in the struggle for racial justice has been tragically etched in all the recent Negro riots. Yesterday, I tried to analyze the riots and deal with their causes. Today I want to give the other side. There is certainly something painfully sad about a riot. One sees screaming youngsters and angry adults fighting hopelessly and aimlessly against impossible odds. And deep down within them, you can see a desire for self-destruction, a kind of suicidal longing.

Occasionally Negroes contend that the 1965 Watts riot and the other riots in various cities represented effective civil rights action. But those who express this view always end up with stumbling words when asked what concrete gains have been won as a result. At best, the riots have produced a little additional antipoverty money allotted by frightened government officials, and a few water-sprinklers to cool the children of the ghettos. It is something like improving the food in the prison while the people remain securely incarcerated behind bars. Nowhere have the riots won any concrete improvement such as have the organized protest demonstrations. When one tries to pin down advocates of violence as to what acts would be effective, the answers are blatantly illogical. Sometimes they talk of overthrowing racist state and local governments and they talk about guerrilla warfare. They fail to see that no internal revolution has ever succeeded in overthrowing a government by violence unless the government had already lost the allegiance and effective control of its armed forces. Anyone in his right mind knows that this will not happen in the United States. In a violent racial situation, the power structure has the local police, the state troopers, the National Guard and, finally, the army to call on—all of which are predominantly white. Furthermore, few if any violent revolutions have been successful unless the violent minority had the sympathy and support of the nonresistant majority. Castro may have had only a few Cubans actually fighting with him up in the hills, but he could never have overthrown the Batista regime unless he had the sympathy of the vast majority of Cuban people.

It is perfectly clear that a violent revolution on the part of American blacks would find no sympathy and support from the white population and very little from the majority of the Negroes themselves. This is no time for romantic illusions and empty philosophical debates about freedom. This is a time for action. What is needed is a strategy for change, a tactical program that will bring the Negro into the mainstream of American life as quickly as possible. So far, this has only been offered by the nonviolent movement. Without recognizing this we will end up with solutions that don't solve, answers that don't answer, and explanations that don't explain.

And so I say to you today that I still stand by nonviolence. And I am still convinced that it is the most potent weapon available to the Negro in his struggle for justice in this country. And the other thing is that I am concerned about a better world. I'm concerned about justice. I'm concerned about brotherhood. I'm concerned about truth. And when one is concerned about these, he can never advocate violence. For through violence you may murder a murderer but you can't murder murder. Through violence you may murder a liar but you can't establish truth. Through violence you may murder a hater, but you can't murder hate. Darkness cannot put out darkness. Only light can do that.

And I say to you, I have also decided to stick to love. For I know that love is ultimately the only answer to mankind's problems. And I'm going to talk about it everywhere I go. I know it isn't popular to talk about it in some circles today. I'm not talking about emotional bosh when I talk about love, I'm talking about a strong, demanding love. And I have seen too much hate. I've seen too much hate on the faces of sheriffs in the South. I've seen hate on the faces of too many Klansmen and too many White Citizens Councilors in the South to want to hate myself, because every time I see it, I know that it does something to their faces and their personalities and I say to myself that hate is too great a burden to bear. I have decided to love. If you are seeking the highest good, I think you can find it through love. And the beautiful thing is that we are moving against wrong when we do it, because John was right, God is love. He who hates does not know God, but he who has love has the key that unlocks the door to the meaning of ultimate reality.

I want to say to you as I move to my conclusion, as we talk about "Where do we go from here," that we honestly face the fact that the movement must address itself to the question of restructuring the whole of American society. There are forty million poor people here. And one day we must ask the question, "Why are there forty million poor people in America?" And when you begin to ask that question, you are raising questions about the economic system, about a broader distribution of wealth. When you ask that question, you begin to question the capitalistic economy. And I'm simply saying that more and more, we've got to begin to ask questions about the whole society. We are called upon to help the discouraged beggars in life's marketplace. But one day we must come to see that an edifice which produces beggars need restructuring. It means that questions must be raised. You see, my friends, when you deal with this, you begin to ask the question, "Who owns the oil?" You begin to ask the question, "Who owns the iron ore?" You begin to ask the question, "Why is it that people have to pay water bills in a world that is two-thirds water?" These are questions that must be asked.

Now, don't think that you have me in a "bind" today. I'm not talking about communism.

What I'm saying to you this morning is that communism forgets that life is individual. Capitalism forgets that life is social, and the kingdom of brotherhood is found neither in the thesis of communism nor the antithesis of capitalism but in a higher synthesis. It is found in a higher synthesis that combines the truths of both. Now, when I say question that whole society, it means ultimately coming to see that the problem of racism, the problem of economic exploitation, and the problem of war are all tied together. These are the triple evils that are interrelated.

If you will let me be a preacher just a little bit—One night, a juror came to Jesus and he wanted to know what he could do to be saved. Jesus didn't get bogged down in the kind of isolated approach of what he shouldn't do. Jesus didn't say, "Now Nicodemus, you must stop lying." He didn't say, "Nicodemus, you must stop cheating if you are doing that." He didn't say, "Nicodemus, you must not commit adultery." He didn't say, "Nicodemus, now you must stop drinking liquor if you are doing that excessively." He said something altogether different, because Jesus realized something basic—that if a man will lie, he will steal. And if a man will steal, he will kill. So instead of just getting bogged down in one thing, Jesus looked at him and said, "Nicodemus, you must be born again."

He said, in other words, "Your whole structure must be changed." A nation that will keep people in slavery for 244 years will "thingify" them—make them things. Therefore they will exploit them, and poor people generally, economically. And a nation that will exploit economically will have to have foreign investments and everything else, and will have to use its military might to protect them. All of these problems are tied together. What I am saying today is that we must go from this convention and say, "America, you must be born again!"

So, I conclude by saying again that we have a task and let us go out with a "divine dissatisfaction." Let us be dissatisfied until America will no longer have a high blood pressure of creeds and an anemia of deeds. Let us be dissatisfied until the tragic walls that separate the outer city of wealth and comfort and the inner city of poverty and despair shall be crushed by the battering rams of the forces of justice. Let us be dissatisfied until those that live on the outskirts of hope are brought into the metropolis of daily security. Let us be dissatisfied until slums are cast into the junk heaps of history, and every family is living in a decent sanitary home. Let us be dissatisfied until the dark yesterdays of segregated schools will be transformed into bright tomorrows of quality, integrated education. Let us be dissatisfied until integration is not seen as a problem but as an opportunity to participate in the beauty of diversity. Let us be dissatisfied until men and women, however black they may be, will be judged on the basis of the content of their character and not on the basis of the color of their skin. Let us be dissatisfied. Let us be dissatisfied until every state capitol houses a governor who will do justly, who will love mercy and who will walk humbly with his God. Let us be dissatisfied until from every city hall, justice will roll, down like waters and righteousness like a mighty stream. Let us be dissatisfied until that day when the lion and the lamb shall lie down together, and every man will sit under his own vine and fig tree and none shall be afraid. Let us be dissatisfied. And men will recognize that out of one blood God made all men to dwell upon the face of the earth. Let us be dissatisfied until that day when nobody will shout "White Power!"—when nobody will shout "Black Power!"—but everybody will talk about God's power and human power.

I must confess, my friends, the road ahead will not always be smooth. There will be still rocky places of frustration and meandering points of bewilderment. There will be inevitable setbacks here and there. There will be those moments when the buoyancy of hope will be transformed into the fatigue of despair. Our dreams will sometimes be shattered and our ethereal hopes blasted. We may again with tear-drenched eyes have to stand before the bier of some courageous civil rights worker whose life will be snuffed out by the dastardly acts of bloodthirsty mobs. Difficult and painful as it is, we must walk on in the days ahead with an audacious faith in the future. And as we continue our charted course, we may gain consolation in the words so nobly left by that great black bard who was also a great freedom fighter of yesterday, James Weldon Johnson:

> Stony the road we trod,
> Bitter the chastening rod
> Felt in the days
> When hope unborn had died.
>
> Yet with a steady beat,
> Have not our weary feet
> Come to the place
> For which our fathers sighed?
>
> We have come over the way
> That with tears hath been watered.
> We have come treading our paths
> Through the blood of the slaughtered,

> Out from the gloomy past,
> Till now we stand at last
> Where the bright gleam
> Of our bright star is cast.

Let this affirmation be our ringing cry. It will give us the courage to face the uncertainties of the future. It will give our tired feet new strength as we continue our forward stride toward the city of freedom. When our days become dreary with low-hovering clouds of despair, and when our nights become darker than a thousand midnights, let us remember that there is a creative force in this universe, working to pull down the gigantic mountains of evil, a power that is able to make a way out of no way and transform dark yesterdays into bright tomorrows. Let us realize the arc of the moral universe is long but it bends toward justice.

Let us realize that William Cullen Bryant is right: "Truth crushed to earth will rise again." Let us go out realizing that the Bible is right: "Be not deceived, God is not mocked. Whatsoever a man soweth, that shall he also reap." This is for hope for the future, and with this faith we will be able to sing in some not too distant tomorrow with a cosmic past tense, "We have overcome, we have overcome, deep in my heart, I did believe we would overcome."

Published in *World View*, April 1972; in James B. Washington, ed., *The Essential Writings and Speeches of Martin Luther King, Jr., op. cit.*, pp. 245–52.

146

"DEEPENING THE AMERICAN CONSCIOUSNESS"

by A. Philip Randolph

In New Orleans in 1968 Randolph was asked his view of the young African-American militant generation. While repeating his opposition to their tactics, he said:

I am persuaded to agree that black militants have been responsible for deepening the American consciousness of the immediacy, magnitude, and danger of the racial crisis in the cities. They have challenged and stirred the American mind and conscience about the exclusion of the cultural achievements of black Americans from the historiography of our

American society. They have vigorously stressed the need for the Negro's interest in self-help. They have accented the search for identity and the Africans' contribution of an ancient glorious historical cultural heritage and endowment to world civilization.

Jervis Anderson, *Randolph* (New York: Harcourt, Brace, 1972), p. 346.

147

UNITY AND MILITANCY FOR FREEDOM AND EQUALITY

by Henry Winston

The chairman of the Communist party—blinded in prison during McCarthyite terror—produced this analysis of conditions facing black people and the nation as the 1960s drew to a close:

The Communist Party, USA, has a proud record of more than forty years of fighting for Negro freedom. For years, almost alone, it led the struggle in the Deep South, under conditions comparable to those faced in Hitler Germany, for full freedom, for the right of black people to vote, to organize, to have equal access to all public places, for the repeal of the poll tax, and for an end to lynching. Many of its members, Negro and white, gave their lives in those early bitter battles.

Benjamin J. Davis, Henry Winston, William L. Patterson, Claude Lightfoot, James W. Ford, Louis Burnham, Claudia Jones, Edward Strong, James E. Jackson, Hosea Hudson, Mildred McAdory, Pettis Perry, Ray Hansborough, Moranda Smith, Cyril Briggs, and Otto Hall—these are but some of the black Communists whose pioneering efforts in the '30s and '40s helped prepare the ground for the great freedom struggles of the '60s.

Scottsboro, Angelo Herndon, the Martinsville Seven, Willie McGee, Rose Lee Ingram, are but a few of the great rallying cries that were later transformed into the battle cries of Selma and Mississippi. In these great traditions, Communists joined in the Scottsboros of the sixties.

We do not claim any special rights for our pioneering efforts, only the right to continue the struggle we will never cease. We frankly admit that we have much to learn from the new courageous leaders who widened and deepened the freedom path from the ground broken in earlier days. But in all modesty, we also offer the rich experiences we have accumulated, to help illuminate the difficult road ahead we must all travel together.

It is in this spirit that we offer our thoughts on some of the crucial problems facing black Americans and, as they do, all Americans.

We, twenty-two million black Americans, have arrived at a point of grave crisis in our history. Clear thinking as well as courage are the needs of the moment. The question posed for us and, indeed, for white America as well is: How shall black people achieve full equality NOW—in these days, not in the dim future of more unborn black generations? Time has run out for leisurely discussion and debate, for "studies" and "reports" by an endless parade of government commissions. The question is on the action agenda now!

It is a question that must be decided by our sober assessment and not by government provocation. And, indeed, we are being provoked.

Rebellions in more than 120 cities against the misery, poverty, and depression in the ghettos are being "studied" in Washington while President Johnson's $74 billion-a-year military budget, including $30 billion for the genocidal war in Vietnam, is hastily rushed through Congress. More riot training for more police and more National Guardsmen; more repressive laws; more racist hysteria whipped up by the press; more police brutality in the black communities, and more than equality in the casualty lists in Vietnam for black soldiers—what are these but the most provocative incitements to violence?

The Real Instigators of Violence

They point to the real instigators of the violence that has erupted in our cities—the men who sit in the White House and in the halls of Congress.

No one—least of all those who have enslaved us for 350 years, who cage us in ghettos, inflict depression and disease upon us, invade and destroy our homes with all the cruel instruments of modern warfare, taunt us by spending billions for bombs and pennies for poverty, and goad us with terror, official violence, and legal lynchings—has the right to caution us to refrain from violence. Twenty-two million black Americans are faced with a struggle for survival. We need ask no one how to defend our inalienable right to live as human beings.

For countless years, countless black people have been lynched and outraged, their basic human rights trampled upon by forces of law and order and by white racist bands, often working as close partners in crime. Today, racist violence against the Negro people has spread to all parts of the United States—Detroit, Watts, and Cicero, as well as Selma, Milwaukee, Newark, Montgomery, and Mississippi. The right, indeed the responsibility, to defend oneself, one's dear ones, one's people, from violent attacks by racists, in or out of uniform, by all means including armed defense if necessary, is inviolable. We support that right.

The continued and increased spread of police brutality against the black community, the growth of the influence of the John Birch Society, the Ku Klux Klan, and racism in the police departments all over the nation, has led to the demand for the right of Negro people to police their communities. We fully support that right.

The Communist Party of the United States, like Communists everywhere, has always affirmed the right of oppressed people to forcibly overthrow an oppressive regime whenever the channels for democratic change are closed to them. That right is also affirmed in the Declaration of Independence. Therefore, there can be no question of the right of the Negro people in the United States to use violence to free themselves from oppression and to win full freedom.

Whether that right to violence should be exercised is determined by time, place, and circumstances, and by a sober estimate of the concrete situation which prevails at the moment. Surely, everyone would prefer to win basic change without the use of force.

Tokenism Will Not Suffice

What is the situation?

The stubborn refusal of the ruling class of our country, and the Johnson Administration in particular, to permit anything but token changes in the unbearable conditions faced by black Americans, especially in the ghettos, despite the massive peaceful demonstrations of recent years, has led to a growing lack of confidence in the possibility to achieve meaningful change through the democratic process.

The meaning of the mass rebellions of 1967 in the black ghettos should be clear: millions of black Americans will no longer live under the condition of the depression '30s while the U.S. boasts of the "affluence" of the '60s.

The failure of most white Americans, including large sections of the liberal and progressive forces, to understand the desperate nature of the crisis in the ghettos, their failure to ally themselves with the black people in their struggle for the necessary radical changes to resolve the crisis, has resulted in an increasing lack of confidence in the ability of white masses to overcome racism and in their readiness to join with black people in the fight for meaningful solutions.

The repeated failure of the Federal government, and those in the cities and state, to take decisive action against the racists who murder and maim black people, has aroused a new awareness of the need for greater reliance on determined self-defense, including armed defense.

The Minutemen, the Birchites, Ku Klux Klan, White Citizens Council, National Riflemen's Association, and American Nazi groups are openly inciting and organizing racial violence with impunity. Alabama's former Governor Wallace is not only given free rein to spread the plague of racist violence, but is rallying the racist and fascist-like forces all over the United States.

Black people, with good cause, smell the flesh-burning stench of the gas chamber in these menacing developments. They have rightly served notice that they have no intention to play the role of passive victims of genocide.

Moreover, an alternative program to violence, radical enough to solve the problems of the ghettos, and possible of achievement, has not been put forward with any conviction.

Furthermore, there is a lack of class consciousness and an understanding of revolutionary tactics, geared to specific U.S. conditions—and not borrowed from other countries—in the ranks of the leadership of the Negro freedom movement. The world liberation struggle of recent years, particularly in Africa, Asia, Latin America, has inspired the determination to fight for full freedom in the United States.

All of these factors have given rise to a new emphasis, on the part of some, on the need for armed struggle particularly in the black ghettos.

Courage is the banner of the fight for black freedom. Communists join all militant black freedom fighters in bearing this banner high. The ghetto uprisings, and countless heroic battles, have made it amply clear that black people are prepared to fight to win full freedom NOW. The task, especially of Negro leaders, is jointly and skillfully to seek the ways to make the best use of our heroic people's militancy. The task is to prevent the power structure, by its provocations, from misusing this militancy and turning it against the black people.

Militancy and Unity—or Guerrilla Tactics

The task ahead is: how to make the most effective use of every position gained, how to exert the utmost skill in rallying allies to our struggle, and in isolating our enemies. It is for this reason we stress courage and clarity of purpose. It is in this spirit that the question of armed struggle should be soberly considered.

Communists believe in the use of violence to achieve political change only when reaction has closed off the channels whereby a majority of the people can realize their objectives by peaceful means. As we see it today, the overwhelming majority of the American people, including black people, are not yet convinced that the system must be changed, much less that it is necessary to do so by armed force.

Armed uprisings for such objectives cannot be undertaken successfully by the black communities alone, no matter how courageously they struggle. They require power allies, in the ranks of the working class— white and black. Therefore, we reject the organizing of armed uprisings in the black communities today. However, it is necessary to issue the warning that there are extremely dangerous pressures to close the channels of democratic process and, in many areas, they have virtually been closed. Should this continue, it would leave the black people no alternative to violent struggle.

We believe that conspiratorial, terroristic actions which are not based upon a program aimed at improving the conditions of life for the masses, and which do not receive the support of the people, are adventurous, provocative, and politically irresponsible, inviting reprisals against the black community. They should, therefore, be rejected.

We also believe that terrorism within the Negro community, directed against so-called Uncle Toms or others who refuse to go along with such tactics is entirely out of place, divisive, and harmful to the struggle for full freedom. It, too, should be rejected.

Although we do not advocate a policy of looting and arson, it is clear that while ghetto uprisings were unable to end the unbearable condition against which the spontaneous revolts were directed, they did achieve certain positive results. These militant actions forcefully exposed to the nation and the entire world the urgent nature of the crisis in the ghettos. They made it painfully clear to many white Americans that life in our great cities will be unbearable for all, unless it is made bearable for the people of the black communities.

Right of Self-Defense Against Organized Violence

Moreover these militant actions have intensified and deepened the mass resistance to the unjust war in Vietnam and inspired to greater militancy the struggle to end it. They greatly stimulated the struggle for Negro representation, spurred the Negro communities to the highest levels of political unity, and contributed to convincing larger sections of the white communities to work for, and accept, black municipal leaders. They have compelled the Administration to respond to the pressure for additional black representation on all levels. Every advance that has been made in Negro representation in the recent period owes much to the message contained in the explosions in the black ghettos in 1967.

However, those who conclude that the task now is to give an organized character to the spontaneous uprisings in the black ghettos gravely misjudge both the mood of the black communities and the relationship of forces such organized armed uprisings would have to contend with. The strength of the 1967 uprisings lay in their spontaneity. It was this quality of the rebellions which rallied the sympathy and support of black communities and jolted large numbers of white Americans into an understanding of the depth of the crisis in the ghettos.

It would be quite a different matter, under present conditions, to win support in the black communities, let alone in the white neighborhoods, for an organized armed uprising. Nor can there be any comparison between the repressive measures employed in the suppression of the spontaneous uprisings, harsh as they were, and the unlimited force that would be used by the ruling class and its government against an organized uprising.

Black communities, of course, have the right to take necessary measures to defend themselves from invasion and assault by armed forces. But the real task at hand is to rally nationwide support of all truly democratic white Americans, especially white workers, to stop the annual "summer slaughter" and to aid the struggle for survival of black Americans.

Inspiring Mass Militancy in Struggle

The Open Letter of the Communist Party, USA, addressed to the President before the "hot summer" of 1967 exploded, called for "united action of all forces on the Left regardless of differences." It called for the "most sacrificing all-out efforts of every Communist to work tirelessly to unite Americans of conscience, black and white, to act at once."

The need for such united struggle cannot wait for another "hot summer." It must be directed NOW toward the elimination of the unbearable conditions that will breed not only more hot summers but even colder winters.

There is an urgent need for organized, militant, and united struggle in every black community in the United States. Its arsenal of tactical weapons should include any and all forms of struggle that will most effectively and most speedily advance the fight for full freedom: mass marches, demonstrations, massive militant civil disobedience, boycotts, and strikes. It should include sit-ins, sit-downs, and sit-outs, and armed defense when necessary. It should include black community mass marches to the polls to elect Negro mayors, U.S. Senators, Congressmen, and Negro public officials on every level.

The door should be wide open to any new and effective forms of struggle forged in the fires of the freedom fight. The only test for tactical weapons of the freedom struggle should be: will they advance or set back the struggle? Will they unite or divide the mass of the black people? Will they aid in winning allies or isolating us?

Militancy, the indispensable ingredient for all effective struggles, has to meet the test. The courage of brave individuals has played, and can play, a significant role in today's freedom struggle. But the militancy of individuals lies in the ability to inspire *mass* militancy. It can never be a substitute for it. Individual courage, therefore, must be synchronized with those forms of struggle to which the mass of black people are ready to respond at any given stage of the struggle.

There is an urgent need, too, for consideration of forms of organization which will unite the people in the black communities and coordinate the communities themselves on a city, state, and national level. The aim should be effectively to bring to bear on the power structure the collective will of the black people, to organize and direct mass actions on every front and at every level.

The objective should be to unite the black communities politically, and to make full use of their strategic position in our cities. From such positions of strength they can, in alliance with other oppressed minorities and progressive sections of the white population, struggle effectively for unprecedented new levels of Negro representation and, thereby, drastically alter political relationships in the country.

Through united action, an effective fight can be waged for black control of black communities, for federal, state, and city responsibility to provide billions for the reconstruction and rehabilitation of the black communities, placing them on a par with the rest of the nation. Jobs, at all skills, in such reconstruction, should go to the people of the black communities, especially to the youth, and at union wages.

To inspire the struggles of today, black communities should be united in commemorating our black heroes, among them Dr. W. E. B. Du Bois and former New York City Councilman Benjamin J. Davis.

Unity of the black communities can truly spell black power.

It is wrong to conclude, as some do, from the stubborn refusal of the power structure and the Johnson Administration to deal adequately with the crisis in the black ghettos, that the channels for democratic change are closed to the black people. It is true, they are being blocked by racist and reactionary forces who are determined to close them. But they are not yet closed. On the contrary, the Negro people have achieved their strongest political position in our country precisely during the past decade.

This is the meaning of the tremendous increase in voter registration in the South, notably in Mississippi. This is the meaning of the Mississippi Freedom Democratic Party—the symbol of new politics in the country. This is the significance of the new level of black-white unity achieved at the convention of the National Conference of New Politics that has given birth to the "Spirit of Chicago."

Keep the Door of Democracy Open

Thus the fateful question: will the channels of democracy be closed to the black people?—from which would result, inevitably, that it would be closed to all Americans—has not as yet been answered in the affirmative. On the contrary, conditions exist for opening wider the door of democracy. This requires a militant fight resolutely to combat every fascist-like attempt to close them. This is the path not only toward winning greater partial aims, but to preparing the best grounds for the fight for revolutionary change—for the establishment of a socialist society.

The costly experience of Hitler fascism should serve to remind revolutionaries, and democrats as well, of the terrible price paid for the failure to defend each precious democratic right to the bitter end.

Many white people, frustrated by the dangerous drift to disaster of our cities, have responded with fear to the uprisings in the black ghettos. The racists have been quick to seize upon these fears to inflame deeply imbedded prejudices that exist. Thus, a serious situation is developing which can turn our streets into bloody battlegrounds of racist strife.

But, it should also be noted, that among increasing numbers of white people there is evident significant new levels of understanding of the real meaning of full equality for black people. This is reflected in the readiness of large numbers of whites to accept and work for increased black representation. The basis for achieving higher levels of black-white unity are present today.

This is especially so because the crisis in the black ghettos has served to put the spotlight on the crisis of our cities. There is no way of resolving one crisis without at the same time resolving the other. Thus, life itself has joined the fate of the black communities with the fate of our cities, including the white communities. Of course, the answer to both crises lies in Washington, in changing federal responsibilities to the cities, to provide adequate funds for decent homes, for schools, hospitals, and transit.

Unity of Black and White Around Common Interests

Above all the answer lies in drastically changing our nation's priorities: from waging aggressive war to providing for the long-neglected needs of peace-time living. That requires the speedy ending of the unjust war in Vietnam.

More and more Americans, white as well as Negro, have come to recognize the interrelation of three crises: the ghetto, our cities, and the war in Vietnam. An irresistible force can be brought into being by uniting the mass of Americans to fight for the resolution of all three unbearable crises. This struggle, by uniting white and black around their common interests, can weaken the dangerous inroads of the racists in the white communities. It is toward the development of this irresistible force that black and white progressives, especially revolutionaries, should bend their efforts.

To achieve such unity in struggle, it is incumbent upon white progressives and revolutionaries to conduct a consistent and courageous battle against racism in their own communities, shops, offices, and schools.

The struggle for black freedom faces not only great trials but great opportunities. Both aspects of the present situation have to be grasped. More, they have to be acted upon, and acted upon unitedly, in time to make the 1968 elections the arena for great and victorious struggles.

Political Affairs, February 1968, pp. 1–9.

148

THE PLATFORM OF THE BLACK PANTHER PARTY

by Bobby Seale

Chairman Bobby Seale speaks, at length:

"Now, when we first organized the Black Panther Party for Self-Defense, Huey said, 'Bobby, we're going to draw up a basic platform...that the mothers who struggled hard to raise us, that the fathers who worked hard to feed us, that the young brothers in school who come out of school semiliterate, saying and reading broken words, that all of these can read....'

"Huey said, 'First we want freedom, we want power to determine the destiny of our black communities.

" 'Number two: We want full employment for our people.

" 'Number three: We want housing fit for shelter of human beings.

" 'Number four: We want all black men to be exempt from military service.

" 'Number five: We want decent education for our black people in our communities that teaches us the true nature of this decadent, racist society and that teaches black people and our young black brothers and sisters their place in the society, for if they don't know their place in society and in the world, they can't relate to anything else.

" 'Number six: We want an end to the robbery by the white racist businessmen of black people in their community.

" 'Number seven: We want an immediate end to police brutality and murder of black people.

" 'Number eight: We want all black men held in city, county, state, and Federal jails to be released because they have not had a fair trial because they've been tried by all-white juries, and that's just like being tried in Nazi Germany, being a Jew.

" 'Number nine: We want black people when brought to trial to be tried by members of their peer group, and a peer being one who comes from the same economic, social, religious, historical, and racial background...they would have to choose black people from the black community to sit up on the jury. They would have to choose some of them mothers who have been working twenty years in Miss Anne's kitchen, scrubbing floors like my mother has done. They'd have to choose some of them hard-working fathers...some of those brothers who stand on the block out there wondering where they're going to get a gig....'

"And number ten: Huey said, let's summarize it: 'We want land, we want bread, we want housing, we want clothing, we want education, we want justice, and we want peace.'"

There is a more formal version of the Panthers' "ten points" than the one quoted, which is from a speech by Seale in February 1968; the content, however, is the same, and the formal version is principally notable because Point Ten includes, word for word, the Declaration of Independence.

From the *Black Panther,* February 1968, quoted in Gene Marine, *The Black Panther,* (New York; Signet Books, 1969), pp. 35–36. The platform was drafted in 1966 by Huey Newton and Bobby Seale.

The immediate background for this was the massacre by police of students at South Carolina State College in Orangeburg in February 1968. The students were protesting various racist acts; thirty-three students were hit by gunfire from police, of whom three died. See Clayborne Carson, *op. cit.,* pp. 249–50. A full account is by Jack Bass and Jack Nelson, *The Orangeburg Massacre,* rev. ed. (Macon, Ga.: Mercer University Press, 1993).

149

HONORING DR. DU BOIS

by Martin Luther King, Jr.

On February 23, 1968—the 100th birthday of W. E. B. Du Bois—an evening in his honor, sponsored by *Freedomways,* was held in Carnegie Hall in New York City. The centennial address was delivered by the Nobel Laureate Dr. King. In less than two months, Dr. King was assassinated. The final section of this address, indicating the radicalism that marked King's last years and characterized Du Bois for almost all his life, follows:

And yet, with all his pride and spirit he did not make a mystique out of blackness. He was proud of his people, not because their color endowed them with some vague greatness but because their concrete achievements in struggle had advanced humanity and he saw and loved progressive humanity in all its hues, black, white, yellow, red, and brown.

Above all he did not content himself with hurling invectives for emotional release and then to retire into smug passive satisfaction. History had taught him it is not enough for people to be angry—the supreme task is to organize and unite people so that their anger becomes a transforming force. It was never possible to know where the scholar Du Bois ended and the organizer Du Bois began. The two qualities in him were a single unified force.

This life style of Dr. Du Bois is the most important quality this generation of Negroes needs to emulate. The educated Negro who is not really part of us and the angry militant who fails to organize us have nothing in common with Dr. Du Bois. He exemplified black power in achievement and he organized black power in action. It was no abstract slogan to him.

We cannot talk of Dr. Du Bois without recognizing that he was a radical all of his life. Some people would like to ignore the fact that he was a Communist in his later years. It is worth noting that Abraham Lincoln warmly welcomed the support of Karl Marx during the Civil War and corresponded with him freely. In contemporary life the English speaking world has no difficulty with the fact that Sean O'Casey was a literary giant of the twentieth century and a Communist or that Pablo Neruda is generally considered the greatest living poet though he also served in the Chilean Senate as a Communist. It is time to cease muting the fact that Dr. Du Bois was a genius and chose to be a Communist. Our irrational obsessive anticommunism has led us into too many quagmires to be retained as if it were a mode of scientific thinking.

In closing it would be well to remind white America of its debt to Dr. Du Bois. When they corrupted Negro history they distorted American history because Negroes are too big a part of the building of this nation to be written out of it without destroying scientific history. White America, drenched with lies about Negroes, has lived too long in a fog of ignorance. Dr. Du Bois gave them a gift of truth for which they should eternally be indebted to him.

Negroes have heavy tasks today. We were partially liberated and then re-enslaved. We have to fight again on old battlefields but our confidence is greater, our vision is clearer, and our ultimate victory surer because of the contributions a militant, passionate black giant left behind him.

Dr. Du Bois has left us but he has not died. The spirit of freedom is not buried in the grave of the valiant. He will be with us when we go to Washington in April to demand our right to life, liberty, and the pursuit of happiness.

We have to go to Washington because they have declared an armistice in the war on poverty while squandering billions to expand a senseless, cruel, unjust war in Vietnam. We will go there, we will demand to be heard, and we will stay until the administration responds. If this means forcible repression of our movement, we will confront it, for we have done this before. If this means scorn or ridicule, we will embrace it for that is what America's poor now receive. If it means jail we accept it willingly, for the millions of poor already are imprisoned by exploitation and discrimination.

Dr. Du. Bois would be in the front ranks of the peace movement today. He would readily see the parallel between American support of the corrupt and despised Thieu-Ky regime and northern support to the southern slavemasters in 1876. The CIA scarcely exaggerates, indeed it is surprisingly honest, when it calculates for Congress that the war in Vietnam can persist for 100 years. People deprived of their freedom do not give up—Negroes have been fighting more than a hundred years and even if the date of full emancipation is uncertain, what is explicitly certain is that the struggle for it will endure.

In conclusion let me say that Dr. Du Bois' greatest virtue was his committed empathy with all the oppressed and his divine dissatisfaction with all forms of injustice. Today we are still challenged to be dissatisfied. Let us be dissatisfied until every man can have food and material necessities for his body, culture and education for his mind, freedom and human dignity for his spirit. Let us be dissatisfied until rat-infested, vermin-filled slums will be a thing of a dark past and every family will have a decent sanitary house in which to live. Let us be dissatisfied until the empty stomachs of Mississippi are filled and the idle industries of Appalachia are revitalized. Let us be dissatisfied until brotherhood is no longer a meaningless word at the end of a prayer but the first order of business on every legislative agenda. Let us be dissatisfied until our brother of the Third World—Asia, Africa, and Latin America—will no longer be the victim of imperialist exploitation, but will be lifted from the long night of poverty, illiteracy, and disease. Let us be dissatisfied until this pending cosmic elegy will be transformed into a creative psalm of peace and "justice will roll down like waters from a mighty stream."

Freedomways 8 (Spring 1968) 104–11; published in part.

150

"THE UGLY ATMOSPHERE"

by Martin Luther King, Jr.

Early in 1968, there was what a *New York Times* reporter called a "burst of violence [which] was not a particularly severe outbreak, as things go nowadays." In it an eighteen-year old student was killed and a number of other black youths "were beaten and gassed." This occurred in Memphis on March 28, a week prior to the murder of King. After this "outburst" King said:

Riots are here. Riots are part of the ugly atmosphere of our society. I cannot guarantee that riots will not take place this summer. I can only guarantee that our demonstrations will not be violent... if riots take place it will not be the responsibility of Martin Luther King or the Southern Christian Leadership Conference.

Walter Rugaber, from Memphis, *New York Times,* Sunday, March 31, 1968, p. E2.

151

"I SEE THE PROMISED LAND"

by Martin Luther King, Jr.

This is the conclusion of Dr. King's last sermon, delivered on April 3, 1968, at the Mason Temple in Memphis. The Mason Temple is the headquarters of the Church of God in Christ, the largest African-American pentecostal denomination in the United States.

Let us rise up tonight with a greater readiness. Let us stand with a greater determination. And let us move on in these powerful days, these days of challenge to make America what it ought to be. We have an opportunity to make America a better nation. And I want to thank God, once more, for allowing me to be here with you.

You know, several years ago, I was in New York City autographing the first book that I had written. And while sitting there autographing books, a demented black woman came up. The only question I heard from her was, "Are you Martin Luther King?"

And I was looking down writing, and I said yes. And the next minute I felt something beating on my chest. Before I knew it I had been stabbed by this demented woman. I was rushed to Harlem Hospital. It was a dark Saturday afternoon. And that blade had gone through, and the X-rays revealed that the tip of the blade was on the edge of my aorta, the main artery. And once that's punctured, you drown in your own blood—that's the end of you.

It came out in the *New York Times* the next morning, that if I had sneezed, I would have died. Well, about four days later, they allowed me, after the operation, after my chest had been opened, and the blade had been taken out, to move around in the wheelchair in the hospital. They allowed me to read some of the mail that came in, and from all over the states, and the world, kind letters came in. I read a few, but one of them I will never forget. I had received one from the President and Vice-President. I've forgotten what those telegrams said. I'd received a visit and a letter from the Governor of New York, but I've forgotten what the letter said. But there was another letter that came from a little girl, a young girl who was a student at the White Plains High School. And I looked at that letter, and I'll never forget it. It said simply, "Dear Dr. King: I am a ninth-grade student at the White Plains High School." She said, "While it should not matter, I would like to mention that I am a white girl. I read in the paper of your misfortune, and of your suffering. And I read that if you had sneezed, you would have died. And I'm simply writing you to say that I'm so happy that you didn't sneeze."

And I want to say tonight, I want to say that I am happy that I didn't sneeze. Because if I had sneezed, I wouldn't have been around here in 1960, when students all over the South started sitting-in at lunch counters. And I knew that as they were sitting in, they were really standing up for the best in the American dream. And taking the whole nation back to those great wells of democracy which were dug deep by the Founding Fathers in the Declaration of Independence and the Constitution. If I had sneezed, I wouldn't have been around in 1962, when Negroes in Albany, Georgia, decided to straighten their back up. And whenever men and women straighten their backs up, they are going somewhere, because a man can't ride your back unless it is bent. If I had sneezed, I wouldn't have been here in 1963, when the black people of Birmingham, Alabama, aroused the conscience of this nation, and brought into being the Civil

Rights Bill. If I had sneezed, I wouldn't have had a chance later that year, in August, to try to tell Americans about a dream that I had had. If I had sneezed, I wouldn't have been down in Selma, Alabama, to see the great movement there. If I had sneezed, I wouldn't have been in Memphis to see a community rally around those brothers and sisters who are suffering. I'm so happy that I didn't sneeze.

And they were telling me, now it doesn't matter now. It really doesn't matter what happens now. I left Atlanta this morning, and as we got started on the plane, there were six of us, the pilot said over the public address system, "We are sorry for the delay, but we have Dr. Martin Luther King on the plane. And to be sure that all of the bags were checked, and to be sure that nothing would be wrong with the plane, we had to check out everything carefully. And we've had the plane protected and guarded all night."

And then I got into Memphis. And some began to say the threats, or talk about the threats that were out. What would happen to me from some of our sick white brothers?

Well, I don't know what will happen now. We've got some difficult days ahead. But it doesn't matter with me now. Because I've been to the mountaintop. And I don't mind. Like anybody, I would like to live a long life. Longevity has its place. But I'm not concerned about that now. I just want to do God's will. And He's allowed me to go up to the mountain. And I've looked over. And I've seen the promised land. I may not get there with you. But I want you to know tonight, that we, as a people will get to the promised land. And I'm happy, tonight. I'm not worried about anything. I'm not fearing any man. Mine eyes have seen the glory of the coming of the Lord.

J. M. Washington, ed., *op cit.*, pp. 285–86.

152

WARNING MARTIN LUTHER KING, JR.

by Roy Wilkins

One day during the spring of 1968 I flew to Cleveland on a speech and inspection tour. I had my briefcase in hand and my raincoat over my arm and I was walking down one of the long corridors at the airport when I bumped into Dr. King. He, too, was traveling through Cleveland, and he had three very large men at his side.

"Roy," he called out in surprise, "are you traveling all alone?"

"Yes," I answered, not thinking much about it one way or another.

"I don't think you should do that," he said. "It's too dangerous. You should always have someone with you."

We talked for a few minutes, and as he and his men walked off, I watched them make their way through the airport crowds. "Have things really gotten that bad?" I asked myself. Then I shook off the depressing thought, grabbed a cab, and drove into town.

Not long afterward, from across the street of the Lorraine Motel in Memphis, James Earl Ray fixed Dr. King in the crosshairs of his telescopic sight and squeezed a trigger. That rifle shot was my answer.

Roy Wilkins, *op. cit.*, p. 326.

153

SHOWDOWN FOR NONVIOLENCE

by Martin Luther King, Jr.

In an article published eight days after his assassination, Dr. King made explicit the profound social transformation he desired and the policy of mass black-white unity, especially of the poor, which he believed might bring it about.

The policy of the federal government is to play Russian roulette with riots; it is prepared to gamble with another summer of disaster. Despite two consecutive summers of violence, not a single basic cause of riots has been corrected. All of the misery that stoked the flames of rage and rebellion remains undiminished. With unemployment, intolerable housing, and discriminatory education a scourge in Negro ghettos, Congress and the administration still tinker with trivial, halfhearted measures.

Yet only a few years ago, there was discernible, if limited, progress through nonviolence. Each year, a wholesome, vibrant Negro self-confidence was taking shape. The fact is inescapable that the tactic of nonviolence, which had then dominated the thinking of the civil rights movement, has in the last two years not been playing its transforming role. Nonviolence was a creative doctrine in the South because it checkmated the rabid segregationists who were thirsting for an opportunity to physically crush Negroes. Nonviolent direct action enabled the Negro to take to the streets in active protest, but it muzzled the guns of the oppressor because even he could not shoot down in daylight unarmed men, women, and children. This is the reason there was less loss of life in ten years of southern protest than in ten days of northern riots.

Today, the northern cities have taken on the conditions we faced in the South. Police, national guard, and other armed bodies are feverishly preparing for repression. They can be curbed not by unorganized resort to force by desperate Negroes but only by a massive wave of militant nonviolence. Nonviolence was never more relevant as an effective tactic than today for the North. It also may be the instrument of our national salvation.

I agree with the President's National Advisory Commission on Civil Disorders that our nation is splitting into two hostile societies and that the chief destructive cutting edge is white racism. We need, above all, effective means to force Congress to act resolutely—but means that do not involve the use of violence. For us in the Southern Christian Leadership Conference, violence is not only morally repugnant, it is pragmatically barren. We feel there is an alternative both to violence and to useless timid supplications for justice. We cannot condone either riots or the equivalent evil of passivity. And we know that nonviolent militant action in Selma and Birmingham awakened the conscience of white America and brought a moribund, insensitive Congress to life.

The time has come for a return to mass nonviolent protest. Accordingly, we are planning a series of such demonstrations this spring and summer, to begin in Washington, D.C. They will have Negro and white participation, and they will seek to benefit the poor of both races.

We will call on the government to adopt the measures recommended by its own commission. To avoid, in the commission's words, the tragedy of "continued polarization of the American community and ultimately the destruction of basic democratic values," we must have "national action—compassionate, massive, and sustained, backed by the resources of the most powerful and the richest nation on earth."

The demonstrations we have planned are of deep concern to me, and I want to spell out at length what we will do, try to do, and believe in. My staff and I have worked three months on the planning. We believe that if this campaign succeeds, nonviolence will once again be the dominant instrument for social change—and jobs and income will be put in the hands of the tormented poor. If it fails, nonviolence will be discredited, and the country may be plunged into holocaust—a tragedy deepened by the awareness that it was avoidable.

We are taking action after sober reflection. We have learned from bitter experience that our government does not correct a race problem until it is confronted directly and dramatically. We also know, as official Washington may not, that the flash point of Negro rage is close at hand.

Our Washington demonstration will resemble Birmingham and Selma in duration. It will be more than a one-day protest—it can persist for two or three months. In the earlier Alabama actions, we set no time limits. We simply said we were going to struggle there until we got a response from the nation on the issues involved. We are saying the same thing about Washington. This will be an attempt to bring a kind of Selma-like movement, Birmingham-like movement, into being, substantially around the economic issues. Just as we dealt with the social problem of segregation through massive demonstrations, and we dealt with the political problem—the denial of the right to vote—through massive demonstrations, we are now trying to deal with the economic problems—the right to live, to have a job and income—through massive protest. It will be a Selma-like movement on economic issues.

We remember that when we began direct action in Birmingham and Selma, there was a thunderous chorus that sought to discourage us. Yet today, our achievements in these cities and the reforms that radiated from them are hailed with pride by all.

We've selected fifteen areas—ten cities and five rural districts—from which we have recruited our initial cadre. We will have two hundred poor people from each area. That would be about three thousand to get the protests going and set the pattern. They are important, particularly in terms of maintaining nonviolence. They are being trained in this discipline now.

In areas where we are recruiting, we are also stimulating activities in conjunction with the Washington protest. We are planning to have some of these people march to Washington. We may have half the group from Mississippi, for example, go to Washington and begin the protest there, while the other half begins walking. They would flow across the South, joining the Alabama group, the Georgia group, right on up through South and North Carolina and Virginia. We hope that the sound and sight of a growing mass of poor people walking slowly toward Washington will have a positive, dramatic effect on Congress.

Once demonstrations start, we feel, there will be spontaneous supporting activity taking place across the country. This has usually happened in campaigns like this, and I think it will again. I think people will start moving. The reasons we didn't choose California and other areas out West are distance and the problem of transporting marchers that far. But part of our strategy is to have spontaneous demonstrations take place on the West Coast.

A nationwide nonviolent movement is very important. We know from past experience that Congress and the president won't do anything until you develop a movement around which people of goodwill can find a way to put pressure on them, because it really means breaking that coalition in Congress. It's still a coalition-dominated, rural-dominated, basically southern Congress. There are southerners there with committee chairmanships, and they are going to stand in the way of progress as long as they can. They get enough right-wing midwestern or northern Republicans to go along with them.

This really means making the movement powerful enough, dramatic enough, morally appealing enough, so that people of goodwill, the churches, labor, liberals, intellectuals, students, poor people themselves begin to put pressure on congressmen to the point that they can no longer elude our demands.

Our idea is to dramatize the whole economic problem of the poor. We feel there's a great deal that we need to do to appeal to Congress itself. The early demonstrations will be more geared toward educational purposes—to educate the nation on the nature of the problem and the crucial aspects of it, the tragic conditions that we confront in the ghettos.

After that, if we haven't gotten a response from Congress, we will branch out. And we are honest enough to feel that we aren't going to get any instantaneous results from Congress, knowing its recalcitrant nature on this issue, and knowing that so many resources and energies are being used in Vietnam rather than on the domestic situation. So we don't have any illusions about moving Congress in two or three weeks. But we do feel that, by starting in Washington, centering on Congress and departments of the government, we will be able to do a real educational job.

We call our demonstration a campaign for jobs and income because we feel that the economic question is the most crucial that black people, and poor people generally, are confronting. There is a literal depression in the Negro community. When you have mass unemployment in the Negro community, it's called a social problem; when you have mass unemployment in the white community, it's called a depression. The fact is, there is a major depression in the Negro community. The unemployment rate is extremely high, and among Negro youth, it goes up as high as forty percent in some cities.

We need an economic bill of rights. This would guarantee a job to all people who want to work and are able to work. It would also guarantee an income for all who are not able to work. Some people are too young, some are too old, some are physically disabled, and yet in order to live, they need income. It would mean creating certain public-service jobs, but that could be done in a few weeks. A program that would really deal with jobs could minimize—I don't say stop—the number of riots that could take place this summer.

Our whole campaign, therefore, will center on the job question, with other demands, like housing, that are closely tied to it. We feel that much more building of housing for low-income people should be done. On the educational front, the ghetto schools are in bad shape in terms of quality, and we feel that a program should be developed to spend at least a thousand dollars per pupil. Often, they are so far behind that they need more and special attention, the best quality education that can be given.

These problems, of course, are overshadowed by the Vietnam war. We'll focus on the domestic problems, but it's inevitable that we've got to bring out the question of the tragic mix-up in priorities. We are spending all of this money for death and destruction, and not nearly enough money for life and constructive development. It's inevitable that the question of the war will come up in this campaign. We hear all this talk about our ability to afford guns and butter, but we have come to see that this is a myth, that when a nation becomes involved in this kind of war, when the guns of war become a national obsession, social needs inevitably suffer. And we hope that as a result of our trying to dramatize this and getting thousands and thousands of people moving around this issue, that our government will be forced to reevaluate its policy abroad in order to deal with the domestic situation.

The American people are more sensitive than Congress. A Louis Harris poll has revealed that fifty-six percent of the people feel that some kind of program should come into being to provide jobs to all who want to work. We had the WPA when the nation was on the verge of bankruptcy; we should be able to do something when we're sick with wealth. That poll also showed that fifty-seven percent of the people felt the slums should be eradicated and the communities rebuilt by those who live in them, which would be a massive job program.

We need to put pressure on Congress to get things done. We will do this with First Amendment activity. If Congress is unresponsive, we'll have to escalate in order to keep the issue alive and before it. This action may take on disruptive dimensions, but not violent in the sense of destroying life or property: it will be militant nonviolence.

We really feel that riots tend to intensify the fears of the white majority while relieving its guilt, and so open the door to greater repression. We've seen no changes in Watts, no structural changes have taken place as the result of riots. We are trying to find an alternative that will force people to confront issues without destroying life or property. We plan to build a shantytown in Washington, patterned after the bonus marches of the thirties, to dramatize how many people have to live in slums in our nation. But essentially, this will be just like our other nonviolent demonstrations. We are not going to tolerate violence. And we are making it very clear that the demonstrators who are not prepared to be nonviolent should not participate in this. For the past six weeks, we've had workshops on nonviolence with the people who will be going to Washington. They will continue through the spring. These people will form a core of the demonstration and will later be the marshals in the protests. They will be participating themselves in the early stages, but after two or three weeks, when we will begin to call larger numbers in, they will be the marshals, the ones who will control and discipline all of the demonstrations.

We plan to have a march for those who can spend only a day or two in Washington, and that will be toward the culminating point of the campaign. I hope this will be a time when white people will rejoin the ranks of the movement.

Demonstrations have served as unifying forces in the movement; they have brought blacks and whites together in very practical situations, where philosophically they may have been arguing about Black Power. It's a strange thing how demonstrations tend to solve problems. The other thing is that it's little known that crime rates go down in almost every community where you have demonstrations. In Montgomery, Alabama, when we had a bus boycott, the crime rate in the Negro community went down sixty-five percent for a whole year. Anytime we've had demonstrations in a community, people have found a way to slough off their self-hatred, and they have had a channel to express their longings and a way to fight nonviolently—to get at the power structure, to know you're doing something, so you don't have to be violent to do it.

We need this movement. We need it to bring about a new kind of togetherness between blacks and whites. We need it to bring allies together and to bring the coalition of conscience together.

A good number of white people have given up on integration too. There are a lot of "White Power" advocates, and I find that people do tend to despair and engage in debates when nothing is going on. But when action is taking place, when there are demonstrations, they have a quality about them that leads to a unity you don't achieve at other times.

I think we have come to the point where there is no longer a choice now between nonviolence and riots. It must be militant, massive nonviolence, or riots. The discontent is so deep, the anger so ingrained, the despair, the restlessness so wide, that something has to be brought into being to serve as a channel through which these deep emotional feelings, these deep angry feelings, can be funneled. There has to be an outlet, and I see this campaign as a way to transmute the inchoate rage of the ghetto into a constructive and creative channel. It becomes an outlet for anger.

Even if I didn't deal with the moral dimensions and question of violence versus nonviolence, from a practical point of view, I don't see riots working. But I am convinced that if rioting continues, it will strengthen the right wing of the country, and we'll end up with a kind of right-wing takeover in the cities and a Fascist development, which will be terribly injurious to the whole nation. I don't think America can stand another summer of Detroit-like riots without a development that could destroy the soul of the nation, and even the democratic possibilities of the nation.

I'm committed to nonviolence absolutely. I'm just not going to kill anybody, whether it's in Vietnam or here. I'm not going to burn down any building. If nonviolent protest fails this summer, I will continue to preach it and teach it, and we at the Southern Christian Leadership Conference will still do this. I plan to stand by nonviolence because I have found it to be a philosophy of life that regulates not only my dealings in the struggle for racial justice but also my dealings with people, with my own self. I will still be faithful to nonviolence.

But I'm frank enough to admit that if our nonviolent campaign doesn't generate some progress, people are just going to engage in more violent activity, and the discussion of guerrilla warfare will be more extensive.

In any event, we will not have been the ones who will have failed. We will place the problems of the poor at the seat of government of the wealthiest nation in the history of mankind. If that power refuses to acknowledge its debt to the poor, it will have failed to live up to its promise to insure "life, liberty, and the pursuit of happiness" to its citizens.

If this society fails, I fear that we will learn very shortly that racism is a sickness unto death.

We welcome help from all civil rights organizations. There must be a diversified approach to the problem, and I think both the NAACP and the Urban League play a significant role. I also feel that CORE and SNCC have played very significant roles. I think SNCC's recent conclusions are unfortunate. We have not given up on integration. We still believe in black and white together. Some of the Black Power groups have temporarily given up on integration. We have not. So maybe we are the bridge, in the middle, reaching across and connecting both sides.

The fact is, we have not had any insurrection in the United States because an insurrection is planned, organized, violent rebellion. What we have had is a kind of spontaneous explosion of anger. The fact is, people who riot don't want to riot. A study was made recently by some professors at Wayne State University. They interviewed several hundred people who participated in the riot last summer in Detroit, and a majority of these people said they felt that my approach to the problem—nonviolence—was the best and most effective.

I don't believe there has been a massive turn to violence. Even the riots have had an element of nonviolence to persons. But for a rare exception, they haven't killed any white people, and Negroes could, if they wished, kill by the hundreds. That would be insurrection. But the amazing thing is that the Negro has vented his anger on property, not persons, even in the emotional turbulence of riots.

But I'm convinced that if something isn't done to deal with the very harsh and real economic problems of the ghetto, the talk of guerrilla warfare is going to become much more real. The nation has not yet recognized the seriousness of it. Congress hasn't been willing to do anything about it, and this is what we're trying to face this spring. As committed as I am to nonviolence, I have to face this fact: if we do not get a positive response in Washington, many more Negroes will begin to think and act in violent terms.

I hope, instead, that what comes out of these nonviolent demonstrations will be an economic bill of rights for the disadvantaged, requiring about ten or twelve billion dollars. I hope that a specific number of jobs is set forth, that a program will emerge to abolish unemployment, and that there will be another program to supplement the income of those whose earnings are below the poverty level. These would be measures of success in our campaign.

It may well be that all we'll get out of Washington is to keep Congress from getting worse. The problem is to stop it from moving backward. We started out with a poverty bill at 2.4 billion dollars, and now it's back to 1.8 billion. We have a welfare program that's dehumanizing, and then Congress adds a Social Security amendment that will bar literally thousands of children from any welfare. Model cities started out; it's been cut back. Rent subsidy, an excellent program for the poor, cut down to nothing. It may be that because of these demonstrations, we will at least be able to hold on to some of the things we have.

There is an Old Testament prophecy of the "sins of the Fathers being visited upon the third and fourth generations." Nothing could be more applicable to our situation. America is reaping the harvest of hate and shame planted through generations of educational denial, political disfranchisement, and economic exploitation of its black population. Now, almost a century removed from slavery, we find the heritage of oppression and racism erupting in our cities, with volcanic lava of bitterness and frustration pouring down our avenues.

Black Americans have been patient people, and perhaps they could continue with but a modicum of hope; but everywhere, "time is winding up," in the words of one of our spirituals, "corruption in the land, people take your stand; time is winding up." In spite of years of national progress, the plight of the poor is worsening. Jobs are on the decline as a result of technological change, schools North and South are proving themselves more and more inadequate to the task of providing adequate education and thereby entrance into the mainstream of the society. Medical care is virtually out of reach of millions of black and white poor. They are aware of the great advances of medical science—heart transplants, miracle drugs—but their children still die of preventable diseases, and even suffer brain damage due to protein deficiency.

In Mississippi, children are actually starving, while large landowners have placed their land in the soil bank and receive millions of dollars annually not to plant food and cotton. No provision is made for the life and survival of the hundreds of thousands of sharecroppers who now have no work and no food. Driven off the land, they are forced into tent cities and ghettos of the North, for our Congress is determined not to stifle the initiative of the poor (though they clamor for jobs) through welfare handouts. Handouts to the rich are given more sophisticated nomenclature such as parity, subsidies, and incentives to industry.

White America has allowed itself to be indifferent to race prejudice and economic denial. It has treated them as superficial blemishes, but now awakes to the horrifying reality of a potentially fatal disease. The urban outbreaks are "a fire bell in the night," clamorously warning that the seams of our entire social order are weakening under strains of neglect.

The American people are infected with racism—that is the peril. Paradoxically, they are also infected with democratic ideals—that is the hope. While doing wrong, they have the potential to do right. But they do not have a millennium to make changes. Nor have they a choice of continuing in the old way. The future they are asked to inaugurate is not so unpalatable that it justifies the evils that beset the nation. To end poverty, to extirpate prejudice, to free a tormented conscience, to make a tomorrow of justice, fair play, and creativity—all these are worthy of the American ideal.

We have, through massive nonviolent action, an opportunity to avoid a national disaster and create a new spirit of class and racial harmony. We can write another luminous moral chapter in American history. All of us are on trial in this troubled hour, but time still permits us to meet the future with a clear conscience.

Look, April 16, 1968, pp. 23–25; in J.M. Washington, ed., cited work, pp. 64–72.

154

"IT IS ALREADY VERY, VERY LATE"

by James Baldwin

In the summer of 1968, after the assassination of King and outbreaks that followed, the editors of *Esquire* (August) interviewed James Baldwin. We conclude this effort with Baldwin's warning "we do have to be free."

Q: Can we still cool it?
BALDWIN: That depends on a great many factors. It's a very serious question in my mind whether or not the people of this country, the bulk of the population of this country, have enough sense of what is really

happening to their black co-citizens to understand why they're in the streets. I know as of this moment they maybe don't know it, and this is proved by the reaction to the civil-disorders report. It came as no revelation to me or to any other black cat that white racism is at the bottom of the civil disorders. It came as a great shock apparently to a great many other people, including the President of the United States and the Vice President. And now you ask me if we can cool it. I think the President goofed by not telling the nation what the civil-disorders report was all about. And I accuse him and the entire administration, in fact, of being largely responsible for this tremendous waste and damage. It was up to him and the Vice President to interpret that report and tell the American people what it meant and what the American people should now begin to think of doing. *Now!* It is already very, very late even to begin to think of it. What causes the eruptions, the riots, the revolts—whatever you want to call them—is the despair of being in a static position, absolutely static, of watching your father, your brother, your uncle, or your cousin—no matter how old the black cat is or how young—who has no future. And when the summer comes, both fathers and sons are in the streets—they can't stay in the houses. I was born in those houses and I know. And it's not their fault.

Q: From a very short-range approach, what should the federal government do, right now, to cool it?

BALDWIN: What do you mean by the federal government? The federal government has come to be, in the eyes of all Negroes anyway, a myth. When you say the federal government, you're referring to Washington, and that means you're referring to a great many people. You're referring to Senator Eastland and many people in Washington who out of apathy, ignorance, or fear have no intention of making any move at all. You're talking about the people who have the power, who intend to keep the power. And all that they can think of are things like swimming pools, you know, in the summertime, and sort of made up jobs simply to protect peace and the public property. But they show no sign whatever of understanding what the root of the problem really is, what the dangers really are. They have made no attempt, whatever, any of them, as far as I know, really to explain to the American people that the black cat in the streets wants to protect his house, his wife, and his children. And if he is going to be able to do this he has to be given his autonomy, his own schools, a revision of the police force in a very radical way. It means in short that if the American Negro, the American black man, is going to become a free person in this country, the people of this country have to give up something. If they don't give it up it will be taken from them.

Q: You say that existing jobs are just make-work jobs. What kind of job program should be adopted?
BALDWIN: It's very difficult to answer that question since the American Republic has created a surplus population. You know it's created not only people who are unemployable but who no longer wish to be employed in this system. A job program involves, first of all, I would think, a real attack on all American industries and on all American labor unions. For example, you're sitting in Hollywood. And there are not any Negroes, as far as I know, in any of the Hollywood craft unions: there is no Negro grip, no Negro crew member, no Negro works in Hollywood on that level or on any higher level either. There are some famous Negroes who work out here for a structure which keeps Negroes out of the unions. Now it's not an Act of God that there aren't any Negroes in the unions. It's not something that is handed down from some mountain. It's a deliberate act on the part of the American people. They don't want the unions broken, because they are afraid of the Negro as a source of competition in the economic market. Of course what they've made him is something much worse than that. You can't talk about job programs unless you're willing to talk about what is really holding the structure together. Eastman Kodak, General Motors, General Electric—all the people who really have the power in this country. It's up to them to open up *their* factories, *their* unions, to let us begin to work.

Q: They would have to begin, say, on-the-job training programs for those....
BALDWIN: Yes, and by the way I know a whole lot of Negroes on the streets, baby, who are much brighter than a lot of cats dictating the policies of Pan American. You know what this country really means by on-the-job training programs is not that they're teaching Negroes skills, though there's that too; what they're afraid of is that when the Negro comes into the factory, into the union, when he comes, in fact, into the American institutions he will change these institutions because no Negro in this country really lives by the American middle-class standards. That's what they really mean by on-the-job training. That's why they pick up a half-dozen Negroes here and there, and polish them up, polish them off, and put them in some ass-hole college someplace, then expect those cats

to be able to go back on the street and cool the other cats. They can't. The price in this country to survive at all still is to become like a white man. More and more people are refusing to become like a white man. That's at the *bottom* of what they mean by on-the-job training. They mean they want to fit you in. And furthermore, let's tell it like it is. The American white man does not really want to have an autonomous Negro male anywhere *near* him.

Q: In on-the-job training programs, the white American structure wants a worker who is trained, who shows up regularly at eight-thirty in the morning and works till five in the afternoon.

BALDWIN: Yeah, well I know an awful lot of cats who did that for a long, long time. We haven't got to be trained to do that. We don't even have to be given an incentive to do that.

Q: Would you say, then, that many black people have been able to go nowhere, so they've lost any feeling that it's worth working regularly?

BALDWIN: That is part of what we're talking about. Though it goes deeper than that, I think. It's not only that. What is happening in this country among the young, and not only the black young, is an overwhelming suspicion that it's not worth it. You know that if you watched your father's life like I watched my father's life, as a kid much younger than I watches his father's life; his father *does* work from eight to five every day and ends up with nothing. He can't protect anything. He has nothing. As he goes to the grave, having worked his fingers to the bone for years and years and years, he still has nothing and the kid doesn't either. But what's worse than that is that one has begun to conclude from the fact that maybe in this Republic—judging now on the evidence of its own performance—maybe there isn't anything. It's easy to see on the other hand what happens to the white people who make it. And that's not a very attractive spectacle either. I mean I'm questioning the values on which this country thinks of itself as being based.

Q: What you are calling for, then, is a radical change in thinking by government and industry.

BALDWIN: Yes.

Q: And given the inertia plus...

BALDWIN: Fear.

Q: ...fear and whatever else there may be, any such changes seem...

BALDWIN: ...seem improbable.

Q: Certainly, they will come slow. A union will not throw open its doors and bring in several hundred people from the black community right away. Now my question is . . .
BALDWIN: You've answered your question.

Q: "Sweeper jobs," then, just won't work?
BALDWIN: No. I'll tell you what you will do. You will do what you did last summer and the summer before that. You'll pour some money into the ghetto and it will end up in the hands of various adventurers. In the first place, thirteen dollars and some change is not *meant* to do anything. And a couple of cats will make it, and the rest will be where they were.

Q: But can you buy time with this kind of program; enough time for the longer term changes?
BALDWIN: You could if you meant it. What's at issue is whether or not you mean it. Black people in this country conclude that you mean to destroy us.

Q: But if industry and government seriously planned job-training programs, and the unions opened up?
BALDWIN: Look, the labor movement in this country has always been based precisely on the division of black and white labor. That is no Act of God either. Labor unions along with the bosses created the Negro as a kind of threat to the white worker. There's never been any real labor movement in this country because there's never been any coalition between black and white. It's been prevented by the government and the industries and the unions.

Q: What would be the first steps a union could take to demonstrate that it seriously wants to correct such inequities? What should the leadership do?
BALDWIN: Educate their own rank and file. Declare themselves. And penalize any member of the union who is against it.

Q: What can industry do on a short-range basis?
BALDWIN: I'm not sure that you should be asking me these questions at all. But I'll do my best to answer them. What can industry do? Well you know, the same as the labor unions. The labor unions won't have Negroes in the unions above a certain level. And they can never rise out of that local, or do what they might be able to do if they weren't trapped in that local at a certain level. Industry is perfectly willing to hire me to dig a ditch or carry a shovel. It isn't going to hire me to build a city or to fly a plane. It is unable to look on me as just another worker. There are

exceptions to this rule, obviously, to be found everywhere. But this is the way it works and the exceptions, in fact, prove the rule.

Q: Do you think it would help if industry were to get involved as cosponsors of low-income housing?
BALDWIN: No. I think we've had far more, more than enough of low-income housing which simply becomes high-rise slums.

Q: Well, if they were not high-rise slums?
BALDWIN: I don't want any more projects built in Harlem, for example. I want someone to attack the real-estate lobby because that's the only way to destroy the ghetto.

Q: But what about building low-income housing out in the suburbs where factories are beginning to move?
BALDWIN: Well, that depends on the will of the American people, doesn't it? That's why they are in the suburbs—to get away from me.

Q: What about certain plans of industry to set up factories or businesses which would be owned by ghetto people? Would you see this as a positive step?
BALDWIN: What would be produced in those factories?

Q: Piecework, small items subcontracted by larger manufacturers.
BALDWIN: It's a perfectly valid idea except that in order to do that you have to eliminate the ghetto. Look, it is literally true that from a physical point of view those houses are unlivable. No one's going to build a factory in Harlem, not unless you intend, you know, *really* to liberate Harlem.

Q: Well, New York State, for example, plans to build a State office building in Harlem.
BALDWIN: In Harlem. I know exactly where they're going to build it, too. And at the risk of sounding paranoiac, I think I know why. It's going to be where the Black Nationalist Bookstore is now, and one of the reasons for it, I am convinced, is simply because the Black Nationalist Bookstore is a very dangerous focal ground—125th Street and Seventh Avenue. You know, it's what in Africa would be called a palaver tree. It's where Negroes get together and talk. It's where all the discontent doesn't begin, exactly, but where it always focuses.

Q: Wouldn't you think that would be a very foolish idea, because you can always pick some other place to meet and talk?

BALDWIN: Yes, but the American white man has proved, if nothing else, he is absolutely, endlessly foolish when it comes to this problem.

Q: Let's talk about the average citizen, the white man who lives on Eighty-ninth Street and Riverside Drive, what should he be doing?
BALDWIN: It depends on what he feels. If he feels he wants to save this country, he should be talking to his neighbors and talking to his children. He shouldn't, by the way, be talking to me.

Q: What should he be telling his neighbors?
BALDWIN: That if I go under in this country, I, the black man, he goes too.

Q: Is there any action he can take? Pressure on the local government?
BALDWIN: Pressure on his landlord, pressure on the local government, pressure wherever he can exert pressure. Pressure, above all, on the real-estate lobby. Pressure on the educational system. Make them change textbooks so that his children and my children will be taught something of the truth about our history. It is run now for the profit motive, and nothing else.

Q: What about the white suburbanite who fled the city, while making sure the blacks stayed there? What does he have to do now?
BALDWIN: If he wants to save his city, perhaps he should consider moving back. They're his cities too. Or just ask himself why he left. I know why he left. He's got a certain amount of money and a certain future, a car, two cars, you know, scrubbed children, a scrubbed wife, and he wants to preserve all that. And he doesn't understand that in his attempt to preserve it he's going to destroy it.

Q: What about the poverty program, does that offer any remedy?
BALDWIN: Are you joking? There has not been a war on poverty in this country yet. Not in my lifetime. The war on poverty is a dirty joke.

Q: How would you improve it?
BALDWIN: By beginning it.

Q: In what fashion?
BALDWIN: Look, there's no way in the world to do it without attacking the power of some people. It cannot be done unless you do that. The power of the steel companies, for example, which can both make and break a town. And they've done it, they're doing it. Everybody knows it. You can't have

a war on poverty unless you are willing to attack those people and limit their profits.

Q: Is it a matter of limiting the profits of industries only, or is it also a matter of limiting the power of the politicians?
BALDWIN: But the politicians are not working for the people; they're working for exactly the people I say we have to attack. That is what has happened to politics in this country. That is why the political machinery now is so vast, and so complex no one seems to be able to control it. It's completely unresponsive to the needs of the American community, completely unresponsive. I'm not talking only as a black man, I mean to the whole needs of the American people.

Q: You mean insofar as it responds to industry?
BALDWIN: It responds to what it considers its own survival.

Q: What would you say ought to be done to improve the relationship of the police with the black community?
BALDWIN: You would have to educate them. I really have no quarrel particularly with the policemen. I can even see the trouble they're in. They're hopelessly ignorant and terribly frightened. They believe everything they see on television, as most people in this country do. They are endlessly respectable, which means to say they are Saturday-night sinners. The country has got the police force it deserves and of course if a policeman sees a black cat in what he considers a strange place he's going to stop him; and you know of course the black cat is going to get angry. And then somebody may die. But it's one of the results of the cultivation in this country of ignorance. Those cats in the Harlem street, those white cops; they are scared to death and they *should* be scared to death. But that's how black boys die, because the police are scared. And it's not the policemen's fault; it's the country's fault.

Q: In the latest civil disorder, there seems to have been a more permissive attitude on the part of the police, much less reliance on firearms to stop looters as compared with last summer when there was such an orgy of shooting by the police and the National Guard.
BALDWIN: I'm sorry, the story isn't in yet, and furthermore, I don't believe what I read in newspapers. I object to the term "looters" because I wonder who is looting whom, baby.

Q: How would you define somebody who smashes in the window of a television store and takes what he wants?

BALDWIN: Before I get to that, how would you define somebody who puts a cat where he is and takes all the money out of the ghetto where he makes it? Who is looting whom? Grabbing off the TV set? He doesn't really want the TV set. He's saying screw you. It's a judgment, by the way, on the value of the TV set. Everyone knows that's a crock of shit. He doesn't want the TV set. He doesn't want it. He wants to let you know he's there. The question I'm trying to raise is a very serious question. The mass media—television and all the major news agencies—endlessly use that word "looter." On television you always see black hands reaching in, you know. And so the American public concludes that these savages are trying to steal everything from us. And no one has seriously tried to get to where the trouble is. After all, you're accusing a captive population who has been robbed of *everything* of looting. I think it's obscene.

Q: Would you make a distinction between snipers, fire bombers, and looters?
BALDWIN: I've heard a lot about snipers, baby, and then you look at the death toll.

Q: Very few white men, granted. But there have been a few.
BALDWIN: I know who dies in the riots.

Q: Well, several white people have died.
BALDWIN: Several, yeah, baby, but do you know how many Negroes have died?

Q: Many more. But that's why we're talking about cooling it.
BALDWIN: It is not the black people who have to cool it.

Q: But they're the ones . . .
BALDWIN: It is not the black people who have to cool it, because they won't.

Q: Aren't they the ones who are getting hurt the most, though?
BALDWIN: That would depend on the point of view. You know, I'm not at all sure that we are the ones who are being hurt the most. In fact I'm sure we are not. We are the ones who are *dying* fastest.

Q: The question posed, however, was whether snipers could be classified as true revolutionaries; fire bombers, as those overwhelmed with frustration and seeking to destroy the symbols of their discontent; looters, as victims of the acquisitive itch?
BALDWIN: I have to ask you a very impertinent question. How in the

world can you possibly begin to categorize the people of a community whom you do not know at all? I disagree with your classifications altogether. Those people are all in the streets for the same reason.

Q: Does some of our problem come from our flaunting the so-called good life, with its swimming pools, cars, suburban living, and so on, before a people whom society denies these things?

BALDWIN: No one has ever considered what happens to a woman or a man who spends his working life downtown and then has to go home uptown. It's too obvious even to go into. We are a nation within a nation, a captive nation within a nation. Yes, and you do flaunt it. You talk about us as though we were not there. The real pain, the real danger is that white people have always treated Negroes this way. You've always treated Sambo this way. We always were Sambo for you, you know, we had no feelings, we had no ears, no eyes. We've lied to you for more than a hundred years and you don't even know it yet. We've lied to you to survive. And we've begun to despise you. We don't hate you. We've begun to despise you. And it is because we can't afford to care what happens to us, and *you* don't care what happens to us. You don't even care what happens to your own children. Because we have to deal with your children too. We don't care what happens to you. It's up to you. To live or to die. Because you made our life that choice all these years.

Q: What about the role of some of the black institutions. Does the church have some meaning still in the black community insofar as the possibility of social progress is concerned?

BALDWIN: You must consider that the fact that we have a black church is, first of all, an indictment of a Christian nation. There shouldn't be a black church. And that's again what you did. We've used it. Martin Luther King used it most brilliantly, you know. That was his forum. It's always been our only forum. But it doesn't exist anywhere in the North anymore, as Martin Luther King himself discovered. It exists in the South, because the black community in the South is a different community. There's still a Negro family in the South, or there was. There is no Negro family essentially in the North, and once you have no family you have no church. And that means you have no forum. It cannot be used in Chicago and Detroit. It can be used in Atlanta and Montgomery and those places. And now since Martin is dead—not before, but certainly since he is dead— that forum is no longer useful because people are repudiating their Christian church in toto.

Q: Are they repudiating Christianity as well?
BALDWIN: No more intensely than you have.

Q: Then the black church is dead in the North?
BALDWIN: Let me rephrase it. It does not attract the young. Once that has happened to any organization, its social usefulness is at least debatable. Now that's one of the great understatements of the century.

Q: In that case, what is the role of Adam Clayton Powell?
BALDWIN: Adam Clayton Powell is not considered a pastor, he is considered a politician. He is considered, in fact, one more victim. People who can't stand Adam would never, never, *never* attack him now. Crimes which Adam is accused of—first of all, the people in Harlem know a great deal more about that than anybody who has written about it. That's one thing. And for another, as long as you don't impeach Senator Eastland, it's a bullshit tip and we know it. We're not fighting for him, we're fighting for us.

Q: What about some of the other leaders of the black community?
BALDWIN: The real leaders now in the black community you've never heard of. Roy's not a leader, Whitney's not a leader.

Q: What does the death of Martin Luther King signify?
BALDWIN: The abyss over which this country hovers now. It's a very complicated question and the answer has to be very complicated too. What it means to the ghetto, what it means to the black people of this country, is that you could kill Martin, who was trying to save you, and you will face tremendous opposition from black people because you choose to consider, you know, the use of violence. If you can shoot Martin, you can shoot all of us. And there's nothing in your record to indicate you won't, or anything that would prevent you from doing it. That will be the beginning of the end, if you do, and that knowledge will be all that will hold your hand. Because one no longer believes, you see—*I* don't any longer believe, and not many black people in this country can afford to believe—any longer a word you say. I don't believe in the morality of this people at all. I don't believe you do the right thing because you think it's the right thing. I think you may be forced to do it because it will be the expedient thing. Which is good enough.

I don't think that the death of Martin Luther King means very much to any of those people in Washington. I don't think they understand what happened at all. People like Governor Wallace and Mister Maddox certainly don't. I would doubt very much if Ronald Reagan does. And that is of course where the problem lies, with people like that, with people we mentioned earlier, and with the institutions we mentioned earlier. But to the black people in this country it means that you have declared war. You have declared war. That you do intend to slaughter us, that you intend to put us in concentration camps. After all, Martin's assassination—whether it was done by one man or by a State Trooper, which is a possibility; or whether it was a conspiracy, which is also a possibility; after all I'm a fairly famous man too, and one doesn't travel around—Martin certainly didn't without the government being aware of every move he made—for this assassination I accuse the American people and all its representatives.

For me, it's been Medgar. Then Malcolm. Then Martin. And it's the same story. When Medgar was shot they arrested some lunatic in Mississippi, but I was in Mississippi, with Medgar, and you don't need a lunatic in Mississippi to shoot a cat like Medgar Evers, you know, and the cat whoever he was, Byron de la Beckwith, slipped out of the back door of a nursing home and no one's ever heard from him since. I won't even discuss what happened to Malcolm, or all the ramifications of that. And now Martin's dead. And every time, you know, including the time the President was murdered, everyone insisted it was the work of one lone madman; no one can face the fact that his madness has been created deliberately. Now Stokely will be shot presently. And whoever pulls that trigger will not have bought the bullet. It is the people and their representatives who are inciting to riot, not Stokely, not Martin, not Malcolm, not Medgar. And you will go on like this until you will find yourself in a place from which you can't turn back, where indeed you may be already. So, if Martin's death has reached the conscience of a nation, well then it's a great moral triumph in the history of mankind, but it's very unlikely that it has.

Q: Some people have said that the instant canonization by white America is the cop-out...
BALDWIN: It's the proof of their guilt, and the proof of their relief. What they don't know is that for every Martin they shoot there will be ten others. You already miss Malcolm and wish he were here. Because Malcolm was the only person who could help those kids in the ghetto. The *only* person.

Q: I was just about to say, we white people...
BALDWIN: ...wished that Malcolm were here? But you, the white people,

no matter how it was done actually, technically, you created the climate which forced him to die.

Q: We have created a climate which has made political assassination acceptable...
BALDWIN: ...which made inevitable that death, and Medgar's, and Martin's. And may make other deaths inevitable too, including mine. And all this in the name of freedom.

Q: Do you think "cooling it" means accepting a culture within a culture, a black culture as separate?
BALDWIN: You mean, white people cooling it?

Q: Yes.
BALDWIN: White people cooling it means a very simple thing. Black power frightens them. White power doesn't frighten them. Stokely is not, you know, bombing a country out of existence. Nor menacing your children. White power is doing that. White people have to accept their history and their actual circumstances, and they won't. Not without a miracle they won't. Goodwill won't do it. One's got to face the fact that we police the globe—we, the Americans, police the globe for a very good reason. We are protecting what we call the free world. You ought to be black, sitting in Harlem, listening to that phrase. We, like the South African black miners, know exactly what you're protecting when you talk about the free world.

Q: Are there some viable black institutions that...
BALDWIN: Why does a white country look to black institutions to save it?

Q: Well, to begin a dialogue, to find out what should be done...
BALDWIN: That is up to you.

Q: But doesn't white America need instruction from...
BALDWIN: ...the streets of any ghetto.

Q: But on the streets of any ghetto can you learn...
BALDWIN: Ask any black junkie what turned him into a junkie.

Q: But what I'm after are programs that you can work with.
BALDWIN: What you mean by programs is a way of alleviating the distress without having it cost you anything.

Q: Well, even if we're willing to spend the money...
BALDWIN: I'm not talking about money.

Q: But if we are willing to change our point of view...
BALDWIN: Well, then, the person to talk to is first of all your own heart, your wife, your child. It's your country too. I've read a great deal about the good white people of this country since I came back to it in 1957. But it's the good white people of this country who forced the black people into the streets.

Q: Do you think it counts for anything having a mayor like John Lindsay walking the streets?
BALDWIN: I like John Lindsay. Just because he walks the streets, perhaps. Or for the same reasons I like J.F.K., you know, with enormous reservations. He's somewhere near the twentieth century at least.

Q: What kind of President should we have? Would a black President help?
BALDWIN: You're going to need somebody who is willing, first of al, to break the stranglehold of what they call the two-party system. John Lewis was right on the day of the March on Washington, when he said we can't join the Republican Party because look who that is made up of. We can't join the Democratic Party—look who's in *that* party. Where's *our* party? What we need is somebody who can coalesce the energies in this country, which are now both black *and* white, into another party which can respond to the needs of the people. The Democratic Party cannot do it. Not as long as Senator Eastland is in it. I name him, to name but one. I certainly will never vote for a Republican as long as Nixon is in that party. You need someone who believes in this country, again to begin to change it. And by the way, while we're on this subject, one of the things we should do is cease protecting all those Texas oil millionaires who are one of the greatest menaces any civilization has ever seen. They have absolutely no brains, and a *fantastic* amount of money, *fantastic* amount of power, *incredible* power. And there's nothing more dangerous than that kind of power in the hands of such ignorant men. And this is done with the consent of the federal government. With the *collusion* of the federal government.

Q: Do you have any hope for the future of this country?
BALDWIN: I have a vast amount of determination. I have a great deal of hope. I think the most hopeful thing to do is to look at the situation. People accuse me of being a doom-monger. I'm not a doom-monger. If you don't look at it, you can't change it. You've got to look at it. And at certain times it cannot be more grim. If we look at it, we can change it. If we don't look at it, we won't. If we don't change it, we're going to die.

We're going to perish, every single one of us. That's a tall order, a hard, hard bill to pay; but you have been accumulating it for a very long time. And now the bill is in. It is in for you and your children and it is in all over the world. If you can't pay your bill, it's the end of you. And you created in this country a whole population which has nothing to lose. It's part of your bill. There's nothing more that you can do to me, nothing more at all. When you, in the person of your President, assure me that you will not tolerate any more violence, you may *think* that frightens me. People don't get frightened when they hear that, they get *mad*. And whereas you're afraid to die, I'm not.

Q: You would say, then, that we have a lot to answer for?
BALDWIN: I'm not trying to accuse you, you know. That's not the point. But you have an awful lot to face. I don't envy any white man in this century, because I wouldn't like to have to face what you have to face. If you don't face it, though, it's a matter of *your* life or death. Everyone's deluded if they think it's a matter of Sambo's life or death. It isn't a matter of Sambo's life or death, and it can't be, for they have been slaughtering Sambos too long. It's a matter of whether or not *you* want to live. And you may think that my death, or my diminution, or my disappearance will save you, but it won't. It can't save you. All that can save you now is your confrontation with your own history . . . which is not your past, but your present. Nobody cares what happened in the past. One can't afford to care what happened in the past. But your history has led you to this moment, and you can only begin to change yourself and save yourself by looking at what you are doing in the name of your history, in the name of your gods, in the name of your language. And what has happened is as though I, having always been outside it—more outside it than victimized by it, really, in a sense; outside it surely, you know, slaughtered by it, victimized by it, but mainly *outside* it—can see it better than you can see it. Because I cannot afford to let you fool me. If I let you fool me, then I die. But I've fooled *you* for a long time. That's why you keep saying, what does the Negro want? It's a summation of your own delusions, the lies you've told yourself. You know *exactly* what I want!

Q: So that when we come to you with the question, How do we cool it?, all we're asking is that same old question, What does the Negro want?
BALDWIN: Yes. You're asking me to help you save it.

Q: Save ourselves?
BALDWIN: Yes. But *you* have to do that.

Q: Speaking strictly, from your point of view, how would you talk to an angry black man ready to tear up the town?
BALDWIN: I only know angry black men. You mean, how would I talk to someone twenty years younger than I?

Q: That's right.
BALDWIN: That would be very difficult to do. I've tried, and I try it, I try it all the time. All I can tell him, really, is I'm with you, whatever that means. I'll tell you what I *can't* tell him. I can't tell him to submit and let himself be slaughtered. I can't tell him that he should not arm, because the white people are armed. I can't tell him that he should let anybody rape his sister, or his wife, or his mother. Because that's where it's at. And what I try to tell him, too, is if you're ready to blow the cat's head off— because it could come to that—try not to hate him, for the sake of your soul's salvation and for no other reason. But let's try to be better, let's try—no matter what it costs us—to be better than they are. You haven't got to hate them though we do have to be free. It's a waste of time to hate them.

On the impact of King's murder upon black people, see Roger Wilkins, *A Man's Life: An Autobiography* (New York: Simon and Schuster, 1982), pp. 211–16.

Index

Ward, Herbert C., 372
Ware, Charles, 332
War on Poverty, 358, 372–73, 411, 471, 541, 560–61
Washington, D.C., 243, 244–45, 547, 550
Washington, Booker T., 9
Washington Prayer Pilgrimage (1957), 56
Watkins, Hollis, 94
Watts, Mazette, 38
Watts uprising, 367–73, 391, 411–13, 456, 523–24
Wayne State University, 552
wealth, redistribution of, 445
Weinberger, Eric, 210
welfare, 553
Wells, Aaron, 338
Wells, James, 94
Wells, Samuel, 332, 333
West, Ben, 20, 21
Wheatley, Phyllis, 7
Wheaton College, Mass., 63
Wheat Street Baptist Church, 67
White, Walter, 54
white backlash, 454–58, 467, 492
White Citizens Councils, 70, 136, 167, 300
Wichita, Kans., 12
Wiles, V. McKinley, 337
Wilkins, Roy, 54, 56–58, 61, 62, 64, 74, 95, 115, 148, 168, 200, 201, 202, 208, 244, 272, 308, 320, 343, 367, 407, 440, 442, 544
Williams, Earl, 493–504

Williams, Hosea, 330–31
Williams, Lloyd, 64
Winfield, Ala., 126–27
Winona, Miss., 464
Winston, Henry, 100, 102, 529
Winters, Shelley, 160
Wisconsin Temporary Housing Project, 501
withholding policy, 64–65
Wofford, Harris, 95
women, 158–59, 179–80, 282, 512
Woodall, Luther, 332, 333
Woods, Anita, 194, 195
Woolworth's, 60, 61, 65, 140
working class, 105–6
world opinion, 338
World War II, 177, 274
Wright, Herbert, 53, 63
Wright, Isaac, 216
Wright, J. Skelley, 92
Wright, Paul S., 34
writers. See artists

Yale University (Conn.), 63
Yorty, Sam, 367
Young, Whitney, Jr., 266, 269, 273, 308, 357, 437, 440, 442
Younge, Mrs., 360–61
Younge, Sammy, 360–61, 395–97, 398
youth. See children

Zimmerman, Charles, 272